Mental Health in a Digital World

Global Mental Health in Practice Series

Mental Health in a Digital World

Edited by

Dan J. Stein
University of Cape Town, South Africa

Naomi A. Fineberg
University of Hertfordshire, United Kingdom

Samuel R. Chamberlain
University of Southampton, England

ACADEMIC PRESS
An imprint of Elsevier

ELSEVIER

Library of Congress Cataloging-in-Publication Data
A catalog record for this book is available from the Library of Congress

British Library Cataloguing-in-Publication Data
A catalogue record for this book is available from the British Library

ISBN 978-0-12-822201-0

For information on all Academic Press publications
visit our website at https://www.elsevier.com/books-and-journals

Publisher: Nikki Levy
Editorial Project Manager: Megan Ashdown
Production Project Manager: Swapna Srinivasan
Cover Designer: Mark Rogers

Typeset by STRAIVE, India

Contents

Contributors

Anzar Abbas AiCure, New York, NY, United States

Shalini Ahuja Centre for Implementation Science, Health Services and Population Research Department Institute of Psychiatry, Psychology and Neurosciences King's College London, London, United Kingdom

Michael Van Ameringen MacAnxiety Research Centre; Department of Psychiatry and Behavioural Neurosciences, McMaster University, Hamilton, ON, Canada

Gerhard Andersson Department of Behavioural Sciences and Learning, Department of Biomedical and Clinical Sciences, Linköping University, Linköping, Sweden

Ole A. Andreassen NORMENT Centre, Institute of Clinical Medicine, University of Oslo and Division of Mental Health and Addiction, Oslo University Hospital, Oslo, Norway

Jason Bantjes Institute for Life Course Health Research, Department of Global Health, Faculty of Medicine and Health Sciences, University of Stellenbosch, Stellenbosch, South Africa

Joël Billieux Institute of Psychology, University of Lausanne (UNIL); Centre for Excessive Gambling, Addiction Medicine, Lausanne University Hospitals (CHUV), Lausanne, Switzerland

Sydney B. Clark Department of Psychological Sciences, Kent State University, Kent, OH, United States

Beáta Bőthe Department of Psychology, Université de Montréal, Montréal, QC, Canada

Matthias Brand Department of General Psychology: Cognition and Center for Behavioral Addiction Research (CeBAR), University of Duisburg-Essen, Duisburg; Erwin L. Hahn Institute for Magnetic Resonance Imaging, Essen, Germany

Valentina Caricasole University of Milan, Department of Mental Health, Department of Biomedical and Clinical Sciences Luigi Sacco, Milan, Italy

Lior Carmi Post Trauma Center, Chaim Sheba Medical Center, Ramat Gan, Israel

Samuel R. Chamberlain Department of Psychiatry, Faculty of Medicine, University of Southampton; Southern Health NHS Foundation Trust, Southampton, United Kingdom

Samantha L. Connolly Center for Healthcare Organization and Implementation Research, VA Boston Healthcare System; Department of Psychiatry, Harvard Medical School, Boston, MA, United States

Allison Crawford Virtual Mental Health, Centre for Addiction and Mental Health Associate Professor, University of Toronto, Toronto, ON, Canada

Vasa Curcin Department of Informatics; School of Population Health and Environmental Sciences, King's College London, London, United Kingdom

Giselle Day Houston VA HSR&D Center for Innovations in Quality, Effectiveness and Safety, Michael E. DeBakey VA Medical Center; VA South Central Mental Illness Research, Education and Clinical Center, Houston, TX, United States

Philippe Delespaul Department of Psychiatry and Neuropsychology, Faculty of Health Medicine and Lifesciences, Maastricht University, Maastricht; Mondriaan Mental Health Trust, Department of Adult Psychiatry, Heerlen, The Netherlands

Paul H. Delfabbro School of Psychology, The University of Adelaide, Adelaide, Australia

Anthony H. Ecker Houston VA HSR&D Center for Innovations in Quality, Effectiveness and Safety, Michael E. DeBakey VA Medical Center; Menninger Department of Psychiatry and Behavioral Sciences, Baylor College of Medicine; VA South Central Mental Illness Research, Education and Clinical Center, Houston, TX, United States

Fernando Fernández-Aranda Department of Psychiatry, Bellvitge University Hospital-IDIBELL, Barcelona; Ciber Fisiopatología Obesidad y Nutrición (CIBERObn), Instituto de Salud Carlos III, Madrid; Department of Clinical Sciences, School of Medicine, University of Barcelona, Barcelona, Spain

Luwishennadige M.N. Fernando Centre for Mental Health, Melbourne School of Population and Global Health, University of Melbourne, Melbourne, VIC, Australia

Naomi A. Fineberg School of Life and Medical Sciences, University of Hertfordshire, Hatfield; Hertfordshire Partnership University NHS Foundation Trust, Welwyn Garden City; University of Cambridge School of Clinical Medicine, Cambridge, United Kingdom

Christopher A. Flessner Department of Psychological Sciences, Kent State University, Kent, OH, United States

Oleksandr Frei NORMENT Centre, Institute of Clinical Medicine, University of Oslo and Division of Mental Health and Addiction; Department of Research, Innovation and Education, Division of Clinical Neuroscience, Oslo University Hospital, Oslo, Norway

Johannes Fuss Institute of Forensic Psychiatry and Sex Research, University Duisburg-Essen, Essen, Germany

Isaac R. Galatzer-Levy Reality Labs, Facebook; Psychiatry, New York University School of Medicine, New York, NY, United States

Theresa R. Gladstone Department of Psychological Sciences, Kent State University, Kent, OH, United States

Gabrielle F. Gloston Houston VA HSR&D Center for Innovations in Quality, Effectiveness and Safety, Michael E. DeBakey VA Medical Center; Menninger Department of Psychiatry and Behavioral Sciences, Baylor College of Medicine, Houston, TX, United States

Pattie P. Gonsalves Sangath, Saket, New Delhi; Sangath, Bardez, Goa, India; School of Psychology, University of Sussex, Brighton, United Kingdom

Jon E. Grant Department of Psychiatry, University of Chicago, Chicago, IL, United States

Anna Hartford Brain-Behaviour Unit, Neuroscience Institute, University of Cape Town, Cape Town, South Africa

Donald Hilty Department of Psychiatry & Behavioral Sciences, Mather, CA, United States

Guy Hindley NORMENT Centre, Institute of Clinical Medicine, University of Oslo and Division of Mental Health and Addiction, Oslo University Hospital, Oslo, Norway; Department of Psychosis Studies, Institute of Psychiatry, Psychology and Neuroscience, King's College London, London, United Kingdom

Julianna B. Hogan Houston VA HSR&D Center for Innovations in Quality, Effectiveness and Safety, Michael E. DeBakey VA Medical Center; Menninger Department of Psychiatry and Behavioral Sciences, Baylor College of Medicine; VA South Central Mental Illness Research, Education and Clinical Center, Houston, TX, United States

Kevin Ing University of California Irvine School of Medicine, Department of Psychiatry & Human Behavior, Orange, CA, United States

Thomas R. Insel Humanest Care, Pleasanton, CA, United States

Konstantinos Ioannidis Department of Psychiatry, University of Cambridge, and Cambridgeshire and Peterborough NHS Foundation Trust, Cambridge, United Kingdom

Madeleine L. Jarrett Child, Youth and Emerging Adult Program, Cundill Centre for Child and Youth Depression, Centre for Addiction and Mental Health; Human Biology Program, Faculty of Arts and Science, University of Toronto, Toronto, ON, Canada

Susana Jiménez-Murcia Department of Psychiatry, Bellvitge University Hospital-IDIBELL, Barcelona; Ciber Fisiopatología Obesidad y Nutrición (CIBERObn), Instituto de Salud Carlos III, Madrid; Department of Clinical Sciences, School of Medicine, University of Barcelona, Barcelona, Spain

Anthony Jorm Centre for Mental Health, Melbourne School of Population and Global Health, University of Melbourne, Melbourne, VIC, Australia

Daniel L. King College of Education, Psychology, & Social Work, Flinders University, Adelaide, Australia

Taishiro Kishimoto Department of Neuropsychiatry, Keio University School of Medicine, Tokyo, Japan

Ashley A. Lahoud Department of Psychological Sciences, Kent State University, Kent, OH, United States

Jan A. Lindsay Houston VA HSR&D Center for Innovations in Quality, Effectiveness and Safety, Michael E. DeBakey VA Medical Center; Menninger Department of Psychiatry and Behavioral Sciences, Baylor College of Medicine; VA South Central Mental Illness Research, Education and Clinical Center, Houston, TX, United States

Christine Lochner SA MRC Unit on Risk & Resilience in Mental Disorders, Department of Psychiatry, Stellenbosch University, Stellenbosch, South Africa

John Luo University of California at Irvine School of Medicine, Director of Emergency and Consultation-Liaison Psychiatry, UCI Medical Center, Health Sciences Clinical Department of Psychiatry & Human Behavior, Orange, CA, United States

Gemma Mestre-Bach Universidad Internacional de La Rioja, Logroño, La Rioja, Spain

Kai Mueller Outpatient Clinic for Behavioral Addictions, Department of Psychosomatic Medicine and Psychotherapy at the University Medical Center, Mainz, Germany

John A. Naslund Department of Global Health and Social Medicine, Harvard Medical School, Boston, MA, United States

Jim van Os Department of Psychiatry and Neuropsychology, Faculty of Health Medicine and Lifesciences, Maastricht University, Maastricht; Department of Psychiatry, Brain Center Rudolf Magnus, University Medical Center Utrecht, Utrecht University, Utrecht, The Netherlands; Department of Psychosis Studies, Institute of Psychiatry, King's College London, King's Health Partners, London, United Kingdom

Beth Patterson MacAnxiety Research Centre; Department of Psychiatry and Behavioural Neurosciences, McMaster University, Hamilton, ON, Canada

Marc N. Potenza Department of Psychiatry; Department of Neuroscience; Yale Child Study Center, Yale University School of Medicine; Connecticut Mental Health Center, New Haven; Connecticut Council on Problem Gambling, Wethersfield; Wu Tsai Institute, Yale University, New Haven, CT, United States

Nicola Reavley Centre for Mental Health, Melbourne School of Population and Global Health, University of Melbourne, Melbourne, VIC, Australia

Katharina Schultebraucks Emergency Medicine, Columbia University, New York, NY, United States

Jay H. Shore Department of Psychiatry and Family Medicine, University of Colorado Anschutz Medical Campus; Centers for American Indian and Alaska Native Health, Colorado School of Public Health, Anschutz Medical Campus, University of Colorado, Aurora, CO, United States

Saher Siddiqui Harvard College, Harvard University, Cambridge, MA, United States

Philip Slabbert Institute for Life Course Health Research, Department of Global Health, Faculty of Medicine and Health Sciences, University of Stellenbosch, Stellenbosch, South Africa

Olav B. Smeland NORMENT Centre, Institute of Clinical Medicine, University of Oslo and Division of Mental Health and Addiction, Oslo University Hospital, Oslo, Norway

Dan J. Stein SA MRC Unit on Risk & Resilience in Mental Disorders, Department of Psychiatry & Neuroscience Institute, University of Cape Town, Cape Town, South Africa

John Strauss Child, Youth and Emerging Adult Program, Cundill Centre for Child and Youth Depression; Shannon Centennial Informatics Lab, Centre for Addiction and Mental Health; Department of Psychiatry, Faculty of Medicine, University of Toronto, Toronto, ON, Canada

John Torous Department of Psychiatry and Director, Division of Digital Psychiatry, Beth Israel Deaconess Medical Center, Harvard Medical School, Boston, MA, United States

Miguel A. Vadillo Department of Psychology, Autonomous University of Madrid, Madrid, Spain; School of Population Health and Environmental Sciences, King's College London, London, United Kingdom

Alberto Varinelli University of Milan, Department of Mental Health, Department of Biomedical and Clinical Sciences Luigi Sacco, Milan, Italy

Simone Verhagen Department of Psychiatry and Neuropsychology, Faculty of Health Medicine and Lifesciences, Maastricht University, Maastricht; Department of Lifespan Psychology, Faculty of Psychology, Open University, Heerlen, The Netherlands

Matteo Vismara University of Milan, Department of Mental Health, Department of Biomedical and Clinical Sciences Luigi Sacco, Milan, Italy

Elisa Wegmann Department of General Psychology: Cognition and Center for Behavioral Addiction Research (CeBAR), University of Duisburg-Essen, Duisburg, Germany

Akkapon Wongkoblap Department of Informatics, King's College London, London, United Kingdom; School of Information Technology; DIGITECH, Suranaree University of Technology, Nakhon Ratchasima, Thailand

Jasmine Zhang MacAnxiety Research Centre; Department of Psychiatry and Behavioural Neurosciences, McMaster University, Hamilton, ON, Canada

Preface

Digital mental health is exploding as a discipline for innovation, research, and investment. It is no longer possible to track all of the new companies innovating in mental health, but at least 1000 start-ups have been launched in the past decade, with $1.8B (USD) invested in 2020 alone, nearly a threefold increase over 2019 (https://rockhealth.com/reports/2020-market-insights-report-chasing-a-new-equilibrium/; https://medium.com/what-if-ventures/approaching-1-000-mental-health-startups-in-2020-d344c822f757). By early 2021, PubMed listed over 2500 references for "digital mental health," a term that was scarcely reported in the literature a decade ago (https://pubmed.ncbi.nlm.nih.gov/). And for the first time there are venture funds and investment vehicles organized specifically to support innovation in this space (https://www.whatif.vc/).

Why all of this interest in digital mental health? There was no technological breakthrough, like CRISPR, that can explain this new fascination. There was no particular discovery or research finding of effectiveness that would shift mental health to this new discipline. Although during the Covid-19 pandemic the focus of the field was on remote care with a rapid transition to telehealth, there was no clear global change in the prevalence or incidence of mental illness, as there was for the virus, which appeared to be a driver of this intense interest.

One explanation for the explosion of digital mental health is more prosaic. In spite of the progress in neuroscience and genomics, the emergence of new interventions, and the increasing awareness of the importance of mental health for overall health, the field has largely stalled in terms of outcomes. Measures of morbidity and mortality for the major mental illnesses have changed little over the past 4 decades, even while outcomes for many chronic noncommunicable diseases are improving globally. As a result, mental health has become a crisis in many parts of the world.

Our failure to bend the curve for mental health outcomes is not due to lack of means or lack of knowledge. Psychiatry and psychology have developed powerful treatments that compare favorably to treatments in the rest of medicine. Rather the crisis in mental health is a crisis of care. We simply have failed to deliver the medical and psychological treatments that we know are effective. Or we deliver them so late in the course of illness or with so little fidelity that they are no longer effective.

To solve this crisis of care we need to address three critical gaps: engagement, quality, and accountability. That's where digital mental health comes in. The nearly ubiquitous tools of modernity—smartphones, sensors, and data science—may be able to bend the curve for mental health by solving for the gaps in engagement, quality, and accountability. This volume describes much of the empirical data to support this potential. These are early days in this new world for mental health, a world that includes unavoidable ethical and practical challenges. But given the imperative for better outcomes, we must navigate through these challenges to find a way to better outcomes. That path leads through engagement, quality, and accountability.

Engagement is more than access. Access is ensuring that anyone can find care when they want it. Access may be enough to improve outcomes in many areas of medicine, but in mental health, many of the people who most need care do not want it or, at least, do not want the care we offer in traditional brick and mortar clinics, emergency rooms, and hospitals. Engagement raises the bar. Engagement builds care that people want because it gives them agency, it is built to serve them not the provider, and involves them continuously not just during a crisis. As described in this volume, digital mental health can learn from the social media revolution which has created products that are so engaging we now worry they are addictive. Digital mental health offers a strategy through community, gamification, and in-the-moment access for building care that is engaging and effective.

For those who access care, quality has been a barrier to recovery. In most of the world, mental health care is fragmented, reactive, and crisis-oriented. Medications and psychological treatments are rarely integrated. Also few providers are trained to provide evidence-based psychological treatments with fidelity. Chapters in this volume describe how digital tools can integrate and democratize care, ensuring that the same high-quality treatment can be delivered remotely in Boston and Botswana. While most of the attention has been focused on remote, transparent therapy, the use of remote tools for training is equally important for building quality.

Finally, accountability has been lacking in mental health care. There has been little focus on outcomes because there is little measurement of outcomes. To borrow a business axiom, we do not manage what we do not measure. Digital mental health via wearable sensors and smartphone data can provide passive, continuous, objective measures of how we think, feel, and behave. Just as HbA1c provides feedback in diabetes and blood pressure helps us manage hypertension, digital phenotyping may give us the accountability essential to improve outcomes for people with mental illness.

The critical question for our field is how we improve outcomes. Beyond reducing acute symptoms, how do we ensure that people with anxiety, mood, or psychotic disorders recover to enjoy a full life? How do we prevent suicide and unnecessary suffering? How do we solve the equity gap and the social determinants that have kept us from reducing morbidity and mortality? Digital mental health may not be able to answer all of these questions, but if we can use these new tools to improve engagement, quality, and accountability, we will be making a good and much needed start in the right direction. This volume provides an important introduction to help readers navigate this new world.

Thomas R. Insel
Humanest Care
Pleasanton, CA, United States

Introduction

1

Dan J. Stein[a], Christine Lochner[b], Samuel R. Chamberlain[c], and Naomi A. Fineberg[d]
[a]SA MRC Unit on Risk & Resilience in Mental Disorders, Department of Psychiatry & Neuroscience Institute, University of Cape Town, Cape Town, South Africa, [b]SA MRC Unit on Risk & Resilience in Mental Disorders, Department of Psychiatry, Stellenbosch University, Stellenbosch, South Africa, [c]Department of Psychiatry, Faculty of Medicine, University of Southampton, Southampton, United Kingdom, [d]School of Life and Medical Sciences, University of Hertfordshire, Hatfield, United Kingdom

Computer studies were introduced into high schools in some parts of the world in the 1970s, and one of us—Dan—was fortunate to be one of the first in line to enroll. It is extraordinary to think that students worked on a massive mainframe computer, writing each line of code using a card-punching machine, and waiting hours for their programs to run. No one had a personal computer, and no mental health clinician was using a computer at work or at home. While that seems forever ago, it is as well to bear in mind that in many parts of the world, many people still do not have ready access to computers.

By the time Dan completed his psychiatric training in the early 1990s, the personal computer was on many desks, and this was starting to impact many aspects of work life (for example, one could conduct electronic searches on a compact disk), and home life (for example, one could use the computer for word processing). Excited by these developments Dan edited a special issue of a continuing medical education journal devoted to "Computers and Psychiatry." It had nothing on the Internet or phone apps, on gaming disorder or cyberchondria, or on computer-delivered psychotherapy.

In high-income countries today, devices with enormous computing power are ubiquitous, constantly relied on at work and at home. They have hugely enriched many aspects of our lives, providing wonderful ways of communicating, and incredible sources of information. For mental health professionals there are many opportunities; the Internet and phone apps provide many sources of information, a way of communication, and new avenues for monitoring mental health and delivering psychotherapy. However, there is an increasing digital divide; in poorly resourced settings where access to online data is less available, or among older age groups unaccustomed to using online technologies, these forms of psychoeducation and psychotherapy are not readily accessible.

At the same time, mental health clinicians are aware that the digital world has had many negative impacts. Email and social media often seem to steal individuals' attention and time, the Internet gives our patients a great deal of false information about medical matters related to their health, and it provides an avenue for many destructive behaviors such as cyberbullying. The accessibility of online platforms has led to a range of putative new disorders, ranging from online gambling and gaming disorder to cyberchondria and cyberhoarding. Appropriately, there is growing attention to the notion of "problematic Internet use," and negative aspects of the digital life comprise a growing public health problem.

It seems timely therefore to review global mental health from a digital perspective. e-Health, or the use of information and communications technology in health services may be particularly useful given the high penetration of mobile phones in the low- and middle-income world. m-Health refers to the use of mobile phones, wearable devices, and related technologies and is a rapidly advancing area. There is an opportunity for clinicians and researchers to consider the intersections between global mental health, e-health, m-health, and problematic Internet use, and to assess their implications for contemporary psychiatric practice and research.

The volume is divided into four sections, each addressing a key aspect of the intersections between global mental health, e-health, m-health, and problematic Internet use. In his introductory preface, Thomas Insel—who on leaving his position as the director of the National Institute of Mental Health, devoted the next phase of his career to digital psychiatry—argues that this field may help bend the curve for mental health by addressing current gaps in engagement of patients, in quality of mental health care, and in accountability of clinicians. In the remainder of this introductory chapter we outline the framework and contents of the volume, and reflect on some of the key issues it raises for global mental health and psychiatry.

Data collection and analysis

Digital technologies have transformed the way in which we collect and analyze data, including medical and psychiatric data. The section has chapters on various aspects of current work on mental health data collection and analysis.

Clinical informatics is a rapidly expanding field. In his chapter on "Electronic medical records and information technology to improve mental health services" Donald Hilty provides an overview of contemporary work in clinical informatics. The chapter covers developments in information systems, electronic health records, electronic communications with patients and staff, behavioral health indicators, and related digital advances to improve practice and research. By understanding how systems are designed and tailored to collect data, clinicians can use technology to inform decisions and facilitate outcomes. Hilty proposes that expert application of information technology allows health care to be both efficient and patient-centered.

The concept of "Big data" is increasingly important in psychiatry research, with large datasets now available in a range of areas including neurogenetics and neuroimaging. In their chapter on "Big data and the goal of personalized health interventions," Guy Hindley, Olav Smeland, Oleksandr Frei, and Ole Andreassen review the key concepts relevant to work on big data, describe how big data are collected and analyzed, and provide examples of the application of big data to mental health research. The authors emphasize some of the key challenges faced in using big data to develop a more personalized medicine that improves outcomes, and they consider how these challenges may be addressed in future work. Notably, they emphasize the importance of ensuring that mental health data are obtained from around the globe.

The development of the Internet has led to a range of online research on various aspects of mental health. In their chapter on "Collecting data from Internet (and other platforms) users for mental health research," Ashley Lahoud, Theresa Gladstone, Sydney Clark, and Christopher Flessner consider the potential advantages and pitfalls of such online research. They provide a brief historical overview of the Internet's use within the context of mental health research, discuss the validity of using the Internet for such investigations, and outline both benefits and costs of such work. They conclude their chapter by describing different tools for conducting research online, as well as where to access research participants on the Internet.

In their chapter on "Ecological momentary assessment and other digital technologies for capturing daily life in mental health," Simone Verhagen, Jim van Os, and Philippe Delespaul emphasize that to advance mental health care, we need innovative strategies that are person-centered, contextually embedded, and able to capture symptom occurrence and nonoccurrence in daily life. They assert that traditional static measures are unable to capture the dynamic variation that is needed to fully understand both vulnerability and resilience. Instead, they argue that m-health digital technologies, such as ecological momentary assessment strategies and passive sensor tracking, provide attractive solutions that may ultimately contribute to more personalized psychiatric approaches.

While digital phenotyping is typically thought of in relation to individual patients, social media analyses provide another level of data that may shed light on a range of phenomena relevant to mental health research and practice. In their chapter on "Social media big data analysis for mental health research" Akkapon Wongkoblap, Miguel Vadillo, and Vasa Curcin review current work in this area. The chapter discusses the potential value of data from a range of different platforms, and also describes a range of approaches to analyzing the big data that are derived from such platforms. The chapter concludes with a framework for the use of social media platforms in health interventions; this brings together different stakeholders, namely, users, social media platforms, research communities, health organizations, and governments.

Communication, psychoeducation, and screening

Digital technologies have transformed the way in which we communicate and seek information, and have the potential to transform the ways in which we screen for mental disorders. The second section of the volume addresses issues around using digital technologies to enhance communication, psychoeducation, and mental disorder screening.

Telepsychiatry is increasingly employed, and in the aftermath of the Covid-19 pandemic has become standard practice in many regions. In their chapter on "Telemental health via videoconferencing," Samantha Connolly, Julianna Hogan, Anthony Ecker, Gabrielle Gloston, Giselle Day, Jay Shore, and Jan Lindsay provide an overview of telemental health, including factors related to effectiveness, safety, and uptake on a global scale. They argue that telemental health can be an effective form of care delivery with high acceptability among patients and providers alike. Telepsychiatry can significantly increase access to care around the world, provided that key factors are in place to ensure successful and sustained uptake.

Social media are not only increasingly central in our social lives, but also increasingly relevant to clinical practice. In their chapter on "Social media and clinical practice" John Luo and Kevin Ing help clinicians to navigate the waters of social media. The chapter provides useful practical advice about mental health practice in the digital world. As the authors emphasize, understanding the use of social media in medical practice, including both its benefits and risks, is key for improving access to clinicians, education about mental health, and delivery of psychiatric services, while minimizing the risk of boundary violations and privacy breaches.

In a very short space of time, the Internet has become the main source of information for many clinicians and patients. In their chapter on "Websites and the quality of mental health information," Nicola Reavley, Luwishennadige Madhawee Fernando, and Anthony Jorm provide evidence from a systematic review that despite the increasing number of websites and social media devoted to mental health, there is overall low quality of online information, with the possible exception of information for mood disorders. They argue that ongoing evaluations of website quality are needed to ensure that individuals with mental disorders are provided with accurate and usable information.

The penetration of mobile cellular phones across the globe has already changed many aspects of daily life (including payment for goods and services), and promises to also change aspects of clinical practice. In their chapter on "Identification, prediction, and intervention via remote digital technology: Digital phenotyping and deployment of clinical interventions in psychiatry," Lior Carmi, Anzar Abbas, Katharina Schultebraucks, and Isaac Galatzer-Levy review the use of mobile phones and other digital devices for screening and assessment of mental disorders. They argue that harnessing smart devices for clinical use holds immense promise for characterizing clinical functioning and intervening remotely. At the same time, they note that much work is needed to understand clinical risk based on digital signals and to develop coordinated systems to deploy useful interventions.

A small but important literature has emerged on the digital therapeutic alliance. In their thoughtful chapter "The digital therapeutic relationship: Retaining humanity in the digital age," Jason Bantjes and Philip Slabbert note the concern that use of technology for mental health delivery has the potential to dehumanize care and to deny the need for human connectedness. The authors go on to suggest that by using a human factor approach to design person-centered e-interventions, humanity and connectedness can be retained. They also explore how e-interventions can be conceptualized within relationship-centered paradigms, considering, for example, the application of attachment theory to guide research and practice in the development of humanistic e-interventions.

Problematic Internet use

While digital technologies hold a great deal of promise for advancing many areas of physical and mental health, there are important public health concerns about the Internet, ranging from the broad construct of "problematic Internet use" to specific conditions that are related to digital technologies. This section of the volume includes chapters on a range of such conditions including Internet gambling and gaming, which are now recognized by the World Health Organization as the ICD-11 diagnoses of gambling disorder and gaming disorder, respectively, and cybersex and cyberchondria. It also addresses developmental aspects of problematic Internet use.

Problematic Internet use is an umbrella term that refers to excessive engagement in and lack of control over online activities, associated with distress or impairment. The term encompasses a wide range of excessive online activities, including online buying, online gambling, online gaming, cybersex, online pornography, online streaming, use of social media, cyberchondria and cyberbulling. In their chapter, Jon Grant, Konstantinos Ioannidis, and Samuel Chamberlain focus on online addictive and impulsive conditions, particularly gambling disorder, gaming disorder, and cybershopping. The prevalence and burden of these conditions is increasingly recognized, and there is a pressing need for appropriate diagnosis and treatment.

There has been growing interest in the phenomenological and psychobiological overlaps and contrasts between impulsive and compulsive psychiatric conditions. In their chapter, Matteo Vismara, Valentina Caricasole, Alberto Varinelli, and Naomi Fineberg go on to address online compulsive disorders including cyberchondria and cyberhoarding. The prevalence of and burden associated with obsessive-compulsive and related disorders has only been recently recognized, but there have been important advances in understanding their neurobiology and treatment; these lessons may be useful in addressing online compulsive conditions.

What is the best way of conceptualizing the spectrum of problematic Internet use, ranging from impulsive to compulsive conditions? In their chapter on "Internet-use disorders: A theoretical framework for their conceptualization and diagnosis," Elisa Wegmann, Joël Billieux, and Matthias Brand address this question. They also discuss the related questions of how best to differentiate between normal, problematic, and disordered use of digital technologies, and how to conceptualize the heterogeneity of different kinds of problematic Internet use. Such work is able to draw on a range of relevant research on offline impulsive and compulsive conditions, and online conditions may in turn also provide unique and important windows onto the relevant questions.

Online sexual activity has likely been a key driver of Internet traffic as well as of advances in Internet technology. While the boundaries between normal and pathological cybersex are invariably controversial, it has been suggested that there are both compulsive and impulsive forms of excessive cybersex, ranging from online consumption of erotic and pornographic material, to sexual interaction and simulation. In their chapter on "Cybersex," Johannes Fuss and Beáta Bőthe cover a broad range of sexual activities using digital technologies, ranging from Internet pornography to sex robots, emphasizing how such technologies have brought about significant changes to how humans experience and express their sexuality.

A developmental perspective is key for understanding the nature and course of psychopathology. In addition, early exposure to digital technologies is increasingly ubiquitous, and may in turn influence a range of developmental processes. In their chapter on "Developmental considerations regarding Internet use," Gemma Mestre-Bach, Fernando Fernández-Aranda, Susana Jiménez-Murcia, and Marc Potenza address not only the positive aspects of social networking, but also key negative aspects such as cyberbullying. The developmental perspective of this chapter usefully complements the content of other chapters in this section.

Interventions

The fourth section of the volume addresses Internet and digital interventions for clinical problems. Such interventions range from online psychotherapy to mobile phone apps and virtual reality adjuncts to psychotherapy. The section includes work not only on online interventions for problematic use of the Internet, but also on health policies to mitigate problematic use of the Internet.

In his chapter on "Internet-based psychotherapies," Gerhard Andersson emphasizes that the evidence base for Internet-based psychotherapies and other technology-based interventions is increasing rapidly. The chapter provides a comprehensive overview of the field, discussing how Internet treatments can be delivered, as well as different treatment formats, target groups, and clinical implementations. He points out that while some guided Internet-based psychotherapies tend to work as well as face-to-face treatments, they are not yet widely implemented, and he outlines future directions for much-needed research on efficacy and implementation.

Smart phones provide a key opportunity for advancing the field of digital mental health. In their chapter on phone apps, John Strauss, Jasmine Zhang, Madeleine Jarretta, Beth Patterson, and Michael van Ameringen provide a comprehensive review of publications in this area. They provide a framework to evaluate mental health apps, and consider the extent to which evidence-based recommendations about such apps are possible. We expect ongoing innovation and implementation in this area; the field seems in its infancy, and deserves careful nurturance.

To address the growing prevalence and burden of digital technology-based mental health problems, a range of clinical and public health interventions are urgently needed. In their chapter on interventions, Daniel L. King, Joël Billieux, Kai Mueller, and Paul Delfabbrod provide a comprehensive review of this key area of work. The authors not only review online psychotherapies for such conditions, but also emphasize that an optimal approach to digital technology-based mental health problems may entail coordinated efforts of stakeholders ranging across families and peers, schools, health providers, government bodies, and the industries that provide online content. Global mental health practitioners and researchers can expect that one of the key public health battles of this century will be between public health advocates and digital industries; this area deserves a great deal of focused attention.

Digital technologies may be a crucial tool for scaling up mental health services around the world. In their chapter on "Scaling-up of mental health services in the digital age: The rise of technology and its application to low- and middle-income countries," Saher Siddiqui, Pattie Pramila Gonsalves, and John Naslund explore five major areas benefitting from these emerging digital technologies: community outreach, challenging stigma, and spreading awareness; youth mental health; mental health in humanitarian settings; clinical care and frontline health workers; and technology for severe mental disorders. Their chapter includes a discussion of broad ethical considerations in low- and middle-income countries, highlighting risks pertaining to misinformation, victimization, and widening health inequities.

In their chapter on "The addictive qualities of the Internet: Some ethical considerations," Anna Hartford and Dan Stein expand on the ethical ramifications of advances in digital technologies. They focus in particular on debates regarding persuasive digital technologies—those which aim to maximize use, or even to encourage compulsive engagement—as well as the difficulty in articulating the harms involved in excessive Internet use. The chapter also addresses practical ethical implications, including regulation of design features, concerns about growing socioeconomic inequality in online services, and whether there should be a "right to disconnect." Hopefully these issues will receive further attention in the future.

Conclusion

A key theme of this volume is the need to balance the immense potential of digital technologies for advancing global mental health versus the psychiatric burden of problematic Internet use. Addressing the pros and cons of technology has been a key feature of modernity, and the need for a balanced approach in health care in particular, encompassing both scientific rigor and a humane focus, has been an increasingly pressing need as health care itself has become more technological over the past century.

Digital technologies, with their incredibly rapid rate of change, and their overwhelming intrusion into all aspects of life, make this key dilemma of modernity a particularly acute one, and one which is highly relevant to global mental health. We hope that this volume, by covering a range of pertinent areas, ranging from the value of electronic medical records for mental health services, to the human right to disconnect, provides a useful resource for global mental health practitioners, researchers, wider stakeholders, and the public, as they grapple with this dilemma.

We are grateful that so many leading clinicians and researchers from around the world have contributed to this volume, endeavoring to provide comprehensive and balanced overviews of their particular areas of work, and outlining future clinical and research directions. Our hope is that the volume will be useful to a broad audience including both clinicians and consumers, as well as academics and policy makers. While we are aware of how quickly the landscape of digital mental health is changing, we are also impressed by the need for immediate and ongoing attention to this area, in order to ensure that our approaches are balanced and rigorous, and that they contribute positively to global mental health. Finally, we wish to acknowledge that some chapters in this publication are based on work from COST Action 16207 "European Network for Problematic Usage of the Internet" supported by COST (European Cooperation in Science and Technology) www.cost.eu.

Section A

Digital Data Collection and Analysis

Information technology and electronic health record to improve behavioral health services

2

Donald Hilty[a], John A. Naslund[b], Shalini Ahuja[c], John Torous[d],
Taishiro Kishimoto[e], and Allison Crawford[f]
[a]Department of Psychiatry & Behavioral Sciences, Mather, CA, United States, [b]Department
of Global Health and Social Medicine, Harvard Medical School, Boston, MA, United States,
[c]Centre for Implementation Science, Health Services and Population Research Department
Institute of Psychiatry, Psychology and Neurosciences King's College London, London,
United Kingdom, [d]Department of Psychiatry and Director, Division of Digital Psychiatry,
Beth Israel Deaconess Medical Center, Harvard Medical School, Boston, MA, United States,
[e]Department of Neuropsychiatry, Keio University School of Medicine, Tokyo, Japan, [f]Virtual
Mental Health, Centre for Addiction and Mental Health Associate Professor, University of
Toronto, Toronto, ON, Canada

Introduction

We continue to increase our exchange of information through health technologies, particularly clinical informatics, used to access, disseminate, and analyze information, and to facilitate patient-centered care (PCC), defined as high-quality, affordable, and timely health care by the Institute of Medicine (IOM) (Hilty, Torous, Parish, et al., 2020; Institute of Medicine, 2001). Health-care systems and governmental agencies across the world are emphasizing quality, evidence-based care, and are trying to set individual and population outcomes that can be evaluated by behavioral health (BH) data/indicators (Proctor, Silmere, Raghavan, et al., 2010). This requires services that are acceptable to patients, with measurable outcomes, and scalable approaches. For feasible and sustainable services, and effectiveness, implementation science and translational approaches are suggested, with input from all stakeholders in health-care settings (Gargon, Gorst, & Williamson, 2019; World Health Organization, 2017a). Technology is a key part of the World Health Organization (WHO) global health strategy, with the expectation of scalable BH interventions, particularly for people in communities affected by adversity (Crawford & Serhal, 2020; World Health Organization, 2020). In our immediate context, care is needed during the COVID pandemic, so that the innovation curve does not reinforce the social gradient of health and worsen health-care inequities (Luo, Hilty, Worley, et al., 2006).

The Health Information Technology for Economic and Clinical Health (HITECH) Act brought a wave of electronic health records (EHRs), and with this, meaningful use of criteria standards in the United States. The EHR or computer-based patient record

(CPR) is credited with improving clinical practice through ease of access and retrieval of information (e.g., clinical guidelines), decision support systems with reminders and alerts and data collection for outcome measurement. CPR notes are more completely documented and have more appropriate clinical decisions compared to handwritten notes (Shanafelt, Dyrbye, West, et al., 2016). Evolution in health care has brought improvements, but it has also created inefficiencies and new challenges, with EHRs linked to high rates of burnout among health professionals (Hilty, Unutzer, Ko, et al., 2019). This may be happening because the impact of technology and related change have not been fully assessed, at least in behavioral health (BH)/psychiatry (Luxton, 2016; Shanafelt et al., 2016).

System management [e.g., health information systems (IS), telemedicine, Information technology (IT)], facilities and clinics (e.g., labs, home health) and delivery structures (e.g., integrated networks) play a key role in health care. IT falls into the categories of clinical information systems, administrative information, and clinical decision support (CDS). CDS is supported by advances in artificial intelligence (AI) to assist patients and clinicians with decision-making in time and across home, in life, in health care and across populations (The National Academy of Sciences, Engineering, and Medicine. Health and Medicine Division, 2020) (Fig. 2.1). Advances in sensing technologies and affective computing have enabled machines to longitudinally analyze data for patterns in time and help users detect, assess, and respond to emotional states. The use of machine learning (ML) and pattern recognition promises to improve public and population health surveillance.

Many assume that good clinicians will adapt in-person care to video, telephone, mobile health, and other technologies, and intermix these options with ease in combination (Hilty, Torous, et al., 2020). But clinician or learner-centered approaches that parallel patient-centered ones are needed to ensure quality care so technologies can complement EHR, CDS, and IS processes. Furthermore, organizational/institutional competencies have been suggested for synchronous and asynchronous technology implementation (Hilty, Torous, et al., 2020; Luxton, 2016), as a way to align work by training directors, faculty, department administrators, and health system leaders. Clinicians/faculty need to embrace technology as part of healthcare reform (Mostaghimi, Olszewski, Bell, et al., 2017; World Health Organization, 2020), so students in health disciplines and other team members can professionally deliver care via technology (Crawford, Sunderji, López, et al., 2016; Hilty, Crawford, Teshima, et al., 2015) and create a positive e-culture for clinics and health systems (Hilty, Torous, et al., 2020). Competencies have been published for video (2015, 2018) (Hilty, Chan, Torous, et al., 2019b; Hilty, Maheu, Drude, et al., 2018), social media (2018) (Hilty, Chan, Torous, et al., 2019a; Hilty, Zalpuri, Stubbe, et al., 2018), mobile health (2019, 2020) (Hilty, Armstrong, Luxton, et al., 2020; Zalpuri, Liu, Stubbe, et al., 2018), wearable sensors (2020) (Aung, Matthews, & Choudhury, 2017), and other asynchronous technologies (2020) (Hilty, Torous, et al., 2020).

This chapter introduces topics primarily from Section A, as well as Sections 2–4 of the book. Section 1 focuses on issues around data collection and analysis, EHRs

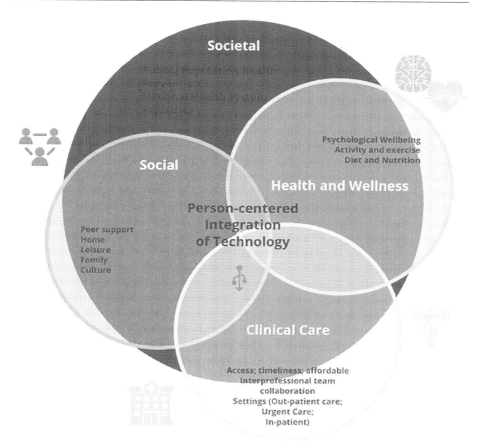

Fig. 2.1 Person-centered health, lifestyle, clinical care, and population health integration via technology.

and information technologies, which improve services and research. It also provides an overview on big data and personalized health interventions, use of the Internet to collect data, and research on the Internet (e.g., social media), as well as new developments in ecological momentary assessment (EMA), digital phenotyping, and social media and tracking (MISST) (Chapters 2–6). Section B addresses issues around e-health to enhance communication, psychoeducation, and screening for mental disorders. It addresses telepsychiatry or telebehavioral health, new options for patient care via mobile health, the role of social media in practice and how to help patients use the Internet—developments that impact the digital therapeutic relationship (Chapters 7–9,11). Section C addresses problematic Internet use, with chapters on topics including Internet gambling and gaming, cybersex, cyberbullying, and cyberchondria, as well as developmental aspects of problematic Internet use (Chapters 12–16).

Section 4 addresses Internet interventions, ranging from online psychotherapy to mobile phone apps and to virtual reality adjuncts to psychotherapy; online interventions for problematic use of the Internet, health policy to mitigate problematic use of the Internet and ethical considerations are also included (Chapters 18–21).

Specifically, this chapter will help the reader:

(1) learn how to set goals toward quality outcomes and be efficient and patient-centered using technology,
(2) adapt to technological components and processes used by clinicians and systems,
(3) consider how systems are designed and tailored to collect data, inform decisions, and evaluate outcomes, and
(4) set priorities in line with clinician, team, system, and institutional/organizational technological competencies for care.

Setting goals to achieve value and quality in practice and the role of technology

Innovation with technology is only as good as the evidence base that supports it, and the evidence-based approaches used by clinicians to provide care, as well as the process/quality improvement and evaluation of outcomes by a health-care system. Technology serves to efficiently collect data to show that quality care was provided, but to date, most of the technology deployed to assess quality has focused on process metrics (e.g., productivity, errors, cost) and many forces besides payment (e.g., population health, economic cost analyses, the linkage between health and other social progress) are propelling the shift to outcome metrics across the world.

Advances in the collection and analysis of big data hold promise to advance BH practice and research. Much of this work aims toward achieving personalized BH interventions, which started in high-income countries and are taking root around the globe (see Chapter 3) (Aung et al., 2017; Naslund, Aschbrenner, Araya, et al., 2017). At a minimum, the treatment of mental illness relies on subjective measurement for diagnosis, treatment/intervention and long-term monitoring. At a maximum, a variety of sensors and wearables offer new options for patient care, clinician decision-making, and population health—via mobile phones and other smart devices. This technology more precisely assesses and captures human behavior through continuous monitoring and can enable personalized digital interventions aligned with clinical outcomes. These options can reduce geographical cost and temporal barriers, with privacy and professionalism risks that are reasonable (Ahuja, Hanlon, Chisholm, et al., 2019; Torous & Roberts, 2017).

Health-care clinics and hospitals can help by identifying BH domains or targets to assess (Hilty, Torous, et al., 2020). Standard quality reporting metrics in the United States come from the Center for Medicare and Medicaid Services (CMS) and National Quality Forum (i.e., G-PRO), as well as the International Consortium for Health Outcomes Measurement (ICHOM), which outlines international standards of health outcome assessment in BH care (Obbarius, van Maasakkers, Baer, et al., 2017). The Mental Health Atlas of 2017 shows discrepancies in availability of data on BH, with almost a quarter of all countries in the African region reporting "no regular collection of BH data in the last 2 years" (World Health Organization, 2017b). To improve monitoring and transparency, in 2014 the Organization of Economic Corporation and Development recommended a list of BH indicators, including those measuring: readmissions; case management and mortality with severe mental disorders; anticholinergic and antidepressant drugs with elderly patients; continuity of care and timeliness of ambulatory follow-up after hospitalization; use of antidepressant medication and visits during the acute phase of treatment; and racial and ethnic disparities and BH follow up rates (Organisation of Economic Corporation and Development, 2014).

In low- and middle-income countries (LIMCs), the lack of BH data from primary care limits the scale-up of community mental health programmes (Ajuah, Shidhaye, Semrau, et al., 2018; Cohen, Eaton, Radtke, et al., 2011). This information gap is responded to by the formulation of contextualized BH indicators, for example, a minimum set of frequently endorsed indicators were codesigned using a Delphi study across five LMICs. These indicators measure mental health coverage and performance covering domains such as needs, utilization, quality, and financial risk protection (Ajuah et al., 2018). While evaluating the use of these new indicators in LMICs, interviewees perceived that new and simpler BH forms led to a better collection of data, monitoring, and documentation (Ajuah et al., 2018; Proctor et al., 2010). Iterative development with input helps with prioritization, customization, and coordination for health and governmental systems (Hilty, Torous, et al., 2020).

Important clinical and administrative outcomes include no-show rates, percentage of treatments completed over time, and proportion of first-time patients presenting for follow-up visits within recommended time frames. Stable, simple and standard measures can directly shape quality evaluation and clinical decision-making—with input by patients on selection and alignment with regulatory and payor metrics and can avoid complexity and burdening care participants. The forms and results should appear in clinician notes to inform decision-making—meaning EHR compatibility is key. The level of knowledge, competence, confidence, and motivation of health workers affects the likelihood of implementation and sustainability (Proctor et al., 2010).

Use of technology for clinical care requires a careful assessment of the type, its feasibility and its fit with a purpose/goal (e.g., need to learn, treatment plan). BH-related, technology-based services exist on a continuum (Table 2.1): Internet information—self-help/support groups and psychoeducation classes—self-assessment and care (e.g., depression)—informal online consultation with a clinician—formal online evaluation with a questionnaire, completion of an app-based mood questionnaire or asynchronous but structured clinical interview—to continuous monitoring fed to clinicians for decisions—video consultation or management—and combinations of the above technologies or with in-person services (i.e., hybrid care) (Hilty, Chan, Torous, et al., 2015; Hilty, Torous, et al., 2020).

Table 2.1 A continuum of technology use in health and clinical care: issues for patients and clinicians.

Level	Source/entry	Initiator goals/aims	Questions and perspectives	Liabilities	Suggestions for programs
1	Website information	Health information: gain perspective, obtain standard, and updated info	Do I need more information? How should I approach the problem? What is out there? Better if referred by clinician who has checked it out	Quality of information and lack of regulation	Provide training on how to evaluate sites and to identify good ones; how to screen for patients' use
2	Online educational materials and self-directed assessment	Person/patient: education, tips to reflect, and make changes Caregiver: education, tips, supports, and advice Clinician: give assignments to care participants	I learn easier this way and I can do good things on my own. What is the next step? I need "sound" info to make decisions for loved ones Patients need "good" sites to get information	Some prefer in-person interaction Not all problems can be self-assessed Limited time to check sites out for quality	Provide advice on good options, how to evaluate the materials, and help patients do likewise Supplement clinical care options
3	Support/chat groups or "communities"	Spontaneous, anonymity, gain answers/tips, and greater perspective Socialization and networking	What should/can I do? What are others doing locally, regionally, or globally? Can I connect easier with others?	Peer compatibility? Information quality? Who is talking on the other end?	Provide curricula in general and how to use at specific clinical sites (e.g., inpatient unit, outpatient care)

4	Social media (SM)/ networking	Person/patient/ caregiver: easy, convenient, and spontaneous Clinician: rarely use; could screen if/what patients are doing, why and impact All: if purposeful and focused on one dimension, it could add to relationship	Can impact therapeutic alliance positively/ negatively Public information may be visible; it cannot be collected for analysis, though Discuss, weigh pros/ cons, address privacy, when to use/not use (e.g., SI) and tracking (if any) Not billable care	Not HIPAA compliant? Undisclosed and/or impulsive use may indicate problems and boundary issues? Personal/professional role diffusion?	Provide skills, knowledge and approaches in curriculum and with case conferences Focus on developing professional role in transition from past personal experience(s)
5	Assisted self-care assessment and decision-making; de-identified	Person/patient/ caregiver: feel ownership of care with a "consult" by a clinician Clinician: distributes my time with help from others and empowers patients	Empowering, in general, and increased self-efficacy/confidence Other team members can help (e.g., mid-levels) Do I have time to discuss issues with patient? Is there time to train team and share decision-making?	Occasional "bad" decision or poor outcome, partly due to lack of context? Doing more without time/quality is a risk?	Provide training on how to screen what patients are doing and when to seek help, and when to make decisions together

Continued

Table 2.1 Continued

Level	Source/entry	Initiator goals/aims	Questions and perspectives	Liabilities	Suggestions for programs
6	eConsult between primary care provider (PCP) and specialist: email or consult within electronic health record (EHR)	PCP (pediatrician, family medicine, nurse practitioner, obstetrician): timely to visit, sense of completion in requests in time	What are the things this is good for?	These may not work for some medium and most severe patient cases	Embed in EHR and monitor timeliness, follow-up implementation and quality control
		Specialist: simple questions (e.g., facts, steps to do) can be answered; avoids setup of video or time to talk	Though I can send a consult quickly, when will I hear back and how is my system helping me remember to follow-up? If I work longitudinally with consultees and a team, they learn over time	These take time to clarify question, review chart and outline plan; easier to talk?	Build into care workflow and culture of care
7	Asynchronous video or one-time synchronous consultation	Person/patient/caregiver: obtain good quality tips for primary provider to use Clinician: distributes time well with help from others and empowers patients	Feels good about getting "better" care; glad primary provider gets an opinion Primary provider learns and develops relationship with psychiatrist?	Can primary provider use tips? They will work for which patients? Learning curve takes some time?	Build into the regular care continuum, like an option on a stepped continuum

8	Asynchronous, longitudinal, between-session patient-clinician contact (e.g., mobile app, e-mail/text, wearable sensor)	Person/patient/caregiver has minor question, forgot a question, or needs a detail Clinician: good for quick advice and simple details All: send/assign apps, questionnaires, reports (e.g., individualized educational plans); use screening/follow-up surveys to track	Convenient to reach the clinician or team member? Easier for teen patients, who prefer texting over calling? Build into the EHR?	Some patients and/or clinicians do not use? Things taken out of context; errors? HIPAA compliant?	Provide training across the curriculum; boost at core training sites; enhance with subspecialty (e.g., child) Faculty development suggested for patient and trainee e-mail/text
9	Continuous mobile health/e-monitoring to database/EHR (e.g., Chronoform)	Person/patient/caregiver agrees Clinician: good for longitudinal monitoring All: set triggers to accelerate care prn; captured in EHR	Is the contact tracked, private, documented and billable? Patient feels glad to be tracked and sense of bigger care plan? Integration with decision-making takes preparation and extra time?	Some see as a nuisance (i.e., extra time) Best in systematic care models with team-based approach?	Team training, coordination, communication, and documentation is important
10	Synchronous or in-person ongoing care	Person/patient: it works and is much more convenient Clinician: if patients like it, it is a good option	Allows synchronous decision-making (patient-clinician); links providers (e.g., primary care psychiatry)	It always has to be scheduled (and paid for); not spontaneous	Provide curriculum, and other experiences

Components and processes of systems used by clinicians

Overview

Evaluation of clinical practice has become increasingly important in *both* the provision of a service *and* demonstration of quality care and improved patient health outcomes. A philosophical shift has occurred from efficacy-based interventions—often under ideal conditions or research protocols—to translational and effective interventions, based on implementation science (i.e., acceptability, adoption, feasibility, cost, sustainability) (Gargon et al., 2019; World Health Organization, 2017a). Methodologies are needed for the development, implementation, and evaluation (quantitative, qualitative) of a technology. Key steps suggested for institutions to integrate video apply to other technologies: (1) assess readiness; (2) create/hardwire the culture; (3) write policies and procedures; (4) establish the curriculum and competencies; (5) train learners and faculty; and (6) evaluate/manage change (Luxton, 2016).

Structural approaches

EHRs. EHRs may be a good example for considering barriers that may interfere with the successful implementation of technology. For users, menu-based user interfaces have been cumbersome, but are evolving into more intuitive graphical interfaces. CPR and integrated voice-recognition software are usually time-saving after the initial investment of time to learn it. For CPRs that require physician typing for data entry and analysis, patient engagement (e.g., eye contact) and rapport may be affected (Hendrickson, Melton, & Pitt, 2019; Shanafelt et al., 2016). EHR guidelines are aimed at preparing clinical practices for reporting within the new health-care delivery and payment models.

   Dictation. Dictation with voice recognition is increasingly common and reduces administrative support costs. While it is a significant adjustment for some clinicians, for systems the costs pay for themselves compared to alternatives (i.e., computer equipment, time, support staff). There are challenges of integration with legacy systems, billing systems, and practice management systems. An undeveloped area appears to be using video and audio dictations more purposely in workflow (e.g., replacing a specialist text e-consultation with a video, since it is more engaging, memorable, synthetic, and user friendly) (Hilty, Randhawa, Maheu, et al., 2020; Hilty, Torous, et al., 2020).

   Kiosks and tablets. Not all clinicians and patients are interested in or able to use their an EHR patient portal due to inexperience with technology, or limited access to high-speed Internet (a common challenge in underserved communities, particularly in rural or low-resource areas, as well as in many regions in LMICs). A popular alternative is to have kiosks within the reception area of the practice where patients can easily complete targeted patient-reported outcomes using a touch screen. These have been used for diagnosis and treatment of depression and alcohol use disorders in primary care clinics in rural and urban settings in Colombia (Torrey, Cepeda, Castro, et al., 2020).

Patient portals. A way to assess outcomes is *a patient portal*, which is a secure electronic website that gives patients access to parts of their EHR within a clinician's EHR. One can administer questionnaires and surveys to patients through these portals, which streamlines assessment, treatment, and integration of patient-reported outcomes.

Functional technologies

e-Consultation (i.e., e-consult or eConsult). This generally involves a primary care provider (PCP) referral for a consultation related to questions about patient care that are outside of their expertise (Archibald, Stratton, Liddy, et al., 2018; Liddy, Drosinis, & Keely, 2016). It requires basic hardware, software, and integration within the EHR, with substantial practice, quality and process improvement supports. e-Consultation resulted in reduced wait times for patients, lower costs, fewer in-person visits, and high satisfaction by users. Store-and-forward/asynchronous technology (ATP). Store-and-forward technologies have been used for dermatology, radiology, and many other specialties—the specialist interprets an image or a video interview for BH while incorporating clinical history from the referring physician—and gives the PCP a plan to implement (Shanafelt et al., 2016). ATP has outcomes comparable to video consultation and can enable collaborative and integrated care (Hilty, Torous, et al., 2020; Yellowlees, Burke Parish, González, et al., 2018).

E-mail. There appear to be several advantages to e-mail interviewing, particularly with young populations, is cost-effective and offers flexibility (Cleary & Walter, 2011). It also provides a transcript for analysis and offers time to reflect on questions, compose answers, and respond at leisure in the comfort of familiar home surroundings. Challenges include verification of self-report, potentially compromised rapport due to lack of visual and auditory cues, privacy, and issues around quality control in studies (e.g., participants' comprehension levels).

Text. Text-based, chat and social media communication pose opportunities and challenges in terms of content and process issues (Hilty, Randhawa, et al., 2020). Mobile health interventions are used in many ways (e.g., reminders, 14%; information, 17%; supportive messages, 42%; self-monitoring procedures, 42%) (Berrouiguet, Baca-García, Brandt, et al., 2016). As keyboard characters have limitations for text, emoticons have been used since 1982 to enrich communication and comprehension (Aldunate & González-Ibáñez, 2017), though they are not always used in a standard way, particularly across cultures (Hilty, Randhawa, et al., 2020).

Apps. A review of apps found scant evidence-based treatment content, few comprehensive anxiety self-management apps and few advanced features that leverage the broader functionalities of smartphone capabilities (e.g., sensors, ecological momentary assessments) (Bry, Chou, Miguel, et al., 2018; Chan, Li, Torous, Gratzer, et al., 2018). The child, adolescent, and family literature show significant research on apps and text interventions related to appointment reminders, treatment adherence, well-being, suicide, and other clinically related topics (Pisani, Wyman, Gurditta, et al., 2018).

Sensors and wearables. Wearable sensors are usually wireless, miniature circuits embedded in patches or bandages, wristbands, rings, or shirts (e.g., smartwatches, heart rate monitors, and smart glasses) (L'Hommedieu, L'Hommedieu, Begay, et al., 2019). These enable the collection of behavioral data, detection, symptom monitoring, accessing, and sharing of data, and providing interventions (Aung et al., 2017). This transforms care by moving from cross-sectional, manual transfer of data to an integrated, longitudinal, minimally intrusive and interactive sharing of data that is based on the ecology of a person or patient in their natural settings, using EMA methods (The National Academy of Sciences, Engineering, and Medicine. Health and Medicine Division, 2020) (see Chapter 4).

Picking the right technologies and models of care and integrating them into practice

How does one best integrate technologies into clinical practice? The application of telehealth modalities to one's practice requires reflection and purpose, discussion with patients, and staying up on the rapidly changing literature. Overarching goals in the integration of technology include *improving access* to care in terms of geography, time, and transportation; *triaging patients* if they need to be seen in between appointments; providing *adjunctive support* to in-person services, and *improving efficiency and continuity* of care. The specific needs and goals, preferences on what technology to use and the requisite behaviors/skills and targeted outcomes can vary among the users: patients; primary care teams; and specialists (Table 2.2). In vivo training on technology can enable the clinician to "fit" the technology with the patient's need, develop a good digital relationship and iteratively improve the process (Fig. 2.2).

(1) *The patient.* Depending on comfort, familiarity with technology and/or the clinician, the individual patient may have varying degrees of receptiveness and skill (i.e., e-literacy). The patient's willingness to engage and favorable opinion may determine the success and effectiveness of the implementation. A social support system consisting of individuals who can assist them with this decision and in navigating the new technology is also helpful.

(2) *The disease and context.* The technology must be appropriate and effective for the course of treatment of the disease. For example, a condition like schizophrenia may be suited to at-home monitoring, if examinations and procedures (e.g., long-acting antipsychotic injections) can be done. Though often very ill, individuals living with schizophrenia should not be excluded from improving quality of life from exercising an online support group chat (Chan et al., 2018; Hilty, Chan, et al., 2015).

(3) *The clinician.* Before offering care accompanied by in-person services with technology, the clinician must ensure that they have the expertise, time, and resources to provide quality and consistent care as is promised and expected through the new modality.

(4) *Cultural factors.* Compassionate care that is competent, and safe—and provided from a place of humility—is increasingly recognized as an instrumental part of health care, including via technology like video (Hilty, Feliberti, Evangelatos, et al., 2018), mobile health (Hilty, Maheu, et al., 2018), and other technologies (Luo et al., 2006). Digital care should be culturally safe—meaning that it aligns with the preferences and values of the recipient of care, as judged by that person rather than by the provider. The corollary for providers is assuming a stance of cultural humility, a reflexive approach as an other-oriented learner, rather than focusing on the development of a competent professional identity (Indigenous Physicians Association of Canada, 2019). Racial and ethnic minorities and marginalized

Table 2.2 Goals and skills for patients, primary care teams, and specialists to use asynchronous technology for behavioral health care.

Patient care	Patient	PC team member	Specialist
Assessment/ evaluation (e.g., text)	Learn from personal experience and via health-care visits	Patient care planning	Include SP/device, apps and other technologies in informed consent
Consent	Reflect on purpose for use	Use a screening questionnaire to assess text use OR	Elicit history/screen for personal vs health-care use
History	Log/diary information?	Have a Team member ask a few screening questions	Use privacy settings
Engagement and communication	Send information to health-care team for their use?	Consider factors to decide if should use text before proceeding	All: reflect and weigh impact
Administration and documentation	Communicate with health-care team: get information or make a decision	Time, skills, and knowhow to use text?	Positives vs negatives?
Medicolegal: privacy, safety, data protection/ integrity, and security	Weigh relative value compared to other technology	Can text be built into information flow (e.g., EHR)?	Impact on care: communication
	If used, what is(are) the purpose(s) for health care?	How do we use text with patients and specialist consultants?	Text vs other technologies
	Does clinic and/ or health system support text use or not?	If used, what is main purpose: log, send or obtain information?	Clarify with patient and PC team about effective communication Instruct on best ways to use an app An evidence-based app with An evidence-based approach Simplicity with purpose
Assessment/ evaluation (e.g., e-consultation)	Learn about it and weigh vs other options (i.e., in-person or video with specialist)	Goals: gain knowledge and skill with CDS for assessment and treatment	Help learners and staff to use decision support tools based on evidence

Continued

Table 2.2 Continued

Patient care	Patient	PC team member	Specialist
	If used, could feel good that the PCP has access to specialists to e-mail, telephone, e-consult, and/or refer for synchronous or in-person care	Gain technical assistance on safety/risk and contingency plan	Research/disseminate procedures to prevent problems and manage workflow
		Triage urgent/emergent issues to synchronous option	Advise on specific specialty consultations with relative/absolute contraindications
		Quickly diagnose and treat to improve system's capacity	Train/supervise to optimize assessment (e.g., preconsult information, tests)
Assessment/evaluation (e.g., asynchronous video or store-and-forward)	Easy to use and glad that PCP confers with a specialist	Clinical care considerations	Train/consult PC team members to improve assessment, triage, and interventions
	Less travel and it gets done faster	What skills are needed?	Diagnostic tests
	Go through a guided interview and add things here and there that provide context (e.g., narrative, verbal and nonverbal behaviors)	What technology is needed?	Concurrent care management
		Training in semistructured interviewing for reliability and validity to improve my (or PC team member's) skills, as well as our workflow	
		Many synchronous video consults are not needed	ATP psychiatrist needs training related to
			Clinical workflow Primary care setting Security, privacy and confidentiality Team-leading, if applicable

Table 2.2   Continued

Patient care	Patient	PC team member	Specialist
Management/ treatment planning (e.g., secure e-mail and text)	Good ways to use e-mail and text if privacy ensured	Care	Select "best" mode for a given task: SP/device and/or apps, e-mail/ text, telephone and/or in-person
Use tools within EHR for clinical decision support (CDS)	Follow-up details needed	Triage simple and/or sequential workflow to target goal; triage complex, urgent/ emergent issues to synchronous option	Triage complex, urgent/emergent issues to synchronous (telephone, in-person) care
Use "best practice" with evidence-based approaches	Send additional documents/ information or complete questionnaires	Obtain clinical information for CDS for assessment/ treatment	Give technical assistance on safety/ risk (e.g., medication) and offer a back-up plan
Monitor and improve	Engage loved one to help	Consultation: gaining knowledge, skill development	Prioritize SP/D and app options, e-mail and tools that integrate into the EHR
	Capture day-to-day accurate accounts of life (e.g., mood, functioning, activity)	Apply knowledge into practice	Learn/teach pre- and intraplatform data feeds (e.g., questionnaire upload) into EHR to improve quality of care and be efficient
	To "stay in contact" with a nurse, mid- level and/or PCP	Gain technical assistance on safety/ risk and back-up plans	
Administrative Issues	Keep information up-to-date	Develop standard consent form, treatment plan and other procedures	Seek input from users to plan
Workflow and documentation	Review patient portal and communicate needs	Adhere to clinic, health system and professional requirements	Help administrators to
Medicolegal: privacy, safety, data protection/ integrity and security	Learn safeguards for privacy, security and confidentiality	Identify and adhere to laws and regulations in the jurisdiction(s) of practice and of that of the patient	Develop language for documentation

Continued

Table 2.2   Continued

Patient care	Patient	PC team member	Specialist
	Use secure forms of communication (e.g., secure e-mail within EHR not Gmail)	Obtain clinical and legal advice	Adapt current practices
			Develop policies/procedures
			Teach/consult
			Adapt legal/regulatory principles
			Assess fit of technology for users
Human factors			
Communication	Be flexible	Be flexible	Teach on scope of communication with technology to clarify expectations and anticipate problems (e.g., feasibility of checking mH device at other sites, clinics)
Attitude	Be brief, clear and spell out communications	Role model willingness to improve	Educate/consult colleagues about asynchronous technology use
Cultural/diversity	Clarify if issues are unclear	Discuss scope, timing and agreed upon plan(s) for use	Clarify expectations with questions about culture
Social determinants	Able to discuss my culture, language and other matters related to use of technologies	Triage to other technology, if needed	Adjust care to culture and preferences, using generalizations not stereotypes
Special populations	Do not want to be stereotyped	Consider preferences	Teach/consult to PC team on cultural complexities to achieve outcomes
		Ask about impact of culture and diversity on use and preferences	

Table 2.2 Continued

Patient care	Patient	PC team member	Specialist
		Promote reflection and discussion; make adjustments and manage language impact	
		Generalize across generations and cultures	

Abbreviations: Application = app; (video); Aysnchronous telepsychiatry = ATP; Electronic health record = EHR; Mobile health = mH; Mental/behavioral health = BH; primary care provider = PCP. Smartphone = SP.

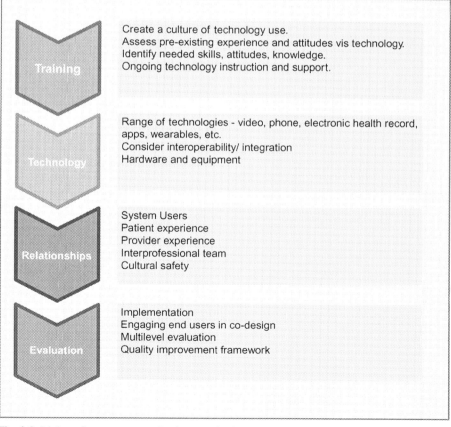

Fig. 2.2 Linkage between person/patient needs, therapeutic relationships, technology, training and evaluation.

populations can be engaged for input about technological fluency, health literacy, language, social, economic, and other cultural issues, and support integration of technology into their care (Doshi, Aseltine, Sabina, et al., 2017; Torous & Roberts, 2017).

Models of care

Another key issue is selecting the best model of care for a patient or population. Models of telepsychiatric care have been framed into low, moderate, or high-intensity levels of care by updating previous work (Hilty, Rabinowitz, McCarron, et al., 2018). The intensity levels are based on patient acuity, technology complexity, specialist time, and the designated primary provider (i.e., a PCP with a secondary telepsychiatrist vs a telepsychiatrist). Low-intensity interventions involve specialists working with PCPs by telephone, text, or e-mail (doctor-to-doctor "curbside" consultations; case reviews) (Hilty, Rabinowitz, et al., 2018). Moderate intensity service interventions usually include a specialist assessment of the patient by specialist via video consultation to adjust PCP diagnoses, develop treatment plans (e.g., ATP), or augment treatment (Hilty, Rabinowitz, et al., 2018; Yellowlees et al., 2018). High-intensity interventions with video include team-based care via collaborative care and stepped care (Hilty, Rabinowitz, et al., 2018).

AI and big data

CDS via AI

Traditional applications of clinical decision support technology that have existed for decades, such as EHRs and expert systems, are being enhanced by newer technologies, such as cloud computing, artificial intelligence (AI), machine learning (ML), and signal processing algorithms (i.e., neural networks, random forests, support vector machines, natural language processing; NLP) (The National Academy of Sciences, Engineering, and Medicine. Health and Medicine Division, 2020). These technologies enable context-aware, live streaming of data, and real-time feedback to enhance the assessment of clinical, lifestyle, and social activities (Shatte, Hutchinson, & Teague, 2019). Temporal modeling leverages dynamical information and extends methods across multiple decision time points, so clinicians iteratively reevaluate, intervene, and make new observations and sequentially make decisions (Greenes, Bates, Kawamoto, et al., 2018; The National Academy of Sciences, Engineering, and Medicine. Health and Medicine Division, 2020). Computing tools can also improve structure, process, and synergy with the way clinicians approach their work (Aung et al., 2017).

Clinicians can monitor, intervene and follow trajectories longitudinally, often with quality of life and economic cost dimensions (Aung et al., 2017). Current studies are investigating smartphone, biological and clinical data to identify markers of risk, diagnosis, state, stage, treatment response, and prognosis in different populations. Virtual reality is safe and can be used to assist researchers in the assessment of neurocognitive function and in capturing impairments associated with psychotic spectrum disorders (Hilty, Randhawa, et al., 2020; Rus-Calafell, Garety, Sason, et al., 2018). Apps and smartphones automatically and quickly collect a variety of "big data" with significant complexity that could provide opportunities for observation, exploration, and hypothesis generation (Torous & Baker, 2016). These approaches can help with patient engagement and enrollment across a variety of international and culturally diverse populations (e.g., age, disorder, ethnicity, generation, immigrant, military, refugee).

New research approaches could reshape lifestyles and health care. AI methods (e.g., computational methods using statistical and mathematical algorithms), nanotechnology and other technologies have the capability to collect, build, and model person-specific, intelligently filtered information presented in a timely manner. It is also possible to explore the link between objectively measured behavioral features [e.g., phone usage, mood rating, short message service (SMS) text messages], location, and social interaction data for patients (e.g., depression) (Faurholt-Jepsen, Munkholm, Frost, et al., 2016). More broadly, digital phenotyping or behavioral markers are being developed for both clinical and nonclinical populations to correlate multimodal sensor data, cognitions and changes in mood. Analyzing large amounts of data will require close collaboration between partners from diverse areas of expertise, such as researchers, clinicians, statisticians, software developers, and engineers (see Chapter 5).

The internet and social media

Internet users seek information on a wide range of diseases or medical problems, treatments or procedures, doctors or other health professionals, and other health-related topics; this includes many caregivers, too (Hilty, Chan, et al., 2015) (see Chapter 3). Teenagers may have few traditional care options and feel more comfortable sharing experiences and try to learn new behaviors anonymously or at a distance. At times, they may express ideas of self-harm and negative affective states, which is concerning if these things are not shared with parents and/or professionals (Hilty, Armstrong, et al., 2020). Anxiety, trauma (e.g., military personnel), and patients with psychotic disorders use the Internet for seeking information related to their illness and medication (Hilty, Chan, et al., 2015) and connecting with others who share similar conditions and experiences (Naslund, Aschbrenner, McHugo, et al., 2019).

Research using social media data is measuring self-report of key symptoms (e.g., suicidal ideation, sexting) and evaluating social media content for diagnostic and predictive analysis. Models assess affect, linguistic style, and context with supervised learning algorithms, random forests, and machine learning to discriminate between healthy, depressed and posttraumatic stress disorder populations (Reece, Reagan, Lix, et al., 2017). Postpartum depression was predicted from a model related to increased social isolation and decreased social capital (i.e., less activity, interaction); this was manifested by fewer status updates, media items, and reaching out to friends compared to others and usual personal patterns (De Choudhury, Counts, Horvitz, et al., 2014). Social media offer popular venues for sharing personal experiences, seeking information, and offering peer-to-peer support among individuals living with mental illness; yet caution is warranted regarding safety, privacy, and viability of these platforms to characterize BH conditions and provide evidence-based services (Naslund, Bondre, Torous, et al., 2020). There may be other risks, too, as research since 2010 shows that teenagers spend more time on new media screen activities, less time on television, and less time on nonscreen activities—and depressive symptoms, suicide-related outcomes, and suicide deaths increased during this period after a long plateau (Twenge, Joiner, Rogers, et al., 2018).

Clinician, team, system, and institutional/organizational competencies

Competency-based medical education (CBME) focuses on skill development and curricula to produce desired outcomes for learners rather than knowledge acquisition (Frank, Mungroo, Ahmad, et al., 2010). Competency frameworks used by faculty, program directors and administrators include the Royal College CanMEDS and US Accreditation Council of Graduate Medical Education (Aung et al., 2017; Hilty, Armstrong, et al., 2020; Hilty, Chan, et al., 2019a, 2019b; Hilty, Crawford, et al., 2015; Hilty, Maheu, et al., 2018; Hilty, Torous, et al., 2020; Hilty, Zalpuri, et al., 2018; Zalpuri et al., 2018). Skill assessment is also a priority of the IOM's Bridge to Quality, "which called on the health professions to examine and redesign future education with PCC, interdisciplinary teams, quality improvement approaches, and informatics " (Institute of Medicine, 2001).

Clinicians' skills need to be adapted from in-person and video care to a wide range of technologies (Tables 2.1 and 2.2). Training for technology should include, but not be limited to: (1) use of medical libraries; (2) use of information technology for Internet-based searches and other work; (3) literature, drug information, and other databases; and (4) video, telephone, mobile health, and other technologies. Active participation, as appropriate, in educational courses, conferences, and other organized educational activities at both local and national level from boards, professional organizations and other institutions *should* be more skills-focused, interactive and fun for learners and use technology. Skill targets, teaching, and assessment methods and observation by faculty help to ensure skill development rather than assuming learners will develop the skills—all of these things are part of building an e-culture for care (Fig. 2.3).

IT, IS, AI, ML, and other informatics topics are increasingly added to the competency sets across technologies, particularly wearable sensors (Aung et al., 2017), and other asynchronous technologies (Hilty, Torous, et al., 2020). Specifically, mobile health competencies should include CDS, prudent selection of technology and management of the flow of information across an EHR platform (Hilty, Chan, et al., 2019a; Hilty, Zalpuri, et al., 2018). The informatics skill/expertise and communication roles were expanded to educational (e.g., using resources for searches, publishing) and administrative/practice management capacity (e.g., licensure, jurisdictional, liability, and prescribing requirements) (Torous, Chan, Boland, et al., 2017).

Fig. 2.3 Dimensions of creating an e-culture for use of technology in clinical care and training.

Many health systems are still working on basic clinical, technological, and administrative workflow, and may benefit from institutional level competencies to prepare to implement new technologies: (1) assess readiness; (2) create/hardwire the culture; (3) write policies and procedures; (4) establish the curriculum and competencies; (5) train learners and faculty; and (6) evaluate/manage change (Hilty, Torous, et al., 2020; Luxton, 2016). Key participants include patients, trainees, faculty and leaders; teams across professions and systems within the institution; and organizational leaders who set priorities and distribute resources (Table 2.3). While both synchronous and asynchronous telepsychiatry services offer numerous benefits, ongoing research is needed to better understand the costs of these technologies for BH, particularly for implementation across diverse settings and integration into existing payment models and healthcare financing (Naslund, Mitchell, Joshi, et al., 2020).

Table 2.3 Competencies for institutions and health-care organizations for synchronous and asynchronous telehealth.

Competency focus	Shifts for synchronous care	Shifts for asynchronous care
Patient-centered care	Educate on in-person and synchronous similarities	Offer selected options (e.g., apps, wearable sensors)
– Screening	Use as one of many care models/treatment options	Design clinical technology workflows
– Points-of-entry	Use templates and adjust policies and procedures	Import social science, health behavior and business ideas
– Teams		
– Data approach		
Evaluation and outcomes	Build video scheduled and on demand options	Organize care on a technology platform (e.g., electronic health record, pre- and postloads)
– Readiness for change	Use disease state measures and adapt, if applicable, aligned with in-person accreditation	Use technology-specific measures, evidence based if available
– Link outcomes with evidence base	Use 360 evaluation	Use 360 evaluation
– Measures and benchmarks		Use artificial intelligence, machine learning and data analytics
Trainee/Student Needs/ Roles	Integrate skill development, care, teaching, supervision	Use quantitative and qualitative approaches
– Learner-centered	Monitor well-being and professionalism	Use observation, video, and simulation
– Resource management	Adjust curricula (e.g., part-time rotations, supervision)	Role model healthy behaviors
– Lifelong learning	Employ quality measures	Capitalize on personal expertise to spur others' use
Clinical care, teaching, and leadership roles	Monitor technology impact on care, well-being/fatigue	Use sustainable, longitudinal approaches
– Skills and attitudes	Integrate part-time use for care, with teaching by champions	Remember that "less is more" and evidence base is key
– Professionalism	Define success based on teams, systems, and populations	Use technology for portfolio, curricula, dissemination, networking, and other purposes
– Technology leader		
– Human factors		

Table 2.3   Continued

Competency focus	Shifts for synchronous care	Shifts for asynchronous care
Teams, professions, and systems	Foster alignment across systems	Align shared outcomes
Assess structure and function	Organize goals and outcomes for success based on teams, systems and professions	Patient/clinician outcomes
Projects to develop skills and culture	Employ team-based care and virtual teams	Learner/teacher
	Use stepped care and interprofessional principles	Clinic/system
		Institution/community
Organizational priorities and resources	Use professional development projects for existing/new leaders, as a gateway to others (e.g., mobile health)	Assess context, pace, scope and drive of/for change
Governance and change	Measure technology in performance evaluations and provide feedback	Monitor private, federal, state, and other sectors for best practices, partner agencies, and grant funding
Human resources	Add or distribute funding and infrastructure for pilot and full-scale projects, to impact health service delivery, and training programs, particularly in the community	Strive for incremental, sustainable solutions
Institutional, community, and societal perspectives		Adapt evidence-based system approaches
Partnerships		Develop strategies for promoting adoption/optimization of clinical information systems

Discussion

E-platforms have traditionally distributed academic networks of like-minded researchers and clinicians into regional health information organizations (Yellowlees, Hogarth, & Hilty, 2006). These empower consumers and clinicians in day-to-day health-care delivery by improving access to evidence-based information at the point of care; facilitate the delivery of a wider range of health services, particularly to primary, and community care; provide accurate data to support research and clinical policy and governance arrangements; and ensure a sustainable, secure, reliable electronic environment, underpinned by strong, policy-driven protections for privacy and other medicolegal matters (Yellowlees et al., 2006).

Many organizations are still reluctant to change, in general, and specifically related to technology despite telemedicine's impact (Hilty, Torous, et al., 2020), and internationally, this tends to appear in three problem areas: (1) technology infrastructure; (2) policy, human resource, and health governance challenges for BH management IS (e.g., data collection, reporting, and dissemination) and infrastructure (e.g., experts, technical support, supervision); (3) inadequate inclusion of BH care in budgets, in general, and limited efforts to integrate BH into medical settings; and (4) limited emphasis on program implementation and sustainability (Mugisha, Abdulmalik, Hanlon, et al., 2017; Upadhaya, Jordans, Abdulmalik, et al., 2016). Greater attention is given to control and eradication of infectious diseases and conditions associated with reproductive, maternal, and child health, as well as to disaster response.

Successful implementation of BH indicators is dependent on their evidence base, and importantly is a function of acceptability, feasibility, and sustainability (Gargon et al., 2019). Unconventional and innovative approaches to collect data on BH indicators (e.g., using community health workers, care coordinators, mid-level providers) (Hoeft, Fortney, Patel, et al., 2018; Singla, Kohrt, Murray, et al., 2017) show promise for integrating BH care in primary care settings. Referred to as task sharing, training nonspecialist providers like community health workers is a robust approach—along with using technology—for scaling up capacity and making evidence-based BH services more available in both higher and lower income countries (Naslund, Gonsalves, Gruebner, et al., 2019; Raviola, Naslund, Smith, et al., 2019). There remain barriers to measuring new BH indicators related to the time consumed in recording (e.g., the severity of illness, functionality), overstretched health workers, poor coordination within and across departments and poor service delivery (Proctor et al., 2010). At the organizational level, utilization-focused evaluation may reduce uncertainties, improve effectiveness, and inform decisions on the goals, concerns, and perspectives of stakeholders (Hilty, Feliberti, et al., 2018; Luo et al., 2006).

Progressive businesses have integrated core business divisions—research and development, operations, marketing and finance—with an IT division (i.e., a shared IT-business framework) to leverage knowledge and capital (Ray, Muhanna, & Barney, 2007). This paradigm has been applied to video as a way to organize/integrate health care rather than adding technology to existing systems (i.e., IT-business-health model) (Hilty, Uno, Chan, et al., 2019). This suggests that *organizing* care with technology will have better outcomes than *appending* it to health care (i.e., building "in" user-friendliness and workflow rather than adding steps for patients and clinicians in existing systems) (Hilty, Torous, et al., 2020). Assessment (e.g., e-literacy) and segmentation of target patient groups in the development, testing, and implementation of digital BH interventions may prevent and overcome limitations in existing digital programs (Mohr, Weingardt, Reddy, et al., 2017).

Conclusions

Various technologies are employed for many types of patient-centered care, with information systems, electronic health records, electronic communication, BH indicators, and related digital advances playing instrumental roles in advancing practice and research. Needs assessments to help in developing appropriate outcomes for patients, clinicians, and systems, which then need to be aligned with technological, quality improvement, and other workflows used by health systems. By grasping how systems are designed and tailored to collect data, patients are empowered to make decisions and clinicians benefit from decision support. Setting priorities involves input from all care participants, and patient, clinician, and institutional competencies for skills, attitudes, and behaviors can align missions and stimulate quality improvement.

Acknowledgments

The authors acknowledge support by American Telemedicine Association and the Telemental Health Interest Group; Department of Psychiatry and Behavioral Sciences, University of California, Davis School of Medicine; European Psychiatric Association; Veteran Affairs Northern California Health Care System and Mental Health Service; and World Health Organization and Psychiatric Association.

Conflicts of interest

None.

References

Ahuja, S., Hanlon, C., Chisholm, D., et al. (2019). Experience of implementing new mental health indicators within information systems in six low- and middle-income countries. *BJPsych Open*, 5(5), e71. Published 2019 Aug 6 https://doi.org/10.1192/bjo.2019.29.

Ajuah, S., Shidhaye, R., Semrau, M., et al. (2018). Mental health information systems in resource-challenged countries: Experiences from India. *BJPsych International*, 15(2), 43–46. https://doi.org/10.1192/bji.2017.6.

Aldunate, N., & González-Ibáñez, R. (2017). An integrated review of emoticons in computer-mediated communication. *Frontiers in Psychology*, 6(7), 2061. https://doi.org/10.3389/fpsyg.2016.02061. eCollection, 2016.

Archibald, D., Stratton, J., Liddy, C., et al. (2018). Evaluation of an electronic consultation service in psychiatry for primary care providers. *BMC Psychiatry*, 18(1), 119. https://doi.org/10.1186/s12888-018-1701-3.

Aung, M. H., Matthews, M., & Choudhury, T. (2017). Sensing behavioral symptoms of mental health and delivering personalized interventions using mobile technologies. *Depression and Anxiety*, 34(7), 603–609. https://doi.org/10.1002/da.22646.

Berrouiguet, S., Baca-García, E., Brandt, S., et al. (2016). Fundamentals for future mobile-health (mHealth): A systematic review of mobile phone and web-based text messaging in mental health. *JMIR, 18*(6), e135. https://doi.org/10.2196/jmir.5066.

Bry, L. J., Chou, T., Miguel, E., et al. (2018). Consumer smartphone apps marketed for child and adolescent anxiety: A systematic review and content analysis. *Behavior Therapy, 49*(2), 249–261. https://doi.org/10.1016/j.beth.2017.07.008.

Chan, S., Li, L., Torous, J., Gratzer, D., et al. (2018). Review of use of asynchronous technologies incorporated in mental health care. *Current Psychiatry Reports, 20*(10), 85. Published 2018 Aug 28 https://doi.org/10.1007/s11920-018-0954-3.

Cleary, M., & Walter, G. (2011). Is e-mail communication a feasible method to interview young people with mental health problems? *Journal of Child and Adolescent Psychiatric Nursing, 24*(3), 150–152. https://doi.org/10.1111/j.1744-6171.2010.00257.x.

Cohen, A., Eaton, J., Radtke, B., et al. (2011). Three models of community mental health services in low-income countries. *International Journal of Mental Health Systems, 5*(1), 3. Published 2011 Jan 25 https://doi.org/10.1186/1752-4458-5-3.

Crawford, A., & Serhal, E. (2020). Digital health equity and COVID-19: The innovation curve cannot reinforce the social gradient of health. *Journal of Medical Internet Research, 22*(6), e19361. Published 2020 Jun 2 https://doi.org/10.2196/19361.

Crawford, A., Sunderji, N., López, J., et al. (2016). Defining competencies for the practice of telepsychiatry through an assessment of resident learning needs. *BMC Medical Education, 16*, 28. Published 2016 Jan 26 https://doi.org/10.1186/s12909-016-0529-0.

De Choudhury, M., Counts, S., Horvitz, E., et al. (2014). Characterizing and predicting postpartum depression from shared Facebook data. In *Presented at: 17th ACM conference on Computer supported cooperative work & social computing—CSCW'14; Feb 15–19, 2014; Baltimore, MD, USA* (pp. 626–638). https://doi.org/10.1145/2531602.2531675.

Doshi, R., Aseltine, R. H., Sabina, A. B., et al. (2017). Interventions to improve management of chronic conditions among racial and ethnic minorities. *Journal of Racial and Ethnic Health Disparities, 4*(6), 1033–1041.

Faurholt-Jepsen, M., Munkholm, K., Frost, M., et al. (2016). Electronic self-monitoring of mood using IT platforms in adult patients with bipolar disorder: A systematic review of the validity and evidence. *BMC Psychiatry, 16*(1), 7. https://doi.org/10.1186/s12888-016-0713-0.

Frank, J. R., Mungroo, R., Ahmad, Y., et al. (2010). Toward a definition of competency-based education in medicine: A systematic review of published definitions. *Medical Teacher, 32*(8), 631–637.

Gargon, E., Gorst, S. L., & Williamson, P. R. (2019). Choosing important health outcomes for comparative effectiveness research: 5th annual update to a systematic review of core outcome sets for research. *PLoS One, 14*(12). https://doi.org/10.1371/journal.pone.0225980, e0225980.

Greenes, R. A., Bates, D. W., Kawamoto, K., et al. (2018). Clinical decision support models and frameworks: Seeking to address research issues underlying implementation successes and failures. *Journal of Biomedical Informatics, 78*, 134–143.

Hendrickson, M. A., Melton, G. B., & Pitt, M. B. (2019). The review of systems, the electronic health record, and billing. *Journal of the American Medical Association, 322*(2), 115–116. https://doi.org/10.1001/jama.2019.5667.

Hilty, D. M., Armstrong, C. M., Luxton, D. D., et al. (2020). A scoping review of sensors, wearables and remote monitoring for behavioral health: Uses, outcomes, clinical competencies and research directions. *The Journal of Technology in Behavioral Science, 6*, 278–313.

Hilty, D. M., Chan, S., Torous, J., et al. (2015). New frontiers in healthcare and technology: Internet- and web-based mental options emerge to complement in-person and telepsychiatric care options. *Journal of Health & Medical Informatics, 6*(4), 1–14.

Hilty, D. M., Chan, S., Torous, J., et al. (2019a). A framework for competencies for the use of mobile technologies in psychiatry and medicine. *JMIR Uhealth and Mobile Health, 8*(2). http://mhealth.jmir.org/2020/2/e12229/.

Hilty, D. M., Chan, S., Torous, J., et al. (2019b). A telehealth framework for mobile health, smartphones and apps: Competencies, training and faculty development. *The Journal of Technology in Behavioral Science, 4*(2), 106–123.

Hilty, D. M., Crawford, A., Teshima, J., et al. (2015). A framework for telepsychiatric training and e-health: Competency-based education, evaluation and implications. *International Review of Psychiatry, 27*(6), 569–592.

Hilty, D. M., Feliberti, J., Evangelatos, G., et al. (2018). Competent cultural telebehavioral healthcare to diverse populations: Administration, evaluation, and financing. *The Journal of Technology in Behavioral Science, 4*(3), 186–200.

Hilty, D. M., Maheu, M., Drude, K., et al. (2018). The need to implement and evaluate telehealth competency frameworks to ensure quality care across behavioral health professions. *Academic Psychiatry, 42*(6), 818–824.

Hilty, D. M., Rabinowitz, T. R., McCarron, R. M., et al. (2018). Telepsychiatry and e-mental health models leverage stepped, collaborative, and integrated services to primary care. *Psychosomatics, 59*(3), 227–250.

Hilty, D. M., Randhawa, K., Maheu, M. M., et al. (2020). A review of telepresence, virtual reality and augmented reality applied to clinical care. *The Journal of Technology in Behavioral Science*. https://doi.org/10.1007/s41347-020-00126-x.

Hilty, D. M., Torous, J., Parish, M., et al. (2020). A literature review comparing clinicians' approaches and skills to in-person, synchronous and asynchronous care: Moving toward asynchronous competencies to ensure quality care. *Telemedicine Journal and E-Health*. https://doi.org/10.1089/tmj.2020.0054.

Hilty, D. M., Uno, J., Chan, S., et al. (2019). Role of technology in professional development. *Psychiatric Clinics of North America, 42*, 493–512.

Hilty, D. M., Unutzer, J., Ko, D. K., et al. (2019). Approaches for departments, schools and health systems to better implement technologies used for clinical care and education. *Academic Psychiatry, 43*(6), 611–616.

Hilty, D. M., Zalpuri, I., Stubbe, D., et al. (2018). Social media/networking as part of e-behavioral health and psychiatric education: Competencies, teaching methods, and implications. *The Journal of Technology in Behavioral Science, 3*(4), 268–293.

Hoeft, T. J., Fortney, J. C., Patel, V., et al. (2018). Task-sharing approaches to improve mental health care in rural and other low-resource settings: A systematic review. *The Journal of Rural Health, 34*(1), 48–62. https://doi.org/10.1111/jrh.12229.

Indigenous Physicians Association of Canada. (2019). *First Nations, Inuit, Metis health core competencies*. https://www.ipac-amac.ca/downloads/core-competencies.pdf. Accessed 01-08-20.

Institute of Medicine. (2001). *Crossing the quality chasm*. http://www.iom.edu/~/media/Files/Report%20Files/2001/Crossing-the-Quality-Chasm/Quality%20Chasm%202001%20%20report%20brief.pdf. Accessed 01-08-20.

L'Hommedieu, M., L'Hommedieu, J., Begay, C., et al. (2019). Lessons learned: Recommendations for implementing a longitudinal study using wearable and environmental sensors in a health care organization. *JMIR mHealth and uHealth, 7*(12). https://doi.org/10.2196/13305, e13305.

Liddy, C., Drosinis, P., & Keely, E. (2016). Electronic consultation systems: Worldwide prevalence and their impact on patient care—A systematic review. *Family Practice, 33*(3), 274–285.

Luo, J. L., Hilty, D. M., Worley, L. L. M., et al. (2006). Considerations in change management related to technology. *Academic Psychiatry, 30*(6), 465–469.

Luxton, D. D. (2016). *Artificial intelligence in behavioral health care.* Boston, MA: Elsevier.

Mohr, D. C., Weingardt, K. R., Reddy, M., et al. (2017). Three problems with current digital mental health research … and three things we can do about them. *Psychiatric Services, 68*(5), 427–429. https://doi.org/10.1176/appi.ps.201600541.

Mostaghimi, A., Olszewski, A. E., Bell, S. K., et al. (2017). Erosion of digital professionalism during medical students' core clinical clerkships. *JMIR Medical Education, 3*(1), e9. https://doi.org/10.2196/mededu.6879.

Mugisha, J., Abdulmalik, J., Hanlon, C., et al. (2017). Health systems context(s) for integrating mental health into primary health care in six Emerald countries: a situation analysis. *International Journal of Mental Health Systems, 11*, 7. Published 2017 Jan 5 https://doi.org/10.1186/s13033-016-0114-2.

Naslund, J. A., Aschbrenner, K. A., Araya, R., et al. (2017). Digital technology for treating and preventing mental disorders in low-income and middle-income countries: A narrative review of the literature. *Lancet Psychiatry, 4*(6), 486–500.

Naslund, J. A., Aschbrenner, K. A., McHugo, G. J., et al. (2019). Exploring opportunities to support mental health care using social media: A survey of social media users with mental illness. *Early Intervention in Psychiatry, 13*(3), 405–413.

Naslund, J. A., Bondre, A., Torous, J., et al. (2020). Social media and mental health: Benefits, risks, and opportunities for research and practice. *The Journal of Technology in Behavioral Science*, 1–13.

Naslund, J. A., Gonsalves, P. P., Gruebner, O., et al. (2019). Digital innovations for global mental health: Opportunities for data science, task sharing, and early intervention. *Current Treatment Options in Psychiatry, 6*(4), 337–351. https://doi.org/10.1007/s40501-019-00186-8.

Naslund, J. A., Mitchell, L. M., Joshi, U., et al. (2020). Economic evaluation and costs of telepsychiatry programmes: A systematic review [published online ahead of print, 2020 Aug 3]. *Journal of Telemedicine and Telecare.* https://doi.org/10.1177/1357633X20938919, 1357633X20938919.

Obbarius, A., van Maasakkers, L., Baer, L., et al. (2017). Standardization of health outcomes assessment for depression and anxiety: Recommendations from the ICHOM depression and anxiety working group. *Quality of Life Research, 26*(12), 3211–3215.

Organisation of Economic Corporation and Development. (2014). *Perspectives on global development 2014: Boosting productivity to meet the middle-income challenge.* https://www.oecd.org/dev/pgd/EN_Pocket%20Edition_PGD2014_web.pdf. 01-08-20. Accessed 01-08-20.

Pisani, A. R., Wyman, P. A., Gurditta, K., et al. (2018). Mobile phone intervention to reduce youth suicide in rural communities: Field test. *JMIR Mental Health, 5*(2), e10425. Published 2018 May 31 https://doi.org/10.2196/10425.

Proctor, E., Silmere, H., Raghavan, R., et al. (2010). Outcomes for implementation research: Conceptual distinctions, measurement challenges, and research agenda. *Administration and Policy in Mental Health, 38*(2), 65–76.

Raviola, G., Naslund, J. A., Smith, S. L., et al. (2019). Innovative models in mental health delivery systems: task sharing care with non-specialist providers to close the mental health treatment gap. *Current Psychiatry Reports, 21*(6), 44. Published 2019 Apr 30 https://doi.org/10.1007/s11920-019-1028-x.

Ray, G., Muhanna, W. A., & Barney, J. B. (2007). Competing with IT: The role of shared IT-business understanding. *Communications of the ACM, 50*(12), 87–91.

Reece, A. G., Reagan, A. J., Lix, K. L. M., et al. (2017). Forecasting the onset and course of mental illness with Twitter data. *Scientific Reports*, 7(1), 13006. Published 2017 Oct 11 https://doi.org/10.1038/s41598-017-12961-9.

Rus-Calafell, M., Garety, P., Sason, E., et al. (2018). Virtual reality in the assessment and treatment of psychosis: A systematic review of its utility, acceptability and effectiveness. *Psychological Medicine*, 48(3), 362–391. https://doi.org/10.1017/S0033291717001945.

Shanafelt, T. D., Dyrbye, L. N., West, C. P., et al. (2016). Potential impact of burnout on the US physician workforce. *Mayo Clinic Proceedings*, 91(11), 1667–1668. https://doi.org/10.1016/j.mayocp.2016.08.016.

Shatte, A. B., Hutchinson, D. M., & Teague, S. J. (2019). Machine learning in mental health: A scoping review of methods and applications. *Psychological Medicine*, 49(9), 1426–1448.

Singla, D. R., Kohrt, B. A., Murray, L. K., et al. (2017). Psychological treatments for the world: Lessons from low- and middle-income countries. *Annual Review of Clinical Psychology*, 13, 149–181. https://doi.org/10.1146/annurev-clinpsy-032816-045217.

The National Academy of Sciences, Engineering, and Medicine. Health and Medicine Division. (2020). http://www.nationalacademies.org/hmd/Global/Meetings.aspx. Accessed 01-08-20.

Torous, J., & Baker, J. T. (2016). Why psychiatry needs data science and data science needs psychiatry: Connecting with technology. *JAMA Psychiatry*, 73(1), 3–4.

Torous, J., Chan, S., Boland, R. J., et al. (2017). Clinical informatics in psychiatric training: Preparing today's trainees for the already present future. *Academic Psychiatry*, 42(5), 694–697.

Torous, J., & Roberts, L. W. (2017). The ethical use of mobile health technology in clinical psychiatry. *The Journal of Nervous and Mental Disease*, 205(1), 4–8. https://doi.org/10.1097/nmd.0000000000000596.

Torrey, W. C., Cepeda, M., Castro, S., et al. (2020). Implementing technology-supported care for depression and alcohol use disorder in primary care in Colombia: Preliminary findings. *Psychiatric Services*, 71(7), 678–683. https://doi.org/10.1176/appi.ps.201900457.

Twenge, J. M., Joiner, T. E., Rogers, M. L., et al. (2018). Increases in depressive symptoms, suicide-related outcomes, and suicide rates among U.S. adolescents after 2010 and links to increased new media screen time. *Clinical Psychological Science: A Journal of the Association for Psychological Science*, 6, 3–17. https://doi.org/10.1177/2167702617723376.

Upadhaya, N., Jordans, M. J. D., Abdulmalik, J., et al. (2016). Information systems for mental health in six low and middle income countries: cross country situation analysis. *International Journal of Mental Health Systems*, 10, 60. Published 2016 Sep 26 https://doi.org/10.1186/s13033-016-0094-2.

World Health Organization. (2017a). *Technology report on scalable psychological interventions for people in communities affected by adversity*. https://www.who.int/mental_health/management/scalable_psychological_interventions/en/. Accessed 01-08-20.

World Health Organization. (2017b). *Mental health ATLAS 2017 report*. https://www.who.int/mental_health/evidence/atlas/mental_health_atlas_2017/en/. Accessed 01-08-20.

World Health Organization. (2020). *Draft global strategy on digital health, 2020–2024*. https://www.who.int/docs/default-source/documents/gs4dhdaa2a9f352b0445bafbc-79ca799dce4d.pdf. Published 26-06-20. Accessed 01-08-20.

Yellowlees, P., Burke Parish, M., González, Á., et al. (2018). Asynchronous telepsychiatry: A component of stepped integrated care. *Telemedicine Journal and E-Health*, 24(5), 375–378.

Yellowlees, P. M., Hogarth, M. A., & Hilty, D. M. (2006). The development of distributed academic networks in America. *Academic Psychiatry*, 30(6), 451–455.

Zalpuri, I., Liu, H., Stubbe, D., et al. (2018). A competency-based framework for social media for trainees, faculty and others. *Academic Psychiatry*, 42(6), 808–817.

Big data and the goal of personalized health interventions

Guy Hindley[a,b], Olav B. Smeland[a], Oleksandr Frei[a,c], and Ole A. Andreassen[a]
[a]NORMENT Centre, Institute of Clinical Medicine, University of Oslo and Division of Mental Health and Addiction, Oslo University Hospital, Oslo, Norway, [b]Department of Psychosis Studies, Institute of Psychiatry, Psychology and Neuroscience, King's College London, London, United Kingdom, [c]Department of Research, Innovation and Education, Division of Clinical Neuroscience, Oslo University Hospital, Oslo, Norway

Introduction/Overview

In 2015, President Barack Obama used his annual "State of the Union" address to announce his new Precision Medicine Initiative (Hey & Kesselheim, 2016). This would revolutionize medicine by introducing personalized approaches to diagnosis and treatment, which would ensure "the right treatment for the right person at the right time." While this goal seemed in reach for several medical specialities, particularly cardiology and oncology (Hey & Kesselheim, 2016), its relevance to mental health was even more aspirational (Kraguljac & Lahti, 2018). Since the introduction of modern psychotropic medication, psychological therapies, and community-based care heralded a revolution in mental health treatment in the second half of the 20th century, progress in the treatment of mental disorders has stalled (Kraguljac & Lahti, 2018). In particular, the translation of research findings from the laboratory to the mental health clinic has proved a stubbornly difficult divide to cross (Kraguljac & Lahti, 2018; Manchia et al., 2020). For example, despite concerted efforts, diagnoses are still made without the support of objective diagnostic tests (Singh & Rose, 2009). This is important since relying on descriptive diagnostic criteria alone allows a large degree of heterogeneity, in addition to considerable comorbidity across diagnoses. Once an individual has received a diagnosis, they are treated with a "one-size-fits-all" approach, whereby the choice of medical or psychological therapy is broadly based on diagnosis, side-effect profile, and the comorbidities of the patient. Little is known about why some patients respond to certain treatments and others do not (Lally & MacCabe, 2016; Manchia et al., 2020). Patients, therefore, often require trials of multiple medications before they achieve the desired response and approximately 30% of patients do not respond to standard treatments at all (Lally & MacCabe, 2016; Manchia et al., 2020). It is, therefore, unsurprising that treatment outcomes remain poor, particularly for those with severe mental disorders such as schizophrenia and bipolar disorder. Combined with high rates of physical comorbidities linked to poor lifestyle and side effects from common psychotropic medication, this contributes to evidence that individuals with a severe mental disorder are expected to die 15–20 years sooner than the average person (Walker, McGee, & Druss, 2015).

Mental Health in a Digital World. https://doi.org/10.1016/B978-0-12-822201-0.00021-6

There are several contributing factors to this lack of progress. Principle among these is the limited understanding of the neurobiological processes underlying mental disorders (Manchia et al., 2020). While there have been important break-throughs, positive findings have often failed to replicate. When they do, differences between patients and controls are often only discernible at the group level, lim-iting the clinical utility of the discovery. Related to this, groups defined by diag-nostic category often exhibit extensive clinical and neurobiological heterogeneity, suggesting that diagnostic categories may incorporate multiple different etiolog-ical processes, which overlap within and across diagnoses (Alnæs et al., 2019). Although there are some evidence supporting key pathological processes, such as increased presynaptic dopamine synthesis in patients with schizophrenia (Howes, McCutcheon, Owen, & Murray, 2017), the emerging understanding of neuropathol-ogy includes the concept of multiple causal factors each with small effects on the development of each disorder. This is particularly true in genetics, whereby each disorder is predicted to be influenced by thousands of genetic variants, each with a tiny effect (Holland et al., 2020).

Given the challenges of clinical complexity and multiple small causal effects, the collection, and analysis of large-scale, complex datasets are a crucial stepping stone toward improved outcomes for people with mental disorders (Manchia et al., 2020). At the simplest level, if there is a causal factor with a small effect, it can only be dis-covered with large datasets. This is best demonstrated in genetics, whereby effective sample sizes of over 100,000 were needed to reliably identify large proportions of the genetic risk factors. Still, only small fractions of the genetic component of com-mon mental disorders such as schizophrenia (Schizophrenia Working Group of the Psychiatric Genomics Consortium, 2014), bipolar disorder (Stahl et al., 2019), and major depressive disorder have been identified (Wray et al., 2018). The same phenom-enon is increasingly evident in other modalities such as neuroimaging. Beyond this, the flexibility and depth of big data and its application to machine learning algorithms mean that unexpected associations and causal relationships can be revealed (Shilo, Rossman, & Segal, 2020). This is even more relevant when attempting to combine data across different domains, including biological, digital, and environmental levels. Given the complex, multifactorial etiologies of mental disorders, such analytical ap-proaches will be necessary to make significant inroads in understanding, prediction, prevention, and personalized treatment. Taken together, big data have the potential to make significant inroads into the understanding of the causes of mental disorders and the development of tools for prediction and risk stratification (Shatte, Hutchinson, & Teague, 2019). While these goals are still far from the clinic, the maturation of large-scale datasets, increased access to electronic health records (EHRs), and novel method development for the mental health setting mean that Barack Obama's view of the future may not be quite so far away.

Here, we shall provide an overview of the key concepts behind big data, de-scribe how it is collected and analyzed, provide examples of its application to mental health research alongside some of the key challenges faced, before looking to the future with a focus on its potential impact on personalized management of mental disorders.

What is big data?

As might be expected given its nonspecific name, there is no precise definition of "big data." It has been defined quantitatively according to how "big" the dataset is (Baro, Degoul, Beuscart, & Chazard, 2015), or qualitatively according to how the size and complexity of the data necessitates the use of unconventional analytical approaches (Gligorijević, Malod-Dognin, & Pržulj, 2016). When characterizing a dataset, it is often helpful to conceptualize it according to its "axes." The following axes are particularly relevant when considering large datasets (Shilo et al., 2020):

1. *Number of participants*: In conventional study design, the target sample size is ideally calculated a priori according to the power required to test a specific hypothesis. While this may be the case for certain large-scale longitudinal studies which set out to study specific rare disorders, the sample sizes of big data projects are often opportunistic and pragmatic. Furthermore, big data projects are often open ended such that sample sizes increase over time (Ngiam & Khor, 2019). While maximizing sample size is often desirable, this is offset by financial and organizational costs and the time required to recruit participants (Shilo et al., 2020).

2. *Depth of phenotyping*: The list of phenotypes of potential relevance to mental disorders is virtually infinite and crosses many disciplines. This includes clinical characteristics such as diagnosis, medication use, contact with health services to psychometric measures including symptom measures; demographic and environmental exposures; -omics data such as gene expression, methylation, proteomics, and metabolomics; physiological measures such as serum metabolite or cytokine levels; and imaging modalities such as structural and functional MRI, MRS, and PET; some big data initiatives may focus specifically on a single modality, for example, large-scale genome-wide association studies (GWAS) primarily collect genotyping data alongside case-control status for specific disorders (Tam et al., 2019). Others, like EHRs, may be limited by the scope of the resource from which data are drawn (Abul-Husn & Kenny, 2019). Biobanks, on the other hand, try to maximize phenotypic depth, even storing samples for the future phenotyping as technology and new hypotheses emerge (Kinkorová & Topolčan, 2020).

3. *Longitudinal follow-up*: There is increasing awareness that high-quality longitudinal studies are required to make meaningful inroads into understanding the etiology of mental disorders, both to provide insights into premorbid neurodevelopmental factors and clinical outcomes (Manchia et al., 2020). While some big data initiatives are cross sectional by design, such as GWAS, most incorporate data collected over several time points. Longitudinal studies may vary greatly according to the length and regularity of follow-up. Given the evidence linking events in utero with risk of severe mental disorders (Ursini et al., 2018), there is a particular onus on initiatives which begin prenatally, even preconception, and follow participants through life, termed as the "prewomb to tomb" approach (Shilo et al., 2020). Studies such as these include the Born in Guangzhou Cohort Study (Qiu et al., 2017), Avon Longitudinal Study of Parents and Children (Boyd et al., 2013), the Norwegian Mother and Child Cohort Study (Magnus et al., 2016), and the ABCD Study (Casey et al., 2018).

4. *Interactions between participants*: Understanding the interactions between participants is essential to identify potential biases within the sample and boost the power to discover causal relationships (Shilo et al., 2020). This includes genetic relatedness within the sample, which may be partially intended as in twin or family studies, or unintended, as in a population-based study such as UK Biobank (Sudlow et al., 2015). This might also include other interactions such as shared environmental factors within a neighborhood or city.

5. *Sample heterogeneity*: Sample heterogeneity has traditionally been deemed something to avoid to reduce noise, enabling easier detection of true associations while minimizing sample size (Shilo et al., 2020). However, homogenous samples do not reflect the real-world population leading to findings with poor generalizability and applicability. This is particularly relevant to mental health research since study samples are often skewed toward older, white, affluent, and well-educated populations. In contrast, mental disorders often present early in life are more prevalent in people from ethnic minorities and lower socioeconomic classes, and are strongly associated with several environmental factors which are underrepresented in the typical research participant, such as substance use and childhood trauma. Combined with big data's ability to identify associations with small effects in the context of high heterogeneity, there is therefore greater appreciation of the need to encourage sample heterogeneity with regard to age, sex, ethnicity, education level, and nationality (Shilo et al., 2020).

6. *Standardization and harmonization*: Big data initiatives increasingly leverage data from multiple disparate sources. It can, therefore, be a challenge to harmonize and standardize phenotypic information across datasets (Shilo et al., 2020). For clinical data, there are several standardized approaches for high-level information such as the International Classification of Diseases (ICD) system for diagnostic categories (World Health Organization, 1993), but more granular data are more challenging. As the importance of these approaches becomes increasingly apparent, initiatives such as the Observational Health Data Sciences and Informatics initiative are attempting to provide unified, standardized approaches to medical data harmonization (Banda, 2019). For biological level data, there are also often challenges related to data acquisition, whereby differences in protocols can introduce problematic confounders into the datasets.

7. *Linkage between datasets*: Similar to harmonization, linking individual participants across multiple data sources can provide additional phenotypic depth and time points to an analysis (Shilo et al., 2020). Some countries, particularly the Nordic countries such as Estonia and Norway, have highly organized and centralized medical health records, which are ideal for data linkage (Andreassen, 2018). Thanks to secure data-sharing and anonymization techniques, health records can be linked to individual cohort studies, greatly amplifying the reach of each individual study (Andreassen, 2018). The benefits of data linkage must, however, be carefully balanced against privacy and data security.

Where does big data come from?

There are several sources of large-scale health data. First, *electronic health records (eHR) and national registries* provide health and sociodemographic data from entire regions or even countries. Several countries, including Nordic nations such as Sweden, Finland, Estonia, Denmark, and Norway, have established secure anonymization of health records for research purposes (Andreassen, 2018). Health records are particularly valuable since they represent entire populations rather than a sample from which inferences about the population are draw (Abul-Husn & Kenny, 2019). This means they are not susceptible to selection bias as with most other datasets, embrace the heterogeneity of the population and incorporate real-world factors such as drug compliance (Ngiam & Khor, 2019). They also provide birth-to-death longitudinal data and the opportunity to incorporate interactions between individuals (Ngiam & Khor,

2019). Key limitations include variable depths of phenotyping beyond demographic information and diagnostic codes and difficulties harmonizing and standardizing data across diverse health systems (Shilo et al., 2020). Ethical implications on privacy and data security are also important considerations. Notable applications of health record research include the use of Denmark's death registry and health records to identify significantly increased mortality from cardiovascular disease among people with severe mental disorders (Laursen et al., 2013).

Biobanks and longitudinal cohort studies are a second key resource. Initially conceived as the systematic collection of biospecimens from a population-based cohort, the concept of a Biobank has grown to incorporate in-depth phenotyping from biological specimens, health records, diagnostic interviews, and questionnaire responses. By deeply phenotyping prospective, population-based samples, Biobanks attempt to provide a wide-reaching resource to improve the understanding of multiple complex, multifactorial diseases within the same sample, as opposed to a hypothesis-driven disorder-specific study (Bycroft et al., 2018). This is ideally suited for common mental disorders such as depression for which the prevalence is high enough to provide a large enough sample of patients (Davis et al., 2020). They are also well suited for the analysis of symptom-level data, such as a GWAS of psychotic-like experiences (Legge et al., 2019). However, their application to mental disorders is limited by the fact that even relatively common disorders such as schizophrenia and bipolar do not yield especially large sample sizes (Davis et al., 2020). Another key consideration is selection bias. In particular, a recent study has shown how both participation and dropout from the UK Biobank can bias both genetic and phenotypic associations (Tyrrell et al., 2021). Some of the most prominent Biobanks include UK Biobank (Bycroft et al., 2018), Norwegian Nord Trondelag Health Study (HUNT) (Krokstad et al., 2013), and Million Veteran Program (USA) (Gaziano et al., 2016). There are also several from middle-income countries including the Mexico City Prospective Study from Mexico and Guangzhou Biobank from China. Longitudinal cohort studies which begin at conception or in utero are especially relevant since most mental disorders present at a young age and are likely influenced by environmental factors from conception. This is particularly important for neurodevelopmental disorders such as ADHD, autism, and, arguably, schizophrenia.

Digital technologies offer opportunities to collect vast datasets, even from relatively few participants. In particular, "digital phenotyping" is the use of data harvested from smartphones, wearable technologies, or personal computers (Melcher, Hays, & Torous, 2020). This is similar to the concept of "ecological momentary assessment," whereby data are iteratively collected in real time from within the individual's natural environment, which reduces recall bias and increases external validity (Busk et al., 2020). Data can be collected actively, whereby the individual consciously provides relevant information, such as responding to a prompted question about their mood, or passively, which leverages data automatically collected by the device, such as geolocation, velocity, heart rate, time using the device, and usage of specific applications (Melcher et al., 2020). Given the breadth and granularity of phenotypic information and the rich longitudinal datasets, such approaches provide an entirely novel insight into the individual patient experience. The feasibility and practicality of smartphone technologies also offer exciting possibilities for novel interventional tools, such as prediction of an episode of mood disturbance in a patient with bipolar disorder (Busk et al., 2020).

For specific modalities, *large-scale international consortia* have enabled the collection of sample sizes that were almost inconceivable just 20 years ago. Prominent among these is the Psychiatric Genetics Consortium (PGC), which has collected vast datasets for several common mental disorders including schizophrenia (Schizophrenia Working Group of the Psychiatric Genomics Consortium, 2014), bipolar disorder (Stahl et al., 2019), major depression (Wray et al., 2018), attention-deficit hyperactivity disorder (Demontis et al., 2019), and autism spectrum disorder (Grove et al., 2019). This approach has also been applied to other modalities such as neuroimaging through initiatives like the Enhancing Neuro-Imaging Genetics through Meta-Analysis (ENIGMA) consortium, which has collected some of the largest samples of structural MRI across many mental and neurological disorders (Thompson et al., 2020). A major limitation of this approach, however, is the lack of additional phenotypic information. Even basic demographics such as sex and age are sometimes not clear given the inclusion of so many diverse substudies. As biobank research continues to mature, the convergence of biobanks, consortia, and health records will hopefully resolve this issue.

Finally, *private-public partnerships* can also contribute large, valuable datasets. For example, the FinnGen (https://www.finngen.fi/en) project aims to provide open-source genome-wide summary statistics across the spectrum of human disease by combining health registries and large-scale population-based genotyping. This was made possible, in part, due to funding from private companies who gain early access to the genetic data in return (FinnGen, 2020). Alternatively, private genotyping companies like 23andMe have collaborated on several high-impact projects around the world, including the largest GWAS of major depression to date (Hyde et al., 2016; Wray et al., 2018). This is possible by providing genetic data from customers who have consented to take part in research studies and have completed self-report questionnaires. This is particularly relevant since 23andMe has one of the largest datasets of people from nonwhite, non-Asian ancestry, which is currently a major limitation to most psychiatric genetics studies (Amariuta et al., 2020). Important limitations include the reliance on self-report measures, which have questionable validity.

Data storage and preprocessing

Before analyzing large datasets, there are several important technical considerations. Foremost among these is data storage. This is a particular challenge for high-throughput -omics data, which often produce huge quantities of information for a single individual. For example, it was estimated that the 20 largest institutions already required over 100 petabytes (10^6 gigabytes) of storage for genomics data alone in 2015, and were predicted to need 2–40 exabytes per year by 2025 (10^9 gigabytes) (Stephens et al., 2015).

Similarly, the computational resources required to analyze large datasets are considerable. Within genomics, even a seemingly simple task such as variant calling, the process which determines the genetic base at each chromosomal position, is a substantial computational challenge. By 2025, this task alone is predicted to require 2 trillion central processing unit hours (CPU hours), which are not only expensive but also has an enormous environmental impact (Stephens et al., 2015). Both storage and analysis of big data, therefore, require the use of specialist computing services such as high-performance computing (HPC) clusters or cloud computing (Navale & Bourne, 2018). Cloud computing, which is increasingly accessible through private providers such as Amazon Web Services and Google Cloud, is a particularly important area for the future growth since it outsources the financial and organizational costs of providing a locally available HPC, which would be prohibitively expensive for most institutes in low- and middle-income countries (Navale & Bourne, 2018). Regulations on data security and privacy are important here though, given the sensitive nature of mental health-related data.

Data preprocessing is also a crucial step for most big data analysis pipelines. Although the details differ according to the dataset and analytical approach, this is particularly important for machine learning, whereby inaccurate labeling of data points can significantly impair the performance of the algorithm (Ngiam & Khor, 2019). Machine learning approaches also require data curation, a process of reclassifying data labels in order to improve the performance of the algorithm. Finally, missing data are an important consideration, particularly when applied to neural networks, which cannot handle missing data, or genotyping which deliberately collects incomplete datasets to reduce costs (Tam et al., 2019). Imputation of missing data is, therefore, often necessary (Ngiam & Khor, 2019).

Data analysis

Big data analyses can broadly be categorized into "descriptive analysis," "prediction analysis," and "counterfactual prediction" (Shilo et al., 2020). At its most basic, descriptive analysis is defined as "using data to provide a quantitative summary of certain features of the world" (Hernán, Hsu, & Healy, 2019). The main advantage of descriptive studies using large datasets is the ability to perform unbiased exploratory analyses from which testable hypotheses can be formulated. Examples of descriptive analysis of big data in mental health include GWAS studies describing associations between common genetic variants and mental disorders or the identification of an association between lithium use and cortical thickness in patients with bipolar disorder (Hibar et al., 2018).

Prediction analyses aim to predict a specific outcome by mapping a set of input data to the outcome in a "training dataset." Its ability to successfully predict the outcome of interest is then tested in an independent dataset, or "test dataset" (Shilo et al., 2020). Examples of prediction analyses for mental health include the prediction of the diagnosis of a mental health disorder or treatment response using GWAS genetic data, or the prediction of an episode of psychosis or mood disturbance using digital pheno-typing from smartphone and wearable technologies (Busk et al., 2020). An important limitation of prediction analyses such as these is that, even if meaningful prediction is achieved, it does not necessarily infer causality since the model may be driven by noncausal associations. While prediction alone is powerful, understanding causation is essential for the development of effective interventions (Shilo et al., 2020).

Counterfactual prediction, in contrast, uses input data to predict certain outcomes under hypothetical scenarios, i.e., counter to the fact. Causal relationships can, there-fore, be inferred by modeling how the change in input variables impacts the outcome (Dickerman & Hernán, 2020). A commonly encountered example of counterfactual prediction is Mendelian randomization, which infers causal relationships between two phenotypes by computing the extent to which one phenotype modulates the association between the second phenotype and its associated genetic determinants. This has indicated causal relationships between prior cannabis use and schizophrenia (Vaucher et al., 2018), raised CRP and decreased risk of schizophrenia (Hartwig et al., 2018), and "confiding in others" and reduced risk of depression (Choi et al., 2020). Mendelian randomization has several important limitations though, and its application to highly polygenic disorders like mental disorders has been questioned (Verbanck, Chen, Neale, & Do, 2018).

Big data analysis is also intimately linked to artificial intelligence and machine learning. While neither are required for big data analysis, nor is big data necessary for their application, there is often overlap since the larger the dataset, the better the ma-chine learning algorithms perform. Briefly, artificial intelligence is the concept that a machine can perform tasks of equivalent or greater complexity than humans. Machine learning is a computational method for achieving artificial intelligence by enabling a machine to solve problems without being problem-specific programming (Samuel, 1959). Machine learning is categorized as supervised, in which data are labeled and classified prior to training the algorithm, or unsupervised in which the data are fed into the model raw (Ngiam & Khor, 2019). "Deep learning," meanwhile, is a particularly type of machine learning which has risen to prominence in recent years thanks to its flexibility handling multiple types of data input (Esteva et al., 2019). Inspired by human neural networks, it comprises multiple interconnected "neural layers" through which input data are filtered. This filtering process allows the model to extract salient features, termed "featurization," from each set of input data. Higher-level networks then merge salient features from multiple different data types with the ultimate goal of mapping diverse input data to the predefined outcome (Esteva et al., 2019).

Deep learning has many applications beyond prediction analyses. For example, natural language processing uses deep learning to interpret the meaning of text or speech. This is particularly relevant to mental health, given that the bulk of clinical information is stored as written text in eHRs. This is therefore an invaluable resource but it is unfeasible for researchers to synthesize entire registries worth of clinical notes. The application of natural language processing to mental health research is in its infancy, but it has already been used to construct a tool for predicted self-harm using eHR notes (Van Le, Montgomery, Kirkby, & Scanlan, 2018) and to identify the psychological construct "mood instability" from eHR notes (Patel et al., 2015). Other machine learning-based approaches of relevance include data mining, which attempts to identify previously unreported patterns or features of a dataset, and transfer learning, which uses algorithms trained for one problem to inform the solution of another, related problem (REFs).

Machine learning algorithms have already been applied extensively to mental health research. A recent review identified a total of 300 studies, most of which were focused on either detection and diagnosis ($n=190$) or prognosis ($n=67$) (Shatte et al., 2019). The vast majority applied supervised learning and classification techniques ($n=267$). While the gap to clinically useful predictive tools remains large, promising results have been reported for the prediction of suicide in army veterans (Kessler et al., 2017), treatment outcome in first-episode psychosis (Koutsouleris et al., 2016), and alcohol use in adolescence (Squeglia et al., 2016).

Insights from genetics, neuroimaging, and eHealth

Genetics

Most mental disorders are highly heritable, with broad-sense heritability between 40% and 80% for common severe mental disorders such as schizophrenia (Hilker et al., 2018), bipolar disorder (Johansson, Kuja-Halkola, Cannon, Hultman, & Hedman, 2019), and major depression (Kendler, Ohlsson, Lichtenstein, Sundquist, & Sundquist, 2018). A comprehensive understanding of the genetic component of these disorders would, therefore, represent a major breakthrough in both understanding the pathobiology of these disorders and in enabling the development of predictive tools and more personalized treatment approaches. Approximately, half of this genetic component has been linked to common genetic variants, also termed as SNPs, which are identified using GWAS (Mullins et al., 2020; Ripke, Walters, & O'Donovan, 2020; Wray et al., 2018). However, it is increasingly recognized that most common mental disorders are highly polygenic, meaning they are influenced by several thousand individual variants, with latest estimates as high as 10,000 or more (Holland et al., 2020). Furthermore, each variant is estimated to influence the risk of developing a disorder by a tiny amount, with the most strongly associated risk alleles rarely increasing an individual's risk by more than a 1%–2% when compared to the general population (Ripke et al., 2020). This means that GWAS studies of hundreds of thousands of patients and controls have still only uncovered a minority of associated variants and explain a minority of the total heritability using standard analytical techniques (Holland et al., 2020). For example, the latest schizophrenia GWAS, which comprised 69,369 patients and 236,642 controls, was able to identify 270 genetic loci, which only explains 2.6% of the variability within the sample (Ripke et al., 2020).

One of the main applications of GWAS findings is the development of genetic prediction tools. The current state of the art for GWAS-based prediction is a polygenic risk score (PRS), which computes a composite score according to the presence of known protective or risk alleles weighted by their effect size. Excitingly, PRSs are close to clinical utility in other fields such as cardiology, where they have been shown to improve risk stratification and early intervention (Mars et al., 2020; Mosley et al., 2020). Unfortunately, mental disorders are still some way off due to their extensive polygenicity. For example, the best-performing PRS from the latest SCZ GWAS accounts for just 7.7% of the SCZ risk (Ripke et al., 2020). The most straightforward solution to this is to continue to increase sample sizes. However, latest estimates suggest that effective sample sizes of 10 million or more are required to identify approximately 80% of the heritability of common mental disorders (Holland et al., 2020). While this is not inconceivable given the rate of progress over the last 20 years, this also places emphasis on the need to develop novel statistical tools to improve discovery and predictive ability. Some examples include methods which leverage information about the functional significance of genomic regions (Schork et al., 2013) and polygenic overlap between related traits to boost statistical power to discover novel loci (Smeland et al., 2019; Turley et al., 2018; van der Meer et al., 2020). Furthermore, a novel technique using causal mixture models has been used to model the overall shared genetic architecture between two traits (Frei et al., 2019). Similar advanced statistical modeling techniques could be applied to locus discovery and polygenic risk prediction to improve performance without the need to huge increases in sample size (Frei et al., 2019).

Beyond GWAS, there is also great mostly untapped potential in other -omic technologies. Foremost among these is large-scale whole genome sequencing projects, which are essential for the identification of rare variants which may have a disproportionately large impact on risk for a given disorder (Gershon, Alliey-Rodriguez, & Liu, 2011). As the cost of whole genome sequencing continues to decrease, this will become increasingly feasible (Stephens et al., 2015). Furthermore, methylomics, transcriptomics, proteomics, and metabolomics, including single-cell -omics, possess great but largely untapped potential (Wörheide, Krumsiek, Kastenmüller, & Arnold, 2021). This may be particularly important for understanding disease progression. An individual's genome stays largely unchanged through the course of their life, however, difference in gene expression, splicing, and posttranslational modifications could be relevant factors for acute changes in mental state. Multiomics approaches are becoming increasingly viable through the development of several tissue-specific large-scale gene-expression and methylation resources, include GTEx (GTEx Consortium, 2017), PsychEncode (Akbarian et al., 2015), and Common Mind Consortium (Common Mind Consortium, n.d.).

The potential applications of genetic risk prediction to the management of mental disorders are far reaching. First, improved risk prediction would provide opportunities for targeted prevention. This would most likely take the form of risk stratification, as is routine practice in the management of cardiovascular risk, for example. An individual would be predicted to have a certain level of risk, which in turn informs preventative interventions. This might include closer observation, earlier access to psychological therapies, or trials of psychotropic medication. Second, genetics could inform the diagnostic process. At its simplest, high genetic risk could provide evidence in favor of a certain diagnosis (Smeland, Frei, Dale, & Andreassen, 2020). More disruptively, an objective genetic risk score could contribute to the diagnostic system itself, helping to redefine mental disorders so that they are better aligned with underlying biological dysfunction (Smeland et al., 2020). Genetic risk scores may also inform interventional trials. It is possible that individuals with different levels of genetic risk respond differently to different pharmacological or psychological therapies (Oedegaard et al., 2016). The ability to know an individual's genetic load a posteriori could, therefore, inform study design and analysis. Finally, and perhaps most importantly, genetic risk scores could be used to predict treatment response to increase the probability that an individual responds to the chosen treatment. Given the rate of nonresponse (Lally & MacCabe, 2015; Manchia et al., 2020) and the evidence showing the negative impact of untreated mental disorder (Schennach-Wolff et al., 2011), this alone could provide considerable impact on the lives of people with mental disorder.

Neuroimaging

While it is widely accepted that mental disorders involve the disturbance of brain functioning to some degree, remarkably little is known about specific, causal abnormalities linking brain structure or function to an individual's experience of mental disorder. There have been several important and replicable discoveries including dopaminergic neurotransmission using PET (Fusar-Poli & Meyer-Lindenberg, 2013), glutamatergic and GABAergic function using MRS (Schür et al., 2016), and convincing evidence of increased ventricles and cortical thinning on structural MRI scans in both schizophrenia and bipolar (Rimol et al., 2012). However, these changes are only evident at the group level, and so these findings have limited significance to an individual in the clinic.

However, there is increasing awareness that one of the main reasons for the failure to identify reliable discoveries in neuroimaging of mental disorders is that, just like genetics, there are many small differences between patients and controls in neuroimaging measures, rather than few differences with large effects. In other words, "small effects is the new normal" (Paulus & Thompson, 2019), which means that big data are required to robustly identify the full landscape of biologically meaningful neuroimaging measures. While this has currently been most clearly demonstrated in structural measures, this is likely to hold true for other modalities too including task-based functional MRI, DTI, and connectivity.

Large-scale, international collaborative projects, such as the ENIGMA consortium alongside biobank imaging initiatives like within the UK Biobank, have started to generate large samples of neuroimaging measures both in patient groups and healthy populations. Beyond providing the power to robustly identify small effects, this has also enabled the application of novel analytical approaches, including machine learning algorithms to brain imaging data (Thompson et al., 2020). For example, Nunes et al. were able to differentiate participants with bipolar disorder from control participants in a large, heterogenous samples using regional brain measures (Nunes et al., 2020). Similarly, individuals with BD were differentiated from individuals with MDD using multiple kernel learning, a form of machine learning, based on multimodal structural images from a relatively small sample (Vai et al., 2020). Finally, machine learning tools have been used to construct normative models for "brain age," which are able to predict chronological age from structural MR images. Interestingly, the model systematically overestimated brain age of patients with schizophrenia, suggesting the model was capable of differentiating patients with schizophrenia from controls despite not being trained to solve this particular problem (Kaufmann et al., 2019).

There have also been several exciting examples of combined analyses of large-scale genetics and imaging datasets. For example, a new statistical approach capable of performing multivariate GWAS of hundreds or thousands of correlated measures was applied to voxel-level MRI data to boost the discovery of genetic loci associated with cortical brain structure by two to three times compared to standard univariate GWAS-based techniques (van der Meer et al., 2020). Furthermore, higher polygenic risk score in a nonclinical population was found to be associated with increased heterogeneity of multiple diverse brain structural brain measures. This is a crucial point since it shows that focusing on the mean may miss important differences between patients and controls, and so more sophisticated analytical approaches, such as the normative model used for brain age, may be required for clinically useful diagnostic tools (Alnæs et al., 2019).

As datasets continue to mature and secure, international data-sharing protocols become more commonplace, there is increasing potential in sharing individual-level raw data which would enable the use of more granular imaging measures and the development of unsupervised machine learning techniques. This may improve the discriminating ability of predictive or diagnostic neuroimaging for mental disorders, raising hopes of developing clinically relevant tools (Manchia et al., 2020).

eHealth

While imaging and genotyping have the potential to provide ground-breaking insights into the underlying biology of mental disorders, eHealth can provide real-world, behavioral, and symptom-level detail, which is missing from many big data initiatives in mental health research. Smartphone-based initiatives are particularly powerful given their prevalence worldwide, including in low- and middle-income countries.

While eHealth initiatives are still somewhat in their infancy, there are several examples of their potential application. In a sample of just 84 patients with bipolar disorder who generated 15,975 individual self-assessments, future mood was predicted with reasonable accuracy 1, 3, and 7 days in the future using hierarchical Bayesian regression models (Busk et al., 2020). There have also been several studies using passive smartphone data collection to track sleep in a variety of mental disorders including depression, anxiety, and psychotic disorders (Aledavood et al., 2019). Given evidence that sleep disturbance may play a causative role in deteriorations in mental state, this may be particularly useful for early recognition and intervention in people with known mental disorders (Aledavood et al., 2019).

eHealth may also have applications beyond symptom tracking and early warning. It has been suggested that ecological momentary assessments may also be able to detect new presentations of mental disorders through distinct digital phenotyping. This idea has been explored in depression (Yim et al., 2020), bipolar disorder (Schwartz, Schultz, Reider, & Saunders, 2016), and psychotic disorders (Bell, Lim, Rossell, & Thomas, 2017), with some evidence of success, although most studies are limited by small sample sizes. Given the novel nature of this research, the need to standardize methodological aspects of data collection and analysis will become increasingly relevant to enable the generation of larger datasets with increased power (Yim et al., 2020).

Key challenges

There are several important limitations and obstacles that need to be navigated before the potential of big data can be fully achieved.

From big data to the individual patient

At the heart of the big data paradigm is the irony that we may need samples comprising millions of participants to develop interventions, which are useful for the individual patient. How findings derived from such large datasets can be translated to single patients remains an open and urgent question in the field. Normative models, as were used in the brain-aging model described above, is an alternative which offers the ability to predict individual disease development or treatment outcomes from complex input data. Whether such approaches are suitable for developing predictive tools with sufficient accuracy for clinical use remains to be seen.

Ethical considerations

Primarily, there are significant issues in relation to generalizability and equity of access. By their very nature, many of these initiatives are costly and require advanced and well-developed health systems. As a result, many of the enormous datasets from large-scale consortia are severely lacking in diversity of ancestral groups (Amariuta et al., 2020). This is a particular issue in genetics since polygenic risk scores developed in the European ancestry samples perform significantly worse in other ancestral groups due to ancestral differences in the pattern of inheritance of common genetic variants. As polygenic risk scores near clinical utility in other fields, the ethical implications of this are coming into stark contrast and so there are increasing efforts to diversify samples and develop tools, which enable the translation of polygenic risk scores across ancestries (Amariuta et al., 2020; Huynh-Le et al., 2021). The implications for other modalities such as imaging are less clear. The global impact of this research will also be limited by cost and lack of access. While genotyping is now relatively cheap and getting cheaper, currently priced at approximately 40 USD per sample (Tam et al., 2019), access to the resources required is limited in low- and middle-income countries. Access to MRI and other imaging modalities is even more inadequate. As of 2016, only one of six regions had access to an MRI scan in Tanzania, representing approximately one scanner for every 10 million people (Ngoya, Muhogora, & Pitcher, 2016). On the other hand, access to the most basic mental health services in low-income countries is equally limited. There are only 0.05 psychiatrists and 0.04 psychologists per 100,000 in low-income countries, compared to 10.50 and 14.00, respectively, in high-income countries (World Health Organization (WHO), 2008). eHealth initiatives using smartphones, which are, unlike psychiatrists, highly prevalent in low-income countries, may therefore represent cheap and easily scalable options for mental health interventions in low-resource settings.

A second important consideration is the need to protect patient confidentiality and privacy. There is currently a trend toward increasing researchers' access to large-scale EHRs, in line with the Nordic model (Andreassen, 2018). As anonymization strategies, data security, and ethico-legal practices mature, this trend is likely to continue, with huge potential benefits to patients (Andreassen, 2018). Nonetheless, in the current climate of mistrust and suspicion of health professionals, which have been amplified by COVID, it is essential that health services ensure the highest ethical standards and maintain open, accessible dialog with the general public.

The acceptability of predictive tools is also a key ethical concern. While there is evidence that polygenic risk scores can have a positive impact on patients by helping to explain their condition and alleviate blame or guilt (Putt et al., 2020), there are potential harms including discrimination by insurers or employers against people with high genetic risks and a loss of autonomy (Chowdhury et al., 2013). Furthermore, there will be potential harm to individuals inaccurately labeled high risk from unnecessary emotional distress and, possibly, unnecessary interventions.

Service-user involvement

It is also essential that the perspectives of individuals with lived experience of mental disorders are incorporated at all stages of big data research initiatives. While this is intuitively needed to ensure acceptability of a clinical tool or intervention, the recent evidence also demonstrates its relevance when defining treatment outcomes, which are particularly relevant for machine learning algorithms. In a survey of over 6000 individuals with depression and bipolar disorder, patient desired outcomes diverged significantly from clinically defined outcomes, with patients prioritizing independence and autonomy over symptom management (Altimus, 2019). This takes on even greater significance in the context of personalized health interventions, which cannot claim to be personalized if they do not incorporate the individual's personal preferences.

Phenotypic depth vs sample breadth

From a scientific perspective, the balance between phenotypic depth and sample scale is critical. While large-scale genetic and neuroimaging studies have advanced the field, the inherent complexity of mental disorders will not fully be understood until we can incorporate longitudinal, multilevel phenotypic data. Novel analytic approaches are, therefore, required that can handle the complexity of the data. For example, alongside the machine learning approaches described earlier, improved statistical modeling techniques have enabled computationally efficient multivariate analysis of hundreds of correlated neuroimaging phenotypes, helping to substantially boost discovery of genetic variants associated with cortical structure (van der Meer et al., 2020).

Reproducibility and replicability

Finally, while big data should improve the reproducibility and replicability in mental health research, there are specific issues in the context of machine learning. Machine learning models, and particularly deep learning models, deliberately leverage randomness to converge on a solution to a problem (Beam, Manrai, & Ghassemi, 2020). This means that training the same algorithm on the same dataset can produce different results, a direct violation of the requirement for reproducible analyses in biomedical sciences. There are solutions to this problem, including the application of "meta-learning" algorithms, which aim to identify the best-performing algorithm for a given task. The cost of meta-learning, however, is currently astronomical. A single model costs up to 3.2 million USD per model in cloud computing resources and contributes five times the amount of carbon emissions produced by an average car over its lifetime (Beam et al., 2020). While this issue of reproducibility is of secondary importance to improvements in patient outcomes derived from machine learning algorithms, this remains an unsolved issue.

Looking to the future

The future for big data and personalized health interventions in mental health is certainly bright. While clinically applicable tools remain out of reach, the rate of progress over the last 5–10 years suggest that it would be foolish to make any confident predictions about the future progress.

With regard to risk stratification, there should be increasing focus on combining modalities across genetics, -omics, imaging, and clinical data in order to approach meaningful predictive accuracy. Combinations of polygenic risk scores, imaging data, and cognitive testing have already been shown to improve the prediction of Alzheimer's disease, providing the analytical template and evidence for the efficacy of such an approach in neuropsychiatric disorders (Kauppi et al., 2018). A similar multimodal approach has also been applied to predict type 1 diabetes in children (Ferrat et al., 2020). The convergence of large international genomic and neuroimaging consortia, EHRs, and biobanks will provide unique opportunities for combined approaches to prediction.

Related to this, there is a need to focus on well-defined clinical problems, which are likely to have the biggest impact on individuals with mental disorders. Given the immediate clinical benefit, stratification approaches including treatment response should be high on this list. Examples include response to lithium among people with bipolar disorder, response to SSRI treatment in depression, or response to first-line antipsychotics in schizophrenia. The latter is of particular relevance since 15% of all people diagnosed with schizophrenia will not respond to first-line treatment, but will respond to clozapine (Lally & MacCabe, 2015). The impact of early clozapine treatment on patients with treatment-resistant schizophrenia could, therefore, be transformative. What's more, large-scale GWAS of treatment nonresponse has been possible due to the fact that patients taking clozapine regularly provide blood samples to monitor potential side effects (Pardiñas et al., 2018). This means that combination of a clear clinical need and readily available large-scale data could provide a unique opportunity to test the application of big data-driven personalized interventions for mental disorders.

It is also likely that big data approaches will contribute to the discovery of new mechanistic insights to improve our understanding of mental disorders. This is necessary to reduce the stigma associated with mental disorders, develop more targeted treatments with fewer side effects, and ultimately improve outcomes. What's more, the combination of improved predictive tools, improved mechanistic understanding, and improved therapeutics are all necessary to achieve the goal of personalized treatment of mental disorders.

Conclusions

In this chapter, we have provided an overview of big data in the context of mental health research. We have described how it is stored, processed, and analyzed; offered insights into the application of big data principles to mental health genetics, neuroimaging, and eHealth; and discussed some of the key challenges facing the field moving forward. While there is certainly much progress still to be made and several important challenges to negotiate, particularly surrounding equity, data security, and privacy, there are clear grounds for optimism that big data may provide the catalyst for the next revolution in mental health care and achieving Obama's vision of providing "the right treatment to the right person at the right time" (Hey & Kesselheim, 2016).

References

Abul-Husn, N. S., & Kenny, E. E. (2019). Personalized medicine and the power of electronic health records. *Cell, 177*, 58–69.

Akbarian, S., et al. (2015). The PsychENCODE project. *Nature Neuroscience, 18*, 1707–1712.

Aledavood, T., et al. (2019). Smartphone-based tracking of sleep in depression, anxiety, and psychotic disorders. *Current Psychiatry Reports, 21*.

Alnæs, D., et al. (2019). Brain heterogeneity in schizophrenia and its association with polygenic risk. *JAMA Psychiatry, 76*, 739–748.

Altimus, C. (2019). *Supporting wellness: A survey of lived experience.[PDF file]*.

Amariuta, T., et al. (2020). Improving the trans-ancestry portability of polygenic risk scores by prioritizing variants in predicted cell-type-specific regulatory elements. *Nat. Genet., 52*, 1346–1354.

Andreassen, O. A. (2018). eHealth provides a novel opportunity to exploit the advantages of the Nordic countries in psychiatric genetic research, building on the public health care system, biobanks, and registries. *American Journal of Medical Genetics, Part B: Neuropsychiatric Genetics, 177*, 625–629.

Banda, J. M. (2019). Fully connecting the observational health data science and informatics (OHDSI) initiative with the world of linked open data. *Genomics and Informatics, 17*.

Baro, E., Degoul, S., Beuscart, R., & Chazard, E. (2015). Toward a literature-driven definition of big data in healthcare. *BioMed Research International, 2015*.

Beam, A. L., Manrai, A. K., & Ghassemi, M. (2020). Challenges to the reproducibility of machine learning models in health care. *Journal of the American Medical Association, 323*, 305–306.

Bell, I. H., Lim, M. H., Rossell, S. L., & Thomas, N. (2017). Ecological momentary assessment and intervention in the treatment of psychotic disorders: A systematic review. *Psychiatr. Serv., 68*, 1172–1181.

Boyd, A., et al. (2013). Cohort profile: The 'Children of the 90s'—The index offspring of the avon longitudinal study of parents and children. *Int. J. Epidemiol., 42*, 111–127.

Busk, J., et al. (2020). Forecasting mood in bipolar disorder from smartphone self-assessments: Hierarchical Bayesian approach. *JMIR mHealth uHealth, 8*, e15028.

Bycroft, C., et al. (2018). The UK Biobank resource with deep phenotyping and genomic data. *Nature, 562*, 203–209.

Casey, B. J., et al. (2018). The adolescent brain cognitive development (ABCD) study: Imaging acquisition across 21 sites. *Developmental Cognitive Neuroscience, 32*, 43–54.

Choi, K. W., et al. (2020). An exposure-wide and mendelian randomization approach to identifying modifiable factors for the prevention of depression. *Am. J. Psychiatry, 177*, 944–954.

Chowdhury, S., et al. (2013). Incorporating genomics into breast and prostate cancer screening: Assessing the implications. *Genetics in Medicine, 15*, 423–432.

Common Mind Consortium. https://www.synapse.org/#!Synapse:syn2759792/wiki/69613.

Davis, K. A. S., et al. (2020). Mental health in UK Biobank—development, implementation and results from an online questionnaire completed by 157 366 participants: A reanalysis. *BJPsych Open, 6*.

Demontis, D., et al. (2019). Discovery of the first genome-wide significant risk loci for attention deficit/hyperactivity disorder. *Nat. Genet., 51*, 63–75.

Dickerman, B. A., & Hernán, M. A. (2020). Counterfactual prediction is not only for causal inference. *European Journal of Epidemiology, 35*, 615–617.

Esteva, A., et al. (2019). A guide to deep learning in healthcare. *Nat. Med., 25*, 24–29.

Ferrat, L. A., et al. (2020). A combined risk score enhances prediction of type 1 diabetes among susceptible children. *Nat. Med., 26*, 1247–1255.

FinnGen. (2020). *FinnGen Documentation of R4 release.* https://finngen.gitbook.io/documentation/.

Frei, O., et al. (2019). Bivariate causal mixture model quantifies polygenic overlap between complex traits beyond genetic correlation. *Nat. Commun., 10*, 1–11.

Fusar-Poli, P., & Meyer-Lindenberg, A. (2013). Striatal presynaptic dopamine in schizophrenia, part II: Meta-analysis of [(18)F/(11)C]-DOPA PET studies. *Schizophr. Bull., 39*, 33–42.

Gaziano, J. M., et al. (2016). Million veteran program: A mega-biobank to study genetic influences on health and disease. *J. Clin. Epidemiol., 70*, 214–223.

Gershon, E. S., Alliey-Rodriguez, N., & Liu, C. (2011). After GWAS: Searching for genetic risk for schizophrenia and bipolar disorder. *Am. J. Psychiatry, 168*, 253–256.

Gligorijević, V., Malod-Dognin, N., & Pržulj, N. (2016). Integrative methods for analyzing big data in precision medicine. *Proteomics, 16*, 741–758.

Grove, J., et al. (2019). Identification of common genetic risk variants for autism spectrum disorder. *Nat. Genet., 51*, 431–444.

GTEx Consortium, et al. (2017). Genetic effects on gene expression across human tissues. *Nature, 550*(204).

Hartwig, C., et al. (2018). Neurodevelopmental disease mechanisms, primary cilia, and endosomes converge on the BLOC-1 and BORC complexes. *Dev. Neurobiol., 78*, 311–330.

Hernán, M. A., Hsu, J., & Healy, B. (2019). A second chance to get causal inference right: A classification of data science tasks. *Chance*, *32*, 42–49.

Hey, S. P., & Kesselheim, A. S. (2016). Countering imprecision in precision medicine. *Science (80–)*, *353*, 448–449.

Hibar, D. P., et al. (2018). Cortical abnormalities in bipolar disorder: an MRI analysis of 6503 individuals from the ENIGMA Bipolar Disorder Working Group. *Mol. Psychiatry*, *23*, 932–942.

Hilker, R., et al. (2018). Heritability of schizophrenia and schizophrenia spectrum based on the nationwide Danish twin register. *Biol. Psychiatry*, *83*, 492–498.

Holland, D., et al. (2020). Beyond SNP heritability: Polygenicity and discoverability of phenotypes estimated with a univariate Gaussian mixture model. *PLoS Genet.*, *16*, e1008612.

Howes, O. D., McCutcheon, R., Owen, M. J., & Murray, R. M. (2017). The role of genes, stress, and dopamine in the development of schizophrenia. *Biol. Psychiatry*, *81*, 9–20.

Huynh-Le, M.-P., et al. (2021). Polygenic hazard score is associated with prostate cancer in multi-ethnic populations. *Nat. Commun.*, *12*, 1236.

Hyde, C. L., et al. (2016). Identification of 15 genetic loci associated with risk of major depression in individuals of European descent. *Nat. Genet.*, *48*, 1031–1036.

Johansson, V., Kuja-Halkola, R., Cannon, T. D., Hultman, C. M., & Hedman, A. M. (2019). A population-based heritability estimate of bipolar disorder—In a Swedish twin sample. *Psychiatry Res.*, *278*, 180–187.

Kaufmann, T., et al. (2019). Common brain disorders are associated with heritable patterns of apparent aging of the brain. *Nat. Neurosci.*, *22*, 1617–1623.

Kauppi, K., et al. (2018). Combining polygenic hazard score with volumetric MRI and cognitive measures improves prediction of progression from mild cognitive impairment to Alzheimer's disease. *Front. Neurosci.*, *12*, 260.

Kendler, K. S., Ohlsson, H., Lichtenstein, P., Sundquist, J., & Sundquist, K. (2018). The genetic epidemiology of treated major depression in Sweden. *Am. J. Psychiatry*, *175*, 1137–1144.

Kessler, R. C., et al. (2017). Predicting suicides after outpatient mental health visits in the Army Study to Assess Risk and Resilience in Servicemembers (Army STARRS). *Mol. Psychiatry*, *22*, 544–551.

Kinkorová, J., & Topolčan, O. (2020). Biobanks in the era of big data: objectives, challenges, perspectives, and innovations for predictive, preventive, and personalised medicine. *EPMA J.*, *11*(3), 333–341. https://doi.org/10.1007/s13167-020-00213-2.

Koutsouleris, N., et al. (2016). Multisite prediction of 4-week and 52-week treatment outcomes in patients with first-episode psychosis: A machine learning approach. *The Lancet Psychiatry*, *3*, 935–946.

Kraguljac, N. V., & Lahti, A. C. (2018). Paving the way for targeted drug development in schizophrenia. *JAMA Psychiatry*, *75*, 19–20.

Krokstad, S., et al. (2013). Cohort profile: The HUNT study, Norway. *Int. J. Epidemiol.*, *42*, 968–977.

Lally, J., & MacCabe, J. H. (2015). Antipsychotic medication in schizophrenia: A review. *Br. Med. Bull.*, *114*, 169–179.

Lally, J., & MacCabe, J. H. (2016). Personalised approaches to pharmacotherapy for schizophrenia. *BJPsych Adv.*, *22*, 78–86.

Laursen, T. M., et al. (2013). Life expectancy and death by diseases of the circulatory system in patients with bipolar disorder or schizophrenia in the Nordic countries. *PLoS One*, *8*, e67133.

Legge, S. E., et al. (2019). Association of genetic liability to psychotic experiences with neuropsychotic disorders and traits. *JAMA Psychiatry*, *76*, 1256–1265.

Magnus, P., et al. (2016). Cohort profile update: The Norwegian mother and child cohort study (MoBa). *Int. J. Epidemiol.*, *45*, 382–388.

Manchia, M., et al. (2020). Translating big data to better treatment in bipolar disorder—a manifesto for coordinated action. *Eur. Neuropsychopharmacol.*, *36*, 121–136.

Mars, N., et al. (2020). Polygenic and clinical risk scores and their impact on age at onset and prediction of cardiometabolic diseases and common cancers. *Nat. Med.*, *26*, 549–557.

Melcher, J., Hays, R., & Torous, J. (2020). Digital phenotyping for mental health of college students: A clinical review. *Evidence-based mental health*, *23*, 161–166.

Mosley, J. D., et al. (2020). Predictive accuracy of a polygenic risk score compared with a clinical risk score for incident coronary heart disease. *J. Am. Med. Assoc.*, *323*, 627–635.

Mullins, N., et al. (2020). Genome-wide association study of over 40,000 bipolar disorder cases provides novel biological insights. *medRxiv*. https://doi.org/10.1101/2020.09.17.20187054.

Navale, V., & Bourne, P. E. (2018). Cloud computing applications for biomedical science: A perspective. *PLoS Comput. Biol.*, *14*.

Ngiam, K. Y., & Khor, I. W. (2019). Big data and machine learning algorithms for health-care delivery. *The Lancet Oncology*, *20*, e262–e273.

Ngoya, P. S., Muhogora, W. E., & Pitcher, R. D. (2016). Defining the diagnostic divide: An analysis of registered radiological equipment resources in a low-income African country. *Pan Afr. Med. J.*, *25*.

Nunes, A., et al. (2020). Using structural MRI to identify bipolar disorders—13 site machine learning study in 3020 individuals from the ENIGMA Bipolar Disorders Working Group. *Mol. Psychiatry*, *25*, 2130–2143.

Oedegaard, K. J., et al. (2016). The pharmacogenomics of bipolar disorder study (PGBD): Identification of genes for lithium response in a prospective sample. *BMC Psychiatry*, *16*.

Pardiñas, A. F., et al. (2018). Common schizophrenia alleles are enriched in mutation-intolerant genes and in regions under strong background selection. *Nat. Genet.*, *50*, 381–389.

Patel, R., et al. (2015). Mood instability is a common feature of mental health disorders and is associated with poor clinical outcomes. *BMJ Open*, *5*.

Paulus, M. P., & Thompson, W. K. (2019). The challenges and opportunities of small effects: The new normal in academic psychiatry. *JAMA Psychiatry*, *76*.

Putt, S., et al. (2020). Exploration of experiences with and understanding of polygenic risk scores for bipolar disorder. *J. Affect. Disord.*, *265*, 342–350.

Qiu, X., et al. (2017). The born in Guangzhou cohort study (BIGCS). *Eur. J. Epidemiol.*, *32*, 337–346.

Rimol, L. M., et al. (2012). Cortical volume, surface area, and thickness in schizophrenia and bipolar disorder. *Biol. Psychiatry*, *71*, 552–560.

Ripke, S., Walters, J. T. R., & O'Donovan, M. C. (2020). Mapping genomic loci prioritises genes and implicates synaptic biology in schizophrenia. *medRxiv*. https://doi.org/10.1101/2020.09.12.20192922.

Samuel, A. L. (1959). Some studies in machine learning using the game of checkers. *IBM J. Res. Dev.*, *3*, 210–229.

Schennach-Wolff, R., et al. (2011). Predictors of response and remission in the acute treatment of first-episode schizophrenia patients—Is it all about early response? *Eur. Neuropsychopharmacol.*, *21*, 370–378.

Schizophrenia Working Group of the Psychiatric Genomics Consortium, et al. (2014). Biological insights from 108 schizophrenia-associated genetic loci. *Nature*, *511*, 421.

Schork, A. J., et al. (2013). All SNPs are not created equal: Genome-wide association studies reveal a consistent pattern of enrichment among functionally annotated SNPs. *PLoS Genet*, *9*, e1003449.

Schür, R. R., et al. (2016). Brain GABA levels across psychiatric disorders: A systematic literature review and meta-analysis of 1H-MRS studies. *Hum. Brain Mapp.*, *37*, 3337–3352.

Schwartz, S., Schultz, S., Reider, A., & Saunders, E. F. H. (2016). Daily mood monitoring of symptoms using smartphones in bipolar disorder: A pilot study assessing the feasibility of ecological momentary assessment. *J. Affect. Disord.*, *191*, 88–93.

Shatte, A. B. R., Hutchinson, D. M., & Teague, S. J. (2019). Machine learning in mental health: A scoping review of methods and applications. *Psychol. Med.*, *49*, 1426–1448.

Shilo, S., Rossman, H., & Segal, E. (2020). Axes of a revolution: Challenges and promises of big data in healthcare. *Nature Medicine*, *26*, 29–38.

Singh, I., & Rose, N. (2009). Biomarkers in psychiatry. *Nature*, *460*, 202–207.

Smeland, O. B., et al. (2019). Discovery of shared genomic loci using the conditional false discovery rate approach. *Hum. Genet.*, 1–10.

Smeland, O. B., Frei, O., Dale, A. M., & Andreassen, O. A. (2020). The polygenic architecture of schizophrenia—rethinking pathogenesis and nosology. *Nature Reviews Neurology*, 1–14. Nature Research. https://doi.org/10.1038/s41582-020-0364-0.

Squeglia, L. M., et al. (2016). Neural predictors of initiating alcohol use during adolescence. *Am. J. Psychiatry*, *174*, 172–185.

Stahl, E. A., et al. (2019). Genome-wide association study identifies 30 loci associated with bipolar disorder. *Nat. Genet.*, *51*, 793–803.

Stephens, Z. D., et al. (2015). Big data: Astronomical or genomical? *PLoS Biol.*, *13*, 1–11.

Sudlow, C., et al. (2015). UK biobank: an open access resource for identifying the causes of a wide range of complex diseases of middle and old age. *Plos med*, *12*, e1001779.

Tam, V., et al. (2019). Benefits and limitations of genome-wide association studies. *Nature Reviews Genetics*, *20*, 467–484.

Thompson, P. M., et al. (2020). ENIGMA and global neuroscience: A decade of large-scale studies of the brain in health and disease across more than 40 countries. *Translational Psychiatry*, *10*, 1–28.

Turley, P., et al. (2018). Multi-trait analysis of genome-wide association summary statistics using MTAG. *Nat. Genet.*, *50*, 229–237.

Tyrrell, J., et al. (2021). Genetic predictors of participation in optional components of UK Biobank. *Nat. Commun.*, *12*, 886.

Ursini, G., et al. (2018). Convergence of placenta biology and genetic risk for schizophrenia article. *Nat. Med.*, *24*, 792–801.

Vai, B., et al. (2020). Predicting differential diagnosis between bipolar and unipolar depression with multiple kernel learning on multimodal structural neuroimaging. *Eur. Neuropsychopharmacol.*, *34*, 28–38.

van der Meer, D., et al. (2020). Understanding the genetic determinants of the brain with MOSTest. *Nat. Commun.*, *11*, 3512.

Van Le, D., Montgomery, J., Kirkby, K. C., & Scanlan, J. (2018). Risk prediction using natural language processing of electronic mental health records in an inpatient forensic psychiatry setting. *J. Biomed. Inform.*, *86*, 49–58.

Vaucher, J., et al. (2018). Cannabis use and risk of schizophrenia: A Mendelian randomization study. *Mol. Psychiatry*, *23*, 1287–1292.

Verbanck, M., Chen, C. Y., Neale, B., & Do, R. (2018). Detection of widespread horizontal pleiotropy in causal relationships inferred from Mendelian randomization between complex traits and diseases. *Nat. Genet.*, *50*, 693–698.

Walker, E. R., McGee, R. E., & Druss, B. G. (2015). Mortality in mental disorders and global disease burden implications. *JAMA Psychiatry*. https://doi.org/10.1001/jamapsychiatry.2014.2502.

Wörheide, M. A., Krumsiek, J., Kastenmüller, G., & Arnold, M. (2021). Multi-omics integration in biomedical research—A metabolomics-centric review. *Analytica Chimica Acta, 1141,* 144–162.

World Health Organization. (1993). *The ICD-10 classification of mental and behavioural disorders: Diagnostic criteria for research. The ICD-10 classification of mental and behavioural disorders: Diagnostic criteria for research.*

World Health Organization (WHO). (2008). Scaling up care for mental, neurological, and substance use disorders. *mhGAP Ment. Heal. Gap Action Program, 44.*

Wray, N. R., et al. (2018). Genome-wide association analyses identify 44 risk variants and refine the genetic architecture of major depression. *Nat. Genet., 50,* 668.

Yim, S. J., et al. (2020). The utility of smartphone-based, ecological momentary assessment for depressive symptoms. *Journal of Affective Disorders, 274,* 602–609.

Collecting data from Internet (and other platform) users for mental health research

Ashley A. Lahoud, Theresa R. Gladstone, Sydney B. Clark, and Christopher A. Flessner
Department of Psychological Sciences, Kent State University, Kent, OH, United States

Introduction/overview

The Internet has been one of the most impactful advances of the 21st century. Today, nearly 60% of people on the planet use the Internet (Internet World Stats. Available online: http://www.internetworldstats.com/stats.htm accessed on July 11, 2020). The digital world has transformed society, impacting everything from basic everyday appliances, like vacuums and cars, to human emotion and behavior. Given the Internet's wide reach and prevalence, it is no surprise that scientists have realized its potential as a tool to both promote and conduct research. Internet use has grown rapidly since its inception (Reips, 2001). Over the first decade of the 21st century alone, academic output on the Internet in refereed journals has increased dramatically (Dutton, 2013). As the Internet becomes a more integral part of users' daily lives, it is imperative to consider the ways the Internet can be used to help conduct psychological research as well as the impact the Internet itself has on the psyche of users. Internet research can be divided into three general categories: translational (implementing traditional methods; e.g., surveys, questionnaires, etc., on the Internet), phenomenological (studying a topic unique to/spawned by the Internet; e.g., social media use, Internet addiction), and novel (providing a new way to study phenomenon already being studied in psychology; e.g., impression formation, media preferences). In this chapter, we aim to provide readers with a brief historical overview of the Internet's use within the context of psychological research, followed by a discussion of the validity of using the Internet to complete said research as well as the costs and benefits to doing so. We end the chapter with a discussion of various tools available to researchers for conducting research online, as well as where to access research participants on the Internet.

A brief historical overview of the Internet's use within psychology

Records of computer use in psychological experiments began as early as the 1970s (Connes, 1972); however, it wasn't until the mid-1990s, as computer technology improved and Internet use became more ubiquitous, that the Internet began to become a

Mental Health in a Digital World. https://doi.org/10.1016/B978-0-12-822201-0.00015-0

major tool in psychology and mental health research (Gosling & Mason, 2015). Some of the first papers to report conducting research on the web were presented as early as 1996 at the Society for Computers in Psychology (Krantz & Reips, 2017). Since then, the aims of psychological research have changed as the ways that people interact with the Internet have evolved and the distinction between online life and "real life" has become more blurred.

Kuś (2014) described three distinguishable eras of the Internet. The first era occurred from the early 1990s to 2002 and was marked by a general pessimistic perception of the Internet. The anonymity of the Internet caused many to view it as having a potentially destructive influence on social relationships. This sentiment was supported by early mental health research by Kraut et al. (1998), which found that the amount of time novice users spent on the web was associated with stronger symptoms of depression, stress, and social isolation. Despite this negative perception of the Internet, researchers also began to focus on examining whether studies utilizing Internet sampling methodology produced valid results. This work helped build trust among the research community and laid the foundation for the conduct of future studies.

The start of the second era of the Internet was marked by the advent of social media sites like MySpace (2003) and Facebook (2004). This era further introduced novel research questions connecting mental health to Internet use (Hawn, 2009) and also introduced new methods for engaging participants in the research enterprise. A full discussion of social media research is outside the scope of this chapter; however, social media use has both assisted in translational research (i.e., via recruitment opportunities as well as direct surveys which can be posted to and completed on the site) and given rise to phenomenological research pertaining to the impact of social media on everything from mental health to behavior. This era also brought with it multiple textbook publications focusing on Internet research, thus, helping to legitimize Internet sampling methods and procedures as a research method (Birnbaum, 2000; Fraley & Brumbaugh, 2004; Joinson, McKenna, Postmes, & Reips, 2007).

The third and final era began in approximately 2012. This final era relates to another wave of pessimism regarding the integration of the Internet into nearly all aspects of human life. It is also closely related to the development and proliferation of Internet accessibility via smartphones and tablets. The ability to access the Internet at nearly any time and on a host of devices has led to what some have referred to as "digital dementia." This term, coined by Spitzer (2013), refers to the Internet's deleterious impact on memory and attention. New sources of data, such as crowdsourcing and big data, have been and continue to be explored. Overall, the Internet has historically exerted a growing impact on psychological research, but in order for research in this domain to advance, reliability and validity of Internet sampling must be evident.

Are the use of Internet sampling procedures reliable and valid?

Can we rely on research conducted via the Internet to be reliable and valid? Fortunately, this was one of the earliest questions asked by investigators within the field of psychology seeking to leverage the Internet for the conduct of scientific research (Krantz, Ballard, & Scher, 1997). Researchers were eager to utilize a method of collecting data that limited issues experienced in the lab (i.e., costliness, small sample sizes, participant response bias, etc.); however, Internet research came with its fair share of critics and mistrust. In the early days of Internet research, much of the skepticism hailed from assumptions about who was online and how the potential participants behaved. For example, concerns that Internet samples (1) were selective and lacking in diversity, (2) failed to generalize across presentation formats, (3) were more easily impacted by data fraud including the same participants completing a study multiple times, and (4) findings would differ from those obtained via more traditional methods (Gosling & Mason, 2015; Gosling, Vazire, Srivastava, & John, 2004; Krantz & Reips, 2017) were frequently cited. Since these earlier days, a plethora of work has largely debunked these concerns.

Researchers studying a diverse array of topics from perceptions of attractiveness and desirability, to health-related messages, or Internet attitudes and behaviors have found that the psychometric properties of the measures utilized across in-person and Internet sampling methodologies exhibit no significant differences (Dodou & de Winter, 2014; Krantz et al., 1997; Lewis, Watson, & White, 2010; Riva, Teruzzi, & Anolli, 2003). The results of Internet studies are generally consistent with those obtained with participants recruited via traditional methods.

Krantz and Dalal (2000) have posited that "validity" is the correspondence of results between experiments conducted on the web and within the laboratory. That is, a data set utilizing the same variables should show trends in data that are similar across formats; thus, the results of the two studies should be highly correlated (Krantz et al., 1997). A majority of studies have found differences between results obtained with Internet and paper-and-pencil versions of questionnaires (Bliven, Kaufman, & Spertus, 2001; Ekman, Dickman, Klint, Weiderpass, & Litton, 2006; Fouladi, McCarthy, & Moller, 2002). For example, Gosling et al. (2004) compared an Internet sample of 361,703 users to a traditional sample comprised of all studies in the *Journal of Personality and Social Psychology* in the year 2002. Their findings were promising and demonstrated that Internet samples were not adversely impacted by scammers (repeat responders or respondents responding too quickly) and were generally more diverse than samples collected via traditional methods (Gosling et al., 2004). Previous and subsequent studies have come to similar conclusions (Lewis et al., 2010; Reips, 1996). This research indicates consistency, if not improvement, in sample collection methods between online and non-Internet methods. The trend throughout this research indicates that Internet and laboratory studies tend to yield the same conclusions (Krantz & Dalal, 2000). Importantly, each research field will have to verify validity among their topics in order to identify what types of research can be conducted over the Internet.

Of course, though there is a tendency for Internet and laboratory studies to yield the same results, this is not always the case. For example, Campos, Zucoloto, Bonafé, Jordani, and Maroco (2011) found that although self-report measures of burnout show good reliability in both paper-and-pencil and online administration formats, the concordance between answers was generally higher in the paper-and-pencil format. Some studies, however, have found nonequivalence of psychometric properties, particularly when measuring areas such as desirability (Barak & Cohen, 2002; Joinson, 1999). These differences were assumed to be a direct result of the mode of administration, rather than sample differences. These variances can be illuminating and meaningful in their own right.

The use of the Internet to collect research data has also opened the door to studies that implement mixed methods to better answer research questions. For example, the People's Internet (PIN) study is utilizing a mixed methods approach in three countries to investigate how people use the Internet in daily life. Data collection includes ethnography with large-scale surveys, document analysis, and digital trace data of online users (Ørmen, Helles, & Bruhn Jensen, 2021). Termed "triangulation," each method illuminates a unique, yet related aspect of Internet use and allows the research to corroborate findings using multiple methods (Blaikie, 1991). Overall, the Internet gives researchers the ability to more easily collect various types of data (i.e., qualitative and quantitative) within one study, which allows for more thorough and nuanced investigations of research questions. Sound data collection methods are imperative to the success of this work.

The research described above suggests that there may be substantially less discrepancy between the psychometric properties of various assessments tools, and, in turn, the results obtained via Internet sampling vs face-to-face procedures than was once hypothesized. When implementing creative and new methods of research, however, it is important to revise and improve methods of data collection as science progresses. Various methods have been developed to further improve the quality of data collected via Internet sampling procedures. For example, a commonly employed tool utilized within the context of Internet research is the instructional manipulation check. This tool involves including one or more question that appear similar to other questions included within the assessment battery/survey; however, this manipulation check item requires the participant to do something unexpected (e.g., click a certain answer; Oppenheimer, Meyvis, & Davidenko, 2009). This item is designed to detect whether the respondent is paying attention to instructions and/or may be responding randomly to study items. Various other strategies have been developed to increase Internet research quality including (1) monitoring the amount of time it takes a participant to complete the study to determine if they completed it significantly quicker or slower than other participants (Johnson, 2010), (2) making participants aware of errors like missing items using automated features (Johnson, 2010), (3) offering appropriate incentives (Göritz, 2010), and (4) recruiting from places that make it hard for individuals to fake their identity or participate in the research multiple times (e.g., studies completed via Facebook, where an individual would have to have multiple accounts to participate more than once; Stillwell & Kosinski, 2012, see more in Gosling & Mason, 2015). By implementing these and other methods, researchers can continue to reap the benefits of online research.

Benefits to utilizing the Internet to answer research questions

The number of research studies completed online has continued to grow, and this, in large part, is due to the many benefits of the use of Internet research to answer important scientific questions. For example, recruitment is perhaps the most often lauded benefit to the use of Internet research. The Internet circumvents transportation issues, allowing participants to participate from a much wider geographic location. Recruitment of large and diverse samples allows researchers to study people besides the WEIRD (Western, educated, industrialized, rich, and democratic) samples that are easy to access on college campuses and typically make up a study's participant pool. Furthermore, recruiting via the Internet allows researchers to target populations of participants that are hard to reach, small, and geographically dispersed (i.e., transgender populations; Miner, Bockting, Romine, & Raman, 2012). The ability of participants to complete a research study from the privacy of one's own home addresses, in part, concerns related to participants responding in a more socially desirable manner (Kraut et al., 2004). Anecdotally, in the last author's (CAF's) own research experiences seeking to understand the phenomenology of trichotillomania (i.e., hair pulling disorder), respondents to a large Internet-based survey reported higher rates of pulling hair from their pubic region than is typically found when conducting face-to-face interviews (Woods et al., 2006). These results have been attributed to the fact that participants may be more comfortable responding to potentially stigmatizing and embarrassing topics when they are alone than when they are face-to-face with someone who may judge them (Franklin et al., 2008). Further, in a study of 96 researchers, cost effectiveness, speed, ease, and statistical power were rated among the most highly valued reasons for conducting a study via the web. Other benefits include that Internet research allows massive amounts of data to be collected easily, it obviates the need for data entry, and provides for the use of skip logic and in-the-moment performance to streamline the process of completing questionnaires while also providing immediate feedback to participants and researchers. In addition, the Internet allows various forms of media such as videos, sounds, animations, etc., to be integrated into studies with relative ease (Gosling & Johnson, 2010).

Method-specific benefits to Internet research also exist. For example, qualitative research conducted using Internet sampling procedures allows researchers to avoid the laborious task of transcription and also provides participants with different methods (e.g., online focus groups, online interviews, message boards) which may be more convenient and conducive to participation (Rodham & Gavin, 2006). As briefly mentioned above, a substantial development in the proliferation of Internet research in the past decade has been the use of smart phones. The ubiquity of smartphones makes them ideal for collecting time sensitive, moment-by-moment data. The ability to quantify these moment-by-moment, individual-level behaviors from smartphones is known as "digital phenotyping" (Torous, Kiang, Lorme, & Onnela, 2016). The data collected from these devices can be combined with electronic medical records, molecular imaging, and neuroimaging to more holistically capture the social and behavioral dimensions of psychiatric and neurological disease. Smartphone data collection also lends itself to easier and simplified longitudinal collection (Harari et al., 2016). Finally, telehealth (i.e., providing mental health services remotely via the Internet) research was spawned with the birth of the Internet and its use in healthcare. The ability to complete this research via the web enhances accessibility and ecological validity of the work (Comer et al., 2015, 2017).

Lastly, the Internet better connects researchers and volunteers interested in their studies. Whereas before, individuals in large part were required to live near medical centers in order to receive information about clinical trials, the Internet capitalizes on the fact that there are people interested in knowing more about themselves and their medical conditions. ClinicalTrials.gov, for example, has thousands of visitors each day. There is significant motivation among patients to seek out new trials, particularly for unmet medical needs (Pulley et al., 2018). Brüggen, de Ruyter, and Wetzels (2005) mention that one of the main motivating factors for participants to contribute to research, besides compensation, is a desire to give opinions and a need for recognition. Internet research uniquely allows participants to engage in the research enterprise. Despite the many benefits inherent to web-based research, several limitations must also be considered.

Risks/costs of Internet research

Although the use of the Internet is largely positive for psychology and mental health researchers, there are costs to conducting research of this nature. As was alluded to previously, study materials need to be validated for online use (Buchanan, 2007; Buchanan, Johnson, & Goldberg, 2005). This can add labor and time to what may otherwise be a very straightforward design. Similarly, many researchers are not specifically instructed how to properly perform online studies before engaging in this type of research (Krantz & Reips, 2017). Many research design textbooks do not include sections about how to conduct research online; thus, finding and receiving this training is an added challenge (Krantz & Reips, 2017). Even studies completed with validated measures by trained researchers can experience challenges.

Some of the major concerns in conducting Internet research pertain to participant drop-out, lack of environmental controls, technical variances, and ethical issues. It is easier for participants to drop out of web-based research, whereas it is rare for a participant to leave an in-person study (Krantz, 2012). Participants completing research independent of experimenters reduce performative responses and the pressures of social desirability, allowing participants more autonomy. It can also lead to incomplete data sets. This issue is magnified if dropout is nonrandom, which can limit generalizability and introduce an important confound to study results. Because participants are not in the laboratory, environmental variations are also not easily controlled. This is particularly true of research conducted via smartphones, which can be used from nearly any place and at any time. Further, technical variance cannot be well-controlled utilizing Internet sampling procedures. For example, how participants view and interact with research tasks can vary depending on whether they are viewing the study on a desktop, laptop, smartphone, or other device. Additional programs running in the background, the ability to listen to audio, network connection, etc. can impact a participant's experience and, thus, the pursuant results. Thankfully, many of these variances can be collected as part of the experiment. Finally, there are ethical issues that need to be considered when running studies online. Because a researcher is not there to explain the study or debrief after it is completed, there is no commonly accepted way to be sure that participants understand the nature of the study (Kraut et al., 2004). This is particularly relevant in work with minors or at-risk populations. Some drawbacks of Internet research, however, are specific to the mode of collection.

One method of collection many researchers are turning to for data is "big data" (see Chapter 2). Big data is the "large scale analysis of log data from digital devices" (Lazer, Kennedy, King, & Vespignani, 2014). In research, this data often comes from social media users and web audiences (Freelon, 2014), Unfortunately, it can be challenging to validate the output and techniques used to generate this data (Rieder, Abdulla, Poell, Woltering, & Zack, 2015) and the data is typically created for commercial and not academic use, thus shaping what data is included and how it is presented (Webster, 2015). Furthermore, big data focuses more on aggregate trends and less on the individual, so there may be large variations in behaviors, causing researchers to overlook meaningful differences. Despite these various factors, the benefits of using the Internet to complete mental health research far outweigh the risks.

How to go about collecting data from Internet users

The Internet can aid in many aspects of research. Study advertisement, survey and study creation, and participant recruitment are some of the domains where the Internet is best poised to assist researchers. The following portion of this chapter discusses various Internet platforms on which to advertise, create, and recruit for studies. Innumerable platforms exist in each of these domains and so this chapter cannot claim to be inclusive of every existing platform. Furthermore, because this industry evolves rapidly, we expect details herein to become quickly outdated. It is the authors' hope that information and resources provided here can be used to help make informed decisions about the best practices of Internet research in clinical psychology. This discussion of various Internet platforms to assist with research will serve as a springboard for researchers considering prevalent and alternative platforms for research in the field. The hope is by increasing awareness of the various modes of task completion, researchers can make better and more informed choices in construction of research designs to better answer their questions. As a final note, many of the to-be mentioned platforms contribute to more than one domain of research (i.e., can be used for a combination of advertisement for, construction of, and recruitment for research).

In the digital age, when people are arguably overloaded with messages and potential ways to spend their time on the Internet, how do mental health researchers break through the clutter and get people interested in participating in their studies? This question has been present long before the advent of the Internet, but the Internet offers unique advertising opportunities for researchers. For many researchers, the obvious answer is to follow the lead of marketers and businesses and use a combination of traditional paper ads, word of mouth, and the Internet. The replication crisis has pushed researchers to recruit non-WEIRD samples. One way to do this is to physically go out into the communities and advertise at highly populated events where the desired participants are likely to congregate. Many of these events have websites where sponsors are recognized, and/or they feature screens at the events that alternately display event information and sponsor advertisements. For a fee, researchers may use the event itself, along with the online sites already being trafficked by guests of the event, to help recruit participants. In a similar vein, this technique can be applied to any situation where a public space is infiltrated by screens, including city buses, kiosks, and more.

There are other creative ways for researchers to use technology to more efficiently make potential participants aware of research studies. The integration of QR codes onto paper advertisement is one such way. QuickResponse or QR codes are matrix bar codes that can be scanned via smartphones to take a participant directly to a website or survey. With normal paper advertising, the impetus is largely on the participant to instigate connecting with researchers. With the use of QR codes, the participant burden is decreased. Participants can fill out a survey agreeing to be contacted by the researcher, which is typically less cumbersome than having to remember and call on their own time and can be done at any time of day rather than just during business hours.

One of the primary ways research advertising has been pursued on the Internet is via electronic ads on social media platforms. Ads on sites like Facebook and YouTube have become a very popular recruitment method. One of the main benefits to this type of advertisement is that the ad can be targeted. Facebook, in particular, has risen in popularity with researchers, as ads can lead directly to online surveys. This type of advertising is particularly beneficial when targeting specific groups, as information can be posted directly on pages to which individuals in those groups subscribe. A more thorough description of the use of social media in mental health research is discussed elsewhere in this book, and thus is outside of the scope of this chapter; but, these forms of advertising should not be overlooked when considering ways to optimize Internet use in research.

The Internet has even been built into how convenience samples of undergraduates are recruited. SONA Systems software is an online cloud-based program designed to help manage research participants. This software is commonly used by psychology researchers, whereby undergraduate students enroll in research studies often in exchange for class participation credit. The generalizability of findings inferred from samples comprised of college students has been long debated. However, it is generally agreed that college students differ from others in the general population in meaningful ways. For example, responses from college students have been found to be more homogeneous compared to nonstudent adults and the effect sizes of college student data differs in magnitude and direction compared to adult samples (Peterson, 2001). Although student samples are considered the initial form of "convenience sample," the advent of the Internet has introduced two new convenience sample methods: online panels and crowdsourcing (Roulin, 2015).

One research exclusive method to recruiting participants via the Internet is the use of online panels. Online panels are a sample of persons who have agreed to complete surveys and provide information via the Internet. Panelists typically provide personal and basic demographic information, which allows researchers to select a pool of potential respondents that falls within the population they are interested in for their specific surveys. Most panel vendors are panel "brokers" meaning they outsource surveys to partners and these partners administer them to their own panels (Craig et al., 2013). Invitations to complete a survey are typically sent to panelists using a generic email invitation. There are two kinds of online panels: probability panels and nonprobability (convenience) panels. Probability panelists are recruited through random, registry-based sampling of the general population (Hays, Liu, & Kapteyn, 2015). Recruitment methods are less selective and may involve random digit dialing or address-based sampling. Examples of some probability-based samples include the GFK Knowledge Panel (now part of Ipsos), which has a panel of 55,000 individuals recruited using address-based sampling. Although the panel has existed for decades, it does not appear to be aiming to increase the number of panelists, as Ipsos only randomly selects a few addresses a year to receive an invitation to join the KnowledgePanel to offset attrition, https://join. knpanel.com/about.html. Other panels include the Longitudinal Internet Studies for Social Sciences (LISS) panel in the Netherlands, which uses population registry-based sampling, or the American Life Panel, which recruits by random digit dialing, face-to-face, and address-based sampling.

Nonprobability samples typically self-enroll in online panels by clicking on pop-up banners or signing up through a website. For this reason, these panels tend to be made up of more educated individuals with higher socioeconomic status compared to nonpanel members (Craig et al., 2013). Because response rates are low, and quota sampling approaches are often used to target respondents with certain characteristics, panel respondents are often weighted to match a target distribution (e.g., the US census; Hays et al., 2015). There are many examples of convenience-based samples online that are most typically used in market-based research, but some noteworthy ones in clinical research include ResearchMatch, MedSurvey, and M3 Global Research. ResearchMatch is a clinical research-specific online panel hosted by Vanderbilt University. It aims to match volunteers throughout the US with researchers actively searching for individuals interested in completing clinical research (Harris et al., 2012). Researchers must be a member of a Clinical and Translational Science Awards (CTSA) consortium institution in order to post studies to ResearchMatch (Harris et al., 2012), and currently their website boasts 146,656 volunteers, 8637 researchers, and 775 studies (accessed July 26, 2020). Other examples of health-specific online convenience panels include MedSurvey and M3 Global Research. When deciding on the use of an online panel, it is important for researchers to consider the pros and cons. Similar to the pros and cons mentioned earlier with regard to Internet-based sampling procedures, online panels can present shortcomings related to responsiveness, sociodemographic diversity and validated data, and participant overlap between panels (Craig et al., 2013; Hays et al., 2015). For example, probability samples are consistently more accurate than nonprobability surveys (Yeager et al., 2011). It is worth noting that many of these panel companies not only offer access to their panels of participants, but also offer help programming surveys and reporting results. Notably, though these recruitment methods occur on the web, the research itself does not have to be hosted online. Online panels are not the only opportunity on the Internet to access research participants.

Crowdsourcing is another popular online recruitment method. The term "crowdsourcing" is often highly debated (Wazny, 2017). Generically, crowdsourcing refers to the use of Internet services to host research opportunities by enlisting the services of large groups of people, who are either paid or unpaid, and submit their data via the Internet. Crowdsourcing and online samples have much in common, and in fact, various sources have referred to the same online research collection sites (i.e., Qualtrics Panels) as both an online panel (Roulin, 2015) and a crowdsourcing service (Buhrmester, Talaifar, & Gosling, 2018). Although they serve much the same function, research conducted via crowdsourcing sites invite participants to complete studies that are administered exclusively online, whereas research advertised via an online platform can either be conducted online, or the invitation can be to an in-person study. Like online platforms, there are hundreds of crowdsourcing sites available, but the most widely used in psychological research is Amazon Mechanical Turk (MTurk).

MTurk is a crowdsourcing platform owned by Amazon. The website, first introduced in 2005, allows researchers ("requesters") to post Human Intelligence Tasks (HITS) that online participants ("workers") can choose to complete for monetary compensation (usually ranging from cents to a couple of dollars depending on the task), though recruitment costs include a 40% commission paid to Amazon (Boas, Christenson, & Glick, 2020). In many fields of psychological research, the number of MTurk studies has increased over time to the point that MTurk studies have started to crowd out studies using college participants (Anderson et al., 2019). Compared to other study methods, MTurk studies are brief (Anderson et al., 2019) and many studies have found no difference between performance of MTurk participants and those recruited via other methods, such as social media or university samples (Buhrmester, Kwang, & Gosling, 2011; Gleibs, 2017). The demographic diversity of MTurk exceeds that of typical undergraduate populations, though the research pool is not representative of the US population (Arditte, Cek, Shaw, & Timpano, 2016; Buhrmester et al., 2011; Casler, Bickel, & Hackett, 2013). Obviously, MTurk has been embraced by the research community and is now a prominent tool in many domains of psychological research. In fact, a 2018 study of the application of crowdsourcing in health cited only four studies that used crowdsourcing in clinical mental health research, all of which had applied the use of MTurk (Wazny, 2018). Although MTurk embodies many of the benefits of Internet research discussed earlier (i.e., fast, large sample sizes, cost-effective, ease, flexible research designs, and longitudinal study capabilities; Buhrmester et al., 2018; Chandler & Shapiro, 2016) there are limitations to MTurk. For example, MTurk provides a convenience sample of workers from primarily the United States and India. Researchers must be careful when generalizing the results of their experiment to persons hailing from other nationalities. Furthermore, research comparing the use of MTurk to in-person survey completion has found significantly higher self-reported levels of distraction among participants using MTurk, but surprisingly few differences in attention between conditions (Clifford & Jerit, 2014). Correcting for some of these limitations may be easier navigated via the use of other crowdsourcing platforms.

The number of crowdsourcing platforms in research continues to grow. For example, there are currently several platforms, such as Prolific Academic, Turkprime, Daemo, and Finding Five specifically created to cater to the needs of academic users.

Prolific Academic (ProA), for instance, has a more diverse participant pool than MTurk, and participants have been found to be comparatively more naïve and less dishonest (Peer, Brandimarte, Samat, & Acquisti, 2017). Other platforms have been geared more toward market research but are still potentially useful for scientific research. These include CrowdFlower, ClickWorker, Research Now, etc. CrowdFlower, for example, is a crowdsourcing platform that has been mentioned as an alternative to MTurk. CrowdFlower is an aggregator platform, meaning that tasks are delegated to multiple partner channels. It has the added benefit of preventing the submission of multiple surveys from the same IP address and has mechanisms to prevent contamination from scammers (de Winter, Kyriakidis, Dodou, & Happee, 2015). Like Prolific Academic, participants have been found to be more naïve and less dishonest than MTurk samples, and exhibit better response rates than MTurk or ProA (Peer et al., 2017). MicroWorkers was identified by Crone and Williams (2017) as a viable crowdsourcing platform for Australians, who make up only a small portion of the MTurk sample. Although Crone and Williams (2017) found recruitment via MicroWorkers to be slower than MTurk and 9% of users were discovered to be minors, participants were relatively new/infrequent users and more diverse than college samples. The above represents just a few examples of the prevailing literature on alternative crowdsourcing platforms. Many other reviews exist highlighting the variance between MTurk and other crowdsourcing sites (Vakharia, 2013; Wazny, 2017). The authors share Buhrmester et al.'s (2018) sentiment that the most prudent course of action when it comes to utilizing an unfamiliar crowdsourcing platform is to seek out work by colleagues who have had experience with that particular platform and learn from it.

Tools to construct surveys and tasks online

Thus far, we have discussed how to use the Internet to advertise and recruit for online studies; however, to collect data from participants via the web, a user must first have demonstrated an ability to construct surveys and tasks, which can be administered online. Most studies conducted online utilize surveys or questionnaires, but more specific tasks can also be created. For example, the implicit social cognition tests on the popular Project Implicit website. These tests use the Internet to measure response speed as an indicator of innate social biases https://www.projectimplicit.net/. As was mentioned briefly above, various online and crowdsourcing platforms have survey construction capabilities integrated into their user interface (i.e., MedSurvey, M3 Global, Finding Five, etc.) making it easier for researchers to organize and streamline the steps of their studies in one place. In the likely case that a researcher decides to utilize a more ubiquitous survey construction tool, there are many options to choose from and capabilities to consider. Does the construction tool allow for multiple response types (i.e., open ended verses multiple choice), can skip logic be implemented, is response time reported, is the respondent's browser recorded, can researchers share, copy, and save questions, can data be exported to the statistical software of choice? These are all relevant considerations when deciding on a survey construction tool. SurveyMonkey, Qualtrics, and SurveyGizmo are all frequently used to construct online surveys and experiments, though they each also have the added benefit of offering access to on-line panels. This latter feature can be expensive. For example, one study found that a Qualtrics panel was more representative than MTurk, but the cost to access it was nearly three times as high (Boas et al., 2020). Qualtrics recruitment and compensation are handled by a third-party firm, giving researchers less say over payment rates (Boas et al., 2020). Google Forms is another platform intended for survey web creation, but it lacks some useful functions, such as the ability to tell how much time was spent on each form. In a recent paper, Zakharov, Nikulchev, Ilin, Ismatullina, and Fenin (2017) note several tools which are particularly popular in countries outside the United States including LimeSurvey, EnKlikAnketa, and PsychoPy.

Online tools have also been created specifically for clinical research. The Research Electronic Data Capture (REDCap) is one such web application. REDCap is used to build and manage online surveys and databases (Harris et al., 2009). Developed in 2004, REDCap was created with a focus on clinical research. REDCap has been used to support basic science research studies, collect data for clinical trials, perform quality reviews for clinical practice, complete comparative effectiveness trials, and more (Harris et al., 2019). In a 2018 report of the top research areas in which REDCap was cited, psychology, psychiatry, and neurosciences were all listed among the top 20 (Harris et al., 2019). REDCap is free to organizations that are a REDCap consortium partner site and software and consortium support are available for free to nonprofit organizations that join the REDCap consortium by submitting an online license agreement, https://projectredcap.org/partners/join/.

Smartphones

Lastly, we would be remiss if we did not include a discussion of the use of smartphones and other portable devices in Internet research (see Chapter 9). Smartphones are mobile devices that can access the Internet and support the use of applications. Smartphones are a promising and multifunctional research mechanism. One way researchers can take advantage of smartphones is by adapting their studies into mobile apps in which anyone who downloads the app to their device is a participant in the experiment (Dufau et al., 2011). This, in theory, allows researchers to gain access to anyone with a smartphone who is willing to participate. Smartphones can also be used to track clinically relevant health behaviors such as amount of physical activity, sleep routines, and recreational habits (Behar, Roebuck, Domingos, Gederi, & Clifford, 2013; BinDhim, McGeechan, & Trevena, 2014; Bort-Roig, Gilson, Puig-Ribera, Contreras, & Trost, 2014). The collection of behavioral data can then be used to predict important outcomes such as psychological illness (e.g., depression, anxiety, or schizophrenia), drug relapse, or manic episodes (Harari et al., 2016).

In the future, behavior patterns gleaned from an individuals' smartphone could help mental health personnel identify individuals in need of psychological interventions, help tailor interventions to the specific needs of the person, and help track therapy outcomes (Harari et al., 2016). Studies requiring accurate reporting of social media use are greatly improved by smartphone data, as smartphones provide an objective measure, rather than relying on less accurate traditional methods like self-report data

(Harari et al., 2016). One disadvantage of smartphone sensing is that, in many cases, it requires a high-level of technological expertise on the part of the researcher (e.g., the ability to use Python or R) and experience managing "big data" (Harari et al., 2016). Another potential issue is that, in certain cases, it may over- or underestimate study-relevant targets (e.g., the phone may be unable to distinguish between in-person conversations versus the television; Harari, Müller, Aung, & Rentfrow, 2017). Smartphone sensing methods are a valuable resource for behavioral research as they can collect vast amounts of real-time data in a way that is virtually undetectable to the participant, thus minimizing potential confounding influences that could alter natural participant behavior (Harari et al., 2017).

Conclusion

Sassenberg, Boos, Postmes, and Reips (2003) asserted that one of modern psychology's most important tasks is to examine the impact of the Internet on its users. Almost two decades later, it is fair to say that the opposite is also true; psychology is using the Internet to impact its users. Since the mid-1990s, the Internet has played an ever-growing and crucial role in the conduct of mental health research. Despite early skepticism and some persisting drawbacks of Internet research, this methodology has ultimately proven beneficial in helping researchers achieve their scientific goals. As trust in online research has grown, so too have the number and quality of platforms created to aid in this endeavor. Currently, hundreds of sites exist to help bring together researchers and the volunteers interested in completing their studies. This technological revolution is having a profound and enduring impact on the way scientists conduct and disseminate their work. Although tools and platforms will quickly change, what should persist is an evaluative discernment of the online platforms in achieving research needs.

References

Anderson, C. A., Allen, J. J., Plante, C., Quigley-McBride, A., Lovett, A., & Rokkum, J. N. (2019). The MTurkification of social and personality psychology. *Personality and Social Psychology Bulletin*, *45*(6), 842–850. https://doi.org/10.1177/0146167218798821.

Arditte, K. A., Cek, D., Shaw, A. M., & Timpano, K. R. (2016). The importance of assessing clinical phenomena in mechanical Turk research. *Psychological Assessment*, *28*(6), 684–691. https://doi.org/10.1037/pas0000217.

Barak, A., & Cohen, L. (2002). Empirical examination of an online version of the self-directed search. *Journal of Career Assessment*, *10*(4), 387–400.

Behar, J., Roebuck, A., Domingos, J. S., Gederi, E., & Clifford, G. D. (2013). A review of current sleep screening applications for smartphones. *Physiological Measurement*, *34*(7), R29–R46. https://doi.org/10.1088/0967-3334/34/7/R29.

BinDhim, N. F., McGeechan, K., & Trevena, L. (2014). Who uses smoking cessation apps? A feasibility study across three countries via smartphones. *JMIR mHealth and uHealth*, *2*(1). https://doi.org/10.2196/mhealth.2841, e4.

Birnbaum, M. H. (2000). *Psychological experiments on the internet*. San Diego, CA: Academic Press.

Blaikie, N. W. H. (1991). A critique of the use of triangulation in social research. *Quality and Quantity, 25*, 115–136.

Bliven, B. D., Kaufman, S. E., & Spertus, J. A. (2001). Electronic collection of health-related quality of life data: Validity, time benefits, and patient preference. *Quality of Life Research, 10*(1), 15–22. https://doi.org/10.1023/a:1016740312904.

Boas, T. C., Christenson, D. P., & Glick, D. M. (2020). Recruiting large online samples in the United States and India: Facebook, mechanical turk, and qualtrics. *Political Science Research and Methods, 8*(2), 232–250.

Bort-Roig, J., Gilson, N. D., Puig-Ribera, A., Contreras, R. S., & Trost, S. G. (2014). Measuring and influencing physical activity with smartphone technology: A systematic review. *Sports Medicine, 44*(5), 671–686. https://doi.org/10.1007/s40279-014-0142-5.

Brüggen, E., de Ruyter, K., & Wetzels, M. (2005). What motivates respondents to participate in online panels? In *Paper presented at the paper presented at the world marketing congress, Meunster, Germany*.

Buchanan, T. (2007). Personality testing on the Internet: What we know and what we do not. In A. N. Joinson, K. McKenna, T. Postmes, & U.-D. Reips (Eds.), *The Oxford handbook of Internet psychology* (pp. 447–459). Oxford University Press.

Buchanan, T., Johnson, J. A., & Goldberg, L. R. (2005). Implementing a five-factor personality inventory for use on the internet. *European Journal of Psychological Assessment, 21*(2), 115–127. https://doi.org/10.1027/1015-5759.21.2.115.

Buhrmester, M., Kwang, T., & Gosling, S. D. (2011). Amazon's mechanical Turk: A new source of inexpensive, yet high-quality, data? *Perspectives on Psychological Science, 6*(1), 3–5. https://doi.org/10.1177/1745691610393980.

Buhrmester, M. D., Talaifar, S., & Gosling, S. D. (2018). An evaluation of Amazon's mechanical Turk, its rapid rise, and its effective use. *Perspectives on Psychological Science, 13*(2), 149–154. https://doi.org/10.1177/1745691617706516.

Campos, J. A. D. B., Zucoloto, M. L., Bonafé, F. S. S., Jordani, P. C., & Maroco, J. (2011). Reliability and validity of self-reported burnout in college students: A cross randomized comparison of paper-and-pencil vs. online administration. *Computers in Human Behavior, 27*(5), 1875–1883.

Casler, K., Bickel, L., & Hackett, E. (2013). Separate but equal? A comparison of participants and data gathered via Amazon's MTurk, social media, and face-to-face behavioral testing. *Computers in Human Behavior, 29*, 2156–2160.

Chandler, J., & Shapiro, D. (2016). Conducting clinical research using crowdsourced convenience samples. *Annual Review of Clinical Psychology, 12*, 53–81. https://doi.org/10.1146/annurev-clinpsy-021815-093623.

Clifford, S., & Jerit, J. (2014). Is there a cost to convenience? An experimental comparison of data quality in laboratory and online studies. *Journal of Experimental Political Science, 1*(2), 120–131. https://doi.org/10.1017/xps.2014.5.

Comer, J. S., Furr, J. M., Cooper-Vince, C., Madigan, R. J., Chow, C., Chan, P., et al. (2015). Rationale and considerations for the internet-based delivery of parent-child interaction therapy. *Cognitive and Behavioral Practice, 22*(3), 302–316. https://doi.org/10.1016/j.cbpra.2014.07.003.

Comer, J. S., Furr, J. M., Miguel, E. M., Cooper-Vince, C. E., Carpenter, A. L., Elkins, R. M., et al. (2017). Remotely delivering real-time parent training to the home: An initial randomized trial of internet-delivered parent-child interaction therapy (I-PCIT). *Journal of Consulting and Clinical Psychology, 85*(9), 909–917. https://doi.org/10.1037/ccp0000230.

Connes, B. (1972). The use of electronic desk computers in psychological experiments. *Journal of Structural Learning*.

Craig, B. M., Hays, R. D., Pickard, A. S., Cella, D., Revicki, D. A., & Reeve, B. B. (2013). Comparison of US panel vendors for online surveys. *Journal of Medical Internet Research, 15*(11). https://doi.org/10.2196/jmir.2903, e260.

Crone, D. L., & Williams, L. A. (2017). Crowdsourcing participants for psychological research in Australia: A test of Microworkers. *Australian Journal of Psychology, 69*, 39–47. https://doi.org/10.1111/ajpy.12110.

de Winter, J. C. F., Kyriakidis, M., Dodou, D., & Happee, R. (2015). Using CrowdFlower to study the relationship between self-reported violations and traffic accidents. *Procedia Manufacturing, 3*, 2518–2525.

Dodou, D., & de Winter, J. C. F. (2014). Social desirability is the same in offline, online, and paper surveys: A meta-analysis. *Computers in Human Behavior, 36*, 487–495. https://doi.org/10.1016/j.chb.2014.04.005.

Dufau, S., Dunabeitia, J. A., Moret-Tatay, C., McGonigal, A., Peeters, D., Alario, F. X., et al. (2011). Smart phone, smart science: How the use of smartphones can revolutionize research in cognitive science. *PLoS ONE, 6*(9). https://doi.org/10.1371/journal.pone.0024974, e24974.

Dutton, W. H. (2013). Internet studies: The foundations of a transformative field. In *The oxford handbook of internet studies* Dutton, W.H.

Ekman, A., Dickman, P. W., Klint, A., Weiderpass, E., & Litton, J. E. (2006). Feasibility of using web-based questionnaires in large population-based epidemiological studies. *European Journal of Epidemiology, 21*(2), 103–111. https://doi.org/10.1007/s10654-005-6030-4.

Fouladi, R. T., McCarthy, C. J., & Moller, N. P. (2002). Paper-and-pencil or online? Evaluating mode effects on measures of emotional functioning and attachment. *Assessment, 9*(2), 204–215. https://doi.org/10.1177/10791102009002011.

Fraley, R. C., & Brumbaugh, C. C. (2004). *A dynamical systems approach to understanding stability and change in attachment security*. New York: Guilford Press.

Franklin, M. E., Flessner, C. A., Woods, D. W., Keuthen, N. J., Piacentini, J. C., Moore, P., et al. (2008). The child and adolescent trichotillomania impact project: Descriptive psychopathology, comorbidity, functional impairment, and treatment utilization. *Journal of Developmental and Behavioral Pediatrics, 29*(6), 493–500. https://doi.org/10.1097/DBP.0b013e31818d4328.

Freelon, D. (2014). On the interpretation of digital trace data in communication and social computing research. *Journal of Broadcasting & Electronic Media, 58*(1), 59–75. https://doi.org/10.1080/08838151.2013.875018.

Gleibs, I. H. (2017). Are all "research fields" equal? Rethinking practice for the use of data from crowdsourcing market places. *Behavior Research Methods, 49*(4), 1333–1342. https://doi.org/10.3758/s13428-016-0789-y.

Göritz, A. S. (2010). Using lotteries, loyalty points, and other incentives to increase participant response and completion. In S. D. Gosling, & J. A. Johnson (Eds.), *Advanced methods for conducting online behavioral research* (pp. 219–233). American Psychological Association.

Gosling, S. D., & Johnson, J. A. (2010). *Advanced methods for conducting online behavioral research*. Washington, DC: Am. Psychol. Assoc.

Gosling, S. D., & Mason, W. (2015). Internet research in psychology. *Annual Review of Psychology, 66*, 877–902. https://doi.org/10.1146/annurev-psych-010814-015321.

Gosling, S. D., Vazire, S., Srivastava, S., & John, O. P. (2004). Should we trust web-based studies? A comparative analysis of six preconceptions about internet questionnaires. *The American Psychologist, 59*(2), 93–104. https://doi.org/10.1037/0003-066X.59.2.93.

Harari, G. M., Lane, N. D., Wang, R., Crosier, B. S., Campbell, A. T., & Gosling, S. D. (2016). Using smartphones to collect behavioral data in psychological science: Opportunities, practical considerations, and challenges. *Perspectives on Psychological Science, 11*(6), 838–854. https://doi.org/10.1177/1745691616650285.

Harari, G. M., Müller, S. R., Aung, M. S., & Rentfrow, P. J. (2017). Smartphone sensing methods for studying behavior in everyday life. *Current Opinion in Behavioral Sciences, 18*, 83–90. https://doi.org/10.1016/j.cobeha.2017.07.018.

Harris, P. A., Scott, K. W., Lebo, L., Hassan, N., Lightner, C., & Pulley, J. (2012). ResearchMatch: A national registry to recruit volunteers for clinical research. *Academic Medicine, 87*(1), 66–73. https://doi.org/10.1097/ACM.0b013e31823ab7d2.

Harris, P. A., Taylor, R., Minor, B. L., Elliott, V., Fernandez, M., O'Neal, L., et al. (2019). The REDCap consortium: Building an international community of software platform partners. *Journal of Biomedical Informatics, 95*, 103208. https://doi.org/10.1016/j.jbi.2019.103208.

Harris, P. A., Taylor, R., Thielke, R., Payne, J., Gonzalez, N., & Conde, J. G. (2009). Research electronic data capture (REDCap)—A metadata-driven methodology and workflow process for providing translational research informatics support. *Journal of Biomedical Informatics, 42*(2), 377–381. https://doi.org/10.1016/j.jbi.2008.08.010.

Hawn, C. (2009). Take two aspirin and tweet me in the morning: How twitter, Facebook, and other social media are reshaping health care. *Health Affairs (Millwood), 28*(2), 361–368. https://doi.org/10.1377/hlthaff.28.2.361.

Hays, R. D., Liu, H., & Kapteyn, A. (2015). Use of internet panels to conduct surveys. *Behavior Research Methods*, (47), 685–690. https://doi.org/10.3758/s13428-015-0617-9.

Johnson, J. A. (2010). In G. Johnson (Ed.), *Web-based self-report personality scales* (pp. 149–166).

Joinson, A. (1999). Social desirability, anonymity, and internet-based questionnaires. *Behavior Research Methods, Instruments, & Computers, 31*(3), 433–438. https://doi.org/10.3758/bf03200723.

Joinson, A. N., McKenna, K. Y. A., Postmes, T., & Reips, U. D. (2007). *Oxford handbook of internet psychology*.

Krantz, J. H. (2012). Internet-based research methods. In *Encyclopedia of research design* (pp. 1–6). Thousand Oaks: Sage Publications, Inc.

Krantz, J. H., Ballard, J., & Scher, J. (1997). Comparing the results of laboratory and World-Wide Web samples on the determinants of female attractiveness. *Behavior Research Methods, Instruments, & Computers, 29*, 264–269. https://doi.org/10.3758/BF03204824.

Krantz, J. H., & Dalal, R. (2000). Validity of web-based psychological research. In M. H. Birnbaum (Ed.), *Psychological experiments on the Internet* (pp. 35–60). Academic Press. https://doi.org/10.1016/B978-012099980-4/50003-4.

Krantz, J. H., & Reips, U. D. (2017). The state of web-based research: A survey and call for inclusion in curricula. *Behavior Research Methods, 49*(5), 1621–1629. https://doi.org/10.3758/s13428-017-0882-x.

Kraut, R., Olson, J., Banaji, M., Bruckman, A., Cohen, J., & Couper, M. (2004). Psychological research online: Report of Board of Scientific Affairs' Advisory Group on the Conduct of Research on the Internet. *The American Psychologist, 59*(2), 105–117. https://doi.org/10.1037/0003-066X.59.2.105.

Kraut, R., Patterson, M., Lundmark, V., Kiesler, S., Mukopadhyay, T., & Scherlis, W. (1998). Internet paradox. A social technology that reduces social involvement and psychological well-being? *The American Psychologist, 53*(9), 1017–1031. https://doi.org/10.1037//0003-066x.53.9.1017.

Kuś, J. (2014). Basic principles of conducting psychological experiments through the Internet. *E-methodology*, 9–16. https://doi.org/10.15503/emeth2014-9-16.

Lazer, D., Kennedy, R., King, G., & Vespignani, A. (2014). Big data. The parable of Google Flu: Traps in big data analysis. *Science, 343*(6176), 1203–1205. https://doi.org/10.1126/science.1248506.

Lewis, I. M., Watson, B., & White, K. M. (2010). Response efficacy: The key to minimizing rejection and maximizing acceptance of emotion-based anti-speeding messages. *Accident; Analysis and Prevention, 42*(2), 459–467. https://doi.org/10.1016/j.aap.2009.09.008.

Miner, M. H., Bockting, W. O., Romine, R. S., & Raman, S. (2012). Conducting internet research with the transgender population: Reaching broad samples and collecting valid data. *Social Science Computer Review, 30*(2), 202–211. https://doi.org/10.1177/0894439311404795.

Oppenheimer, D. M., Meyvis, T., & Davidenko, N. (2009). Instructional manipulation checks: Detecting satisficing to increase statistical power. *Journal of Experimental Social Psychology, 45,* 867–872.

Ørmen, J., Helles, R., & Bruhn Jensen, K. (2021). Converging cultures of communication: A comparative study of Internet use in China, Europe, and the United States. *New Media & Society, 23*(7), 1751–1772.

Peer, E., Brandimarte, L., Samat, S., & Acquisti, A. (2017). Beyond the Turk: Alternative platforms for crowdsourcing behavioral research. *Journal of Experimental Social Psychology, 70,* 153–163.

Peterson, R. A. (2001). On the use of college students in social science research: Insights from a second-order meta-analysis. *Journal of Consumer Research, 28*(3), 450–461.

Pulley, J. M., Jerome, R. N., Bernard, G. R., Olson, E. J., Tan, J., Wilkins, C. H., et al. (2018). Connecting the public with clinical trial options: The ResearchMatch Trials Today tool. *Journal of Clinical and Translational Science, 2*(4), 253–257. https://doi.org/10.1017/cts.2018.327.

Reips, U. D. (1996). Experimenting in the world wide web. In *Paper presented at the in proceedings of the 26th society for computers in psychology conference (SCiP—96), Chicago, USA.*

Reips, U. D. (2001). The web experimental psychology lab: Five years of data collection on the internet. *Behavior Research Methods, Instruments, & Computers, 33*(2), 201–211. https://doi.org/10.3758/bf03195366.

Rieder, B., Abdulla, R., Poell, T., Woltering, R., & Zack, L. (2015). Data critique and analytical opportunities for very large Facebook Pages: Lessons learned from exploring "We are all Khaled Said. *Big Data & Society, 2*(2). 2053951715614980.

Riva, G., Teruzzi, T., & Anolli, L. (2003). The use of the internet in psychological research: Comparison of online and offline questionnaires. *Cyberpsychology & Behavior, 6*(1), 73–80. https://doi.org/10.1089/109493103321167983.

Rodham, K., & Gavin, J. (2006). The ethics of using the internet to collect qualitative research data. *Research Ethics, 2*(3), 92–97.

Roulin, N. (2015). Don't throw the baby out with the bathwater: Comparing data quality of crowdsourcing, online panels, and student samples. *Industrial and Organizational Psychology, 8*(2), 190–196. https://doi.org/10.1017/iop.2015.24.

Sassenberg, K., Boos, M., Postmes, T., & Reips, U. D. (2003). Studying the Internet: A challenge for modern psychology. *Swiss Journal of Psychology, 62*(2), 75–77. https://doi.org/10.1024//1421-0185.62.2.75.

Spitzer, M. (2013). *Demencia digital (Digital dementia).* Ediciones B.

Stillwell, D. J., & Kosinski, M. (2012). myPersonality project: Use of online social networks for large-scale social research. In *1st ACM Workshop Mobile Syst. Comput. Soc. Sci. (MobiSys).*

Torous, J., Kiang, M. V., Lorme, J., & Onnela, J. P. (2016). New tools for new research in psychiatry: A scalable and customizable platform to empower data driven smartphone research. *JMIR Mental Health, 3*(2). https://doi.org/10.2196/mental.5165, e16.

Vakharia, D.a. L.,. M. (2013). Beyond AMT: An analysis of crowd work platforms. *Arxiv Online*.

Wazny, K. (2017). "Crowdsourcing" ten years in: A review. *Journal of Global Health, 7*(2). https://doi.org/10.7189/jogh.07.020602, 020602.

Wazny, K. (2018). Applications of crowdsourcing in health: An overview. *Journal of Global Health, 8*(1). https://doi.org/10.7189/jogh.08.010502, 010502.

Webster, M. (2015). Big data, bad data, good data: The link between information governance and big data outcomes. *IBM offering information white paper January*.

Woods, D. W., Flessner, C. A., Franklin, M. E., Keuthen, N. J., Goodwin, R. D., Stein, D. J., et al. (2006). The trichotillomania impact project (TIP): Exploring phenomenology, functional impairment, and treatment utilization. *The Journal of Clinical Psychiatry, 67*(12), 1877–1888. https://doi.org/10.4088/jcp.v67n1207.

Yeager, D. S., Krosnick, J. A., Chang, L., Javitz, H. S., Levendusky, M. S., Simpser, A., et al. (2011). Comparing the accuracy of RDD telephone surveys and internet surveys conducted with probability and non-probability samples. *Public Opinion Quarterly, 75*, 709–747.

Zakharov, I., Nikulchev, E., Ilin, D., Ismatullina, V., & Fenin, A. (2017). Web-based platform for psychology research. In *ITM web of conferences* (p. 10). https://doi.org/10.1051/itmconf/20171004006.

Ecological momentary assessment and other digital technologies for capturing daily life in mental health

Simone Verhagen[a,e], Jim van Os[a,b,c], and Philippe Delespaul[a,d]
[a]Department of Psychiatry and Neuropsychology, Faculty of Health Medicine and Lifesciences, Maastricht University, Maastricht, The Netherlands, [b]Department of Psychiatry, Brain Center Rudolf Magnus, University Medical Center Utrecht, Utrecht University, Utrecht, The Netherlands, [c]Department of Psychosis Studies, Institute of Psychiatry, King's College London, King's Health Partners, London, United Kingdom, [d]Mondriaan Mental Health Trust, Department of Adult Psychiatry, Heerlen, The Netherlands, [e]Department of Lifespan Psychology, Faculty of Psychology, Open University, Heerlen, The Netherlands

Introduction

Mental health services require reorientation (van Os, Delespaul, Wigman, Myin-Germeys, & Wichers, 2013). Conventional interventions fail to match the demand and the need for services is growing. Efficiency improvement is much needed. The classic strategy to improve knowledge uses group-based diagnoses as a point of departure to access research knowledge about working mechanisms of change. Unfortunately, this results in insufficient new insights. It also offers only marginal relief in clinical practice (Kapur, Phillips, & Insel, 2012; McGorry & Van Os, 2013; van Os, Guloksuz, Vijn, Hafkenscheid, & Delespaul, 2019). Personalized medicine and precision diagnostics are an attempt to better profile individuals and more efficiently select interventions to optimize outcome (Collins & Varmus, 2015). This strategy might potentially be successful when assessments lead to the detection of a problem in the etiological track and interventions solve its cause. However, psychiatric classification fails to realize this (McGorry & Van Os, 2013).

Treatment choices are defined by probabilistic rules at best. However, rules defined to optimize decisions for large groups, miss the precision needed for individual cases. Possibly, person-to-person heterogeneity and within-person individual variation should not be viewed as sources of noise that hide the underlying core pathology, but be re-appreciated as elements of clinical characterization, useful in person-centered care. Relevant processes are not deterministically related to core pathologies. A different perspective on assessment is required with a strategy that tries to understand variability.

Mental Health in a Digital World. https://doi.org/10.1016/B978-0-12-822201-0.00017-4

Digital technology is widely accessible. It is ideally suited to support the mental health-care reorientation toward person-centered clinical characterization (Luxton, McCann, Bush, Mishkind, & Reger, 2011; Maj, 2020; Marzano et al., 2015). Patient participation is now a central tenet in health care, not just at the level of clinical decision-making but also at the level of health-care organization and participatory citizen science (Storm & Edwards, 2013). Granted, treatment should take group-based findings from randomized controlled trials into account. Nevertheless, knowledge of personal variability, values, and preferences are essential elements for successful shared decision-making. Genuine interest in the individual's input tempers the mechanical expert application of group-based trial findings (Maj, 2020). Intriguingly, shared decision-making in psychiatry lags behind with acceptance compared to somatic medicine. This delay remains, despite an increasingly active recovery movement demanding more focus on personal, social, and existential outcomes (Davidson, 2016; Zomer et al., 2020).

In this chapter, personalized medicine is conceptualized, not as a profile-based fine-tuned strategy that optimizes the selection of best-suited individuals for specific interventions, but as an iterative process of assessment, implementation, and follow-up, to optimize goal-directed care, preferably through shared decision-making. It emphasizes understanding variability in a mental state rather than simply the stable core underlying vulnerability. The paper introduces a contextual and ecological approach to mental health that, with the help of digital technology, can guide the field forward toward more personal care strategies.

Mental health revolution

Mental disorders are highly prevalent and an increasing number of people need professional care (Patel et al., 2018). Resources, however, remain scarce and insufficient to provide one-on-one treatment for most people with mental health problems. Societal costs are rising with a high economic burden for health care and welfare systems. Likewise, the personal burden for patients and relatives is high (Patel et al., 2018; Whiteford et al., 2013). A different approach is needed with a focus on better resource efficiency, a more enduring impact, and broader societal reach.

The World Health Organization (WHO) originally defined health as "a state of complete physical, mental, and social well-being and not merely the absence of disease or infirmity" (World Health Organization, 1948). A newer WHO definition is more nuanced: "health is a state of well-being in which the individual realizes his or her abilities, can cope with the normal stresses of life, can work productively and fruitfully, and is able to make contributions to his or her community" (WHO, 2001). Huber and colleagues define positive health as "the ability to adapt and to self-manage, in the face of social, physical, and emotional challenges" and emphasize that resilience is a central concept in health (Huber et al., 2011). The updated health definitions imply a holistic approach in the assessment and treatment of mental distress, beyond symptom reduction and noticing daily life functioning. Individual well-being is now central to recovery and forms an essential target for research (Slade, 2010).

Mental health research traditionally focused on the nature of psychopathology, trying to find parallel phenotypes in "objective" biology that help explain the occurrence of symptoms and provide targets for treatment. These avenues have yielded limited results (Kapur et al., 2012). For example, genetic research has shown that thousands of genetic variants only explain a fraction of largely transdiagnostic mental suffering. There is suggestive evidence that nature and nurture are interdependent systems (Reis, Collins, & Berscheid, 2000). This finding confirms the key concept that behavior arises at the interface of person-environment interactions (Hergenhahn & Henley, 2013; Lewin, 2013). Focusing too much on a single aspect of such interactions can lead to incorrect conclusions and, in clinical practice, to unnecessary treatments with minimal effects.

Precision medicine

Somatic health care has embraced a precision medicine approach: treatment and prevention take into account the person's profile defined by genetic variations, environment, and lifestyle (Jameson & Longo, 2015; National Research Council, 2011). The idea is that by defining subgroups of responders and nonresponders, treatment effectivity becomes predictive. Precise phenotyping can then inform solutions tailored to the individual (instead of a one-size-fits-all approach). A more precise diagnosis leads to better differentiation and to treatments that are more efficient. For example, research has found that genetic makeup influences how cancer attacks cells and as a consequence determines growth and metastases. Knowledge of the individual's genetic variation then provides clues to target medication accordingly (Pauli et al., 2017). In mental health care, however, the application of precision medicine is much more challenging given the lack of definite patterns of association between biology and mental health (Insel, 2017; Kapur et al., 2012). One reason for this is that subjective experience is not directly measurable in the physical domain. As a consequence, a knowledge gap exists, and more systematic research is required.

There are still no satisfying models available to predict the onset of mental problems. The etiology is often multicausal and how psychological variation occurs, is unknown (Brietzke et al., 2019). Stochasticity—or randomness—likely plays an important role. Genes interact with the environment, the impact of which becomes imbued with meaning according to the personal value system of the person (Tsuang, Bar, Stone, & Faraone, 2004). The list of factors that potentially can play a role in worsening mental health is without limit. The identification of subgroups to aid clinical decision-making, therefore, has yielded limited results. Research only provides evidence for broad mental health syndromes that may have some validity, such as anxiety/depression or psychosis.

Furthermore, no intervention is a panacea but most psychotherapies have some therapeutic effect, and pharmacotherapy may provide benefit (Huhn et al., 2014). However, results derived from group comparisons in randomized control trials using well-defined (and restricted) patient samples only apply to the *average person* (van Os et al., 2019; Wolfers et al., 2018). Not everyone benefits from evidence-based treatment.

Consequently, researchers have tried to differentiate between responders and nonresponders. In reality, this has not yielded workable results for clinical practice. Although many attempts at stratification have been published (through biology, cognition, demographics, and course), there are still no tests that predict the diagnosis or treatment response of any mental disorder or syndrome (Kapur et al., 2012).

Patients form a heterogeneous group, even within the same diagnostic category (i.e., interindividual variability) (Nandi, Beard, & Galea, 2009; Wolfers et al., 2018). They differ in the level of symptoms, impact, severity, age of onset, clinical course, and treatment response. Moreover, people differ in how they attribute meaning to their experiences and how it affects their life goal perspective. Within individuals, longitudinal patterns vary across time (i.e., intraindividual variability) (Trull, Lane, Koval, & Ebner-Priemer, 2015). Interventions that fail at a specific moment in the illness history of a specific person can often be applied successfully later. Etiological knowledge is mostly lacking, and research has had limited success in finding relevant patterns in symptom variation, interactions, and mechanisms in environmental responsiveness (Ebner-Priemer, Eid, Kleindienst, Stabenow, & Trull, 2009; Maj, 2020; van Os et al., 2013). Although replicated statistical associations exist (e.g., between anxiety and depression, between cannabis use and psychosis, between genetic variation and psychopathology), we remain far from reliable tests providing likelihood ratios that are sufficiently discriminating to apply systematically in clinical practice (Kapur et al., 2012).

The variability between- and within-person remains highly challenging for clinicians (Fried, 2017). Their reference for treatment avenues is based on research outcomes and traditional classification systems. A system that is said to be evidence-based but in which the individual rarely fits in. Moreover, available diagnostic tools lack sensitivity to detect dynamic patterns over time (van Os et al., 2019). A translation is needed from research to clinical practice so that clinicians obtain access to contextualized knowledge of underlying mechanisms specific to their patients.

The importance of context

Mental health problems are embedded within an environmental context as well as within a context of meaning, the personal attribution of significance and value to internal and external events. Most people will intuitively grasp that after a fight, emotions tend to linger and influence the level of functioning. For example, a subsequent task might be performed half-heartedly (with the mind still wandering back to the incident) or a conversation tenser than intended. A person might retreat or, in contrast, seek social contacts. Emotion dysregulation is widely recognized to play a crucial role in mental distress, influencing people's level of overall functioning (Gross & Muñoz, 1995). Events in daily life, combined with a preexisting vulnerability (e.g., because of trauma or prolonged stress during childhood), can trigger emotional dysregulation and increase negative affect (Hofmann, Sawyer, Fang, & Asnaani, 2012). An ecological approach would help to grasp the intricacies and variabilities of mental distress.

Moreover, it can shed light on the often-neglected positive influences of context on mood or general well-being. For example, people feel more relaxed when on holiday. A contributing factor may be the increased time spent outside and being active. If so, relaxation could be increased by increasing the level of outside time during routine daily life. Most monitoring instruments assess levels of distress, with treatment focusing on vulnerability and symptom reduction. The standard implementation of positive health with equal attention to aspects of resilience lags behind (Slade, 2010).

Although intuitive, the attention to personal context and individual meaning (an integrative approach) has suffered in the evidence-based, reductionist context of mental health science (van Os et al., 2019). The most important reason is that clinical decision-making using an ideographic strategy became suspect, as it often proved biased and lacking in scientific evidence (Hurlburt & Schwitzgebel, 2011). The field is in need of a reliable science of the individual, where diversity is explored and patterns are grounded in empirical evidence.

Instead of relying on biomarkers to explain psychopathology, clinical characterization is a useful method to arrive at a plausible theory and treatment plan for the individual (Aedo et al., 2018; Brietzke et al., 2019; Maj, 2020). Unlike classic models that break up a theory into components to be examined separately, clinical characterization investigates the current context and builds a personalized theory around this information. Multiple sources are used to arrive at this point. It is valuable to know someone's previous history (with respect to both life events as well as genetic risks), personality traits, intellectual functioning, and general health. However, information on the current situation is even more crucial. How is someone functioning right now, what are struggles or hassles, what creates uplifts, does a positive social network exists, is the person able to function at home, at work? Does he enjoy it? Clinical observations are a useful source of information to determine the level of distress and to unravel underlying causal factors (Maj, 2020). What is required are instruments that help to support holistic information building, preferably in a process of cocreation between patients and professionals.

Modern care practices

In the context of treatment, dialog between the patient and therapist is central (Van Audenhove & Vertommen, 2000). Most treatments—psychotherapeutic and psychopharmacological—have similar and moderate effect sizes when compared to each other (the so-called "dodo bird verdict") (Luborsky et al., 2002). Common elements such as the therapeutic alliance and perceived level of control contribute significantly to positive outcomes (Huibers & Cuijpers, 2014; Wampold, 2015). This means that irrespective of the treatment approach, adequate fit and good metacommunication between therapist and patient are crucial for success. Communication in the clinical setting and associated roles have shifted because of technological advances. The internet makes it possible to examine symptoms and signs and explanations and solutions. Now that knowledge is in the public domain, patients have opportunities to

be informed (Tambuyzer, Pieters, & Van Audenhove, 2014). The professional's identity, therefore, has shifted from bearer of knowledge to coach in a process of shared
decision-making. This definition requires a shift from passive consumption toward a
balanced process in which the patient is an expert of his or her own life.

The importance of patient involvement in health-care practice is increasingly recognized. Patients acquired a voice in shaping political agendas and individually became
much more active in their own care. Key elements of involvement are participation
in decision-making as well as active involvement in a range of health-care activities,
cocreating care processes (Tambuyzer et al., 2014).

Achieving mental health change takes time. Consequently, longer treatment trajectories are needed. These should not result in increased dependency but in contrast
foster autonomy and empowerment. Psychologically, this refers to the sense of control someone has over their own health and the experience of ownership (Aujoulat,
d'Hoore, & Deccache, 2007). An enduring care impact is influenced by motivation
and tools that strengthen this. Technology can empower patients to collect personal
data, which in turn stimulates engagement. Individual findings can thus become part
of a common language that is shared with the health-care professional, serving as an
aid in the decision-making process.

The relevant time window

The primary diagnostic focus in mental health aims to detect vulnerable individuals
(i.e., between-subject variation) and grant them access to care. Sometimes detection
occurs before the first onset with the intention to start preventive measures and avoid
spiraling down toward increased vulnerability and ultimately a chronic state. At best,
detection occurs using cross-sectional assessments during risk periods, for instance,
adolescence (Arango et al., 2018; Maj, 2020; McGorry & Van Os, 2013; McGorry,
Hartmann, Spooner, & Nelson, 2018).

Sometimes the diagnostic focus is on detecting episodic symptom exacerbation.
This knowledge can help to target medication regimes or other anticipatory actions.
Detection of episodic occurrences often requires long-term monitoring (depending
on the period or cyclic nature of the changes) and strategies to do so are ideally carried out automatically or autonomously by patients or their relatives, thus minimizing
professional involvement. Relevant triggers can be external (e.g., life events, seasonal
effects), internal (e.g., hormonal, autoimmune) or both. Ideally, the assessment leads
to a better understanding of the personal mechanisms of vulnerability (and resilience),
with professionals supporting a learning process that optimizes coping. At times, understanding the actual working mechanisms is impossible or irrelevant and aims are
adjusted to detect warning signals, thereby activating protective measures.

Person-environment interaction patterns that focus on infrequently occurring life
events, yield insufficient variation to engage in learning processes. From the point
of view of learning and understanding one's personal vulnerability profile, the assessment of so-called micro-life events (hassles and uplifts), is more promising

(van Os et al., 2017). These events are valuable risk indicators and trigger relevant micro-changes in behavior, perception, affect, and cognition. They can be assessed in smaller time frames and catch relevant dynamic, moment-to-moment changes (i.e., minutes and hours, not days or weeks) (Havermans, Nicolson, & deVries, 2007).

What makes someone vulnerable is part of the personal makeup (e.g., genes and accumulated personal experiences), their life circumstances, and corresponding challenges (Suls & Rothman, 2004). When variability in cognition, affect, perception, and behavior is collected in daily life, it can be analyzed to understand its relation to contextual challenges. These micro-life challenges or hassles, or circumstances of uplifts provide hypotheses that are tracked for therapeutic experimentation. Effects can be monitored and over time yield a personal, fingerprint-analog of the dynamics of an individual's vulnerability. When adequately applied, an iterative personal medicine emerges that avoids increasing vulnerability and realizes improved resilience.

Ecological validity

Vulnerability and resilience for mental health occur in context. In research, it is crucial to encompass this phenomenon and include contextualized information in theory and model building. Moreover, in the therapy office (being a restricted environment) the relevant lived experience of daily struggle is missing. Ecologically valid measures can provide a solution, helping therapy to move to the daily life domain and thus potentially providing treatment with round the clock impact (Bos, Snippe, Bruggeman, Wichers, & van der Krieke, 2019). Pharmacological treatment (when adequately applied) has a continuous enduring impact but with psychotherapy, this continuous impact is less apparent. New skills and insights learned in therapy often generalize poorly (Higgs, Jones, Loftus, & Christensen, 2008; Smith et al., 2005). As a result, a relaxing breathing technique learned and totally mastered in the safe context of the therapist's office, often fails to activate in a busy or stressful environment. The area of mental health care is in need of tools that help improve generalizability in the challenging moment-to-moment situations that compose the reality of normal daily life.

Profiled vs iterative personalized medicine

Personalized medicine often aims to profile subjects to subgroups that optimally respond to specific interventions (Collins & Varmus, 2015). The implicit rationale is that the procedure selects subgroups that are more likely to have problems in a specific etiological track. The intervention piggybacks on causal mechanisms or on specific individual characteristics, which improves the likelihood of success of the intervention. A more fruitful approach to personalized medicine would be to focus on iterative optimization of the individual trajectory in care. In this strategy, the patient and clinician collaboratively monitor experiential dynamics over time, discuss potential interpretations, and make choices to apply changes (collaborative empiricism). The process of shared learning is replicated iteratively. Optionally, in-the-moment feedback, relevant to the individual, is provided to optimize the learning process. Treatment optimization is likely achieved when feedback can be provided on the spot, allowing both the patient and clinician to adapt their approach when evidence shows that it has no or limited effect. Finding empirical ways to differentiate between a successful treatment and an unsuccessful treatment, for each individual separately is perhaps a more realistic approach for precision psychiatry.

In sum, there are a number of challenges in the field of mental health. Shifts in care practice suggest the need for a holistic and individual approach with attention to symptom dynamics across the psychopathology spectrum. We believe that mobile health solutions are highly promising in meeting these challenges. They can provide accessible solutions for self-management, just-in-time interventions, and support outside the therapy office. Research benefits from more accurate, personalized measurements that can shed light on lived experience in daily life.

Digital health solutions

Modern technological advances can move assessments fluently into the daily domain. Smartphones offer an ever-widening array of functionalities and are now part of our behavioral routine (e.g., as an alarm clock, agenda, navigation system, communication medium, and personal coach). Smartphones are personal devices and consequently can support the autonomy of people as extensions (or prostheses) in the process of better health. Apps play an increasingly important role in behavioral change toward increased health and better lifestyles. This ambition generally requires personal information, collected through both passive (e.g., movement-trackers) and active strategies (e.g., logging of fluid- or calorie intake). Algorithms allow the reinforcement of healthy behavior ("you reached your goal of 10.000 steps!") or nudge people in the right direction ("it's time to drink water or move around") (Anderson, Burford, & Emmerton, 2016; Kao & Liebovitz, 2017). In applications for mental health, solutions are often complex and require multidomain informational integration. They differ from health apps with an easy-to-track, singular focus (e.g., to alter sedentary behavior). Technological innovations already exist for the evaluation, prediction, decision-making, and management of mental health complaints (Mehrotra & Tripathi, 2018; Price et al., 2014). To provide reliable and accurate solutions for individual recovery, empirical rigor, and scientific backing is imperative. The necessary science is emerging slowly.

Ecological momentary assessment

A promising research method for "precision psychiatry" is Ecological Momentary Assessment (EMA)(van Os et al., 2013). EMA, or Experience Sampling Method (ESM), is a structured diary approach aimed to capture different mental state domains (e.g., cognition, affect, perception, and behaviors) and contextual information in the flow of daily life (Csikszentmihalyi & Larson, 2014). Administered with the support of digital technology, it is a mHealth tool with ecological validity (van Os et al., 2017). A smartphone app (through auditory or visual signals, notifications, or text messages) can indicate users to complete a short questionnaire (usually within 1–2 min) that is made available for a limited time. EMA uses a time-based assessment protocol in which assessments are programmed either to occur randomly, semirandomly, or at a fixed time during the day. Most EMA Apps also allow event-based sampling, for example, to capture smoking or drinking behavior. Event sampling requires participants to initiate an assessment based on occurrence. Over time and with repetition (e.g., for a week, month, or even a year), a rich dataset is created with unique situational information. A representation of momentary time-based sampling with respect to mood and context dynamics is presented in Fig. 5.1 (van Os et al., 2017). The data exploration method yields valuable insights into microlevel occurrences and underlying psychological mechanisms, through sophisticated analytical techniques or through distributions and summary statistics (as is common in clinical practice). There is increasing recognition that mental health symptoms occur in relation to context and that it is necessary to capture these contexts. EMA is a good method to gain insight into these cooccurrences and thus complements conventional nonecological research methods (Myin-Germeys et al., 2018).

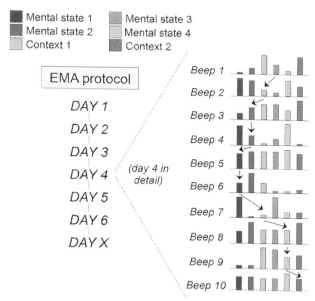

Fig. 5.1 Ecological Momentary Assessment (EMA) uses repeated assessments across days, assessing mental states and contextual information. Zooming in on a micro-epoch shows that answers fluctuate and covary over the day.
From van Os, J., Verhagen, S., Marsman, A., Peeters, F., Bak, M., Marcelis, M., et al. (2017). The experience sampling method as an mHealth tool to support self-monitoring, self-insight, and personalized health care in clinical practice. *Depression and Anxiety, 34*(6), 481–493.

Added value to cross-sectional methods

Our knowledge of psychopathology has expanded to the microscale of daily life. Cross-sectional research provides limited insight into dynamics, while there is increased awareness of its importance to understand the mechanisms of psychopathological development and maintenance over time. EMA with its longitudinal, repeated assessment design can fulfill this knowledge gap (Myin-Germeys et al., 2009). It allows the collection of fine-grained information in real-life settings.

One constraint of cross-sectional methods to assess psychopathology using questionnaires or structured interviews is that they rely on retrospection. EMA uses in-the-moment assessments, thereby limiting recall bias ["a systematic caused by differences in the accuracy or completeness of the recollections retrieved ('recalled') by participants regarding events or experiences from the past" (John, 2001)] (Csikszentmihalyi & Larson, 2014). Accuracy is especially important for the assessment of mental symptom variation since people are often inclined to remember negative events, herewith losing the required specificity (Watkins, 2002). Additionally, well-being information is essential to counterbalance the negativity bias, allowing users to learn about personal resilience and figure out under which conditions they are feeling well, so shifting their focus (van Os et al., 2017). The ability to assess relevant health domains in a single questionnaire and the potential to make implicit patterns between these domains tangible for users uniquely adds to conventional assessment strategies. Moreover, multiple assessments increase the chance to detect change (with heightened sensitivity) and yields less random error variance compared to conventional methods. Stress reactivity, emotional dysregulation, coping, self-esteem, vulnerability, or resilience are complex psychological constructs that are assumed to regulate daily life (van Os et al., 2017). Assessment requires large batteries of traditional questionnaires. The EMA strategy can be a substitute for these assessments. EMA thus fundamentally adds to information accuracy and excels in unraveling the subtle interplay between psychopathology and environmental context (Myin-Germeys et al., 2009).

Learning from group-level research

EMA has made a significant contribution to the mental health field. Group-level findings using random sampling techniques of mental state in context, provides solid guidance for the interpretation of single-case ($n=1$) data in personal recovery trajectories. To illustrate a symptom severity ("I feel down") the between-subjects (grouped in healthy controls, patients with residual depressive symptoms, and patients diagnosed with depression) and within-subject variation (the first to the last responded beep in a week) are visualized in Fig. 5.2 (van Os et al., 2017). Patients with depressive complaints show increased variation and higher base levels of feeling down compared to the control group. From this, one could form the hypothesis that an increase in negativity and an increase in variation might provide warning signals to individuals. Temporal stability reflects that the subject is in the safe zone. Contextualization of

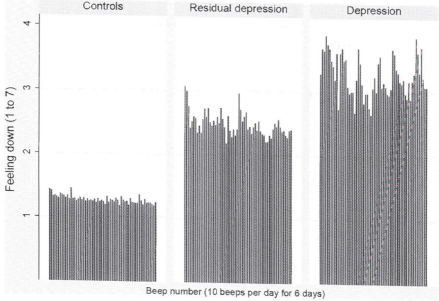

Fig. 5.2 Group level results of a momentary assessment protocol with 10 questionnaires a day for 6 consecutive days, displaying mean scores on the item "I feel down" in controls ($N=251$, $n=12,394$ moments), patients with residual depression ($N=129$, $n=6420$ moments), and depression ($N=45$, $n=2287$ moments), rated on a seven-point Likert scale (ranging from $1=$ not at all to $7=$ very much).

From van Os, J., Verhagen, S., Marsman, A., Peeters, F., Bak, M., Marcelis, M., et al. (2017). The experience sampling method as an mHealth tool to support self-monitoring, self-insight, and personalized health care in clinical practice. *Depression and Anxiety, 34*(6), 481–493.

these findings can provide further clues for personal theories or hypotheses. Fig. 5.3 displays the same group findings, now as a function of location ("where am I"). Here, location seems to have a limited impact on feeling down for controls but becomes increasingly important in the patient groups. Symptom severity increases especially in health-care locations and during transport (van Os et al., 2017). Individuals may need additional support in these situations. Subjects differ from each other. To understand individual trajectories long monitoring trajectories are required, herewith challenging the endurance of the subjects. The unique patterns of mood states over the course of the week, combined with contextual information, provides a unique insight into the severity of problems and clues for change strategies (e.g., you feel less down when being outdoors).

Time series analysis and prospective modeling techniques are useful to understand how symptoms influence each other and to anticipate what might happen at the next time point. For example, in large samples, the experience of feeling anxious at the previous moment (time point $t-1$) predicts "feeling down" at the following moment (time point t) as presented in Fig. 5.4 (van Os et al., 2017).

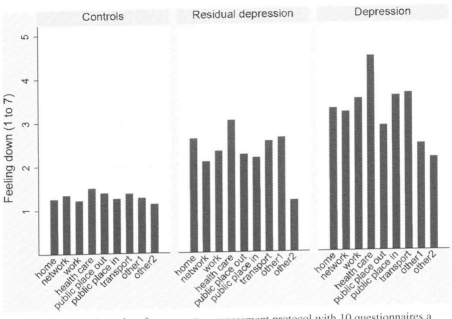

Fig. 5.3 Group level results of a momentary assessment protocol with 10 questionnaires a day for 6 consecutive days, displaying mean scores on the item "I feel down" summarized per location ("Where am I at the moment") in controls ($N = 251$, $n = 12,394$ moments), patients with residual depression ($N = 129$, $n = 6420$ moments), and depression ($N = 45$, $n = 2287$ moments), rated on a seven-point Likert scale (ranging from 1 = not at all to 7 = very much). From van Os, J., Verhagen, S., Marsman, A., Peeters, F., Bak, M., Marcelis, M., et al. (2017). The experience sampling method as an mHealth tool to support self-monitoring, self-insight, and personalized health care in clinical practice. *Depression and Anxiety, 34*(6), 481–493.

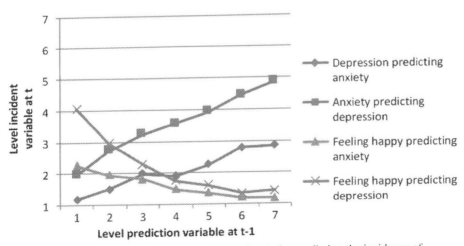

Fig. 5.4 Prospective analysis of mean mood state levels for predicting the incidence of depression (i.e., feeling down) or anxiety (i.e., feeling anxious) in patients with residual depression ($N = 233$, $n = 10,582$ EMA moments), rated on a seven-point Likert scale (ranging from 1 = not at all to 7 = very much). For instance, those with higher scores on feeling happy at $t - 1$ (previous time point) predict lower scores of feeling down at t (current time point). From van Os, J., Verhagen, S., Marsman, A., Peeters, F., Bak, M., Marcelis, M., et al. (2017). The experience sampling method as an mHealth tool to support self-monitoring, self-insight, and personalized health care in clinical practice. *Depression and Anxiety, 34*(6), 481–493.

A prospective examination of mood dynamics has extended our knowledge on how symptomatology is maintained over time in different psychopathology clusters (Myin-Germeys et al., 2009; Sperry, Walsh, & Kwapil, 2020). More in-debt (prospective) examinations of multiple symptoms and their impact on each other are possible using network analysis techniques (Borsboom & Cramer, 2013). These type of analyses are useful on the group level (informing on general patterns specific to patient groups), but also on the individual level (informing on within-person dynamics). Modeling individual trajectories in mental health care could then provide tailored clues on where to intervene during treatment (Bak, Drukker, Hasmi, & van Os, 2016). When anxiety predicts visual hallucination, psychotherapy can focus on anxiety treatment.

Toward a paradigm shift in clinical practice

Group level research provides the building blocks for within-person research. Complex data-collection logistics required in EMA has delayed the wide application of this promising technology in clinical practice for decades. Although digital technology is possible through smartphones, technology alone is insufficient to disseminate innovative care practices or change routine care. In our traditional approach to mental illness, symptom variability is considered irrelevant, assuming the underlying latent concept contains the relevant information. This approach results in a model that characterizes the individual based on its stable underlying vulnerability. Treatment options are selected using scientific knowledge collected on the group level characteristic of the individual. The resulting options are limited and often fail to fit the person's individual needs. This reductionist strategy is the central rationale of programs that aim to improve the quality of care and the transparency of clinical decision-making. It has shaped the mindset of clinicians for more than five decades (van Os et al., 2019). Most clinicians feel shifting assessment from detecting the core unified underlying handicap or illness—a strategy that disregards variability—to focusing on changes over time—a strategy that emphasizes differences—is unnatural and not very professional. However, it is in fact a reconnection with the basic research question of psychology: understanding behavior, cognition, affect, and perception from the point of view of an individual (with its stable characteristics of genes and learning history) in its daily adaptation process with the requirements of a meaningful environment (Hergenhahn & Henley, 2013). The group-based strategy that the field adopted was a second-choice option that worked for some years and improved the field but fell short of the ambitions to optimize care for most individuals (Thomas, Bracken, & Timimi, 2012).

Reliable assessment of subjective experiences

The availability of tools to understand the person during dynamic interaction with a meaningful context dramatically changes with EMA as a mHealth solution. The logistic challenges are huge. Behavior can be observed in the public domain, but it is challenging to follow someone at all times, leading the observer to be blind to what happens during private moments. Often, the mere external observation does not improve the quality of the data, but alters the observed reality (thereby creating reactivity) (Hufford, Shields, Shiffman, Paty, & Balabanis, 2002). From an ecological psychology point of view, the original, unaltered situations are relevant and often crucial. In contrast and by their nature, cognition, affect, and perception, are private phenomena. There is no "objective" control condition to validate them.

This "inconvenient truth" is the reason why psychology moved to behaviorism (develop the scientific field by exclusively relying on externally observable behavior) almost a century ago. It is also the reason why psychology developed psychometric theory when the need emerged to focus again on the subjective domains: cognition, affect, and perception. The idea was to use item redundancy to limit error variance in the assessment of a latent construct (Hurlburt, 1993).

While the field moved to trust reports of private subjective experiences as scientific input, one should not disregard the critiques formalized almost a century ago. The design of EMA intends to reduce biases in the selection of relevant moments by using a random unpredictable time-based algorithm, to ascertain a representative sample of daily life experiences and contexts. The unpredictability of assessment moments makes them unavoidable and helps subjects maintain their regular daily life routines. Mental state assessment is limited to the moment, avoiding the need for retrospection or aggregation. This maximizes the adequate reflection of the current, contextually embedded mood, cognition, perception, and behavior. These elements help us overcome the biased unreliable assessment of subjective experiences.

Individual EMA use in clinical practice

EMA is designed to follow the abovementioned guidelines for reliable assessment in situ. The method is useful for treatment monitoring and can even replace daily diaries used in therapy or routine outcome monitoring used to collect management information. By doing so, it increases the ecological validity and personal relevance of information (van Os et al., 2017; Verhagen et al., 2017). Data explorations help to discover what clinical improvement means for individual patients. Barge-Schaapveld, Nicolson, van der Hoop, and De Vries (1995), for example, showed that clinical improvement was reflected in behavioral changes such as increased activation (e.g., spending more time on varying activities and less time on passive leisure) and mood changes (e.g., more positive and less negative affect). Other indicators of improvements are decreases in stress sensitivity and increases in perceived reward (Wichers et al., 2009). Ecological Momentary Intervention (EMI) goes a step further, where EMA is enhanced with exercises to promote behavioral change and increase skill generalization in daily life (Myin-Germeys, Klippel, Steinhart, & Reininghaus, 2016). For example, Hanssen et al. (2020) provided initial evidence that an interactive smartphone application with personalized feedback (i.e., two tailored suggestions based on previous EMA scores per day) helped to reduce momentary psychotic experiences in patients suffering from a psychosis-spectrum disorder, whereas EMA alone did not.

Recent mental health views propose to activate and empower patients through self-management and shared decision-making (Huber et al., 2011). Self-monitoring facilitates these processes, allowing patients to engage actively in data collection, learn from the results, and discuss them with others (e.g., health-care professional). Personalization is ensured because treatment choices are informed by personal experiences and circumstances (i.e., within-person variation) instead of traditional between-group results. The dialog to plan the treatment process is enriched by the personal data provided through the EMA method, herewith empowering the patient to participate on an equal basis in the guiding process of care (van Os et al., 2017; Verhagen, 2020). Patient and clinician work together in this shared decision-making process, with the professional as a coach who brings in general mental health knowledge and the patient as an expert on his or her own life. This collaborative process empowers and motivates (Verhagen, 2020). Shifting from the traditional approach where the professional is a mental health expert and the patient passively follows instructions became possible with technological advances. The internet brings expert knowledge to the public domain. Now, everyone can look up the basic symptoms of depression and corresponding treatment options. Patients are often very much aware of what might be wrong, but just need guidance in exploring strategies to learn and build resilience to manage mental state challenges autonomously.

Case example

An interesting case example of long-term EMA use illustrates its clinical utility. In this lived-experience story, a patient tells her journey toward finding meaning in depression. During a 2-year period, she monitored her recovery with a personalized EMA protocol (with added items such as "I feel numbed" and medication tracking). Weekly sessions with an EMA expert aimed to explore the data and discuss its implications. Data was continuously available and presented in interactive graphs and figures through an online reporting module. Item combinations were possible to visually examine their interactions and dynamics over time (both at aggregated levels as well as the individual level; see Fig. 5.5). Pie charts represented the contextual items, showing their distribution over selected time windows ("what am I doing," "where am I," and "with whom am I") (Lenssen & Verhagen, 2019). The reporting software allows exploring combinations of mood states and context, thus enabling hypothesis testing. One could, for example, assume that spending time in the company of others provides some symptom relief. However, does this hypothesis hold when examining the personal data? People do not learn from books. It is much more powerful to see evidence from your own data (see Fig. 5.6 as an example). The experience to explore her own life provided meaning and anchoring during challenging times. During the distinct stages of recovery, the technology acquired different meaning: an easy tracking function in the beginning; providing a solid base for suggestions to change

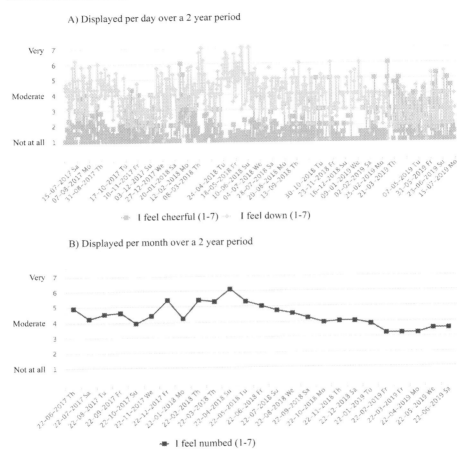

Fig. 5.5 Online feedback graph showing personal EMA data collected over a period of 2 years. Part (A) displays the mood items cheerful and down over time with answers averaged by day. Mood fluctuations can be seen, next to how the feelings relate to each other (e.g., high scores on down are accompanied by low scores on cheerfulness). Part (B) displays the item numbed over time with answers averaged by month. A general decline can be seen, showing overall recovery.
From Lenssen, J., & Verhagen, S.J. (2019). Monitoring my journey from doctor, to patient, to doctor with lived experience. *Schizophrenia Bulletin*.

in the middle phase, and a synthesis providing the "bigger picture" in the final phase (Lenssen & Verhagen, 2019).

Not everyone is able to collect daily observations for months or years, but some certainly do and experience how rewarding it can be. To improve enduring engagement, data collection can be targeted to sensitive periods that are relevant for the patient. The burden becomes less of an issue when digital technology provides new insight and results have personal meaning.

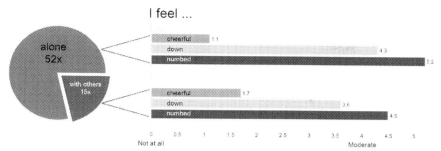

Fig. 5.6 The pie chart *(left)* displays answers to the question "Who am I with" during 2 weeks of sampling, indicating that this person was alone 52 times and with others 15 times. The bar graph *(right)* shows how cheerful, down, and numbed the person was when alone vs when with others. Here, the person felt more cheerful, less down, and less numb when with others. From Lenssen, J., & Verhagen, S.J. (2019). Monitoring my journey from doctor, to patient, to doctor with lived experience. *Schizophrenia Bulletin.*

Leveraging the full potential of technologies

Not all domains are represented equally within these ecological attempts toward precision psychiatry. Psychology recognizes cognition, mood, perception, and behavior as central elements in its theory (Hergenhahn & Henley, 2013). The original implementations of EMA included verbatim descriptions of cognition content (i.e., "what were you thinking just before the notification?"). These were coded on context, timing (past, present, future), context-relatedness (on/off-line) and pathology (clear thoughts up to delusional thinking) (Delespaul, 1995). Open answer formats were less used when moving from paper-and-pencil to smartphone data collection. Additional coding requirements added to the logistic complexity. Formal aspects of cognition were self-rated on Likert scales, for example, assessing guilt, obsessive thoughts, and racing thoughts (Kimhy et al., 2006). Direct behavioral assessment of cognitive functioning (e.g., memory, problem-solving, and concentration) is an underrepresented but clinically relevant domain. Function impairments are common across disorders and tend to linger after symptom reduction, thereby challenging recovery (Millan et al., 2012). Knowing someone's varying cognitive capacity provides guidance for psychosocial or pharmacological interventions. Insight into cognition fluctuations can furthermore shed light on daily struggles and facilitate self-understanding (e.g., allowing daily routine adjustments according to performance peaks). To date, most information on cognition stems from cross-sectional test batteries that inform cognitive capabilities. Test administration occurs under standardized and controlled conditions (Casaletto & Heaton, 2017). Far less is known about cognitive fluctuations and their relation with changes in mental state and contextual challenges. To develop resilience, it is helpful to know when and under which circumstances someone struggles. Novel technological innovations allow in vivo assessments of cognitive functioning (Swendsen, Schweitzer, & Moore, 2019). Short cognition tasks are developed as an add-on to EMA monitoring (e.g., a 30-s momentary Digit Symbol Substitution or a Visuospatial

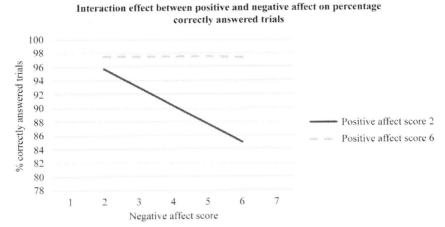

Fig. 5.7 This figure shows that the influence of negative affect on correctness (on a 30-s momentary Digit Symbol Substitution Task) is limited when positive affect is low, but stronger when positive affect is high. Data are gathered in the general population ($N=40$, $n=1293$) within an eight times per day, 6-day EMA protocol.

Memory Task) to allow assessing the relation between affect (e.g., mood) and cognition (e.g., percentage of correct items in a processing speed task) (Daniëls et al., 2020; Verhagen et al., 2019), see Fig. 5.7 for an example. Insight into the patterns of cognitive reactivity on affect or context provides the necessary dynamic information that is lacking in golden-standard assessments. The inclusion of short, objectively and unbiased (with minimal training effect) cognition tasks in EMA assessments is relatively new. However, important questions remain. It is, for instance, unclear which specific cognitive function is targeted by the momentary test operationalization. For example, does the momentary Digit Symbol Substitution Task genuinely reflect processing speed or is performance more related to coping in different environments? Additional research is needed to answer these questions.

Digital phenotyping

Mental suffering follows distinct but unique phases. Instruments that are sensitive to subtle state changes help the clinical characterization, allowing appropriate treatment choices that fit the individual. Machine learning techniques can be useful, as they might help to predict what the critical markers are that signal a relapse or state change. The sheer amount of personal data in a repeated high-sampling EMA protocol enables the possibility of personal predictions on a single-case level.

Most EMA applications make use of subjective assessments that require active participation of users, for example, asking how somebody is feeling now, where they are and what they are doing. This inevitably reduces the usefulness of EMA in processes that evolve over longer time frames (weeks, months, years). The passive assessment of, for example, location can lower the assessment burden and time needed for completing questionnaires. Sensor-based data and ambulatory physiological measures are future candidates to complement EMA assessments, but research still needs to determine their reliability and benefit for use in routine clinical practice (van Os et al., 2017).

The above-described approaches toward precision psychiatry attempt to reunite biological, behavioral, and social information into a strategy that is useful as communication in care. Smartphones or other wearable technologies facilitate data collection in daily life. Digital phenotyping harvests information recorded by the sensors that are embedded in mobile devices (Insel, 2017). It bears the promise of avoiding the disruptive user input that limits the long-term applicability of EMA. It potentially allows passive monitoring of behavior and uses smart algorithms to derive indicators of affect, cognition, and perception for use in psychiatry. The human interaction with technology becomes informative for health, similar to how imaging or physical exams inform on health states. Smartphone sensors (activity, location, social contact tracking), keyboard interactions (cognition tracking), voice and speech analyses (prosody, sentiment, coherence tracking) can be used to inform on behavior, cognition and mood in order to improve diagnosis, monitoring, and risk prediction (Insel, 2017; Jain, Powers, Hawkins, & Brownstein, 2015; Onnela & Rauch, 2016; Torous, Kiang, Lorme, & Onnela, 2016). Some research evidence supports these avenues, but practical implementation is still in its infancy.

Continually harvesting behavioral indicators in the background of a device even when subjects granted permission, has important ethical aspects related to patient privacy as well as the privacy of peers, family, friends, and other contacts. In addition, an overload of fuzzy data is unhelpful, especially since clinicians are often already strained in time and resource allocation (Fry, 2018). Care solutions can only be successful when data interpretation is simple and the added personal value is apparent from the start (Huckvale, Venkatesh, & Christensen, 2019). Moreover, overreliance on passive interactions with smartphones might lead to missed chances for change. Clinical characterization that includes several sources of information—blending self-rating with additional sources of information—is in our opinion the way forward.

Unobtrusive mental health assessments

Contrary to active EMA methods that require user input, digital phenotyping mines data passively, generated automatically without user involvement in the background of sensor devices. Smartphones and smartwatches such as FitBit collect all kinds of information without the conscious effort of their owners (Hicks et al., 2019). Sensor data are behavioral assessments that become meaningful data using algorithms (Ravi, Wong, Lo, & Yang, 2016). It helps to track personal activity patterns (e.g., number of steps taken a day), informs on sleep quality (e.g., 7 h of effective sleep) and even mobilizes users by sending movement reminders when they remain inactive for a while. In terms of general health improvement, this can be very helpful (Price et al.,

2014). A few tools have made it to mental care practices, where patients and clinicians informally explore applications. Psychiatrists ask their patients to monitor the blood pressure with their smartwatches to assess potential hazardous side effects after prescribing new medication. These simple off-the-shelf technologies offer additional information to complement more rigorous assessments methods (such as blood measures in the treatment office).

Sensor-based information is quickly becoming more accessible and provides an unobtrusive way to collect naturalistic behavior on activity patterns, mobility, and social interactions in the flow of daily life (Harari et al., 2016). Monitoring regular human-computer interaction is another promising source of data. Here, the content of actions on the smartphone is irrelevant but for instance, the typing speed when composing a message is. The underlying assumption is that raw sensor data reflects state-level performance indicative of relevant behavioral change (Insel, 2017). Sudden changes in processing speed could, for instance, indicate motor problems or concentration difficulties. Much research is necessary to determine the reliability and validity of the raw data and applied algorithms that generate mental health indicators of psychopathology in daily life, symptom occurrence and severity, mobility, social contacts or indicators of recovery processes (Ben-Zeev, Scherer, Wang, Xie, & Campbell, 2015). Subtle changes in the data, interpreted as early-warning signs could trigger just-in-time interventions via (in-app) feedback. Reliable algorithms or data rules are needed to detect those changes. Clinical information and statistical analyses are essential to build data-driven rules that are applicable in practice (Vaidyam, Halamka, & Torous, 2019). Large datasets are helpful to test novel conceptualizations and validate these rules. Aggregated group findings will not be sufficient, as the idea behind digital phenotyping is to develop personalized psychiatry. Individual users form central tenets around which behavioral predictions should be built.

Research is imperative to improve care practices and interesting work is ongoing. For example, it was hypothesized that passive sensing information could potentially help signal psychotic relapse in patients diagnosed with schizophrenia (Ben-Zeev et al., 2015; Wang et al., 2016). Initial evidence from an ongoing RCT shows associations between sleep patterns, smartphone usage, mobility, conversations, and self-report indices for psychopathology in this group (Wang et al., 2016). Social dysfunction in psychosis-spectrum patients provides another potential avenue for relapse prevention of patients suffering from psychosis. Using the microphone function, call histories, and message logs, information was captured on social communications. Results yielded some indicators of behavior change, showing an association between fewer calls and message and relapse (Buck et al., 2019).

Making sense of complex sensor data is promising, but not easy to realize in a reliable manner. Some strategies can yield useful results in the short run (so-called low hanging fruit). Complementing EMA methods with passive geographical location tracking is a promising application (Dao, Ravesloot, Greiman, & Hargrove, 2019; Duncan et al., 2019). A recent study has tested GPS sensors as a proxy for psychopathological problems in patients with schizophrenia and related their findings to EMA self-report measures (Depp et al., 2019). GPS information can be used to compute how much time is spent at home, how many locations are visited or how far someone travels.

The study showed high correlations between GPS-based information and self-reported location. Less movement was associated with higher negative symptom severity and to a lesser degree with lower community functioning (Depp et al., 2019).

Activity trackers are often applied alongside EMA monitoring in mental health. Patients who show alterations in their activity level can be more depressed or manic (Kim et al., 2019; Minaeva et al., 2020). Using the current algorithms, EMA monitoring of depression better detects depressed individuals than actigraphy alone. The combination of both yields slightly better predictions. The added value of passive tracking was low, but the method is promising for situations where EMA is inconvenient or too obtrusive (Minaeva et al., 2020). These preliminary findings indicate a possible application of mobility and movement indicators, but widespread use in clinical practice is still far off.

Biosensors are another emerging field. Stress and stress sensitivity are important generic factors in mental illness. EMA studies have examined subjective stress levels in people suffering from mental health complaints and compared these outcomes with the cortisol fluctuations (Collip et al., 2011). Unfortunately, cortisol assessments and other biomarkers add another burden to the EMA protocol. Users have to carry swaps that need analysis in a lab. Physiological parameters from wearable devices could provide an attractive alternative, with stress activating the autonomous nerve system that in turn influences heart rate, temperature, skin conductance, and the respiratory system (Draghici & Taylor, 2016; Hinrichs et al., 2017). This is very novel and trials are on their way to identify reliable unobtrusive markers for a stress reaction in daily life (Egger et al., 2020).

Conclusion

We are on the verge of dramatic changes in providing support to people who have a mental illness. Up until recently, all interventions relied on the so-called transference effects: psychopharmacological treatments as well as psychotherapy intend to provide an impact beyond the intervention moment itself. For psychopharmacology, this transference is clear. Optimal daily dosages should result in stable 24-h protection; depot titration intends a weeklong shield. The intention of psychotherapy is similar. The ultimate aim is not limited to the goal, for instance, of relaxing or detecting automatic disturbing thoughts during a therapy session. In contrast, we hope that patients can apply new insights and skills in daily life. Unfortunately, this is not obvious. There is often a gap between therapy and everyday life.

Most clinicians are aware of this gap. The ultimate reference for successful mental health care is for an individual to function and realize self-selected daily life goals. For years, this has been the motivation to substitute clinical inpatient care for ambulatory care. However, changing the location of care alone is insufficient. Of course, ambulatory care increases flexibility. It provides comprehensive options for coping. Society offers options for distraction, versatile solutions for loneliness, or purposeful activities that are not available during hospitalization. Nevertheless, the relocated solutions do not solve the disabilities that patients experience, for example, avoidance of anxiety-inducing situations, withdrawal due to lack of energy, or demotivation due to depression.

Often patients get a home assignment to collect relevant events from their everyday life. During the sessions, the therapist and patient mutually explore the details of the vulnerability. Antecedent and consequent situations are analyzed to define risk patterns and challenges for learning. Often, the set of documented moments is limited, and the reporter's scope biases the interpretation of the context. In the worst-case scenario, patients complete the home assignments in the parking lot or the therapist's waiting room.

For the first time in psychotherapy history, the patient can provide the clinician with unbiased information about their daily real-life challenges and optimal functioning moments. The Ecological Momentary Assessment (EMA) or experience sampling method optimizes these procedures. Subjects randomly report their contextualized mental states. They do not make interpretations, do not have to detect patterns, they only have to respond to short questionnaires that collated reflect vulnerabilities and resilience. Subsequent learning in situ avoids the challenges and pitfalls of generalized skills learning. Even more, clinicians and peers are designing protocols that coach individuals to navigate their daily life challenges. When well designed, they avoid having to rely on professional help that might not always be available (even using a telephone help desk). The method then offers an ever-present "therapist in the pocket" that radically improves the individual's autonomous development of resilience.

No intervention in mental health works without the active engagement and motivation of the concerned persons. People will even refuse to take medication when they doubt it will help them. However, getting control of one's fears or challenge negative thoughts is impossible without being aware of the aim to alter, the confidence that changes are possible, and the exploration of alternative solutions. Cognitive behavior therapy and the recovery movement stress the importance that patients and clinicians engage in a collaborative empiricism strategy. Engagement guarantees the motivation that makes change possible. Moreover, exploring a shared reality is crucial to ascertain the required commitment.

The traditional expert-patient approach to clinical practice does not create the context needed for collaborative empirical exploration. Horizontal relations require transparency and exploration. The communication does not improve with content that is inaccessible or alien to patients. The risk that patients cannot engage fully in the collaborative dialog is real for most expert content, such as psychiatric diagnoses. It also occurs in assessments generated by smart algorithms applied to sensor data collected by smartphones in subjects' daily lives. This technical input can reduce personal engagement. Being able to rewind the film of everyday life, using the narratives and words used by the patients when he/she recorded data, helps to understand better why mood improves or deteriorates. The process further improves when we include the perception of all those engaged in the process (or those sharing similar experiences).

Technology should be like pencils, not a solution for which we have to create a need, but the answer to a need. Smartphone data collection using the EMA methodology can solve one of the long-lasting clinical care challenges: building solutions for daily life functioning. EMA is not a panacea, and challenges remain. In the future, new possibilities undoubtedly will emerge. Innovative technologies develop at a rapid speed. It is tempting to apply technology when it becomes available. Nevertheless, the collection of large amounts of data does not guarantee reliable and valid use. Science has to provide the necessary evidence to ground the new applications. Meanwhile, this evidence exists and improves for EMA. We believe that this already offers a significant improvement for regular clinical practice.

References

Aedo, A., Murru, A., Sanchez, R., Grande, I., Vieta, E., & Undurraga, J. (2018). Clinical characterization of rapid cycling bipolar disorder: Association with attention deficit hyperactivity disorder. *Journal of Affective Disorders*, *240*, 187–192.

Anderson, K., Burford, O., & Emmerton, L. (2016). Mobile health apps to facilitate self-care: A qualitative study of user experiences. *PLoS ONE*, *11*(5), e0156164.

Arango, C., Díaz-Caneja, C. M., McGorry, P. D., Rapoport, J., Sommer, I. E., Vorstman, J. A., et al. (2018). Preventive strategies for mental health. *The Lancet Psychiatry*, *5*(7), 591–604.

Aujoulat, I., d'Hoore, W., & Deccache, A. (2007). Patient empowerment in theory and practice: Polysemy or cacophony? *Patient Education and Counseling*, *66*(1), 13–20.

Bak, M., Drukker, M., Hasmi, L., & van Os, J. (2016). An n = 1 clinical network analysis of symptoms and treatment in psychosis. *PLoS ONE*, *11*(9), e0162811.

Barge-Schaapveld, D. Q., Nicolson, N. A., van der Hoop, R. G., & De Vries, M. W. (1995). Changes in daily life experience associated with clinical improvement in depression. *Journal of Affective Disorders*, *34*(2), 139–154.

Ben-Zeev, D., Scherer, E. A., Wang, R., Xie, H., & Campbell, A. T. (2015). Next-generation psychiatric assessment: Using smartphone sensors to monitor behavior and mental health. *Psychiatric Rehabilitation Journal*, *38*(3), 218.

Borsboom, D., & Cramer, A. O. (2013). Network analysis: An integrative approach to the structure of psychopathology. *Annual Review of Clinical Psychology*, *9*, 91–121.

Bos, F. M., Snippe, E., Bruggeman, R., Wichers, M., & van der Krieke, L. (2019). Insights of patients and clinicians on the promise of the experience sampling method for psychiatric care. *Psychiatric Services*, *70*(11), 983–991.

Brietzke, E., Hawken, E. R., Idzikowski, M., Pong, J., Kennedy, S. H., & Soares, C. N. (2019). Integrating digital phenotyping in clinical characterization of individuals with mood disorders. *Neuroscience & Biobehavioral Reviews*, *104*, 223–230.

Buck, B., Scherer, E., Brian, R., Wang, R., Wang, W., Campbell, A., et al. (2019). Relationships between smartphone social behavior and relapse in schizophrenia: A preliminary report. *Schizophrenia Research*, *208*, 167–172.

Casaletto, K. B., & Heaton, R. K. (2017). Neuropsychological assessment: Past and future. *Journal of the International Neuropsychological Society: JINS*, *23*(9–10), 778.

Collins, F. S., & Varmus, H. (2015). A new initiative on precision medicine. *New England Journal of Medicine*, *372*(9), 793–795.

Collip, D., Nicolson, N., Lardinois, M., Lataster, T., Van Os, J., & Myin-Germeys, I. (2011). Daily cortisol, stress reactivity and psychotic experiences in individuals at above average genetic risk for psychosis. *Psychological Medicine*, *41*(11), 2305.

Csikszentmihalyi, M., & Larson, R. (2014). Validity and reliability of the experience-sampling method. In *Flow and the foundations of positive psychology* (pp. 35–54). Springer.

Daniëls, N., Bartels, S., Verhagen, S., Van Knippenberg, R., De Vugt, M., & Delespaul, P. A. (2020). Digital assessment of working memory and processing speed in everyday life: Feasibility, validation, and lessons-learned. *Internet Interventions, 19*, 100300.

Dao, T. H. D., Ravesloot, C., Greiman, L., & Hargrove, T. (2019). Mining spatial associations between daily activities and health using EMA–GPS data. *Transactions in GIS, 23*(3), 515–537.

Davidson, L. (2016). The recovery movement: Implications for mental health care and enabling people to participate fully in life. *Health Affairs, 35*(6), 1091–1097.

Delespaul, P. (1995). *Assessing schizophrenia in daily life*. Maastricht: Universitaire Pers Maastricht.

Depp, C. A., Bashem, J., Moore, R. C., Holden, J. L., Mikhael, T., Swendsen, J., et al. (2019). GPS mobility as a digital biomarker of negative symptoms in schizophrenia: A case control study. *npj Digital Medicine, 2*(1), 1–7.

Draghici, A. E., & Taylor, J. A. (2016). The physiological basis and measurement of heart rate variability in humans. *Journal of Physiological Anthropology, 35*(1), 22.

Duncan, D. T., Park, S. H., Goedel, W. C., Sheehan, D. M., Regan, S. D., & Chaix, B. (2019). Acceptability of smartphone applications for global positioning system (GPS) and ecological momentary assessment (EMA) research among sexual minority men. *PLoS ONE, 14*(1), e0210240.

Ebner-Priemer, U. W., Eid, M., Kleindienst, N., Stabenow, S., & Trull, T. J. (2009). Analytic strategies for understanding affective (in) stability and other dynamic processes in psychopathology. *Journal of Abnormal Psychology, 118*(1), 195.

Egger, S. T., Knorr, M., Bobes, J., Bernstein, A., Seifritz, E., & Vetter, S. (2020). Real-time assessment of stress and stress response using digital phenotyping: A study protocol. *Frontiers in Digital Health, 2*, 18.

Fried, E. (2017). *Moving forward: How depression heterogeneity hinders progress in treatment and research*. Taylor & Francis.

Fry, H. (2018). *Hello world: How to be human in the age of the machine*. Random House.

Gross, J. J., & Muñoz, R. F. (1995). Emotion regulation and mental health. *Clinical Psychology: Science and Practice, 2*(2), 151–164.

Hanssen, E., Balvert, S., Oorschot, M., Borkelmans, K., van Os, J., Delespaul, P. A. E. G., et al. (2020). An ecological momentary intervention incorporating personalised feedback to improve symptoms and social functioning in schizophrenia spectrum disorders. *Psychiatry Research, 284*, 112695.

Harari, G. M., Lane, N. D., Wang, R., Crosier, B. S., Campbell, A. T., & Gosling, S. D. (2016). Using smartphones to collect behavioral data in psychological science: Opportunities, practical considerations, and challenges. *Perspectives on Psychological Science, 11*(6), 838–854.

Havermans, R., Nicolson, N. A., & deVries, M. W. (2007). Daily hassles, uplifts, and time use in individuals with bipolar disorder in remission. *The Journal of Nervous and Mental Disease, 195*(9), 745–751.

Hergenhahn, B. R., & Henley, T. (2013). *An introduction to the history of psychology*. Cengage Learning.

Hicks, J. L., Althoff, T., Kuhar, P., Bostjancic, B., King, A. C., Leskovec, J., et al. (2019). Best practices for analyzing large-scale health data from wearables and smartphone apps. *npj Digital Medicine, 2*(1), 1–12.

Higgs, J., Jones, M. A., Loftus, S., & Christensen, N. (2008). *Clinical reasoning in the health professions E-book*. Elsevier Health Sciences.

Hinrichs, R., Michopoulos, V., Winters, S., Rothbaum, A. O., Rothbaum, B. O., Ressler, K. J., et al. (2017). Mobile assessment of heightened skin conductance in posttraumatic stress disorder. *Depression and Anxiety, 34*(6), 502–507.

Hofmann, S. G., Sawyer, A. T., Fang, A., & Asnaani, A. (2012). Emotion dysregulation model of mood and anxiety disorders. *Depression and Anxiety*, *29*(5), 409–416.

Huber, M., Knottnerus, J. A., Green, L., van der Horst, H., Jadad, A. R., Kromhout, D., et al. (2011). How should we define health? *BMJ*, *343*, d4163.

Huckvale, K., Venkatesh, S., & Christensen, H. (2019). Toward clinical digital phenotyping: A timely opportunity to consider purpose, quality, and safety. *npj Digital Medicine*, *2*(1), 1–11.

Hufford, M. R., Shields, A. L., Shiffman, S., Paty, J., & Balabanis, M. (2002). Reactivity to ecological momentary assessment: An example using undergraduate problem drinkers. *Psychology of Addictive Behaviors*, *16*(3), 205–211.

Huhn, M., Tardy, M., Spineli, L. M., Kissling, W., Förstl, H., Pitschel-Walz, G., et al. (2014). Efficacy of pharmacotherapy and psychotherapy for adult psychiatric disorders: A systematic overview of meta-analyses. *JAMA Psychiatry*, *71*(6), 706–715.

Huibers, M. J., & Cuijpers, P. (2014). Common (nonspecific) factors in psychotherapy. In *The Encyclopedia of Clinical Psychology* (pp. 1–6).

Hurlburt, R., & Schwitzgebel, E. (2011). *Describing inner experience?: Proponent meets skeptic*. Mit Press.

Hurlburt, R. T. (1993). *Sampling inner experience in disturbed affect*. Springer Science & Business Media.

Insel, T. R. (2017). Digital phenotyping: Technology for a new science of behavior. *JAMA*, *318*(13), 1215–1216.

Jain, S. H., Powers, B. W., Hawkins, J. B., & Brownstein, J. S. (2015). The digital phenotype. *Nature Biotechnology*, *33*(5), 462–463.

Jameson, J. L., & Longo, D. L. (2015). Precision medicine—Personalized, problematic, and promising. *Obstetrical & Gynecological Survey*, *70*(10), 612–614.

John, M. (2001). *A dictionary of epidemiology* (p. 153). Oxford University Press.

Kao, C.-K., & Liebovitz, D. M. (2017). Consumer mobile health apps: Current state, barriers, and future directions. *PM & R : The Journal of Injury, Function, and Rehabilitation*, *9*(5), S106–S115.

Kapur, S., Phillips, A. G., & Insel, T. R. (2012). Why has it taken so long for biological psychiatry to develop clinical tests and what to do about it? *Molecular Psychiatry*, *17*(12), 1174–1179.

Kim, H., Lee, S., Lee, S., Hong, S., Kang, H., & Kim, N. (2019). Depression prediction by using ecological momentary assessment, Actiwatch data, and machine learning: Observational study on older adults living alone. *JMIR mHealth and uHealth*, *7*(10), e14149.

Kimhy, D., Delespaul, P., Corcoran, C., Ahn, H., Yale, S., & Malaspina, D. (2006). Computerized experience sampling method (ESMc): Assessing feasibility and validity among individuals with schizophrenia. *Journal of Psychiatric Research*, *40*(3), 221–230.

Lenssen, J., & Verhagen, S. J. (2019). Monitoring my journey from doctor, to patient, to doctor with lived experience. *Schizophrenia Bulletin*.

Lewin, K. (2013). *Principles of topological psychology*. Read Books Ltd.

Luborsky, L., Rosenthal, R., Diguer, L., Andrusyna, T. P., Berman, J. S., Levitt, J. T., et al. (2002). The dodo bird verdict is alive and well—Mostly. *Clinical Psychology: Science and Practice*, *9*(1), 2–12.

Luxton, D. D., McCann, R. A., Bush, N. E., Mishkind, M. C., & Reger, G. M. (2011). mHealth for mental health: Integrating smartphone technology in behavioral healthcare. *Professional Psychology: Research and Practice*, *42*(6), 505.

Maj, M. (2020). Beyond diagnosis in psychiatric practice. *Annals of General Psychiatry*, *19*, 1–6.

Marzano, L., Bardill, A., Fields, B., Herd, K., Veale, D., Grey, N., et al. (2015). The application of mHealth to mental health: Opportunities and challenges. *The Lancet Psychiatry, 2*(10), 942–948.

McGorry, P., & Van Os, J. (2013). Redeeming diagnosis in psychiatry: Timing versus specificity. *The Lancet, 381*(9863), 343–345.

McGorry, P. D., Hartmann, J. A., Spooner, R., & Nelson, B. (2018). Beyond the "at risk mental state" concept: Transitioning to transdiagnostic psychiatry. *World Psychiatry, 17*(2), 133–142.

Mehrotra, S., & Tripathi, R. (2018). Recent developments in the use of smartphone interventions for mental health. *Current Opinion in Psychiatry, 31*(5), 379–388.

Millan, M. J., Agid, Y., Brüne, M., Bullmore, E. T., Carter, C. S., Clayton, N. S., et al. (2012). Cognitive dysfunction in psychiatric disorders: Characteristics, causes and the quest for improved therapy. *Nature Reviews Drug Discovery, 11*(2), 141–168.

Minaeva, O., Riese, H., Lamers, F., Antypa, N., Wichers, M., & Booij, S. H. (2020). Screening for depression in daily life: Development and external validation of a prediction model based on actigraphy and experience sampling method. *Journal of Medical Internet Research, 22*(12), e22634.

Myin-Germeys, I., Klippel, A., Steinhart, H., & Reininghaus, U. (2016). Ecological momentary interventions in psychiatry. *Current Opinion in Psychiatry, 29*(4), 258–263.

Myin-Germeys, I., Kasanova, Z., Vaessen, T., Vachon, H., Kirtley, O., Viechtbauer, W., et al. (2018). Experience sampling methodology in mental health research: New insights and technical developments. *World Psychiatry, 17*(2), 123–132.

Myin-Germeys, I., Oorschot, M., Collip, D., Lataster, J., Delespaul, P., & Van Os, J. (2009). Experience sampling research in psychopathology: Opening the black box of daily life. *Psychological Medicine, 39*(9), 1533–1547.

Nandi, A., Beard, J. R., & Galea, S. (2009). Epidemiologic heterogeneity of common mood and anxiety disorders over the lifecourse in the general population: A systematic review. *BMC Psychiatry, 9*(1), 31.

National Research Council. (2011). *Toward precision medicine: Building a knowledge network for biomedical research and a new taxonomy of disease*. National Academies Press.

Onnela, J.-P., & Rauch, S. L. (2016). Harnessing smartphone-based digital phenotyping to enhance behavioral and mental health. *Neuropsychopharmacology, 41*(7), 1691–1696.

Patel, V., Saxena, S., Lund, C., Thornicroft, G., Baingana, F., Bolton, P., et al. (2018). The Lancet Commission on global mental health and sustainable development. *The Lancet, 392*(10157), 1553–1598.

Pauli, C., Hopkins, B. D., Prandi, D., Shaw, R., Fedrizzi, T., Sboner, A., et al. (2017). Personalized in vitro and in vivo cancer models to guide precision medicine. *Cancer Discovery, 7*(5), 462–477.

Price, M., Yuen, E. K., Goetter, E. M., Herbert, J. D., Forman, E. M., Acierno, R., et al. (2014). mHealth: A mechanism to deliver more accessible, more effective mental health care. *Clinical Psychology & Psychotherapy, 21*(5), 427–436.

Ravi, D., Wong, C., Lo, B., & Yang, G.-Z. (2016). A deep learning approach to on-node sensor data analytics for mobile or wearable devices. *IEEE Journal of Biomedical and Health Informatics, 21*(1), 56–64.

Reis, H. T., Collins, W. A., & Berscheid, E. (2000). The relationship context of human behavior and development. *Psychological Bulletin, 126*(6), 844.

Slade, M. (2010). Mental illness and well-being: The central importance of positive psychology and recovery approaches. *BMC Health Services Research, 10*(1), 26.

Smith, P. C., Araya-Guerra, R., Bublitz, C., Parnes, B., Dickinson, L. M., Van Vorst, R., et al. (2005). Missing clinical information during primary care visits. *JAMA, 293*(5), 565–571.

Sperry, S. H., Walsh, M. A., & Kwapil, T. R. (2020). Emotion dynamics concurrently and pro-spectively predict mood psychopathology. *Journal of Affective Disorders*, *261*, 67–75.

Storm, M., & Edwards, A. (2013). Models of user involvement in the mental health context: Intentions and implementation challenges. *Psychiatric Quarterly*, *84*(3), 313–327.

Suls, J., & Rothman, A. (2004). Evolution of the biopsychosocial model: Prospects and chal-lenges for health psychology. *Health Psychology*, *23*(2), 119.

Swendsen, J., Schweitzer, P., & Moore, R. C. (2019). Mobile cognitive testing using experience sampling. In *Experience sampling in mental health research* (pp. 142–155). Routledge.

Tambuyzer, E., Pieters, G., & Van Audenhove, C. (2014). Patient involvement in mental health care: One size does not fit all. *Health Expectations*, *17*(1), 138–150.

Thomas, P., Bracken, P., & Timimi, S. (2012). The limits of evidence-based medicine in psychi-atry. *Philosophy, Psychiatry, & Psychology*, *19*(4), 295–308.

Torous, J., Kiang, M. V., Lorme, J., & Onnela, J.-P. (2016). New tools for new research in psychiatry: A scalable and customizable platform to empower data driven smartphone re-search. *JMIR Mental Health*, *3*(2), e16.

Trull, T. J., Lane, S. P., Koval, P., & Ebner-Priemer, U. W. (2015). Affective dynamics in psy-chopathology. *Emotion Review*, *7*(4), 355–361.

Tsuang, M. T., Bar, J. L., Stone, W. S., & Faraone, S. V. (2004). Gene-environment interactions in mental disorders. *World Psychiatry*, *3*(2), 73.

Vaidyam, A., Halamka, J., & Torous, J. (2019). Actionable digital phenotyping: A framework for the delivery of just-in-time and longitudinal interventions in clinical healthcare. *mHealth*, *5*.

Van Audenhove, C., & Vertommen, H. (2000). A negotiation approach to intake and treatment choice. *Journal of Psychotherapy Integration*, *10*(3), 287–299.

van Os, J., Delespaul, P., Wigman, J., Myin-Germeys, I., & Wichers, M. (2013). Beyond DSM and ICD: Introducing "precision diagnosis" for psychiatry using momentary assessment technology. *World Psychiatry*, *12*(2), 113.

van Os, J., Guloksuz, S., Vijn, T. W., Hafkenscheid, A., & Delespaul, P. (2019). The evidence-based group-level symptom-reduction model as the organizing principle for mental health care: Time for change? *World Psychiatry*, *18*(1), 88–96.

van Os, J., Verhagen, S., Marsman, A., Peeters, F., Bak, M., Marcelis, M., et al. (2017). The experience sampling method as an mHealth tool to support self-monitoring, self-insight, and personalized health care in clinical practice. *Depression and Anxiety*, *34*(6), 481–493.

Verhagen, S. J. W. (2020). *The power of individual landscapes: A clinical exploration of per-sonal experience sampling and new horizons*. Ridderprint BV.

Verhagen, S. J. W., Daniëls, N. E., Bartels, S. L., Tans, S., Borkelmans, K. W., de Vugt, M. E., et al. (2019). Measuring within-day cognitive performance using the experience sampling method: A pilot study in a healthy population. *PLoS One*, *14*(12), e0226409.

Verhagen, S. J. W., Berben, J. A., Leue, C., Marsman, A., Delespaul, P. A. E. G., van Os, J., et al. (2017). Demonstrating the reliability of transdiagnostic mHealth Routine Outcome Monitoring in mental health services using experience sampling technology. *PLoS One*, *12*(10), e0186294.

Wampold, B. E. (2015). How important are the common factors in psychotherapy? An update. *World Psychiatry*, *14*(3), 270–277.

Wang, R., Aung, M. S., Abdullah, S., Brian, R., Campbell, A. T., Choudhury, T., et al. (2016). CrossCheck: Toward passive sensing and detection of mental health changes in people with schizophrenia. In *Proceedings of the 2016 ACM international joint conference on pervasive and ubiquitous computing* (pp. 886–897).

Watkins, P. C. (2002). Implicit memory bias in depression. *Cognition & Emotion*, *16*(3), 381–402.

Whiteford, H. A., Degenhardt, L., Rehm, J., Baxter, A. J., Ferrari, A. J., Erskine, H. E., et al. (2013). Global burden of disease attributable to mental and substance use disorders: Findings from the Global Burden of Disease Study 2010. *The Lancet, 382*(9904), 1575–1586.

WHO. (2001). *Mental health: New understanding, new hope*. The World Health Report Geneva: World Health Organization.

Wichers, M. C., Barge-Schaapveld, D. Q. C. M., Nicolson, N. A., Peeters, F., de Vries, M., Mengelers, R., et al. (2009). Reduced stress-sensitivity or increased reward experience: The psychological mechanism of response to antidepressant medication. *Neuropsychopharmacology, 34*(4), 923–931.

Wolfers, T., Doan, N. T., Kaufmann, T., Alnæs, D., Moberget, T., Agartz, I., et al. (2018). Mapping the heterogeneous phenotype of schizophrenia and bipolar disorder using normative models. *JAMA Psychiatry, 75*(11), 1146–1155.

World Health Organization. (1948). *Preamble to the constitution of the World Health Organization as adopted by the international health conference, New York, 19-22 June, 1946; signed on 22 July 1946 by the representatives of 61 States*. (Official Records of the World Health Organization, no. 2, p. 100) and entered into force on 7 April 1948 http://www.who.int/governance/eb/who_constitution_en.Pdf.

Zomer, L. J., Voskes, Y., Van Weeghel, J., Widdershoven, G. A., Van Mierlo, T. F., Berkvens, B. S., et al. (2020). The active recovery triad model: A new approach in Dutch long-term mental health care. *Frontiers in Psychiatry, 11*.

Social media big data analysis for mental health research

Akkapon Wongkoblap[a,d,e], Miguel A. Vadillo[b,c], and Vasa Curcin[a,c]
[a]Department of Informatics, King's College London, London, United Kingdom,
[b]Department of Psychology, Autonomous University of Madrid, Madrid, Spain, [c]School
of Population Health and Environmental Sciences, King's College London, London,
United Kingdom, [d]School of Information Technology, Suranaree University of Technology,
Nakhon Ratchasima, Thailand, [e]DIGITECH, Suranaree University of Technology, Nakhon
Ratchasima, Thailand

Mental health problems are widely recognized as a major public health challenge worldwide. This highlights the need for effective tools for detecting mental health disorders in the population. Social media data is a promising source of information where people publish rich personal information that can be mined to extract valuable psychological information. However, social media data poses its own set of challenges, such as the specific terms and expressions used on different platforms, interactions between different users through likes and shares, and the need to disambiguate between statements about oneself and about third parties. Traditionally, social media natural language processing (NLP) techniques have looked at text classifiers and user classification models separately, which presents a challenge for researchers wanting not only to combine text sentiment and user sentiment analysis but also to extract user's narratives from the textual content.

Mental disorders

Mental illness is one of the leading contributors to the global burden of disease. Figs. 6.1 and 6.2 shows disability-adjusted life years (DALYs)—measured from years of life lost and years lived with disability—(as displayed in Fig. 6.3) caused by diseases between 1990 and 2019. As can be seen, mental and substance abuse disorders are constantly growing from ranked ninth in 1990 to fourth cause of DALYs in 2019 globally. The number of global patients suffering from mental disorders was estimated to be over 970 million in 2019 (Institute for Health Metrics and Evaluation, 2019).

In terms of an economic burden, the global cost of mental health problems was approximated to be US$2.5 trillion in 2010, and is expected to reach US$6.1 trillion by 2030 (see Fig. 6.4A). It disrupts economic growth in many countries, especially in low- and middle-income countries. The calculation of the costs normally takes no account of indirect costs such as *national level*: mental, human capital, and economic growth losses; *workplace level*: work productivity losses, worker replacement costs, and earlier retirement; and *individual level*: income losses and poverty, poor

Mental Health in a Digital World. https://doi.org/10.1016/B978-0-12-822201-0.00018-6

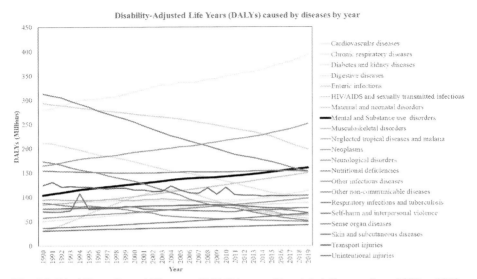

Fig. 6.1 Disability-adjusted life years (DALYs) caused by global diseases from 1990 to 2019. Data from Institute for Health Metrics and Evaluation. (c. 2019). *Global Burden of Disease Study 2019 (GBD 2019) Data Resources.* http://ghdx.healthdata.org/gbd-results-tool/.

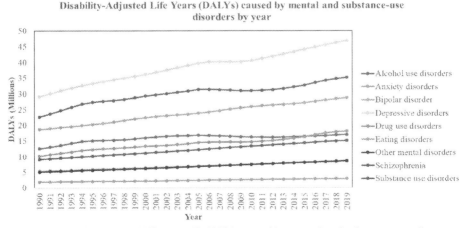

Fig. 6.2 Disability-adjusted life years (DALYs) caused by mental and substance-use diseases from 1990 to 2019.
Data from Institute for Health Metrics and Evaluation. (c. 2019). *Global Burden of Disease Study 2019 (GBD 2019) Data Resources.* http://ghdx.healthdata.org/gbd-.

educational attainment, and lower life expectancy (Bloom et al., 2011; Razzouk, 2017). Fig. 6.4A indicates that the indirect costs of mental illness are greater than direct costs. Mental disorder costs also contribute to the largest proportion of economic losses among the leading diseases (Trautmann et al., 2016) as shown in Fig. 6.4B and C.

Fig. 6.3 DALY disability affected life year infographic retrieved from Wikimedia Commons. From Wikipedia. (c. 2012). *Infographic for DALY disability adjusted life year*. https:// commons.wikimedia.org/wiki/File:DALY_disability_affected_life_year_infographic.svg.

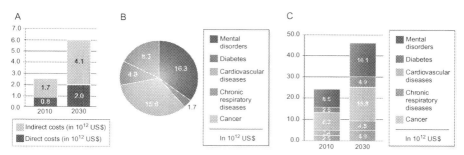

Fig. 6.4 Economic costs of mental disorders in trillion US$ using three different approaches: direct and indirect costs of mental disorders (A), the cumulative economic output loss between 2011 and 2030 (B), and risks and money to quantify the risk of disability or death (C). From Trautmann, S., Rehm, J., & Wittchen, H. (c. 2016). The economic costs of mental disorders: Do our societies react appropriately to the burden of mental disorders? *EMBO Reports, 17*(9), 1245–1249. https://doi.org/10.15252/embr.201642951.

These data highlight the need for novel and effective approaches to early detection and treatment of individuals with mental disorders. In the remainder of this chapter, we review how analysis of social media data usefully contributes to such work.

Social media data

Social media are online platforms that allow users to create, discuss, modify, and exchange content. Users registering on such platform can present their identities to others, communicate with others, form a wide variety of interest groups, and establish or maintain relationships (Kietzmann, Hermkens, McCarthy, & Silvestre, 2011). Social media contains various types of social media whose characteristics are different. This helps define a profile-based platform to collect user's data and annotate those users associated with mental disorders.

Social media typology

Based on the above definition, social media can be classified into 13 different types. Table 6.1 describes the definitions of each social media (Aichner & Jacob, 2015). Another social media typology is based on the nature of connection (profile-based vs content-based) and the level of customization of messages (broadcast vs customized). Table 6.2 provides details of the nature of the connection. Profile-based vs content-based and customized vs broadcast dimensions can be used to define four types of social media using a 2×2 matrix, as shown in Table 6.3 (Zhu & Chen, 2015).

Despite the variety of types, many studies are focused only on an individual's content on profile-based social media platforms. These can potentially detect users with mental disorder from their textual content. Profile-based social media platforms include microblogs like *Twitter* and social networks like *Facebook*. Unlike other types of social media, social networking, and microblog platforms allow users to create personal profiles, establish new relationships as well as maintain close friendships, publish status updates and have interactions with other users. Those users openly express a variety of thoughts, feelings, and emotions every day.

In 2020 there are over 3.6 billion social network users (Statista, 2016). Just the most popular social networking site, Facebook, contains over 1.79 billion active users in July 2020 (Facebook Inc., 2020). The most popular microblog, Twitter, contains more than 330 million monthly active accounts (Twitter Inc., 2019).

Studies by De Choudhury, Counts, Horvitz, and Hoff (2014), Eichstaedt et al. (2018), Marengo, Azucar, Longobardi, and Settanni (2020), Park, Lee, Kwak, Cha, and Jeong (2013), Sungkyu Park et al. (2015), and Wu, Shen, Wang, and Chen (2020) have explored data from Facebook and Twitter (Almouzini, Khemakhem, & Alageel, 2019; Alsagri & Ykhlef, 2020; Amir, Coppersmith, Carvalho, Silva, & Wallace, 2017; Bollen, Gonçalves, Ruan, & Mao, 2011; Braithwaite, Giraud-Carrier, West, Barnes, & Hanson, 2016; Burnap, Colombo, & Scourfield, 2015; Chandra Guntuku, Preotiuc-Pietro, Eichstaedt, & Ungar, 2019; Chen, Sykora, Jackson, & Elayan, 2018; Coppersmith, Dredze, & Harman, 2014; Coppersmith, Ngo, Leary, & Wood, 2016; Coppersmith, Leary, Crutchley, & Fine, 2018; Coppersmith, Harman, & Dredze, 2014; De Choudhury, Counts, & Horvitz, 2013b; De Choudhury, Gamon, Counts, & Horvitz, 2013; De Choudhury, Counts, & Horvitz, 2013a; Fodeh et al., 2019; Guan, Hao, Cheng, Yip, & Zhu, 2015; Gui et al., 2019; Homan et al., 2014; Jamison-Powell, Linehan, Daley, Garbett, & Lawson, 2012; Kang, Yoon, & Kim, 2016; Lin et al., 2020; Lin et al., 2014; Mbarek, Jamoussi, Charfi, & Ben Hamadou, 2019; O'Dea et al., 2015; Prieto, Matos, Álvarez, Cacheda, & Oliveira, 2014; Ramírez-Cifuentes et al., 2020; Reece et al., 2017; Roy et al., 2020; Saravia, Chang, De Lorenzo, & Chen, 2016; Schwartz et al., 2013; Schwartz et al., 2014; Shen et al., 2017; Tsugawa et al., 2015; Tsugawa et al., 2013; Volkova, Han, & Corley, 2016; Wang, Brede, Ianni, & Mentzakis, 2017; Wilson, Ali, & Valstar, 2014; Resnik et al., 2014; Yazdavar et al., 2020). Studies have also examined profile-based social media data from Instagram

Table 6.1 Definitions of social media types.

Type of social media	Description
Blogs	A blog shortened from web and log is a list of ordered posts published by a poster. Other users can read and comment. *Example:* wordpress.com, medium.net
Business networks	A business network is a platform where individuals create a professional profile to connect and maintain professional contacts. Companies seek new employees based on professional profiles. *Example:* linkedin.com, xing.com
Collaborative projects	A platform facilitates users with a common interest to collaborate to develop a new project. The result from the project is released as open source. *Example:* wikipedia.org, mozilla.org
Enterprise social networks	Enterprise social network is a private platform for employees in a specific company to connect to one another and exchange knowledge in the company. *Example:* yammer.com, socialcast.com
Forums	A forum is an online discussion board where users can create topics to ask or exchange with other users and reply to user's topics. *Example:* quora.com, reddit.com
Microblogs	Microblogs are like blogs but there is a word limitation of the length of posting, e.g., 280 characters. Posts may contain pictures, videos, and URLs. Users can follow other accounts. *Example:* twitter.com, weibo.com
Photo sharing	Photo sharing is a platform where users can upload, caption and share photos. Other users can comment the shared photos. *Example:* flickr.com, instagram.com
Products/services review	Product and service review platforms are websites where users can evaluate products and write or read reviews. The sites often sell or provide product information. *Example:* amazon.com, yelp.com
Social bookmarking	Social bookmarking is a centralized platform for users to create and arrange bookmarks in order to share with others. *Example:* delicious.com, pinterest.com
Social gaming	Social gaming refers to online games that users can interact and collaborate with other players. *Example:* gameloft.com, steam.com
Social networks	Social networking platforms allow users to create profiles and connect to others who know each other or have common interests. Users can post text, pictures, videos, and URLs. *Example:* facebook.com, vk.com
Video sharing	Video sharing refers to an online platform where users can upload and share videos. The platform may allow users to comment on the videos. *Example:* youtube.com, tiktok.com
Virtual worlds	Virtual worlds are online places where users can create a customized avatar to represent themselves. These avatars are used to interact and communicate with other avatars. *Example:* secondlife.com, twinity.com

Table 6.2   Profile-based vs. content-based social media.

	Profile-based	**Content-based**
Focal point	The individual member	Contents posted
Nature of information	Topics are typically related to the person	Discussions and comments are based around contents posted
Main purpose	Users make connections mainly because they are interested in the user behind the profile	Users make connections because they like the contents a certain profile provides
Examples	Facebook, Twitter, Line, Whatsapp	Flickr, Instagram, Pinterest, YouTube

Taken from Zhu, Y.-Q., & Chen, H.-G. (2015). Social media and human need satisfaction: Implications for social media marketing. *Business Horizons*, *58*(3), 335–345. https://doi.org/10.1016/j.bushor.2015.01.006.

Table 6.3   Social media matrix.

	Customized message	*Broadcast message*
Profile-based	Relationship Allowing users to connect, reconnect, communicate, and build relationships. (e.g., Facebook, LinkedIn, Line, Whatsapp)	Self-media Allowing users to broadcast their updates and others to follow. (e.g., Twitter, Weibo)
Content-based	Collaboration Allowing users to collaboratively find answers, advice, help, and reach consensus. (e.g., Quora, Reddit, Yahoo! Answers)	Creative outlets Allowing users to share their interest, creativity, and hobbies with each other. (e.g., YouTube, Flickr, Foodily, Pinterest)

Taken from Zhu, Y.-Q., & Chen, H.-G. (2015). Social media and human need satisfaction: Implications for social media marketing. *Business Horizons*, *58*(3), 335–345. https://doi.org/10.1016/j.bushor.2015.01.006.

(Chancellor, Lin, Goodman, Zerwas, & De Choudhury, 2016; Chiu, Lane, Koh, & Chen, 2021; Huang, Chiang, & Chen, 2019; Mann, Paes, & Matsushima, 2020; Reece & Danforth, 2017), Sina Wiebo APIs (Almouzini et al., 2019; Alsagri & Ykhlef, 2020; Amir et al., 2017; Bollen et al., 2011; Braithwaite et al., 2016; Burnap et al., 2015; Chandra Guntuku et al., 2019; Chen et al., 2018; Coppersmith, Dredze, & Harman, 2014; Coppersmith et al., 2016, 2018; Coppersmith, Harman, & Dredze, 2014; De Choudhury, Counts, & Horvitz, 2013b; De Choudhury, Gamon, et al., 2013; De Choudhury, Counts, & Horvitz, 2013a; Fodeh et al., 2019; Guan et al., 2015; Gui et al., 2019; Homan et al., 2014; Jamison-Powell et al., 2012; Kang et al., 2016; Lin et al., 2020; Lin et al., 2014; Mbarek et al., 2019; O'Dea et al., 2015; Prieto et al., 2014; Ramírez-Cifuentes et al., 2020; Reece et al., 2017; Roy et al., 2020; Saravia et al., 2016; Schwartz et al., 2013; Schwartz et al., 2014; Shen et al., 2017; Tsugawa et al., 2015; Tsugawa et al., 2013; Volkova et al., 2016; Wang et al., 2017; Wilson et al., 2014; Yazdavar et al., 2020), and Vkontakte APIs (Maxim, Ignatiev, & Smirnov, 2020; Stankevich, Latyshev, Kuminskaya, Smirnov, & Grigoriev, 2019; Stankevich, Smirnov, Kiselnikova, & Ushakova, 2020).

Data collection from social media users

Data collection is normally considered the first step in developing a predictive model. Within the context of research on personal data from social media, data collection can be considered as one of the hardest steps, due to ethical issues, transparent data processing, and data privacy (Ford, Curlewis, Wongkoblap, & Curcin, 2019). A dataset can be obtained by two approaches: (1) direct collection from subjects and (2) data aggregation from a social media site. The choice of approach depends on the purpose of each study and the relevant target platform.

Directly collecting from subjects

In medical and social sciences, human subject research is a systematic approach to observing and analyzing humans agreeing to take part in a study by Schultz (1969) and World Medical Association (2013). De Choudhury, Gamon, et al. (2013) adapted the human subject research method to observe and collect data from social network users suffering from mental disorder symptoms (De Choudhury, Gamon, et al., 2013). They recruited participants and used a questionnaire to screen them for mental disorders. Eichstaedt asked patients to participate in their study and used medical records to classify the patients as being depressed (Eichstaedt et al., 2018). After screening, both studies asked participants for access to their social media data to collect social network profiles.

Studies have also posted project information on relevant websites inviting participants to take part in their research (Cheng, Li, Kwok, Zhu, & Yip, 2017; De Choudhury et al., 2014; Lv, Li, Liu, & Zhu, 2015; Mann et al., 2020; Marengo et al., 2020; Tsugawa et al., 2015), and published tasks on crowdsourcing platforms asking for research participants (Braithwaite et al., 2016; Chandra Guntuku et al., 2019; De Choudhury, Counts, & Horvitz, 2013b; De Choudhury, Gamon, et al., 2013; Reece et al., 2017; Reece & Danforth, 2017; H.A. Schwartz et al., 2016).

Aggregating data extracted from public posts

Another method is searching target users using keywords. This approach is considered an easy and cost-time effective approach to identify participants with mental disorders from social network platforms. In 2014, Coppersmith et al. introduced an automatic data collection method to search target users with mental health disorders (Coppersmith, Dredze, & Harman, 2014). They used regular expressions or keywords to search for a set of target tweets mentioning the diagnosis of mental health diseases. The returned tweets were investigated and verified as genuine tweets, which spoke to the mental health diagnosis of the tweet owners.

Several subsequent studies (Almouzini et al., 2019; Alsagri & Ykhlef, 2020; Amir et al., 2017; Bollen et al., 2011; Braithwaite et al., 2016; Burnap et al., 2015; Chandra Guntuku et al., 2019; Chen et al., 2018; Coppersmith, Dredze, & Harman, 2014; Coppersmith et al., 2016, 2018; Coppersmith, Harman, & Dredze, 2014; De Choudhury, Counts, & Horvitz, 2013b; De Choudhury, Gamon, et al., 2013; De

Choudhury, Counts, & Horvitz, 2013a; Fodeh et al., 2019; Guan et al., 2015; Gui et al., 2019; Homan et al., 2014; Jamison-Powell et al., 2012; Kang et al., 2016; Lin et al., 2020; Lin et al., 2014; Mbarek et al., 2019; O'Dea et al., 2015; Prieto et al., 2014; Ramírez-Cifuentes et al., 2020; Reece et al., 2017; Roy et al., 2020; Saravia et al., 2016; Schwartz et al., 2013; Schwartz et al., 2014; Shen et al., 2017; Tsugawa et al., 2015; Tsugawa et al., 2013; Volkova et al., 2016; Wang et al., 2017; Wilson et al., 2014; Yazdavar et al., 2020) used the aggregating data approach to collect data from profile-based social media platforms.

User verification and annotation

After receiving a set of target users or posts, every user and every owner of the returned posts from a social network platform needs to be annotated. This step is an important one because correctly labeled users can help to distinguish between user groups and to analyze differences between them. There are two main approaches to user annotation. The first method is screening users with a questionnaire and another is manual annotation.

Screening users with a questionnaire

A traditional and medical method to screen patients for mental health disorders is the use of a self-report questionnaire. This method has been applied to screen online users with depression (De Choudhury, Gamon, et al., 2013). Common questionnaires used to screen users with depression include *Center for Epidemiological Study Depression Scale (CES-D)* (Almouzini et al., 2019; De Choudhury, Counts, & Horvitz, 2013b; De Choudhury, Gamon, et al., 2013; S. Park et al., 2013; Park et al., 2015; Reece et al., 2017; Reece & Danforth, 2017; Tsugawa et al., 2015; Wu et al., 2020; Yang, McEwen, Ong, & Zihayat, 2020), the Patient Health Questionnaire-9 (PHQ-9) (Almouzini et al., 2019; De Choudhury et al., 2014), and Beck's Depression Inventory (BDI) (Chandra Guntuku et al., 2019; De Choudhury, Gamon, et al., 2013; Mann et al., 2020; Maxim et al., 2020; Park et al., 2013; Sungkyu Park et al., 2015; Stankevich et al., 2019, 2020; Tsugawa et al., 2015).

Manual annotation

Another approach to annotating users with mental disorders is manual annotation. This method is usually associated with the approach of searching users by keywords (see Aggregating data extracted from public posts Section). Researchers investigate every returned message from a social network platform and manually annotate the messages. Several studies (Almouzini et al., 2019; Alsagri & Ykhlef, 2020; Amir et al., 2017; Bollen et al., 2011; Braithwaite et al., 2016; Burnap et al., 2015; Chandra Guntuku et al., 2019; Chen et al., 2018; Coppersmith, Dredze, & Harman, 2014; Coppersmith et al., 2016, 2018; Coppersmith, Harman, & Dredze,

2014; De Choudhury, Counts, & Horvitz, 2013b; De Choudhury, Gamon, et al., 2013; De Choudhury, Counts, & Horvitz, 2013aFodeh et al., 2019; Guan et al., 2015; Gui et al., 2019; Homan et al., 2014; Jamison-Powell et al., 2012; Kang et al., 2016; Lin et al., 2020; Lin et al., 2014; Mbarek et al., 2019; O'Dea et al., 2015; Prieto et al., 2014; Ramírez-Cifuentes et al., 2020; Reece et al., 2017; Roy et al., 2020; Saravia et al., 2016; Schwartz et al., 2013; Schwartz et al., 2014; Shen et al., 2017; Tsugawa et al., 2015; Tsugawa et al., 2013; Volkova et al., 2016; Wang et al., 2017; Wilson et al., 2014; Yazdavar et al., 2020) have manually annotated genuine messages that mention diagnosis of a mental disorder.

Klein provided detailed processes of collecting data for health-related events on social network (Klein, Sarker, Cai, Weissenbacher, & Gonzalez-Hernandez, 2018). Fig. 6.5 depicts the workflow of annotating users with depression. First, a set of regular expressions is created to search messages mentioning self-expressions or self-declaration related to mental disorder diagnosis via a search API. It returns a set of matching messages, which must be manually verified to identify genuine messages exactly mentioning diagnosis. The profiles of verified users who disclosed their mental illness diagnoses are annotated as *positive*. Public pages publishing mental health information are removed or annotated as *negative*.

Data collection from social media platforms

There are different methods for collecting profile-based social media data depending on platforms and policies. This section focuses on common and popular social network platforms in which users can update statuses on their timelines and have interactions with friends. In particular, data collection from *Facebook* and *Twitter* will be discussed.

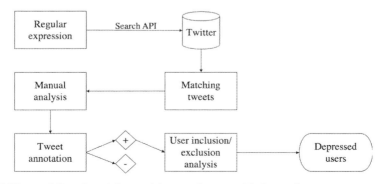

Fig. 6.5 The workflow for mining social network users with depression.

Facebook

Facebook allows a developer or a company to use their services such as artificial intelligence, gaming, virtual reality, and business tools. One service that researchers are interested in and consider valuable for research is called "*Facebook Login*."[a] An API is provided for a developer to develop an app, which allows users to log in using their Facebook account and to provide permissions to access their profiles.

To use this function, the developer needs to provide app descriptions and how the app uses user's data in order to get approval from Facebook before releasing the app for public use. There are two approval states: (i) app review and (ii) business verification or individual verification.[b]

App review is a general review process that an app must pass before being published. Apps that request to access Facebook name, an email, and a current profile picture may not go through this process. *One permission that is valuable* for observing user's behaviors is "user posts," which must pass the review process and get approved. *Business verification or individual verification* is another process to allow Facebook to verify a business or an individual developer before accessing sensitive user's data, such as user posts, friend lists, and location check-ins.

Some permissions are available at both business and individual verification levels, but some are available only at the business verification level. For example, the user post permission is only available with business verification. This means that any app requesting access to users' posts needs to pass both *app review* and *business verification* processes. Facebook provides a new channel for accessing public Facebook data for researchers. However, the access allows only for public content across Facebook Pages and Groups, as well as verified profiles and public Instagram accounts. However, profiles of target users cannot be collected. Currently, Facebook focuses on misinformation, elections, COVID-19, racial justice, well-being only. Any of the other categories listed cannot be accessed these services.[c]

Twitter

Twitter provides many API channels ranging from publishing tweets to advertising. The most useful APIs that researchers can use to collect user's data are *search tweets* API[d] and *get timelines* API.[e]

Search tweet API allows developers to search or query a set of matching tweets using keywords and operators. This API can retrieve tweets since the first tweets in March 2006. Twitter offers three different types of search APIs:

1. *Standard* API provides a sampling of recent Tweets published in the past 7 days.

---

[a] https://developers.facebook.com/docs/facebook-login/overview.
[b] https://developers.facebook.com/docs/facebook-login/review.
[c] https://help.crowdtangle.com/en/articles/4302208-crowdtangle-for-academics-and-researchers.
[d] https://developer.twitter.com/en/docs/tweets/search/overview.
[e] https://developer.twitter.com/en/docs/tweets/timelines/overview.

2. *Premium* API has free and paid access to either the last 30 days of tweets or full access to tweets since 2006.

3. *Enterprise* API is a paid version, which can access both the last 30 days of tweets and full access to tweets since 2006.

The difference between *premium* and *enterprise* APIs is that the former has more restrictions. For example, the enterprise API allows a single query of up to 2048 characters per request, while the premium API can use up to 1024 characters. Enterprise API retrieves up to 500 tweets per request and premium API returns the maximum of 100 tweets. Currently, Twitter is releasing the new version of Twitter API v2. This API also includes "academic research product track," which allows researchers to access Twitter's real-time and full historical public data with no cost.[f]

Get tweet timeline API is an end point to retrieve tweets on the timeline of a user. This API provides up to 3200 recent tweets on the timeline.

Natural language processing (NLP)

Natural language processing (NLP) is the field of studying and understanding human languages using computers. NLP studies speech recognition, understanding, machine translation, and generation. It is a multidisciplinary approach consisting of linguistics, computer science, cognitive science, and artificial intelligence (Deng & Liu, 2018). This study focuses on natural language understanding to investigate textual content published on social network profiles. The following section will explain descriptions of text processing to process written languages.

Text processing is used to interpret written languages in an appropriate format understandable by a machine. It includes a simple step like separating the given text into smaller parts to a complicated approach. This section reviews segmentation, tokenization, and word embedding.

Segmentation

Segmentation is the process of separating a given text into smaller segments (Dalianis, 2018). It includes two types: one for *sentence segmentation*, and another for *word segmentation*. Sentence segmentation separates a given text into several sentences. It can use a question mark, comma, or conjunction words to separate the sentences. This example shows how sentence segmentation segments an English text:

"*I am not feeling well these days, since I have massive workloads.*"

This can be segmented into two sentences: one for "*I am not feeling well these days,*" and another for "*since I have massive workloads.*" It uses a comma to separate the sentences.

Tokenization

A sentence or a text contains many words, numbers white spaces, punctuation, and special characters like emoticons. Each token is represented each of the elements in

---

[f] https://developer.twitter.com/en/products/twitter-api/academic-research.

the text. To enable a machine to understand the information in the text, *tokenization* is used to separate a given text into smallest parts (Dalianis, 2018). The simplest way of performing word tokenization is by using white spaces, commas, and question marks. From the above example, a tokenizer extracts the text as.

"*I*" "*am*" "*not*" "*feeling*" "*well*" "*these*" "*days*" "*,*" "*since*" "*I*" "*have*" "*massive*" "*workloads*" "*"*" "*"*" "*"*" "*.*"

Linguistic inquiry and word count (LIWC)

Linguistic Inquiry and Word Count (LIWC) is a text analysis program used to extract relevant psychological meanings and linguistic styles from the text (Tausczik & Pennebaker, 2010). This tool provides up to 93 dimensions from a given text. The psychologically meaningful categories and function words include, for instance, *affect words* (positive emotion, negative emotion, and sadness), *parts of speech* (1st personal singular pronoun, impersonal pronouns, negations, and regular verbs), *personal concerns* (work, death, and money), and *punctuation* (commas, question marks, and parentheses). For instance, Table 6.4 shows the example of extracted dimensions from the sentence in the above section by LIWC.

As can be seen, the extracted values of each category are computed from the percentage of words in the sentence. For example, the word "I" appears twice, and the sentence has 12 words. Therefore, 1st personal singular pronoun is 16.67% (2/12).

Various studies (Braithwaite et al., 2016; Chandra Guntuku et al., 2019; Chen et al., 2018; Cheng et al., 2017; Coppersmith, Harman, & Dredze, 2014; De Choudhury, Counts, & Horvitz, 2013a; De Choudhury, Counts, & Horvitz, 2013b; De Choudhury, Gamon, et al., 2013; De Choudhury et al., 2014; Eichstaedt et al., 2018; Hao, Li, Gao, Li, & Zhu, 2014; Homan et al., 2014; Jamison-Powell et al., 2012; Kuang, Liu, Sun, Yu, & Ma, 2014; Lin et al., 2014; Liu, Tov, Kosinski, Stillwell, & Qiu, 2015; Lv et al., 2015; Marengo et al., 2020; Mbarek et al., 2019; Ramírez-Cifuentes et al., 2020; Reece et al., 2017; Reis & Culotta, 2015; Schwartz et al., 2013, 2016; Shen et al., 2017; Wang et al., 2017; Wilson et al., 2014; Yang et al., 2020; Yazdavar et al., 2020; Zhang et al., 2015) used LIWC to extract psychological meanings and signs of mental health issues from the textual content.

Table 6.4 Extracted dimensions from LIWC.

Dimensions	Extracted values
1st personal singular pronoun (*I*)	16.67
Positive emotion	8.33
Negative emotion	0.00
Negations	8.33
Cognitive Processes (cause)	8.33
Time Orientation - Present focus	16.67

Word embedding

Word embedding is another text processing technique to transform the words or vocabulary of a document into vectors. The main idea of word embedding is to determine word similarity. In other words, a pair of words that frequently cooccurs in the same context tends to share similar meanings. Word embeddings was used by (Amir et al. (2017), Chiu et al. (2021), Coppersmith et al. (2018), Gui et al. (2019), Huang et al. (2019), Li, Li, Huang, and Hou (2020), Lin et al. (2020), Ma and Cao (2020), Mann et al. (2020), Orabi, Buddhitha, Orabi, and Inkpen (2018), Ramírez-Cifuentes et al. (2020), Shen et al. (2017), Wang et al. (2020), Wongkoblap, Vadillo, and Curcin (2021), and Wu et al. (2020)). *word2vec* and *GloVe* are common techniques used in deep learning.

Global Vectors (GloVe) is an unsupervised learning method for constructing vector space representations of words (Pennington, Socher, & Manning, 2014). GloVe is based on a count-based method, which computes the aggregated distributions of word cooccurrence from a given corpus and performs dimensionality reduction.

Anaphora resolution

Anaphora resolution is a linguistic method that determines which previously mentioned person is the subject of a subsequent statement (Mitkov, 2012). It is the problem of resolving that a reference or an *anaphor* refers to an earlier or later entity or an *antecedent*. For example, the anaphora resolution of the message shown below:

"*My friend got diagnosed with depression. He was suffering from his exam failure.*"
This can determine "He" is the anaphor and "My friend" is the antecedent.

Machine learning

Machine learning is a method that allows a computer to learn from a dataset and uses this experience to make a decision (Goodfellow et al., 2016). Mitchell (1997) defined the term "*learning*" as follows "A computer program is said to learn from experience E with respect to some class of tasks T and performance measure P, if its performance at tasks in T, as measured by P, improves with experience E". In other words, it means that a computer program is given a task and its performance can improve with experience.

This section begins with important and necessary terminologies in machine learning. This can help to understand basic concepts in this study.

- An *instance* or an *input* x means a specific object or an observed event. The instance consists of at least one-dimensional feature vector $x = (x_1, x_2, ..., xD) \in RD$, where D represents the number of dimensions.
- The term "*feature*" denotes a set of observations that is relevant to the modeling problem, typically represented numerically (Chaoji, Hoonlor, & Szymanski, 2008). Each dimension is often called a feature (Zhu & Chen, 2015).
- A *label* or an *output* y is a real value associated with an instance x. Labels can be either continuous values R or, e.g., a finite set of values. From the example, these categorical values are often called classes and can be represented as $y \in \{0, 1\}$, where 0 denotes nondepressed and 1 presents depressed. Two classes can be called binary labels. Some problems can have

more than two classes and represented as $y \in \{0, \ldots, C\}$, where C denotes the number of classes (Zhu & Goldberg, 2009).

- A *training sample* consists of a set of instances $X = \{x_1, x_2, \ldots, xn\}$, where *n* represents the number of samples or observed objects. Recall that, each instance *xi* consists of D -dimensional feature vectors (Zhu & Goldberg, 2009). So, the training sample with *n*-instances and *D*-dimensions can be represented as $X = \{(x_{11}, x_{12}, \ldots, x_1 D), (x_{21}, x_{22}, \ldots, x_2 D), \ldots, (xn_1, xn_2, \ldots, xnD)\}$.
- *Labeled data* contains *(instance, label)* pairs, while *unlabeled data* contains instances alone (Zhu & Goldberg, 2009).

Machine learning algorithms

Machine learning algorithms can be broadly divided into two main categories: one for *supervised learning* and another for *unsupervised learning*. Another learning paradigm is *semisupervised learning*.

Supervised machine learning

Supervised machine learning is an algorithm that can learn from a set of inputs supervised by a set of labels paired with the inputs. In other words, it refers to the method followed by a machine able to learn a set of patterns from provided data with the pair of their labels and to make a prediction based on the learnt patterns (Goodfellow et al., 2016). The training sample $\{(xi, yi)\}i_{=1}n$ contains a set of pairs between instances $X = \{x_1, x_2, \ldots, xi\}$ and labels $Y = \{y_1, y_2, \ldots, yi\}$. The learning algorithm can then learn from the training sample and try to make a prediction.

Many supervised machine learning algorithms were used to detect social media users with mental disorders in several studies. Support Vector Machine (SVM) was used in studies (Cheng et al., 2017; Hao et al., 2014; Hu, Li, Heng, Li, & Zhu, 2016; Huang et al., 2014; Kuang et al., 2014; Li et al., 2020; Lin et al., 2014; Lv et al., 2015; Ma & Cao, 2020; Wang et al., 2013; Wang, Zhang, & Sun, 2013; Wang et al., 2020; Zhang et al., 2015), Linear SVM in (Almouzini et al., 2019; Alsagri & Ykhlef, 2020; Homan et al., 2014; Kang et al., 2016; Preotiuc-Pietro, Sap, Schwartz, & Ungar, 2015; Resnik, Armstrong, Claudino, & Nguyen, 2015; Wang et al., 2017; Yang et al., 2020), SVM with a Radial Basis Function (RBF) kernel in (Alsagri & Ykhlef, 2020; De Choudhury, Counts, & Horvitz, 2013a, De Choudhury, Counts, & Horvitz, 2013b; De Choudhury, Gamon, et al., 2013; Huang et al., 2014; Kang et al., 2016; Resnik et al., 2015; Wang et al., 2017). Regression techniques included Ridge regression (Schwartz et al., 2016), Linear regression (Chandra Guntuku et al., 2019; Hu et al., 2016; Schwartz et al., 2014), Loglinear regression (Coppersmith, Dredze, & Harman, 2014; Coppersmith, Harman, & Dredze, 2014), Logistic regression (Almouzini et al., 2019; Alsagri & Ykhlef, 2020; Amir et al., 2017; Bollen et al., 2011; Braithwaite et al., 2016; Burnap et al., 2015; Chandra Guntuku et al., 2019; Chen et al., 2018; Coppersmith, Dredze, & Harman, 2014; Coppersmith et al., 2016, 2018; Coppersmith, Harman, & Dredze, 2014; De Choudhury, Counts, & Horvitz, 2013b; De Choudhury, Gamon, et al., 2013; De Choudhury, Counts, & Horvitz, 2013a; Fodeh et al., 2019; Guan et al., 2015; Gui et al., 2019; Homan et al., 2014; Jamison-Powell et al., 2012; Kang et al., 2016; Lin et al., 2020; Lin et al., 2014; Mbarek et al., 2019; O'Dea et al., 2015; Prieto et al., 2014; Ramírez-Cifuentes et al., 2020; Reece et al., 2017; Roy et al., 2020; Saravia et al., 2016; Schwartz et al., 2013; Schwartz et al., 2014; Shen et al., 2017; Tsugawa et al., 2015; Tsugawa et al., 2013; Volkova et al., 2016; Wang et al., 2017; Wilson et al., 2014; Yazdavar et al., 2020), Regularized multinomial logistic regression (Chancellor et al., 2016), Linear Support Vector Regression (SVR) (Almouzini et al., 2019; Alsagri & Ykhlef, 2020; Homan et al., 2014; Kang et al., 2016; Preotiuc-Pietro et al., 2015; Resnik et al., 2014, 2015; Wang et al., 2017; Yang et al., 2020), Least Absolute Shrinkage and Selection Operator (LASSO) (Hao et al., 2014; Schwartz et al., 2013), and Multivariate Adaptive Regression Splines (MARS) (Hao et al., 2014). Other algorithms used for binary classification covered Decision trees (Alsagri & Ykhlef, 2020; Burnap et al., 2015; Fodeh et al., 2019; Huang et al., 2014; Li et al., 2020; Mbarek et al., 2019; Prieto et al., 2014; Wang, Zhang, & Sun, 2013; Wang, Zhang, Ji, et al., 2013), Random forest (Almouzini et al., 2019; Chen et al., 2018; Guan et al., 2015; Huang et al., 2014; Li et al., 2020; Marengo et al., 2020; Maxim et al., 2020; Mbarek et al., 2019; Reece et al., 2017; Reece & Danforth, 2017; Roy et al., 2020; Saravia et al., 2016; Stankevich et al., 2019, 2020; Yang et al., 2020), Rules decision (Wang, Zhang, Ji, et al., 2013), and Classification and Regression Trees (Yang et al., 2020).

Unsupervised machine learning

Unsupervised machine learning is a method that captures unknown patterns or features in a dataset and then produces the most suitable representation associated with the dataset (Goodfellow et al., 2016). Unsupervised machine learning is the chain rule of probability from inputs $X = \{ x_1, x_2, \ldots, xi \}$.

To distinguish between supervised and unsupervised machine learning, the former requires both a feature and a label, while the latter may require only a feature. Unsupervised learning algorithms include *principal components analysis* used in studies (Burnap et al., 2015; De Choudhury, Counts, & Horvitz, 2013a; De Choudhury, Counts, & Horvitz, 2013b; De Choudhury, Gamon, et al., 2013; Maxim et al., 2020; Schwartz et al., 2014; Stankevich et al., 2020), and *k-means clustering* in (Fodeh et al., 2019; Maxim et al., 2020; Prieto et al., 2014; Wang et al., 2017; Yang et al., 2020).

Semisupervised learning

Semisupervised learning is the combination of *supervised* and *unsupervised* learning. Semisupervised classification is an extension to the supervised learning in which the training data contains both labeled and unlabeled instances. This reflects partially labeled data learning. One of the well-known semisupervised learning algorithms is *multiple instance learning (MIL)*, which shown the successful detection of depressed users from social media data in studies (Wongkoblap, Vadillo, & Curcin, 2019a, 2019b, 2021).

Multiple instance learning (MIL) is a weakly supervised learning algorithm first proposed by (Keeler, Rumelhart, & Leow, 1991). As mentioned above, supervised learning requires instances and labels associated with the instances to learn during the training process. The main advantage of MIL is that instead of requiring a single instance, MIL can learn from instances bags { $X_1, X_2, \cdots, Xi$ } and labeled bag $y_1, y_2, \ldots, yi$, where each Xi contains instances { $xi_1, xi_2, \ldots, xin$ }, $xin \in X$. Each instance can be independent. In such way, each instance can have its own individual label { $yi_1, yi_2, \cdots, yin$ }, where each $yin \in \{0, 1\}$. It is assumed that each yin is unknown during the training process.

MIL can then be trained as either an instance classifier $f(X): X \rightarrow Y$ or a bag classifier $F(X): Xi \rightarrow Y$. From the assumption above, MIL can provide an extreme result $yi = 1$ in the case of having an instance xin predicted as a positive label $yin = 1$.

Deep learning

Machine learning techniques have been successfully developed, improved, and applied in many studies. However, classical machine learning algorithms may need handed feature engineering, which is time expensive. Sometimes they cannot perform well on high-dimensional datasets. A new type of machine learning algorithm implemented to overcome this problem is *deep learning* or *deep neural networks* (Goodfellow et al., 2016).

Deep learning has a long history of implementations, usually referred to with different names. A neural network trained with one or two hidden layers was introduced (Rumelhart, Hinton, & Williams, 1986). The name *"deep learning"* is given, due to the depth of many connected layers in a model. The term *neural* is borrowed from neuroscience. Each next hidden layer of a neural network is connected and represented hidden vector values sent to the next layer. This is assumed to be similar to how a brain neuron works, where each cell receives a signal from a previous cell and sends it to the next cell.

Deep learning is useful to simplify representations from raw data, which may contain complex concepts such as high-level and abstract features. Fig. 6.6 shows the illustration of a deep learning model extracting components from pixels of pictures/inputs and then map extractable representations to outputs/labels. Different parts of the deep learning model represent edges, corners, contours, and object parts extracted from the picture. Those components are then mapped to the output *"person"* (Goodfellow et al., 2016).

This section introduces the variety of deep learning techniques intensively and successfully used to build a prediction model. A family of neural architectures includes the basic layer of deep learning called *multiple layer perceptron (MLP)*. Other type of layers used in computer vision is *convolutional neural network (CNN)* and in natural language processing is *recurrent neural network (RNN)*. The improved version of RNN is *long short-term memory (LSTM)*.

Multiple layer perceptron (MLP)

Multiple layer perceptron (MLP) or *deep feedforward network* is a basic and essential deep learning layer. It computes the approximation of a function f^* via parameters $è$ to provide an output associated with the learnt function and a provided input. In other words, a classifier with the MLP is a function $y = f(x; è)$ which maps an input x to an output y and computes the best approximation value of the parameters $è$ suitable for the output y (Goodfellow et al., 2016). MLP was used in studies (Benton, Coppersmith, and Dredze,

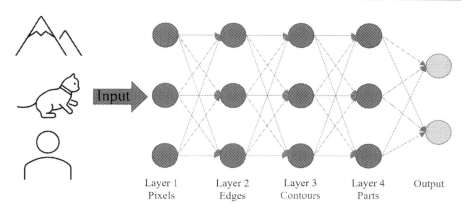

Fig. 6.6 A deep learning model to extract high-level and abstract features from pictures. From Goodfellow, I., Bengio, Y., & Courville, A. (c. 2016). Deep Learning. MIT Press. p. 6. http://www.deeplearningbook.org.

2017; Benton, Mitchell, and Hovy, 2017; Hao, Li, Li, & Zhu, 2013; Maxim et al., 2020; Stankevich et al., 2020; Yang et al., 2020) to detect users with mental disorders.

Developing a deep learning model requires the design of an *output unit* to compute the form of a desired output and a *cost function* to measure the differences between provided outputs and predicted results in the network. An *activation function* is chosen to compute hidden values in each layer. The overall architecture of the model needs to be taken into account in order to design how many layers should have in the network, how each layer is connected to each other, and how many units should have in each layer (Goodfellow et al., 2016).

The designed deep learning is then trained to produce an approximated output *y* from the provided input *x*. This results in the flow of information of *x* throughout the network. This is called *forward preparation*. During training, the cost (an error result occurs between a provided output and a predicted value) is computed and then is flowed backward through the network to improve the predicted result. This process is called the *back-propagation* algorithm or *backprop*.

Fig. 6.6 shows how a neural network works. However, deep learning consists of various types of layers. Each layer of a neural network model can be replaced by *CNN*, *RNN*, and *LSTM*. Studies (Chiu et al., 2021; Coppersmith et al., 2018; Gui et al., 2019; Huang et al., 2019; Lin et al., 2020; Lin et al., 2014; Ma & Cao, 2020; Mann et al., 2020; Orabi et al., 2018; Ramírez-Cifuentes et al., 2020; Wang et al., 2020; Wu et al., 2020) used those algorithms to detect social media users with mental disorders.

Convolutional neural network (CNN)

Convolutional network or *Convolutional neural network (CNN)* was introduced by LeCun (Le Cun et al., 1989; Lecun, Bottou, Bengio, & Haffner, 1998) and first implemented by Fukushima (Fukushima, 1980; Goodfellow et al., 2016). CNN is one among several well-known neural networks introduced to process data like a grid topology.

CNN normally performs two operations. The first step is called a *convolutional layer/operation*. CNN creates a *kernel* or *filter* with the size of width and height. The *kernel* is shifted spatially along with the size of an *input*. After shifting the kernel along all the area of the input, the convolution operation provides an *output*, sometimes called a *feature map*. The size of the *kernel* is assumed to be smaller than the size of the input, which helps the *kernel* to provide a set of learnable features.

Receiving the feature map, a *pooling layer/operation* is applied to reduce the spatial size of input and preserve the originality of the input. The reduction also helps to reduce the number of parameters in the networks and avoid overfitting. The pooling layer consists of two operations. The *MAX pooling* operation provides the maximum value in the local region where the filter is hovering over. The *AVERAGE pooling* operation computes the average value in the region in which the filter is hovering over.

Recurrent neural network (RNN)

Recurrent neural network (RNN) was implemented by Rumelhart et al. (Goodfellow et al., 2016; Rumelhart et al., 1986). The main purpose of RNN is to process the sequence of data. RNN provides the output members of the network by learning from the outputs of the previous state (Fig. 6.7).

The RNN structure has a few drawbacks. Its computation is slow and cannot properly learn long-term dependencies of an input. One way of dealing with these issues is to design a model that partitions the long-term dependencies into small parts and processes with multiple time scales. In this way, the model can transfer information from the distant past to the present.

Long short-term memory (LSTM)

Long short-term memory (LSTM) was introduced by Hochreiter and Schmidhuber in 1997 to eliminate the above problems (Hochreiter & Schmidhuber, 1997). Instead of a fixed loop, LSTM decides the weight on its self-loop depending on another previously

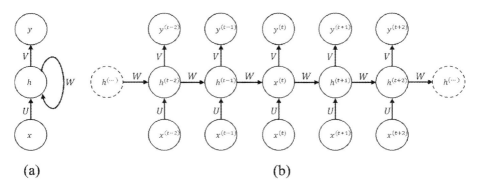

(a)   (b)

Fig. 6.7 The computational graph of an RNN. (A) The RNN structure with recurrent connections. (B) The time-unfolded computational graph of the RNN.

hidden unit in the context of its inputs. In this way, LSTM is more flexible and can change the time scale dynamically. An LSTM cell consists of *a forget gate* $f^{(t)}$, *an input gate* $i^{(t)}$, *an output gate* $o^{(t)}$, *new cell content* $\tilde{C}^{(t)}$, *a cell state* $C^{(t)}$, and *a hidden state* $h^{(t)}$.

Evaluating ML models

This section explains evaluation methods to measure the performance of a model, including evaluation matrices and model selection.

Cross-validation

Cross-validation is a technique to split a dataset into different training and test sets (Chollet, 2017). In machine learning settings, a *training set* is a dataset used to develop or train a machine learning model. A *test set* is separated to evaluate the model, and the test set is unseen during the training step. Cross-validation randomly partitions a dataset into n equal subsets and proceeds to iterate n times, with each subset used for validation or testing exactly once, while the remaining $n-1$ subsets are used as the training data. For instance, illustrates 10-fold cross-validation, which splits a dataset into 10 equal subsets. In each iteration, the $n-1$ training subsets are used to train a model and then the unique test set is used to evaluate the performance of the model.

Classification evaluation

Classification evaluation is an approach to measure the performance of a classifier. Classification problems include *binary classification* and *multiclass classification*. Binary classification is the task of classifying samples into one of only two different classes, while multiclass classification means a method of determining instances as one of more than two different classes. For example, classifying users with and without depression is binary classification, and classifying a message into one of the negative, positive, and neutral classes reflects a multiclass classification problem.

The number of each class represented in the confusion matrix can be used to measure the performance of a classifier. A set of common tools for a binary classification problem consist of accuracy, precision, recall (sensitivity), specificity, f1-score, receiver operating characteristic (ROC), and area under the curve (AUC).

Ethics surrounding profiling social media for mental health

The current performance of predictive models is still improving, and reliable predictive models may eventually allow early detection and pave the way for health interventions in the forms of offering relevant health services or delivering useful health information links. By harnessing the capabilities offered to commercial entities on profile-based social media platforms, there is a potential to deliver real health benefits to users. However, ethical concerns have been raised about the use of publicly available data sources, profile-based social media data for health research, advertisements for mental health services, and social media platforms to report suicidal behavior.

Several studies are particularly useful in highlighting the importance of ethical issues in this area of research. In a well-known example, researchers from Facebook and Cornell University (Kramer, Guillory, & Hancock, 2014) collected and used datasets from Facebook, without offering the possibility to opt out. This study was not approved by the Cornell University Institutional Review Board (IRB) either, "because this experiment was conducted by Facebook, Inc. for internal purposes, the Cornell University IRB determined that the project did not fall under Cornell's Human Research Protection Program" (Verma, 2014).

Also, another prominent study collected public Facebook posts and made the dataset publicly available to other researchers on the internet (Lewis, Kaufman, Gonzalez, Wimmer, & Christakis, 2008). The posts were manually collected by accessing friend's profiles, and then they were anonymized. But even so, the posts could still be easily identified (Zimmer, 2010).

The above examples of collecting profile-based social media data from users and publicly available data on profile-based social media platforms raise concerns about *privacy* and *informed consent*. This affects trust for social media users in the transparency of research and ethics of researchers.

General Data Protection Regulation (GDPR) helps to raise confidence in data safety and transparent analysis. However, *GDPR Article 9: Processing of special categories of personal data* specifically mentions that consent is not required if permission relates to personal data which are manifestly made public by the data subject. A core problem is a perception of whether any data in the public domain is automatically available for research. This is controversial from an ethical point of view, as the disruption presented by the wide availability of social network data impacts the norms that guide our perception on the use of our data for research (Zarsky, 2016). Ultimately, GDPR is focused on process, not on the *objective* of the research, which is fundamental to shaping any research consent and the social consensus around it.

The ethical research practices of using profile-based social media data for research remain clearly undefined, incomplete, and inconsistent, particularly when working with information that is publicly available (Ford et al., 2019; Sykora, Elayan, Barbour, & Jackson, 2020; Taylor & Pagliari, 2018). From those ethical concerns, we frame a set of challenges to be overcome by different stakeholders. The next section will provide and explain a framework to deal with ethical considerations and practices when working with profile-based social media data for health analytics.

A framework for the use of social media for health intervention

We now propose a framework for the use of profile-based social media platforms in health interventions involving five groups of stakeholders including users, social

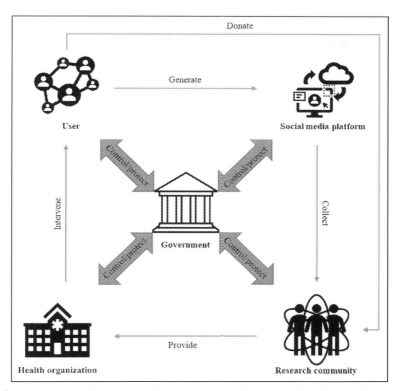

Fig. 6.8 A framework of key stakeholders associated with the use of profile-based social media platforms for health intervention.

media platforms, research communities, health organizations, and governments. Fig. 6.8 shows the framework and relevant stakeholders.

User

This group includes all users currently using profile-based social media platforms. These people are considered as the most active and affected group because they mainly are *providers* and *receivers* in this framework. In terms of providers, users generate data on the platforms and provide permissions to other relevant stakeholders to use their data for academic research and societal benefits. Receivers are clients who receive health services from stakeholders.

This group of people is aware that their data may be misused and analyzed out of the context of research. For example, their data may be analyzed for health issues that affected the individual's insurance premiums (Ford et al., 2019) or explored by officers for prosecution (Golder, Ahmed, Norman, & Booth, 2017).

In terms of informed consent for using their data, users have different ideas about their data privacy and can be divided into two groups: one for whom understanding the public nature of social media; and another for whom needing data ownership and private data. The former prefers not to receive informed consent but should be anonymized. The latter needs to be informed to use their generated data (Ford et al., 2019; Golder et al., 2017; Sykora et al., 2020).

Users also concern over the accuracy of methods of analyzing the data. Due to concerns about data privacy, users are aware that they should not publish everything they think (Golder et al., 2017). They also avoid posting when feeling uneasy or low (Ford et al., 2019). Users believe that these issues may affect the performance of predictive models and analytics results (Ford et al., 2019; Golder et al., 2017).

Sykora et al. conducted an online survey and a focus group. Three main ethical concerns from the participants were: (1) what information is being collected and processed, (2) what are the purposes of the analysis, and (3) whether users are informed about the data collection and analysis (Sykora et al., 2020). These concerns emphasize ethical practices for researchers to inform users before starting research from their data.

To overcome these issues, other stakeholders in the framework need to build trust for profile-based social media users to ensure not only that their data will be safe from misuse but also benefits outweigh the risks to privacy. This will make users feel comfortable and provide their data for research. They would also prefer to receive health analytics results and health services from stakeholders.

Social media platform

Profile-based social media is an online platform that allows users to publish posts, interact with other users, and communicate with others. The platform is not just an infrastructure but includes development, management, and policy teams. They need to maintain the stability of the infrastructures and create a good environment for users. The policy team should set a set of policies to support user's trust and safeguard user's privacy. For example, the company should prevent someone from accessing sensitive data (Almouzini et al., 2019; Alsagri & Ykhlef, 2020; Amir et al., 2017; Benton, Mitchell, & Hovy, 2017; Chen et al., 2018; Chiu et al., 2021; Coppersmith, Dredze, & Harman, 2014; Coppersmith et al., 2015, 2018; Fodeh et al., 2019; Gui et al., 2019; Huang et al., 2019; Li et al., 2020; Lin et al., 2020; Mitchell et al., 2015; Orabi et al., 2018; Preoţiuc-Pietro et al., 2015; Ramírez-Cifuentes et al., 2020; Roy et al., 2020; Shen et al., 2017; Yazdavar et al., 2020).

A well-known example highlighting this issue is that related to Facebook data scandals. The company allowed researchers to access sensitive information and the data was subsequently used for the 2016 US presidential election. Data was not used for the initial purpose of the research (Fuller, 2019). This contributed to users losing trust in the use of their social media data for research (Ford et al., 2019). Social media providers need to safeguard the privacy of users and protect them from risks of data misuse.

Another concern for profile-based social media providers is publicly available data. This issue may undermine the trust and satisfaction of users to publish content on the platforms, because their data may be retrieved by researchers without their consent. However, it is difficult and challenging for researchers to receive informed consent

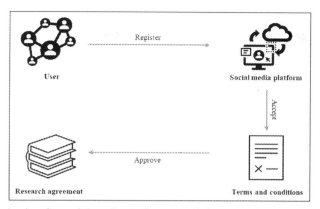

Fig. 6.9 A mechanism for social media platforms to ask for research agreement from users.

from millions of users (Benton, Coppersmith, & Dredze, 2017). We suggest those platforms should develop a mechanism to restrict access to sensitive information and obtain informed consent from users before researchers can use user's data. Fig. 6.9 depicts a mechanism for social media platforms to ask for research agreement from users. First, users register accounts on social media platforms, and then they accept with terms and conditions of using the platforms. The sites should develop an additional page to ask the users whether they agree to participate in research studies already approved by the platforms and IRBs. In this way, the users agree to provide their right to the platforms to screen forthcoming research and the platforms need to screen ethical and transparent research for their users.

However, the previous approach may make users feel uneasy because they do not know in which studies they are taking parts. The platforms may develop an additional function to notify users which studies are collecting your data. Consequently, the users can notify research teams conducting the research to remove their data from the studies. This additional mechanism provides an option for the users to opt out of undesired studies. Due to the affiliation of researchers, users trust studies from some organizations such as universities (Golder et al., 2017).

These approaches would help researchers to access publicly available data ethically and at the same time, it would allow users to feel comfortable to participate in research. This can increase public trust for users in transparent and ethical research and platforms can safeguard data privacy. The companies can also support societal benefits and development for public health research (Richterich, 2018).

Researcher

Within the present framework, researchers are a group of academics from universities or people from nonprofit research organizations who conduct studies on health analytics from profile-based social media data. Users trust not-for-profit researchers and academics rather than government and commercial organizations to use their profile-based social media data for research (Golder et al., 2017).

We surveyed a set of 82 studies analyzing mental health from profile-based social media data and analyzed those study methods of how they adopted a wide range of approaches to handle ethical constraints.

Eighteen percent of them (15 studies) were approved by their IRBs (Braithwaite et al., 2016; Chandra Guntuku et al., 2019; Cheng et al., 2017; Coppersmith et al., 2015; Guan et al., 2015; Lv et al., 2015; Marengo et al., 2020; Mitchell et al., 2015; O'Dea et al., 2015; Park et al., 2013; Park et al., 2015; Reece et al., 2017; Reece & Danforth, 2017; Tsugawa et al., 2015; Yazdavar et al., 2020). Sixteen percent of them (13 studies) reported receiving informed consent from participants prior to data analysis (Chandra Guntuku et al., 2019; Cheng et al., 2017; De Choudhury et al., 2014; Guan et al., 2015; Hao et al., 2014; Hu et al., 2016; Liu et al., 2015; Marengo et al., 2020; Park et al., 2013; Park et al., 2015; Reece et al., 2017; Reece & Danforth, 2017; Tsugawa et al., 2015). For public data collected from crowdsourcing platforms, participants who opted in provided their consent to data sharing (De Choudhury, Gamon, et al., 2013; Reece et al., 2017; Reece & Danforth, 2017). For myPersonality data, the study by Liu et al. (2015) stated that the dataset itself had IRB approval, so the project did not report obtaining any further approval from the author's institution. The study by Youyou, Kosinski, and Stillwell (2015) also considered that no IRB approval was needed for using myPersonality data. The study by Chancellor et al. (2016) did not seek IRB approval, because of its reliance on Instagram data without personally identifiable information.

In studies (Burnap et al., 2015; Chandra Guntuku et al., 2019; Coppersmith et al., 2016; Coppersmith, Harman, & Dredze, 2014; Jamison-Powell et al., 2012; O'Dea et al., 2015; Reece et al., 2017; Reece & Danforth, 2017; Wilson et al., 2014; Yazdavar et al., 2020), the researchers reported the social network datasets collected from participants were anonymized. The study by O'Dea et al. (2015) removed names, user identifiers, and user identities, and the data collected had to be analyzed after 3 months. All names were deleted from collected data before analysis (O'Dea et al., 2015). The tweet containing names or usernames were removed or replaced with other text (Coppersmith et al., 2016; Coppersmith, Harman, & Dredze, 2014; Wilson et al., 2014). A study by Jamison-Powell et al. (2012) reported that they removed user identifiers from tweets illustrated in the published paper.

Another concern for researchers is the accuracy and biases of methods of using social media data for health analytics. Users are aware of the analytics results which may not reflect faithfully their health conditions or public health (Ford et al., 2019; Golder et al., 2017). So, researchers need to prove the accuracy of predictive models and analytics results to increase the trust of users to be profiled for health conditions.

It can be seen that those studies protected user's privacy by removing all identities and asking for informed consent to access profiles of users. These are ethical practices for researchers, as they can make participants feel comfortable to take parts in studies and gain trust from researchers.

Health organization

Another group of stakeholders is nonprofit and licensed health organizations that intervene with people with certain health conditions and provide health services.

Not-for-profit and licensed health organizations should be middlemen between social media platform providers and users because users are feeling distrustful of social media providers and commercial organizations (Golder et al., 2017). They feel that academics are more ethical and not exploitative (Golder et al., 2017), while social media platforms have lost trust as data custodians and monetary profits (Ford et al., 2019), as can be seen from Facebook scandals (Fuller, 2019).

Studies focused on the perspectives of participants in using social media for population health monitoring (Mikal, Hurst, & Conway, 2016) and mental health disorders (Ford et al., 2019). The authors reported that most research participants agreed to have their public posts used for health monitoring, with anonymized data although they also thought that informed consent would be necessary in some cases. Participants of these studies also believed that profiling for certain health conditions could help to increase access to health services, improve the diagnosis of health conditions, and target advertising for the provision of mental health care (Ford et al., 2019).

In this way, we suggest that nonprofit and licensed health organizations should be representatives of other stakeholders to use health analytics results and target advertisements to users with certain health conditions. However, participants agreed that their privacy must outweigh societal benefits. If the organizations can reassure social media users that their privacy is safe and the top priority, this would make users feel more comfortable to receive health services and interventions (Ford et al., 2019).

Government

Governments and authorities are a group of people who create laws and are responsible for managing the duties and services of stakeholders in the framework to use social media data for health analytics ethically and transparently. Governments and authorities should facilitate researchers, platform providers, and health organization to generate public health, economic, scientific, and societal value for stakeholders. Authorities should also focus on the protection of unwanted surveillance and intrusion affecting their citizens (Richterich, 2018; Taylor & Pagliari, 2018). They also need to penalize stakeholders who break the rules.

Ethical considerations and practices

Stakeholders relevant to using profile-based social media data for health analytics should be aware of ethical considerations and practices. All stakeholders should respect a code of conduct and any policy changes affecting their roles.

Identity and user protection

As explained in Researcher Section, few studies have focused on ethical issues. The study by Conway (2014) provided a taxonomy of ethical concepts to bear in mind when using Twitter data for public health studies. Studies by Conway (2014) and McKee (2013) reviewed and presented normative rules for using public Twitter data, including paraphrasing collected posts, receiving informed consent from participants, hiding participant's identity, and protecting collected data.

One possibility for reducing any conflict in this area of research is to anonymize the collected datasets to prevent the identification of users (Sula, 2016; Wilkinson & Thelwall, 2011). In the United States and United Kingdom, any research involving human participants must provide project information to IRBs or ethics committees for revision and obtain approval prior to data collection (British Psychological Society, 2014; Markham & Buchanan, 2012).

Additionally, according to the Federal Policy for the Protection of Human Subjects ("Common Rule"), all studies conducted in the United States are required to offer an opt-out for participants. However, private companies do not fall under this rule (Verma, 2014). These ethical practices help to safeguard the right of the participants and their data privacy (Benton, Coppersmith, & Dredze, 2017).

Changing policy

Policies and terms of service on social network platforms may be changed to respond to government regulations and some ethical concerns. This may have a big impact on using profile-based social media data for research. Researchers have to follow the terms of service of the social media platforms. When they change their policies, this may have an effect by restricting their services and sensitive information to protect data privacy. For instance, the Facebook scandal and data misuse occurred in March 2018 (Fuller, 2019). This highly impacted Facebook, which had to change its policy and terms of service (O'Neil, 2019). Those changes restricted researchers' and developers' access to Facebook data. They had to change their app mechanisms to comply with the terms and pass couple of review processes (as explained in Facebook Section). This may prevent the researchers from accessing social network data and delay progress in research.

Identifying health conditions from social media behavior

In a recent survey on using social media data to identify users with depression, UK social network users expressed serious concerns about privacy risks and did not see the potential societal benefits outweighing these risks (Ford et al., 2019). Thus, if these technologies are to have a meaningful impact on people's lives, increased importance must be placed on the transparency and trust of the analytics performed.

Achieving this trust is, to an extent, helped by the required compliance of any research with ethical codes and with our above framework, which would help to raise confidence in data safety and transparent analysis.

Other users on profile-based social media sites need to be open-minded. Users who posted about suffering from influenza, for instance, received sympathy, while users publishing about their infection with the human immunodeficiency virus (HIV) experienced stigma and discrimination from other users (Richterich, 2018). This means that users with certain medical conditions cannot openly express their health issues.

It would affect the effectiveness of health analytics from social media data because people cannot disclose their conditions.

To be successful, all stakeholders in our proposed framework need to facilitate each other and comply with ethical codes. Researchers, social media providers, and health organizations should collaborate together to provide better societal benefits for social media users. Governments and authorities need to protect their citizens by providing laws and regulations to control stakeholders to be ethical. All stakeholders need to ensure that societal benefits outweigh the risks to the privacy of users. Other third parties such as publishers should also monitor researchers and research studies to be ethical and transparent, requiring IRB approvals for publication.

Finally, profiling for mental health conditions and targeting advertisements for mental health services can be achieved by the collaboration of all stakeholders. There is still a question as to how we can persuade all parties to protect the privacy of users and so build their trust. As researchers, we have an obligation to be ethical and transparent and build trust for other stakeholders.

References

Aichner, T., & Jacob, F. (2015). Measuring the degree of corporate social media use. *International Journal of Market Research, 57*(2), 257–275. https://doi.org/10.2501/IJMR-2015-018.

Almouzini, S., Khemakhem, M., & Alageel, A. (2019). Detecting Arabic depressed users from twitter data. In *Vol. 163. Procedia computer science* (pp. 257–265). Elsevier B.V. https://doi.org/10.1016/j.procs.2019.12.107.

Alsagri, H. S., & Ykhlef, M. (2020). Machine learning-based approach for depression detection in twitter using content and activity features. *IEICE Transactions on Information and Systems, E103D*(8), 1825–1832. https://doi.org/10.1587/transinf.2020EDP7023.

Amir, S., Coppersmith, G., Carvalho, P., Silva, M. J., & Wallace, B. C. (2017). Quantifying mental health from social media with neural user embeddings. *Proceedings of the 2nd Machine Learning for Healthcare Conference, 68*, 306–321.

Benton, A., Coppersmith, G., & Dredze, M. (2017). Ethical research protocols for social media health research. In *Proceedings of the first ACL workshop on ethics in natural language processing* (pp. 94–102).

Benton, A., Mitchell, M., & Hovy, D. (2017). Multitask learning for mental health conditions with limited social media data. In *Vol. 1. 15th conference of the European chapter of the association for computational linguistics, EACL 2017 – proceedings of conference* (pp. 152–162). Association for Computational Linguistics (ACL). https://doi.org/10.18653/v1/e17-1015.

Bloom, D. E., Cafiero, E., Jané-Llopis, E., Abrahams-Gessel, S., Bloom, R. L., Fathima, S., et al. (2011). The global economic burden of noncommunicable diseases. In *World economic forum*.

Bollen, J., Gonçalves, B., Ruan, G., & Mao, H. (2011). Happiness is assortative in online social networks. *Artificial Life, 17*(3), 237–251. https://doi.org/10.1162/artl_a_00034.

Braithwaite, S. R., Giraud-Carrier, C., West, J., Barnes, M. D., & Hanson, C. L. (2016). Validating machine learning algorithms for twitter data against established measures of suicidality. *JMIR Mental Health, 3*(2). https://doi.org/10.2196/mental.4822, e21.

British Psychological Society. (2014). *Code of human research ethics*. British Psychological Society.

Burnap, P., Colombo, G., & Scourfield, J. (2015). Machine classification and analysis of suicide-related communication on Twitter. In *HT 2015 – Proceedings of the 26th ACM conference on hypertext and social media* (pp. 75–84). Association for Computing Machinery, Inc. https://doi.org/10.1145/2700171.2791023.

Chancellor, S., Lin, Z. J., Goodman, E. L., Zerwas, S., & De Choudhury, M. (2016). Quantifying and predicting mental illness severity in online pro-eating disorder communities. In *Vol. 27. Proceedings of the ACM conference on computer supported cooperative work, CSCW* (pp. 1171–1184). Association for Computing Machinery. https://doi.org/10.1145/2818048.2819973.

Chandra Guntuku, S., Preotiuc-Pietro, D., Eichstaedt, J. C., & Ungar, L. H. (2019). What twitter profile and posted images reveal about depression and anxiety. *Proceedings of the International AAAI Conference on Web and Social Media, 13*(1), 236–246. https://ojs.aaai.org/index.php/ICWSM/article/view/3225.

Chaoji, V., Hoonlor, A., & Szymanski, B. K. (2008). Recursive data mining for role identification. In *5th International conference on soft computing as transdisciplinary science and technology, CSTST'08 – proceedings* (pp. 218–225). https://doi.org/10.1145/1456223.1456270.

Chen, X., Sykora, M. D., Jackson, T. W., & Elayan, S. (2018). What about mood swings: Identifying depression on Twitter with temporal measures of emotions. In *The web conference 2018 – companion of the world wide web conference, WWW 2018* (pp. 1653–1660). Association for Computing Machinery, Inc. https://doi.org/10.1145/3184558.3191624.

Cheng, Q., Li, T. M., Kwok, C. L., Zhu, T., & Yip, P. S. (2017). Assessing suicide risk and emotional distress in Chinese social media: A text mining and machine learning study. *Journal of Medical Internet Research, 19*(7). https://doi.org/10.2196/jmir.7276.

Chiu, C. Y., Lane, H. Y., Koh, J. L., & Chen, A. L. P. (2021). Multimodal depression detection on instagram considering time interval of posts. *Journal of Intelligent Information Systems, 56*(1), 25–47. https://doi.org/10.1007/s10844-020-00599-5.

Chollet, F. (2017). *Deep learning with python*. Manning Publications Company.

Conway, M. (2014). Ethical issues in using twitter for public health surveillance and research: Developing a taxonomy of ethical concepts from the research literature. *Journal of Medical Internet Research, 16*(12), e290. https://doi.org/10.2196/jmir.3617.

Coppersmith, G., Dredze, M., & Harman, C. (2014). Quantifying mental health signals in twitter. In *Proceedings of the workshop on computational linguistics and clinical psychology: From linguistic signal to clinical reality* (pp. 51–60). https://doi.org/10.3115/v1/W14-3207.

Coppersmith, G., Dredze, M., Harman, C., & Hollingshead, K. (2015). From ADHD to SAD: Analyzing the language of mental health on twitter through self-reported diagnoses. In *Proceedings of the 2nd workshop on computational linguistics and clinical psychology: From linguistic signal to clinical reality* (pp. 1–10). https://doi.org/10.3115/v1/W15-1201.

Coppersmith, G., Leary, R., Crutchley, P., & Fine, A. (2018). Natural language processing of social media as screening for suicide risk. *Biomedical Informatics Insights, 10*. https://doi.org/10.1177/1178222618792860, 1178222618792860.

Coppersmith, G., Ngo, K., Leary, R., & Wood, A. (2016). Exploratory analysis of social media prior to a suicide attempt. In *Proceedings of the third workshop on computational linguistics and clinical psychology* (pp. 106–117).

Coppersmith, G. A., Harman, C. T., & Dredze, M. H. (2014). Measuring post traumatic stress disorder in twitter. In *Vol. 2. Proceedings of the 7th international AAAI conference on weblogs and social media (ICWSM)* (pp. 23–45).

Dalianis, H. (2018). Clinical text mining: Secondary use of electronic patient records. In *Clinical text mining: Secondary use of electronic patient records* (pp. 1–181). Springer International Publishing. https://doi.org/10.1007/978-3-319-78503-5.

De Choudhury, M., Counts, S., & Horvitz, E. (2013a). Predicting postpartum changes in emotion and behavior via social media. In *Conference on human factors in computing systems - proceedings* (pp. 3267–3276). https://doi.org/10.1145/2470654.2466447.

De Choudhury, M., Counts, S., & Horvitz, E. (2013b). Social media as a measurement tool of depression in populations. In *Proceedings of the 5th annual ACM web science conference, WebSci'13* (pp. 47–56). Association for Computing Machinery. https://doi.org/10.1145/2464464.2464480.

De Choudhury, M., Counts, S., Horvitz, E. J., & Hoff, A. (2014). Characterizing and predicting postpartum depression from shared Facebook data. In *Proceedings of the ACM conference on computer supported cooperative work, CSCW* (pp. 625–637). Association for Computing Machinery. https://doi.org/10.1145/2531602.2531675.

De Choudhury, M., Gamon, M., Counts, S., & Horvitz, E. (2013). Predicting depression via social media. In *Proceedings of the 7th international conference on weblogs and social media, ICWSM 2013* (pp. 128–137). AAAI Press.

Deng, L., & Liu, Y. (2018). Deep learning in natural language processing. In *Deep learning in natural language processing* (pp. 1–327). Springer International Publishing. https://doi.org/10.1007/978-981-10-5209-5.

Eichstaedt, J. C., Smith, R. J., Merchant, R. M., Ungar, L. H., Crutchley, P., Preoţiuc-Pietro, D., et al. (2018). Facebook language predicts depression in medical records. *Proceedings of the National Academy of Sciences of the United States of America, 115*(44), 11203–11208. https://doi.org/10.1073/pnas.1802331115.

Facebook Inc. (2020). *Facebook reports second quarter 2020 results*. https://investor.fb.com/investor-news/press-release-details/2020/Facebook-Reports-Second-Quarter-2020-Results/default.aspx.

Fodeh, S., Li, T., Menczynski, K., Burgette, T., Harris, A., Ilita, G., et al. (2019). Using machine learning algorithms to detect suicide risk factors on twitter. In *Vol. 2019. IEEE international conference on data mining workshops, ICDMW* (pp. 941–948). IEEE Computer Society. https://doi.org/10.1109/ICDMW.2019.00137.

Ford, E., Curlewis, K., Wongkoblap, A., & Curcin, V. (2019). Caring or creepy? A mixed-methods survey of public opinions on using social media content for identifying users with depression and targeting mental health-care advertising. *JMIR Mental Health*. https://doi.org/10.2196/preprints.12942.

Fukushima, K. (1980). Neocognitron: A self-organizing neural network model for a mechanism of pattern recognition unaffected by shift in position. *Biological Cybernetics, 36*(4), 193–202. https://doi.org/10.1007/BF00344251.

Fuller, M. (2019). Big data and the Facebook scandal: Issues and responses. *Theology, 122*(1), 14–21. https://doi.org/10.1177/0040571X18805908.

Golder, S., Ahmed, S., Norman, G., & Booth, A. (2017). Attitudes toward the ethics of research using social media: A systematic review. *Journal of Medical Internet Research, 19*(6). https://doi.org/10.2196/jmir.7082.

Goodfellow, I., Bengio, Y., & Courville, A. (2016). *Deep learning*. MIT Press. http://www.deeplearningbook.org.

Guan, L., Hao, B., Cheng, Q., Yip, P. S., & Zhu, T. (2015). Identifying Chinese microblog users with high suicide probability using internet-based profile and linguistic features: Classification model. *JMIR Mental Health, 2*(2). https://doi.org/10.2196/mental.4227, e17.

Gui, T., Zhang, Q., Zhu, L., Zhou, X., Peng, M., & Huang, X. (2019). Depression detection on social media with reinforcement learning. In *Vol. 11856. Lecture Notes in computer science (including subseries lecture notes in artificial intelligence and lecture notes in bioinformatics)* (pp. 613–624). Springer. https://doi.org/10.1007/978-3-030-32381-3_49.

Hao, B., Li, L., Gao, R., Li, A., & Zhu, T. (2014). Sensing subjective well-being from social media. In *Vol. 8610. Lecture notes in computer science (including subseries lecture notes in artificial intelligence and lecture notes in bioinformatics)* (pp. 324–335). Springer Verlag. https://doi.org/10.1007/978-3-319-09912-5_27.

Hao, B., Li, L., Li, A., & Zhu, T. (2013). *Predicting mental health status on social media* (pp. 101–110). Berlin, Heidelberg: Springer.

Hochreiter, S., & Schmidhuber, J. (1997). Long short-term memory. *Neural Computation, 9*(8), 1735–1780. https://doi.org/10.1162/neco.1997.9.8.1735.

Homan, C., Johar, R., Liu, T., Lytle, M., Silenzio, V., & Alm, C. O. (2014). Toward macro-insights for suicide prevention: Analyzing fine-grained distress at scale. In *Proceedings of the workshop on computational linguistics and clinical psychology: From linguistic signal to clinical reality* (pp. 107–117).

Hu, Q., Li, A., Heng, F., Li, J., & Zhu, T. (2016). Predicting depression of social media user on different observation windows. In *Vol. 1. Proceedings – 2015 IEEE/WIC/ACM international joint conference on web intelligence and intelligent agent technology, WI-IAT 2015* (pp. 361–364). Institute of Electrical and Electronics Engineers Inc. https://doi.org/10.1109/WI-IAT.2015.166.

Huang, X., Zhang, L., Chiu, D., Liu, T., Li, X., & Zhu, T. (2014). Detecting suicidal ideation in Chinese microblogs with psychological lexicons. In *Proceedings - 2014 IEEE international conference on ubiquitous intelligence and computing, 2014 IEEE international conference on autonomic and trusted computing, 2014 ieee international conference on scalable computing and communications and associated symposia/workshops, UIC-ATC-ScalCom 2014* (pp. 844–849). Institute of Electrical and Electronics Engineers Inc. https://doi.org/10.1109/UIC-ATC-ScalCom.2014.48.

Huang, Y. C., Chiang, C. F., & Chen, A. L. P. (2019). Predicting depression tendency based on image, text and behavior data from Instagram. In *DATA 2019 - Proceedings of the 8th international conference on data science, technology and applications* (pp. 32–40). SciTePress. https://doi.org/10.5220/0007833600320040.

Institute for Health Metrics and Evaluation. (2019). *Global burden of disease study 2019 (GBD 2019) data resources*. http://ghdx.healthdata.org/gbd-results-tool.

Jamison-Powell, S., Linehan, C., Daley, L., Garbett, A., & Lawson, S. (2012). "I can't get no sleep": Discussing #insomnia on Twitter. In *Conference on human factors in computing systems – proceedings* (pp. 1501–1510). https://doi.org/10.1145/2207676.2208612.

Kang, K., Yoon, C., & Kim, E. Y. (2016). Identifying depressive users in Twitter using multimodal analysis. In *2016 International conference on big data and smart computing, BigComp 2016* (pp. 231–238). Institute of Electrical and Electronics Engineers Inc. https://doi.org/10.1109/BIGCOMP.2016.7425918.

Keeler, J. D., Rumelhart, D. E., & Leow, W. K. (1991). Integrated segmentation and recognition of hand-printed numerals. In *Vol. 3. Advances in neural information processing systems* (pp. 557–563).

Kietzmann, J. H., Hermkens, K., McCarthy, I. P., & Silvestre, B. S. (2011). Social media? Get serious! Understanding the functional building blocks of social media. *Business Horizons, 54*(3), 241–251. https://doi.org/10.1016/j.bushor.2011.01.005.

Klein, A. Z., Sarker, A., Cai, H., Weissenbacher, D., & Gonzalez-Hernandez, G. (2018). Social media mining for birth defects research: A rule-based, bootstrapping approach to collecting data for rare health-related events on Twitter. *Journal of Biomedical Informatics*, *87*, 68–78. https://doi.org/10.1016/j.jbi.2018.10.001.

Kramer, A. D. I., Guillory, J. E., & Hancock, J. T. (2014). Experimental evidence of massive-scale emotional contagion through social networks. *Proceedings of the National Academy of Sciences of the United States of America*, *111*(24), 8788. https://doi.org/10.1073/pnas.1320040111.

Kuang, C., Liu, Z., Sun, M., Yu, F., & Ma, P. (2014). Quantifying Chinese happiness via large-scale microblogging data. In *Proceedings - 11th web information system and application conference, WISA 2014* (pp. 227–230). Institute of Electrical and Electronics Engineers Inc. https://doi.org/10.1109/WISA.2014.48.

Le Cun, Y., Jackel, L. D., Boser, B., Denker, J. S., Graf, H. P., Guyon, I., et al. (1989). Handwritten digit recognition: Applications of neural network chips and automatic learning. *IEEE Communications Magazine*, *27*(11), 41–46. https://doi.org/10.1109/35.41400.

Lecun, Y., Bottou, L., Bengio, Y., & Haffner, P. (1998). Gradient-based learning applied to document recognition. *Proceedings of the IEEE*, *86*(11), 2278–2324. https://doi.org/10.1109/5.726791.

Lewis, K., Kaufman, J., Gonzalez, M., Wimmer, A., & Christakis, N. (2008). Tastes, ties, and time: A new social network dataset using Facebook.com. *Social Networks*, *30*(4), 330–342. https://doi.org/10.1016/j.socnet.2008.07.002.

Li, G., Li, B., Huang, L., & Hou, S. (2020). Automatic construction of a depression-domain lexicon based on microblogs: Text mining study. *JMIR Medical Informatics*, *8*(6). https://doi.org/10.2196/17650.

Lin, C., Hu, P., Su, H., Li, S., Mei, J., Zhou, J., et al. (2020). SenseMood: Depression detection on social media. In *ICMR 2020 - Proceedings of the 2020 international conference on multimedia retrieval* (pp. 407–411). Inc: Association for Computing Machinery. https://doi.org/10.1145/3372278.3391932.

Lin, H., Jia, J., Guo, Q., Xue, Y., Li, Q., Huang, J., et al. (2014). User-level psychological stress detection from social media using deep neural network. In *MM 2014 - Proceedings of the 2014 ACM conference on multimedia* (pp. 507–516). Inc: Association for Computing Machinery. https://doi.org/10.1145/2647868.2654945.

Liu, P., Tov, W., Kosinski, M., Stillwell, D. J., & Qiu, L. (2015). Do Facebook status updates reflect subjective well-being? *Cyberpsychology, Behavior and Social Networking*, *18*(7), 373–379. https://doi.org/10.1089/cyber.2015.0022.

Lv, M., Li, A., Liu, T., & Zhu, T. (2015). Creating a Chinese suicide dictionary for identifying suicide risk on social media. *PeerJ*, *2015*(12), e1455. https://doi.org/10.7717/peerj.1455.

Ma, Y., & Cao, Y. (2020). Dual attention based suicide risk detection on social media. In *Proceedings of 2020 IEEE international conference on artificial intelligence and computer applications, ICAICA 2020* (pp. 637–640). Institute of Electrical and Electronics Engineers Inc. https://doi.org/10.1109/ICAICA50127.2020.9182380.

Mann, P., Paes, A., & Matsushima, E. H. (2020). See and read: Detecting depression symptoms in higher education students using multimodal social media data. In *Proceedings of the 14th international AAAI conference on web and social media, ICWSM 2020* (pp. 440–451). AAAI Press.

Marengo, D., Azucar, D., Longobardi, C., & Settanni, M. (2020). Mining Facebook data for quality of life assessment. *Behaviour and Information Technology*, *40*, 597–607. https://doi.org/10.1080/0144929X.2019.1711454.

Markham, A., & Buchanan, E. (2012). *Ethical decision-making and internet research: Version 2.0*. Association of Internet Researchers.

Maxim, S., Ignatiev, N., & Smirnov, I. (2020). Predicting depression with social media images. In *ICPRAM 2020 - Proceedings of the 9th international conference on pattern recognition applications and methods* (pp. 235–240). SciTePress. http://www.scitepress.org/DigitalLibrary/HomePage.aspx.

Mbarek, A., Jamoussi, S., Charfi, A., & Ben Hamadou, A. (2019). Suicidal profiles detection in twitter. In *WEBIST 2019 – Proceedings of the 15th international conference on web information systems and technologies* (pp. 289–296). SciTePress. https://doi.org/10.5220/0008167602890296.

McKee, R. (2013). Ethical issues in using social media for health and health care research. *Health Policy, 110*(2–3), 298–301. https://doi.org/10.1016/j.healthpol.2013.02.006.

Mikal, J., Hurst, S., & Conway, M. (2016). Ethical issues in using twitter for population-level depression monitoring: A qualitative study. *BMC Medical Ethics, 17*(1), 22. https://doi.org/10.1186/s12910-016-0105-5.

Mitchell, M., Hollingshead, K., & Coppersmith, G. (2015). Quantifying the language of schizophrenia in social media. In *Proceedings of the 2nd workshop on computational linguistics and clinical psychology: From linguistic signal to clinical reality* (pp. 11–20).

Mitchell, T. M. (1997). *Machine learning.* McGraw-Hill, Inc.

Mitkov, R. (2012). Anaphora resolution. In *Vol. 9780199276349. The oxford handbook of computational linguistics* Oxford University Press. https://doi.org/10.1093/oxfordhb/9780199276349.013.0014.

O'Dea, B., Wan, S., Batterham, P. J., Calear, A. L., Paris, C., & Christensen, H. (2015). Detecting suicidality on twitter. *Internet Interventions, 2*(2), 183–188. https://doi.org/10.1016/j.invent.2015.03.005.

O'Neil, E. (2019). *API updates and important changes.* Facebook. https://developers.facebook.com/blog/post/2019/04/25/api-updates/.

Orabi, A. H., Buddhitha, P., Orabi, M. H., & Inkpen, D. (2018). Deep learning for depression detection of twitter users. In *Proceedings of the fifth workshop on computational linguistics and clinical psychology: From keyboard to clinic* (pp. 88–97).

Park, S., Lee, S. W., Kwak, J., Cha, M., & Jeong, B. (2013). Activities on Facebook reveal the depressive state of users. *Journal of Medical Internet Research, 15*(10), e217. https://doi.org/10.2196/jmir.2718.

Park, S., Kim, I., Lee, S. W., Yoo, J., Jeong, B., & Cha, M. (2015). Manifestation of depression and loneliness on social networks: a case study of young adults on Facebook. In *Proceedings of the 18th ACM conference on computer supported cooperative work & social computing* (pp. 557–570).

Pennington, J., Socher, R., & Manning, C. D. (2014). GloVe: Global vectors for word representation. In *EMNLP 2014–2014 Conference on empirical methods in natural language processing, proceedings of the conference* (pp. 1532–1543). Association for Computational Linguistics (ACL). https://doi.org/10.3115/v1/d14-1162.

Preoţiuc-Pietro, D., Eichstaedt, J., Park, G., Sap, M., Smith, L., Tobolsky, V., et al. (2015). The role of personality, age, and gender in tweeting about mental illness. In *Proceedings of the 2nd workshop on computational linguistics and clinical psychology: From linguistic signal to clinical reality.* https://doi.org/10.3115/v1/W15-1203.

Preotiuc-Pietro, D., Sap, M., Schwartz, H. A., & Ungar, L. H. (2015). Mental illness detection at the world well-being project for the CLPsych 2015 shared task. In *CLPsych@ HLT-NAACL* (pp. 40–45).

Prieto, V. M., Matos, S., Álvarez, M., Cacheda, F., & Oliveira, J. L. (2014). Twitter: A good place to detect health conditions. *PLoS One, 9*(1). https://doi.org/10.1371/journal.pone.0086191.

Ramírez-Cifuentes, D., Freire, A., Baeza-Yates, R., Puntí, J., Medina-Bravo, P., Velazquez, D. A., et al. (2020). Detection of suicidal ideation on social media: Multimodal, relational, and behavioral analysis. *Journal of Medical Internet Research*, *22*(7). https://doi.org/10.2196/17758.

Razzouk, D. (2017). Burden and indirect costs of mental disorders. In *Mental health economics: The costs and benefits of psychiatric care* (pp. 381–391). Springer International Publishing. https://doi.org/10.1007/978-3-319-55266-8_25.

Reece, A. G., & Danforth, C. M. (2017). Instagram photos reveal predictive markers of depression. *EPJ Data Science*, *6*(1), 1–12. https://doi.org/10.1140/epjds/s13688-017-0110-z.

Reece, A. G., Reagan, A. J., Lix, K. L. M., Dodds, P. S., Danforth, C. M., & Langer, E. J. (2017). Forecasting the onset and course of mental illness with twitter data. *Scientific Reports*, *7*(1). https://doi.org/10.1038/s41598-017-12961-9, 13006.

Reis, V. L. D., & Culotta, A. (2015). Using matched samples to estimate the effects of exercise on mental health from twitter. In *Vol. 1*. *Proceedings of the national conference on artificial intelligence* (pp. 182–188). AI Access Foundation.

Resnik, P., Armstrong, W., Claudino, L., & Nguyen, T. (2015). The University of Maryland CLPsych 2015 shared task system. In *Proceedings of the 2nd workshop on computational linguistics and clinical psychology: from linguistic signal to clinical reality* (pp. 54–60).

Resnik, P., Armstrong, W., Claudino, L., Nguyen, T., Nguyen, V., & Boyd-graber, J. (2014). *Beyond LDA: Exploring supervised topic modeling for depression-related language in Twitter*, *Vol. 1*, 99–107.

Richterich, A. (2018). *The big data agenda: Data ethics and critical data studies*. London: University of Westminster Press. https://doi.org/10.16997/book14.

Roy, A., Nikolitch, K., McGinn, R., Jinah, S., Klement, W., & Kaminsky, Z. A. (2020). A machine learning approach predicts future risk to suicidal ideation from social media data. *NPJ Digital Medicine*, *3*(1), 1–12. https://doi.org/10.1038/s41746-020-0287-6.

Rumelhart, D. E., Hinton, G. E., & Williams, R. J. (1986). Learning representations by back-propagating errors. *Nature*, *323*(6088), 533–536. https://doi.org/10.1038/323533a0.

Saravia, E., Chang, C. H., De Lorenzo, R. J., & Chen, Y. S. (2016). MIDAS: Mental illness detection and analysis via social media. In *Proceedings of the 2016 IEEE/ACM international conference on advances in social networks analysis and mining, ASONAM 2016* (pp. 1418–1421). Institute of Electrical and Electronics Engineers Inc. https://doi.org/10.1109/ASONAM.2016.7752434.

Schultz, D. P. (1969). The human subject in psychological research. *Psychological Bulletin*, *72*(3), 214–228. https://doi.org/10.1037/h0027880.

Schwartz, H. A., Eichstaedt, J., Kern, M., Park, G., Sap, M., Stillwell, D., et al. (2014). Towards assessing changes in degree of depression through Facebook. In *Proceedings of the workshop on computational linguistics and clinical psychology: from linguistic signal to clinical reality* (pp. 118–125).

Schwartz, H. A., Eichstaedt, J. C., Kern, M. L., Dziurzynski, L., Agrawal, M., Park, G. J., et al. (2013). Characterizing geographic variation in well-being using tweets. In *Proceedings of the 7th international conference on weblogs and social media, ICWSM 2013* (pp. 583–591). AAAI Press.

Schwartz, H. A., Sap, M., Kern, M. L., Eichstaedt, J. C., Kapelner, A., Agrawal, M., et al. (2016). Predicting individual well-being through the language of social media. In *Pacific symposium on biocomputing* (pp. 516–527). World Scientific Publishing Co. Pte Ltd. https://doi.org/10.1142/9789814749411_0047.

Shen, G., Jia, J., Nie, L., Feng, F., Zhang, C., Hu, T., et al. (2017). Depression detection via harvesting social media: A multimodal dictionary learning solution. In *IJCAI international joint conference on artificial intelligence* (pp. 3838–3844). https://doi.org/10.24963/ijcai.2017/536.

Stankevich, M., Latyshev, A., Kuminskaya, E., Smirnov, I., & Grigoriev, O. (2019). Depression detection from social media texts. In *Vol. 2523. CEUR workshop proceedings* (pp. 279–289). CEUR-WS. http://ceur-ws.org/.

Stankevich, M., Smirnov, I., Kiselnikova, N., & Ushakova, A. (2020). Depression detection from social media profiles. In *Vol. 1223. Communications in computer and information science* (pp. 181–194). Springer. https://doi.org/10.1007/978-3-030-51913-1_12.

Statista. (2016). *Number of social media users worldwide from 2010 to 2020 (in billions).* https://www.statista.com/statistics/278414/number-of-worldwide-social-network-users/.

Sula, C. A. (2016). Research ethics in an age of big data. *Bulletin of the Association for Information Science and Technology, 42*, 17–21. https://doi.org/10.1002/bul2.2016.1720420207.

Sykora, M., Elayan, S., Barbour, N., & Jackson, T. (2020). A survey of the ethics of social media analytics. In *Proceedings of the 7th European conference on social media, ECSM 2020* (pp. 298–305). Academic Conferences International. https://doi.org/10.34190/ESM.20.047.

Tausczik, Y. R., & Pennebaker, J. W. (2010). The psychological meaning of words: LIWC and computerized text analysis methods. *Journal of Language and Social Psychology, 29*(1), 24–54. https://doi.org/10.1177/0261927X09351676.

Taylor, J., & Pagliari, C. (2018). Mining social media data: How are research sponsors and researchers addressing the ethical challenges? *Research Ethics, 14*(2), 1–39. https://doi.org/10.1177/1747016117738559.

Trautmann, S., Rehm, J., & Wittchen, H. U. (2016). The economic costs of mental disorders: Do our societies react appropriately to the burden of mental disorders? *EMBO Reports, 17*(9), 1245–1249. https://doi.org/10.15252/embr.201642951.

Tsugawa, S., Kikuchi, Y., Kishino, F., Nakajima, K., Itoh, Y., & Ohsaki, H. (2015). Recognizing depression from twitter activity. In *Vol. 2015. Conference on human factors in computing systems – proceedings* (pp. 3187–3196). Association for Computing Machinery. https://doi.org/10.1145/2702123.2702280.

Tsugawa, S., Mogi, Y., Kikuchi, Y., Kishino, F., Fujita, K., Itoh, Y., et al. (2013). On estimating depressive tendencies of twitter users utilizing their tweet data. In *2013 IEEE virtual reality (VR)* (pp. 1–4). IEEE.

Twitter Inc. (2019). *Q1 2019 earnings report.* https://s22.q4cdn.com/826641620/files/doc_financials/2019/q1/Q1-2019-Slide-Presentation.pdf.

Verma, I. M. (2014). Editorial expression of concern: Experimental evidence of massive-scale emotional contagion through social networks. *Proceedings of the National Academy of Sciences of the United States of America, 111*(29), 10779. https://doi.org/10.1073/pnas.1412469111.

Volkova, S., Han, K., & Corley, C. (2016). Using social media to measure student wellbeing: A large-scale study of emotional response in academic discourse. In *Vol. 10046. Lecture notes in computer science (including subseries lecture notes in artificial intelligence and lecture notes in bioinformatics)* (pp. 510–526). Springer Verlag. https://doi.org/10.1007/978-3-319-47880-7_32.

Wang, T., Brede, M., Ianni, A., & Mentzakis, E. (2017). Detecting and characterizing eating-disorder communities on social media. In *WSDM 2017 - proceedings of the 10th ACM international conference on web search and data mining* (pp. 91–100). Association for Computing Machinery, Inc. https://doi.org/10.1145/3018661.3018706.

Wang, X., Chen, S., Li, T., Li, W., Zhou, Y., Zheng, J., et al. (2020). Depression risk prediction for Chinese microblogs via deep-learning methods: Content analysis. *JMIR Medical Informatics, 8*(7), e17958. https://doi.org/10.2196/17958.

Wang, X., Zhang, C., Ji, Y., Sun, L., Wu, L., & Bao, Z. (2013). A depression detection model based on sentiment analysis in micro-blog social network. In *Vol. 7867. Lecture notes in computer science (including subseries lecture notes in artificial intelligence and lecture notes in bioinformatics)* (pp. 201–213). https://doi.org/10.1007/978-3-642-40319-4_18.

Wang, X., Zhang, C., & Sun, L. (2013). An improved model for depression detection in micro-blog social network. In *Proceedings – IEEE 13th international conference on data mining workshops, ICDMW 2013* (pp. 80–87). IEEE Computer Society. https://doi.org/10.1109/ICDMW.2013.132.

Wilkinson, D., & Thelwall, M. (2011). Researching personal information on the public web: Methods and ethics. *Social Science Computer Review*, 29(4), 387–401. https://doi.org/10.1177/0894439310378979.

Wilson, M. L., Ali, S., & Valstar, M. F. (2014). Finding information about mental health in microblogging platforms: A case study of depression. In *Proceedings of the 5th information interaction in context symposium, IIiX 2014* (pp. 8–17). Association for Computing Machinery. https://doi.org/10.1145/2637002.2637006.

Wongkoblap, A., Vadillo, M. A., & Curcin, V. (2019a). Modeling depression symptoms from social network data through multiple instance learning. In *AMIA joint summits on translational science proceedings. AMIA joint summits on translational science* (pp. 44–53).

Wongkoblap, A., Vadillo, M. A., & Curcin, V. (2019b). Predicting social network users with depression from simulated temporal data. In *EUROCON 2019 - 18th international conference on smart technologies*Institute of Electrical and Electronics Engineers Inc. https://doi.org/10.1109/EUROCON.2019.8861514.

Wongkoblap, A., Vadillo, M. A., & Curcin, V. (2021). Deep Learning With Anaphora Resolution for the Detection of Tweeters With Depression: Algorithm Development and Validation Study. *JMIR Ment Health*. https://doi.org/10.2196/19824.

World Medical Association. (2013). World medical association declaration of Helsinki: Ethical principles for medical research involving human subjects. *JAMA*, 2191–2194. https://doi.org/10.1001/jama.2013.281053.

Wu, M. Y., Shen, C. Y., Wang, E. T., & Chen, A. L. P. (2020). A deep architecture for depression detection using posting, behavior, and living environment data. *Journal of Intelligent Information Systems*, 54(2), 225–244. https://doi.org/10.1007/s10844-018-0533-4.

Yang, X., McEwen, R., Ong, L. R., & Zihayat, M. (2020). A big data analytics framework for detecting user-level depression from social networks. *International Journal of Information Management*, 54, 102141.

Yazdavar, A. H., Mahdavinejad, M. S., Bajaj, G., Romine, W., Sheth, A., Monadjemi, A. H., et al. (2020). Multimodal mental health analysis in social media. *PLoS One*, 15(4). https://doi.org/10.1371/journal.pone.0226248.

Youyou, W., Kosinski, M., & Stillwell, D. (2015). Computer-based personality judgments are more accurate than those made by humans. *Proceedings of the National Academy of Sciences of the United States of America*, 112(4), 1036–1040. https://doi.org/10.1073/pnas.1418680112.

Zarsky, T. Z. (2016). Incompatible: The GDPR in the age of big data. *The Seton Hall Law Review*, 47, 995.

Zhang, L., Huang, X., Liu, T., Li, A., Chen, Z., & Zhu, T. (2015). Using linguistic features to estimate suicide probability of Chinese microblog users. In *Vol. 8944. Lecture notes in computer science (including subseries lecture notes in artificial intelligence and lecture notes in bioinformatics)* (pp. 549–559). Springer Verlag. https://doi.org/10.1007/978-3-319-15554-8_45.

Zhu, X., & Goldberg, A. B. (2009). Introduction to semi-supervised learning. In *Synthesis lectures on artificial intelligence and machine learning* (pp. 1–130). https://doi.org/10.2200/s00196ed1v01y200906aim006.

Zhu, Y.-Q., & Chen, H.-G. (2015). Social media and human need satisfaction: Implications for social media marketing. *Business Horizons*, 58(3), 335–345. https://doi.org/10.1016/j.bushor.2015.01.006.

Zimmer, M. (2010). "But the data is already public": On the ethics of research in Facebook. *Ethics and Information Technology*, 12(4), 313–325. https://doi.org/10.1007/s10676-010-9227-5.

Section B

Communication, psychoeducation, screening

Telepsychiatry and video-to-home (including security issues)

Samantha L. Connolly[a,b], Julianna B. Hogan[c,d,e], Anthony H. Ecker[c,d,e], Gabrielle F. Gloston[c,d], Giselle Day[c,e], Jay H. Shore[f,g], and Jan A. Lindsay[c,d,e]
[a]Center for Healthcare Organization and Implementation Research, VA Boston Healthcare System, Boston, MA, United States, [b]Department of Psychiatry, Harvard Medical School, Boston, MA, United States, [c]Houston VA HSR&D Center for Innovations in Quality, Effectiveness and Safety, Michael E. DeBakey VA Medical Center, Houston, TX, United States, [d]Menninger Department of Psychiatry and Behavioral Sciences, Baylor College of Medicine, Houston, TX, United States, [e]VA South Central Mental Illness Research, Education and Clinical Center, Houston, TX, United States, [f]Department of Psychiatry and Family Medicine, University of Colorado Anschutz Medical Campus, Aurora, CO, United States, [g]Centers for American Indian and Alaska Native Health, Colorado School of Public Health, Anschutz Medical Campus, University of Colorado, Aurora, CO, United States

Introduction

Telemental health (TMH) conducted via videoconferencing allows for the real-time delivery of mental health care when patients and providers are at a distance. TMH can be provided from larger hospitals to smaller clinics lacking mental health services, as well as to nonclinical locations such as prisons, schools, community centers, and increasingly, directly to patients' homes. Patients and providers can connect via a variety of video-enabled devices, including smartphones, tablets, and desktop or laptop computers. A full spectrum of mental health services has been successfully provided via TMH, ranging from individual and group psychotherapy, to psychiatric medication management, diagnostic consultation, and neuropsychological assessment.

Over its 60-year history, TMH has evolved from a relative novelty to a common mode of care delivery that is becoming increasingly integrated into health-care systems worldwide. The first recorded instance of TMH took place in 1961 in the United States, when a therapist at the Nebraska Psychiatric Institute provided group therapy to patients located in a different room via closed-circuit television (Brown, 1998; Wittson, Affleck, & Johnson, 1961). The Massachusetts General Hospital used this same method to provide psychiatric consultation to employees of the Logan International Airport, approximately 3 miles away, in 1968, and to the Bedford Massachusetts Veterans Administration Hospital, approximately 20 miles away, in 1970 (Dwyer, 1973). Interest waned somewhat in the following decades due to high costs, poor video quality, and difficulty integrating services into health-care systems (Darkins, Darkins, Darkins, Cary, & Cary, 2000). However, TMH saw a resurgence in

Mental Health in a Digital World. https://doi.org/10.1016/B978-0-12-822201-0.00014-9

the early 1990s in Norway, as the country sought to provide specialty services to remote locations. Norway's successes sparked interest in the United Kingdom, Australia, and the United States, among other locations (Darkins et al., 2000). TMH has seen considerable growth in the past decade across private and publicly funded healthcare systems worldwide, including the Australian and Canadian national health-care systems and the United States Department of Veterans Affairs (VA) (Doarn, 2018; Australian Government Department of Health, 2019; Godleski, Darkins, & Peters, 2012; Health, 2019; O'Gorman, Hogenbirk, & Warry, 2016). Notably, the rates of TMH rose exponentially in response to the COVID-19 pandemic, which dramatically limited the provision of in-person mental health care (Kannarkat, Smith, & McLeod-Bryant, 2020; Wind, Rijkeboer, Andersson, & Riper, 2020). This chapter will provide an overview of TMH, including factors related to effectiveness, safety, and uptake on a global scale.

Effectiveness

Overall, TMH has been found to be an effective modality for delivering mental health services (Berryhill, Culmer et al., 2019; Berryhill, Halli-Tierney et al., 2019; Fletcher et al., 2018; Gros et al., 2013). In fact, several studies have used noninferiority designs to specifically evaluate the equivalence of TMH and in-person care. In traditional randomized controlled trials (RCTs), a central goal is to identify differences between groups, and nonstatistically significant findings cannot be interpreted as the groups being equivalent (i.e., there was only a failure to detect a difference). In noninferiority designs, the statistical tests are designed to determine whether TMH is no worse than other modalities in terms of clinical effects (Greene, Morland, Durkalski, & Frueh, 2008). Multiple studies have shown that TMH is noninferior to in-person care in reducing mental health disorder symptoms (Acierno et al., 2016; Egede et al., 2015; Liu et al., 2019; Morland et al., 2010, 2014; Yuen et al., 2015). One study using an equivalence design (i.e., hypothesizing that TMH would be neither worse nor better than the comparator group) found that TMH was equivalent to in-person psychotherapy for PTSD (Maieritsch et al., 2016). Taken together, these studies suggest that psychotherapy can be delivered via TMH with outcomes comparable to standard in-person care.

Psychiatric care delivered via TMH has also been examined. An equivalence study of psychiatric follow-up appointments, which included medication management and supportive therapy, found that TMH was equivalent to in-person visits (O'Reilly et al., 2007). Similarly, an RCT conducted in the Canary Islands found that cognitive behavioral therapy combined with medication management delivered via TMH was equivalent to in-person care (De Las Cuevas, Arredondo, Cabrera, Sulzenbacher, & Meise, 2006). Collectively, these studies suggest that the effectiveness of psychiatric care delivered via TMH is noninferior or equivalent to in-person care.

TMH has been shown to be effective in reducing mental health disorder symptoms. Much work has focused on TMH's effectiveness in mood, anxiety, and trauma-related disorders. Among individuals with depression, TMH was found to decrease depression symptoms while reducing barriers to receiving care (Choi, Hegel et al., 2014; Choi, Marti et al., 2014; Egede et al., 2015; Khatri, Marziali, Tchernikov, & Shepherd, 2014). TMH has been shown to improve insomnia and hopelessness occurring in the context of depression (Luxton et al., 2016; Scogin et al., 2018). In rural clinics without on-site psychiatrists, a TMH psychiatry program produced greater reductions in depression symptoms, improved quality of life, and importantly, greater depression remission rates at 12-month follow-up compared to clinics without the program (Fortney et al., 2007). Psychiatric follow-up visits conducted via TMH produced significant decreases in depression symptoms; although this reduction did not differ from an in-person control group, the TMH group had lower dropout rates (Hungerbuehler, Valiengo, Loch, Rössler, & Gattaz, 2016). These findings suggest that TMH is an effective modality for the treatment of depression and may have some advantages over in-person treatment.

TMH has been researched extensively as a PTSD treatment modality. One study found that TMH produced significant reductions in PTSD symptoms that were largely maintained at 6-month follow-up; there were no significant differences between in-person care versus TMH delivered to the patient's home or to a clinic (Morland et al., 2020). Overall, TMH has been shown to be an effective modality for delivering psychotherapy for PTSD, with significant reduction in symptoms (Germain, Marchand, Bouchard, Drouin, & Guay, 2009; Gros, Lancaster, López, & Acierno, 2018; Hassija & Gray, 2011; Tuerk, Yoder, Ruggiero, Gros. & Acierno, 2010), and improvements have been sustained 3 months after treatment (Murphy & Turgoose, 2019). Given that dropout rates for PTSD psychotherapies are high, TMH delivered to patients' homes may improve treatment retention by reducing barriers to care. A review of medical record data found that individuals who received TMH for PTSD from home attended more treatment sessions than those attending in-person (Boykin et al., 2019).

TMH is effective in treating anxiety and obsessive-compulsive disorders, demonstrating reductions in symptoms and high rates of remission (Gros et al., 2013). Exposure is a hallmark feature of evidence-based psychotherapies for PTSD, obsessive-compulsive disorders, and anxiety disorders, and treatment modality (i.e., in-person, TMH, telephone) can determine the types of exposures that are possible. TMH, especially to the home, could allow exposures that are not possible in a clinic (i.e., having a patient with OCD "contaminate" themselves by touching a feared stimulus in their home, such as the lid of their garbage can, and then touching their kitchen table) (Goetter et al., 2013). As such, TMH enables effective exposure therapy while increasing access to evidence-based psychotherapy (Alcañiz et al., 2003; Goetter et al., 2013; Goetter, Herbert, Forman, Yuen, & Thomas, 2014; Himle et al., 2006).

Although most work has investigated the effectiveness of TMH for mood, anxiety, and anxiety-related disorders (e.g., OCD, PTSD), emerging research suggests that TMH also shows promise as an effective treatment modality for serious mental illness (e.g., schizophrenia) (Kasckow et al., 2014), eating disorders (Gros et al., 2013), and substance use disorders (Lin et al., 2019). These encouraging findings support TMH's ability to effectively treat underserved conditions, by connecting patients with specialized providers who may be located at a considerable distance.

The use of TMH has also been evaluated among pediatric populations. A prior review found that TMH is an effective treatment for childhood depression and can be used to accurately conduct psychiatric and psychological assessments (Boydell et al., 2014). In one randomized trial of CBT for childhood depression, participants reported reduced depression posttreatment in both the TMH and in-person conditions, but gains were made faster via TMH (Nelson, Barnard, & Cain, 2003). Behavioral TMH treatment for autism reduced problem behaviors and was highly acceptable to parents (Wacker et al., 2013). Finally, there is evidence that TMH can help children cope with medical illness and other behavioral health concerns included feeding issues (Van Allen, Davis, & Lassen, 2011). In sum, TMH has a large and growing evidence base demonstrating its effectiveness in providing psychiatric and psychotherapeutic services.

Patient satisfaction

Patient satisfaction with TMH is generally found to be high (Jenkins-Guarnieri, Pruitt, Luxton, & Johnson, 2015). This is the case when TMH is provided to clinics or directly to patients' homes (Fletcher et al., 2018; Jenkins-Guarnieri et al., 2015). High satisfaction with TMH has been reported among older adult, military veteran, incarcerated, and indigenous populations, as well as by parents of children receiving mental health treatment via TMH (Brooks, Manson, Bair, Dailey, & Shore, 2012; Jenkins-Guarnieri et al., 2015; Mayworm et al., 2020; Morgan, Patrick, & Magaletta, 2008). Notably, multiple studies have found no difference in patient satisfaction and working alliance between TMH and in-person care (Jenkins-Guarnieri et al., 2015). Furthermore, a recent study reported that patients with generalized anxiety disorder rated working alliance as significantly higher in the TMH condition compared to in-person; the authors hypothesized that TMH may feel more comfortable and less intrusive to patients and may give them an increased sense of control (Watts et al., 2020). However, some work suggests that working alliance ratings may be lower for group therapy delivered via TMH as compared to in-person; further research is needed to understand potential differences between group and individual therapy delivered via TMH (Jenkins-Guarnieri et al., 2015).

Benefits of TMH include its convenience, by saving patients time and money in not having to travel far distances to their appointment or account for delays due to traffic or parking (Lindsay et al., 2017). TMH can increase access to services that may have otherwise been out of reach, and can increase acceptability among those who may feel stigmatized or uncomfortable presenting to a mental health clinic in person (Shore, Goranson, Ward, & Lu, 2014). TMH can be particularly advantageous for patients with physical health concerns, childcare, or eldercare responsibilities that make leaving the home difficult (Lindsay et al., 2017; Moreau et al., 2018). However, some patients report difficulties successfully using TMH technology, which can negatively impact satisfaction with this modality. These difficulties are often related to a lack of digital literacy or device ownership, particularly among older patients, as well as poor broadband connectivity, especially in more rural areas (Cowan, McKean,

Gentry, & Hilty, 2019; Richardson, Christopher Frueh, Grubaugh, Egede, & Elhai, 2009). Improved access to video-enabled devices, high-speed internet connectivity, and patient training in technology use is necessary to address these barriers to use.

Provider satisfaction

Providers similarly report being satisfied with TMH, noting its ability to improve access to care for patients, increase efficiency of services, and save time and money (Connolly, Miller, Lindsay, & Bauer, 2020). Providers may find TMH to be more effective than in-person care in some circumstances, such as for patients with PTSD, agoraphobia, or social anxiety who may feel more comfortable speaking from the safety of their home and may not be willing to receive care in-person (Connolly et al., 2020; Cowan et al., 2019; Lindsay et al., 2017). Providers are also able to view their patient in their home environment, which can provide valuable contextual information regarding the patient's current level of functioning and factors that may be contributing to impairment.

While providers feel positive toward TMH overall, they still report multiple drawbacks, including technological difficulties, increased hassles of adjusting to a new care modality, and the need for training and technical support. Providers have also reported that TMH can feel more impersonal or impede the detection of nonverbal cues. Some providers reported beliefs that patients would not like TMH or that certain patients would not be appropriate to receive care remotely (Connolly et al., 2020; Cowan et al., 2019).

However, providers' attitudes are generally positive despite these drawbacks, suggesting that the advantages of TMH may outweigh the disadvantages. Furthermore, providers' attitudes tend to improve with experience, as they become more comfortable, adapt to new workflows, and find that worst-case scenarios may not prove to be true (Brooks et al., 2012; Glover, Williams, Hazlett, & Campbell, 2013; Whitten & Kuwahara, 2004). That being said, providers may report lower satisfaction with TMH than their patients (Cruz, Krupinski, Lopez, & Weinstein, 2005; Shulman, John, & Kane, 2017; Thomas et al., 2018). The perceived drawbacks of establishing a therapeutic relationship via TMH may be of greater concern to providers than to patients; indeed, one study found that providers reported lower working alliance scores for TMH versus in-person sessions, while patient scores did not differ across modalities (Ertelt et al., 2011). Using TMH may require more effort on the provider end versus the patient end, which may also contribute to this difference in satisfaction. Providers must undergo training in how to schedule, conduct and document their sessions, as well as maintain safety and confidentiality, while patients are often only required to log on to their appointment, whether from the comfort of their home or another more convenient location.

Although previous work has found that providers tend to favor in-person care over TMH when given the choice, this question must be revisited in light of the COVID-19 pandemic, in which in-person appointments introduce infection risk. In addition, reimbursement of TMH services has increased during COVID-19, which may also alter provider perceptions of the relative advantages and drawbacks of this modality (Centers for Medicare & Medicaid Services, 2020). Many providers are now permitted to conduct TMH sessions from their own home, versus from their place of work (Békés & Aafjes-van Doorn, 2020). TMH has been proposed as a way to prevent provider burnout and improve flexibility and work-life balance by allowing providers to work from home and remove time spent commuting (Vogt, Mahmoud, & Elhaj, 2019). The potential benefits of conducting TMH from home will need to be assessed more thoroughly moving forwards, but initial findings suggest providers have responded largely positively to this shift in care provision during the COVID-19 pandemic (Békés & Aafjes-van Doorn, 2020). It will be important to track the extent to which these changes in reimbursement and telework policies will persist beyond the initial response to the COVID-19 pandemic.

Regulatory and safety issues

With technological advances in delivering mental health remotely, so too have there been substantive changes regarding the regulation and security of health information. Specifically, advances in technology have allowed providers and patients to connect anywhere, anytime. However, ethical and legal guidelines have not necessarily moved at the same pace (Kramer, Kinn, & Mishkind, 2015). The discrepancies between the range of technology-enabled care modalities that are available and the rules surrounding the delivery of that care have created gaps between what providers *can* do and what they *should* do as mental health professionals.

The expansion of ethical and legal guidelines aims to increase the safety of TMH. These regulations encourage the delivery of high-quality, patient-centered services while mitigating risks to both patients and providers. At the same time, despite the helpful spirit of regulations to protect the health, safety, and welfare of patients (US Department of Health and Human Services, 2020), these rules may also present barriers to care. Furthermore, rules and governing structures differ across jurisdictions. Here, we will focus on three different governing structures: the United States, Canada, and the European Union. First, we will review regulatory issues surrounding the portability of licensure across jurisdictions. Next, security and privacy of health information and technologies will be discussed. Lastly, we will introduce best practices for ensuring patient safety during TMH visits.

Licensure portability and reciprocity

TMH removes geographic barriers to care, and therefore invites questions regarding provision of services across jurisdictions. This can be especially relevant for providers who live or practice near to the border of two or more states, provinces, or countries, and for providers or patients who relocate permanently or temporarily.

Within the United States, the issuing and maintenance of mental health licenses is regulated on the state level. Licensure regulations often vary from state to state, with very few states offering reciprocity between jurisdictions. Under reciprocity, a provider licensed in a participating jurisdiction is eligible to be licensed in another participating jurisdiction via an expedited process. Reciprocity can also ease restrictions on access to medical services and allow for a more competitive market from which patients may choose a provider. The Psychology Interjurisdictional Compact (PSYPACT) allows for the provision of TMH across state lines without requiring psychologists to be licensed in each state; to date, 15 states have enacted the necessary legislation and an additional 16 states have introduced such legislation in 2020 (psypact.org).

Psychiatrists must hold a medical license from the state where they practice (i.e., where the resident resides); the Interstate Medical Licensure Compact includes 29 states and attempts to streamline the issuing of multiple licenses to providers (www.imlcc.org). There can be considerable state-level variability with regards to documentation, mandated reporting, and exam requirements, so it is important for the provider to be familiar with relevant differences in the states where their patients reside (Federation of State Medical Boards, 2020). Psychiatrists should also be well informed of regulations regarding the prescribing of controlled substances, which historically required the provider to have first examined the patient in-person [see, Ryan Haight Online Pharmacy Consumer Protection Act of 2008; Hageseth vs Superior Court, 150 Cal. App. 4th 1399 (Cal. Ct. App. 2007)]; however, regulations have been loosened during COVID-19 (Wicklund, 2020). As such, it is imperative that providers stay up to date with the most recent guidance at the time of practice.

While commenting on malpractice and liability is beyond the scope of this chapter, it is critical for providers to be aware of the current regulatory climate and to seek consultation when necessary to prevent negative outcomes (Cowan et al., 2019). It is also worth noting that exceptions to certain state-level regulations exist for providers working within federal systems such as the Veterans Health Administration, Department of Defense, or the Indian Health Service; these providers are able to practice across state lines without needing additional licenses (Shore, n.d.).

Jurisdictional issues are common in other countries as well, including Canada (Fistein, Holland, Clare, & Gunn, 2009). Psychiatrists practicing in Canada must hold a medical degree in their province and must also seek specialist certification in psychiatry by either the Royal College of Physicians and Surgeons of Canada or a provincial college (Canadian Psychiatric Association, 2020). For psychologists in Canada, educational requirements can vary from province to province, with some areas offering master-level providers charters to practice independently and other areas requiring a doctoral degree in psychology (Canadian Psychological Association, 2020).

The European Union (EU) represents a unique challenge when delivering care across countries, where multiple languages are spoken and many different cultures are represented (Van Daele et al., 2020). Common standards for psychiatrist training and certification help to ensure patient safety (Brittlebank et al., 2016). The European Certificate in Psychology (EuroPsy) is not a license to practice, but a set of standards for education, professional training, and competence, used as a benchmark for independent practice and to uphold the standards of the European Federation of Psychologists' Associations (EFPA).

While international practice can relieve local shortages in mental health care, providers must often navigate complex regulatory processes (Stevens & Gielen, 2007). Education and training required as a precursor to licensure can differ substantially between countries. For example, some countries may require a doctorate in a specific specialty, a degree from an accredited institution, or to pass competency exams, while others do not. In addition to limitations of licensure portability when practicing internationally, there are additional clinical considerations, including cultural competency, stigma toward mental health treatment, and language barriers. Wherever a mental health provider chooses to practice, careful attention should be paid to the rules and regulations that surround the provision of mental health care in that area. Providers should consult the guidelines put forth by a country's psychological or psychiatric association (e.g., see APA's Office of International Affairs for a list of international psychological associations; www.apa.org/international/natlorgs.html).

Security and privacy of patient information

Security and privacy of technologies and information also differ by jurisdictional boundaries. For example, the Health Insurance Portability and Accountability Act (HIPAA; 1996) and Health Information Technology for Economic and Clinical Health Act (HITECH; 2009) represent the United States' efforts to protect healthcare information and virtual patient data. Similar efforts exist in Canada [the Personal Information Protection and Electronic Documents Act (PIPEDA), introduced in 2000] (Canada, 2000) and in the European Union (the Directive on Data Protection, introduced in 1998) (Birnhack, 2008).

Under HIPAA, "covered entities," such as health plans, health-care providers, or health-care clearinghouses, are required by federal law to keep health information private. HITECH addresses the privacy and security concerns associated with the electronic transmission of health information, in part through language that strengthens the civil and criminal enforcement of HIPAA rules. In Canada, the PIPEDA directs covered organizations to obtain an individual's consent when their personal information is collected, used, or disclosed. It also states the right of an individual to access their personal information, which is held by a covered organization, and the right to challenge its accuracy. Within Europe, the Data Protection Directive protects individuals with regard to how their personal data may be moved or processed, ensuing the right to privacy according to the European Court of Human Rights.

Such guidelines often indicate which TMH video platforms are deemed compliant, in that the adequate security and encryption safeguards are in place to protect patients' privacy and prevent bad actors from gaining access to TMH sessions. However, some restrictions have been loosened during the COVID-19 pandemic; for example, at the time of this writing, providers in the United States are temporarily able to use non-HIPAA compliant TMH platforms (Notification of Enforcement Discretion for

Telehealth Remote Communications During the COVID-19 Nationwide Public Health Emergency, 2020). Providers should frequently review regulatory guidance regarding the protection of patient information during TMH encounters, given often rapidly changing directives.

Patient safety during TMH encounters

Providers must be prepared to respond in clinical emergencies from a distance and be informed about local or national policies or laws that govern mandated reporting, emergency responding, and involuntary commitment. This can include awareness of resources that can be leveraged in times of crisis, such as the National Suicide Prevention Hotline within the United States (https://suicidepreventionlifeline.org/), the Canada Suicide Prevention Service (https://www.crisisservicescanada.ca/en/), or the International Association for Suicide Prevention in Europe (IASP; https://www.iasp.info/resources/Crisis_Centres/Europe/). Such resources typically offer both phone and text options allowing both patients and providers to initiate support, as well as information on mental health awareness and the prevention of suicide for the general public.

To properly engage in emergency planning, providers should obtain the patient's address at each visit so that they can appropriately respond in case of a clinical emergency (Luxton, Pruitt, & Osenbach, 2014). Providers should gather contact information of a family member or friend who can be reached in case of an emergency and should be aware of available emergency services in the patient's area. This is particularly important when working with patients in more remote locations with minimal first responder resources; providers should be cognizant of these issues and develop an adequate safety plan well in advance of a potential clinical emergency.

It is imperative that patients and providers feel safe and well informed during TMH appointments. Providers should confirm that they are conducting the session from a private location, and some patients may feel more comfortable if providers are able to pan their camera to show that there are no other individuals in the room listening to their session (Burgess et al., 2020). Similarly, providers should assess the relative privacy of the patient's location, including whether there are family members nearby who may be able to hear portions of the session. If at all possible, patients should be encouraged to find a private space to best replicate the confidentiality of an in-person appointment; for some patients, this could include sitting in a parked car (Moring et al., 2020). Such precautions are particularly important in instances of suspected or confirmed intimate partner violence. Providers should take care in asking any questions that may have negative repercussions if heard by a partner; if the patient is able to wear headphones, providers may be able to ask simple yes-or-no questions to determine whether it is safe to discuss sensitive topics at a given time (Rossi et al., 2020). Providers should also discuss a backup plan with patients at the start of the TMH session in the case that the videoconferencing technology fails and ends a session prematurely; this is particularly critical if the patient is deemed to be at high risk and in need of safety planning prior to concluding a session. Back-up plans can include trying an alternative TMH platform or having the provider call the patient via phone to complete the remainder of the session.

In sum, there are substantial regulatory and safety considerations to account for when providing TMH to ensure high-quality provision of mental health care. Providers are encouraged to seek guidance when needed and take advantage of helpful resources; organizations such as the American Telemedicine Association (https://www.ameri-cantelemed.org/resource/) provide practice guidelines that reflect the current TMH policies and regulations. Such tools are imperative in helping to inform providers' decisions given the complex and fast-changing nature of the virtual care landscape.

Global telemental health

By transcending geographic barriers, TMH is in many ways poised to expand and improve the provision of mental health care on a global scale. Its benefits may be particularly critical in areas that are low resourced or impacted by ongoing war and conflict, natural disasters, or large-scale health crises such as the COVID-19 pandemic. Technological advances, increased health funding and infrastructure within the developing countries, and widespread use of mobile devices make TMH an obvious choice for increasing availability of mental health services (Kim & Zuckerman, 2019).

TMH is a growing delivery modality in low- and middle-income countries. Across 19 studies, Acharibasam and Wynn (2018) found that "user-centered" telehealth programs were more easily implemented than programs not recognizing the unique local context. User-centered programs engaged local organizations and health-care workers and were context sensitive, which strengthens Bischoff, Springer, and Taylor (2017) argument that approaches to global mental health initiatives must be nonconventional and integrate traditions of the communities being served. While there is high need for global TMH (Acharibasam et al., 2018), local providers were less prepared to deliver mental health care via TMH than other delivery modalities. Further, providers from low- and middle-income countries were found to benefit from communities of practice using online networks, highlighting the need for collaboration and support among local mental health providers. Patient perspectives and attitudes must also be considered, as there may be considerable skepticism or stigma surrounding mental health care; providers should be prepared to discuss barriers to treatment and provide reassurance regarding the safety, effectiveness, and confidentiality of TMH (Naal, Whaibeh, & Mahmoud, 2020).

Task sharing is a critical strategy that can optimize efficiency, maximize expertise, and increase access to care in resource-constrained communities (Hoeft, Fortney, Patel, & Unützer, 2018; Patel, 2012; World Health Organization, 2008). Task sharing, also referred to as task shifting, involves the transfer of tasks from a highly trained professional to an individual who is less skilled to ensure that everyone is working at the top of their scope of practice. This process reserves the skilled professional for tasks that require more specialized training and skill. TMH is well positioned to facilitate task sharing; for instance, allowing a mental health provider at a remote location to deliver care to patients being seen at a clinic without specialized providers; mental health clinicians can also offer education and consultation to community workers or primary care providers at these sites (Hoeft et al., 2018).

While increasing adoption of global TMH will require further expansion of infrastructure, funding, and capacity, special considerations must also be made for countries affected by crises. Many developing countries have been or are currently subject to unrest and extreme circumstances that directly impact quality of life and mental well-being. In the wake of conflict resulting in long-term damage, many resource-constrained countries are not prepared to address mental health needs, which can perpetuate and exacerbate major economic losses due to death or disability associated with severe mental illness. Large-scale social dislocations, whether caused by an economic crisis, war, or violence, may also worsen or trigger mental illness. Approximately one-third of all countries lack a mental health policy, plan, or laws (World Health Organization, 2015). Among countries rebuilding postconflict, there is great need for mental health services and coordination with primary care services. Previous disaster response efforts that integrated mental health support such as the earthquakes of Great East Japan in 2011, Hanshin-Awaji in 1995, and Niigata Chuetsu in 2006 demonstrate the feasibility of this approach. Disaster response projects funded by organizations such as the World Bank Group underscore the opportunity that emergencies present to improve mental health systems. It is important that disasters not only be used as a catalyst for temporary mental health infrastructure but also serve as a launchpad for sustained mental health programs that serve communities (Marquez & Saxena, 2016).

TMH offers a unique opportunity to rapidly provide disaster relief services from a distance (Augusterfer, Mollica, & Lavelle, 2018). Following two natural disasters in 2015, a telepsychiatry network was established in a remote region of Pakistan that previously had little to no mental health services; refugees displaced by conflict in Syria have also expressed great interest in receiving mental health services via TMH. Based on the previous case examples, Augusterfer et al. (2018) recommend a collaborative TMH model that connects on-site primary care providers with remote mental health professionals to address the needs of local communities. Not only does the model provide expert consultation to areas of great need, but also it still centers on native providers, who are well acquainted with the traditions and practices of the community being served. This model is the framework for the Global Mental Health Program's Harvard Program in Refugee Trauma and has been successfully deployed in over 85 countries. It features face-to-face collaboration between site primary care providers and mental health providers, followed by routine TMH sessions (Augusterfer et al., 2018). TMH enables providers to deliver evidence-based psychotherapy to individuals in remote regions that are traditionally underserved or difficult to reach due to disasters or conflict. Combined with increased accessibility to internet and mobile devices across the world, global TMH has great potential to address the mental health treatment gap in resource-constrained countries in crisis (Augusterfer, Mollica, & Lavelle, 2015).

Social distancing and quarantine practices, implemented by countries and local authorities to promote public health and prevent spread during the COVID-19 pandemic, have introduced new barriers to receiving mental health care (Wright & Caudill, 2020). Mental health treatment during the pandemic is needed to address preexisting mental health conditions and to manage psychological impacts of COVID-19 (Whaibeh, Mahmoud, & Naal, 2020). Sustained isolation from support systems has the potential to increase loneliness and exacerbate anxiety and depressive symptoms. Acknowledging the importance of mental health during a pandemic, Australia and China have made diligent efforts to prioritize mental health services for individuals directly impacted by COVID-19. TMH services have been made available to front-line workers and those who test positive for COVID-19 in China, and TMH funding originally allocated in response to Australian brush fires has been increased to further support citizens impacted by COVID-19 (Zhou et al., 2020).

Countries of lower socioeconomic status face legal restrictions, lack infrastructure, technology or access to technology, and have limited digital literacy among potential users. Consequently, widespread adoption of TMH in low- and middle-income countries has been limited, and individuals with high need lack access to virtually delivered care (Ramalho et al., 2020). The variability in responses to the COVID-19 pandemic makes clear the harsh realities endured by resource-constrained countries in need of TMH. For long-standing crises, innovative technologies such as TMH that promote continuity of care are essential. Although 50% of the world does not use the internet, 97% live in an area that is within range of a cellular signal (International Telecommunication Union (ITU), 2020). Beyond establishing global TMH programs, additional effort must be made to maximize accessibility to predominantly offline populations located within African, Asian, and Pacific regions (Zhai, 2020). Scholars have stressed the importance of proactive implementation of global TMH as opposed to reactive implementation in observation of the varied response to COVID-19 (Smith et al., 2020).

Future directions in global TMH

As video technology and access to broadband internet improves, TMH will increasingly become a viable alternative to in-person, traditional mental health treatment. Despite the improved feasibility of TMH, several key gaps in the current research were identified that must be addressed for successful deployment. There is a need to develop and test implementation strategies specific to global TMH (Jefee-Bahloul, 2014), specifically approaches to implement urgent, rapid uptake of TMH in response to large-scale disasters and health crises. Building infrastructure, plans, and policies to support TMH for the long term and not just during a crisis or disaster will help both scalability and sustainability. In addition, collaborating with local experts to integrate culturally adapted treatments can increase uptake and improve outcomes. Research teams might also consider collecting qualitative feedback from key players involved in delivering care via TMH in different settings to better inform future global TMH implementation strategies.

In addition to creating structural changes and reconceptualizing models for implementing global TMH, initiatives must also consider underserved populations in need of innovative modes of treatment delivery. Indigenous populations worldwide uphold unique practices and traditions distinct from the dominant societies around them.

Although they account for approximately 5% of the world's population, indigenous peoples are more likely to live in poverty and have a life expectancy up to 20 years shorter than that of nonindigenous people (Dawson, Walker, Campbell, Davidson, & Egede, 2020). Global TMH, which can be tailored to address the unique needs of communities, could greatly benefit indigenous populations who often live in remote areas, but empirical evidence is still needed. Some Veteran and civilian indigenous populations have participated in trials investigating the efficacy of TMH (Day et al., 2020; Mishkind, 2020); however, further testing is warranted to better understand the effectiveness, feasibility, and necessity of tailored TMH programs (Dawson et al., 2020). Literature has shown that individuals from indigenous populations benefit from culturally adapted mental health treatment, which is likely the case for TMH as well (Jones, Jacklin, & O'Connell, 2017). Adapting mental health treatments can increase the relevance and engagement for individuals seeking help, thus improving clinical outcomes. However, as is the case for many other underserved, remote populations, there is a considerable workforce deficit. Future research should also test the most optimal structure and delivery method for mental health treatment in indigenous populations (Dawson et al., 2020).

The posttrauma experience is another area of interest for the future global TMH research. For example, despite identified psychosocial needs caused by massive displacements since 2011, the response to Syrian refugees has been lacking. This population, along with others living in postcrisis and disaster settings, has great need of mental health care yet lacks resources and access to adequate care (Yalim & Kim, 2018). In addition to local awareness, there must also be global awareness to catalyze organizations to address mental health needs in a scalable, cost-effective, and accessible manner. In creating global TMH programs for postcrisis settings, it is important to consider cultural customs and practices to promote well-being and engagement with any treatment deployed (Acharibasam & Wynn, 2018). Prioritization of mental health services to prevent retraumatization is a necessary complement to short-term, reactive TMH treatment programs (Marquez & Saxena, 2016). The widespread damage caused by civil conflict and massive displacements endured by Syrian refugees underscores the importance of a holistic understanding of these populations and trauma-informed care in postdisaster settings (Yalim & Kim, 2018).

Future developments for global TMH might expand beyond addressing postcrisis mental health concerns to specifically tailoring programs to treat highly prevalent mental health conditions preemptively or on an ongoing basis. Worldwide, depression and substance use disorders are common mental health conditions, with approximately 15% of individuals having at least one mental health or substance use disorder (SUD; Arthur, 2014). Consequently, both disorders may increase the likelihood for suicidal ideation (Ferrari et al., 2014), particularly when left untreated. As low- and middle-income countries often lack mental health infrastructure, proactively increasing widespread implementation of treatments for these disorders would likely decrease the current gap in treatment in underserved areas of the world. Once global TMH programs are established, additional concerns could easily be addressed. For example, one article characterized tele-SUD current usage as more of a supplementary treatment delivery system, citing it as a missed opportunity given the opioid crisis

(Huskamp et al., 2018). Employing a mixed-methods evaluation of qualitative and quantitative data may provide a more holistic perspective on key treatment elements for various settings and populations, enabling improved access to care for a variety of mental health concerns to historically underserved populations worldwide.

Conclusion

TMH is an effective form of care delivery that demonstrates high acceptability among patients and providers alike. It can dramatically increase access to care for those who are unable or unwilling to receive services in-person, whether due to geographic barriers, childcare or eldercare responsibilities, stigma toward mental health treatment, or infection risk during a global pandemic. However, a multitude of factors must be in place to ensure successful and sustained uptake of TMH. This includes access to the necessary technologies and internet connectivity, patient and provider training, TMH-friendly reimbursement and licensure structures, and buy-in across all levels of healthcare systems regarding the effectiveness and value of providing mental health care remotely. Indeed, important work has begun to define and develop strategies to improve TMH implementation (Lindsay et al., 2019; Mahmoud, Whaibeh, & Mitchell, 2020). The value of TMH in improving mental health outcomes on a global scale is clear, and opportunities for its use are growing exponentially. Future work must continue to prioritize the improvement and expansion of this critical treatment modality to ensure that those in need of quality mental health care are able to receive it.

References

Acharibasam, J. W., & Wynn, R. (2018). Telemental health in low-and middle-income countries: A systematic review. *International Journal of Telemedicine and Applications*, *2018*, 9602821.

Acierno, R., Gros, D. F., Ruggiero, K. J., Hernandez-Tejada, M. A., Knapp, R. G., Lejuez, C. W., ... Tuerk, P. W. (2016). Behavioral activation and therapeutic exposure for posttraumatic stress disorder: A noninferiority trial of treatment delivered in person versus home-based telehealth. *Depression and Anxiety*, *33*(5), 415–423.

Alcañiz, M., Botella, C., Baños, R., Perpiñá, C., Rey, B., Lozano, J. A., ... Gil, J. A. (2003). Internet-based telehealth system for the treatment of agoraphobia. *Cyberpsychology & Behavior*, *6*(4), 355–358.

Arthur, M. (2014). Institute for health metrics and evaluation. *Nursing Standard*, *28*(42), 32.

Augusterfer, E. F., Mollica, R. F., & Lavelle, J. (2015). A review of telemental health in international and post-disaster settings. *International Review of Psychiatry*, *27*(6), 540–546.

Augusterfer, E. F., Mollica, R. F., & Lavelle, J. (2018). Leveraging technology in post-disaster settings: The role of digital health/telemental health. *Current Psychiatry Reports*, *20*(10), 88.

Australian Government Department of Health (2019). Better Access Telehealth Services for people in rural and remote areas. Retrieved from https://www1.health.gov.au/internet/main/publishing.nsf/Content/mental-ba-telehealth.

Békés, V., & Aafjes-van Doorn, K. (2020). Psychotherapists' attitudes toward online therapy during the COVID-19 pandemic. *Journal of Psychotherapy Integration*, *30*(2), 238.

Berryhill, M. B., Culmer, N., Williams, N., Halli-Tierney, A., Betancourt, A., Roberts, H., & King, M. (2019). Videoconferencing psychotherapy and depression: A systematic review. *Telemedicine and e-Health*, *25*(6), 435–446.

Berryhill, M. B., Halli-Tierney, A., Culmer, N., Williams, N., Betancourt, A., King, M., & Ruggles, H. (2019). Videoconferencing psychological therapy and anxiety: A systematic review. *Family Practice*, *36*(1), 53–63.

Birnhack, M. D. (2008). The EU data protection directive: An engine of a global regime. *Computer Law and Security Review*, *24*(6), 508–520.

Bischoff, R. J., Springer, P. R., & Taylor, N. (2017). Global mental health in action: Reducing disparities one community at a time. *Journal of Marital and Family Therapy*, *43*(2), 276–290.

Boydell, K. M., Hodgins, M., Pignatiello, A., Teshima, J., Edwards, H., & Willis, D. (2014). Using technology to deliver mental health services to children and youth: A scoping review. *Journal of the Canadian Academy of Child and Adolescent Psychiatry*, *23*(2), 87.

Boykin, D. M., Keegan, F., Thompson, K. E., Voelkel, E., Lindsay, J. A., & Fletcher, T. L. (2019). Video to home delivery of evidence-based psychotherapy to veterans with posttraumatic stress disorder. *Frontiers in Psychiatry*, 10.

Brittlebank, A., Hermans, M., Bhugra, D., Da Costa, M. P., Rojnic-Kuzman, M., Fiorillo, A., … van der Gaag, R. J. (2016). Training in psychiatry throughout Europe. *European Archives of Psychiatry and Clinical Neuroscience*, *266*(2), 155–164.

Brooks, E., Manson, S. M., Bair, B., Dailey, N., & Shore, J. H. (2012). The diffusion of telehealth in rural American Indian communities: A retrospective survey of key stakeholders. *Telemedicine and e-Health*, *18*(1), 60–66.

Brown, F. W. (1998). Rural telepsychiatry. *Psychiatric Services*, *49*(7), 963–964.

Burgess, C., Miller, C., Franz, A., Abel, E. A., Gyulai, L., Osser, D., … Godleski, L. (2020). Practical lessons learned for assessing and treating bipolar disorder via telehealth modalities during the COVID-19 pandemic. *Bipolar Disorders*.

Canada. (2000). Personal Information Protection and Electronic Documents Act. S.C. 2000, c. 5. URL: https://laws-lois.justice.gc.ca/PDF/P-8.6.pdf [June 06, 2021].

Canadian Psychiatric Association. (2020). Retrieved from July 21, 2020 https://www.cpa-apc.org/.

Canadian Psychological Association. (2020). Retrieved from July 21, 2020 https://cpa.ca/practice/practiceregulation/.

Centers for Medicare & Medicaid Services. (2020). *Press release Trump Administration Issues Second Round of Sweeping Changes to Support U.S. Healthcare System During COVID-19 Pandemic*. Retrieved from July 21, 2020 https://www.cms.gov/newsroom/press-releases/trump-administration-issues-second-round-sweeping-changes-support-us-healthcare-system-during-covid.

Choi, N. G., Hegel, M. T., Marti, C. N., Marinucci, M. L., Sirrianni, L., & Bruce, M. L. (2014). Telehealth problem-solving therapy for depressed low-income homebound older adults. *The American Journal of Geriatric Psychiatry*, *22*(3), 263–271.

Choi, N. G., Marti, C. N., Bruce, M. L., Hegel, M. T., Wilson, N. L., & Kunik, M. E. (2014). Six-month postintervention depression and disability outcomes of in-home telehealth problem-solving therapy for depressed, low-income homebound older adults. *Depression and Anxiety*, *31*(8), 653–661.

Connolly, S. L., Miller, C. J., Lindsay, J. A., & Bauer, M. S. (2020). A systematic review of providers' attitudes toward telemental health via videoconferencing. *Clinical Psychology: Science and Practice*, e12311.

Cowan, K. E., McKean, A. J., Gentry, M. T., & Hilty, D. M. (2019, December). Barriers to use of telepsychiatry: Clinicians as gatekeepers. *Mayo Clinic Proceedings*, *94*(12), 2510–2523.

Cruz, M., Krupinski, E. A., Lopez, A. M., & Weinstein, R. S. (2005). A review of the first five years of the University of Arizona telepsychiatry programme. *Journal of Telemedicine and Telecare*, *11*(5), 234–239.

Cuevas, C. D. L., Arredondo, M. T., Cabrera, M. F., Sulzenbacher, H., & Meise, U. (2006). Randomized clinical trial of telepsychiatry through videoconference versus face-to-face conventional psychiatric treatment. *Telemedicine Journal & e-Health*, *12*(3), 341–350.

Darkins, A., Darkins, A. W., Darkins, W. A., Cary, M. A., & Cary, M. (2000). *Telemedicine and telehealth: Principles, policies, performances and pitfalls*. Springer Publishing Company.

Dawson, A. Z., Walker, R. J., Campbell, J. A., Davidson, T. M., & Egede, L. E. (2020). Telehealth and indigenous populations around the world: A systematic review on current modalities for physical and mental health. *mHealth*, *6*.

Day, S., Day, G., Keller, M., Touchett, H., Amspoker, A., Martin, L., & Lindsay, J. (2020). Personalized implementation of video telehealth for rural veterans (PIVOT-R). *mHealth*. https://doi.org/10.21037/mhealth.2020.03.02.

Doarn, C. R. (2018). Telemedicine and psychiatry—A natural match. *mHealth*, *4*.

Dwyer, T. F. (1973). Telepsychiatry: Psychiatric consultation by interactive television. *American Journal of Psychiatry*, *130*(8), 865–869.

Egede, L. E., Acierno, R., Knapp, R. G., Lejuez, C., Hernandez-Tejada, M., Payne, E. H., & Frueh, B. C. (2015). Psychotherapy for depression in older veterans via telemedicine: A randomised, open-label, non-inferiority trial. *The Lancet Psychiatry*, *2*(8), 693–701.

Ertelt, T. W., Crosby, R. D., Marino, J. M., Mitchell, J. E., Lancaster, K., & Crow, S. J. (2011). Therapeutic factors affecting the cognitive behavioral treatment of bulimia nervosa via telemedicine versus face-to-face delivery. *International Journal of Eating Disorders*, *44*(8), 687–691.

Federation of State Medical Boards. (2020). Retrieved from July 21, 2020 https://www.fsmb.org/advocacy/telemedicine-policies/.

Ferrari, A. J., Norman, R. E., Freedman, G., Baxter, A. J., Pirkis, J. E., Harris, M. G., … Whiteford, H. A. (2014). The burden attributable to mental and substance use disorders as risk factors for suicide: Findings from the Global Burden of Disease Study 2010. *PLoS ONE*, *9*(4), e91936.

Fistein, E. C., Holland, A. J., Clare, I. C. H., & Gunn, M. J. (2009). A comparison of mental health legislation from diverse commonwealth jurisdictions. *International Journal of Law and Psychiatry*, *32*(3), 147–155.

Fletcher, T. L., Hogan, J. B., Keegan, F., Davis, M. L., Wassef, M., Day, S., & Lindsay, J. A. (2018). Recent advances in delivering mental health treatment via video to home. *Current Psychiatry Reports*, *20*(8), 56.

Fortney, J. C., Pyne, J. M., Edlund, M. J., Williams, D. K., Robinson, D. E., Mittal, D., & Henderson, K. L. (2007). A randomized trial of telemedicine-based collaborative care for depression. *Journal of General Internal Medicine*, *22*(8), 1086–1093.

Germain, V., Marchand, A., Bouchard, S., Drouin, M. S., & Guay, S. (2009). Effectiveness of cognitive behavioural therapy administered by videoconference for posttraumatic stress disorder. *Cognitive Behaviour Therapy*, *38*(1), 42–53.

Glover, J. A., Williams, E., Hazlett, L. J., & Campbell, N. (2013). Connecting to the future: Telepsychiatry in postgraduate medical education. *Telemedicine and e-Health*, *19*(6), 474–479.

Godleski, L., Darkins, A., & Peters, J. (2012). Outcomes of 98,609 US Department of Veterans Affairs patients enrolled in telemental health services, 2006–2010. *Psychiatric Services*, *63*(4), 383–385.

Goetter, E. M., Herbert, J. D., Forman, E. M., Yuen, E. K., Gershkovich, M., Glassman, L. H., ... Goldstein, S. P. (2013). Delivering exposure and ritual prevention for obsessive–compulsive disorder via videoconference: Clinical considerations and recommendations. *Journal of Obsessive-Compulsive and Related Disorders, 2*(2), 137–145.

Goetter, E. M., Herbert, J. D., Forman, E. M., Yuen, E. K., & Thomas, J. G. (2014). An open trial of videoconference-mediated exposure and ritual prevention for obsessive-compulsive disorder. *Journal of Anxiety Disorders, 28*(5), 460–462.

Greene, C. J., Morland, L. A., Durkalski, V. L., & Frueh, B. C. (2008). Noninferiority and equivalence designs: Issues and implications for mental health research. *Journal of Traumatic Stress, 21*(5), 433–439.

Gros, D. F., Lancaster, C. L., López, C. M., & Acierno, R. (2018). Treatment satisfaction of home-based telehealth versus in-person delivery of prolonged exposure for combat-related PTSD in veterans. *Journal of Telemedicine and Telecare, 24*(1), 51–55.

Gros, D. F., Morland, L. A., Greene, C. J., Acierno, R., Strachan, M., Egede, L. E., ... Frueh, B. C. (2013). Delivery of evidence-based psychotherapy via video telehealth. *Journal of Psychopathology and Behavioral Assessment, 35*(4), 506–521.

Hassija, C., & Gray, M. J. (2011). The effectiveness and feasibility of videoconferencing technology to provide evidence-based treatment to rural domestic violence and sexual assault populations. *Telemedicine and e-Health, 17*(4), 309–315.

Himle, J. A., Fischer, D. J., Muroff, J. R., Van Etten, M. L., Lokers, L. M., Abelson, J. L., & Hanna, G. L. (2006). Videoconferencing-based cognitive-behavioral therapy for obsessive-compulsive disorder. *Behaviour Research and Therapy, 44*(12), 1821–1829.

Hoeft, T. J., Fortney, J. C., Patel, V., & Unützer, J. (2018). Task-sharing approaches to improve mental health care in rural and other low-resource settings: A systematic review. *The Journal of Rural Health, 34*(1), 48–62.

Hungerbuehler, I., Valiengo, L., Loch, A. A., Rössler, W., & Gattaz, W. F. (2016). Home-based psychiatric outpatient care through videoconferencing for depression: A randomized controlled follow-up trial. *JMIR Mental Health, 3*(3), e36.

Huskamp, H. A., Busch, A. B., Souza, J., Uscher-Pines, L., Rose, S., Wilcock, A., ... Mehrotra, A. (2018). How is telemedicine being used in opioid and other substance use disorder treatment? *Health Affairs (Project Hope), 37*(12), 1940–1947. https://doi.org/10.1377/hlthaff.2018.05134.

International Telecommunication Union (ITU). (2020). *Measuring digital development Facts and figures. 2019.* Retrieved from https://www.itu.int/en/ITU-D/Statistics/Documents/facts/FactsFigures2019.pdf.

Jefee-Bahloul, H. (2014). Telemental health in the Middle East: Overcoming the barriers. *Frontiers in Public Health, 2,* 86.

Jenkins-Guarnieri, M. A., Pruitt, L. D., Luxton, D. D., & Johnson, K. (2015). Patient perceptions of telemental health: Systematic review of direct comparisons to in-person psychotherapeutic treatments. *Telemedicine and e-Health, 21*(8), 652–660.

Jones, L., Jacklin, K., & O'Connell, M. E. (2017). Development and use of health-related technologies in indigenous communities: Critical review. *Journal of Medical Internet Research, 19*(7), e256.

Kannarkat, J. T., Smith, N. N., & McLeod-Bryant, S. A. (2020). Mobilization of telepsychiatry in response to COVID-19—Moving toward 21st century access to care. *Administration and Policy in Mental Health and Mental Health Services Research,* 1–3.

Kasckow, J., Felmet, K., Appelt, C., Thompson, R., Rotondi, A., & Haas, G. (2014). Telepsychiatry in the assessment and treatment of schizophrenia. *Clinical Schizophrenia & Related Psychoses, 8*(1), 21–27A.

Khatri, N., Marziali, E., Tchernikov, I., & Shepherd, N. (2014). Comparing telehealth-based and clinic-based group cognitive behavioral therapy for adults with depression and anxiety: A pilot study. *Clinical Interventions in Aging*, *9*, 765.

Kim, T., & Zuckerman, J. E. (2019). Realizing the potential of telemedicine in global health. *Journal of Global Health*, *9*(2).

Kramer, G. M., Kinn, J. T., & Mishkind, M. C. (2015). Legal, regulatory, and risk management issues in the use of technology to deliver mental health care. *Cognitive and Behavioral Practice*, *22*(3), 258–268.

Lin, L. A., Casteel, D., Shigekawa, E., Weyrich, M. S., Roby, D. H., & McMenamin, S. B. (2019). Telemedicine-delivered treatment interventions for substance use disorders: A systematic review. *Journal of Substance Abuse Treatment*, *101*, 38–49.

Lindsay, J. A., Day, S. C., Amspoker, A. B., Fletcher, T. L., Hogan, J., Day, G., … Martin, L. A. (2019). Personalized implementation of video telehealth. *Psychiatric Clinics*, *42*(4), 563–574.

Lindsay, J. A., Hudson, S., Martin, L., Hogan, J. B., Nessim, M., Graves, L., … White, D. (2017). Implementing video to home to increase access to evidence-based psychotherapy for rural veterans. *Journal of Technology in Behavioral Science*, *2*(3–4), 140–148.

Liu, L., Thorp, S. R., Moreno, L., Wells, S. Y., Glassman, L. H., Busch, A. C., … Agha, Z. (2019). Videoconferencing psychotherapy for veterans with PTSD: Results from a randomized controlled non-inferiority trial. *Journal of Telemedicine and Telecare*. https://doi.org/10.1177/1357633X19853947.

Luxton, D. D., Pruitt, L. D., & Osenbach, J. E. (2014). Best practices for remote psychological assessment via telehealth technologies. *Professional Psychology: Research and Practice*, *45*(1), 27.

Luxton, D. D., Pruitt, L. D., Wagner, A., Smolenski, D. J., Jenkins-Guarnieri, M. A., & Gahm, G. (2016). Home-based telebehavioral health for US military personnel and veterans with depression: A randomized controlled trial. *Journal of Consulting and Clinical Psychology*, *84*(11), 923.

Mahmoud, H., Whaibeh, E., & Mitchell, B. (2020). Ensuring successful telepsychiatry program implementation: Critical components and considerations. *Current Treatment Options in Psychiatry*, 1–12.

Maieritsch, K. P., Smith, T. L., Hessinger, J. D., Ahearn, E. P., Eickhoff, J. C., & Zhao, Q. (2016). Randomized controlled equivalence trial comparing videoconference and in person delivery of cognitive processing therapy for PTSD. *Journal of Telemedicine and Telecare*, *22*(4), 238–243.

Marquez, P. V., & Saxena, S. (2016, July). Making mental health a global priority. In *Vol. 2016*. *Cerebrum: The Dana forum on brain science* Dana Foundation.

Mayworm, A. M., Lever, N., Gloff, N., Cox, J., Willis, K., & Hoover, S. A. (2020). School-based telepsychiatry in an urban setting: Efficiency and satisfaction with care. *Telemedicine and e-Health*, *26*(4), 446–454.

Mishkind, M. C. (2020). Serving remote locations and isolated population. *mHealth*, *6*.

Moreau, J. L., Cordasco, K. M., Young, A. S., Oishi, S. M., Rose, D. E., Canelo, I., … Hamilton, A. B. (2018). The use of telemental health to meet the mental health needs of women using department of veterans affairs services. *Women's Health Issues*, *28*(2), 181–187.

Morgan, R. D., Patrick, A. R., & Magaletta, P. R. (2008). Does the use of telemental health alter the treatment experience? Inmates' perceptions of telemental health versus face-to-face treatment modalities. *Journal of Consulting and Clinical Psychology*, *76*(1), 158.

Moring, J. C., Dondanville, K. A., Fina, B. A., Hassija, C., Chard, K., Monson, C., … Galovski, T. E. (2020). Cognitive processing therapy for posttraumatic stress disorder via telehealth: Practical considerations during the COVID-19 pandemic. *Journal of Traumatic Stress*.

Morland, L. A., Greene, C. J., Rosen, C. S., Foy, D., Reilly, P., Shore, J., … Frueh, B. C. (2010). Telemedicine for anger management therapy in a rural population of combat veterans with posttraumatic stress disorder: A randomized noninferiority trial. *Journal of Clinical Psychiatry, 71*(7), 855–863.

Morland, L. A., Mackintosh, M. A., Glassman, L. H., Wells, S. Y., Thorp, S. R., Rauch, S. A., … Sohn, M. J. (2020). Home-based delivery of variable length prolonged exposure therapy: A comparison of clinical efficacy between service modalities. *Depression and Anxiety, 37*(4), 346–355.

Morland, L. A., Mackintosh, M. A., Greene, C. J., Rosen, C. S., Chard, K. M., Resick, P., & Frueh, B. C. (2014). Cognitive processing therapy for PTSD delivered to rural combat veterans via telemental health: A randomized non-inferiority trial. *The Journal of Clinical Psychiatry, 75*, 470–476.

Murphy, D., & Turgoose, D. (2019). Evaluating an Internet-based video cognitive processing therapy intervention for veterans with PTSD: A pilot study. *Journal of Telemedicine and Telecare.* https://doi.org/10.1177/1357633X19850393.

Naal, H., Whaibeh, E., & Mahmoud, H. (2020). Guidelines for primary health care-based telemental health in a low-to middle-income country: The case of Lebanon. *International Review of Psychiatry,* 1–9.

Nelson, E. L., Barnard, M., & Cain, S. (2003). Treating childhood depression over videoconferencing. *Telemedicine Journal and E-Health, 9*(1), 49–55.

Notification of Enforcement Discretion for Telehealth Remote Communications During the COVID-19 Nationwide Public Health Emergency. (2020). Retrieved from https://www.hhs.gov/hipaa/for-professionals/special-topics/emergency-preparedness/notification-enforcement-discretion-telehealth/index.html.

O'Gorman, L. D., Hogenbirk, J. C., & Warry, W. (2016). Clinical telemedicine utilization in Ontario over the Ontario telemedicine network. *Telemedicine and e-Health, 22*(6), 473–479.

O'Reilly, R., Bishop, J., Maddox, K., Hutchinson, L., Fisman, M., & Takhar, J. (2007). Is telepsychiatry equivalent to face-to-face psychiatry? Results from a randomized controlled equivalence trial. *Psychiatric Services, 58*(6), 836–843.

Patel, V. (2012). Global mental health: From science to action. *Harvard Review of Psychiatry, 20*(1), 6–12.

Ramalho, R., Adiukwu, F., Bytyçi, D. G., El Hayek, S., Gonzalez-Diaz, J. M., Larnaout, A., … da Costa, M. P. (2020). Telepsychiatry and healthcare access inequities during the COVID-19 pandemic. *Asian Journal of Psychiatry.*

Richardson, L. K., Christopher Frueh, B., Grubaugh, A. L., Egede, L., & Elhai, J. D. (2009). Current directions in videoconferencing tele-mental health research. *Clinical Psychology: Science and Practice, 16*(3), 323–338.

Rossi, F. S., Shankar, M., Buckholdt, K., Bailey, Y., Israni, S. T., & Iverson, K. M. (2020). Trying times and trying out solutions: Intimate partner violence screening and support for women veterans during CoViD-19. *Journal of General Internal Medicine,* 1–4.

Scogin, F., Lichstein, K., DiNapoli, E. A., Woosley, J., Thomas, S. J., LaRocca, M. A., … Parton, J. (2018). Effects of integrated telehealth-delivered cognitive-behavioral therapy for depression and insomnia in rural older adults. *Journal of Psychotherapy Integration, 28*(3), 292.

Shore, J. (n.d.). State Licensure. Retrieved from https://www.psychiatry.org/psychiatrists/practice/telepsychiatry/toolkit/state-licensure.

Shore, P., Goranson, A., Ward, M. F., & Lu, M. W. (2014). Meeting veterans where they're@: A VA Home-Based Telemental Health (HBTMH) pilot program. *The International Journal of Psychiatry in Medicine, 48*(1), 5–17.

Shulman, M., John, M., & Kane, J. M. (2017). Home-based outpatient telepsychiatry to improve adherence with treatment appointments: A pilot study. *Psychiatric Services*, *68*(7), 743–746.

Smith, A. C., Thomas, E., Snoswell, C. L., Haydon, H., Mehrotra, A., Clemensen, J., & Caffery, L. J. (2020). Telehealth for global emergencies: Implications for coronavirus disease 2019 (COVID-19). *Journal of Telemedicine and Telecare*. https://doi.org/10.1177/13576 33X20916567.

Stevens, M. J., & Gielen, U. P. (Eds.). (2007). *Toward a global psychology: Theory, research, intervention, and pedagogy* Psychology Press.

Thomas, J. F., Novins, D. K., Hosokawa, P. W., Olson, C. A., Hunter, D., Brent, A. S., ... Libby, A. M. (2018). The use of telepsychiatry to provide cost-efficient care during pediatric mental health emergencies. *Psychiatric Services*, *69*(2), 161–168.

Tuerk, P. W., Yoder, M., Ruggiero, K. J., Gros, D. F., & Acierno, R. (2010). A pilot study of prolonged exposure therapy for posttraumatic stress disorder delivered via telehealth technology. *Journal of Traumatic Stress: Official Publication of The International Society for Traumatic Stress Studies*, *23*(1), 116–123.

US Department of Health and Human Services. (2020). Retrieved from July 21, 2020 https://www.hhs.gov/.

Van Allen, J., Davis, A. M., & Lassen, S. (2011). The use of telemedicine in pediatric psychology: Research review and current applications. *Child and Adolescent Psychiatric Clinics*, *20*(1), 55–66.

Van Daele, T., Karekla, M., Kassianos, A. P., Compare, A., Haddouk, L., Salgado, J., ... De Witte, N. A. (2020). Recommendations for policy and practice of telepsychotherapy and e-mental health in Europe and beyond. *Journal of Psychotherapy Integration*, *30*(2), 160.

Vogt, E. L., Mahmoud, H., & Elhaj, O. (2019). Telepsychiatry: Implications for psychiatrist burnout and well-being. *Psychiatric Services*, *70*(5), 422–424.

Wacker, D. P., Lee, J. F., Dalmau, Y. C. P., Kopelman, T. G., Lindgren, S. D., Kuhle, J., ... Waldron, D. B. (2013). Conducting functional communication training via telehealth to reduce the problem behavior of young children with autism. *Journal of Developmental and Physical Disabilities*, *25*(1), 35–48.

Watts, S., Marchand, A., Bouchard, S., Gosselin, P., Langlois, F., Belleville, G., & Dugas, M. J. (2020). Telepsychotherapy for generalized anxiety disorder: Impact on the working alliance. *Journal of Psychotherapy Integration*, *30*(2), 208.

Whaibeh, E., Mahmoud, H., & Naal, H. (2020). Telemental health in the context of a pandemic: The COVID-19 experience. *Current Treatment Options in Psychiatry*, 1–5.

Whitten, P., & Kuwahara, E. (2004). A multi-phase telepsychiatry programme in Michigan: Organizational factors affecting utilization and user perceptions. *Journal of Telemedicine and Telecare*, *10*(5), 254–261.

Wicklund, E. (2020). *DEA gives providers leeway to use telehealth for substance abuse care.* Retrieved from https://mhealthintelligence.com/news/dea-gives-providers-leeway-to-use-telehealth-for-substance-abuse-care.

Wind, T. R., Rijkeboer, M., Andersson, G., & Riper, H. (2020). The COVID-19 pandemic: The 'black swan' for mental health care and a turning point for e-health. *Internet Interventions*, *20*.

Wittson, C. L., Affleck, D. C., & Johnson, V. (1961). Two-way television in group therapy. *Mental Hospitals*.

World Health Organization. (2008). *Task shifting: Global recommendations and guidelines.* Geneva: World Health Organization.

World Health Organization. (2015). *Mental health atlas—2014.* Retrieved from https://www.who.int/mental_health/evidence/atlas/mental_health_atlas_2014/en/.

Wright, J. H., & Caudill, R. (2020). Remote treatment delivery in response to the COVID-19 pandemic. *Psychotherapy and Psychosomatics. 89*(3), 1.

Yalim, A. C., & Kim, I. (2018). Mental health and psychosocial needs of Syrian refugees: A literature review and future directions. *Advances in Social Work, 18*(3), 833–852.

Yuen, E. K., Gros, D. F., Price, M., Zeigler, S., Tuerk, P. W., Foa, E. B., & Acierno, R. (2015). Randomized controlled trial of home-based telehealth versus in-person prolonged exposure for combat-related PTSD in veterans: Preliminary results. *Journal of Clinical Psychology, 71*(6), 500–512.

Zhai, Y. (2020). A call for addressing barriers to telemedicine: Health disparities during the COVID-19 pandemic. *Psychotherapy and Psychosomatics, 1.*

Zhou, X., Snoswell, C. L., Harding, L. E., Bambling, M., Edirippulige, S., Bai, X., & Smith, A. C. (2020). The role of telehealth in reducing the mental health burden from COVID-19. *Telemedicine and e-Health, 26*(4), 377–379.

Social Media and Clinical Practice

8

John Luo[a] and Kevin Ing[b]
[a]University of California at Irvine School of Medicine, Director of Emergency and Consultation-Liaison Psychiatry, UCI Medical Center, Health Sciences Clinical Department of Psychiatry & Human Behavior, Orange, CA, United States, [b]University of California Irvine School of Medicine, Department of Psychiatry & Human Behavior, Orange, CA, United States

Introduction

Social media has transformed how people utilize the Internet in a significant way. Today, checking one's social media account on Facebook, Instagram, Twitter, or on LinkedIn is part of a daily routine and for many it has displaced the morning newspaper. Social media has become more than just a tool to keep in touch with friends and family; it has become integral to both personal and professional activities. In fact, to eschew having any social media account is tantamount to embracing being called a "Luddite." Social media; mobile devices such as smartphones, tablets, and computers; and increasing availability and access to high-speed Internet both at home and on the road have become one integrated and all-consuming experience, and many today cannot fathom how they managed in the heyday of pencil and paper.

In the beginning of social media use around the late 1990s, it was clearly designed for consumer or public use. Facebook was started as a way for college students on campus to connect with one another in 2004. MySpace was at the time the most popular social media website, with tools to connect with friends and share things such as music. Professional or commercial use of social media has evolved over the years. Professional social media site LinkedIn was launched around the same time and grew to outpace other professional social media sites such as Within3, Sermo, and Google Orkut. In 2010, the American Association for Directors of Psychiatry Residency Training (AADPRT) programs developed a model curriculum to help medical school faculty to educate resident physicians and medical students about the appropriate use of social media by health professionals. At the time, there was a clear separation between personal and professional use. It has taken time for the health-care industry to become comfortable with adopting social media use professionally but now it has become standard practice and practically expected.

Background

Social media has its humble beginnings with the concept of Web 2.0 (O'Reilly, 2005). With Web 2.0, the Internet was no longer just a collection of websites but an opportunity to harness the knowledge of the masses. For example, Amazon with its product

Mental Health in a Digital World. https://doi.org/10.1016/B978-0-12-822201-0.00012-5

reviews posted by purchasers, has captured and refined user engagement as a sales tool in addition to providing a voice and opportunity. Many reviewers have been able to parlay their voice in reviewing products into a second career, much like the movie reviewer, food critic, and wine ratings. YouTube started out as a mechanism to share personal videos, and now has become both a personal and professional destination for entertainment as well as education. The key difference with Web 2.0 is that there are now platforms that promote all of this "content" beyond just hyperlinks from a website to another website. Adding the concept of "hashtags" from Twitter in addition to the long reach of search engines such as Google, social media has created an integrated world where everyone can share their thoughts, opinions, and a vast array of content such as web sites, photos, GIFs, and documents.

From the 2000s onwards, social media use has expanded from personal use to business use. There was initial hesitation in the medical community to commingle professional and personal use of the different social media platforms. The model curriculum developed by AADPRT has vignette and discussion points that highlight distinct boundaries of professional use. For example, some psychiatry residency training directors took the stance that they could not be "friends" with their trainees on social media platforms because of their employer-employee relationship. More definitive boundaries were the rule, including not establishing connections between provider and patient. However, the question of whether a physician colleague in the health system could also be a professional connection if the individuals also had a clinician-patient relationship tested these boundaries.

At first, professional social media use was limited to marketing and mostly mirrored content already available on the organization or practice website. For example, physician authors would use Twitter and Facebook to highlight their recent publication, but not the practice or professional services. In a parallel fashion, Facebook usage began to grow, in part due to games such as FarmVille (https://zynga.com/games/farmville-2/) that promoted social aspects of the game with gifts to friends, cooperative crafting tasks, and trading goods. Twitter became very popular to share opinions and tidbits of information, and local television news often presented Twitter posts of users comments on events. Facebook began to expand its reach by encouraging business use to reach customers, and likewise LinkedIn took on a more personal feel with the inclusion of posts and the ability to share and "like" them. Physician review platforms such as Healthgrades.com and Vitals.com began to grow in popularity, and likewise health-care providers, health-care systems, and organizations began to incorporate social media for brand awareness and to manage their reputation online. Over time, social media usage has become integrated into personal daily lives as well as being increasingly used for educational, clinical, and research purposes in health care.

Clinical Use

Physician Training, Medical Education, and Professional Development

Digital trends in recent years have elided the distinction between personal and professional social media use that existed in the early 2000s. Whereas original recommendations promoted a strict abstinence of professional social media use in order to avoid Health Information Portability and Accountability Act of 1996 aka HIPAA (Health Information Privacy, n.d.) violations or the crossing of boundaries with patients (e.g., revealing too much personal information), it is now the case that health-care providers and organizations have fully embraced social media use in professional practice. Many now forcefully argue that there is no longer a debate about whether or not health-care providers should engage on social networking sites; rather the question at hand is how these technologies may best be used for positive change (Inkster, Stillwell, Kosinski, & Jones, 2016).

Social media can be used to great effect in physician training and medical education (Cheston, Flickinger, & Chisolm, 2013). Microblogging platforms may be utilized as pedagogical tools to increase learner engagement and accessibility while responding to both real-time and asynchronous learner feedback. A teacher can use Twitter hashtags to create interactive content, poll students, and gather responses (Cheston et al., 2013; Forgie, Duff, & Ross, 2013). Blogs can promote professional virtues such as reflection, creativity, and collaboration (Diug, Kendal, & Ilic, 2016). For example, George and Dellasega demonstrate how Twitter-based and blog-based writing prompts support the process of graduate-level medical humanities education by enabling learners to engage in group-writing process, read and respond in real time, and connect students to subject experts (George & Dellasega, 2011). Through teleconferencing, trainees can "meet" experts around the world. Internet-based continuing medical education has been demonstrated to be effective (Wutoh, Boren, & Balas, 2004). In one study, the number of internet postings and engagement with social media teaching components correlates with final grades (Carvas, Imamura, Hsing, Dewey-Platt, & Fregni, 2010).

Top-ranking podcasts (e.g., MDedge Psychcast, Psychiatric Secrets Revealed, The Carlat Psychiatry Podcast, American Journal of Psychiatry Audio, Mad in America, Psychiatry & Psychotherapy Podcast, Psychopharmacology and Psychiatry Updates) disseminate mental health information to patients and clinicians alike throughout the world. This information may be of high quality, though there are also concerns about dissemination of incorrect information (see Chapter 9).

Patient Care and Advocacy

Patient education and advocacy is a primary role of the psychiatrist (Peters, Uible, & Chisolm, 2015). Some have argued that for clinicians in the Web 2.0 age, social media should be seen as an entrustable or day-to-day professional activity (Kind, 2014). Generally speaking, the literature suggests there is a difference between interacting directly with one's own patients versus advising and educating the general public or other individuals. While providers are generally recommended not to directly engage with their own patients through social media, the ethical question emerges of whether this may be seen as an act of omission given the rising landscape and responsibilities of global digital citizenry (Grajales 3rd et al., 2014). An analysis of 2000 randomly selected tweets from a collection of 14,701 suicide-related tweets found that 14% of these were "strongly concerning" for suicide (O'Dea et al., 2015). Others have suggested that digital platforms can be used to monitor substance abuse, behaviors, and mood states in real time, provide mental health information and improved provider-patient communication (Demartini et al., 2013). Guidelines for provider-patient communication revolving around suicidal ideation arguably remain ethically and legally ambiguous. Peters, Uible, and Chisolm recommend not entering into clinical discussions with individuals through Twitter, whether publicly or through private direct messaging (Peters et al., 2015). Rather they encouraged acting as a "good Samaritan" and referring the individual with thoughts of suicide to a local emergency department, as well as consider reporting to Twitter's internal mechanism for dealing with suicidal messages (https://support.twitter.com/forms/suicide).

Social media provides an opportunity to communicate with patients from their vantage point, in their own time and place (Decamp, 2013) At least 70%–80% of adults seek health information on the Internet and many patients seek psychiatric information on social media (Shepherd et al., 2015). Social media can provide free resources that patients can access at their own pace and discretion (Mehta & Atreja, 2015). Such widely available resources may increase access to basic health information, especially invaluable in low-resource settings for the purposes of rectifying inequities in global health (Leow et al., 2012). Such efforts can increase patients' awareness to standards of care (DeCamp, 2015).

Finally, by increasing social media presence, psychiatrists can help the public understand mental health problems and available resources and treatments. Psychiatrist can help to address biased and blatant misinformation found on the Internet in real time (Lafferty & Manca, 2015). The 24/7 news cycle offers a continuous stream of media opportunities to comment on current events, natural disasters, terrorist attacks, school shootings, racial and systemic injustices, and other issues pertaining to public mental health. An analysis of 176 million tweets from 2011 to 2014 demonstrates that there is a 48-h period after a suicide or depression-related news event during which the public expresses heightened interest to the topic of mental illness, providing a prime window of opportunity for psychiatrists to convey informed perspectives and to offer the public evidence and direction to reputable sources of information (McClellan, Ali, Mutter, Kroutil, & Landwehr, 2017). Psychiatrists also play an important role in communicating to social and economic institutions, politicians, and advocacy groups. Various advocacy groups such as the American Foundation for Suicide Prevention, Mental Health America, National Institute of Mental Health (NIMH), The Centers for Disease Control and Prevention (CDC), National Alliance on Mental Illness (NAMI), National Council for Behavioral Health, and Child Mind Institute are invaluable for public education, policy advocacy, and promoting fundraising and research efforts.

In the proper context, social media can also facilitate clinician-patient communication (Hawn, 2009). Tan and Goonawardene review how the proper use of internet health information can improve the physician-patient relationship, particularly when there is a "prior, positive relationship," when the internet information is directly discussed with the physician, such that the physician continues the traditional role of health educator (Tan & Goonawardene, 2017).

Patient Support Groups

In addition to psychiatrists' presence on social media, an increasing phenomenon is the presence of self-organized patient online networks (Mehta & Atreja, 2015). Over and against static information websites, patient networks are seen as more helpful and supportive due to their reciprocal feedback and collaborative, interactive nature. Individual patients are able to share their mental health journeys within a flexible and easily accessible, socially adaptive community. Such participation provides emotional support, reduces stigma, and increases health-seeking behaviors (Demartini et al., 2013). Clinicians and other professionals can also have a role in such patient-organized online support networks; however, professional comments must be timely, informative, and not superficial (Mehta & Atreja, 2015). Mehta and Atreja describe that ideally, these networks achieve a balance of flexibility vs security, anonymity vs authenticity, and openness vs moderation. Additionally, such groups must be "patient-centered... and patient-powered" while also encouraging health-care professional participation where appropriate (Mehta & Atreja, 2015).

Marketing and Networking

Social media plays an indisputable role in advertisement, marketing, and networking among clinical and health-care institutions. YouTube, Twitter, Facebook, and LinkedIn provide opportunities for health-care organizations, hospitals, and professional associations to exhibit their clinical services, humanitarian efforts, academical achievements, and various honors. Social media promotes professional networking (Giordano & Giordano, 2011). Many student- and doctor-dedicated social networking sites promote networking (e.g., studentdoctor.net, sermo.com, doximity.com, osmosis.org) (Table 8.1). The Facebook group Psychiatry Network at 11,300 members is the largest group of psychiatrists on Facebook and dedicated to discussing difficult cases, networking, advocacy efforts, as well as giving and receiving referrals throughout different geographic regions. A content analysis of 15,000 tweets in 58 health organizations illustrated that social-support-related tweets exchanged by health organizations can arranged in into: (1) informational (e.g., medical or health-related advice, guidance, news, findings), (2) emotional (e.g., encouragement, comfort, congratulations, praise, empathy, concern, gratitude), and (3) instrumental (e.g., giving a tangible aid) (Rui, Chen, & Damiano, 2013).

At least one in 40 scholars participate in "academic Twitter" for scholarly dialogue and mutual promotion and collaboration (Gregory & Singh, 2018). Liu, Beresin, and Chisolm discuss the advantages of such activity and offer guidance on the use of tweeting for networking purposes (Liu, Beresin, & Chisolm, 2019). For example, tweeting a conference hashtag when attending a national meeting can alert other attendees to one's attendance, rapidly identify one to other thought leaders and vice versa, and allow for direct interaction with speakers, celebrities, public figures, and advocates via replies, retweets, and direct messaging. Microblogging and blogging can be used to promote one's own career, lift up the accomplishments of colleagues and trainees, and amplify or show support for messages.

Physician Wellness

Social media provides opportunities for clinician social support, continuing medical education, and the promotion of professional virtues that contribute to wellness and

Table 8.1 Social media for networking in psychiatric organizations.

Organization	Twitter handle	Facebook	YouTube	Instagram	LinkedIn
Association of American Medical Colleges (AAMC)	@AAMCToday	https://www.facebook.com/aamctoday		https://instagram.com/aamctoday	https://www.linkedin.com/company/aamc
Accreditation Council for Graduate Medical Education (ACGME)	@acgme				https://www.linkedin.com/company/acgme
National Institute of Mental Health (NIMH)	@NIMHgov	http://www.facebook.com/nimhgov	http://www.youtube.com/nimhgov	https://www.instagram.com/nimhgov/	
National Institute of Drug Abuse (NIDA)	@NIDAnews	https://www.facebook.com/nih.gov	https://www.youtube.com/user/nihod	https://www.instagram.com/nihgov/	
Substance Abuse and Mental Health Services Administration (SAMHSA)	@samhsagov	https://www.facebook.com/samhsa	http://www.youtube.com/samhsa		
The New England Journal of Medicine (NEJM)	@NEJM	https://www.facebook.com/TheNewEnglandJournalofMedicine?	https://www.youtube.com/user/NEJMvideo	https://www.instagram.com/nejm/	https://www.linkedin.com/company/nejm-group
The Journal of the American Medical Association Psychiatry (JAMA Psychiatry)	@JAMAPsych	https://www.facebook.com/JAMAPsychiatry/	https://ja.ma/psyyt	https://www.instagram.com/jamanetwork/	https://www.linkedin.com/showcase/jamapsychiatry/
Elsevier Psychiatry	@els_psychiatry	https://www.facebook.com/ElsevierConnect	https://www.youtube.com/c/elsevier/		https://www.linkedin.com/company/elsevier
The American Journal of Psychiatry	@AmJPsychiatry	https://www.facebook.com/APAPublishing			https://www.linkedin.com/company/american-psychiatric-association/

Organization	Twitter	Facebook	YouTube	Instagram	LinkedIn
The Journal of the American Academy of Child & Adolescent Psychiatry (JAACAP)	@JAACAP	http://www.facebook.com/jaacap/			
American Psychiatric Association (APA)	@APAPsychiatric	https://www.facebook.com/AmericanPsychiatricAssociation		https://www.instagram.com/apapsychiatric/	https://www.linkedin.com/company/american-psychiatric-association/
American Society of Addiction Medicine (ASAM)	@ASAMorg	http://www.facebook.com/AddictionMedicine	http://www.youtube.com/addictionmedicine	https://www.instagram.com/asamorg/	https://www.linkedin.com/company/american-society-of-addiction-medicine/
American Academy of Child & Adolescent Psychiatry (AACAP)	@AACAP	https://www.facebook.com/pages/American-Academy-of-Child-Adolescent-Psychiatry/			
American Academy of Addiction Psychiatry (AAAP)	@AAAP1985	https://www.facebook.com/AAAP1985	https://www.youtube.com/channel/UCJotzGdUV-p2Jtsc5nkVzaQ	https://www.instagram.com/aaap1985/	https://www.linkedin.com/company/aaap
American Association For Geriatric Psychiatry (AAGP)	@GeriPsyc	http://www.facebook.com/pages/American-Association-for-Geriatric-Psychiatry-AAGP/			http://www.linkedin.com/company/american-association-for-geriatric-psychiatry

Sampling of social media use by professional psychiatric organizations.

reduction of burnout. Blogging has been shown to enhance clinical practice as well as promote thoughtful reflection upon difficult patient care scenarios (Lowney & O'Brien, 2012). Blogging can promote empathy and compassion (Fischer, Haley, Saarinen, & Chretien, 2011; Rosenthal et al., 2011). Blogging personal experiences also provides a unique opportunity to exhibit enthusiasm and passion for clinical care—characteristics that are essential to the skillsets of master clinicians (Christmas, Kravet, Durso, & Wright, 2008). Another study of third year medical students who participated in a humanism and professionalism course that included blog participation demonstrated no decline in empathy over the course of a yearlong clerkship, contrasting with previous studies that have shown decline in empathy over the course of the third year of medical school (Rosenthal et al., 2011). In another study, faculty-moderated course blogging was as effective in foster medical student reflective-writing skills as traditional formats of essay writing in small-group discussions (Fischer et al., 2011).

Treatment

The eliding of distinctions between profession and personal social media use raises the question of to what degree self-disclosure facilitates or hinders the therapeutic process with patients. Given the pervasiveness and accessibility of social media, a patient or would-be patient may have access to knowledge about a clinician's hobbies, music tastes, interests and pastimes, political leanings, family members, vacations, and as many personal details as have been made publicly available. Such knowledge may potentially lead to negative, split decisions. A patient may choose in a moment to not work with a physician for any number of reasons (e.g., personal details are misaligned) and thus decide to not work with a competent clinician for reasons unrelated to the clinician's potential effectiveness. Moreover, Applebaum and Kopelman raise concerns about "unreflective and excessive self-disclosure by psychiatrists," sometimes unwittingly (Appelbaum & Kopelman, 2014). While psychotherapy has shifted from the Freudian model of a "blank slate" therapist who never discloses any personal details, it is now widely agreed on that some level of personal disclosure may be appropriate, as long as this is rare, careful, and likely to have a positive therapeutic impact on the treatment process (Henretty & Levitt, 2010). However, online social media disclosures typically lack these characteristics. A psychiatrist may not even be aware of the extent of Internet disclosure and so unable to address such disclosure and its significance in the clinical encounter.

Sabin and Harland describe four major ethical challenges for the use of digital technologies in patient care: managing of clinical boundaries, maintaining privacy and confidentiality, establishing realistic expectations regarding digital communications, and upholding professional ideals (Sabin & Harland, 2017). New technologies offer both technical challenges (e.g., privacy settings and encryption) as well as psychological challenges (e.g., boundary confusion regarding the concept of "friending" on Facebook or unrealistic expectations about digital communication with a provider). In their summary of boundaries on clinical practice, Gabbard and Gutheil discuss a number of areas critical to the therapeutic process that can also be applied to the ethics of treatment in social media: roles, time, place, payment, and self-disclosure (Gutheil &

Gabbard, 1993). The landscape of social media invites new boundary-confusing challenges into the framework in which a therapeutic relationship is conducted. Sabin and Harland offer as an example the concept of how clinicians might respond to "friend requests" on Facebook (Sabin & Harland, 2017). Because responses are binary—one can either accept the request or deny it—any action undertaken has potential to confuse and introduce ambiguity into the relationship. An acceptance might be understood as the establishment of a "friendship" that supersedes the patient-therapist relationship; likewise a Facebook rejection might be understood as rejection of the patient as person, i.e., "my therapist doesn't like me." For these reasons, 85.8% of psychiatry residents when polled state that they just ignore such "friending" attempts from patients (Ginroy, Sabatier, & Eth, 2012). Rather, such scenarios should not be avoided, but regarded as opportunities to discuss and explore motivations for "friending" activity, and clarify misunderstandings. Discussion of such boundaries between patient and therapist may provide useful grist for the mill of helping the patient understand one's behavior and identity and a citizen of the digital age, navigating the relational ramifications of social media use in their rest of their life.

Zur offers a number of practical tips for exploring the range of clinical and relational dynamics at work in patient-therapist social media interaction and how they affect the therapeutic process (Zur, 2015). Professional boundaries should be regularly and consistently maintained and clarified whenever potential confusion occurs, and explicit protocols for emergencies should be discussed and preferably made explicit in a patient contract at the onset of treatment. Once a consistent online treatment presence has been established on social media, websites and platforms should be regularly reviewed and modified with most current updates for how online communication is best conducted (with attention paid to times when the clinician is not available). Despite potential ethical issues, social media technologies provide a useful tool for promoting mental health treatment and distributing accurate information, especially for technology-savvy younger generations that are familiar with searching for, finding, and sharing information online (Frankish, Ryan, & Harris, 2012).

Research

In health care, social media has recently become a focus of research studying its potential clinical efficacy as well as aspects of public health (see Chapter 6). A check of PubMed.gov on the search "social media" produced over 31,000 results, with more articles published every day. Many of these articles focus on the use of social media in health care as highlighted in this chapter. In addition, social media has been used for recruitment of participants in medical research studies. Recruitment of research subjects makes sense online as the pool of potential subject is deep as well as appropriate. However, much still needs to be determined with regards to the ethics of recruitment over social media as well as the maintaining of privacy for study participants. Patients with health conditions on social media are potentially quite vulnerable as many are on social media platforms for support as well as identifying treatments that may be more relevant and synchronous for their values in care. Without the intermediary health-care provider to facilitate whether a research study is relevant and to facilitate the discussion of potential benefits and risks, direct access to participants by study investigators puts a great deal of faith on the recruitment process. Nonetheless, patients online on social media platforms are a treasure trove for research regarding attitudes and awareness of medical information. For example, there is so much information openly shared by patients on health care-focused social media sites such as Patientslikeme. com. People share their symptoms, medications, types of treatment, as well as age of onset of symptoms and their demographics. Patients have participated in many published research studies such as how patients with mental health issues reported treatment history and tolerability, captured through the PatientsLikeMe survey tool correspond with genetic profiling (Patientslikeme Publications, n.d.).

Concerns

Privacy

Therapeutic trust in the relationship and the vital importance of patient confidentiality are crucial aspects of psychiatry. As such, concerns about privacy (for both the physician and the patient) may partially explain why psychiatry is a relatively late adopter of social media compared to other medical specialties (Chisolm, 2015). While the American Medical Association has published opinions recommending a strict separation of personal and professional use of social media (American Medical Association, 2011), such distinctions are increasingly impossible to achieve. An analysis of 700 tweets by health-care professionals found that 31% of tweets where of a personal nature and 70% were unrelated to one's job (Lee et al., 2014). Other voices recommend a more realistic approach of recognizing that nothing posted to the internet is truly private or personal. Rather, one should consider whether everything one might express on social media is in fact appropriate for a health-care professional (DeCamp, Koenig, & Chisolm, 2013). Grajales recommends four guiding principles to guide social media use at all times: (1) maintain professionalism at all times; (2) be authentic, have fun, and don't be afraid; (3) ask for help; and (4) focus, grab attention, and engage (Grajales 3rd et al., 2014). Regarding clinician privacy, physicians are recommended to activate all privacy settings, particularly of platforms with a more personal nature (e.g., Facebook) (Gabbard, Kassaw, & Perez-Garcia, 2011). For a patient, excess personal knowledge about one's psychiatrist can cloud the therapeutic process with a case of "TMI" ("too much information") (Petrow, 2014).

Additional ethical challenges revolve around efforts to maintain patient confidentiality and privacy. For example, the American Psychiatric Association has commented on the ethics of clinicians using Google, other search engines, and social media platforms to search for information about a patient (American Medical Association, 2016). When conducting such activities, clinicians do well to avoid hastily drawn conclusions from such searches. Information found on the internet may not be accurate, may reveal only a facet of information rather than a holistic portrayal, or may be misinterpreted when decontextualized from the original setting. Clinicians must thus be careful about the clinical utility of making inferences from patient social media information (Cox-George, 2015). Frankish, Ryan, and Harris make a distinction between three general groups of information found on the internet: (1) "public-public information" ("publicly available on the net that was obviously placed there with the purpose of it being accessed by anyone") found on online newspapers and accessible opinion blogs; (2) "private-public information" that is "publicly available but was clearly never intended for a general audience" (e.g., personal details found from accessing private and family photos and captions, comments and conversations on personal Facebook pages, entries from an defined online community); and (3) "private-private information," i.e., emails or direct message exchanges that have the same claims to full privacy as would be expected of any private paper letter exchange (Yan, 2009). While public-public information on social media bears the same marks of intended reach and audience as information found on any widely accessible public newspaper, private-public information would appear to be more analogous to overhearing a private exchange that took place while listening close to someone's porch or backyard or even clearly intentionally private conversation conducted in a public park: "It is generally regarded as wrong to access information that was clearly not intended as public information, whether it was accessible publicly or not (Frankish et al., 2012)." Of course, there may be extraordinary circumstances in which a breach of confidentiality of private-public information would be ethically permissible: An attempted overdose by a patient might constitute sufficient reason to view the suicide note left on his Facebook page if it were thought that his note contain information vital to the patient's treatment plan (Desai, Patwardhan, & Coore, 2014). Such circumstances are the exception to the rule. The authors conclude with clinician recommendations for conducting such search activity: Patient confidentiality should be maintained at all times and online searches for patient information should be done only out of intent to provide care as effectively as possible, preferably with their knowledge and consent (Frankish et al., 2012).

In recent years, Facebook has utilized artificial intelligence-empowered algorithms to identify whether posts can identify suicide risk (Anon, 2017). Such new suicide prevention efforts walk a fine line between maintaining data protection and privacy on the one hand, while fulfilling the societal obligations of responsible digital citizenry by mitigating unintended consequences of social media's impact, on the other hand.

Security

Whereas privacy is the safeguarding of user identity and related information, security involves the protection of unauthorized access to the data (https://www.hiv.gov/blog/difference-between-security-and-privacy-and-why-it-matters-your-program). Security is the responsibility of both the social media site and the individual user. People should follow general security guidelines to maintain the integrity of their social media account. First is the use of a password with sufficient difficulty to guess or generate randomly. Operating systems such as the Mac OS have built-in features to generate and secure passwords for website accounts. Password generators and management programs both online and on a smartphone application offer convenient access to the multitude of difficult-to-remember passwords. Many social media sites offer login alerts, which send an email or text to the user to identify when and where their account was accessed. Two-factor authentication is an additional layer of security that demands both something you know such as the password and something you have such as a hardware security token or time-limited access code sent via text. With the ease of use and temptation to use a Facebook or Gmail account as the login for many other website accounts, great caution should be exercised in deciding whether convenience outweighs higher level of security. It may be hazardous to allow third-party websites to have access to social media accounts without checking their privacy policy and security measures. Convenience versus security is a challenging decision to be made. However, with the potential damage that inappropriate access to social media accounts may bring, less convenience for more security should strongly be considered.

On the system side, social media companies are responsible for maintaining sufficient security measures such as encryption, physical security to their data centers, proper authentication, and log reviews of access to databases as well as vetting third-party data analytics firms. The United States presidential election in 2016 may have been influenced by targeted Facebook ads generated by psychological profiles created by Cambridge Analytica (Sherr, 2018). Cambridge Analytica acquired data from Alexsandr Kogan, who was conducting research on personality profiles with an app which asked users to log into their Facebook accounts. It asked for access to profiles, locations, and their friends' information as well, which allowed Cambridge Analytica to then create targeted ads to change political opinion of the 2016 US election as well as Brexit. Google account passwords have surfaced on cybercrime forums, which puts access to linked social media accounts at risk (Schwartz, 2014). While security is a responsibility of social media companies, account holders should check their accounts from time to time to discover if there is a breach, especially if due to the social media platform.

Reputation

The proliferation of social media has generated an evolving landscape that in many ways challenges the traditional approaches of respectability and authority when it comes to what constitutes an authority on a subject. The proliferation of news blogging and independent journalists raises challenges for legacy media institutions that once monopolized a corner on journalistic integrity and public perception as the sole source of legitimate information (Carlson, 2017; Hermida, 2012). In the predigital age, institutional access to expensive print and recording equipment, infrastructure, supply chains and distribution channels provided for the capacity to propagate materials and messages to a large audience. Thanks to widespread internet use, any individual with a smartphone now has the capacity to dispense information into the public with as theoretically wide a reach as the oldest and most respected institutions. This democratization of distributional power means that in a sense "anyone can become an expert," or at least, anyone can be perceived as one, as long as one's social media voice is large and loud enough to challenge traditional sense-making apparatuses. Any individual with a clear and persuasive delivery, respectable graphic design choices, and an understanding of how to manipulate search engine results and newsfeed trending algorithms can amass enough Twitter followers that it becomes difficult to distinguish her from a true expert in a particular subject matter. In this sense, the social media landscape may exert competitive pressures that select for the success of persons who may be experts in the skill set of social media use without equivalent medical expertise. Navigating this environmental feature will require a more observant and informed digital citizenry. Psychiatrists as advocates must respond to such challenges by equipping the populace to detect legitimately accurate voices from others. As such, a sufficient level of social media competence within the psychiatric profession is necessary to craft and curate a reputable online presence.

Traditionally, one's scholarly recognition and impact is largely measured by traditional metrics such as number of citations in peer-reviewed journals and the impact factors of those journals (Eysenbach, 2011). This track record of publications and citations is the current accepted measure of recognition and impact for advancement in academic medicine. It may take decades to build such an academic reputation and track record. However, such metrics of academic impact may miss important dynamics of impact in the social media era. Criteria for impact may need to be "reviewed and reimagined" for the digital age (Lafferty & Manca, 2015). In an environment where the ever-increasing amount of literature stands always to outpace its readers, a scholar who might not cite an article may bookmark, tweet it, or blog about it. Altmetrics ("alternative metrics" or "article level metrics") provide a means of measuring the impact and influence of such social media activities that would otherwise be missed by traditional metrics (Priem and Hemminger, 2010). These altmetrics consist of "relatively real-time measures of online dissemination" and include frequency of readings, times saved on reference managers, mentions, and discussions in media (Priem and Hemminger, 2010). Many have argued that these metrics may more accurately reflect past and current readership (Thelwall et al., 2013) as well as better predict future readership and citations (Desai et al., 2014; Djuricich, 2014; Piwowar, 2013). Different social media platforms and activities may correlate different with traditional measures: in an analysis of 2486 articles related to health profession education, blogging was associated with the greatest increase in citations (13%), while tweets were associated with an increase in citations of only 1.2% (Maggio, Leroux, Meyer, et al., 2018). Altmetrics have been dubbed measures of "disseminative impact" in contradistinction to "scholarly impact" (Trueger et al., 2015). Of course, if the online influence of one's work outweighs its scholarly import, potential negative downstream effects can be imagined. Social media is indisputably "an amplifier that raises the volume on a message, be it good or bad" (Thoma, 2015). Altmetrics are thus measures of *quantity* of attention (whether good or bad), if not necessarily *quality* of attention (Maggio, Meyer, & Artino, 2017). Nevertheless, altmetrics as measures of disseminative impact may perhaps be relevant measures of academic achievement and advancement in the field as well as important signposts of social and cultural importance. They may measure and predict levels of public engagement, advocacy, and outreach (Chisolm, 2017). As such, altmetrics are now being adopted and reported in numerous journals such as JAMA and Academic Medicine.

Addiction

Widespread social media in society has contributed to a number of problems with social media and its harmful effects in society. Social media addiction involves habitual or excessive use that may interfere with other life tasks and may be employed to escape negative moods (see other chapters in this volume on Internet addiction) (Ryan, Chester, Reece, & Xenos, 2014). Hariman et al. have commented on the negative impact of social media on public mental health (Hariman, Ventriglio, & Bhugra, 2019), particularly on (but not exclusive to) adolescents who are broadly influenced by what is seen online in ways that can lead to a number of mood and anxiety symptoms (Woods and Scott, 2016). A number of theories have been advanced for social media's harmful effects: overly negative comparisons with one's peers, poor sleep, influence on body image which may contribute to unrealistic and critical self-evaluation and self-hatred, derogatory speech, online bullying and "trolling" (Kelly, Zilanawala, Booker, & Sacker, 2018). In one systematic review of 10 studies of social media use disorder (SNUD) in Asia and particularly China, statistically significant associations have been found between SNUD and depression (Hussain, Wegmann, Yang, & Montag, 2020). Qzone is one of the most common social networking sites among Chinese adolescents with 517 million monthly active users as of July 16, 2020 (Data Reportal, 2020). Researchers have used Qzone to explore the mediating role of negative social comparison and the moderating roles of self-esteem, risk of depression, and increased social distress (Niu et al., 2018). There is evidence that the depressogenic effect is mediated by social media network interactions of rumination and corumination with peers, in which problems are extensively discussed and revisited and overly negative themes and feelings are intensified and exacerbated (Davila et al., 2012).

Other lines of research have explored the role of social media not only as tools with which we do something, but also tools that *do something to* us, particularly as instruments for shaping and transforming habits of human perception, thinking, and information foraging. In his Pulitzer Prize finalist *The Shallows*, Nicholas Carr explores the conclusion drawn from dozens of psychologists, neurobiologists, educators, and Web designers: "when we go online, we enter an environment that promotes cursory reading, hurried and distracted thinking, and superficial learning" (Carr, 2020, p. 118). Social media has the tendency to seize our attention, only to scatter it, leaving readers as "mindless consumers of data" (Carr, 2020, p. 125). And while there is nothing wrong with browsing and scanning (as humans have done with skimming of newspapers, books, and other print media for hundreds of years), ".... What is different, and troubling, is that skimming is becoming our dominant mode of reading" (Carr, 2020, p. 138). As Carr describes, "the strip-mining of 'relevant content' replaces the slow excavation of meaning" resulting in entire generations that have not had their powers of attention and slow deliberative thought process trained to resist the attention-dispersing tendencies of social media-driven information onslaught (Carr, 2020, p. 166). This implicit idea that technical efficiency of information exchange as the key to progress runs counterpoint to the wisdom of numerous other traditions, from the American transcendentalists to the earlier English Romantics, to Buddhist and Hindu philosophies or the ancient Stoics—all of whom agree that rather, true enlightenment or well-being comes through contemplation and introspection. As Seneca put it 2000 years ago: "To be everywhere is to be nowhere" Carr, 2020, p. 144). In this way, social media may contribute to a fractured, neoplatonized, and disorienting existence in which one's attention is increasingly diverted from the stabilizing forces and meaning-generating activities of slow deliberative thought and contemplation, human interaction, and community building. Such activities are vital for human development and stress resilience, and best occur through shared time, place, and physical contact and proximity with others.

Sociologist Pierre Bourdieu has commented on how microhabits of practice become "disciplinary formations that reconfigure and shape the world in which we live" and "the hidden persuasion of an implicit pedagogy… can instill a whole cosmology, through injunctions as insignificant as 'sit up straight' or 'don't hold your knife in your left hand'" (Bourdieu, 1990). The material rituals of physical manipulating and handling an iPhone are loaded with an implicit social imaginary. "To become habituated to an iPhone is to implicitly treat the world as 'available' to *me* and at my disposal—to constitute the world as 'at-hand' for me, to be selected, scaled, scanned, tapped, and enjoyed" (Smith, 2013). James Smith comments on the pedagogy hidden in this practice: unconsciously, we may expect the world to conform to our preferences in same way the digital world does through our smart devices. "I am the center of my own environments, and that which surrounds me exists *for* me. In short, my relation to my iPhone— which seems insignificant—is writ large as an iPhone-ized relation to *the world*, an iPhone-ization of my world(view)" (Smith, 2013). Even more so, this iPhone-ization of the world has amplified competitive self-display and self-consciousness to a paralyzing degree. Wallace points out the difference in the American generation born after 1955 as a generation shaped by the sense that "television is something to be *lived with*, not just looked at." Indeed, "We quite literally cannot 'imagine' life without [television]. As it does for so much of today's developed world, it presents and so defines our common experience; but we, unlike any elders, have no memory of a world without such electronic definition. It's built in" (Wallace, 1988). In the same way, social media augments this ever-present sense of all space as hypercompetitive mutual display and comparison. To be is to be seen. "We, the audience, receive unconscious reinforcement of the thesis that the most significant feature of persons is *watchableness*, and that contemporary human worth is not just isomorphic with but rooted in the phenomenon of watching" (Wallace, 1988). The ever-present sense of watchfulness intensifies self-consciousness and comparison, in a sense hyperactivating the intensely ruminative activities of the dorsal lateral prefrontal cortex in ways that render us susceptible to ruminative and overly negative cognitive tendencies.

Suicidologists have commented on the "double edged sword" nature of social media when it comes to suicide (Robert, Suelves, Armayones, & Ashley, 2015). Social media as an amplifying communicative tool has the potential to facilitate the Werther effect, a phenomenon in which news of a prominent or highly publicized suicide is distributed to others at risk and raises the feasibility of the taking one's life, resulting in copycat suicides and suicide clusters (Robinson et al., 2015). Yet, at the same time, social media may prove a source of potential identification and prevention of suicide. Machine-learning techniques suggest that markers of depression are observable in Instagram users' behaviors even before depression is clinically diagnosed (Reece & Danforth, 2017). Similar technologies with Twitter and Facebook have led to the development of algorithms that may help doctors become more aware of those at highest risk (Reece & Danforth, 2017; Gomes de Andrade, Pawson, Muriello, Donahue, & Guadagno, 2018; De Choudhury, Gamon, Counts, & Horvitz, 2013). Multiple suicidologists propose the use of artificial intelligence to determine high-risk messages on Twitter (Burnap, Colombo, & Scourfield, 2015), Weibo (Lv, Li, Liu, & Zhu, 2015), and Facebook (Thompson, Bryan, & Poulin, 2014). Finally, social media can be the source of amplifying the Papageno effect to help others overcome suicide crises (Notredame, Grandgenèvre, Vaiva, & Séguin, 2017; Notredame et al., 2018). Public health researchers have commented on creative uses of social networks to maximize the potential for suicide-preventive communication (Luxton, June, & Fairall, 2012). Educative professional suicide prevention websites increase suicide prevention-related knowledge and may be associated with a reduction in suicidal ideation among vulnerable individuals (Till, Tran, Voracek, et al., 2017).

Discussion

It is no longer a debate whether social media is to be used in the practice of medicine. This change in attitude is related to several driving forces. At first, there was caution and a desire to better understand the impact of technology much along the lines of recommendations in the late 1990s regarding e-mail communication with patients (Kane & Sands, 1998). Technology use in health care was not as prevalent back then, and communication primarily was via phone and facsimile. Understandably, the health-care industry and health-care providers treaded slowly into electronic communication adoption, and now with secure messaging portals via the electronic health record, voicemail has become less popular as a form of communication with a preference for secure messaging whether via e-mail, text, or messaging application. Along those lines, as both patients and the health-care industry have increasingly used technology in their daily lives, over time the reticence and barriers have shifted. Internet access and the availability of vast amounts of health-care information as well as tools to communicate with one another as well as interact with such information has transformed the practice of medicine. Paper has given way to electronic medical records, and the newspaper has been displaced by social media for news and entertainment.

Additionally, time and the ubiquity of technology have helped to drive this change. Desktop computers have mostly given way to laptop computers and tablets. Personal digital assistants are no longer the rage and smartphones are now in the hands of practically all generations young and old. The rise of social media use as a central hub for communication and discovery of information has led to new career options as brand ambassadors and influencers. The knowledge of the masses and the interactivity of the Internet have been fully embraced as people have found that the platform of social media has led to profound changes in how we interact with the world and one another.

Likewise, the practice of health care has begun to adopt and adapt social media plat-forms beyond use predominantly as a marketing platform.

Education, peer support, research, and direct care via social media have become the extension in the delivery and access of health care that the public now demands. Health-care providers, organizations, and systems are now embracing social media for professional use as well. While boundaries still exist, they are quietly shifting with the tide of information, access, and connectivity that social media offers. In turn, health-care providers have embraced social media for their own wellness, to conduct advocacy via Twitter and Instagram, and study its use by patients for scholarly activity in the form of research for publication and presentation. Providers have often used professional medical education vendors to facilitate explanation for procedures, but now can create their own videos and host them on their YouTube channel. Posts from a Twitter feed not only serve as marketing, but help establish a reputation for advocacy, expertise in treatment, as well as improving professional reputation as a well-rounded and erudite clinician.

As reviewed above, the boundary and ethics of social media use in medical practice are still evolving. Many psychiatrists and mental health providers are now comfort-able with their patients having their mobile phone number provided there are clearly established expectations regarding availability and escalation in times of emergency. Educating the patient about the privacy risks of texting is important and it is also critical to refrain from returning such text unless there has been a signed consent and agreement regarding the potential privacy risk. Using the direct messaging feature of social media platforms is not advised for patient-provider communication due to privacy concerns as well as the risk of boundary crossings given the typical blend of both professional and personal use on these social media platforms. Monitoring a patient's post on social media is not only burdensome to the provider, but may impact the patient-provider relationship with content on social media not meant for discus-sion in session. These issues of privacy and appropriate use of social media tools in patient care continue to evolve over time as new norms and practice expectations are established.

Conclusion

It is difficult to imagine a world nowadays without computing devices and the Internet. Certainly, in rural parts of multiple countries there are many citizens who do not have a smartphone and Internet access. However, the landscape of mo-bile devices and Internet access is constantly improving in speed and availability. Social-media use is certainly contingent on the developing pervasiveness of these interactivity and communication tools. It has helped craft a sense of connected-ness to one another and to information, and it is exciting to see the potential that social media has to transform delivery of health-care education, patient care, and communication across the globe. Social media has great promise to improve the understanding of mental illness in society and finally break down the stigma that surrounds it.

References

American Medical Association. 2011 Opinion 9.124—professionalism in the use of social media. [cited 2015 June]; Available from: http://www.ama-assn.org/ama/pub/physician-resources/medical-ethics/code-medical-ethics/opinion9124.page.

American Psychiatric Association. (2016). *Opinion A.1.h. in Opinions of the Ethics Committee on the principles of medical ethics: With annotations especially applicable to psychiatry: 2017 Edition*. Retrieved 4/15/2017 from http://www.psychiatry.org/psychiatrists/practice/ethics.

Anon. (2017). Editorial. You have a new friend request. *Lancet, 389*, 983.

Appelbaum, P. S., & Kopelman, A. (2014). Social media's challenges for psychiatry. *World Psychiatry, 13*(1), 21.

Bourdieu, P. (1990). *The logic of practice* (p. 69). Stanford University Press.

Burnap, P., Colombo, W., & Scourfield, J. (2015). *Machine classification and analysis of suicide-related communication on twitter* (pp. 75–84). New York, NY: ACM Press. https://doi.org/10.1145/2700171.2791023.

Carlson, M. (2017). *Journalistic authority: Legitimating news in the digital era*. Columbia University Press.

Carr, N. (2020). *The shallows: What the internet is doing to our brains*. WW Norton & Company.

Carvas, M., Imamura, M., Hsing, W., Dewey-Platt, L., & Fregni, F. (2010). An innovative method of global clinical research training using collaborative learning with Web 2.0 tools. *Medical Teacher, 32*, 270.

Cheston, C. C., Flickinger, T. E., & Chisolm, M. S. (2013). Social media use in medical education. *Academic Medicine, 88*(6), 893–901. https://doi.org/10.1097/ACM.0b013e31828ffc23.

Chisolm, M. S. (2015). Social media in medicine: The volume that twitter built. *International Review of Psychiatry, 27*(2), 83–84.

Chisolm, M. S. (2017). Altmetrics for medical educators. *Academic Psychiatry, 41*, 460–466. https://doi.org/10.1007/s40596-016-0639-3.

Christmas, C., Kravet, S. J., Durso, S. C., & Wright, S. M. (2008). Clinical excellence in academia: Perspectives from masterful academic clinicians. *Mayo Clinic Proceedings, 83*, 989–994.

Cox-George, C. (2015). The changing face(book) of psychiatry: Can we justify 'following' patients' social media activity? *BJPsych Bulletin, 39*, 283–284.

Data Reportal. (2020). *Global Social Media Overview*. https://datareportal.com/social-media-users#:~:text=QZone%20has%20517%20million%20monthly%20active%20users. (Accessed 29 July 2020).

Davila, J., Hershenberg, R., Feinstein, B. A., Gorman, K., Bhatia, V., & Starr, L. R. (2012). Frequency and quality of social networking among young adults: Associations with depressive symptoms, rumination, and corumination. *Psychology of Popular Media Culture, 1*(2), 72–86. https://doi.org/10.1037/a0027512.

De Choudhury, M., Gamon, M., Counts, S., & Horvitz, E. (2013, June). Predicting depression via social media. In *Proc Seventh Int AAAI Conf Weblogs Soc Media*. https://www.aaai.org/ocs/index.php/ICWSM/ICWSM13/paper/vie.

Decamp, M. (2013). Physicians, social media, and conflict of interest. *Journal of General Internal Medicine, 28*(2), 299–303.

DeCamp, M. (2015). Ethical issues when using social media for health outside professional relationships. *International Review of Psychiatry, 27*(2), 97–105.

DeCamp, M., Koenig, T. W., & Chisolm, M. S. (2013). Social media and physicians' online identity crisis. *Journal of the American Medical Association, 310*(6), 581–582.

Demartini, T. L., et al. (2013). Access to digital technology among families coming to urban pediatric primary care clinics. *Pediatrics, 132*(1), e142–e148.

Desai, T., Patwardhan, M., & Coore, H. (2014). Factors that contribute to social media influence within an internal medicine Twitter learning community. *F1000Res, 3*, 120.

Diug, B., Kendal, Y., & Ilic, D. (2016). Evaluating the use of twitter as a tool to increase engagement in medical education. *Education and Health, 29*(3), 223–230.

Djuricich, A. M. (2014). Social media, evidence-based tweeting, and JCEHP. *The Journal of Continuing Education in the Health Professions, 34*(4), 202–204.

Eysenbach, G. (2011). Can tweets predict citations? Metrics of social impact based on twitter and correlation with traditional metrics of scientific impact. *Journal of Medical Internet Research, 13*(4), e123.

Fischer, M. A., Haley, H.-. L., Saarinen, C. L., & Chretien, K. C. (2011). Comparison of blogged and written reflections in two medicine clerkships. *Medical Education, 45*, 166–175.

Forgie, S. E., Duff, J. P., & Ross, S. (2013). Twelve tips for using twitter as a learning tool in medical education. *Medical Teacher, 35*(1), 8–14.

Frankish, K., Ryan, C., & Harris, A. (2012). Psychiatry and online social media: Potential, pitfalls and ethical guidelines for psychiatrists and trainees. *Australasian Psychiatry, 20*(3), 181–187. https://doi.org/10.1177/1039856212447881.

Gabbard, G. O., Kassaw, K. A., & Perez-Garcia, G. (2011). Professional boundaries in the era of the internet. *Academic Psychiatry, 35*, 168–174.

George, D. R., & Dellasega, C. (2011). Use of social media in graduate-level medical humanities education: Two pilot studies from Penn State College of Medicine. *Medical Teacher, 33*, e429–e434.

Ginroy, A., Sabatier, L. M., & Eth, S. (2012). Addressing therapeutic boundaries in social networking. *Psychiatry, 75*, 40–48.

Giordano, C., & Giordano, C. (2011). Health professions students' use of social media. *Journal of Allied Health, 40*, 78–81.

Gomes de Andrade, N. N., Pawson, D., Muriello, D., Donahue, L., & Guadagno, J. (2018). Ethics and Artificial intelligence: Suicide prevention on Facebook. *Philosophy & Technology, 31*, 669–684.

Grajales, F. J., 3rd, et al. (2014). Social media: A review and tutorial of applications in medicine and health care. *Journal of Medical Internet Research, 16*(2), e13.

Gregory, K., & Singh, S. S. (2018). Anger in academic Twitter: Sharing, caring and getting mad online. *TripleC, 16*(1), 176–193. Available at: https://www.triple-c.at/index.php/tripleC/article/view/890/1102. Social Media Skills for Professional Development 491.

Gutheil, T. G., & Gabbard, G. O. (1993). The concept of boundaries in clinical practice: Theoretical and risk-management dimensions. *The American Journal of Psychiatry, 150*(2), 188–196. https://doi.org/10.1176/ajp.150.2.188.

Hariman, K., Ventriglio, A., & Bhugra, D. (2019). The future of digital psychiatry. *Current Psychiatry Reports, 21*, 88. https://doi.org/10.1007/s11920-019-1074-4.

Hawn, C. (2009). Take two aspirin and tweet me in the morning: How twitter, Facebook, and other social media are reshaping health care. *Health Affairs (Millwood), 28*, 361–368.

Health Information Privacy. (n.d.). Retrieved February 6, 2021, from https://www.hhs.gov/hipaa/index.html.

Henretty, J. R., & Levitt, H. M. (2010). The role of therapist self-disclosure in psychotherapy: A qualitative review. *Clinical Psychology Review, 30*, 63–77.

Hermida, A. (2012). Tweets and truth: Journalism as a discipline of collaborative verification. *Journalism Practice, 6*(5–6), 659–668.

Hussain, Z., Wegmann, E., Yang, H., & Montag, C. (2020). Social networks use disorder and associations with depression and anxiety symptoms: A systematic review of recent research in China. *Frontiers in Psychology, 11*, 211.

Inkster, B., Stillwell, D., Kosinski, M., & Jones, B. (2016). A decade into Facebook: Where is psychiatry in the digital age? *Lancet Psychiatry*, *3*, 1087–1090.

Kane, B., & Sands, D. Z. (1998). Guidelines for the clinical use of electronic mail with patients. The AMIA Internet Working Group, task force on guidelines for the use of clinic-patient electronic mail. *Journal of the American Medical Informatics Association*, *5*(1), 104–111. https://academic.oup.com/jamia/article/5/1/104/766196.

Kelly, Y., Zilanawala, A., Booker, C., & Sacker, A. (2018). Social media use and adolescent mental health: Findings from the UK Millennium Cohort Study. *EClinicalMedicine*, *6*, 59–68. Elsevier Ltd; Available from https://doi.org/10.1016/j.eclinm.2018.12.005.

Kind, T. (2014). Social media milestones: Entrusting trainees to conduct themselves responsibly and professionally. *Journal of Graduate Medical Education*, *6*(1), 170–171.

Lafferty, N. T., & Manca, A. (2015). Perspectives on social media in and as research: A synthetic review. *International Review of Psychiatry*, *27*(2), 85–96.

Lee, J. L., et al. (2014). What are health-related users tweeting? A qualitative content analysis of health-related users and their messages on twitter. *Journal of Medical Internet Research*, *16*(10), e237.

Leow, J. J., et al. (2012). Social media in low-resource settings: A role for twitter and Facebook in global surgery? *Surgery*, *151*(6), 767–769.

Liu, H. Y., Beresin, E. V., & Chisolm, M. S. (2019). Social media skills for professional development in psychiatry and medicine. *The Psychiatric Clinics of North America*, *42*(3), 483–492. https://doi.org/10.1016/j.psc.2019.05.004.

Lowney, A. C., & O'Brien, T. (2012). The landscape of blogging in palliative care. *Palliative Medicine*, *26*, 858–859.

Luxton, D. D., June, J. D., & Fairall, J. M. (2012). Social media and suicide: A public health perspective. *American Journal of Public Health*, *102*, S195–S200. https://doi.org/10.2105/AJPH.2011.300608.

Lv, M., Li, A., Liu, T., & Zhu, T. (2015). Creating a Chinese suicide dictionary for identifying suicide risk on social media. *PeerJ*, *3*. https://doi.org/10.7717/peerj.1455, e1455.

Maggio, L. A., Leroux, T. C., Meyer, H. S., et al. (2018). #MedEd: Exploring the relationship between altmetrics and traditional measures of dissemination in health professions education. *Perspectives on Medical Education*, *7*, 239–247. https://doi.org/10.1007/s40037-018-0438-5.

Maggio, L. A., Meyer, H. S., & Artino, A. R. (2017). Beyond citation rates: A real-time impact analysis of health professions education research using altmetrics. *Academic Medicine*, *92*(10), 1449–1455.

McClellan, C., Ali, M. M., Mutter, R., Kroutil, L., & Landwehr, J. (2017). Using social media to monitor mental health discussions— evidence from twitter. *Journal of the American Medical Informatics Association*, *24*(3), 496–502.

Mehta, N., & Atreja, A. (2015). Online social support networks. *International Review of Psychiatry*, *27*(2), 118–123.

Niu, G. F., Luo, Y. J., Sun, X. J., Zhou, Z. K., Yu, F., Yang, S. L., et al. (2018). Qzone use and depression among Chinese adolescents: A moderated mediation model. *Journal of Affective Disorders*, *231*, 58–62.

Notredame, C. E., Grandgenèvre, P., Pauwels, N., Morgiève, M., Wathelet, M., Vaiva, G., et al. (2018). Leveraging the web and social media to promote access to care among suicidal individuals. *Frontiers in Psychology*, *9*, 1338.

Notredame, C.-E., Grandgenèvre, P., Vaiva, G., & Séguin, M. (2017). At least one more reason why. *European Child & Adolescent Psychiatry*, *27*, 259–260. https://doi.org/10.1007/s00787-017-1033-8.

O'Dea, B., et al. (2015). Detecting suicidality on twitter. *Internet Interventions*, *2*, 183–188.

O'Reilly, T. (2005). *What is Web 2.0*. https://www.oreilly.com/pub/a/web2/archive/what-is-web-20.html.

Patientslikeme Publications. Available at https://patientslikemebibliography.s3.amazonaws.com/PLM_Research_Manuscripts_Bibliography.pdf.

Peters, M. E., Uible, E., & Chisolm, M. S. (2015). A twitter education: Why psychiatrists should tweet. *Current Psychiatry Reports*, *17*(12), 94.

Petrow, S. (2014). When psychiatrists are on Facebook, their patients can get a case of TMI. *The Washington Post*. Available at https://www.washingtonpost.com/national/health-science/when-psychiatrists-are-on-facebook-their-patients-can-get-a-case-of-tmi/2014/08/25/ed31e522-110a-11e4-9285-4243a40ddc97_story.html?utm_term=.e13fcc210f53. (Accessed April 11, 2017).

Piwowar, H. (2013). Altmetrics: Value all research products. *Nature*, *493*(7431), 159.

Priem, J., & Hemminger, B. M. (2010). *Scientometrics 2.0: Towards new metrics of scholarly impact on the social web*. [cited 2015 June 21]; Available from: http://firstmonday.org/ojs/index.php/fm/artic.

Reece, A. G., & Danforth, C. M. (2017). Instagram photos reveal predictive markers of depression. *EPJ Data Science*, *6*, 1–12. [internet]. The author(s). Available from https://doi.org/10.1140/epjds/s13688-017-0110-z.

Robert, A., Suelves, J. M., Armayones, M., & Ashley, S. (2015). Internet use and suicidal behaviors: Internet as a threat or opportunity? *Telemed E Health*, *21*, 306–311. https://doi.org/10.1089/tmj.2014.0129.

Robinson, J., Cox, G., Bailey, E., Hetrick, S., Rodrigues, M., Fisher, S., et al. (2015). Social media and suicide prevention: A systematic review. *Early Intervention in Psychiatry*, *10*, 103–121. https://doi.org/10.1111/eip.12229.

Rosenthal, S., Howard, B., Schlussel, Y. R., Herrigel, D., Smolarz, B. G., Gable, B., et al. (2011). Humanism at heart: Preserving empathy in third-year medical students. *Academic Medicine*, *86*, 350–358.

Rui, J. R., Chen, Y., & Damiano, A. (2013). Health organizations providing and seeking social support: A twitter-based content analysis. *Cyberpsychology, Behavior and Social Networking*, *16*(9), 669–673.

Ryan, T., Chester, A., Reece, J., & Xenos, S. (2014). The uses and abuses of Facebook: A review of Facebook addiction. *Journal of Behavioral Addictions*, *3*(3), 133–148.

Sabin, J. E., & Harland, J. C. (2017). Professional ethics for digital age psychiatry: Boundaries, privacy, and communication. *Current Psychiatry Reports*, *19*, 55. https://doi.org/10.1007/s11920-017-0815-5.

Schwartz, M. (2014). 5 Million Google Passwords Leaked. https://www.bankinfosecurity.com/5-million-google-passwords-leaked-a-7299.

Shepherd, A., et al. (2015). Using social media for support and feedback by mental health service users: Thematic analysis of a twitter conversation. *BMC Psychiatry*, *15*, 29.

Sherr, I. (2018). Facebook, Cambridge Analytica and data mining: What you need to know. https://www.cnet.com/news/facebook-cambridge-analytica-data-mining-and-trump-what-you-need-to-know/.

Smith, J. K. (2013). Imagining the kingdom (cultural liturgies): How worship works. *Baker Books*, *143*.

Tan, S. S. L., & Goonawardene, N. (2017). Internet health information seeking and the patient-physician relationship: A systematic review. *Journal of Medical Internet Research*, *19*(1), e9. http://www.jmir.org/2017/1/e9/. https://doi.org/10.2196/jmir:5729. 28104579.

Thelwall, M., et al. (2013). Do altmetrics work? Twitter and ten other social web services. *PLoS One*, *8*(5), e64841.

Thoma, B. (2015). Personal reflections on exploring social media in medicine. *International Review of Psychiatry*, *27*(2), 161–166.

Thompson, P., Bryan, C., & Poulin, C. (2014). Predicting military and veteran suicide risk: Cultural aspects. In *Proceedings of the workshop on computational linguistics and clinical psychology: From linguistic signal to clinical reality, Baltimore, MD* (pp. 1–6). https://doi.org/10.3115/v1/W14-3201.

Till, B., Tran, U. S., Voracek, M., et al. (2017). Papageno vs Werther effect online: Randomized controlled trial of beneficial and harmful impacts of educative suicide prevention websites. *British Journal of Psychiatry*, *211*, 109–115.

Trueger, N. S., et al. (2015). The Altmetric Score: A new measure for article-level dissemination and impact. *Annals of Emergency Medicine*. Alternative metrics capture "disseminative impact." Although this may or may not correlate with "scholarly impact," the proprietary Altmetrics™ score is increasingly being adopted and reported by journals such as JAMA and Academic Medicine (http://altmetrics.org/manifesto). One can track the Altmetrics™ score of one's articles at http://www.altmetric.com/bookmarklet.php.

Wallace, D. F. (1988). Fictional futures and the conspicuously young. *Review of Contemporary Fiction*, *8*(3), 36–53. quoted in *Imagining the Kingdom*, 146.

Woods, H. C., & Scott, H. (2016). Sleepyteens: Social media use in adolescence is associated with poor sleep quality, anxiety, depression and low self-esteem. *Journal of Adolescence [Internet]*, *51*, 41–49. Academic Press; [cited 2019 May 29]. Available from: https://www.sciencedirect.com/science/article/pii/S0140197116300343.

Wutoh, R., Boren, S. A., & Balas, E. A. (2004). eLearning: A review of internet-based continuing medical education. *The Journal of Continuing Education in the Health Professions*, *24*, 20–30.

Yan, J. (2009). Psychiatrists must beware of the perils of cyberspace. *Psychiatric News*, 9.

Zur, O. (2015). To accept or not to accept? How to respond when clients send "Friend Request" to their psychotherapists or counselors on social networking sites. Available at http://www.zurinstitute.com/socialnetworking.html. (Accessed April 10, 2017).

Websites and the validity of mental health care information

Nicola Reavley, Luwishennadige M.N. Fernando, and Anthony Jorm
Centre for Mental Health, Melbourne School of Population and Global Health, University of Melbourne, Melbourne, VIC, Australia

As many as 65%–80% of adults in high-income countries use websites as their primary source of health information. US surveys conducted between 2003 and 2012 showed that the use of the Internet to access health information steadily increased (Prestin, Vieux, & Chou, 2015), although there are concerns about whether access is increasing equitably across populations. Older people and those with lower levels of education are less likely to access health information online (Alvarez-Galvez et al., 2020). Increasing smartphone access in developing economies has also led to growing use of the Internet to obtain health information (Pew Research Center, 2019).

Web-based information on mental health conditions is provided by governments, non-profit organizations, corporations, and private individuals. In February 2021, a Google search for "depression information" returned 366,000,000 hits in 0.74 s. As searches can be anonymous, the Internet may be a particularly attractive option for people seeking information about stigmatized health conditions, including mental health conditions (Berger, Wagner, & Baker, 2005). A recent systematic review found that, on average, 1 in 3 university students searched the Internet for mental health-related information and 1 in 10 students accessed an online mental health support platform (Montagni et al., 2020). A German study of psychiatric patients showed that just over 70% used the Internet to access mental health-related information (Kalckreuth, Trefflich, & Rummel-Kluge, 2014), most often to search for information about medication (44%), to search for mental health services (39%), to communicate with other patients in forums and chats (20%), or to communicate with mental health professionals (17%).

Given that the Internet has become a widely used source of information on mental disorders, it is essential to understand the quality of available information. This is likely to be particularly important in the "fake news" or "post-truth" era, in which misinformation, generated intentionally or unintentionally, spreads rapidly (Lewandowsky, Ecker, & Cook, 2017). While misinformation about health and scientific issues has always existed, the recent rapid growth of social media, which enables almost instantaneous communication, has increased the trend. Accurate information about complex issues, such as mental illness and its treatments, may be easily ignored in favor of sensationalized news (Wang et al., 2019). Thus, the spread of false, inaccurate, or incomplete information on mental health conditions may decrease the likelihood of help seeking, adherence to treatment interventions, and may increase the risk of harm,

Mental Health in a Digital World. https://doi.org/10.1016/B978-0-12-822201-0.00009-5

particularly in younger people, who are at higher risk of mental health conditions, and are also more frequent users of social media (Gupta & Ariefdjohan, 2020).

This chapter seeks to explore the quality of online mental health information. It is based on systematic reviews of the quality of online information on mental health conducted in 2011 and 2020 (Fernando & Reavley, 2020; Reavley & Jorm, 2011). The earlier review found that the overall quality of mental disorder information available online was poor, except for that on affective disorders which showed trends toward improvement over time. The findings reported here largely draw on those of the 2020 review.

Quality assessment methods

A broad range of methods and measures have been used to assess the quality of health information online. Quality is variously defined but typically includes ratings of completeness, credibility, accuracy, bias, and assessments of readability. Some methods require expert rating while others are automated, including Google's PageRank, which takes into account incoming links, and is based on volume and quality, ranking positions for websites and corresponding keywords (Strzelecki, 2020). There is also an increasing interest in the use of algorithms to automate ratings previously done by humans, although there is some evidence that this is not particularly effective (Allam, Schulz, & Krauthammer, 2017).

However, there is limited consensus on reliability, validity, and utility of these measures. A review of 98 different measures for rating the quality of health information online concluded that there were persistent issues with interrater reliability and construct validity (Gagliardi & Jadad, 2002). The most widely used instrument is the DISCERN rating tool (Charnock et al., 1999), a standardized instrument consisting of 16 questions covering relevance, source, bias, treatment choices, and overall quality of written information. The DISCERN has been shown to be a reliable and valid indicator of website quality in some studies (Ademiluyi, Rees, & Sheard, 2003; Griffiths & Christensen, 2005) but not others (Dueñas-Garcia et al., 2015; Cerminara et al., 2014) and has been criticized as a subjective measure that captures the completeness of presented information rather than its accuracy (Beaunoyer et al., 2017). It is therefore possible to get a high rating on "quality" on the DISCERN even in the presence of misinformation.

Some studies evaluated the accuracy of information using content checklists (Grohol, Slimowicz, & Granda, 2014; Hardy & Sillence, 2016). Grohol et al. (2014) demonstrated strong correlations (ranging from 0.78 to 0.89) between general website quality as measured by the DISCERN, and accuracy of content-specific information. However, in their review of information on premenstrual dysphoric disorder, Hardy and Sillence (2016) found that general website quality was not a good indicator of completeness or accuracy of information.

Several quality assessment studies involved the development of custom tools for website evaluation by combining variables from multiple existing measures (Athanasopoulou et al., 2016; Guardiola-Wanden-Berghe et al., 2011) or developing new rating systems (Alnemary et al., 2017; Nour et al., 2017). These typically involved varying combinations of measures of credibility of sources (Athanasopoulou et al., 2016; Robillard & Feng, 2017), accuracy of information (Nour et al., 2017), and completeness of content (Montoya et al., 2013). However, the reliability and validity of these tools was mostly left unexplored.

Studies that explored readability of website content consistently found reading ages set at a grade 11 level or above (Grohol et al., 2014; Ma et al., 2017; Reynolds, Walker, & Walsh, 2015), which is considered "difficult." Only one study explored usability of information (Kirby et al., 2018), that is, whether consumers of diverse backgrounds and varying levels of health literacy could comprehend key messages and identify specific actions that they could take (Shoemaker, Wolf, & Brach, 2014). This study showed that even when websites provide high quality, understandable information, actionability may still be limited.

Types of mental disorders

Neurodevelopmental disorders

Studies have assessed the quality of information on neurodevelopmental disorders on websites in English (Akram et al., 2008; Kisely, Ong, & Takyar, 2003; Reichow, Shefcyk, & Bruder, 2013; Thapa et al., 2018), Arabic (Alnemary et al., 2017), Spanish (Montoya et al., 2013), and German (Kamp-Becker et al., 2020). Three studies reported findings on ADHD (Montoya et al., 2013; Reichow et al., 2013; Thapa et al., 2018) and five on autism (Alnemary et al., 2017; Grant, Rodger, & Hoffmann, 2015; Kamp-Becker et al., 2020; Reichow, 2012; Reichow et al., 2013).

Across both disorders most studies found that the quality of Internet information was low or insufficient (Alnemary et al., 2017; Kamp-Becker et al., 2020; Reichow, 2012; Thapa et al., 2018) although a study that involved evaluation of the quality of information on multiple developmental disabilities found that the quality of information on ADHD, Autism, intellectual disability, and learning disorders was high (Reichow et al., 2013). Grohol et al. (2014) found the overall quality of ADHD information to be fair across 40 websites while Grant et al. (Reichow, 2012) found the overall quality of autism information to be fair across 20 sites (DISCERN M = 46.5).

Mood and anxiety disorders

In general, mood disorder websites are more likely to contain higher quality information than anxiety disorder websites. Grohol et al. (2014) assessed the quality of mental health information on 11 mental disorders and found that websites for schizophrenia, bipolar disorder, dysthymia, PTSD, and depression contained good-quality information (based on DISCERN ratings) while websites for social phobia, attention deficit hyperactivity disorder (ADHD), generalized anxiety disorder (GAD), and panic disorder contained fair quality information. The earlier review identified 10 studies assessing the quality of information on depression, with a trend of increasing quality seen in later studies (Berland et al., 2001; Christensen, Griffiths, & Medway, 2000; Ferreira-Lay & Miller, 2008; Griffiths et al., 2005; Griffiths & Christensen, 2000, 2002, 2005; Lissman & Boehnlein, 2001; Stjernsward & Ostman, 2007; Zermatten et al., 2010). Higher quality information tended to come from websites of government, professional, and charitable organizations (Ferreira-Lay & Miller, 2008; Lissman & Boehnlein, 2001). Studies assessing the quality of information on antidepressant drugs found that information on pharmaceutical company sites was of lower quality (Morgan & Montagne, 2011). Overall, the quality of information on e-commerce websites selling St John's Wort was rated as low (Thakor et al., 2011).

Five studies included in the earlier review assessed information on anxiety disorders or trauma, with most concluding that information quality was poor. These included information on a range of anxiety disorders (Ipser, Dewing, & Stein, 2007), social phobia (Khazaal et al., 2008a), and Dutch language information on obsessive compulsive disorder (OCD) (Serdobbel, Pieters, & Joos, 2006). In a more recent study, Klila et al. (2013) assessed the quality of information on OCD and concluded that this was relatively good.

A study of the quality of websites providing information on psychological trauma showed that such information was often not useful, and sometimes inaccurate and potentially harmful (Bremner et al., 2006).

Five later studies evaluated Internet information on mood and anxiety disorders, three of which had a focus on parents and parenting-related topics, including perinatal anxiety (Kirby et al., 2018), postnatal mental health (Moore & Ayers, 2011), and treatment choices for parents on child anxiety (Reynolds et al., 2015). Websites on the topic of postnatal mental health generally provided insufficient or incomplete information (Kirby et al., 2018; Moore & Ayers, 2011). Other topics included premenstrual dysphoric disorder (Hardy & Sillence, 2016), for which the specific information was considered incomplete or insufficient.

A study comparing user-contributed mental health-related information on Wikipedia with centrally controlled information sources, as rated by experts, concluded that the quality of information on depression on Wikipedia is generally as good as, or better than, that provided by centrally controlled websites, Encyclopedia Britannica, and a psychiatry textbook (Reavley et al., 2012a).

Bipolar disorder

Three studies assessed quality of information on bipolar disorder, with two studies assessing English language information and concluding that the overall quality of information was good (Barnes et al., 2009; Morel et al., 2008) and another drawing similar conclusions from assessing German language information (Seyringer et al., 2007).

Substance use

Four studies included in the earlier review assessed the quality of information on substance misuse, with all concluding that information quality was poor. They included studies of French language information on alcohol dependence (Coquard et al., 2011;

Coquard, Fernandez, & Khazaal, 2008), cannabis addiction (Khazaal et al., 2008b), and cocaine addiction (Khazaal et al., 2008c). A study by US college online alcohol policy information concluded that information accessibility had improved between 2002 and 2007 (Faden et al., 2002).

Eating disorders

Earlier studies assessing online information on eating disorders revealed that the overall quality of information was of poor or variable quality and did not adequately address diagnostic criteria or treatment options (Guardiola-Wanden-Berghe et al., 2011; Murphy et al., 2004; Perdaens & Pieters, 2011; Smith et al., 2011a). Guardiola-Wanden-Berghe, Sanz-Valero, and Wanden-Berghe (2010) assessed content quality and the relationship with authorship and/or affiliation in blogs covering the topic of eating disorders. Their results showed that indication of authorship (as opposed to anonymity) and affiliation to an institution were associated with higher quality.

Later studies have also shown information to be of fair (Arts, Lemetyinen, & Edge, 2020) or poor quality (Guardiola-Wanden-Berghe et al., 2011; Hernández-Morante et al., 2015), with a recent study finding the presence of misinformation around diagnostic criteria and treatment choices on a number of sites (Smith et al., 2011b). Hernández-Morante et al. (2015) found that Internet information on bulimia nervosa was of superior quality to information on anorexia nervosa but this was not replicated in other studies.

Schizophrenia

Two studies included in the earlier review assessed the quality of information on schizophrenia/psychosis. The first assessed the quality of information on schizophrenia treatment and concluded that accountability, presentation, and readability were poor (Kisely et al., 2003). A later study of information on German websites found that evidence-based medical information was provided by more than half of the sites resulting from the search term "schizophrenia" and by less than one-third of "psychosis" hits (Schrank et al., 2006). Greek and Finnish websites were found to have low-quality information when assessed for accountability and completeness of content (Athanasopoulou et al., 2016). In contrast, Guada and Venable (2011) found that for-profit sites provided good-quality information on schizophrenia while the information on not-for-profit sites was of average quality. The study comparing user-contributed mental health-related information on Wikipedia with centrally controlled information sources also concluded that the quality of information on schizophrenia on Wikipedia is generally as good as, or better than, that provided by centrally controlled websites, Encyclopaedia Britannica, and a psychiatry textbook (Reavley et al., 2012a).

Other disorders

Insomnia websites provided good-quality information but there was variability across sites (Ma et al., 2017). Quality of online information on Alzheimer's disease prevention was variable (Robillard & Feng, 2017). While high-quality websites presented information on modifiable risk factors adopting a balanced tone, low-quality websites tended to emphasize nutrition as a method of prevention, endorse products and services, and make strong recommendations (Robillard & Feng, 2017).

Individual websites with high-quality information

Even in instances in which the overall quality of Internet information was poor across a certain topic, individual websites that contained high-quality information were identified. For example, even though the general quality of treatment information on ADHD was low, the national library of medicine website contained high-quality information (Montoya et al., 2013). Similarly, even though perinatal anxiety was not covered adequately in most websites, Beyond Blue Australia was rated as providing good-quality information (Kirby et al., 2018). Table 9.1 provides a list of websites recommended by study authors that may facilitate patient education.

Websites in languages other than English

Although studies in languages other than English were limited on websites, where available the overall quality was found to be low for Spanish (Hernández-Morante et al., 2015; Montoya et al., 2013), Arabic (Alnemary et al., 2017), German (Kamp-Becker et al., 2020), and Greek and Finish (Athanasopoulou et al., 2016).

Highly rated sites

A number of the studies listed the top-rated websites for the topic area. For studies carried out since 2012, these are given in Table 9.1. They can be used as a guide for consumers searching for high-quality information.

Quality of mental disorder information on social media

A small number of studies have assessed the quality of mental health information presented on YouTube. One focused on ADHD (Thapa et al., 2018) and the other on schizophrenia (Nour et al., 2017). The study of schizophrenia-related content found that this was often inaccurate, overemphasizing persecutory delusions and negative symptoms (Nour et al., 2017). A study of ADHD-related content showed that few had useful information (Thapa et al., 2018).

Longitudinal changes in website quality

Guada and Venable (2011) assessed the quality of Internet information on schizophrenia from 2009 to 2010 and found minimal changes in quality ratings. Reynolds et al. (2015) explored changes to website quality at two time points over a 5-year period

Table 9.1 Websites as recommended by study authors with quality and readability information where available.

Topic	Websites
Child anxiety treatment choices for parents	Association of behavioral and cognitive therapies Anxiety and Depression Association of America Anxiety UK Canadian Mental Health Association-British Columbia Worrywise kids http://www.worrywisekids.org/
Perinatal anxiety websites recommended by Kirby et al. (2018)	Beyond blue (Australia) Oregon.gov (USA) Tommy's.org (GBR)
ADHD treatment websites recommended by Montoya et al. (2013)	National Library of Medicine
Anorexia Nervosa	Royal College of Psychiatrists British Medical Journal Best Practice **Very well mind** Mayo clinic
Schizophrenia Websites as shown in Guada and Venable (2011)	WebMD Schizophrenia MedicineNet: Schizophrenia Psych Central: Schizophrenia and Psychosis *E*-Medicine: Schizophrenia http://emedicine.medscape.com/article/805988- overview MayoClinic.com: Schizophrenia http://www.mayoclinic.com/health/schizophrenia/DS00196
Premenstrual dysphoria information websites as recommended by Hardy and Sillence (2016)	Cleveland Clinic Journal of Medicine Medscape National Centre for Biotechnology Information Up to date WebMD
Postnatal mental health websites for mothers as recommended by Moore and Ayers (2011)	Panda.org postpartum.net Baby blues connection Royal College of Psychiatrists
Postnatal mental health websites for health-care professionals as recommended by Moore and Ayers (2011)	Postpartum health alliance Postpartum support Virginia
Insomnia websites as recommended in Ma et al. (2017)	Medscape Reference Mayo Clinic Wikipedia eMedicineHealth National Sleep Foundation

from 2008 to 2013 and found that only 6 out of 26 websites had updated content. In an attempt to assess the effect of feedback on website quality improvement, Jorm, Fisher, and Oh (2010) scored 52 suicide prevention websites against expert consensus guidelines. Half the websites received feedback on how to improve the sites and half did not. Websites were evaluated again 6 months later. However, feedback did not lead to improvement.

Summary

Evidence suggests that across categories of neurodevelopmental disorders, eating disorders, psychotic disorders, and mood and anxiety disorders, it is more common for the quality of information on mental disorders websites to be rated poor or insufficient. However, the quality of available information varies according to mental health condition, with websites giving information on mood disorders that are generally of higher quality than those giving information about other conditions. While information on mood disorders seems to have improved, variability in methodology and measurement tools across studies mostly makes it difficult to draw conclusions about changes in website quality over time.

Since the original review in 2011, there has been a drop in the total number of studies evaluating quality of Internet information on mental disorders. However, given the relatively low quality identified in this review, there is a need for ongoing efforts to improve this, given that the quality has not kept pace with the volume of available Internet information. The methodology used by Grohol et al. (2014) that involved evaluating the first 20 search results for multiple disorders simultaneously may represent an efficient way of quickly assessing quality and highlighting areas where deeper investigation is needed.

There has been a shift in focus from studies of mood disorders toward studies of the quality of online information about ADHD and autism spectrum disorder, particularly in contents aimed at parents (Montoya et al., 2013; Reichow et al., 2013; Thapa et al., 2018). This has likely occurred in parallel with the increased interest and public discourse around these conditions (Frances & Batstra, 2013). There has also been increased parental awareness and involvement in early intervention (Oono, Honey, & McConachie, 2013; Zwi et al., 2011) and previous studies have shown that parents commonly use the Internet as source of information but may feel overwhelmed or confused by the information obtained (Gibson, Kaplan, & Vardell, 2017). Given the relatively low quality of online information on these conditions, parents may require more specific guidance in accessing accurate and useful information.

Credibility of information continues to be an important aspect of quality assessments. The studies reviewed here attempted to capture this construct using ratings of ownership, authorship, attributions, and presence of HonCode certification (a code of conduct developed by the Health on the Net Foundation). In the context of evidence that consumers may give more weight to expert endorsement of website information over testimonies of those with lived experience, greater emphasis could be placed on such endorsements (Mcinnes & Haglund, 2011; Scanlan et al., 2017).

Across the studies reviewed, the relatively high average reading scores (Walsh & Volsko, 2008) suggests that website providers may be struggling to produce high-quality mental disorder information that is accessible to less educated readers. Greater efforts should be made to address this in order not to increase the digital divide and resulting inequalities in access to health information (Beaunoyer et al., 2017).

Future research should place greater emphasis on the "usability" aspects of health information quality (Shoemaker et al., 2014), extending beyond conventional constructs of completeness, accuracy, and credibility of information and explore whether consumers with diverse backgrounds and health literacy are able to comprehend key messages conveyed based on factors such as content, language, visual material, and layout (understandability) and take specific actions based on the information encountered (actionability). The Patient Education Material Assessment Tool (PEMAT) provides a reliable measure of understandability and actionability of information that may be worth routinely incorporating into website evaluation toolkits. Only one study cited here explored understandability and actionability of information using the PEMAT (Kirby et al., 2018) and found this to be poor even in websites with high levels of content quality.

However, as the goal of much health education is behavioral change, it can be argued that the extent to which a website applies recognized behavior change theories is an indicator of quality that has largely been ignored in the research. Very few studies have assessed links with behavior. A small number of older studies examining the links between Internet use and help seeking has provided mixed results, with one study showing that providing information about depression improved symptoms on the depression scale (Christensen et al., 2006), while another study showed that visits to an adolescent mental health website was associated with visits to school's health centers (Santor et al., 2007).

There is therefore a need for further research on identifying consumers of mental health information on the Internet and how the various aspects of quality affect health behavior such as help seeking and use of evidence-based treatments. Such research should consider factors uniquely relevant to the Internet such as privacy, usability, and accessibility.

Future assessments of quality might use criteria informed by key behavior change theories. A possible approach to this might be to develop an evaluation framework incorporating strategies from behavior change models [such as the Health Belief Model, Theory of Reasoned Action and Planned Behavior, Transtheoretical (Stages of Change) Model and Social Learning Theory], key mental health literacy elements, and health outcomes relevant to mental health promotion. This has parallels in the recent calls for a shift from thinking mental health literacy to mental health action or "action that individuals or groups take to benefit their own mental health or that of others" (Jorm, 2020).

Mental health website quality assessment could be extended to cover the extent to which sites meet the evaluation criteria arising out of such a framework and might include naturalistic reports of user behavior (Frost et al., 2008; Sillence et al., 2007). Such assessments might involve the development of innovative ways of assessing health-related behaviors and outcomes. The move toward greater interactivity, information sharing, and collaboration on the Internet may offer such opportunities.

Information on social media

Social media has become an increasingly significant online venue for the exchange of health-related information and advice, with social media platforms such as TikTok, Twitter, and Instagram increasingly being harnessed to convey public health message (Basch, Hillyer, & Jaime, 2020) and for mental health advocacy (Koteyko & Atanasova, 2018). This raises particular issues in relation to information quality and trustworthiness. Two studies that evaluated mental disorder content on YouTube reported incomplete and potentially misleading information (Nour et al., 2017; Thapa et al., 2018). Studies of the quality of a broad range of health information on online discussion forums show mixed results with Wikipedia generally receiving higher trustworthiness ratings than Facebook or Twitter (Reavley et al., 2012b; Zhao & Zhang, 2017). Other studies suggest that health forums produce information on reasonable quality, although it depends on the topic and relatively little attention has been focused on mental health (Cole, Watkins, & Kleine, 2016).

Two studies that reviewed mental disorder information on YouTube, concluding that the information (on either schizophrenia or ADHD) was generally of poor quality, with the former emphasizing persecutory delusions (Nour et al., 2017). This presents risks relating to the promotion of stigmatizing attitudes to people with diagnoses of mental illness, to which media portrayals of dangerousness contribute (Reavley, Jorm, & Morgan, 2016). While guidelines exist for coverage of mental illness and suicide in a number of countries, with a notable example being the Mindframe guidelines in Australia (https://mindframe.org.au/industry-hubs/for-media), there is relatively little research on how these may be used to improve information quality on social media, although recent efforts to help young people communicate safely about suicide on social media offer a potential way forward (Robinson et al., 2018). Further research is needed to understand the quality of mental disorder information on social media platforms. Tools for evaluating social media content may need to specifically consider the audio-visual nature of the material as well as emotional tone.

Implications for practice

Given the overall low quality of mental disorder information available online, health professionals should be aware that consumers may have accessed incomplete or erroneous information prior to help seeking. Misinformation may need to be identified and corrected and accurate information may need to be provided, including that from the websites identified in this review as providing good-quality information which may be helpful for patient education. For consumers who do not have at least a grade 10 reading level, additional resources may be needed. A widely held assumption based on prior research is that consumers seeking health information would only visit the first 10 websites that appear in search results (Eysenbach & Kohler, 2002). Interestingly, Reynolds and colleagues' study (Reynolds et al., 2015) found that the highest quality information might not be found in the first 10 website ranked by google. Therefore, both researchers and consumers may need to be encouraged to look beyond the first page of search results when accessing mental disorder information.

The poor quality of information on mental health conditions on the Internet raises concerns about the potential for misinformation to contribute to delays in treatment seeking, accessing harmful or ineffective treatments, poor engagement with treatments, and perpetuation of stigma. This potential is an even greater concern in relation to mental health information on social media.

Such concerns are obviously not limited to mental health conditions and there have been a number of calls to combat health-related misinformation online involving (a) improving e-health literacy, (b) encouraging consumers to use Internet collaboratively with clinicians, (c) signaling credibility and endorsement by experts clearly, (d) creating and distributing better quality online information, (e) actively correcting misinformation more frequently, and (f) educating clinicians and patients about particularly reliable and comprehensive websites (Swire-Thompson & Lazer, 2020).

Conclusion

The Internet continues to be a widely used resource to access mental health information. However, the overall low quality of online mental disorder information, with the possible exception of that for mood disorders, raises concerns that consumers may be receiving an incomplete or inaccurate picture of their disorder of interest or concern. Ongoing evaluations of website quality are needed to ensure that consumers are empowered with accurate and usable information. Evaluation of the quality of mental disorder information available on social media is an emerging field that may warrant further efforts in the development of methodology.

References

Ademiluyi, G., Rees, C. E., & Sheard, C. E. (2003). Evaluating the reliability and validity of three tools to assess the quality of health information on the internet. *Patient Education and Counseling, 50*(2), 151–155.

Akram, G., et al. (2008). Characterisation and evaluation of UK websites on attention deficit hyperactivity disorder. *Archives of Disease in Childhood, 93*(8), 695–700.

Allam, A., Schulz, P. J., & Krauthammer, M. (2017). Toward automated assessment of health web page quality using the DISCERN instrument. *Journal of the American Medical Informatics Association, 24*(3), 481–487.

Alnemary, F. M., et al. (2017). Characteristics of Arabic websites with information on autism. *Neurosciences (Riyadh), 22*(2), 143–145.

Alvarez-Galvez, J., et al. (2020). The persistence of digital divides in the use of health information: A comparative study in 28 European countries. *International Journal of Public Health, 65*(3), 325–333.

Arts, H., Lemetyinen, H., & Edge, D. (2020). Readability and quality of online eating disorder information—Are they sufficient? A systematic review evaluating websites on anorexia nervosa using DISCERN and Flesch readability. *The International Journal of Eating Disorders, 53*(1), 128–132.

Athanasopoulou, C., et al. (2016). Attitudes towards schizophrenia on YouTube: A content analysis of Finnish and Greek videos. *Informatics for Health & Social Care*, *41*(3), 307–324.

Barnes, C., et al. (2009). Review of the quality of information on bipolar disorder on the internet. *The Australian and New Zealand Journal of Psychiatry*, *43*(10), 934–945.

Basch, C. H., Hillyer, G. C., & Jaime, C. (2020). COVID-19 on TikTok: Harnessing an emerging social media platform to convey important public health messages. *International Journal of Adolescent Medicine and Health*. https://doi.org/10.1515/ijamh-2020-0111. Published online: August 11 2020.

Beaunoyer, E., et al. (2017). Understanding online health information: Evaluation, tools, and strategies. *Patient Education and Counseling*, *100*(2), 183–189.

Berger, M., Wagner, T. H., & Baker, L. C. (2005). Internet use and stigmatized illness. *Social Science & Medicine*, *61*(8), 1821–1827.

Berland, G. K., et al. (2001). Health information on the internet: Accessibility, quality, and readability in English and Spanish. *JAMA*, *285*(20), 2612–2621.

Bremner, J. D., et al. (2006). Surfing the net for medical information about psychological trauma: An empirical study of the quality and accuracy of trauma-related websites. *Medical Informatics and the Internet in Medicine*, *31*(3), 227–236.

Cerminara, C., et al. (2014). Use of the DISCERN tool for evaluating web searches in childhood epilepsy. *Epilepsy & Behavior*, *41*, 119–121.

Charnock, D., et al. (1999). DISCERN: An instrument for judging the quality of written consumer health information on treatment choices. *Journal of Epidemiology and Community Health*, *53*(2), 105–111.

Christensen, H., Griffiths, K. M., & Medway, J. (2000). Sites for depression on the web: A comparison of consumer, professional and commercial sites. *Australian and New Zealand Journal of Public Health*, *24*(4), 396–400.

Christensen, H., et al. (2006). The effect of web based depression interventions on self reported help seeking: Randomised controlled trial [ISRCTN77824516]. *BMC Psychiatry*, *6*, 13.

Cole, J., Watkins, C., & Kleine, D. (2016). Health advice from internet discussion forums: How bad is dangerous? *Journal of Medical Internet Research*, *18*(1), e4.

Coquard, O., Fernandez, S., & Khazaal, Y. (2008). Assessing the quality of French language web sites pertaining to alcohol dependency. *Santé Mentale au Québec*, *33*(2), 207–224.

Coquard, O., et al. (2011). A follow-up study on the quality of alcohol dependence-related information on the web. *Substance Abuse Treatment, Prevention and Policy*, *6*, 13.

Dueñas-Garcia, O. F., et al. (2015). Patient-focused websites related to stress urinary incontinence and pelvic organ prolapse: A DISCERN quality analysis. *International Urogynecology Journal*, *26*(6), 875–880.

Eysenbach, G., & Kohler, C. (2002). How do consumers search for and appraise health information on the world wide web? Qualitative study using focus groups, usability tests, and in-depth interviews. *BMJ*, *324*(7337), 573–577.

Faden, V. B., Corey, K., & Baskin, M. (2009). An evaluation of college online alcohol-policy information: 2007 compared with 2002. *Journal of Studies on Alcohol and Drugs. Supplement*, (16), 28–33.

Fernando, L. M. N., & Reavley, N. J. (2020). *How good is internet information about mental disorders? A systematic review (submitted)*.

Ferreira-Lay, P., & Miller, S. (2008). The quality of internet information on depression for lay people. *Psychiatric Bulletin*, *32*, 170–173.

Frances, A., & Batstra, L. (2013). Why so many epidemics of childhood mental disorder? *Journal of Developmental and Behavioral Pediatrics*, *34*(4), 291–292.

Frost, J. H., et al. (2008). How the social web supports patient experimentation with a new therapy: The demand for patient-controlled and patient-centered informatics. *American Medical Informatics Association Annual Symposium Proceedings*, 217–221.

Gagliardi, A., & Jadad, A. R. (2002). Examination of instruments used to rate quality of health information on the internet: Chronicle of a voyage with an unclear destination. *BMJ*, *324*(7337), 569–573.

Gibson, A. N., Kaplan, S., & Vardell, E. (2017). A survey of information source preferences of parents of individuals with autism spectrum disorder. *Journal of Autism and Developmental Disorders*, *47*(7), 2189–2204.

Grant, N., Rodger, S., & Hoffmann, T. (2015). Evaluation of autism-related health information on the web. *Journal of Applied Research in Intellectual Disabilities*, *28*(4), 276–282.

Griffiths, K. M., & Christensen, H. (2000). Quality of web based information on treatment of depression: Cross sectional survey. *BMJ*, *321*(7275), 1511–1515.

Griffiths, K. M., & Christensen, H. (2002). The quality and accessibility of Australian depression sites on the World Wide Web. *Med J Aust*, *176*(Suppl), S97–S104.

Griffiths, K. M., & Christensen, H. (2005). Website quality indicators for consumers. *J Med Internet Res*, *7*(5), e55.

Griffiths, K. M., et al. (2005). Automated assessment of the quality of depression websites. *Journal of Medical Internet Research*, *7*(5), e59.

Grohol, J. M., Slimowicz, J., & Granda, R. (2014). The quality of mental health information commonly searched for on the internet. *Cyberpsychology, Behavior and Social Networking*, *17*(4), 216–221.

Guada, J., & Venable, V. (2011). A comprehensive analysis of the quality of online health-related information regarding schizophrenia. *Health & Social Work*, *36*(1), 45–53.

Guardiola-Wanden-Berghe, R., Sanz-Valero, J., & Wanden-Berghe, C. (2010). Eating disorders blogs: Testing the quality of information on the internet. *Eating Disorders*, *18*(2), 148–152.

Guardiola-Wanden-Berghe, R., et al. (2011). Evaluating the quality of websites relating to diet and eating disorders. *Health Information and Libraries Journal*, *28*(4), 294–301.

Gupta, R., & Ariefdjohan, M. (2020). Mental illness on Instagram: a mixed method study to characterize public content, sentiments, and trends of antidepressant use. *Journal of Mental Health*, 1–8.

Hardy, C., & Sillence, E. (2016). What are women being exposed to? A review of the quality, content and ownership of websites on premenstrual dysphoric disorder. *Womens Health Issues*, *26*(2), 183–189.

Hernández-Morante, J. J., et al. (2015). Analysis of information content and general quality of obesity and eating disorders websites. *Nutrición Hospitalaria*, *32*(2), 606–615.

Ipser, J. C., Dewing, S., & Stein, D. J. (2007). A systematic review of the quality of information on the treatment of anxiety disorders on the internet. *Current Psychiatry Reports*, *9*(4), 303–309.

Jorm, A. F. (2020). We need to move from "mental health literacy" to "mental health action". *Mental Health and Prevention*, *18*, 200179. https://doi.org/10.1016/j.mhp.2020.200179.

Jorm, A. F., Fisher, J., & Oh, E. (2010). Effect of feedback on the quality of suicide prevention websites: Randomised control trial. *Br J Psychiatry*, *197*(1), 73–74.

Kalckreuth, S., Trefflich, F., & Rummel-Kluge, C. (2014). Mental health related Internet use among psychiatric patients: a cross-sectional analysis. *BMC Psychiatry*, *14*, 368.

Kamp-Becker, I., et al. (2020). Blessing or curse? The world wide web as information source for autism and Asperger syndrome. *Zeitschrift für Kinder- und Jugendpsychiatrie und Psychotherapie*, *48*(2), 133–143.

Khazaal, Y., et al. (2008a). Quality of web-based information on social phobia: A cross-sectional study. *Depression and Anxiety*, *25*(5), 461–465.

Khazaal, Y., et al. (2008b). Quality of web-based information on cannabis addiction. *Journal of Drug Education*, *38*(2), 97–107.

Khazaal, Y., et al. (2008c). Quality of web-based information on cocaine addiction. *Patient Education and Counseling*, *72*(2), 336–341.

Kirby, P. L., et al. (2018). Evaluating the quality of perinatal anxiety information available online. *Archives of Women's Mental Health*, *21*(6), 813–820.

Kisely, S., Ong, G., & Takyar, A. (2003). A survey of the quality of web based information on the treatment of schizophrenia and attention deficit hyperactivity disorder. *The Australian and New Zealand Journal of Psychiatry*, *37*(1), 85–91.

Klila, H., et al. (2013). Quality of web-based information on obsessive compulsive disorder. *Neuropsychiatric Disease and Treatment*, *9*, 1717–1723.

Koteyko, N., & Atanasova, D. J. D. (2018). *Context, and media, mental health advocacy on twitter: Positioning in depression awareness week tweets*.

Lewandowsky, S., Ecker, U. K. H., & Cook, J. (2017). Beyond misinformation: Understanding and coping with the "Post-Truth" era. *Journal of Applied Research in Memory and Cognition*, *6*, 353–369.

Lissman, T. L., & Boehnlein, J. K. (2001). A critical review of internet information about depression. *Psychiatric Services*, *52*(8), 1046–1050.

Ma, Y., et al. (2017). Quality and readability of online information resources on insomnia. *Frontiers in Medicine*, *11*(3), 423–431.

Mcinnes, N., & Haglund, B. J. (2011). Readability of online health information: implications for health literacy. *Inform Health Soc Care*, *36*(4), 173–189.

Montagni, I., et al. (2020). Mental health-related digital use by university students: A systematic review. *Telemedicine Journal and E-Health*, *26*(2), 131–146.

Montoya, A., et al. (2013). Evaluating internet information on attention-deficit/hyperactivity disorder (ADHD) treatment: Parent and expert perspectives. *Education for Health (Abingdon, England)*, *26*(1), 48–53.

Moore, D., & Ayers, S. (2011). A review of postnatal mental health websites: Help for healthcare professionals and patients. *Archives of Women's Mental Health*, *14*(6), 443–452.

Morel, V., et al. (2008). Quality of web-based information on bipolar disorder. *Journal of Affective Disorders*, *110*(3), 265–269.

Morgan, M., & Montagne, M. (2011). Drugs on the internet, part II: Antidepressant medication web sites. *Substance Use and Misuse*, *46*(13), 1628–1641.

Murphy, R., et al. (2004). An evaluation of web-based information. *The International Journal of Eating Disorders*, *35*(2), 145–154.

Nour, M. M., et al. (2017). Schizophrenia on YouTube. *Psychiatric Services*, *68*(1), 70–74.

Oono, I. P., Honey, E. J., & McConachie, H. (2013). Parent-mediated early intervention for young children with autism spectrum disorders (ASD). *Cochrane Database Syst Rev*, (4), CD009774.

Perdaens, S., & Pieters, G. (2011). Eating disorders on the internet. A review of the quality of Dutch websites. *Tijdschrift voor Psychiatrie*, *53*(10), 695–703.

Pew Research Center. (2019). *Mobile connectivity in emerging economies*. Washington, DC: Pew Research Center.

Prestin, A., Vieux, S. N., & Chou, W. Y. (2015). Is online health activity alive and well or Flatlining? Findings from 10 years of the health information National Trends Survey. *Journal of Health Communication*, *20*(7), 790–798.

Reavley, N. J., & Jorm, A. F. (2011). The quality of mental disorder information websites: A review. *Patient Education and Counseling*, *85*(2), e16–e25.

Reavley, N. J., Jorm, A. F., & Morgan, A. J. (2016). Beliefs about dangerousness of people with mental health problems: The role of media reports and personal exposure to threat or harm. *Social Psychiatry and Psychiatric Epidemiology*, *51*(9), 1257–1264.

Reavley, N. J., et al. (2012a). Quality of information sources about mental disorders: A comparison of Wikipedia with centrally controlled web and printed sources. *Psychological Medicine*, *42*(8), 1753–1762.

Reavley, N. J., et al. (2012b). Quality of information sources about mental disorders: A comparison of Wikipedia with centrally controlled web and printed sources. *Psychological Medicine*, *42*(8), 1753–1762.

Reichow, B., et al. (2012). Characteristics and quality of autism websites. *J Autism Dev Disord*, *42*(6), 1263–1274.

Reichow, B., Shefcyk, A., & Bruder, M. B. (2013). Quality comparison of websites related to developmental disabilities. *Research in Developmental Disabilities*, *34*(10), 3077–3083.

Reynolds, K. A., Walker, J. R., & Walsh, K. (2015). How well do websites concerning children's anxiety answer parents' questions about treatment choices? *Clinical Child Psychology and Psychiatry*, *20*(4), 555–569.

Robillard, J. M., & Feng, T. L. (2017). Health advice in a digital world: Quality and content of online information about the prevention of Alzheimer's disease. *Journal of Alzheimer's Disease*, *55*(1), 219–229.

Robinson, J., et al. (2018). The #chatsafe project. Developing guidelines to help young people communicate safely about suicide on social media: A Delphi study. *PLoS One*, *13*(11), e0206584.

Santor, D. A., et al. (2007). Online health promotion, early identification of difficulties, and help seeking in young people. *Journal of the American Academy of Child and Adolescent Psychiatry*, *46*(1), 50–59.

Scanlan, F., et al. (2017). Treatment choices for depression: Young people's response to a traditional e-health versus a Health 2.0 website. *Digit Health*, *3*, 2055207617690260.

Schrank, B., et al. (2006). Schizophrenia and psychosis on the internet. *Psychiatrische Praxis*, *33*(6), 277–281.

Serdobbel, Y., Pieters, G., & Joos, S. (2006). Obsessive compulsive disorder and the internet. An evaluation of Dutch-language websites and quality indicators. *Tijdschrift voor Psychiatrie*, *48*(10), 763–773.

Seyringer, M. E., et al. (2007). Bipolar disorder and manic-depressive disorder on the internet. *Neuropsychiatrie*, *21*(2), 172–178.

Shoemaker, S. J., Wolf, M. S., & Brach, C. (2014). Development of the patient education materials assessment tool (PEMAT): A new measure of understandability and actionability for print and audiovisual patient information. *Patient Education and Counseling*, *96*(3), 395–403.

Sillence, E., et al. (2007). How do patients evaluate and make use of online health information? *Social Science & Medicine*, *64*(9), 1853–1862.

Smith, A. T., et al. (2011a). Quality of eating disorders websites: What adolescents and their families need to know. *Journal of Child and Adolescent Psychiatric Nursing*, *24*(1), 33–37.

Smith, A. T., et al. (2011b). Quality of eating disorders websites: What adolescents and their families need to know. *Journal of Child and Adolescent Psychiatric Nursing*, *24*(1), 33–37.

Stjernsward, S., & Ostman, M. (2007). Depression, e-health and family support. What the internet offers the relatives of depressed persons. *Nordic Journal of Psychiatry*, *61*(1), 12–18.

Strzelecki, A. (2020). Google medical update: Why is the search engine decreasing visibility of health and medical information websites? *Int J Environ Res Public Health, 17*(4).

Swire-Thompson, B., & Lazer, D. (2020). Public health and online misinformation: Challenges and recommendations. *Annual Review of Public Health, 41*, 433–451.

Thakor, V., et al. (2011). The quality of information on websites selling St. John's wort. *Complement Ther Med, 19*(3), 155–160.

Thapa, P., et al. (2018). YouTube lens to attention deficit hyperactivity disorder: A social media analysis. *BMC Research Notes, 11*(1), 854.

Walsh, T. M., & Volsko, T. A. (2008). Readability assessment of internet-based consumer health information. *Respiratory Care, 53*(10), 1310–1315.

Wang, Y., et al. (2019). Systematic literature review on the spread of health-related misinformation on social media. *Social Science & Medicine, 240*, 112552.

Zermatten, A., et al. (2010). Quality of web-based information on depression. *Depression and Anxiety, 27*(9), 852–858.

Zhao, Y., & Zhang, J. (2017). Consumer health information seeking in social media: A literature review. *Health Information and Libraries Journal, 34*(4), 268–283.

Zwi, M., et al. (2011). Parent training interventions for attention deficit hyperactivity disorder (ADHD) in children aged 5 to 18 years. *Cochrane Database Syst Rev, 2011*(12), CD003018.

Digital phenotyping

10

Lior Carmi[a,], Anzar Abbas[b,*], Katharina Schultebraucks[c],
and Isaac R. Galatzer-Levy[d,e]*

[a]Post Trauma Center, Chaim Sheba Medical Center, Ramat Gan, Israel, [b]AiCure, New York, NY, United States, [c]Emergency Medicine, Columbia University, New York, NY, United States, [d]Reality Labs, Facebook, New York, NY, United States, [e]Psychiatry, New York University School of Medicine, New York, NY, United States

The importance of measurement

Reliable measurement of a patient's health is central to medical care and scientific research. Fortunately, clinicians have access to tools that allow them to diagnose disease and assess symptom severity with great accuracy—tools such as blood tests, biopsies, MRI scans, ultrasounds, and gene sequencing—all of which provide objective measures of physical health. However, in the context of mental and behavioral health, measurement is far from straightforward.

Psychiatrists rely on rater-based scales or patient-report questionnaires to diagnose disease and assess symptom severity. These tools have well-established shortcomings, both in their clinical validity and the practical logistics of their use (Cuthbert, 2015). Indeed, in the context of medical care and scientific research in mental health, clinicians must not only focus on treatment, but also carefully consider the measurement tools used to assess treatment. In this chapter, we discuss measurement challenges in psychiatry and the emergence of digital phenotyping as a solution toward objective characterization of mental disorders.

The challenge of measurement in mental health

Measurement has historically been recognized a challenge in psychiatry. Before efforts such as the *Diagnostic and Statistical Manual of Mental Disorders* (DSM) by the American Psychiatric Association or the *International Classification of Diseases* (ICD) by the World Health Organization, the same patient could get two different diagnoses from two different clinicians on the same day with little overlap in recorded symptomatology: diagnosing psychiatric patients was a rather subjective exercise, affording little reliability or validity.

With the DSM and ICD, a standardization in symptom classification and measurement emerged (American Psychiatric Association, 2013; World Health Organization, 2020). This allowed for the establishment of standardized approaches to diagnosis as well as scales for the assessment of disease severity. Semistructure interviews were developed, including the structured interview for the HAM-D for depression

---

*Equally contributed.

Mental Health in a Digital World. https://doi.org/10.1016/B978-0-12-822201-0.00002-2

(Williams, 1988), the PANSS for schizophrenia (Kay, Fiszbein, & Opler, 1987), and the CARS for autism spectrum disorder (Schopler, Reichler, DeVellis, & Daly, 1980). It also led to the creation of patient self-report scales, where a patient responds to questions, and answers are indicative of disease severity. Examples of such scales include the BPRS for schizophrenia (Overall & Gorham, 1962), the ASRS for attention-deficit/hyperactivity disorder (Kessler et al., 2005), and the PHQ-9 for depression (Kroenke, Spitzer, & Williams, 2001). A range of clinician-administered and self-report measures have become widely used.

While reliability may have improved over the years, the question of validity remains. Despite the progress made in the standardization of measurement, both rater-based and patient-report scales are prone to varying degrees of observer and patient bias (Fuchs, 2010). Moreover, considering recent developments in neuroscience, the symptom classification efforts themselves are grounded in an outdated disease nosology (Cuthbert & Insel, 2010). There is a need to increase the validity of assessments of mental health, using measures that more accurately reflect patient functioning (Pallagrosi, Fonzi, Picardi, & Biondi, 2016). Indeed, a core motive behind this book is to highlight the potential of new technologies for improving clinical assessment.

In addition to clinical challenges, current assessment tools present practical and logistical barriers (van Eijk, 2020). Every time a rater-based assessment is needed, the patient may have to appear in the clinic in person. They may have to take time off work or set aside part of their weekend. In many cases, they must depend on public transportation or drive long distances to get to the clinic. Then, in what may be an unfamiliar environment, they are interviewed by a clinician they may or may not feel comfortable with, who probes into their health and psychiatric functioning as part of an assessment that can at times take as long as 90 min to administer. The experience can be no less frustrating when the patient is asked to come into the clinic to participate in paper-based patient-report questionnaires. Not only do such experiences lead to measurements that are not reflective of a patient's day-to-day functioning (Schmuckler, 2001), but also the burden associated—both for the patient and the clinician—renders assessment of mental health impractical, so the clinicians have little or no visibility into patient health and behavior once they step outside the clinic.

Virtual care and electronic patient self-report

A natural solution to the logistical challenges associated with clinical assessment has been the use of technology. Indeed, remote patient self-report is the most obvious use of current technologies (Coons et al., 2015). Self-report scales can easily be digitized and completed electronically. This has led to the emergence of ecological momentary assessments, a departure from the rigidity of some traditional self-report scales (Burke et al., 2017). Initial concerns regarding the validity of remote self-report in comparison to in-person assessment have decreased over time, with a plethora of studies confirming their accuracy and reliability (Areán, Ly, & Andersson, 2016; Cavelti, Kvrgic, Beck, Kossowsky, & Vauth, 2012; Löwe, Kroenke, Herzog, & Gräfe, 2004), and they have become widely used in clinical research (Moskowitz & Young, 2006; Shiffman, Stone, & Hufford, 2008). The chapter on ecological momentary assessments for digital phenotyping in Section I of this book describes these developments in detail.

More recently, with broader adoption of telemedicine and virtual care, clinician-administered psychiatric assessments are also being conducted remotely (Barnett & Huskamp, 2020; LaFrance Jr et al., 2020; Wright, 2020). Some traditional scales are even being adopted so they can be conducted over video calls (Dorsey, Bloem, & Okun, 2020). Adoption of virtual care and its impact on measurement are further discussed in the chapter on telepsychiatry in Section II of this book. Through digitization of self-report and virtual care, practical and logistical challenges associated with clinical assessment are being addressed. However, the clinical shortcomings stemming from the still-subjective nature of these assessments remain. And with technology becoming a core component of clinical assessment, its potential to enable objective measurement is becoming more apparent—and digital phenotyping is coming into play.

Digital phenotyping of mental health

Mental illness manifests itself in a range of signs and symptoms. The aim of an assessment tool is to measure such phenomena in a standardized manner. Clinicians do just that during clinical assessments, i.e., they observe aspects of the patient's behavior, including their facial expressivity, characteristics of their speech, acoustics of their voice, patterns of movement, and the manner in which they respond to questions and stimuli. They then use these behavioral characteristics to make judgments regarding the patient's health and clinical functioning. Advances in machine learning, supported by computer vision, natural language processing, and digital signal processing tools have led to the development of tools that allow for quantification of the same behavioral characteristics (Boersma & Weenink, 2018; Goyal, Agarwal, & Kumar, 2017; Hardeniya, Perkins, Chopra, Joshi, & Mathur, 2016). Similarly, these behavioral characteristics can be used to measure health, forming the foundation for the field of digital phenotyping.

Digital phenotyping of mental health proposes solutions to many of the challenges presented by traditional clinical assessment tools (Insel, 2017). Given that a clinician doesn't need to be directly involved in the observation of behavior, i.e., the collection of data, the patient may participate in the assessment on their own time and in their natural environment, removing many of the logistical barriers associated with clinical assessment. Most importantly, digital assessment of behavior leads to reliable, valid, and sensitive measurements, removing clinician and patient bias from the assessment.

Digital medicine is based on four major pillars:

Continuous Passive Monitoring (CPM) of behavioral parameters or Smart Active Monitoring (SAM).
Identification of behavioral patterns that lead to an Individualized Digital Phenotype (IDP) of a disorder.

Accurate detection of clinically relevant changes and accordingly Timely Precise Intervention (TPI), e.g., secondary prevention.
Optimized communication for assessment and intervention.

CPM refers to the efficient measurement of behavioral patterns manifested through mobile phone usage. The information to be measured may consist of communication patterns, activity patterns, and diurnal variation, including changes during sleep. Active data sources such as Smart Active Monitoring may consist of voice prosody, facial and eye coding, linguistic analysis, and remote surveys.

The remainder of this chapter provides an overview of recent developments in digital phenotyping, focusing primarily on the use of consumer devices that do not require specialized hardware. There have been several attempts to classify digital phenotyping tools and the biomarkers they measure (Coravos, Khozin, & Mandl, 2019). Here, we categorize digital phenotyping methods into those that rely on passive monitoring and those that require active assessments. Digital phenotyping efforts that depend on nonconsumer devices have been omitted, including application of machine learning to datasets from medical imaging, electronic medical records, and genetic sequencing data (Abbas, Schultebraucks, & Galatzer-Levy, 2021). Patient self-report, though indeed a form of digital phenotyping, has been mostly omitted from this chapter given detailed discussion of its merits and shortcomings in other chapters of this book.

Passive monitoring

Digital phenotyping through passive monitoring involves recording of an individual's behavior while they go about their days as they would regularly. It is based on the notion that certain passively observable behavioral characteristics can serve as proxies of health. The most popular form of passive monitoring is measurement of actigraphy through wearables (Piau, Wild, Mattek, & Kaye, 2019). This section also discusses how monitoring of an individual's electronic behavior can provide useful behavioral measures. There has been the use of specially designed in-home sensors to measure patient behavior and consequently health (e.g., Adib, Mao, Kabelac, Katabi, & Miller, 2015). However, since these devices are not necessarily consumer grade or meant for broad adoption, a discussion of in-home sensors has been omitted from this chapter. Passively collected measures through digital phenotyping are a relatively novel area of research, partially due to the recent popularity of health-focused consumer devices and accessible data on individual's online behavior. However, they have demonstrated marketed success as effective measurement tools.

Significant efforts have been made both in industry and in academia to develop novel digital phenotypes for remote monitoring health status including mental health. Areas of research interest include the use of GPS to characterize behavioral activation and avoidance (Glenn & Monteith, 2014; Torous, Onnela, & Keshavan, 2017), monitoring of physiology and sleep through smartphones and wearables, e.g., Fitbit, Garmin, or Apple watches (Onnela, Keshavan, Staples, Barnett, & Torous, 2018), and passive measurement of cognitive functioning based on keystroke activity, taps, and swipes via smartphone apps (Dagum, 2018). Such approaches show promise but require significant infrastructure investment to capture data, to process high data volumes, to develop theoretical and machine learning models to map digital signals to behavioral phenotypes, and finally to communicate results in an efficient and comprehensible manner. While significant research and development in the area of digital phenotyping has occurred in academia, attempts to fully develop and maintain such technologies has occurred primarily in industry with both startups and major technology and insurance companies (Google/Verily, Amazon, Kaiser Permanente), each of which has made large investments in digital phenotyping technologies.

Actigraphy and tremor

Actigraphy, a term generally used to refer the movement activity measured through a wearable device (e.g., smartwatches, accelerometers, pedometers), has gained popularity alongside the devices that offer the measurements (Wright, Collier, Brown, & Sandberg, 2017). The use of this technology is perhaps most promising for direct measures of fine motor behavior such as tremor and gait that are difficult to assess simply through observation, whether it be through purpose-built sensors (Jeon et al., 2017) or commercially available devices (Lamont, Daniel, Payne, & Brauer, 2018). However, movement abnormalities form part of the symptomatology of a range of mental disorders, such as depression (Santomas, 2020) and schizophrenia (Shin et al., 2016). Hence, actigraphy has been utilized as a proxy measure of overall movement in a wide range of patient populations (Depp et al., 2019; Wright et al., 2017).

Human-computer interaction

Given the integration of technology into most aspects of daily living, human-computer interaction could refer to any aspect of how a patient interacts with their devices or online. Intuitively, the concept behind using human-computer interactions is that such activity reflects multiple aspects of functioning that are clinically relevant in psychiatry such as motor functioning and cognition reflected in typing behavior to social functioning reflected in social media activity. Keystroke activity-based biomarkers use passively collected keyboard activity, whether on mobile phones or computer keyboards, as correlates of mental health (Epp, Lippold, & Mandryk, 2011; Zulueta et al., 2018). Efforts to use social media activity overlap with efforts to understand natural language (also discussed in "Voice and speech" section), utilizing an individual's online behavior, including the posts they generate and the posts they interact with, as indicators of their health and functioning (Coppersmith, Dredze, & Harman, 2014; McClellan, Ali, Mutter, Kroutil, & Landwehr, 2017). Although measurements derived from an individual's electronic behavior have shown promise as measures of health—particularly in the context of assessing social and cognitive functioning—the question of how they can be integrated into patient care and clinical research remains to be fully addressed.

Active assessments

In contrast to passively acquired data, active assessments ask individuals to engage in predesigned tasks or interactions that collect short bursts of data on their behavior, which can then be used to derive measures of health. These are closest to traditional clinical assessments in that they are meant to elicit behavior for targeted measurement of health, rather than deriving inferences from passive monitoring. They are different from traditional clinical assessments in that the collected data is used to objectively quantify behavioral characteristics to derive measures of health.

Facial expressivity

Facial expressivity is an important measure during assessments of psychiatric functioning (e.g., passive assessment of a depressed patient's emotional experience or active evaluation of blunted affect in an individual with schizophrenia). Recognizing the subjectivity of such observation, efforts to standardize facial measurements date back decades (Ekman & Friesen, 1978). The Facial Action Coding System, which catalogs all possible combinations of facial musculature arrangements, formed the foundation for objective labeling of facial activity and subsequently emotional expressivity (Ekman, 1997). Although facial coding in this manner showed strong direct relationships between facial expressivity and psychiatric functioning (such as in Cohn et al., 2009), manually coding facial activity is not scalable as a clinical measure given the effort required.

With advances in computer vision, the same coding of facial activity can be conducted except using automated tools that are openly available to researchers (Baltrušaitis, Robinson, & Morency, 2016; Baltrušaitis, Zadeh, Lim, & Morency, 2018). As a result, measurement of facial expressivity to assess psychiatric health and functioning has become simple to integrate into clinical research. Several studies have used these methods in the laboratory to demonstrate the relationship between facial expressivity as measured through computer vision and symptom severity across psychiatric disorders (Corcoran & Cecchi, 2018; Haque, Guo, Miner, & Fei-Fei, 2018; Jiang et al., 2020). More recent efforts have built smartphone-based platforms to do so in the real world in patients receiving treatment (Galatzer-Levy, Abbas, Koesmahargyo, et al., 2020; Galatzer-Levy, Abbas, Yadav, et al., 2020). If the collection of video of patient can be made scalable and secure, computer vision-based measurement of facial expressivity can be a valuable assessment of psychiatric functioning.

Voice and speech

Similar to facial expressivity, assessing a patient's speech is a critical part of clinical assessment. The clinician makes observations not only on what the patient is saying, but also *how* they are saying it. They then use their judgment as clinicians to respond to items in the clinical assessment that may refer to the patient's speech, such as verbal fluency or social withdrawal (Kay et al., 1987). Yet, this measurement is unreliable and efforts have long been under way in laboratory research to standardize analysis of voice (Oğuz, Kiliç, & Şafak, 2011). Consequently, a field of vocal acoustics has emerged which uses techniques in digital signal processing to identify features of a voice's waveform that are related to the speaker's health (Godino-Llorente et al., 2008; Jadoul, Thompson, & De Boer, 2018). As a result, several acoustic properties of voice have been related to psychiatric functioning (Hashim, Wilkes, Salomon, Meggs, & France, 2017; Parola, Simonsen, Bliksted, & Fusaroli, 2020), including measures as simple as the loudness or fundamental frequency of voice (Quatieri & Malyska, 2012) to properties such as the harmonics-to-noise ratio (Shama, Krishna, & Cholayya, 2006) and normalized amplitude quotient (Airas & Alku, 2006).

In addition to the acoustics of an individual's voice, recent advances in machine learning tools have allowed for widespread adoption of natural language processing in clinical research (Chowdhary, 2020). With these tools, the analysis can focus on *what* the patient is saying by transcribing their speech or analyzing written text to automatically analyze characteristics of language that are indicative of psychiatric functioning (Althoff, Clark, & Leskovec, 2016; Cook et al., 2016; Stewart & Velupillai, 2020). This includes simple measurements like the lengths of pauses between words to complex language characteristics such as emotional valence of speech, lexical diversity, and deriving cognitive measures based on speech (He, Veldkamp, Glas, & de Vries, 2017; Patel et al., 2015). Several efforts have utilized vocal and speech measures to quantify disease severity in the context of medical care and clinical research and have built software platforms to collect such data from patients in a scalable manner (Komeili et al., 2019). If the collection of such data, which is still considered Protected Health information when collected to assess patient health, can be collected securely in a scalable manner, digital measurements of voice and speech can contribute significantly to efforts in digital phenotyping.

Movement

Measurement of movement through actigraphy is discussed in the "Passive monitoring" section on passive monitoring of behavior. However, measurements of movement through active assessments expands the data through which motor functioning can be assessed. Primarily, such assessments use computer vision to more directly measure an individual's movement activity during active assessments, similar to how motor functioning would be assessed as part of a traditional clinical evaluation (Goetz et al., 2008).

As with actigraphy, one of the primary reasons to utilize such technology is to obtain more sensitive quantification of motor abnormalities. Traditional clinical assessments such as the UPDRS (Goetz et al., 2008) or the TETRAS (Elble, 2016) classify tremor into discrete scores, given the limits of rater observation. In comparison, when computer vision is used on videos of patients performing similar assessments, the quantification of tremor can be made using a continuous measure and by definition be a more sensitive assessment in addition to not being reliant on potentially biased clinician observation (Nieto-Hidalgo, Ferrández-Pastor, Valdivieso-Sarabia, Mora-Pascual, & García-Chamizo, 2018; Pang et al., 2020; Williams et al., 2019).

Moving beyond tremor, computer vision-based measurement of movement can identify other clinically meaningful aspects of an individual's behavior. Head movement has been shown to reflect motor retardation and in some cases overall disease severity in psychiatric populations (Abbas et al., 2020). If oculomotor activity is considered as an aspect of movement, then eye gaze directionality, eye blink behavior, pupil dilation, etc., can serve as important measures of psychiatric functioning. Examples of this include measuring saccades for the assessment of schizophrenia (Huang et al., 2020), blink durations for the assessment of fatigue (Wang, Guo, & Chen, 2017), pupil dilations for the assessments of attention and arousal (Miller, Gross, & Unsworth, 2019), and eye gaze directionality in response to predesigned stimuli designed to measure aspects of social and attentional functioning (Hashemi et al., 2012).

Cognitive functioning

Digital measurement of cognitive functioning requires a special mention as it is perhaps farthest ahead in its adoption in clinical research and medical care, with several commercial efforts making it easily accessible (Kaser, Zaman, & Sahakian, 2017). This is partially due to the fact that traditional paper-based cognitive assessments, similar to patient report questionnaires, have been relatively simple to digitize and can be performed over computers, tablets, and smartphones (Au, Piers, & Devine, 2017; Hafiz et al., 2019; Lancaster et al., 2019). In fact, the experience of cognitive assessments has in some cases been enhanced significantly by the creativity possible with digitization that was not the case with traditional paper-based assessments.

In addition to performance-based cognitive testing, some of the digital measurements discussed above have also been either shown to be correlates of cognition or in themselves are directly reflective of cognitive functioning. The most common example of this has been the use of text or speech data to extract characteristics of language that are indicative of cognitive functioning (Clarke, Foltz, & Garrard, 2020; Thapa et al., 2020). In fact, studies using natural language processing to extract speech characteristics have shown that speech can be indicative of cognitive decline in individuals with Alzheimer's disease years before diagnosis and noticeable cognitive impairment (Beltrami et al., 2018; Filiou et al., 2020; Lopez-de-Ipina et al., 2018; Shibata et al., 2018).

Challenges faced by digital phenotyping

Each of the efforts in digital phenotyping discussed are associated with their own merits and drawbacks. However, novel digital measures of mental health share common obstacles before their potential can be fully realized. First, routes to validation of methods remain unclear. Any methods developed or code utilized must be made open for evaluation, which is often not the case with commercial efforts. A potential solution is a common repository of methods to be established for the sharing of methods between academia, medicine, and industry. Without it, the fields remain disconnected, skepticism persists, and progress is slowed. Second, all efforts must take into consideration regulations pertaining to data privacy, particularly when working with Protected Health Information. Most digital phenotyping methods discussed above require collection of identyfied data, which requires special handling (Cohen & Mello, 2018). Third, there is a need for clear routes to the approval of novel tools from regulatory authorities such as the Food and Drug Administration. Without this, a digital measurement may accumulate widespread scientific support yet still not be accepted as a clinical decision-making tool in the contexts of medical care and clinical research (Manta, Patrick-Lake, & Goldsack, 2020). Finally, novel tools must adapt the way in which data is collected and presented in order to integrate with the existing health-care ecosystem. By doing so, they enable clinicians to make informed decisions without having to allocate extra time toward independent software tools or being inundated with additional of data streams with information that may be difficult to interpret (Abbas et al., 2021).

Privacy and anonymity

A major issue related to this kind of monitoring is the issue of anonymity and the need to keep personal privacy confidential (Insel, 2017). An authorized app must ensure that all the data gathered by the app will be completely anonymous, i.e., with no personal information stored on servers.

All data acquired during the day are encrypted directly inside the smartphone memory. Personal information, e.g., telephone numbers, person names, or specific location, is "whitened" by coding it into hash values. By doing so, behavioral patterns such as communication patterns, diurnal variation, movement patterns, etc., may be recognized without abrogating privacy. The use of this strategy allows counting the number of calls or messages that are sent but not their content or the actual digits. Similarly, one could also measure the distance traveled in a certain time frame. Thus, digital medicine aims to measure and compare the amount of activity done using the smartphone without saving specific personal data.

Promise and future of digital measurement

It is important to distinguish between measurement of behavioral characteristics, measurement of clinically meaningful symptomatology, and measurement of overall disease severity. Computer vision-based quantification of facial activity is a measurement of a behavioral characteristic. The use of facial activity to derive blunted affect in a patient with schizophrenia, for example, is a measurement of clinically meaningful symptomatology. However, to arrive at a composite measure of disease severity, one must successfully integrate several measures of clinically meaningful symptomatology to make a prediction. So far, this chapter has discussed individual clinical measures, i.e., disparate digital markers, which may serve as proxies of overall disease severity. However, the promise of digital phenotyping lies beyond isolated application of individual measures. Ultimately, mental illness is defined by manifestation of a group of symptoms that characterize a disease. Traditional clinical assessments aim to quantify the severity of all such symptoms to arrive at composite measures of disease severity, However, this is not as simple in the context of digital measurement—and for good reason.

Traditional clinical assessments typically call for scoring of symptom severity on equally weighted discrete scales (e.g., on a scale of 0–4, how severe is the patient's tremor?; Elble, 2016). Each of the scores are then combined using simple arithmetic operations such as addition or averaging. In the case of digital measurement, each symptom may be quantified on a continuous scale with its own range of expected values and likely have separate units of measurement (Galatzer-Levy, Abbas, Yadav, et al., 2020). Hence, amalgamation of individual measures into a single composite score is less straightforward. The natural solution here is the application of machine learning to train models that make "predictions" of overall disease severity. However, a significant amount of data must be collected to train such models and their applicability universally must be thoroughly examined before their use. Just as importantly, such a project would require significant technological effort to integrate data streams from individual measurement tools into a unified data infrastructure, as any single academic group or digital assessment tool is unlikely to collect all relevant measures. Past efforts to combine even two such data streams have demonstrated the challenge associated with amalgamation of multimodal digital measurements (Schultebraucks et al., 2020). However, if such challenges are overcome so that accurate, reliable, and sensitive digital measurements can be acquired using consumer devices in large patient populations, this may lead to novel models of disease severity, that are a significant departure from reliance on paper-pencil clinician assessments.

A final remark regarding the software engineering aspects of digital phenotyping is relevant. Apps are not magical. Both their development and maintenance require large infrastructure investments in computing power as well as storage and movement of data. They also require large teams of software engineers to build front end, backend, "plumbing," and delivery systems. These systems must be maintained and updated on the basis of changes in user needs and the software platforms they depend on (i.e., iOS/Android). As such, both the development and maintenance of tools for the identification and intervention require significant initial and sustained investments and efforts to be of clinical value. Our view is that such investment will yield large dividends for the field of mental health over time.

References

Abbas, A., Schultebraucks, K., & Galatzer-Levy, I. R. (2021). Digital measurement of mental health: Challenges, promises, and future directions. *Psychiatric Annals*, *51*(1).

Abbas, A., Yadav, V., Smith, E., Ramjas, E., Rutter, S. B., Benavides, C., … Perez-Rodriguez, M. M. (2020). Computer vision-based assessment of motor functioning in schizophrenia: Use of smartphones for remote measurement of schizophrenia symptomatology. *medRxiv*.

Adib, F., Mao, H., Kabelac, Z., Katabi, D., & Miller, R. C. (2015). Smart homes that monitor breathing and heart rate. In *Proceedings of the 33rd annual ACM conference on human factors in computing systems* (pp. 837–846).

Airas, M., & Alku, P. (2006). Emotions in vowel segments of continuous speech: Analysis of the glottal flow using the normalised amplitude quotient. *Phonetica, 63*(1), 26–46.

Althoff, T., Clark, K., & Leskovec, J. (2016). Large-scale analysis of counseling conversations: An application of natural language processing to mental health. *Transactions of the Association for Computational Linguistics, 4*, 463–476.

American Psychiatric Association. (2013). *Diagnostic and statistical manual of mental disorders* (5th ed.). https://doi.org/10.1176/appi.books.9780890425596.

Areán, P. A., Ly, K. H., & Andersson, G. (2016). Mobile technology for mental health assessment. *Dialogues in Clinical Neuroscience, 18*(2), 163.

Au, R., Piers, R. J., & Devine, S. (2017). How technology is reshaping cognitive assessment: Lessons from the Framingham heart study. *Neuropsychology, 31*(8), 846.

Baltrušaitis, T., Robinson, P., & Morency, L. P. (2016). Openface: An open source facial behavior analysis toolkit. In *2016 IEEE winter Conference on applications of computer vision (WACV)* (pp. 1–10). IEEE.

Baltrušaitis, T., Zadeh, A., Lim, Y. C., & Morency, L. P. (2018). Openface 2.0: Facial behavior analysis toolkit. In *2018 13th IEEE international conference on automatic face & gesture recognition (FG 2018)* (pp. 59–66). IEEE.

Barnett, M. L., & Huskamp, H. A. (2020). Telemedicine for mental health in the United States: Making progress, still a long way to go. *Psychiatric Services, 71*(2), 197–198.

Beltrami, D., Gagliardi, G., Rossini Favretti, R., Ghidoni, E., Tamburini, F., & Calzà, L. (2018). Speech analysis by natural language processing techniques: A possible tool for very early detection of cognitive decline? *Frontiers in Aging Neuroscience, 10*, 369.

Boersma, P., & Weenink, D. (2018). *Praat: Doing phonetics by computer*. [Computer program]. Version 6.0 (p. 37). http://www.praat.org/. Retrieved March, 14, 2018.

Burke, L. E., Shiffman, S., Music, E., Styn, M. A., Kriska, A., Smailagic, A., … Mancino, J. (2017). Ecological momentary assessment in behavioral research: Addressing technological and human participant challenges. *Journal of Medical Internet Research, 19*(3), e77.

Cavelti, M., Kvrgic, S., Beck, E. M., Kossowsky, J., & Vauth, R. (2012). Assessing recovery from schizophrenia as an individual process. A review of self-report instruments. *European Psychiatry, 27*(1), 19–32.

Chowdhary, K. R. (2020). Natural language processing. In *Fundamentals of Artificial Intelligence* (pp. 603–649). New Delhi: Springer.

Clarke, N., Foltz, P., & Garrard, P. (2020). How to do things with (thousands of) words: Computational approaches to discourse analysis in Alzheimer's disease. *Cortex*.

Cohen, I. G., & Mello, M. M. (2018). HIPAA and protecting health information in the 21st century. *JAMA, 320*(3), 231–232.

Cohn, J. F., Kruez, T. S., Matthews, I., Yang, Y., Nguyen, M. H., Padilla, M. T., … De la Torre, F. (2009). Detecting depression from facial actions and vocal prosody. In *2009 3rd international conference on affective computing and intelligent interaction and workshops* (pp. 1–7). IEEE.

Cook, B. L., Progovac, A. M., Chen, P., Mullin, B., Hou, S., & Baca-Garcia, E. (2016). Novel use of natural language processing (NLP) to predict suicidal ideation and psychiatric symptoms in a text-based mental health intervention in Madrid. *Computational and Mathematical Methods in Medicine*.

Coons, S. J., Eremenco, S., Lundy, J. J., O'Donohoe, P., O'Gorman, H., & Malizia, W. (2015). Capturing patient-reported outcome (PRO) data electronically: The past, present, and promise of ePRO measurement in clinical trials. *The Patient-Patient-Centered Outcomes Research, 8*(4), 301–309.

Coppersmith, G., Dredze, M., & Harman, C. (2014). Quantifying mental health signals in Twitter. In *Proceedings of the workshop on computational linguistics and clinical psychology: From linguistic signal to clinical reality* (pp. 51–60).

Coravos, A., Khozin, S., & Mandl, K. D. (2019). Developing and adopting safe and effective digital biomarkers to improve patient outcomes. *npj Digital Medicine, 2*(1), 1–5.

Corcoran, C. M., & Cecchi, G. A. (2018). Computational approaches to behavior analysis in psychiatry. *Neuropsychopharmacology, 43*(1), 225.

Cuthbert, B. N. (2015). Research domain criteria: Toward future psychiatric nosologies. *Dialogues in Clinical Neuroscience, 17*(1), 89.

Cuthbert, B. N., & Insel, T. R. (2010). *Toward new approaches to psychotic disorders: The NIMH research domain criteria project.*

Dagum, P. (2018). Digital biomarkers of cognitive function. *npj Digital Medicine, 1*(1), 10. https://doi.org/10.1038/s41746-018-0018-4.

Depp, C. A., Bashem, J., Moore, R. C., Holden, J. L., Mikhael, T., Swendsen, J., … Granholm, E. L. (2019). GPS mobility as a digital biomarker of negative symptoms in schizophrenia: A case control study. *npj Digital Medicine, 2*(1), 1–7.

Dorsey, E. R., Bloem, B. R., & Okun, M. S. (2020). A New Day: The role of telemedicine in reshaping care for persons with movement disorders. *Movement Disorders, 35*(11), 1897–1902.

Ekman, P., & Friesen, W. V. (1978). *Manual for the facial action coding system.* Consulting Psychologists Press.

Ekman, R. (1997). *What the face reveals: Basic and applied studies of spontaneous expression using the Facial Action Coding System (FACS).* USA: Oxford University Press.

Elble, R. J. (2016). The essential tremor rating assessment scale. *Journal of Neurology & Neuromedicine, 1*(4).

Epp, C., Lippold, M., & Mandryk, R. L. (2011, May). Identifying emotional states using keystroke dynamics. In *Proceedings of the sigchi conference on human factors in computing systems* (pp. 715–724).

Filiou, R. P., Bier, N., Slegers, A., Houzé, B., Belchior, P., & Brambati, S. M. (2020). Connected speech assessment in the early detection of Alzheimer's disease and mild cognitive impairment: A scoping review. *Aphasiology, 34*(6), 723–755.

Fuchs, T. (2010). Subjectivity and intersubjectivity in psychiatric diagnosis. *Psychopathology, 43*(4), 268–274.

Galatzer-Levy, I., Abbas, A., Koesmahargyo, V., Yadav, V., Perez-Rodriguez, M. M., Rosenfield, P., … Hansen, B. J. (2020). Facial and vocal markers of schizophrenia measured using remote smartphone assessments. *medRxiv.*

Galatzer-Levy, I., Abbas, A., Yadav, V., Koesmahargyo, V., Aghjayan, A., Marecki, S., … Sauder, C. (2020). Remote digital measurement of visual and auditory markers of Major Depressive Disorder severity and treatment response. *medRxiv.*

Glenn, T., & Monteith, S. (2014). New measures of mental state and behavior based on data collected from sensors, smartphones, and the Internet. *Current Psychiatry Reports, 16*(12), 523.

Godino-Llorente, J. I., Osma-Ruiz, V., Sáenz-Lechón, N., Cobeta-Marco, I., González-Herranz, R., & Ramírez-Calvo, C. (2008). Acoustic analysis of voice using WPCVox: A comparative study with Multi Dimensional Voice Program. *European Archives of Oto-Rhino-Laryngology, 265*(4), 465–476.

Goetz, C. G., Tilley, B. C., Shaftman, S. R., Stebbins, G. T., Fahn, S., Martinez-Martin, P., … Dubois, B. (2008). Movement Disorder Society-sponsored revision of the Unified Parkinson's Disease Rating Scale (MDS-UPDRS): Scale presentation and clinimetric testing results. *Movement Disorders: Official Journal of the Movement Disorder Society*, *23*(15), 2129–2170.

Goyal, K., Agarwal, K., & Kumar, R. (2017). Face detection and tracking: Using OpenCV. In *vol. 1. 2017 International conference of Electronics, Communication and Aerospace Technology (ICECA)* (pp. 474–478). IEEE.

Hafiz, P., Miskowiak, K. W., Kessing, L. V., Jespersen, A. E., Obenhausen, K., Gulyas, L., ... Bardram, J. E. (2019). The internet-based cognitive assessment tool: System design and feasibility study. *JMIR Formative Research*, *3*(3), e13898.

Haque, A., Guo, M., Miner, A. S., & Fei-Fei, L. (2018). Measuring depression symptom severity from spoken language and 3D facial expressions. *arXiv*. Preprint arXiv:1811.08592.

Hardeniya, N., Perkins, J., Chopra, D., Joshi, N., & Mathur, I. (2016). *Natural language processing: Python and NLTK*. Packt Publishing Ltd.

Hashemi, J., Spina, T. V., Tepper, M., Esler, A., Morellas, V., Papanikolopoulos, N., & Sapiro, G. (2012). A computer vision approach for the assessment of autism-related behavioral markers. In *2012 IEEE international conference on development and learning and epigenetic robotics (ICDL)* (pp. 1–7). IEEE.

Hashim, N. W., Wilkes, M., Salomon, R., Meggs, J., & France, D. J. (2017). Evaluation of voice acoustics as predictors of clinical depression scores. *Journal of Voice*, *31*(2), 256–e1.

He, Q., Veldkamp, B. P., Glas, C. A., & de Vries, T. (2017). Automated assessment of patients' self-narratives for posttraumatic stress disorder screening using natural language processing and text mining. *Assessment*, *24*(2), 157–172.

Huang, L., Wei, W., Liu, Z., Zhang, T., Wang, J., Xu, L., ... Le Meur, O. (2020). Effective schizophrenia recognition using discriminative eye movement features and model-metric based features. *Pattern Recognition Letters*, *138*, 608–616.

Insel, T. R. (2017). Digital phenotyping: Technology for a new science of behavior. *JAMA*, *318*(13), 1215–1216.

Jadoul, Y., Thompson, B., & De Boer, B. (2018). Introducing parselmouth: A python interface to praat. *Journal of Phonetics*, *71*, 1–15.

Jeon, H., Lee, W., Park, H., Lee, H. J., Kim, S. K., Kim, H. B., ... Park, K. S. (2017). Automatic classification of tremor severity in Parkinson's disease using a wearable device. *Sensors*, *17*(9), 2067.

Jiang, Z., Harati, S., Crowell, A., Mayberg, H., Nemati, S., & Clifford, G. (2020). Classifying major depressive disorder and response to deep brain stimulation over time by analyzing facial expressions. *IEEE Transactions on Biomedical Engineering*.

Kaser, M., Zaman, R., & Sahakian, B. J. (2017). Cognition as a treatment target in depression. *Psychological Medicine*, *47*(6), 987–989.

Kay, S. R., Fiszbein, A., & Opler, L. A. (1987). The positive and negative syndrome scale (PANSS) for schizophrenia. *Schizophrenia Bulletin*, *13*(2), 261–276.

Kessler, R. C., Adler, L., Ames, M., Demler, O., Faraone, S., Hiripi, E. V. A., ... Ustun, T. B. (2005). The World Health Organization adult ADHD self-report scale (ASRS): A short screening scale for use in the general population. *Psychological Medicine*, *35*(2), 245.

Komeili, M., Pou-Prom, C., Liaqat, D., Fraser, K. C., Yancheva, M., & Rudzicz, F. (2019). Talk2Me: Automated linguistic data collection for personal assessment. *PLoS ONE*, *14*(3), e0212342.

Kroenke, K., Spitzer, R. L., & Williams, J. B. (2001). The PHQ-9: Validity of a brief depression severity measure. *Journal of General Internal Medicine*, *16*(9), 606–613.

LaFrance, W. C., Jr., Ho, W. L. N., Bhatla, A., Baird, G., Altalib, H. H., & Godleski, L. (2020). Examination of potential differences in reporting of sensitive psychosocial measures via diagnostic evaluation using computer video telehealth. *The Journal of Neuropsychiatry and Clinical Neurosciences*. appi-neuropsych.

Lamont, R. M., Daniel, H. L., Payne, C. L., & Brauer, S. G. (2018). Accuracy of wearable physical activity trackers in people with Parkinson's disease. *Gait & Posture*, *63*, 104–108.

Lancaster, C., Koychev, I., Blane, J., Chinner, A., Wolters, L., & Hinds, C. (2019). The Mezurio smartphone application: Evaluating the feasibility of frequent digital cognitive assessment in the PREVENT dementia study. *medRxiv*, 19005124.

Lopez-de-Ipina, K., Martinez-de-Lizarduy, U., Calvo, P. M., Mekyska, J., Beitia, B., Barroso, N., ... Ecay-Torres, M. (2018). Advances on automatic speech analysis for early detection of Alzheimer disease: A non-linear multi-task approach. *Current Alzheimer Research*, *15*(2), 139–148.

Löwe, B., Kroenke, K., Herzog, W., & Gräfe, K. (2004). Measuring depression outcome with a brief self-report instrument: Sensitivity to change of the Patient Health Questionnaire (PHQ-9). *Journal of Affective Disorders*, *81*(1), 61–66.

Manta, C., Patrick-Lake, B., & Goldsack, J. C. (2020). Digital measures that matter to patients: A framework to guide the selection and development of digital measures of health. *Digital Biomarkers*, *4*(3), 69–77.

McClellan, C., Ali, M. M., Mutter, R., Kroutil, L., & Landwehr, J. (2017). Using social media to monitor mental health discussions—Evidence from Twitter. *Journal of the American Medical Informatics Association*, *24*(3), 496–502.

Miller, A. L., Gross, M. P., & Unsworth, N. (2019). Individual differences in working memory capacity and long-term memory: The influence of intensity of attention to items at encoding as measured by pupil dilation. *Journal of Memory and Language*, *104*, 25–42.

Moskowitz, D. S., & Young, S. N. (2006). Ecological momentary assessment: What it is and why it is a method of the future in clinical psychopharmacology. *Journal of Psychiatry and Neuroscience*, *31*(1), 13.

Nieto-Hidalgo, M., Ferrández-Pastor, F. J., Valdivieso-Sarabia, R. J., Mora-Pascual, J., & García-Chamizo, J. M. (2018). Gait analysis using computer vision based on cloud platform and mobile device. *Mobile Information Systems*.

Oğuz, H., Kiliç, M. A., & Şafak, M. A. (2011). Comparison of results in two acoustic analysis programs: Praat and MDVP. *Turkish Journal of Medical Sciences*, *41*(5), 835–841.

Onnela, J.-P., Keshavan, M., Staples, P., Barnett, I., & Torous, J. (2018). 150. Automated longitudinal latent interval estimation with applications to sleep. *Biological Psychiatry*, *83*(9 Supplement), S61. https://doi.org/10.1016/j.biopsych.2018.02.168.

Overall, J. E., & Gorham, D. R. (1962). The brief psychiatric rating scale. *Psychological Reports*, *10*(3), 799–812.

Pallagrosi, M., Fonzi, L., Picardi, A., & Biondi, M. (2016). Association between clinician's subjective experience during patient evaluation and psychiatric diagnosis. *Psychopathology*, *49*(2), 83–94.

Pang, Y., Christenson, J., Jiang, F., Lei, T., Rhoades, R., Kern, D., ... Liu, C. (2020). Automatic detection and quantification of hand movements toward development of an objective assessment of tremor and bradykinesia in Parkinson's disease. *Journal of Neuroscience Methods*, *333*, 108576.

Parola, A., Simonsen, A., Bliksted, V., & Fusaroli, R. (2020). Voice patterns in schizophrenia: A systematic review and Bayesian meta-analysis. *Schizophrenia Research*, *216*, 24–40.

Patel, R., Jayatilleke, N., Broadbent, M., Chang, C. K., Foskett, N., Gorrell, G., ... Roberts, A. (2015). Negative symptoms in schizophrenia: A study in a large clinical sample of patients using a novel automated method. *BMJ Open*, *5*(9).

Piau, A., Wild, K., Mattek, N., & Kaye, J. (2019). Current state of digital biomarker technologies for real-life, home-based monitoring of cognitive function for mild cognitive impairment to mild Alzheimer disease and implications for clinical care: Systematic review. *Journal of Medical Internet Research*, *21*(8), e12785.

Quatieri, T. F., & Malyska, N. (2012). Vocal-source biomarkers for depression: A link to psychomotor activity. In *Thirteenth annual conference of the international speech communication association*.

Santomas, K. (2020). *Passive monitoring of physical activity using a fitbit charge 3 in individuals at risk for depression*.

Schmuckler, M. A. (2001). What is ecological validity? A dimensional analysis. *Infancy*, *2*(4), 419–436.

Schopler, E., Reichler, R. J., DeVellis, R. F., & Daly, K. (1980). Toward objective classification of childhood autism: Childhood Autism Rating Scale (CARS). *Journal of Autism and Developmental Disorders*.

Schultebraucks, K., Shalev, A. Y., Michopoulos, V., Grudzen, C. R., Shin, S. M., Stevens, J. S., … Marmar, C. R. (2020). A validated predictive algorithm of post-traumatic stress course following emergency department admission after a traumatic stressor. *Nature Medicine*, *26*(7), 1084–1088.

Shama, K., Krishna, A., & Cholayya, N. U. (2006). Study of harmonics-to-noise ratio and critical-band energy spectrum of speech as acoustic indicators of laryngeal and voice pathology. *EURASIP Journal on Advances in Signal Processing*, *2007*, 1–9.

Shibata, D., Ito, K., Nagai, H., Okahisa, T., Kinoshita, A., & Aramaki, E. (2018). Idea density in Japanese for the early detection of dementia based on narrative speech. *PLoS ONE*, *13*(12), e0208418.

Shiffman, S., Stone, A. A., & Hufford, M. R. (2008). Ecological momentary assessment. *Annual Review of Clinical Psychology*, *4*, 1–32.

Shin, S., Yeom, C. W., Shin, C., Shin, J. H., Jeong, J. H., Shin, J. U., & Lee, Y. R. (2016). Activity monitoring using a mHealth device and correlations with psychopathology in patients with chronic schizophrenia. *Psychiatry Research*, *246*, 712–718.

Stewart, R., & Velupillai, S. (2020). Applied natural language processing in mental health big data. *Neuropsychopharmacology*, *46*(1), 252.

Thapa, S., Adhikari, S., Naseem, U., Singh, P., Bharathy, G., & Prasad, M. (2020, November). Detecting Alzheimer's disease by exploiting linguistic information from Nepali transcript. In *International conference on neural information processing* (pp. 176–184). Cham: Springer.

Torous, J., Onnela, J., & Keshavan, M. (2017). New dimensions and new tools to realize the potential of RDoC: Digital phenotyping via smartphones and connected devices. *Translational Psychiatry*, *7*(3), e1053.

van Eijk, R. P. (2020). Frequent self-assessments in ALS clinical trials: Worthwhile or an unnecessary burden for patients? *Annals of Clinical Translational Neurology*, *7*(10), 2074.

Wang, M., Guo, L., & Chen, W. Y. (2017). Blink detection using Adaboost and contour circle for fatigue recognition. *Computers and Electrical Engineering*, *58*, 502–512.

Williams, J. B. (1988). A structured interview guide for the Hamilton Depression Rating Scale. *Archives of General Psychiatry*, *45*(8), 742–747.

Williams, S., Shepherd, S., Fang, H., Alty, J., O'Gorman, P., & Graham, C. D. (2019). Computer vision of smartphone video has potential to detect functional tremor. *Journal of the Neurological Sciences*, *401*, 27–28.

World Health Organization. (2020). *International statistical classification of diseases and related health problems* (11th ed.). https://icd.who.int/.

Wright, A. J. (2020). Equivalence of remote, digital administration and traditional, in-person administration of the Wechsler Intelligence Scale for Children, (WISC-V). *Psychological Assessment*.

Wright, S. P., Collier, S. R., Brown, T. S., & Sandberg, K. (2017). An analysis of how consumer physical activity monitors are used in biomedical research. *The FASEB Journal*, *31*(1_supplement), 1020–1024.

Zulueta, J., Piscitello, A., Rasic, M., Easter, R., Babu, P., Langenecker, S. A., … Leow, A. (2018). Predicting mood disturbance severity with mobile phone keystroke metadata: A biaffect digital phenotyping study. *Journal of Medical Internet Research*, *20*(7), e241.

The digital therapeutic relationship: Retaining humanity in the digital age

Jason Bantjes and Philip Slabbert
Institute for Life Course Health Research, Department of Global Health, Faculty of Medicine and Health Sciences, University of Stellenbosch, Stellenbosch, South Africa

Introduction

Rapid technological advances in information and communication technologies have spurred the development of a range of digital psychological interventions (hereafter referred to simply as e-interventions), including internet-based treatments (IBTs), mental health mobile device applications (apps), online therapy, and wearables that facilitate collection of diagnostic patient information (Hill et al., 2017). There is growing evidence to support the use of e-interventions, suggesting that these may be as effective as conventional psychotherapy for most common mental disorders (Olthuis, Watt, Bailey, Hayden, & Stewart, 2016; Reyes-Portillo et al., 2014; Vallury, Jones, & Oosterbroek, 2015). Furthermore, e-interventions have considerable potential to close the mental health treatment gap by improving access to affordable personalized treatments that enable service users to choose when and how they access care (Hill et al., 2017). There is of course a danger that the increasing use of technology to deliver mental health interventions will dehumanize mental health care, particularly if mental disorders are conceptualized as problems that require technological solutions, without the need for any human interaction. The challenge is to build digital mental health-care systems that employ technology effectively, without dehumanizing patients and denying people's need for human contact.

Two potential solutions to the problem of how to retain humanity in a digital mental health-care system are: (1) using a human factor approach to design person-centered e-interventions and (2) conceptualizing e-interventions within a relationship-centered paradigm. In this chapter, we explore what it means to design person-centered and relationship-centered mental health e-interventions. We begin by discussing how human factor science is being utilized to design e-interventions around the needs of individual users. We propose the concept of a relationship-centered paradigm for conceptualizing e-interventions and argue that therapeutic relationships are central to facilitating enduring personal change. We critically discuss some of the philosophical and theoretical problems of conceptualizing a therapeutic relationship in cyberspace and assert that attachment theory might be an appropriate theoretical framework for understanding and researching relationship-centered e-interventions.

Human factor science and the design of person-centered e-interventions

Human factors science (also known as ergonomics) is the application of psychology, engineering, anatomy, and physiology to the design of products, processes, and systems that are resilient to unanticipated events, support human performance, and promote safety (Scanlon & Karsh, 2010). Utilizing human factor science to engineer human-centric digital interventions is essential for improving functionality, usability, and patient safety (Kushniruk, 2002). Understanding how people engage with digital devices is key to human factor optimization in the design of e-mental health interventions (Schwab & Langell, 2018). A human factor approach entails placing the individual user at the center of the design process by taking account of all the ergonomic, psychological, esthetic, and environmental factors that shape users' experience and interaction with the "machine" (Russ et al., 2013).

The evolution of digital mental health has partly been shaped by insights from human factor science into the typical barriers individuals encounter when accessing face-to-face mental health-care services, including stigma, patients' desire for autonomy, and patients' preference for immediate real-time psychological support (Huckvale, Wang, Majeed, & Car, 2019). Indeed, awareness of these human factors has precipitated the design of among other things machine learning-based chatbots, like *Woebot*, that offer real-time convenient and anonymous support for individuals experiencing psychological distress via interaction with an electronic "companion" that provides CBT coaching (Sachan, 2018).

Adopting a human factor approach entails more than just conceptualizing e-interventions as user-friendly products. Rather it seeks to create person-centered technologies that humanize the user by enlisting them as cocreators of digital interventions (Russ et al., 2013). There is growing appreciation that the success of e-interventions is linked to the extent to which human factors are considered during design, development, and implementation (Huckvale et al., 2019). The basic design principles for building person-centered technological solutions to mental health problems are summarized in Table 11.1.

Beyond the generic principles of human factor design listed above, we would also like to highlight three additional more pointed (albeit less often discussed) factors that need to be considered in the design of person-centered e-interventions, namely:

(1) *Consider the specific needs of particular populations.* Mental health problems are not equally distributed across the population, there are clearly delineated groups of individuals at increased risk of psychopathology. Rather than only being designed for the average "person-in-the-street," e-interventions should also be designed for ease of use by high-risk populations (e.g., older adults who may not be proficient at using digital technologies or forensic patients in confinement who may not have access to information and communication technologies) (Schwab & Langell, 2018).

(2) *Use universal design principals to ensure e-interventions are accessible to all users.* Universal design was originally defined as "design of products and environments to be usable by all people, to the greatest extent possible, without the need for adaptation or specialized design" (Mace, 1988). In the context of digital interventions, universal design entails

Table 11.1 Basic design principles for person-centered e-interventions.

Ensure user privacy and data security. Incorporate measures to improve patient safety and plan for clinical crises (e.g., what would happen if a user is acutely suicidal or discloses their intent to complete suicide). Understand the clinical problem that the e-intervention intends to solve and the typical characteristics of people who experience these kinds of problems (e.g., when designing an app to help people overcome phobias, developers need to understand the mechanisms that precipitate and maintain fears as well as the behaviors that characterize anxious individuals). Ensure ease of navigation. Utilize anthropometric data and knowledge of human anatomy to ensure ease of use (e.g., make the intervention easier to use by taking account of the dexterity of the thumb in relation to the size and shape of the electronic device that will be used). Consider the environment in which the e-intervention will be used (e.g., in low-and middle-income countries users may have difficulties with internet connectivity and bandwidth). Provide effective and efficient user support, especially for novel applications designed for populations who are not familiar with the technology

developing e-interventions that are inclusive of all people by meeting the usability needs of individuals with atypical bodies (Kascak, Rebola, & Sanford, 2014; Ruzic, Lee, Liu, & Sanford, 2016), including individuals with motor and sensory impairments.

(3) *Consider the cultural context in which e-interventions will be used.* Low-cost mobile health (m-health) interventions are being rapidly adopted in low- and middle-income countries (LMICs) and have transformed the health-care delivery landscape in many resource-constrained communities (Kaplan, 2006; Meara et al., 2015). It has been suggested that the same advances in mental health-care delivery may be achieved through e-interventions, especially given that over 1 billion people in LMICs will gain access to smartphones within the next decade (Huckvale et al., 2019). Once they are developed, e-interventions are globally available with few barriers to entry or acquisition, potentially offering affordable mental health care to populations that previously had little access to formal psychiatric treatments. However, most mental health e-interventions are developed in Western industrialized democratic countries, where users tend to be rich and educated (Hill et al., 2017), raising critical questions about their cultural applicability in other settings and the ease with which they can be exported (Opoku, Stephani, & Quentin, 2017). Indeed it may be easier to culturally translate an m-health intervention than to import a digital mental health intervention into an LMIC, particularly given all that has been written about the need for culturally informed mental health care (Kirmayer & Jarvis, 2019). It seems improbable that any e-intervention can be culturally neutral, nonetheless developers need to be sensitive to the cultural context in which e-interventions will be used. This includes being sensitive to identity politics and issues of gender, sexuality, and race that may make e-interventions less or more acceptable to some users. For example, see Bivens and Haimson's discussion of how gender categories are reinforced in the design of social media platforms (Bivens & Haimson, 2016), and Daniels' discussion of cyberfeminism and the politics of race, gender, and embodiment in cyberspace (Daniels, 2009). Developers of mental health e-interventions have a responsibility to take cognizance of how their products can inadvertently reinforce or disrupt sociocultural stereotypes and maintain or challenge the hegemony and marginalization that contribute to psychological distress.

A human factor approach to developing e-interventions humanizes the individual user and places them at the center of the design process, thus creating person-centric mental health-care solutions that are usable, effective, safe, and fit for purpose. Huckvale et al. have noted; "Digital health research will create most value by retaining a clear focus on the role of human factors in maximizing health benefit, by helping health systems to anticipate and understand the person-centered effects of technology changes and by advocating strongly for the autonomy, rights and safety of consumers" (Huckvale et al., 2019). Putting individuals at the center of a design process is, however, not necessarily the same as putting the therapeutic relationship at the center of e-interventions. In the sections that follow, we propose the concept of *relationship-centered e-interventions*, as a heuristic to illustrate a design paradigm that places the therapeutic relationship at the center of e-intervention development. We critically consider what might be entailed by developing e-interventions in which technology is used not simply as a medium to deliver content and replace therapists, but rather as a medium for establishing a relationship and facilitating human-to-human therapeutic interaction.

Conceptualizing e-interventions within a relationship-centered paradigm

Content-centered vs relationship-centered e-interventions

Broadly speaking, we can differentiate between content- and relationship-centered digital interventions. Content-centered e-interventions focus primarily on using technology to teach users effective skills and techniques for regulating emotions and changing behavior, by trying to obviate the need for users to interact with a human therapist. By comparison, relationship-centered e-interventions seek to use technology to facilitate therapeutic contact and interaction between the user and another person. In relationship-centered e-interventions, technology is conceptualized as a conduit for enhancing access to and interaction with a human therapist. A summary of the key differences between a content-centered paradigm and a relationship-centered paradigm in the development of e-interventions is provided in Table 11.2.

Synchronous online therapies conducted via videoconferencing or instant messaging are probably the clearest example of relationship-centered e-interventions. Online therapy developed as a natural evolution of telepsychiatry, which was first used more than half a century ago at the University of Nebraska in 1959 (Shore, 2015). Subsequently, telepsychiatry and online psychological consultation services have been established in many countries (Mucic & Hilty, 2020), highlighting the potential for technology to be used to deliver mental health interventions within a relationship-centered paradigm (see chapter on telepsychiatry for more detail).

The extent to which one adopts a relationship-centered paradigm in the conceptualization of e-interventions is a function of the degree to which one believes

(1) technology is a potential substitute for human therapists;
(2) the therapeutic relationship and human connection are integral to effective psychotherapy; and
(3) a therapeutic alliance can be established in cyberspace.

Table 11.2 Essential differences between content-centered and relationship-centered paradigms in the conceptualization of e-interventions.

Content-centered paradigm	Relationship-centered paradigm
Uses evidence from clinical trials to design digital interventions focused on teaching users skills and techniques for dealing with emotional and behavioral problems. Seeks to create e-interventions that are usable, effective, safe, and fit for purpose. e-Interventions are products that can replace or stand in for the therapist. e-Interventions are either a therapy in and of themselves, or a means of collecting ecological data to aid patient monitoring and diagnosis. Potentially well suited to: psychological skills training; delivering structured CBT interventions; teaching the principles of mindfulness; and digital phenotyping of patients. Examples include: the gamification of psychotherapy; online self-guided interventions; and wearables that collect diagnostic patient data	Uses psychological concepts borrowed from psychoanalytic theory, humanistic psychology, interpersonal psychotherapy, and intersubjectivity to place the therapeutic relationship at the center of the intervention. Seeks to use technology to facilitate communication between therapist and patient. e-Interventions are an interface for deepening the therapeutic alliance. e-Interventions are conduits for delivering psychotherapy. Potentially suited to: depth orientated and interpersonal psychotherapies; couples therapy; online support groups; and online group therapy. Examples include: online therapy via videoconferencing; telepsychiatry; utilizing instant messaging platforms to deliver therapy; and conducting therapy via email

How important is human interaction in e-interventions?

A wide range of Internet-based interventions (IBIs) have been developed and tested for common mental disorders (Andersson & Titov, 2014), with studies of the effectiveness of these interventions becoming increasingly sophisticated over time. Internet-based cognitive behavioral therapy (iCBT) for depressive disorders progressed from proof-of-concept studies in 2002 (Jones et al., 2013) to well-controlled randomized clinical trials demonstrating the effectiveness of this mode of treatment (Karyotaki et al., 2017). Several systematic reviews have confirmed IBIs are as effective as conventional face-to-face psychotherapy for the treatment of common mental disorders (Andrews, Cuijpers, Craske, McEvoy, & Titov, 2010; Baumeister, Reichler, Munzinger, & Lin, 2014; Lin, Ebert, Lehr, Berking, & Baumeister, 2013; Richards & Richardson, 2012), suggesting that digital media may be at least as effective as humans in delivering CBT. However, a more careful examination of the literature highlights the importance of therapist factors and human interaction in iCBT interventions. As Richards and Richardson (2012) note, there is a clear hierarchy of effectiveness within IBIs; therapist-supported interventions are the most efficacious ($g = 0.78$), followed by interventions supported by nonclinical staff ($g = 0.58$), with unguided interventions being the least effective ($g = 0.36$). In addition, asynchronously provided support (e.g., via email contact) showed a larger pooled standardized mean difference (SMD) than studies with synchronous support (e.g., via live chat) ($g = 0.70$ vs $g = 0.28$) (Richards & Richardson, 2012).

Taken together, these data indicate that iCBT interventions that include interaction with a human therapist are more effective than those that are devoid of personal interaction. This prompts interesting questions about the role of the therapeutic relationship in e-interventions, whether there is a need for any human-to-human communication in digital therapies, and whether technology should be conceptualized as a way of replacing human therapists? Attempting to answer these questions takes one deeper into a thicket of even more thorny questions, including: *Does the concept of a therapeutic relationship even have meaning in the context of using an app or talking to a chatbot? How does the cyber therapeutic relationship develop and how does it differ from the conventional therapeutic alliance? How does a therapeutic relationship in cyberspace facilitate a therapeutic outcome? Can the relationship that develops between a user and a superhuman AI chatbot be considered a therapeutic relationship?* Unfortunately, psychological research and the development of theory in the field of e-interventions have not kept pace with the speed of technological advance and the development of innovative online treatments. Consequently, important theoretical questions about the mechanisms of change and the role of the therapeutic relationship in e-interventions remain largely unexplored. This lack of theory could thwart the development of e-interventions by ignoring the need for technological solutions that retain humanity and honor personhood.

Toward a theoretical conceptualization of relationship-centered e-interventions

Conventional notions of the therapeutic relationship

In many forms of conventional psychotherapy (i.e., face-to-face talking therapies), the therapeutic relationship is understood to be an integral component of facilitating change (Lambert & Barley, 2001). Traditionally, psychotherapy has been conceptualized as a talking cure in which client and therapist engage with one another in pursuit of a shared goal to reduce patients' disease and suffering. This person-to-person engagement inevitably results in a therapeutic relationship that can either hinder or facilitate personal growth and change. There is an extensive theoretical literature describing the prominence and dynamics of the therapeutic relationship in conventional therapy (Gaston, 1990). Freud, writing in 1914, noted the profound impact of the therapeutic relationship on the process of psychotherapy (Freud, 1938). As early as 1936, Rosenzweig speculated that the outcomes of all psychotherapies were likely to be more or less equivalent (a conclusion that has come to be known as the "Dodo bird verdict") (Rosenzweig, 1936), because of common underlying mechanisms in psychotherapy that includes the quality of the therapeutic relationship (Drisko, 2004). Building on the ideas of John Bowlby, proponents of attachment theory speculated about the need for felt security and physical proximity in establishing the therapeutic relationship as a secure base for patients (Bowlby, 1988). By the 1950s, Carl Rogers theorized that the therapist's capacity for genuineness, empathy and warmth were necessary and sufficient conditions for therapeutic change (Rogers, 1957) and by the 1960s convincing empirical research demonstrated that therapeutic outcomes were determined not simply by the theoretical orientation of the therapy, but rather by distinct therapist factors that included the therapist's experience, attitude toward and interest in the patient, capacity for empathy and sincerity, and similarity to the patient (Luborsky, Auerbach, Chandler, Cohen, & Bachrach, 1971).

But what, if anything, is the significance of this for mental health e-interventions? Do ideas about the centrality of the therapeutic relationship belong to a bygone era in the history of psychotherapy or do they still have salience in a digital age? Of course, these are philosophical questions that cut to the heart of what we consider to be a "relationship" and whether or not we believe superhuman AI could ever be seen as "human." But these are also theoretical and practical questions that profoundly shape how we think about the place of technology in mental health interventions and how we might develop relationship-centered e-interventions. Unfortunately, research in this area is still in a fledgling state and there is a lack of sophisticated theoretical frameworks for conceptualizing cyber therapeutic relationships. There is, however, a small emerging literature in the field of online therapy and teleanalysis in psychoanalytic practice, which provides some insight into what possibilities might exist for establishing a therapeutic alliance in cyberspace. Examining this literature provides some insight into the possibilities for establishing a therapeutic alliance in cyberspace.

Possibilities for establishing therapeutic relationships in cyberspace

The quality of a therapeutic relationship is a function of the patient and therapist's ability to establish a therapeutic alliance (also referred to as the working alliance).

The therapeutic alliance is defined as "an emergent quality of partnership and mutual collaboration between therapist and client" (Horvath, Del Re, Flückiger, & Symonds, 2011), characterized by collaboration in the moment-to-moment interactions between therapist and patient (Flückiger, Wampold, & Horvath, 2018). The therapeutic alliance is thus an emergent intersubjective phenomena that is cocreated by therapist and patient and is not the outcome of a specific mode of therapy (Flückiger et al., 2018). A positive therapeutic alliance is not necessarily curative in and of itself, nonetheless it is what motivates the client to steadfastly follow and accept treatment (Horvath & Luborsky, 1993). The therapeutic alliance is considered a robust predictor of patients' response to conventional psychotherapy, independent of the duration or type of psychotherapy (Flückiger et al., 2018; Glueck, 2013).

Conceptualizing the therapeutic alliance from a pantheoretical perspective, Bordin (1979) identified three core components of an effective therapeutic alliance, namely:

(1) consensus on the specific goals of therapy;
(2) agreement on the therapeutic tasks; and
(3) the bond between the therapist and client.

Bordin's assertion that the therapeutic alliance is shaped by three factors (i.e., goals, task, and bond) is echoed by Horvath and Luborsky (1993) in their delineation of the common elements of instruments widely used to measure the therapeutic alliance.

It seems unlikely that the goals and tasks of therapy would be adversely affected by using technology to deliver remote psychotherapy, however, the third element of the therapeutic alliance (i.e., the bond between therapist and patient) may be vulnerable in online psychotherapies (Simpson & Reid, 2014). This is significant, given that the attachment between patient and therapist forms the fulcrum of a trusting relationship and the basis of the client's ability to face personal fears and anxieties. Of concern here is whether physical proximity is a necessary condition for the development of a meaningful therapeutic attachment and whether the felt security required for a therapeutic alliance can be achieved in cyberspace. Attachment theory has yet to provide definitive answers to these questions, nonetheless research suggests that the therapeutic alliance and rapport established in remote psychotherapy is equivalent to that achieved in conventional in-person therapies (Flückiger et al., 2018; Goldstein & Glueck, 2016; Simpson & Reid, 2014). A recent systematic review and noninferiority meta-analysis concluded that an effective working alliance can be achieved in online psychotherapies, although the therapeutic alliance established through videoconferencing is inferior to that established in in-person therapy (Norwood, Moghaddam, Malins, & Sabin-Farrell, 2018). Norwood et al. have, however, cautioned against overinterpreting research on the online therapeutic alliance since the measures commonly used to assess the quality of the patient-therapist relationship were developed for in-person psychotherapy and may not take account of the kind of online therapeutic relationships that develop in remote psychotherapies (Norwood et al., 2018). Bordin has hypothesized that various therapeutic modalities would develop their own ideal profile of the alliance (Bordin, 1979), highlighting the need for technology-specific studies of the therapeutic alliance and the development of technology-specific instruments to measure the cyber therapeutic alliance.

It has been suggested that remote psychotherapy offers the potential for clients to feel more empowered, safe, and autonomous, which could compensate for any adverse impact technology may have on the therapeutic relationship (Norwood et al., 2018). Technology may, however, threaten some aspects of the therapeutic alliance (Glueck, 2013), consequently it has been suggested that when conducting online therapy the therapists should take concrete steps to optimize opportunities to establish rapport. There are practical strategies that therapists can adopt to compensate for technological threats to the therapeutic relationship (see Table 11.3). What is interesting about the strategies listed in Table 11.3 is that many of these are directed toward establishing and maintaining Bordin's third dimension of a therapeutic alliance (i.e., the bond between the patient and therapist), rather than supporting the first two dimensions of the therapeutic alliance (i.e., the goals and tasks of therapy) (Bordin, 1979), highlighting the potential application of attachment theory to understanding cyber therapeutic relationships. In the section that follows, we explore how attachment theory might be fruitfully applied to promote the development of relationship-centered e-interventions.

Table 11.3   Practical strategies for establishing rapport in online psychotherapy.

Keep in mind the central importance of eye contact, speech, and observation of facial expressions by ensuring that the position of the camera, screen, and microphone optimize opportunities for the patient and therapist to see and hear each other clearly (Glueck, 2013). Maintain eye contact by reducing "eye-gaze distortions" that sometimes occur because of the position of the camera and screen (Goldstein & Glueck, 2016). Maintain a constant gaze into the camera. Braking eye contact, being distracted by papers on your desk or other objects in the room and looking around your screen are all very obvious in a videoconference call (Seager, Kroll, Martinez, Emerson, & Bursch, 2020). To help you stay focused on the patient, turn off all notifications and pop-ups (e.g., email notifications). Ensure a stable internet connection and sufficient bandwidth to maximize the transmission of uninterrupted real-time information between the therapeutic dyad (Goldstein & Glueck, 2016). Time lapses in verbal transmission should be avoided so that online communication approximates face-to-face therapy as far as possible (Glueck, 2013). The video frame rate and resolution should be high so as to allow even minor movements and facial expressions to be observable (Goldstein & Glueck, 2016). This will facilitate therapists' attunement and responsiveness to patients' emotions, and appropriate mirroring (Goldstein & Glueck, 2016). The "picture-in-picture function" available in most videoconferencing platforms allows therapists to self-monitor and receive real-time feedback, thus providing a unique opportunity for therapists to modulate their own body language and expressions (Glueck, 2013). Seek clarity from the patients when poor picture quality or a disruption in transmission distorts visual cues and nonverbal communication (Glueck, 2013). Make sure microphones are strategically placed and are sensitive enough to ensure that both the therapist and client's speech (including speech pattern, tone, etc.) are accurately conveyed (Glueck, 2013). Use a secure platform and, if necessary, be prepared to explain encrypted technology to the patient. Explicitly discuss issues of cyber security and confidentiality in the use of videoconference calls (Seager et al., 2020). Discuss the various options for remote psychotherapy with the patient (including the pros and cons of each medium) and decide with the patient which medium and platform to use (Seager et al., 2020). Discuss with the patient where they will be for the online sessions and encourage them to ensure that they are in a private space free of distractions (Seager et al., 2020). Ensure your camera is optimally positioned and focused so that the patient can clearly see your facial expressions (Seager et al., 2020). Pay attention to the lighting in order to optimize your visibility. Be conscious of what patients can and cannot see in your video frame. Give patients a visual context of where you are sitting and ask them if they would like to see your office. Provide reassurance that no one else is present and that no one else can hear the conversation (the use of earphones is a concrete way to signal that no one else can hear what the client is saying) (Seager et al., 2020). Give patients an opportunity to ask questions about the use of technology in the process at the outset of therapy (Seager et al., 2020). As you would in face-to-face therapy, use paraphrasing, mirroring, and reflections frequently to communicate that you are engaged and responsive. This will be particularly important if you are using a nonvisual medium (i.e., voice calls) as the patient will have no nonverbal cues to work from (Seager et al., 2020). It is inevitable that there will be technical problems (for example, interruptions in signal strength and lost connections). When these happen, acknowledge them with patience and an appropriate dose of humor (Seager et al., 2020). Anticipate and plan for technical difficulties. Discuss these with the patient at the outset of therapy and where possible have a backup system in place (Glueck, 2013).

Future directions for theory and research

Ongoing technological innovations and the evolution of digital mental health solutions will undoubtedly prompt us to continuously reconceptualize psychotherapy and reconsider the relational dimension of e-interventions. Attachment theory may offer some promise to understand *if*, *when*, and *how* e-interventions can harness the potential potency of a therapeutic relationship to facilitate change. In particular, attachment theory may aid the development of relationship-centered e-interventions by giving us an evidence-based psychological framework for engaging with the following questions:

(**1**) *What are the bounds of the therapeutic frame in cyberspace?* It is well understood in many conventional modes of psychotherapy that the formation of a productive therapeutic relationship requires a clearly demarcated and consistently maintained set of boundaries within which safety and security can be established. In psychodynamically informed psychotherapy, this set of boundaries is typically referred to as the therapeutic frame (Merchant, 2016). At a conscious level, the therapeutic frame is established and maintained through the articulation of a clear set of agreed rules, including the negotiation of fees, regular appointments at a consistent location, and a fixed duration for each appointment (Spruiell, 1983). From the perspective of attachment theory, the safety created by the therapeutic frame is a prerequisite for establishing the secure base on which a therapeutic alliance is built. But because of the nature of cyberspace, the therapeutic frame required for an e-intervention is not the same as that of a conventional psychotherapy. Cyberspace is an unbounded space characterized by: seemingly limitless possibilities for interconnectedness; indistinct (and perhaps unenforceable) rules of ownership and privacy; virtual (as opposed to physical) existence; and ambiguity and increasing complexity. These characteristics create the distinct impression that anything is possible in cyberspace and that the normal rules of the physical world are not necessarily applicable. Certainly, it would appear that the norms for relating and communicating in cyberspace are distinctly different from those in the physical world—see, for example, the discussion of sex and social media in the recently published book by Katrin Tiidenberg and Emily van der Nagel (Katrin & van der Nagel, 2020). Cyberspace offers people the freedom to drop their bodies and assume new (and multiple) identities. The apparent freedom of cyberspace can give rise to disinhibition (Suler, 2004) spawning behavior that might never be contemplated in "real life." As such, the normal boundaries of the therapeutic frame may be stretched or become indistinct in cyberspace, requiring the therapist to exercise a different set of strategies for maintaining the frame. It also seems likely that different modes of digital communication may require different therapeutic frames. Understanding what the optimal therapeutic frame is for different digital media and the strategies needed to maintain this frame will be important as we seek to develop a variety of relationship-centered e-interventions.

(**2**) *How does the attachment style of a user shape the way they engage with and respond to e-interventions?* Attachment theory could shed light on why the use of technology-based communication channels within intimate relationships take on different meanings for different people (Morey, Gentzler, Creasy, Oberhauser, & Westerman, 2013). As noted by Marmarosh (2015): "Attachment theory has an important place in understanding how technology can benefit and inhibit patient change depending on the patients' attachments and presenting concerns." For example, patients and therapists with a more avoidant attachment style may initially be drawn toward e-interventions because the physical distance can create a sense of relational security which precipitates the felt security required for a therapeutic alliance (Marmarosh, 2015). At the same time some modes of digital communication may appeal more to patients with an avoidant attachment style, because they allow the patient to regulate distance from the therapist and thus avoid dependency. Morey et al. (2013) noted how in romantic relationships digital communication may meet the particular needs of insecurely attached individuals because it creates the perception of easier and more regular access to a partner, something which may also be relevant in digital therapeutic relationships. These kinds of insights could aid the development of precision medicine algorithms that can predict why e-interventions work for some people and not others.

(3) *How are therapeutic attachments established in the absence of physical proximity?* In conventional psychological theory, attachment has been thought of primarily as a face-to-face, body-to-body phenomenon that is shaped by sensory and somatosensory stimuli perceived in the moment-to-moment interactions between two people. Diamond (2018) noted that it is relatively recently that technological advances have enabled opportunities for people to experience real-time verbal and visual contact with other people, at little to no cost. There is already tentative evidence to suggest that this kind of verbal and visual digital contact can facilitate attachment (see, for example, the study by Otway et al. (Otway, Carnelley, & Rowe, 2014) showing how texting can boost felt security) but it is as yet unclear if and how secure attachments can be formed in the absence of three-dimensional (3D) somatosensory and olfactory experiences. Crucially for psychotherapy this raises questions about whether a two-dimensional (2D) experience of a therapeutic relationship is sufficient for a patient to construct a stable and enduring internal mental representation of the therapist. It seems plausible that digital communication could "stand-in" for an attachment figure in the absence of physical proximity (i.e., that digital communication can activate existing internal mental representations of the other that were previously established by physical proximity, as, for example, it does when separated romantic couples use technology to maintain and satisfy their attachment needs) (Diamond, 2018). Indeed, evidence from online psychoanalysis indicates that transference and countertransference reactions that emulate the patient's previous significant attachment experiences can occur even when therapy is delivered remotely (Fishkin, Fishkin, Leli, Katz, & Snyder, 2011). This suggests that digital communication can facilitate the activation of existing internal representations and the reenactment of old attachment patterns. But this is not the same as facilitating a new internal representation or establishing a new mental model of attachment. More research is needed to understand if and how patients create internal mental representations of the digital therapist and whether patients see therapeutic chatbots as "people" that can also become internalized attachment figures.

(4) *Can a therapeutic relationship be maintained indefinitely with no physical proximity?* Research suggests that for romantic couples periodic remote communication may be sufficient for maintaining a secure attachment, but that this form of interaction becomes ineffective if the attachment bond is not nourished with intermittent real-time somatosensory, olfactory, and neuroendocrine input from the attachment figure (Diamond, 2018). This prompts questions about the capacity of patients and therapists to maintain a therapeutic alliance over a protracted period of time, in the absence of intermittent physical proximity, suggesting that perhaps technology may be better suited to the delivery of time-limited and brief interventions that do not require a sustained therapeutic alliance, or as an adjunct to face-to-face therapy when patient and therapists are temporarily geographically separated. Research is needed to establish the particular form and duration of physical and psychological proximity necessary to maintain attachment and hence a therapeutic alliance.

Conclusion

In his book, *Deep Medicine*, physician Eric Topol describes how technology can be used in the everyday practice of medicine not to replace doctors, but rather to create opportunities and time for deeper more meaningful human interaction between patient and doctor (Topol, 2019). It remains to be seen whether we will be able to achieve Topol's ideal in mental health care as we rush toward providing technological solutions in the form of e-interventions. To retain humanity and preserve personhood in a digital mental health-care system, we need to give careful and critical attention to the development of person- and relationship-centered e-interventions. This will require a sound evidence-based theoretical framework within which to conceptualize and research *if, when*, and *how* technology can be used to facilitate a therapeutic relationship in cyberspace. Attachment theory may hold the most promise for advancing theory and practice in the development of humanistic e-interventions.

Funding

This work was made possible through financial support provided to Jason Bantjes by the South African Medical Research Council (SAMRC) through its Division of Research Capacity Development under the Mid-Career Scientist Programme (MCSP). The content hereof is the sole responsibility of the authors and does not necessarily represent the official views of the SAMRC.

References

Andersson, G., & Titov, N. (2014). Advantages and limitations of internet-based interventions for common mental disorders. *World Psychiatry, 13*(1), 4–11.

Andrews, G., Cuijpers, P., Craske, M. G., McEvoy, P., & Titov, N. (2010). Computer therapy for the anxiety and depressive disorders is effective, acceptable and practical health care: A meta-analysis. Baune BT, ed. *PLoS ONE, 5*(10), e13196.

Baumeister, H., Reichler, L., Munzinger, M., & Lin, J. (2014). The impact of guidance on internet-based mental health interventions: A systematic review. *Internet Interventions, 1*(4), 205–215.

Bivens, R., & Haimson, O. L. (2016). Baking gender into social media design: How platforms shape categories for users and advertisers. *Social Media + Society, 2*(4), 205630511667248.

Bordin, E. S. (1979). The generalizability of the psychoanalytic concept of the working alliance. *Psychotherapy: Theory Research and Practice, 16*(3), 252–260.

Bowlby, J. (1988). *A secure base: Parent-child attachment and healthy human development*. London: Routledge.

Daniels, J. (2009). Rethinking cyberfeminism(s): Race, gender, and embodiment. *Women's Studies Quarterly, 37*(1/2), 101–124.

Diamond, L. M. (2018). Physical separation in adult attachment relationships. *Current Opinion in Psychology*.

Drisko, J. W. (2004). Common factors in psychotherapy outcome: Meta-analytic findings and their implications for practice and research. *Families in Society*, *85*(1), 81–90.

Fishkin, R., Fishkin, L., Leli, U., Katz, B., & Snyder, E. (2011). Psychodynamic treatment, training, and supervision using internet-based technologies. *The Journal of the American Academy of Psychoanalysis and Dynamic Psychiatry*, *39*(1), 155–168.

Flückiger, C., Wampold, B. E., & Horvath, A. O. (2018). The alliance in adult psychotherapy: A meta-analytic synthesis. *Psychotherapy (Chicago, Ill.)*, *55*(4), 316–340.

Freud, S. (1938). On the beginning of treatment: Further recommendations on the technique of psychoanalysis. In J. Strachey (Ed.), *Vol. 12. Standard edition of the complete psychological works of Sigmund Freud* (pp. 122–144). London: Hogarth Press.

Gaston, L. (1990). The concept of the alliance and its role in psychotherapy: Theoretical and empirical considerations. *Psychotherapy: Theory, Research, Practice, Training*, *27*(2), 143–153.

Glueck, D. (2013). Establishing therapeutic rapport in telemental health. In *Telemental health* (1st ed., pp. 29–46). Elsevier Inc. https://doi.org/10.1016/B978-0-12-416048-4.00003-8.

Goldstein, F., & Glueck, D. (2016). Developing rapport and therapeutic alliance during telemental health sessions with children and adolescents. *Journal of Child and Adolescent Psychopharmacology*, *26*(3), 204–211.

Hill, C., Martin, J. L., Thomson, S., Scott-Ram, N., Penfold, H., & Creswell, C. (2017). Navigating the challenges of digital health innovation: Considerations and solutions in developing online and smartphone-application-based interventions for mental health disorders. *The British Journal of Psychiatry*, *211*(2), 65–69.

Horvath, A. O., Del Re, A. C., Flückiger, C., & Symonds, D. (2011). Alliance in individual psychotherapy. *Psychotherapy*, *48*(1), 9–16.

Horvath, A. O., & Luborsky, L. (1993). The role of the therapeutic alliance in psychotherapy. *Journal of Consulting and Clinical Psychology*, *61*(4), 561–573.

Huckvale, K., Wang, C. J., Majeed, A., & Car, J. (2019). Digital health at fifteen: More human (more needed). *BMC Medicine*, *17*(1), 62.

Jones, B. A., Griffiths, K. M., Christensen, H., Ellwood, D., Bennett, K., & Bennett, A. (2013). Online cognitive behaviour training for the prevention of postnatal depression in at-risk mothers: A randomised controlled trial protocol. *BMC Psychiatry*, *13*, 265.

Kaplan, W. A. (2006). Can the ubiquitous power of mobile phones be used to improve health outcomes in developing countries? *Globalization and Health*, *2*(9).

Karyotaki, E., Riper, H., Twisk, J., Hoogendoorn, A., Kleiboer, A., Mira, A., et al. (2017). Efficacy of self-guided internet-based Cognitive Behavioral Therapy in the treatment of depressive symptoms. *JAMA Psychiatry*, *74*(4), 351.

Kascak, L. R., Rebola, C. B., & Sanford, J. A. (2014). Integrating universal design (UD) principles and mobile design guidelines to improve design of mobile health applications for older adults. In *2014 IEEE international conference on healthcare informatics* (pp. 343–348). IEEE.

Katrin, T., & van der Nagel, E. (2020). *Sex and social media*. Bingley, United Kingdom: Emerald Publishing Limited.

Kirmayer, L., & Jarvis, G. (2019). Culturally responsive services as a path to equity in mental healthcare. *Healthcare Papers*, *18*(2), 11–23.

Kushniruk, A. (2002). Evaluation in the design of health information systems: Application of approaches emerging from usability engineering. *Computers in Biology and Medicine*, *32*(3), 141–149.

Lambert, M. J., & Barley, D. E. (2001). Research summary on the therapeutic relationship and psychotherapy outcome. *Psychotherapy: Theory, Research, Practice, Training*, *38*(4), 357–361.

Lin, J., Ebert, D. D., Lehr, D., Berking, M., & Baumeister, H. (2013). Internet based cognitive behavioral interventions: State of the art and implementation possibilities in rehabilitation. *Rehabilitation (Stuttg)*, *52*(3), 155–163.

Luborsky, L., Auerbach, A. H., Chandler, M., Cohen, J., & Bachrach, H. M. (1971). Factors influencing the outcome of psychotherapy: A review of quantitative research. *Psychological Bulletin*, *75*(3), 145–185.

Mace, R. (1988). *Universal design: Housing for the lifespan of all people*. Nort Carolina, USA: The Center for Universal Design, Nort Carolina State Universit.

Marmarosh, C. L. (2015). Emphasizing the complexity of the relationship: The next decade of attachment-based psychotherapy research. *Psychotherapy*, *52*(1), 12–18.

Meara, J. G., Leather, A. J. M., Hagander, L., Alkire, B. C., Alonso, N., Ameh, E. A., et al. (2015). Global surgery 2030: Evidence and solutions for achieving health, welfare, and economic development. *Lancet*, *386*(9993), 569–624.

Merchant, J. (2016). The use of skype in analysis and training: A research and literature review. *The Journal of Analytical Psychology*, *61*(3), 309–328.

Morey, J. N., Gentzler, A. L., Creasy, B., Oberhauser, A. M., & Westerman, D. (2013). Computers in human behavior young adults' use of communication technology within their romantic relationships and associations with attachment style. *Computers in Human Behavior*, *29*(4), 1771–1778.

Mucic, D., & Hilty, D. M. (2020). Psychotherapy using electronic media. In *Intercultural psychotherapy* (pp. 205–229). Cham: Springer.

Norwood, C., Moghaddam, N. G., Malins, S., & Sabin-Farrell, R. (2018). Working alliance and outcome effectiveness in videoconferencing psychotherapy: A systematic review and non-inferiority meta-analysis. *Clinical Psychology & Psychotherapy*, *25*(6), 797–808.

Olthuis, J. V., Watt, M. C., Bailey, K., Hayden, J. A., & Stewart, S. H. (2016). Therapist-supported internet cognitive behavioural therapy for anxiety disorders in adults. *Cochrane Database of Systematic Reviews*, *3*, 1–205.

Opoku, D., Stephani, V., & Quentin, W. (2017). A realist review of mobile phone-based health interventions for non-communicable disease management in sub-Saharan Africa. *BMC Medicine*, *15*(1), 24.

Otway, L. J., Carnelley, K. B., & Rowe, A. C. (2014). Texting "boosts" felt security. *Attachment & Human Development*, *16*(1), 93–101.

Reyes-Portillo, J. A., Mufson, L., Greenhill, L. L., Gould, M. S., Fisher, P. W., Tarlow, N., et al. (2014). Web-based interventions for youth internalizing problems: A systematic review. *Journal of the American Academy of Child and Adolescent Psychiatry*, *53*(12), 1254–1270.e5.

Richards, D., & Richardson, T. (2012). Computer-based psychological treatments for depression: A systematic review and meta-analysis. *Clinical Psychology Review*, *32*(4), 329–342.

Rogers, C. R. (1957). The necessary and sufficient conditions of therapeutic personality change. *Journal of Consulting Psychology*, *21*(2), 95–103.

Rosenzweig, S. (1936). Some implicit common factors in diverse methods of psychotherapy. *The American Journal of Orthopsychiatry*, *6*(3), 412–415.

Russ, A. L., Fairbanks, R. J., Karsh, B.-T., Militello, L. G., Saleem, J. J., & Wears, R. L. (2013). The science of human factors: Separating fact from fiction. *BMJ Quality and Safety*, *22*(10), 802–808.

Ruzic, L., Lee, S. T., Liu, Y. E., & Sanford, J. A. (2016). *Development of universal design mobile interface guidelines (UDMIG) for aging population* (pp. 98–108).

Sachan, D. (2018). Self-help robots drive blues away. *The Lancet Psychiatry.*, *5*(7), 547.

Scanlon, M. C., & Karsh, B.-T. (2010). Value of human factors to medication and patient safety in the intensive care unit. *Critical Care Medicine*, *38*, S90–S96.

Schwab, T., & Langell, J. (2018). Human factors–based mobile application design for global health. *Surgical Innovation*, *25*(6), 557–562.

Seager, I., Kroll, J., Martinez, R., Emerson, N., & Bursch, B. (2020). Covid-19 tips: Building rapport with youth via telehealth. In *UCLA Pediatr Psychol Consult Liaison Serv* (pp. 1–3).

Shore, J. (2015). The evolution and history of telepsychiatry and its impact on psychiatric care: Current implications for psychiatrists and psychiatric organizations. *International Review of Psychiatry*, *27*(6), 469–475.

Simpson, S. G., & Reid, C. L. (2014). Special Issue: Psychology in the bush original research therapeutic alliance in videoconferencing psychotherapy: A review. *Australian Journal of Rural Health*, 280–299.

Spruiell, V. (1983). The rules and frames of the psychoanalytic situation. *The Psychoanalytic Quarterly*, *52*(1), 1–33.

Suler, J. (2004). The online disinhibition effect. *CyberPsychology and Behaviour*, *7*(3), 321–326.

Topol, E. (2019). *Deep medicine: How artificial intelligence can make healthcare human again.* New York, United States: Basic Books.

Vallury, K. D., Jones, M., & Oosterbroek, C. (2015). Computerized cognitive behavior therapy for anxiety and depression in rural areas: A systematic review. *Journal of Medical Internet Research*, *17*(6), e139. Available from: http://www.jmir.org/2015/6/e139/.

Section C

Problematic use of the Internet

Gambling disorder, gaming disorder, cybershopping, and other addictive/impulsive disorders online

Jon E. Grant[a], Konstantinos Ioannidis[b], and Samuel R. Chamberlain[c,d]
[a]Department of Psychiatry, University of Chicago, Chicago, IL, United States, [b]Department of Psychiatry, University of Cambridge, and Cambridgeshire and Peterborough NHS Foundation Trust, Cambridge, United Kingdom, [c]Department of Psychiatry, Faculty of Medicine, University of Southampton, Southampton, United Kingdom, [d]Southern Health NHS Foundation Trust, Southampton, United Kingdom

Introduction

Problematic use of the Internet is an umbrella term, now used globally, referring to excessive engagement in online activities known to be associated with marked functional impairment. This term encapsulates a variety of online activities, including: compulsive online buying, online gambling, cybersex, excessive use of online pornography, excessive use of online streaming, excessive use of social media, cyberbullying, and cyberchondria. But how did we get to this point?

From the Internet's inception in the 1980s to the global domination of online-based life applications during the new millennium, the Internet has become an integral part of modern life (Gackenbach, 1998; Young, 1998). The "cyber-cosmos" has insidiously invaded our workplaces, interpersonal interactions, as well as family and private lives, including our most intimate moments. It rapidly became apparent to some researchers that specific vulnerable groups of adolescents and adults experienced a lack of control over the use of the Internet, leading to marked functional impairment (e.g., lower quality of life, worse academic performance, mental health struggles, interpersonal and vocational difficulties) (Kuss, Griffiths, Karila, & Billieux, 2014). In the mid-1990s, the term "Internet addiction disorder" was coined (Gackenbach, 1998; Young, 1998) to describe a maladaptive pattern of the use of online resources that shared the characteristics of an addictive ("Internet addiction") or compulsive disorder ("compulsive Internet use disorder").

Since these initial proposals, multiple diagnostic criteria, classifications, and conceptualizations of the phenomena at hand have been proposed; this has led to a wide array of inconsistent and often poorly validated diagnostic criteria, assessment tools, and conceptual formulations (Kardefelt-Winther, 2014). For example, a recent review revealed how prolific the field of gaming disorder had been in producing more than 300 studies, including 2.5 new gaming disorder diagnostic tools per annum in the last

Mental Health in a Digital World. https://doi.org/10.1016/B978-0-12-822201-0.00011-3

few years (King et al., 2020). The general "Internet addiction" field has been similarly prolific (Laconi, Rodgers, & Chabrol, 2014). Regarding terminology, different views on problematic use of the Internet were suggested, as exemplified by the terms referred to, e.g., compulsive Internet use, problematic Internet use, Internet addiction, etc.

The fifth edition of the Diagnostic and Statistical Manual of Mental Disorders (DSM-5) (American Psychiatric Association, APA, 2013) featured Internet Gaming Disorder (IGD) in Section III, as a condition in need of further study. The DSM-5 highlighted that Internet Gaming Disorder appeared to be most common in male adolescents, aged 12–20 years (APA, 2013). Following that, gaming disorder (GD) appeared in the 11th Revision of the International Classification of Diseases (ICD-11) as a pattern of gaming behavior ("digital gaming" or "video gaming") characterized by impaired control over gaming, increasing priority given to gaming over other activities to the extent that gaming takes precedence over other interests and daily activities, and continuation or escalation of gaming despite the occurrence of negative consequences (World Health Organization, WHO, 2019). There is some new empirical evidence that as compared to DSM-5, the ICD-11 GD classification may put more weighting on impairment and severity (Jo et al., 2019), which may be helpful to help avoid "overpathologizing." The need to identify functional impairment as a necessary aspect of the classification has been discussed extensively—see Billieux et al. (2017).

Whereas gaming gained initial traction and has been the focus of DSM-5, ICD-11, research, assessment tools, and therapeutic programs (King et al., 2017), the wider concept of problematic use of the Internet (PUI) was coined to avoid classification with addictions until more about the disorder was understood (Aboujaoude, 2010; Shapira et al., 2003) as well as to allow the wider range of behavioral phenotypes observed to be conceptualized, investigated, and understood, without having an implicit bias about the underlying neurobiological drivers of this behavior (Ioannidis et al., 2016). According to this line of investigation, studies identified a broad range of behaviors characterized by substantial and excessive interaction with the online milieu (Fineberg et al., 2018), behaviors that were then associated with marked functional impairment as well as with profound psychiatric sequalae in adolescents (Kuss, van Rooij, Shorter, Griffiths, & van de Mheen, 2013), adults (Ho et al., 2014), and across the age span (Ioannidis et al., 2018). These data raise the fundamental question: why focus on gaming in terms of nosological classification systems, rather than other types of online behavior that is linked with marked (and indeed, in some cases greater) functional impairment?

Based on empirical evidence, PUI is characterized by excessive online activities likely to be associated with marked functional impairment, in various facets of the human-online environment interaction: including, but not necessarily exhaustively, compulsive online buying, online gambling, cybersex, excessive use of online pornography, excessive use of online streaming, and excessive use of social media (Ioannidis et al., 2018). Other facets that have been investigated have been cyberbullying victimization and cyberchondria (Fineberg et al., 2018). Age influences the presentation of PUI and its comorbidities (Hampshire et al., 2020; Ioannidis et al., 2018). Rather than just focusing on the "addiction" model, a rigorous understanding of PUI needs to nsider addictive, impulse control (Beard & Wolf, 2001), and obsessive-compulsive-related phenomena (Block, 2008; Grant & Chamberlain, 2016; Zohar, 2010). Without a comprehensive approach cutting across these traditionally disparate psychiatric disciplines, important neurobiological models and treatment options are likely to be overlooked, to the detriment of patients.

This chapter will consider in turn three forms of PUI, which are relatively more studied than other areas of PUI, namely: gambling disorder, gaming disorder, and compulsive buying-shopping disorder (cybershopping). Because these have been mostly studied as stand-alone disorders/conditions in their own right, we also highlight their relationship to PUI in general where appropriate. It is important to note that whereas gambling disorder is a well-established mental disorder with considerable empirical support, other putative conditions are less well studied and debate continues as to whether they should be considered as formal mental disorders; and if so, using which criteria, and in which diagnostic category.

Phenomenology, comorbidity, and clinical assessment tools

Gambling disorder

Gambling disorder, is characterized by persistent and repetitive maladaptive patterns of gambling, leading to impaired functioning, and reduced quality of life (Hodgins, Stea, & Grant, 2011). It has a lifetime prevalence rate 0.4%–4%, and disproportionally affects young adults (Black & Shaw, 2019). Consequences of gambling disorder can include marital problems, financial hardship, increased suicidality, and undertaking criminal acts to fund gambling (such as embezzlement) (Grant & Kim, 2001). Gambling disorder is a primary mental disorder and is not contingent on whether the behavior is conducted online, using other technology, or in person (e.g., by visiting slot machines, casinos, or race events). However, online gambling is a common activity. In a report by the United Kingdom Gambling Commission (2019), 82% of previous 4-week gamblers had gambled in person, whereas 40% of previous 4-week gamblers had gambled online. As such, while most gambling—at present—may not be online, online gambling is commonplace. In a study examining gamblers, approximately 20% of the sample had significant PUI. PUI in gambling was associated with higher severity of gambling problems, worse quality of life, lower self-esteem, and higher rates of comorbid symptoms of ADHD, antisocial personality, intermittent explosive disorder, and posttraumatic stress disorder (Chamberlain, Redden, Leppink, & Grant, 2017; Chamberlain, Stochl, Redden, Odlaug, & Grant, 2017).

Gambling disorder, including online gambling, shows high rates of comorbidity, including with anxiety disorders, substance use disorders, depression, and attention-deficit hyperactivity disorder (ADHD) (Lorains, Cowlishaw, & Thomas, 2011; Petry, Stinson, & Grant, 2005). Overlap with compulsive disorders, such as obsessive-compulsive disorder, and obsessive-compulsive personality tendencies, is common. Because of the especially pronounced overlap with substance use disorders at many levels (including phenomenological, but also neurobiological), gambling disorder is currently listed in the Diagnostic and Statistical Manual Version 5 (DSM-5) category of "Substance Related and Addictive Disorders" (American Psychiatric Association, APA, 2013). It is the only behavioral addiction currently listed in that DSM-5 section.

While the trajectories of development of gambling disorder differ between people, overall there are high rates especially in adolescents and young adults, and the typical course is that of periods of abstinence and relapse (Leeman & Potenza, 2012). Interestingly, young adults with some degree of disordered gambling falling short of a full diagnosis have been found to show natural remission of symptoms as they get older (Grant, Derbyshire, Leppink, & Chamberlain, 2014). This may reflect changes in lifestyle—e.g., opportunities to gamble when mixing with peer groups at university, but more focus on careers later on; or changes arising during natural brain development, such as reducing levels of impulsivity over time (Grant et al., 2014). Extremely little is known about variables that predict, from people who gamble recreationally, who will develop disordered gambling; and of those, who will develop a chronic problem or experience remission. In the abovementioned study, persistence of disordered gambling overtime was statistically predicted by older age, and by gambling more money at baseline. Large-scale longitudinal cohorts are needed to further examine vulnerability and resilience markers.

For a diagnosis of gambling disorder to be made, DSM-5 (APA, 2013) requires that participants meet at least four of nine listed criteria—examples of criteria include: escalating amounts gambled over time, difficulty cutting back on gambling, and "chasing losses" (i.e., gambling more money or more frequently after losing, in the mistaken belief that a "win" is due—a type of cognitive distortion). These criteria are largely (but not entirely) adapted from work on substance use disorder. Typically, endorsing 1–3 criteria, but not more, is referred to as "problem gambling"; whereas "disordered gambling" refers to any criteria being met (i.e., problem gambling and gambling disorder). Generally speaking, the focus to date has been on full gambling disorder. However, it is worth considering that even endorsement of a few criteria has been linked to functional impairment similar that observed in people meeting the full diagnostic criteria (Chamberlain, Redden, et al., 2017; Chamberlain, Stochl, et al., 2017); and linked to decision-making deficits typically seen in people who fulfill complete diagnostic criteria (Grant, Chamberlain, Schreiber, Odlaug, & Kim, 2011).

Well-validated instruments exist to screen for gambling disorder, and to diagnose this condition. The Southampton-Chicago Impulsive Screener (S-CIS) is a convenient 1-page screener not only for gambling disorder, but also for many other commonly overlooked impulsive disorders (including compulsive buying, kleptomania, hair-pulling disorder, skin-picking disorder, nail biting, gambling disorder, pyromania, compulsive sex behavior disorder, binge-eating disorder, problematic Internet Use, intermittent explosive disorder, and nonsuicidal self-injury disorder) (Grant & Chamberlain, 2020). It can be used by clinicians or as a self-report instrument. The South Oaks Gambling Screen (SOGS) (Lesieur & Blume, 1987) is a 20-question instrument designed to identify individuals likely to have gambling disorder. These are screening instruments and are not appropriate to make full diagnoses. For a diagnosis of gambling disorder, one of the most used instruments is the Structured Clinical

Interview for Pathological Gambling, which has been further modified for DSM-5 gambling disorder (Grant, Steinberg, Kim, Rounsaville, & Potenza, 2004). To diagnose gambling disorder (as well as a wide array of other impulsive disorders), the Minnesota Impulse Disorders Inventory v1.1 (MIDI v1.1) is a well-validated diagnostic interview (Chamberlain, Ioannidis, & Grant, 2018; Grant, 2008). The MIDI exhibits strong concurrent validity against other gold standards (vs gambling disorder detailed interview, $P < .001$), has high test-retest reliability (95%), and discriminant validity vs primarily nonimpulsive symptoms, including against anxiety, depression, and obsessive-compulsive symptoms (all $P > .05$) (Chamberlain et al., 2018). It is important for clinicians to carefully assess for differential diagnoses—such as bipolar disorder (i.e., gambling in the context of one or more manic episodes).

Internet gaming disorder

Internet gaming disorder (IGD) has been conceptualized as a behavioral addiction, which involves excessive or poorly controlled preoccupation, urge, or behavior directed at engaging in videogame play leading to impairment or distress (Grant, Odlaug, Potenza, Hollander, & Kim, 2010; Grant, Potenza, Weinstein, & Gorelick, 2010). Both major classification systems have working criteria for IGD (or gaming disorder in ICD-11) (Jo et al., 2019). DSM-5 requires five or more of nine criteria be met (e.g., preoccupation, loss of control, and tolerance) concurrently within the past year (APA, 2013). On the other hand, the ICD-11 makes a distinction between online and offline gaming (WHO, 2019) and the disorder is characterized by impaired control over gaming, increasing priority given to gaming over other activities, continuation or escalation of gaming despite the occurrence of negative consequences, while gaming happens over a period of at least 12 months and is severe enough to result in significant impairment in interpersonal and psychosocial functioning.

Prevalence of IGD has mainly been studied in adolescent samples: in a meta-analysis, the pooled prevalence of IGD among adolescents was 4.6% (95% CI = 3.4%–6.0%) with IGD being more prevalent in males (6.8%, 95% CI = 4.3%–9.7%), and lower in females (1.3%, 95% CI = 0.6%–2.2%). Furthermore, prevalence estimates were highest for studies that were conducted in the 1990s using DSM criteria adapted from pathological gambling, and for those examining IGD in Asia and using relatively small samples (Fam, 2018). More recent meta-analysis also suggests higher rates in Asia but notes caveats about the lack of rigorous culture and country-specific validation for screening tools (Stevens, Dorstyn, Delfabbro, & King, 2020). The impact of gaming in the general population and the prevalence of IGD is still unclear and confounded by lack of comparable demographic data, comorbidity data, and of longitudinal studies. Of course, it is problematic to consider prevalence when the criteria for diagnosing IGD are provisional and have not been extensively validated. It is possible that while the Internet gaming has exploded on the global scene, prevalence rates of IGD may have remained relatively unchanged.

Despite any potential benefits that gaming might confer for some individuals, when gaming becomes compulsive, it has the potential to dominate someone's life to the degree of becoming highly absorbing in terms of their normal routine and interactions and highly time consuming to the detriment of other activities (Higuchi et al., 2017; King and Gaming Industry Response Consortium, 2018; King et al., 2019). As a consequence, individuals with GD may miss out on crucial life opportunities (e.g., academic progress, vocational goals) and experience a degree of interference with normal life routine including sometimes basic self-care (disrupted pattern of sleep-awake cycle, disordered eating, lack of adequate personal hygiene). Concerns also may arise from family and loved ones around the individual's pattern of real-world social interactions; for example, those with GD may chose virtual socialization over meeting friends and family in person (Griffiths, 2010; Koo, Han, Park, & Kwon, 2017). Gaming may be undertaken in response to negative emotional states (i.e., as a form of negative urgency) (Dong, Wang, Du, & Potenza, 2017) or even to manage "withdrawal-like" symptoms, e.g., negative states in the absence of gaming stimuli (Kaptsis, King, Delfabbro, & Gradisar, 2016). Negative feelings of missing the gaming environment may be quite complex, and might relate to the direct lack of rewarding stimuli of the gaming interface, or might relate to "fear of missing out" concerns, due to the social dimension of the gaming experience as a mean of communication with others around us (Wegmann, Oberst, Stodt, & Brand, 2017).

Little is known in terms of the longitudinal course of IGD, but the natural course of the illness seems to be more stable in adolescents rather than in adults (Mihara & Higuchi, 2017). In a recent review of 13 longitudinal studies of IGD (follow-up from 6 months up to 5 years), the severity of IGD was a predictive factor for having IGD in the future (King, Delfabbro, & Griffiths, 2013). Other candidate risk factors were identified: being male and being from a single-parent family (Rehbein & Baier, 2013); personality and psychological factors: loneliness (Lemmens, Valkenburg, & Peter, 2011), impulsivity, and problematic conduct; and social factors: lower involvement in sport (Gentile, 2009; Henchoz et al., 2016). Longitudinally, violent video gaming may be correlated with aggressive behavior in children, but the direction of the causal relationship is unknown. Conversely, higher self-esteem and social integration seem to protect from a longitudinal occurrence of IGD (Lemmens et al., 2011; Rehbein & Baier, 2013).

With respect to IGD comorbidities, affective disorders, substance use disorders, and ADHD are commonly reported. An eight-study ($n = 12,861$) meta-analysis of problematic users of the Internet, including online gaming, vs controls (Ho et al., 2014) found high associations with alcohol use disorder (OR = 3.05), depression (OR = 2.77), anxiety disorders (OR = 2.70) (e.g., generalized anxiety disorder, social anxiety disorder, obsessive-compulsive disorder), and ADHD (OR = 2.85). The longitudinal aspect of IGD is important when considering comorbid disorders: for example, those classified as having moderate to severe risk of IGD are about 2.5 times more likely to develop depressive symptoms at follow-up (Mihara & Higuchi, 2017).

While there is an abundance of instruments to screen and diagnose IGD (King et al., 2020), their coverage of the DSM-5 and ICD-11 criteria has been inconsistent. "Continued use despite harm" has specifically been assessed inconsistently. While there is no "gold standard" screening or diagnostic tool for IGD, a number of tools show reasonably good psychometric properties, which support the validity for their use (for a review see King et al., 2020). Those include the AICA-S (Wölfling, Beutel, & Müller, 2012),

GAS-7 (Lemmens, Valkenburg, & Peter, 2009), IGDT-10 (Király, Tóth, Urbán, Demetrovics, & Maraz, 2017), IGDS9-SF (Pontes & Griffiths, 2015), and Lemmens IGD-9 (Lemmens, Valkenburg, & Gentile, 2015) scales. Overall, these currently have greater evidential support for their psychometric properties than other scales, though the authors of the review paper highlight the need for a standard international tool to identify gaming-related harms across the spectrum of maladaptive gaming behaviors (King et al., 2020).

Compulsive buying disorder

Buying and shopping are normal, culturally accepted activities. While the vast majority of shoppers have no major problem inhibiting their impulses to shop, vulnerable individuals can develop compulsive buying disorder. Though not currently recognized in the DSM-5, this condition was included in an earlier version of the DSM as an impulse-control disorder not otherwise specified; and was described clinically in the 20th century by Bleuler and Kraepelin (Black, 2007). The core feature of compulsive buying disorder is the excessive, persistent, uncontrollable purchase of products despite functional impairment (Müller, Mitchell, & de Zwaan, 2015). This functional impairment can include psychological as well as social, financial, or occupational consequences. Financial difficulties are often the initial problem, such as credit card debt, and overdrawn bank accounts. This in turn can fuel other aspects of impairment such as consequent relationship problems, or development of depression.

Compulsive buying disorder has a point prevalence of approximately 5%–5.8% (Koran, Faber, Aboujaoude, Large, & Serpe, 2006; Maraz, Griffiths, & Demetrovics, 2016), though with considerable variation depending on the nature of the sample examined—being higher in young adults, for example. The Internet constitutes an extremely convenient method for purchasing items and hence it is not surprising that compulsive buying disorder would be related to PUI. In a large study examining types of Internet use activities in PUI, one of the strongest statistical associations was for shopping, which was larger than PUI's association with gaming, gambling, use of pornography, and social networking (Ioannidis et al., 2018). A high proportion of treatment-seeking individuals with compulsive buying disorder endorse online shopping as being prominent; and the online form is associated with worse symptom severity (Müller et al., 2019).

In terms of comorbidities, one study found that two-thirds of people with compulsive buying disorder had experienced another major mental disorder at some point in life, especially mood disorders, anxiety disorders, substance use disorders, and personality disorder (especially obsessive-compulsive, avoidant, and borderline types) (Schlosser, Black, Repertinger, & Freet, 1994). Another study reported similar results, also noting high prevalence of eating disorders compared to community controls (Mueller et al., 2009). Very little is known about the longitudinal course of compulsive buying disorder.

Compulsive buying disorder can be briefly screened for using the previously described Southampton-Chicago Impulsive Screener (S-CIS) (Grant & Chamberlain, 2020). More detailed screening tools focusing on compulsive buying disorder include the compulsive buying scale (CBS) (Faber & O'Guinn, 1992), and the pathological buying screener (PBS) (Müller, Trotzke, Mitchell, de Zwaan, & Brand, 2015). The CBS has seven items and uses a five-point scale for responses; two items consider emotional reactions to shopping, and five consider financial consequences. The PBS has 30 questions, each answered in terms of frequency on a 5-point scale. Compulsive buying disorder can be diagnosed using the relevant module from the Minnesota Impulse Disorders Inventory v1.1 (MIDI v1.1) (Chamberlain et al., 2018; Grant, 2008). As with many of the emerging areas of mental health research (and as for PUI itself), a multitude of other instruments exist [reviewed by Mueller, Mitchell, and Peterson (2012)]. It is important to consider differential diagnoses such as mania, kleptomania (compulsive stealing disorder); and to be careful to delineate recreational buying activities from true compulsive buying disorder.

Psychobiology

Our urges and habits are driven by fronto-striatal brain circuitry. In particular, the ventral striatum (nucleus accumbens) plays a crucial role in reward drive, whereas the dorsal striatum (caudate/putamen) is thought to be more important in driving our habits. The cortex exerts top-down control over these evolutionarily ancient systems in order to regulate these urges and habits appropriately. Dysregulation of these cortical and subcortical regions is central to understanding a range of symptom types, including PUI, gambling disorder, gaming disorder, and buying/shopping disorder. While of course overly simplistic in attempting to capture the richness of human behavior and impulsive/compulsive problems, this model—originally applied to OCD (Chamberlain, Blackwell, Fineberg, Robbins, & Sahakian, 2005; Graybiel & Rauch, 2000) and substance use disorders (Everitt & Robbins, 2005)—constitutes a useful vantage point for the wider spectrum of conditions. Certain behaviors are intrinsically prone to repetition, and thus for vulnerable individuals can become ingrained and consequently impairing. It is theorized that behaviors that are initially rewarding can switch over time to become essentially habitual, and not necessarily still driven by reward. At the same time, it is important to appreciate that neurobiological research into many of these putative conditions is limited, despite such data informing recent changes to diagnostic classification systems, viz., the inclusion of gambling disorder in the DSM-5 section on substance use and addictive disorders, and the inclusion of gaming disorder in the International Classification of Diseases 11 (ICD-11).

Objective cognitive tests provide one means of exploring the status of underlying fronto-striatal brain circuitry. Typical studies in this area would use a case-control design to compare cognitive performance between a group of people with a given putative disorder and matched healthy controls. Given that the definitions of mental disorders are not based on neurobiology, but rather on expert consensus, and in view of the heterogeneity of these disorders, it is to be expected that cognitive findings would not be consistent across studies. This is also the case because individual case-control studies differ considerably in the extent to which they control for confounding variables across groups. One key way of synergizing the data is to conduct meta-analysis of case-control studies for a given disorder, and this has been possible for some of these conditions. We focus on such distilled evidence here when possible; if metaanalyses are not available, we provide an overview of individual case-control studies of particular relevance. It should be noted that while meta-analysis provides a convenient means of synergizing evidence, it is contingent on the methodological quality of included data studies. As a caveat, it should be considered that much of the cognitive and imaging literature for these disorders had major methodological issues, such as not screening for the most common comorbidities, and not controlling for confounding variables.

Gambling disorder

Gambling disorder has been relatively widely studied in terms of its neurocognitive underpinnings. Consistent with the above overarching neurobiological model, tasks have typically focused on impulsivity (loss of top-down inhibitory control over behavior, measured, for example, using stop-signal, decision-making, and discounting tasks); and compulsivity (inflexible responding, measured, for example, using set-shifting tasks). In a meta-analysis of tasks of impulsivity, gambling disorder was associated with impairments in motor inhibition, attentional inhibition, discounting, and decision-making (Ioannidis, Hook, Goudriaan, et al., 2019; Ioannidis, Hook, Wickham, Grant, & Chamberlain, 2019). Problem gambling (referring to endorsement of some criteria but not meeting full diagnostic criteria) had not been much studied, but there was initial evidence to indicate impaired decision-making compared to controls. Study quality was reasonable overall, but the vast majority of studies did not screen for comorbid impulsive and related disorders. For compulsivity (van Timmeren, Daams, van Holst, & Goudriaan, 2018), gambling disorder was associated with impairments in cognitive flexibility, attentional set-shifting, and attentional bias. Meta-analysis of studies using functional imaging versions of cognitive tasks indicated abnormal activation patterns in the frontal lobes and basal ganglia, in gambling disorder vs controls (Luijten, Schellekens, Kühn, Machielse, & Sescousse, 2017; Quaglieri et al., 2020).

Gaming disorder (and PUI)

On a neurocognitive level, PUI (including online gaming disorder) has been associated with significant cognitive deficits in attentional inhibition, motor inhibition (and prepotent motor inhibition), decision-making, and working memory, in meta-analysis (Ioannidis, Hook, Goudriaan, et al., 2019; Ioannidis, Hook, Wickham, et al., 2019). When specifically examined, moderation analysis did not separate the umbrella PUI from gaming-specific PUI suggesting that the neurocognitive signature of PUI does not appear to be significantly moderated by whether or not online gaming was the predominant form of online behavior. Further analysis indicated that the impairments were not significantly moderated by geographical site, age, gender, or comorbidities. In an initial case-control study, the presence of impulse-control disorders was shown as a potentially significant confounder in exploring cognitive determinants in the background of mental health comorbidity (Chamberlain et al., 2018), highlighting the need to examine such comorbidities in parallel with PUI.

Taken together, there exist a substantial number of neurocognitive studies to support the existence of underlying fronto-striatal dysfunction in PUI and gaming disorder, at the magnitude of a medium effect size. This identified dysfunction not moderated by gaming being the predominant activity suggests a common neurobiological vulnerability across PUI behaviors. Initial meta-analysis of imaging findings using cognitive tasks in Internet gaming disorder suggested distributed abnormal cortical activation patterns vs controls (Yao et al., 2017).

Compulsive buying disorder

For compulsive buying disorder, there is very little research indeed regarding whether such patients experience objective cognitive problems. In nontreatment-seeking compulsive buyers, significant impairments were found compared to matched controls on response inhibition, risk adjustment during decision-making, and spatial working memory (Derbyshire, Chamberlain, Odlaug, Schreiber, & Grant, 2014). This suggests that there may be some overlapping problems with gambling disorder, gaming disorder, and PUI itself, in terms of impulsivity. Neuroimaging studies for compulsive buying disorder are lacking.

Treatment: Pharmacotherapy and psychotherapy

Gambling disorder

Various medications have been investigated, to some extent, in the context of treating gambling disorder, including antidepressants (particularly serotonin reuptake inhibitors), glutamate modulators, opioid antagonists, and mood-stabilizing agents. Placebo response in gambling disorder is often high (approximately 50%) (Grant & Chamberlain, 2017), and so data from open-label studies need to be viewed with particular caution. There have been approximately 20 randomized, double-blind placebo-controlled clinical trials in gambling disorder, often with mixed findings. Here, we focus on those studies conducted using opioid antagonists and glutamate modulators, as these appear to yield the most therapeutically consistent data; and are also particularly relevant to neurobiological models implicating dysregulation of reward and habit pathways.

In a 12-week study using naltrexone in gambling disorder, superiority was shown over placebo (Kim, Grant, Adson, & Shin, 2001). Another gambling disorder study, this time over 18-weeks, again showed superiority of naltrexone over placebo (Grant, Kim, & Hartman, 2008). In a study in patients with gambling and alcohol use disorder, naltrexone did not differentiate significantly from placebo when used in addition to cognitive behavioral therapy (CBT) (Toneatto, Brands, & Selby, 2009). This is unsurprising because CBT is a first-line treatment for both disorders, and would be expected to lead to symptom improvement in itself. Findings from a gambling disorder study where participants used naltrexone "as needed" were negative, which could reflect the relatively low use of the medication (typically two to three times per week) (Kovanen, Basnet, Castrén, et al., 2016).

Two multicenter studies have further demonstrated the efficacy of opioid antagonists in gambling disorder, this time with nalmefene. In a 16-week multicenter trial, 59% of those assigned to nalmefene showed significant improvements in gambling symptoms as compared to 34% taking placebo (Grant et al., 2006). A second 16-week multicenter study using nalmefene failed to show benefit in the intention-to-treat population compared to placebo, but posthoc analyses of those who received a full titration of the medication for at least 1 week demonstrated significantly greater reductions in gambling symptoms compared to placebo (Grant, Odlaug, et al., 2010; Grant, Potenza, et al., 2010).

In terms of glutamate modulators, n-acetyl cysteine (NAC) has been examined in gambling disorder. Based on preclinical work, NAC is thought to modulate nucleus accumbens glutamate release and, therefore, to dampen down reward-seeking behaviors (Kalivas, Peters, & Knackstedt, 2006). In one study, NAC was given open label for 8 weeks, with responders then randomized double blind to NAC or placebo for a further 6 weeks. At the end of the double-blind phase, 83% of those assigned to NAC were still classified as responders compared to 28.6% of those assigned to placebo (Grant, Kim, & Odlaug, 2007). A second 12-week, double-blind placebo-controlled study combined NAC with imaginal desensitization (a type of psychotherapy) in nicotine-dependent gambling disordered patients. NAC provided significant benefit compared to placebo on nicotine-dependence symptoms during treatment and on gambling symptoms after formal treatment ended, 3 months later (Grant et al., 2014).

In terms of psychotherapy for gambling disorder, the evidence base has recently been extensively reviewed (Petry, Ginley, & Rash, 2017). Approximately 10 studies have evaluated multisession in-person therapy (such as cognitive behavioral therapy, and motivational interviewing) for gambling disorder, and a similar number examined brief interventions (such as workbooks or brief advice) (Petry et al., 2017). Overall, benefits were found for active treatments over control conditions in the short term, but long-term benefits were not clearly established in most cases. Studies generally lacked rigorous control conditions.

Gaming disorder (and PUI)

The majority of research into candidate treatments for any PUI form, to date, focused on gaming disorder. We do not yet know whether treatments that may work for gaming disorder could readily be adapted, and be effective for, other forms of PUI. Survey data indicate that there is substantial demand for the treatment of IGD, that the majority of clinicians are not confident on how to treat it, and that clinicians would tend to view psychotherapy as an initial option (Dullur & Hay, 2017), even with a paucity of controlled therapy trials (but see a group-based mindfulness trial—Li et al., 2017).

To date, there are no high-quality double-blinded placebo-controlled pharmacological treatment trials for gaming disorder. There are a number of agents that have been trialed in an exploratory fashion, providing some support for efficacy, but substantially confounded by comorbid coexisting disorders. For example, citalopram and bupropion have been tried in the context of comorbid depression (Nam, Bae, Kim, et al., 2017) and atomoxetine and methylphenidate in comorbid ADHD (Park, Lee, Sohn, et al., 2016). Robust randomized controlled trials with appropriate sample sizes, diagnostic assessment, and control of confounding comorbidities are nonexistent.

An international systematic review appraising the quality standards of the Internet addiction treatment literature (King, Delfabbro, Griffiths, & Gradisar, 2011) was performed according to the 2010 Consolidating Standards of Reporting Trials (CONSORT) statement for quality ascertainment. This review identified several key limitations in the quality of study design and reporting to that date. Almost a decade later, another review by King et al. (2017)—also using CONSORT—reaffirmed major issues in therapeutic trials for IGD. These included: inconsistencies of definition, diagnostic criteria, and measurement of IGD; lack of randomization and blinding in the study design; insufficient collateral data to affirm quality of recruitment processes; and inadequate reporting, e.g., lack of effect sizes. These issues are concerning given that there are a range of providers across the world now offering inpatient and outpatient treatment programs. In effect, the systematic review revealed that study design quality had not improved over 10 years, highlighting a pressing need for high-quality research to be conducted.

Compulsive buying disorder

Knowledge regarding effective psychological and medication treatments for compulsive buying disorder is quite limited at this time. Most individuals with compulsive buying disorder do not seek treatment; there is a lack of evidence-based treatments, and many geographical jurisdictions do not offer any treatments. This problem is likely compounded by the failure to include compulsive buying disorder in DSM-5, and by the relatively low number of high-quality treatment studies in the literature.

In terms of randomized double-blind placebo-controlled clinical trials, one small study examined the serotonin reuptake inhibitor fluvoxamine vs placebo over 9-weeks in compulsive buying disorder (Black, Gabel, Hansen, & Schlosser, 2000). Fluvoxamine did not differentiate from placebo. Similar negative results were obtained in another study using fluvoxamine for 13 weeks (Ninan et al., 2000). In a trial examining topiramate over 12-week vs placebo, with all subjects also receiving psychoeducation (Nicoli de Mattos et al., 2020), topiramate did not differentiate from placebo on the primary outcome measures. In a small study involving open-label treatment then double-blind discontinuation for 9-week (i.e., continuation of active treatment or switch to placebo), escitalopram did not differentiate from placebo (Koran, Aboujaoude, Solvason, Gamel, & Smith, 2007).

Overall then, randomized controlled trials to date to not support a particular medication as being demonstrably effective in compulsive buying disorder. Trials of medications found to be effective in other related conditions, such as opioid antagonists or glutamate modulators, would be valuable in the future research.

For psychological interventions, in a systematic review of treatment studies for compulsive buying disorder, several studies were found that yielded significant improvements in compulsive buying using group CBT (typically 12 weeks duration); with some evidence also for telephone-guided self-help (12 weeks duration) (Hague, Hall, & Kellett, 2016). However, rigorous control conditions were generally lacking, with studies relying instead typically only on waiting list control. There was one exception: one high-quality study compared group CBT ($n=22$) to telephone-guided self-help ($n=20$), and waiting list ($n=14$). Face-to-face CBT was superior to both other conditions (Müller, Arikian, de Zwaan, & Mitchell, 2013). Overall then, initial evidence suggests that group CBT shows promise in compulsive buying disorder, but more high-quality treatment trials are required before any particular treatment can be categorically recommended.

Discussion and concluding remarks

This chapter considered gambling disorder, gaming disorder, and compulsive buying/shopping disorder within an overarching framework of Problematic Use of the Internet (PUI). While the majority of people can undertake online activities (such as gambling, gaming, and shopping) without untoward impact, abundant evidence indicates that some people are vulnerable to developing habitual, functionally impairing forms of these behaviors. At the same time, it is acknowledged that the Internet offers major societal advantages, and can also play a vital role in treatments. The question remains on the individual level as to whether the person has a problem with the Internet per se or whether the Internet is merely a conduit for some other form of impulsive behavior such as gaming, gambling, or shopping. Answering this question is important as the above-referenced literature suggests that treatment may differ depending upon what drives the maladaptive behavior (CBT or an opioid antagonist if gambling, group CBT if shopping, etc.).

Research into these conditions has typically assessed them in isolation, often not measuring established mental disorders or other online activities in the PUI umbrella, which are likely to be important determinants of impairment. There is also a poverty of longitudinal research, which is necessary to understand vulnerability and resilience factors as to who develops these disorders; and to better understand how symptoms change over time and are affected by personal and environmental variables. In terms of treatment studies, there have been a number of high-quality studies for gambling disorder, but we still need larger studies using a broader range of pharmacological agents and other psychosocial treatment approaches. Longer-term treatment outcomes for all of these disorders need more research. For gaming disorder, there are no high-quality pharmacological trials, and despite a number of psychotherapy studies, major methodological weaknesses are evident. For buying/shopping disorder, only a handful of high-quality studies were identified, but these indicate promise for group CBT.

Disclosures

Dr. Chamberlain previously consulted for Promentis. He receives honoraria from Elsevier for editorial work at Comprehensive Psychiatry, and at Neuroscience & Biobehavioral Reviews. Dr. Chamberlain's research is funded by a Wellcome Trust Clinical Fellowship

(110049/Z/15/Z & A). Dr. Grant has received research grants from NIMH, National Center for Responsible Gaming, and Forest and Roche Pharmaceuticals. Dr. Grant receives yearly compensation from Springer Publishing for acting as Editor-in-Chief of the Journal of Gambling Studies and has received royalties from Oxford University Press, American Psychiatric Publishing, Inc., Norton Press, and McGraw Hill.

References

Aboujaoude, E. (2010). Problematic internet use: An overview. *World Psychiatry*, *9*, 85–90.

American Psychiatric Association. (2013). *Diagnostic and statistical manual of mental disorders version 5 (DSM-5)*.

Beard, K. W., & Wolf, E. M. (2001). Modification in the proposed diagnostic criteria for internet addiction. *CyberPsychology & Behavior*, *4*, 377–383.

Billieux, J., King, D., Higuchi, S., Achab, S., Bowden-Jones, H., Hao, W., et al. (2017). Functional impairment matters in the screening and diagnosis of gaming disorder. *Journal of Behavioral Addictions*, *6*, 285–289.

Black, D. W. (2007). A review of compulsive buying disorder. *World Psychiatry*, *6*(1), 14–18.

Black, D. W., Gabel, J., Hansen, J., & Schlosser, S. (2000). A double-blind comparison of fluvoxamine versus placebo in the treatment of compulsive buying disorder. *Annals of Clinical Psychiatry*, *12*(4), 205–211.

Black, D. W., & Shaw, M. (2019). The epidemiology of gambling disorder. *Gambling Disorder*, 29–48.

Block, J. J. (2008). Issues for DSM-V: Internet addiction. *The American Journal of Psychiatry*, *165*, 306–307.

Chamberlain, S. R., Blackwell, A. D., Fineberg, N. A., Robbins, T. W., & Sahakian, B. J. (2005). The neuropsychology of obsessive compulsive disorder: The importance of failures in cognitive and behavioural inhibition as candidate endophenotypic markers. *Neuroscience and Biobehavioral Reviews*, *29*(3), 399–419.

Chamberlain, S. R., Ioannidis, K., & Grant, J. E. (2018). The impact of comorbid impulsive/compulsive disorders in problematic internet use. *Journal of Behavioral Addictions*, *7*(2), 269–275.

Chamberlain, S. R., Redden, S. A., Leppink, E., & Grant, J. E. (2017). Problematic internet use in gamblers: Impact on clinical and cognitive measures. *CNS Spectrums*, *22*(6), 495–503.

Chamberlain, S. R., Stochl, J., Redden, S. A., Odlaug, B. L., & Grant, J. E. (2017). Latent class analysis of gambling subtypes and impulsive/compulsive associations: Time to rethink diagnostic boundaries for gambling disorder? Version 2. *Addictive Behaviors*, *72*, 79–85.

Derbyshire, K. L., Chamberlain, S. R., Odlaug, B. L., Schreiber, L. R., & Grant, J. E. (2014). Neurocognitive functioning in compulsive buying disorder. *Annals of Clinical Psychiatry*, *26*(1), 57–63.

Dong, G., Wang, L., Du, X., & Potenza, M. N. (2017). Gaming increases craving to gaming-related stimuli in individuals with internet gaming disorder. *Biological Psychiatry: Cognitive Neuroscience and Neuroimaging*, *2*, 404–412.

Dullur, P., & Hay, P. (2017). Problem internet use and internet gaming disorder: A survey of health literacy among psychiatrists from Australia and New Zealand. *Australasian Psychiatry*, *25*(2), 140–145.

Everitt, B. J., & Robbins, T. W. (2005). Neural systems of reinforcement for drug addiction: From actions to habits to compulsion. *Nature Neuroscience*, *8*(11), 1481–1489.

Faber, R. J., & O'Guinn, T. C. (1992). A clinical screener for compulsive buying. *Journal of Consumer Research*, *19*(3), 459–469.

Fam, J. Y. (2018). Prevalence of internet gaming disorder in adolescents: A meta- analysis across three decades. *Scandinavian Journal of Psychology*, *59*(5), 524–531.

Fineberg, N. A., Demetrovics, Z., Stein, D. J., Ioannidis, K., Potenza, M. N., Grünblatt, E., et al. (2018). Manifesto for a European research network into problematic usage of the internet. Version 2. *European Neuropsychopharmacology*, *28*(11), 1232–1246.

Gackenbach, J. (1998). *Psychology and the Internet. Intrapersonal, interpersonal, and transpersonal implications* (1st ed.). Academic Press.

Gambling Commission (UK). (2019). *Gambling participation in 2018: Behaviour, awareness and attitudes*. Annual Report www.gamblingcommission.gov.uk.

Gentile, D. (2009). Pathological video-game use among youth ages 8 to 18: A national study. *Psychological Science*, *20*, 594–602.

Grant, J. E. (2008). *Impulse control disorders*. New York: Norton Press.

Grant, J. E., & Chamberlain, S. R. (2016). Expanding the definition of addiction: DSM-5 vs. ICD-11. *CNS Spectrums*, *21*(4), 300–303.

Grant, J. E., & Chamberlain, S. R. (2017). The placebo effect and its clinical associations in gambling disorder. *Annals of Clinical Psychiatry*, *29*(3), 167–172.

Grant, J. E., & Chamberlain, S. R. (2020). *Validation of the Southampton-Chicago Impulsive Screener (S-CIS) across gambling disorder and impulsive disorders: psychometric findings*. Unpublished data, on file.

Grant, J. E., Chamberlain, S. R., Schreiber, L. R., Odlaug, B. L., & Kim, S. W. (2011). Selective decision-making deficits in at-risk gamblers. *Psychiatry Research*, *189*(1), 115–120.

Grant, J. E., Derbyshire, K., Leppink, E., & Chamberlain, S. R. (2014). One-year follow-up of subsyndromal gambling disorder in non-treatment-seeking young adults. *Annals of Clinical Psychiatry*, *26*(3), 199–205.

Grant, J. E., & Kim, S. W. (2001). Demographic and clinical features of 131 adult pathological gamblers. *Journal of Clinical Psychiatry*, *62*, 957–962.

Grant, J. E., Kim, S. W., & Hartman, B. K. (2008). A double-blind, placebo-controlled study of the opiate antagonist, naltrexone, in the treatment of pathological gambling urges. *Journal of Clinical Psychiatry*, *69*, 783–789.

Grant, J. E., Kim, S. W., & Odlaug, B. L. (2007). N-acetyl cysteine, a glutamate-modulating agent, in the treatment of pathological gambling: A pilot study. *Biological Psychiatry*, *62*(6), 652–657.

Grant, J. E., Odlaug, B. L., Potenza, M. N., Hollander, E., & Kim, S. W. (2010). Nalmefene in the treatment of pathological gambling: Multi-Centre, double-blind, placebo-controlled study. *British Journal of Psychiatry*, *197*, 330–331.

Grant, J. E., Potenza, M. N., Hollander, E., Cunningham-Williams, R., Nurminen, T., Smits, G., et al. (2006). A multicenter investigation of the opioid antagonist nalmefene in the treatment of pathological gambling. *American Journal of Psychiatry*, *163*, 303–312.

Grant, J. E., Potenza, M. N., Weinstein, A., & Gorelick, D. A. (2010). Introduction to behavioral addictions. *The American Journal of Drug and Alcohol Abuse*, *36*(5), 233–241.

Grant, J. E., Steinberg, M. A., Kim, S. W., Rounsaville, B. J., & Potenza, M. N. (2004). Preliminary validity and reliability testing of a structured clinical interview for pathological gambling. *Psychiatry Research*, *128*(1), 79–88.

Graybiel, A. M., & Rauch, S. L. (2000). Toward a neurobiology of obsessive-compulsive disorder. *Neuron*, *28*(2), 343–347.

Griffiths, M. D. (2010). The role of context in online gaming excess and addiction: Some case study evidence. *International Journal of Mental Health and Addiction, 8,* 119–125.

Hague, B., Hall, J., & Kellett, S. (2016). Treatments for compulsive buying: A systematic review of the quality, effectiveness and progression of the outcome evidence. *Journal of Behavioral Addictions, 5*(3), 379–394.

Hampshire, A., Hellyer, P., Soreq, E., Trender, W., Mehta, M. A., Ioannidis, K., et al. (2020). Dimensions and modulators of behavioural and mental-health changes during the Covid-19 pandemic: An N = 343,017 study. *MedRxiv.* https://doi.org/10.1101/2020.06.18.20134635. Pre-print (prior to peer review).

Henchoz, Y., Studer, J., Deline, S., N'Goran, A. A., Baggio, S., & Gmel, G. (2016). Video gaming disorder and sport and exercise in emerging adulthood: A longitudinal study. *Behavioral Medicine, 42,* 105–111.

Higuchi, S., Nakayama, H., Mihara, S., Maezono, M., Kitayuguchi, T., & Hashimoto, T. (2017). Inclusion of gaming disorder criteria in ICD-11: A clinical perspective in favor: Commentary on: Scholars' open debate paper on the World Health Organization ICD-11 gaming disorder proposal (Aarseth et al.). *Journal of Behavioral Addictions, 6,* 293–295.

Ho, R. C., Zhang, M. W. B., Tsang, T. Y., Toh, A. H., Pan, F., & Lu, Y. (2014). The association between internet addiction and psychiatric co-morbidity: A meta-analysis. *BMC Psychiatry, 14,* 183.

Hodgins, D. C., Stea, J. N., & Grant, J. E. (2011). Gambling disorders. *Lancet, 378,* 1874–1884.

Ioannidis, K., Chamberlain, S. R., Treder, M. S., Kiraly, F., Leppink, E., Redden, S., et al. (2016). Problematic internet use (PIU): Associations with the impulsive-compulsive spectrum. An application of machine learning in psychiatry. *Journal of Psychiatric Research, 83,* 94–102.

Ioannidis, K., Hook, R., Goudriaan, A. E., Vlies, S., Fineberg, N. A., Grant, J. E., et al. (2019). Cognitive deficits in problematic internet use: Meta-analysis of 40 studies. Version 2. *The British Journal of Psychiatry, 215*(5), 1–8.

Ioannidis, K., Hook, R., Wickham, K., Grant, J. E., & Chamberlain, S. R. (2019). Impulsivity in gambling disorder and problem gambling: A meta-analysis. Version 2. *Neuropsychopharmacology, 44*(8), 1354–1361.

Ioannidis, K., Treder, M. S., Chamberlain, S. R., Kiraly, F., Redden, S. A., Stein, D. J., et al. (2018). Problematic internet use as an age-related multifaceted problem: Evidence from a two-site survey. Version 2. *Addictive Behaviors, 81,* 157–166.

Jo, Y. S., Bhang, S. Y., Choi, J. S., Lee, H. K., Lee, S. Y., & Kweon, Y. S. (2019). Clinical characteristics of diagnosis for internet gaming disorder: Comparison of DSM-5 IGD and ICD-11 GD diagnosis. *Journal of Clinical Medicine, 8*(7), 945.

Kalivas, P. W., Peters, J., & Knackstedt, L. (2006). Animal models and brain circuits in drug addiction. *Molecular Interventions, 6,* 339–344.

Kaptsis, D., King, D. L., Delfabbro, P. H., & Gradisar, M. (2016). Withdrawal symptoms in internet gaming disorder: A systematic review. *Clinical Psychology Review, 43,* 58–66.

Kardefelt-Winther, D. (2014). A conceptual and methodological critique of internet addiction research: Towards a model of compensatory internet use. *Computers in Human Behavior, 31,* 351–354.

Kim, S. W., Grant, J. E., Adson, D. E., & Shin, Y. C. (2001). Double-blind naltrexone and placebo comparison study in the treatment of pathological gambling. *Biological Psychiatry, 49,* 914–921.

King, D. L., Chamberlain, S. R., Carragher, N., Billieux, J., Stein, D., Mueller, K., et al. (2020). Screening and assessment tools for gaming disorder: A comprehensive systematic review. *Clinical Psychology Review, 77,* 101831.

King, D. L., Delfabbro, P. H., Deleuze, J., Perales, J. C., Király, O., Krossbakken, E., et al. (2019). Maladaptive player-game relationships in problematic gaming and gaming disorder: A systematic review. *Clinical Psychology Review*, *73*, 101–777.

King, D. L., Delfabbro, P. H., & Griffiths, M. D. (2013). Trajectories of problem video gaming among adult regular gamers: An 18-month longitudinal study. *Cyberpsychology, Behavior and Social Networking*, *16*, 72–76.

King, D. L., Delfabbro, P. H., Griffiths, M. D., & Gradisar, M. (2011). Assessing clinical trials of internet addiction treatment: A systematic review and CONSORT evaluation. *Clinical Psychology Review*, *31*(7), 1110–1116.

King, D. L., Delfabbro, P. H., Wu, A. M. S., Doh, Y. Y., Kuss, D. J., Pallesen, S., et al. (2017). Treatment of Internet gaming disorder: An international systematic review and CONSORT evaluation. *Clinical Psychology Review*, *54*, 123–133.

King, D. L., & Gaming Industry Response Consortium. (2018). Comment on the global gaming industry's statement on ICD-11 gaming disorder: A corporate strategy to disregard harm and deflect social responsibility? *Addiction*, *113*(11), 2145–2146.

Király, O., Tóth, D., Urbán, R., Demetrovics, Z., & Maraz, A. (2017). Intense video gaming is not essentially problematic. *Psychology of Addictive Behaviors*, *31*, 807–817.

Koo, H. J., Han, D. H., Park, S. Y., & Kwon, J. H. (2017). The structured clinical interview for DSM-5 internet gaming disorder: Development and validation for diagnosing IGD in adolescents. *Psychiatry Investigation*, *14*(1), 21–29.

Koran, L. M., Aboujaoude, E. N., Solvason, B., Gamel, N. N., & Smith, E. H. (2007). Escitalopram for compulsive buying disorder: A double-blind discontinuation study. *Journal of Clinical Psychopharmacology*, *27*(2), 225–227.

Koran, L. M., Faber, R. J., Aboujaoude, E., Large, M. D., & Serpe, R. T. (2006). Estimated prevalence of compulsive buying behavior in the United States. *The American Journal of Psychiatry*, *163*(10), 1806–1812.

Kovanen, L., Basnet, S., Castrén, S., et al. (2016). A randomised, double-blind, placebo-controlled trial of as-needed naltrexone in the treatment of pathological gambling. *European Addiction Research*, *22*(2), 70–79. https://doi.org/10.1159/000435876.

Kuss, D. J., Griffiths, M. D., Karila, L., & Billieux, J. (2014). Internet addiction: A systematic review of epidemiological research for the last decade. *Current Pharmaceutical Design*, *20*, 4026–4052.

Kuss, D. S., van Rooij, A., Shorter, G. W., Griffiths, M. D., & van de Mheen, D. (2013). Internet addiction in adolescents: Prevalence and risk factors. *Computers in Human Behavior*, *29*(5), 1987–1996.

Laconi, S., Rodgers, R. F., & Chabrol, H. (2014). The measurement of internet addiction: A critical review of existing scales and their psychometric properties. *Computers in Human Behavior*, *41*, 190–202.

Leeman, R. F., & Potenza, M. N. (2012). Similarities and differences between pathological gambling and substance use disorders: A focus on impulsivity and compulsivity. *Psychopharmacology*, *219*, 469–490.

Lemmens, J. S., Valkenburg, P. M., & Gentile, D. A. (2015). The internet gaming disorder scale. *Psychological Assessment*, *27*, 567–582.

Lemmens, J. S., Valkenburg, P. M., & Peter, J. (2009). Development and validation of a game addiction scale for adolescents. *Media Psychology*, *12*(1), 77–95.

Lemmens, J. S., Valkenburg, P. M., & Peter, J. (2011). Psychosocial causes and consequences of pathological gaming. *Computers in Human Behavior*, *27*, 144–152.

Lesieur, H. R., & Blume, S. B. (1987). The south oaks gambling screen (SOGS): A new instrument for the identification of pathological gamblers. *The American Journal of Psychiatry*, *144*(9), 1184–1188.

Li, W., Garland, E. L., McGovern, P., O'Brien, J. E., Tronnier, C., & Howard, M. O. (2017). Mindfulness-oriented recovery enhancement for internet gaming disorder in U.S. adults: A stage I randomized controlled trial. *Psychology of Addictive Behaviors, 31*(4), 393–402.

Lorains, F. K., Cowlishaw, S., & Thomas, S. A. (2011). Prevalence of comorbid disorders in problem and pathological gambling: Systematic review and meta-analysis of population surveys. *Addiction, 106*, 490–498.

Luijten, M., Schellekens, A. F., Kühn, S., Machielse, M. W., & Sescousse, G. (2017). Disruption of reward processing in addiction: An image-based meta-analysis of functional magnetic resonance imaging studies. *JAMA Psychiatry, 74*(4), 387–398.

Maraz, A., Griffiths, M. D., & Demetrovics, Z. (2016). The prevalence of compulsive buying: A meta analysis. *Addiction, 111*(3), 408–419.

Mihara, S., & Higuchi, S. (2017). Cross-sectional and longitudinal epidemiological studies of internet gaming disorder: A systematic review of the literature. *Psychiatry and Clinical Neurosciences, 71*(7), 425–444.

Mueller, A., Mitchell, J., & Peterson, L. A. (2012). Assessment and treatment of compulsive buying. In J. E. Grant, & M. N. Potenza (Eds.), *The oxford handbook of impulse control disorders* Oxford University Press.

Mueller, A., Mühlhans, B., Silbermann, A., Müller, U., Mertens, C., Horbach, T., et al. (2009). Pathologisches Kaufen und psychische Komorbidität [Compulsive buying and psychiatric comorbidity]. *Psychotherapie, Psychosomatik, Medizinische Psychologie*.

Müller, A., Arikian, A., de Zwaan, M., & Mitchell, J. E. (2013). Cognitive-behavioural group therapy versus guided self-help for compulsive buying disorder: A preliminary study. *Clinical Psychology & Psychotherapy, 20*(1), 28–35.

Müller, A., Mitchell, J. E., & de Zwaan, M. (2015). Compulsive buying. *The American Journal on Addictions, 24*(2), 132–137.

Müller, A., Steins-Loeber, S., Trotzke, P., Vogel, B., Georgiadou, E., & de Zwaan, M. (2019). Online shopping in treatment-seeking patients with buying-shopping disorder. *Comprehensive Psychiatry, 94*, 152120.

Müller, A., Trotzke, P., Mitchell, J. E., de Zwaan, M., & Brand, M. (2015). The pathological buying screener: Development and psychometric properties of a new screening instrument for the assessment of pathological buying symptoms. *PLoS ONE, 10*(10), e0141094.

Nam, B., Bae, S., Kim, S. M., et al. (2017). Comparing the effects of bupropion and escitalopram on excessive internet game play in patients with major depressive disorder. *Clinical Psychopharmacology and Neuroscience, 15*, 361–368.

Nicoli de Mattos, C., Kim, H. S., Marasaldi, R. F., Requião, M. G., de Oliveira, E. C., Zambrano Filomensky, T., et al. (2020). A 12-week randomized, double-blind, placebo- controlled clinical trial of topiramate for the treatment of compulsive buying disorder. *Journal of Clinical Psychopharmacology, 40*(2), 186–190.

Ninan, P. T., McElroy, S. L., Kane, C. P., Knight, B. T., Casuto, L. S., Rose, S. E., et al. (2000). Placebo-controlled study of fluvoxamine in the treatment of patients with compulsive buying. *Journal of Clinical Psychopharmacology, 20*(3), 362–366.

Park, J. H., Lee, Y. S., Sohn, J. H., et al. (2016). Effectiveness of atomoxetine and methylphenidate for problematic online gaming in adolescents with attention deficit hyperactivity disorder. *Human Psychopharmacology, 31*, 427–432.

Petry, N. M., Ginley, M. K., & Rash, C. J. (2017). A systematic review of treatments for problem gambling. *Psychology of Addictive Behaviors, 31*(8), 951–961.

Petry, N. M., Stinson, F. S., & Grant, B. F. (2005). Comorbidity of DSM-IV pathological gambling and other psychiatric disorders: Results from the National Epidemiologic Survey on alcohol and related conditions. *Journal of Clinical Psychiatry, 66*, 564–574.

Pontes, H. M., & Griffiths, M. D. (2015). Measuring DSM-5 Internet Gaming Disorder: Development and validation of a short psychometric scale. *Computers in Human Behavior*, *45*, 137–143.

Quaglieri, A., Mari, E., Boccia, M., Piccardi, L., Guariglia, C., & Giannini, A. M. (2020). Brain network underlying executive functions in gambling and alcohol use disorders: An activation likelihood estimation meta-analysis of fMRI studies. *Brain Sciences*, *10*(6), 353.

Rehbein, F., & Baier, D. (2013). Family-, media-, and school-related risk factors of video game addiction. *Journal of Media Psychology*, *25*, 118–128.

Schlosser, S., Black, D. W., Repertinger, S., & Freet, D. (1994). Compulsive buying. Demography, phenomenology, and comorbidity in 46 subjects. *General Hospital Psychiatry*, *16*(3), 205–212.

Shapira, N. A., Lessig, M. C., Goldsmith, T. D., Szabo, S. T., Lazoritz, M., Gold, M. S., et al. (2003). Problematic internet use: Proposed classification and diagnostic criteria. *Depression and Anxiety*, *17*, 207–216.

Stevens, M. W., Dorstyn, D., Delfabbro, P. H., & King, D. L. (2020). Global prevalence of gaming disorder: A systematic review and meta-analysis. *The Australian and New Zealand Journal of Psychiatry*, 4867420962851 (Epub ahead of print).

Toneatto, T., Brands, B., & Selby, P. (2009). A randomized, double-blind, placebo-controlled trial of naltrexone in the treatment of concurrent alcohol use disorder and pathological gambling. *The American Journal on Addictions*, *18*(3), 219–225.

van Timmeren, T., Daams, J. G., van Holst, R. J., & Goudriaan, A. E. (2018). Compulsivity-related neurocognitive performance deficits in gambling disorder: A systematic review and meta-analysis. *Neuroscience & Biobehavioral Reviews*, *84*, 204–217.

Wegmann, E., Oberst, U., Stodt, B., & Brand, M. (2017). Online-specific fear of missing out and internet use expectancies contribute to symptoms of internet-communication disorder. *Addictive Behaviors Reports*, *5*, 33–42.

Wölfling, K., Beutel, M. E., & Müller, K. W. (2012). Construction of a standardized clinical interview to assess internet addiction: First findings regarding the usefulness of AICA-S. *Journal of Addiction Research and Therapy*, *6*, 1–7.

World Health Organization. (2019). *International Statistical Classification of Diseases and Related Health Problems (ICD-11): New Release*. Geneva: World Health Assembly. Available from: https://www.who.int/news-room/detail/25-05-2019-world-health-assembly-update.

Yao, Y. W., Liu, L., Ma, S. S., Shi, X. H., Zhou, N., Zhang, J. T., et al. (2017). Functional and structural neural alterations in internet gaming disorder: A systematic review and meta-analysis. *Neuroscience and Biobehavioral Reviews*, *83*, 313–324.

Young, K. S. (1998). Internet addiction: The emergence of a new clinical disorder. *CyberPsychology & Behavior*, *1*, 237–244.

Zohar, J. (2010). Addiction, impulsivity and obsessive-compulsive disorder: New formulation revealing ancient wisdom. *The Israel Medical Association Journal*, *12*, 233.

Further reading

Carli, V., Durkee, T., Wasserman, D., Hadlaczky, G., Despalins, R., & Kramarz, E. (2013). The association between pathological internet use and comorbid psychopathology: A systematic review. *Psychopathology*, *46*(1), 1–13.

Chamberlain, S. R., & Grant, J. E. (2018). Minnesota impulse disorders interview (MIDI): Validation of a structured diagnostic clinical interview for impulse control disorders in an enriched community sample. Version 2. *Psychiatry Research*, *265*, 279–283.

Ioannidis, K., Redden, S. A., Valle, S., Chamberlain, S. R., & Grant, J. E. (2020). Problematic internet use: An exploration of associations between cognition and COMT rs4818, rs4680 haplotypes. *CNS Spectrums*, *25*(3), 409–418.

Stevens, M. W. R., King, D. L., Dorstyn, D., & Delfabbro, P. H. (2019). Cognitive-behavioral therapy for internet gaming disorder: A systematic review and meta-analysis. *Clinical Psychology & Psychotherapy*, *26*(2), 191–203.

Weinstein, A. M. (2017). An update overview on brain imaging studies of Internet gaming disorder. *Frontiers in Psychiatry*, *8*, 185.

Cyberchondria, cyberhoarding, and other compulsive online disorders

Matteo Vismara[a], Valentina Caricasole[a], Alberto Varinelli[a], and Naomi A. Fineberg[b,c,d]

[a]University of Milan, Department of Mental Health, Department of Biomedical and Clinical Sciences Luigi Sacco, Milan, Italy, [b]School of Life and Medical Sciences, University of Hertfordshire, Hatfield, United Kingdom, [c]Hertfordshire Partnership University NHS Foundation Trust, Welwyn Garden City, United Kingdom, [d]University of Cambridge School of Clinical Medicine, Cambridge, United Kingdom

Introduction

The continual growth of Internet usage has encouraged a wide range of problematic behaviors conducted online, some of which are similar to those observed in obsessive-compulsive and related disorders (OCRDs). OCRDs are a disabling group of conditions sharing urges to perform distressing and time-consuming obsessive-compulsive acts (American Psychiatric Association, 2013; World Health Organization, 2018) that lie at the extreme pole of a continuum linking normal behavior to pathological and dysregulated obsessive-compulsive behaviors. Obsessions are defined as recurrent, distressing, exaggerated, or irrational harm-related thoughts and compulsions as repetitive, unwanted, stereotyped, precautionary behaviors, performed according to rigid rules and designed to reduce or avoid unpleasant consequences but either not realistically achieving this goal or performed to excess. Recognition of the behavioral overlap across these disorders ultimately led to their reclassification in the new OCRDs chapters, both in the Diagnostic and Statistical Manual of Mental Disorder (DSM-5) (American Psychiatric Association, 2013) and the International Classification of Disease (ICD) 11th version (World Health Organization, 2018). Whereas the DSM-5 has included as OCRDs obsessive-compulsive disorder (OCD), body dysmorphic disorder (BDD), trichotillomania (hair-pulling disorder), excoriation (skin-picking) disorder, and hoarding disorder, in the ICD-11, the OCRDs group also comprises olfactory reference disorder and hypochondriasis.

OCD represents the archetypal OCRD. Individuals with OCD repeat a wide repertoire of compulsions, e.g., washing, checking, alongside related obsessions, e.g., of spreading contamination, acting aggressively. In other OCRDs, the obsessions and compulsions are focused more specifically on the body, e.g., in the case of BDD, with urge-driven and unpleasant checking of appearance and attempts at cosmetic remediation of perceived bodily flaws, in olfactory reference syndrome with the fear of causing offense by smelling bad, in hypochondriasis by the fear of contracting

Mental Health in a Digital World. https://doi.org/10.1016/B978-0-12-822201-0.00001-0

serious illness and the need to seek medical reassurance, and in skin-picking disorder or trichotillomania, with the irresistible urge to pick skin or pull out hair. In the case of hoarding disorder, the symptoms extend to possessions, and are characterized by urges to compulsively acquire items or, once acquired, the inability to discard them, usually associated with a perceived need for completeness or to make their environment "feel right."

Aside from the OCRDs, compulsivity, i.e., the tendency to act in a compulsive way, has been linked to a wide range of other behavioral problems and psychiatric conditions (e.g., addictive disorders such as gambling or gaming disorder, neuro-developmental disorders such as autism spectrum disorder) (Fineberg et al., 2014; Fineberg, Apergis-Schoute, et al., 2018). Clinical compulsivity is thus an "umbrella" construct and reflects a combination of multiple and separable symptoms and traits variably represented across these disorders, including anxiety or fear, perfectionism, need for completeness, certainty and control, cognitive rigidity, and poor impulse control. Accordingly, a sound and clinically relevant assessment of compulsivity need to take into account its multidimensional nature (Hellriegel, Barber, Wikramanayake, Fineberg, & Mandy, 2017).

At a preclinical level, compulsivity can be conceptualized as a transdiagnostic ae-tiological factor, underpinned by a cluster of separable neuropsychological components. These include impairment in attentional set-shifting, motor inhibition, flexible, and goal-directed behavioral control (underpinned by poor executive planning and excessive habit formation), as well as increased sensitivity to error (Bandelow et al., 2016; Fineberg et al., 2014, 2010; Fineberg, Apergis-Schoute, et al., 2018). Taking these psychological processes into consideration may enhance case formulation, e.g., by contributing to the elucidation of the function of the pathological behavior or iden-tifying specific "subtargets" for treatment (e.g., behavioral flexibility) and thereby allowing the tailoring of adapted interventions (Sachdev et al., 2019).

The Internet represents a fertile ground for the development of a range of new and emerging digital forms of compulsive behavior (Fineberg, Demetrovics, et al., 2018). Some of these behaviors seem to be online manifestations of similar offline activity. Cyberchondria (CYB), a digital manifestation of hypochondriasis, is one such behav-ior. In CYB, individuals compulsively search online for medical information. These searches are aimed at reducing distressing hypochondriacal obsessions, i.e., that there is something seriously wrong with their health, but instead "backfire" and increase anxiety and distress (Starcevic, Berle, Arnáez, Vismara, & Fineberg, 2020; Vismara et al., 2020). Cyberhoarding, another compulsive online behavior, closely resembles hoarding disorder, but instead of cluttering their physical environment with hoarded material, subjects with cyberhoarding collect digital material, probably sharing with hoarding disorder the need to make their virtual environment "feel right."

Additional poorly defined and less well-understood digital forms of OCRDs may include "information overload," which is characterized by persistent, compulsive, and exhausting online research for different kinds of information that are not only health related. Repetitive use of social network sites (e.g., Instagram, Facebook) defines another form of pathological online behavior known as problematic social network sites use that does not have a recognizable offline representation. This behavior is often driven by an obsessional "fear of missing out," is associated with a need for completeness (in terms of online material viewed), and therefore could be considered compulsive. Compulsive online trading has also recently been described, and it is a maladaptive behavior characterized by compulsive checking and investing in online stock exchange transactions with exaggerated amounts of time dedicated to these operations that disrupt the family, personal, and/or professional activities (Guglielmo, Ioime, & Janiri, 2016).

Different characteristics associated with Internet use are thought to be responsible for the development and escalation of these pathological behaviors. Importantly, the Internet offers various schedules of reinforcement that could induce behavioral repetition. In the case of OCRDs, the performance of the compulsive act initially leads to a temporary reduction of distress or anxiety (rather than reward per se), thereby providing "negative" reinforcement and encouraging the behavior to be repeated. In a similar way, the Internet might provide negative reinforcement for online compulsive behaviors such as CYB, cyberhoarding, problematic social network sites use, etc. by serving as a pseudo-limitless source of reassuring information in the face of unbearable anxiety linked to, respectively, hypochondriacal, hoarding, or "fear of missing out" preoccupations. Moreover, other Internet characteristics, such as its boundless possibilities for action, and its easy accessibility, affordability, and anonymity further increase the likelihood of repeated performance (Young & Nabuco de Abreu, 2010).

This chapter will review, from a clinical perspective, the obsessive-compulsive Internet-related conditions of CYB, cyberhoarding, and the above-mentioned emerging online forms of OCRDs. These disorders are grouped in the present chapter as they share important symptomatic and etiological features, implying a common approach to assessment, diagnosis, and treatment.

Cyberchondria

Nowadays, most people access the Internet, instead of relying on medical books and encyclopedias or even consulting medical professionals, to answer questions about health or illness. In a survey of more than 12,000 people across many different countries, 12%–40% reported searching the Internet frequently for medical information (McDaid & Park, 2010). In the United States, a 2010 general population poll revealed that 88% of Internet users searched for medical information online, while 62% of users had searched for such information in the past month (The Harris Pool, 2010). The growth of this behavior is likely to be associated with the ease with which this information can be accessed via the Internet. Searching online for health-related information allows millions of people worldwide to quickly and easily obtain the information they need, with a generally empowering effect. However, some individuals report experiencing a higher level of anxiety or distress during or after searches for health information. This behavior, associated with the development of a pattern of excessive or repetitive searching, has been described as CYB (Starcevic, 2017; Starcevic & Berle, 2013; Vismara et al., 2020). In this context, digital checking of medical information is thought to have a specific reinforcing effect on CYB, leading to increased symptom severity, distress, functional impairment, and health-care utilization, with overall significant public health implications and costs (Mathes, Norr, Allan, Albanese, & Schmidt, 2018).

The name CYB was originally coined from a combination of the terms "cyber" and "hypochondriasis" (Loos, 2013) and was embraced by the popular media and later in scientific publications, initially referring to anyone excessively seeking information online about health or illness on the Internet and latterly denoting those with a potentially definable mental disorder. Indeed, on one hand, some authors consider the Internet as simply a modern conduit for medical checking (Bodoh-Creed, 2014; White & Horvitz, 2009), while on the other the clinical importance of CYB as a potentially novel form of compulsive digital behavior has been emphasized (Vismara et al., 2020).

Although the phenomenology of CYB has been described in several recent investigations, there is as yet no consensus on the definition of CYB (Vismara et al., 2020). Moreover, CYB is not specifically mentioned in the Diagnostic and Statistical Manual of Mental Disorders, 5th Edition (DSM-5), but is generally referred to in the description of the diagnostic features of an illness anxiety disorder (akin to hypochondriasis), where it is reported that subjects "research their suspected disease excessively (e.g., on the Internet)" (American Psychiatric Association, 2013, p. 316). In the International Classification of Diseases, 11th Revision (ICD-11), CYB is again not specifically addressed, but "information seeking" is included as one of the behaviors associated with the preoccupation or fear of having a disease within the core diagnostic features of hypochondriasis (World Health Organization, 2018).

So far, CYB has been mainly investigated in nonclinical samples, exclusively with descriptive and cross-sectional studies, with samples recruited from the general population or university students, mainly via online surveys. To the best of our knowledge, only three studies have recruited a clinical sample, two of which recruited nonpsychiatric outpatients from general hospitals (Wijesinghe et al., 2019) or orthopedic clinics (Blackburn et al., 2019), while the last included patients with DSM-5 illness anxiety disorder and/or somatic symptom disorder (Newby & McElroy, 2020). In a recent review, this group of authors proposed a working definition of CYB that took the available literature data into account and combined the most recent published conceptualizations (Vismara et al., 2020) (Fig. 13.1).

Assessment of Cyberchondria

Cyberchondria severity scale

The Cyberchondria Severity Scale (CSS), developed in 2014 by McElroy and Shevlin (2014), was the first self-report questionnaire to measure CYB. It was designed as a continuous severity measure, aimed to assess anxiety resulting from online health searches. Indeed, the CSS is not a screening tool for CYB, and corresponding threshold scores to defining the disorder are not established.

The original version of the CSS consisted of 43 items describing behaviors and emotions generated from a review of existing literature on CYB or conceptually similar behaviors. The current version includes 33 questions, each with a five-point scale response (1—Never, 2—Rarely, 3—Sometimes, 4—Often, 5—Always). The CSS is

A pattern of excessive searching on the Internet for medical or health-related information with the following features:
- Searching is compulsive i.e. repetitive, unwanted, stereotyped, performed according to rigid rules and hard to resist, and serves the purpose of seeking reassurance;
- Initial relief, if obtained, through online searching is short-lived and anxiety or distress usually worsens during these searches and persists afterwards;
- Online searching takes precedence over other interests or daily activities and continues or escalates despite the occurrence of negative consequences associated with the searching.

Fig. 13.1 Proposed working definition of Cyberchondria.

divided into five factors or subscales: (1) compulsion, describing how excessive on-line medical research interfere with both online and offline activities; (2) distress, derived from researching health-related information online; (3) excessiveness, describing the extent of the multiple and repetitive researches for medical information; (4) reassurance, indicated by the need to consult with a medical professional about the information found online; and (5) mistrust of medical professionals, reflecting greater confidence in medical information from the Internet than from doctors.

The CSS has been translated into several languages (German, Italian, Polish, Turkish, Croatian, Iranian), but the psychometric properties have been assessed only for the German (Barke, Bleichhardt, Rief, & Doering, 2016), Polish (Bajcar, Babiak, & Olchowska-Kotala, 2019), Italian (Marino et al., 2020), and two Turkish (Selvi, Turan, Sayin, Boysan, & Kandeger, 2018; Uzun & Zencir, 2018) versions.

Starcevic and colleagues conducted in 2020 a systematic literature review of the available tools to measure CYB (Starcevic et al., 2020), providing a comprehensive and detailed overview of CYB assessment instruments. Considering all the studies that adopted the CSS, the internal consistency for the total score was reported as excellent, with Cronbach's α ranging between 0.91 and 0.89. Likewise, internal consistency was excellent for the compulsion subscale (0.96–0.88), and distress subscale (0.92–0.95), good for the excessiveness subscale (0.91–0.74) and for the reassurance subscale (0.89–0.76). Only two studies assessed test-retest reliability of the CSS using translated versions. For one of the Turkish versions, a reliability figure over a 2-week period was 0.65 for the total CSS, and the corresponding figures for the CSS subscales ranged from 0.53 to 0.71 (Uzun & Zencir, 2018). The test-retest reliability figures (over a period of 3 months) for the Polish version of the CSS subscales ranged from 0.58 to 0.76 (Bajcar et al., 2019).

Different studies have shown a solid convergent validity of the CSS with measures of health anxiety (measured with the Short Health Anxiety Inventory or the Modified Version of the Short Health Anxiety Inventory) ranging between 0.53 and 0.59. In one study, however, the correlation between the total CSS and the Health Anxiety Inventory was only 0.23 (Selvi et al., 2018). The CSS also showed a good convergent validity with measures of the severity of problematic usage of the Internet (PUI), as assessed in one study that reported a correlation of 0.45 between the total CSS and the Internet Addiction Test (Selvi et al., 2018). Lastly, although at a lower level, the correlations between measures of OCD (assessed with the Dimensional Obsessive-Compulsive Scale or the Maudsley Obsessive-Compulsive Inventory), showed good convergent validity (*rs* ranging from 0.27 to 0.49).

Different subsequent studies found contradictions in the "Mistrust of medical professionals" subscale, which consists of three reverse-scored items. The performance of this subscale was different from other CSS subscales, reporting lower or negative correlations with other CSS subscales and with the total CSS. Moreover, the internal consistency of this subscale was considerably lower compared to the other CSS subscales. Lastly, the correlations with measures of health anxiety, PUI, OCD, other anxiety-related variables and depression were generally weak, often nonsignificant and at times negative. These findings suggested that the "mistrust of medical professionals" subscale may not assess the same construct of CYB as the other CSS subscales, and it has even been suggested that these items should be calculated separately from the rest of the CSS (Fergus, 2014). Indeed, this led to different studies assessing CYB with or without the subscale and to the further development of shorter, modified versions of the CSS that might be more practical to use in clinical settings. These versions include a German 15 items version (Barke et al., 2016) and a 12 items version from the authors of the original CSS (CSS-12; McElroy et al., 2019). This shorter version displayed a more conceptually coherent version of the instrument, without sacrificing its solid psychometric properties.

Alternative instruments

Four additional CYB instruments have been developed in recent times: the Cyberchondria Scale (CS) (Durak-Batigun, Gor, Komurcu, & Erturk, 2018), the Short Cyberchondria Scale (SCS) (Jokić-Begić, Mikac, Čuržik, & Sangster Jokić, 2019), the Brief Cyberchondria Scale (BCS) (González-Rivera, Santiago-Olmo, Cruz-Rodríguez, Pérez-Ojeda, & Torres-Cuevas, 2020), and the Cyberchondria Tendency Scale (CTS) (Tatli, Tatli, & Kokoc, 2019), developed in non-English speaking population. As the CSS, these instruments consider CYB a multidimensional construct with different overlapping dimensions but are not equivalent to the CSS. Moreover, these new instruments were created for different purposes (Starcevic et al., 2020). The CS was developed to assess the magnitude of CYB focusing on information-seeking behavior and the characteristics of online health searches that both increase or decrease anxiety. On the other hand, the SCS considers anxiety exacerbation following health-related searching as the core of CYB. In the BCS, CYB represents online health research driven by health anxiety. Lastly, the purpose of the CTS is to assess Internet users' CYB tendencies, i.e., the extent to which individuals seek a solution online when a health problem is encountered and how they use health information obtained online.

Epidemiology of Cyberchondria

Prevalence

Considering that no consensus definition and no diagnostic criteria exist for CYB, no reliable epidemiological data on the prevalence of CYB are present in the literature.

However, some population-based studies have investigated behaviors that resemble CYB and show remarkably high levels of self-reported obsessive-compulsive online medical searching. For example, in an online survey of 515 volunteers (White & Horvitz, 2009), escalation of concerns about common symptomatology (defined as the intensification of searching for common symptoms to serious concerns during online searching) and the correlation with anxiety and searching behaviors were explored. Internet-based escalation of concerns occurred frequently ("Always" or "Often") in around 20% of participants with a low level of health anxiety at baseline, and 40% of the participants reported that interactions with the Internet increased their anxiety about medical concerns. Additionally, 40% of participants reported experiencing different behavioral changes related to online searches (i.e., more web pages visited, increased searches, more frequent engagement with medical professionals).

In a more recent investigation (Wijesinghe et al., 2019), a CYB prevalence rate of 16.3% was reported in a sample of 300 outpatients from two general hospitals in Sri Lanka. The Authors considered the presence of any CSS factors as being indicative of CYB, however, they did not specify the threshold they used to endorse the presence of any factors. In addition, the assessment was made using only self-report questionnaires and no characterization of anxiety disorder or other mental disorder was made. In another investigation (Makarla, Gopichandran, & Tondare, 2019), 205 employees working in various information technology companies in India were recruited and assessed with the CSS-15 items. Using cluster analysis, two clusters emerged. Individuals with higher cluster scores centered on all the four CSS factors were classified as "cyberchondria." This cluster accounted for 55.6% of the total sample and was referred to by the authors as CYB prevalence. Another survey-based cross-sectional study conducted on graduate students with no current diagnosed medical condition reported that nearly a quarter of the sample (23.33%) experienced high levels of CYB, corresponding to a CSS score at or above the 75 percentile (Akhtar & Fatima, 2020).

Once agreement is reached on a working definition of CYB, a more accurate validation of the true population prevalence of CYB using observer-rated methods becomes possible.

Demographics

The gender and age distribution of CYB is also not well understood. Some studies found a correlation between CSS scores and sociodemographic variables. For instance, a higher CSS total score was positively correlated with the female gender in one study (Barke et al., 2016), but with the male gender in another (Akhtar & Fatima, 2020). Gender differences were reported also in CSS subscales, with men scoring higher on compulsion, distress, excessiveness, and reassurance subscales, whereas women scored slightly higher than men on the "Mistrust of medical professions" subscale (Akhtar & Fatima, 2020). The CSS total score negatively correlated with age in one study (Bajcar et al., 2019), but not another (Barke et al., 2016). In another investigation, older participants were less likely to experience worsening anxiety during and after online searching for medical information than younger participants (Doherty-Torstrick, Walton, & Fallon, 2016). Moreover, a higher "Mistrust of medical professionals" subscale score was associated with older participants (Barke et al., 2016).

Taken together, this data suggests the "Mistrust of medical professionals" items of the CSS should not be automatically excluded, particularly when measuring CYB either in females or the older age group.

Course

No prospective long-term studies of CYB have been conducted so far.

Cost and burden

A few cross-sectional studies have measured the cost and burden of CYB, using self-reported questionnaires. CYB (defined using the CSS) was found to be moderately correlated with health-care utilization, measured by the number of visits to general practitioners and a range of other health professionals during the previous year, in one study (Barke et al., 2016). In a further study, when accounting for the overlap between CYB and health anxiety, CYB was strongly associated with greater functional impairment, but interestingly not with decreased quality of life (Mathes et al., 2018).

Clinical comorbidity

Different investigations have aimed to understand the extent to which CYB represents a new, separate, and autonomous disorder or a syndrome that is commonly present in a range of established psychiatric disorders (Starcevic et al., 2020; Starcevic & Berle, 2013, 2015). Indeed, CYB shares phenomenology with a variety of psychiatric disorders. As a form of safety behavior, the reassurance seeking of CYB may be motivated either by increased state anxiety, similar to an anxiety disorder such as panic disorder or generalized anxiety disorder, or by doubt and uncertainty about having a serious disease, suggestive of illness anxiety disorder/hypochondriasis. The association between CYB and health anxiety broadly defined has been extensively investigated in different studies. A literature review and meta-analysis of 20 studies, including 7373 participants, showed strong positive correlations between health anxiety and online health searches ($r=0.34$), and between health anxiety and CYB ($r=0.62$), although a high level of heterogeneity between the studies was found (McMullan, Berle, Arnáez, & Starcevic, 2019). Individuals with elevated health anxiety usually experienced greater anxiety during and after online health searches and reported more frequent and longer searches, compared to those with lower or normal levels of health anxiety (Doherty-Torstrick et al., 2016; Eichenberg & Schott, 2019; McManus, Leung, Muse, & Williams, 2014; te Poel, Baumgartner, Hartmann, & Tanis, 2016). However, some studies reported that even individuals with low levels of health anxiety may experience increased anxiety when searching online (Tyrer, Cooper, Tyrer, Wang, & Bassett, 2019), shedding light on the importance of other vulnerability factors, apart from health anxiety, contributing to the development of CYB.

Alternatively, CYB may be conceptualized as a repetitive, and time-consuming, compulsion, more closely similar to the compulsions of an OCRD—such as ICD-11 hypochondriasis or even OCD (Fergus & Russell, 2016; Vismara et al., 2020). Indeed, individuals with hypochondriasis manifesting obsessive (intrusive, unwanted, distressing) thoughts about the catastrophic consequences of not checking for illnesses, often also engage in CYB, i.e., compulsive online medical searches and compulsive checking aimed at neutralizing these obsessional thoughts. In the context of OCD, repeated searches for medical information may otherwise function as a safety behavior designed to alleviate obsessive responsibility for preventing harm, contamination concerns, or other somatic obsessions. Additionally, the need for certainty, which drives some forms of CYB, may reflect an underlying obsessive-compulsive personality disorder, which has been reported to accompany hypochondriasis (Farrow & Fineberg, 2008; Starčević, 1990). Although no investigation so far has investigated CYB in clinical samples of OCD patients, several reports have found a moderate to high ($rs = 0.27–0.49$) correlation between the CSS and OCD symptoms (Bajcar et al., 2019; Fergus, 2014; Fergus & Russell, 2016; Norr et al., 2015).

Importantly, CYB also shows common characteristics with an emerging group of disorders involving PUI, such as Internet gaming disorder or gambling disorder that is currently conceptualized within a framework of behavioral addiction and in which framework loss of inhibitory cognitive control over impulsive as well as compulsive responding is emphasized. Indeed, CYB and PUI share in common the distressing loss of control over urge-driven online activity, resulting in time-consuming, compulsive behavior, representing a major source of negative interference with functioning. Various exploratory studies have found a correlation between CSS and PUI severity in participants from community samples (Fergus & Dolan, 2014; Selvi et al., 2018; Starcevic, Baggio, Berle, Khazaal, & Viswasam, 2019). Additionally, the relationship between CYB and PUI was reported to be even stronger than the one between CYB and health anxiety (Starcevic et al., 2019), suggesting a strong association between CYB and PUI, which merits further exploration in clinical samples.

Neuropsychology, neurocircuitry, neurochemistry, and neurogenetics

Investigations assessing the psychobiology of CYB are scarce. Some authors have investigated the association between CYB and neuropsychological constructs, using online surveys and collecting self-report data from community samples. The constructs investigated that reported a correlation with CYB (measured with the CSS) are low self-esteem (Bajcar & Babiak, 2019), anxiety sensitivity (Fergus, 2015; Norr, Albanese, Oglesby, Allan, & Schmidt, 2014), intolerance of uncertainty (Fergus, 2015; Fergus & Spada, 2017; Norr et al., 2014), pain catastrophizing (Gibler, Jastrowski Mano, O'Bryan, Beadel, & McLeish, 2019), and metacognitive beliefs (Fergus & Spada, 2017). These results might help in understanding the psychological models and mechanisms responsible for CYB and determine individuals at higher risk.

So far, no studies of the neurocircuitry, neurochemistry, or neural genes involved in CYB have been published. Considering the phenomenological link between CYB and the compulsive behaviors of other OCRDs, it would be reasonable to hypothesize that similar neuropsychological mechanisms and neural circuits apply. Growing evidence suggests that compulsivity is mediated by neuropsychological mechanisms responsible for behavioral inhibition (motor inhibition, cognitive inflexibility) reversal learning and habit formation (shift from goal-directed to habitual responding) (Fineberg, Apergis-Schoute, et al., 2018). Aberrant reward-processing and top-down executive control might be involved as well in subjects who manifest a high level of CYB (Brand et al., 2020; Grant et al., 2014). These manifestations are related to a distributed perturbation of neural networks focused around the prefrontal cortex, caudate, putamen, and associated neural-circuitry, in particular the cortico-striato-thalamo-cortical circuits. Thus, to further elucidate the neurobiology and neurochemistry of CYB, the application of neuropsychological paradigms targeting this circuitry is likely to be informative.

Therapeutic interventions

CYB is poorly recognized and knowledge about evidence-based treatment is limited. Two major treatment modalities have been studied: psychological therapies and pharmacotherapy. Only one randomized controlled trial (Newby & McElroy, 2020) has been conducted so far. The investigation compared the effect on CYB of an Internet-delivered cognitive behavioral approach (including components directly targeting excessive online health searches) and psychoeducation, monitoring, and clinical support, in a sample of patients with DSM-5 illness anxiety disorder and/or somatic symptom disorder. CYB severity decreased significantly in patients whose levels of health anxiety were reduced in the course of therapy, reaffirming the relationship between CYB and health anxiety in treatment-seeking individuals. Moreover, this is the first clinical study in which the psychometric properties of the CSS-33 were assessed in patients with diagnosed psychiatric disorders.

Other reports have also proposed a cognitive-behavioral approach to managing CYB (Fergus & Dolan, 2014; Starcevic & Berle, 2013, 2015) or targeting OCD symptoms, PUI, intolerance of uncertainty, or metacognitive beliefs related to CYB (i.e., obsessive thoughts about health, misinterpretation of bodily symptoms, fear of uncertainty, perfectionist tendencies, and ambivalence about what should be perceived as trustworthy advice) (Vismara et al., 2020). Additionally, behavioral approaches involving exposure and response prevention, found to be particularly helpful for treating OCD (Hezel & Simpson, 2019), may be of value in targeting CYB-related reassurance-seeking behaviors and the urge to access the Internet. These interventions would each merit validation under randomized controlled trial conditions.

As far as pharmacological treatments are concerned, no studies have directly addressed CYB. Considering the overlap between CYB and hypochondriasis, it would be rational to consider the use of selective serotonin reuptake inhibitors (SSRIs) as these agents have shown positive results in reducing symptoms of hypochondriasis in patients diagnosed with illness anxiety disorders and/or somatic symptom disorders in three randomized controlled trials (Fallon et al., 2008, 2017; Greeven et al., 2009). In these studies, the largest benefit was associated with SSRI doses at the upper end of the therapeutic range.

In the absence of specific evidence-based interventions, psychoeducation represents another potentially helpful interventional strategy for CYB (Starcevic &

Berle, 2013). While it may be generally helpful for the public at large to learn how to critically appraise online health-related information and understand the impact of such information, patients with CYB may additionally benefit from specific information about the negative consequences of excessive or unnecessary online health searches and encouragement to resist the urge to check the Internet in order to break the vicious cycle of reassurance seeking.

Moreover, other public health interventions such as targeting the way medical information is presented on the Internet may also be of value. Last but not least, the clinician-patient relationship offers other considerable opportunities for positive intervention to reduce the risk or impact of CYB (Vismara et al., 2020). See Table 13.1 for a summary of proposed therapeutic interventions for CYB.

Table 13.1 Proposed therapeutic interventions for cyberchondria.

Psychological interventions	Pharmacological interventions	Public health interventions	Clinician-patient relationship
− Internet-delivered CBT (Newby & McElroy, 2020). − CBT approach to managing CYB (Fergus, 2014; Starcevic & Berle, 2013, 2015). − CBT approach to targeting OCD symptoms, PUI, intolerance of uncertainty, or metacognitive beliefs related to CYB (Vismara et al., 2020). − Psychoeducation (Starcevic & Berle, 2013).	− Selective serotonin reuptake inhibitors (SSRIs), at maximal doses, based on evidence of efficacy in hypochondriasis (Fallon et al., 2008, 2017; Greeven et al., 2009; Vismara et al., 2020).	− Target the way medical information is presented on the Internet. − Increase the amount of more precise, user-friendly and unambiguous medical information on the Internet. − Avoid prioritization of rare or dangerous diseases on the Internet. − Realistically present on the Internet the probabilities of the links between certain symptoms and illnesses.	− Foster a trusting relationship by the same clinician seeing the patient over time to reduce the anxiety associated with inter-clinician differences. − Use clinical judgment to deliver care that is most likely to reduce reassurance-seeking behaviors. − Schedule regular but infrequent visits to reduce the need for emergency presentations. − Avoid unnecessary medical investigations/interventions.

CBT, cognitive behavioral therapy; *OCD*, obsessive compulsive disorder; *PUI*: problematic usage of the Internet.

Cyberhoarding

With the development of technological innovation and limitless possibilities for digital storage, a new subtype of hoarding emerged known as cyberhoarding or digital hoarding. Cyberhoarding has been defined as the compulsive acquisition of digital files to the point of loss of perspective, leading to disorganization and stress, occurring across the workplace and in personal settings (Van Bennekom, Blom, Vulink, & Denys, 2015). Although cyberhoarding does not necessarily interfere with the cluttering of living spaces, it can have a major impact on everyday functioning. Growing evidence suggests that digital hoarders can become as strongly attached to nonphysical data as "nondigital" hoarders do with physical possessions. In the same way, cyberhoarding becomes an extension of the subjects' identity, defines their "sense of self" and is linked with the fear of losing important items. The potential emotional and psychological costs of cyberhoarding are becoming apparent only in recent years. While research on cyberhoarding is novel and scarce, this behavior has been frequently reported by professionals and described by patients themselves.

A clinical case study by Van Bennekom et al. (2015) described a male with physical hoarding compulsions who extended his accumulation in the form of digital photography. His hobby had taken over his life with obsessive taking, editing, categorizing, and copying of pictures onto various external hard drives. Though he never looked at the photographs, organizing them took between 2 and 5 h a day and had severely affected his daily life, leading to overwhelming stress and anxiety. The authors suggested that cyberhoarding may be comparable to physical hoarding as it also involves the accumulation of items, leading to increased digital clutter and disorganization, difficulties in discarding or deleting due to intense emotional attachment, distress, and loss of normal functioning. Lastly, they proposed that this type of hoarding should be added to screening instruments for hoarding disorder.

In a qualitative assessment of cyberhoarding behaviors in 43 individuals, Sweeten, Sillence, and Neave (2018) found a clear overlap between physical and digital domains, with cyberhoarding behavior also reflecting excessive accumulation, difficulties with deleting, emotional distress, and poor insight. Another study, by Schiele and Hughes (2013), explored possession rituals of digital consumers on Pinterest, a social media service with a photo-sharing and bookmarking website. This study showed a high level of emotional attachment to digital possessions and evidence for hoarding of "pinned" items, including a sense of private ownership of discovered items in a public forum. Similarly, cyberhoarding behavior of social media users can lead to hoarding increasing numbers of friends on social media platforms (e.g., Facebook) often without personally knowing the people involved.

Since very little is known about the psychological characteristics of individuals who hoard digital items and the kinds of material they hoard, a new questionnaire has been designed hoping to enhance future work in this field: The Digital Behaviors Questionnaire (DBQ). This tool comprises two sections: the Digital Hoarding Questionnaire (DHQ), assessing two key components of physical hoarding (accumulation and difficulty discarding), and the Digital Behaviors in the Workplace Questionnaire (DBWQ), measuring the extent of cyberhoarding in the workplace.

The term "personal information management" has been coined to describe the ways individuals collect, store, organize, and retrieve their digital items, which is often described as time-consuming and burdensome. Massey, TenBrook, Tatum, and Whittaker (2014) have shown that an individual's "personal information management" is linked to their "Big Five" personality characteristics and that individuals who are more neurotic respond to work pressure by storing more information available to hand (akin to cyberhoarding) on their personal computers. An interview study of 35 adult video gamers revealed that participants could form emotional attachments to digital items within video games, regardless of lack of legal ownership and materiality (Watkins & Molesworth, 2012).

The existing literature does not address the psychobiology of cyberhoarding—neither are there interventional studies to guide treatment or clinical service development. Since cyberhoarding might be less evident than other subtypes of hoarding, it requires precise attention in screening from caregivers. Future researches and clinical trials are necessary to gain further insight into the phenomenology and focused treatment strategy.

Other digital forms of OCRDs

Information overload

Information overload is a compulsive online disorder firstly described by Young and colleagues (1998) as a subtype of Internet addiction disorder. This pathological behavior is characterized by constant, compulsive, and exhausting online research for information. Affected subjects surf from one site to another, spending many hours a day, without any specific topics, from news and information sites to large generalist portals and specialized or thematic sites. In this online time-consuming disorder, patients fail to reduce time spent online looking for information even if this issue impairs work and family and social life.

The existing literature lacks studies specifically inquiring about this disorder since it is very difficult to characterize and assess. Furthermore, there are no psychometric tests to evaluate information overload presence or severity. The definition itself may have changed and evolved from Young's first proposition, due to continuous technological development, the societal increase in online data mining, and the phenomenological overlap with topic-related information overload disorder (e.g., CYB), in which individuals focused their research only on a specific topic. However, simply by googling "information overload," multiple references, blogs, or websites pop up underling the diffusion of this topic in popular media and the presence of this disorder at least as a "nonclinical" entity.

Lastly, literature data about prevalence, gender and age distribution, disease course, or specific treatment for this behavior are lacking.

Problematic social network sites use

Globally, the use of social network sites involves over 3 billion users and this number is constantly increasing. In the last few years, the spreading of social network sites has affected all countries (Clement, 2020). A recent study showed that among American teenagers YouTube, Instagram, and Snapchat are the most popular social network sites and 45% of teenagers affirmed to be online almost (Pew Research Center, 2018). Considering the prolonged use of social network sites and the related impact on everyday life activities, it is important to understand the potential risks of problematic social network sites use. The World Health Organization raised health concerns regarding the propensity of problematic social network sites behaviors associated with addiction among a minority of users (World Health Organization, 2014). Problematic social network sites use prevalence have been reported in different countries: 1.6% in Nigeria (Folaranmi, 2013), 4.5% in Hungary (Bányai et al., 2017), 8.6% in Perù (Wolniczak et al., 2013), and 12% in China (Wu, Cheung, Ku, & Hung, 2013). All these studies analyzed students with the exception of the Hungarian study, which is representative of a general population sample. In this investigation, the data collected from 15 to 22 years old subjects showed that females were at higher risk of problematic social network sites use and reported the greatest amount of Internet and social media use compared to males.

Andreassen and Pallesen defined problematic social network sites use as "being overly concerned about social network sites, driven by a strong motivation to log on to or use social network sites, and to dedicate time and effort to social network sites to the extent that it impairs other social activities, education and/or occupation, interpersonal relationships and/or psychological health and well-being" (Andreassen & Pallesen, 2014). To assess problematic social network sites use severity, the Bergen Social Media Addiction Scale and its previous form, the Bergen Facebook Addiction Scale (Andreassen et al., 2016; Andreassen, Torbjørn, Brunborg, & Pallesen, 2012), have been developed, showing a good reliability (Andreassen et al., 2013; Monacis, De Palo, Griffiths, & Sinatra, 2017).

Although there is only limited research into the association between psychiatric disorders and problematic social network sites use, likely because of the novelty of this form of compulsive behavior, growing evidence showed overlap between problematic social network sites use and mental disorders. A recent systematic review confirms that problematic social network sites use is associated with anxiety disorders, depressive disorders, attention deficit hyperactivity disorder, and OCD (Hussain & Griffiths, 2018). A study collecting self-report survey data from 10,904 14-year-old participants (Kelly, Zilanawala, Booker, & Sacker, 2018) found an association between social network sites use and depressive symptoms (assessed with the Child self-report mood and feelings questionnaires), and the magnitude of the association between social network sites use and depressive symptoms was larger for girls than for boys. Moreover, girls were more likely to present low self-esteem (12.8% vs 8.9%), to have bodyweight dissatisfaction (78.2% vs 68.3%), and to be unhappy with their appearance (15.4% vs 11.8%). The longer time spent on social media sites was associated with a reduction of hours slept per night and increased sleep latency and sleep disruptions. These data are in line with a previous meta-analysis of 16 studies (127.714 participants aged 5–18 years) that concluded that screen time in children and adolescents was associated with risk of depression (OR = 1.12; 95% CI: 1.03–1.22) in a nonlinear dose-response manner (Liu, Wu, & Yao, 2016).

Additionally, in two nationally representative surveys of 388.275 adolescents in grades 8 through 12 and national statistics on suicide deaths for those aged 13–18, a positive correlation was reported between time spent on "screen activities" and mental health issues (Twenge, Joiner, Rogers, & Martin, 2018). Overall, these surveys reported that adolescents' depressive symptoms, suicide-related outcomes, and suicide rates increased between 2010 and 2015, especially among females. All these variables positively correlated with the amount of time spent on digital activities or electronic device use. Indeed, among subjects using electronic devices 5 or more hours daily, 48% had at least one suicide-related outcome. Moreover, these subjects were 66% more likely to have at least one suicide-related outcome compared to participants who used electronic devices ≥ 1 h per day. Focusing on depressive symptoms, adolescents using social media almost every day showed the highest levels of depressive symptoms, especially if associated with reduced in-person social interaction. Specifically, social media use was significantly correlated with depressive symptoms among girls but not among boys. Overall, these results suggest that social network sites use shows a likely exposure-response relationship with depressive symptoms and suicidal behaviors in young people.

Focusing on OCD, Carli et al. (2012) reported an association between various forms of PUI including problematic social network sites use and OCD symptoms. In a second study (Andreassen et al., 2016), a significant and positive correlation between problematic social network sites use and OCD was reported comparing the Obsessive-Compulsive Inventory-Revised scores with Bergen Social Media Addiction Scale scores. In this study, OCD was positively related to problem use of both video games ($\beta=0.071$) and social media ($\beta=0.147$). In particular, OCD symptoms were more strongly associated with problematic social networking, and the authors suggested that individuals overusing social media may experience a constant urge to compulsively check their social networks for new information and updates due to the "fear of missing out".

Supporting evidence of these associations is reported in a study by Van Bennekom, De Koning, and Denys (2018), who described two clinical cases in which social media and smartphone technology became incorporated as key symptoms of OCD. In particular, both patients experienced the obsessional fear of losing control while entering search terms or reactions to posts on social media, while one patient used smartphone technology (i.e., repetitive filming, screen records) for performing compulsions. Additionally, the authors underlined the finding that the content of contemporary obsessions and compulsions often concerns modern technologies (e.g., social media and smartphone features) which are not specifically represented in standard OCD assessment instruments such as the Yale-Brown Obsessive-Compulsive Scale (Y-BOCS). This work provides evidence of how this new digital substrate may affect and modify OCD symptomatology itself as opposed to representing a cooccurring comorbid problem.

Conversely, another paper (Qudrat Abas & Jaff, 2018) documented the positive effects of social media platforms use (e.g., Facebook Messenger) to manage the symptoms of a young female OCD patient in a war scenario. The study is just one of many examples of how the use of social media may also represent a useful adjunctive therapeutic tool, especially for situations where socio-environmental features do not allow person-to-person consultation and not just pathological factors.

Problematic social network sites use remains a poorly researched and potentially highly clinically relevant disorder for the 21st century, especially among the young. Future research should be performed to determine if it represents a digital form of OCRD, or whether it is more strongly associated with social anxiety or other forms of mental disorder, as the first step toward clinical recognition and treatment development.

To the best of our knowledge, no specific intervention that specifically targets problematic social network sites use has been investigated. However, since this behavior shares some clinical features with Internet Gaming Disorder, it may benefit cognitive behavioral therapy (Stevens, King, Dorstyn, & Delfabbro, 2019). Moreover, in young people with problematic social network sites use, clinical assessment and appropriate treatment of the common comorbidities such as disorders of anxiety and depression, as well as risk management in the case of suicidality, is indicated.

Compulsive online trading

Online trading involves the high-paced conduct of online stock exchange transactions. This phenomenon has recently changed the world of the stock exchange, as the implementation of digital technologies and telematics is adapted to support the high-speed acquisition and sale of shares, allowing both the small investor and the high finance operator to intervene on the main world markets instantly and with relative ease. Online financial operations may, however, become pathological if compulsive behavior supervenes.

Compulsive online trading involves the urge-driven, compulsive checking and investing in stock exchange transactions and the expansion of time dedicated to these operations. It may affect patients' life to the extent that it seems to revolve around stock exchange issues, impairing all the domains of individual life. A neuroimaging study provided some preliminary evidence that compulsive online trading may be alternatively considered principally a disorder of addiction with the associated compulsive behavior as secondary: During financial investment, the ventral striatum, which is strongly implicated in addictive disorders, was activated and thought to determine a positive reinforcement effect that ultimately led to compulsion (Knutson & Bossaerts, 2007). Indeed, online trading shares other phenomenological features with disorders of behavioral addiction such as gambling disorder. Clinical profiles of problem gamblers and problematic stock traders have been found to be comparable (Shin, Choi, Ha, Choi, & Kim, 2015) and a propensity for high levels of financial risk is a common conceptual attribute driving both activities (Arthur, Williams, & Delfabbro, 2016). The differences between the two disturbances lie in the fact that stock exchange operations require individual knowledge and skills (creation or purchase of an asset). In addition, investment usually presents a longer-term perspective, while gambling always involves an outcome with a particular event (Arthur et al., 2016). However, this aspect may lead to decreased perceived guilt, with online trading justified as a kind of work activity and, because of that, underestimated and performed more frequently. Based on these assumptions, pathological online trading is likely to be an underestimated but significant issue for public health (Guglielmo et al., 2016). More studies are required to evaluate the prevalence, gender and age distribution, clinical course, and possible biopsychosocial influences of online trading. Clinicians need to be aware of this form of PUI, since it may be unnoticed until the presence of significant financial loss and obligations.

With respect to the treatment of online trading, no specific compounds or psychological interventions have been investigated. Considering the common psychopathological mechanisms with gambling disorder, the therapeutic use of treatments found to be effective in reducing gambling urges and behaviors such as naltrexone (Grant, Suck, & Hartman, 2008; Ward, Smith, & Bowden-Jones, 2018) may be of value.

Conclusions

The increasing use of the Internet and the ready availability of technologies that provide access to the Internet provides new and fertile ground for a wide range of obsessive-compulsive behaviors to be conducted online. Some forms of this behavior are performed almost exclusively online. Considering the existing literature, we know more about CYB and problematic social network sites use, while knowledge about cyberhoarding, information overload, and online trading is very limited. While these syndromes resemble OCRDs in some respects, they also variously share phenomenology with other forms of mental disorder such as behavioral addiction (e.g., online trading) or anxiety disorder (e.g., CYB). In general, understanding of the clinical aspects of these behaviors is scarce or absent, with most information derived from general population surveys. The recent reports of the mental health impact of problematic social network sites use on the young merits particular attention. Therefore, further epidemiological, translational neuroscience, and clinical research is needed to understand the extent to which these behaviors characterize autonomous disorders or represent transdiagnostic behavioral syndromes, to explore their cost and impact on health and well-being and, where relevant, to develop new therapeutic interventions and public health approaches.

Declaration statement

Dr. Fineberg has in the past 12 months held research or networking grants from the ECNP, NIHR, EU H2020 (COST), accepted travel and hospitality expenses from the BAP, ECNP, RCPsych, Indian Association for Biological Psychiatry, received honoraria from Elsevier for editorial duties. She leads an NHS treatment service for OCD and holds Board membership (or similar) for various registered charities linked to OCD. Dr. Vismara, Dr. Caricasole, Dr. Varinelli have nothing to disclose.

References

Akhtar, M., & Fatima, T. (2020). Exploring cyberchondria and worry about health among individuals with no diagnosed medical condition. *JPMA. The Journal of the Pakistan Medical Association*, 70(1), 90–95. https://doi.org/10.5455/JPMA.8682.

American Psychiatric Association. (2013). *Diagnostic and statistical manual of mental disorders: DSM-5*. Arlington, VA: American Psychiatric Publishing.

Andreassen, C. S., Billieux, J., Griffiths, M. D., Kuss, D. J., Demetrovics, Z., Mazzoni, E., et al. (2016). The relationship between addictive use of social media and video games and symptoms of psychiatric disorders: A large-scale cross-sectional study. *Psychology of Addictive Behaviors, 30*(2), 252–262. https://doi.org/10.1037/adb0000160.

Andreassen, C. S., Griffiths, M. D., Gjertsen, S. R., Krossbakken, E., Kvam, S., & Pallesen, S. (2013). The relationships between behavioral addictions and the five-factor model of personality. *Journal of Behavioral Addictions, 2*(2), 90–99. https://doi.org/10.1556/JBA.2.2013.003.

Andreassen, C. S., & Pallesen, S. (2014). Social network site addiction—An overview. *Current Pharmaceutical Design, 20*(25), 4053–4061. https://doi.org/10.2174/13816128113199990616.

Andreassen, C. S., Torbjørn, T., Brunborg, G. S., & Pallesen, S. (2012). Development of a facebook addiction scale. *Psychological Reports, 110*(2), 501–517. https://doi.org/10.2466/02.09.18.PR0.110.2.501-517.

Arthur, J. N., Williams, R. J., & Delfabbro, P. H. (2016). The conceptual and empirical relationship between gambling, investing, and speculation. *Journal of Behavioral Addictions, 5*(4), 580–591. https://doi.org/10.1556/2006.5.2016.084.

Bajcar, B., & Babiak, J. (2019). Self-esteem and cyberchondria: The mediation effects of health anxiety and obsessive–compulsive symptoms in a community sample. *Current Psychology*. https://doi.org/10.1007/s12144-019-00216-x.

Bajcar, B., Babiak, J., & Olchowska-Kotala, A. (2019). Cyberchondria and its measurement. The polish adaptation and psychometric properties of the cyberchondria severity scale CSS-PL. *Psychiatria Polska, 53*(1), 49–60. https://doi.org/10.12740/PP/81799.

Bandelow, B., Baldwin, D., Abelli, M., Altamura, C., Dell'Osso, B., Domschke, K., et al. (2016). Biological markers for anxiety disorders, OCD and PTSD - a consensus statement. Part I: Neuroimaging and genetics. *The World Journal of Biological Psychiatry: The Official Journal of the World Federation of Societies of Biological Psychiatry, 17*(5), 321–365. https://doi.org/10.1080/15622975.2016.1181783.

Bányai, F., Zsila, Á., Király, O., Maraz, A., Elekes, Z., Griffiths, M. D., et al. (2017). Problematic social media use: Results from a large-scale nationally representative adolescent sample. *PLoS ONE, 12*(1). https://doi.org/10.1371/journal.pone.0169839, e0169839.

Barke, A., Bleichhardt, G., Rief, W., & Doering, B. K. (2016). The cyberchondria severity scale (CSS): German validation and development of a short form. *International Journal of Behavioral Medicine, 23*(5), 595–605. https://doi.org/10.1007/s12529-016-9549-8.

Blackburn, J., Fischerauer, S. F., Talaei-Khoei, M., Chen, N. C., Oh, L. S., & Vranceanu, A.-M. (2019). What are the implications of excessive internet searches for medical information by orthopaedic patients? *Clinical Orthopaedics and Related Research, 1*. https://doi.org/10.1097/corr.0000000000000888.

Bodoh-Creed, J. A. (2014). When pfizer met mcdreamy: A classic American love story between medicine and the media. *Dissertation Abstracts International Section A: Humanities and Social Sciences, 75*(5-A(E)). No-Specified.

Brand, M., Rumpf, H., Demetrovics, Z., Muller, A., Stark, R., King, D., et al. (2020). Which conditions should be considered as disorders in the international classification of diseases (ICD-11) designation of "other specified disorders due to addictive behaviors"? *Journal of Behavioral Addictions*. https://doi.org/10.1556/2006.2020.00035.

Carli, V., Durkee, T., Wasserman, D., Hadlaczky, G., Despalins, R., Kramarz, E., et al. (2012). The association between pathological internet use and comorbid psychopathology: A systematic review. *Psychopathology*. https://doi.org/10.1159/000337971.

Clement, J. (2020). *Number of global social network users 2017–2025—Statista.* Retrieved from July 21, 2020 https://www.statista.com/statistics/278414/number-of-worldwide-social-network-users/.

Doherty-Torstrick, E. R., Walton, K. E., & Fallon, B. A. (2016). Cyberchondria: Parsing health anxiety from online behavior. *Psychosomatics, 57*(4), 390–400. https://doi.org/10.1016/j.psym.2016.02.002.

Durak-Batigun, A., Gor, N., Komurcu, B., & Erturk, I. S. (2018). Cyberchondria scale (CS): Development, validity and reliability study. *Dusunen Adam, 31*(2), 148–162. https://doi.org/10.5350/DAJPN2018310203.

Eichenberg, C., & Schott, M. (2019, June 10). Use of web-based health services in individuals with and without symptoms of hypochondria: Survey study. *Journal of Medical Internet Research.* https://doi.org/10.2196/10980.

Fallon, B. A., Ahern, D. K., Pavlicova, M., Slavov, I., Skritskya, N., & Barsky, A. J. (2017). A randomized controlled trial of medication and cognitive-behavioral therapy for hypochondriasis. *American Journal of Psychiatry, 174,* 756–764. https://doi.org/10.1176/appi.ajp.2017.16020189.

Fallon, B. A., Petkova, E., Skritskaya, N., Sanchez-Lacay, A., Schneier, F., Vermes, D., et al. (2008). A double-masked, placebo-controlled study of fluoxetine for hypochondriasis. *Journal of Clinical Psychopharmacology, 28*(6), 638–645. https://doi.org/10.1097/JCP.0b013e31818d21cf.

Farrow, J., & Fineberg, N. A. (2008). Obsessive compulsive personality disorder and hypochondriasi. *Progress in Neurology and Psychiatry, 12*(8), 26–29.

Fergus, T. A. (2014). The Cyberchondria severity scale (CSS): An examination of structure and relations with health anxiety in a community sample. *Journal of Anxiety Disorders, 28*(6), 504–510. https://doi.org/10.1016/j.janxdis.2014.05.006.

Fergus, T. A. (2015). Anxiety sensitivity and intolerance of uncertainty as potential risk factors for cyberchondria: A replication and extension examining dimensions of each construct. *Journal of Affective Disorders, 184,* 305–309. https://doi.org/10.1016/j.jad.2015.06.017.

Fergus, T. A., & Dolan, S. L. (2014). Problematic internet use and internet searches for medical information: The role of health anxiety. *Cyberpsychology, Behavior and Social Networking, 17*(12), 761–765. https://doi.org/10.1089/cyber.2014.0169.

Fergus, T. A., & Russell, L. H. (2016). Does cyberchondria overlap with health anxiety and obsessive-compulsive symptoms? An examination of latent structure and scale interrelations. *Journal of Anxiety Disorders, 38,* 88–94. https://doi.org/10.1016/j.janxdis.2016.01.009.

Fergus, T. A., & Spada, M. M. (2017). Cyberchondria: Examining relations with problematic internet use and metacognitive beliefs. *Clinical Psychology & Psychotherapy, 24*(6), 1322–1330. https://doi.org/10.1002/cpp.2102.

Fineberg, N. A., Apergis-Schoute, A., Vaghi, M., Banca, P., Gillan, C., Voon, V., et al. (2018). Mapping compulsivity in the DSM-5 obsessive compulsive and related disorders: Cognitive domains, neural circuitry, and treatment. *The International Journal of Neuropsychopharmacology, 21*(1), 42–58.

Fineberg, N. A., Chamberlain, S. R., Goudriaan, A. E., Stein, D. J., Vanderschuren, L. J. M. J., Gillan, C. M., et al. (2014). New developments in human neurocognition: Clinical, genetic, and brain imaging correlates of impulsivity and compulsivity. *CNS Spectrums.* https://doi.org/10.1017/S1092852913000801.

Fineberg, N. A., Demetrovics, Z., Stein, D. J., Ioannidis, K., Potenza, M. N., Grünblatt, E., et al. (2018). Manifesto for a European research network into problematic usage of the internet. *European Neuropsychopharmacology, 28*(11), 1232–1246. https://doi.org/10.1016/j.euroneuro.2018.08.004.

Fineberg, N. A., Potenza, M. N., Chamberlain, S. R., Berlin, H. A., Menzies, L., Bechara, A., et al. (2010). Probing compulsive and impulsive behaviors, from animal models to endophenotypes: A narrative review. *Neuropsychopharmacology*. https://doi.org/10.1038/npp.2009.185.

Folaranmi, O. (2013). A survey of facebook addiction level among selected Nigerian University undergraduates. *New Media and Mass Communication*, *10*, 70–80.

Gibler, R. C., Jastrowski Mano, K. E., O'Bryan, E. M., Beadel, J. R., & McLeish, A. C. (2019). The role of pain catastrophizing in cyberchondria among emerging adults. *Psychology Health and Medicine*, *24*(10), 1267–1276. https://doi.org/10.1080/13548506.2019.1605087.

González-Rivera, J., Santiago-Olmo, K., Cruz-Rodríguez, A., Pérez-Ojeda, R., & Torres-Cuevas, H. (2020). Development and validation of the brief cyberchondria scale in Puerto Rico. *International Journal of Recent Scientific Research*, *11*(1 (A)), 36734–36737.

Grant, J. E., Atmaca, M., Fineberg, N. A., Fontenelle, L. F., Matsunaga, H., Janardhan Reddy, Y. C., et al. (2014). Impulse control disorders and "behavioural addictions" in the ICD-11. *World Psychiatry*. https://doi.org/10.1002/wps.20115.

Grant, J. E., Suck, W. K., & Hartman, B. K. (2008). A double-blind, placebo-controlled study of the opiate antagonist naltrexone in the treatment of pathological gambling urges. *Journal of Clinical Psychiatry*, *69*(5), 783–789. https://doi.org/10.4088/JCP.v69n0511.

Greeven, A., van Balkom, A. J. L. M., van der Leeden, R., Merkelbach, J. W., van den Heuvel, O. A., & Spinhoven, P. (2009). Cognitive behavioral therapy versus paroxetine in the treatment of hypochondriasis: An 18-month naturalistic follow-up. *Journal of Behavior Therapy and Experimental Psychiatry*, *40*(3), 487–496. https://doi.org/10.1016/j.jbtep.2009.06.005.

Guglielmo, R., Ioime, L., & Janiri, L. (2016). Is pathological trading an overlooked form of addiction? *Addiction and Health*, *8*(3), 207–209.

Hellriegel, J., Barber, C., Wikramanayake, M., Fineberg, N. A., & Mandy, W. (2017). Is not just right experience (NJRE) in obsessive-compulsive disorder part of an autistic phenotype? *CNS Spectrums*, *22*(1), 41–50. https://doi.org/10.1017/S1092852916000511.

Hezel, D., & Simpson, H. (2019). Exposure and response prevention for obsessive-compulsive disorder: A review and new directions. *Indian Journal of Psychiatry*. https://doi.org/10.4103/psychiatry.IndianJPsychiatry_516_18.

Hussain, Z., & Griffiths, M. D. (2018). Problematic social networking site use and comorbid psychiatric disorders: A systematic review of recent large-scale studies. *Frontiers in Psychiatry*. https://doi.org/10.3389/fpsyt.2018.00686.

Jokić-Begić, N., Mikac, U., Čuržik, D., & Sangster Jokić, C. (2019). The development and validation of the short Cyberchondria scale (SCS). *Journal of Psychopathology and Behavioral Assessment*, *41*(4), 662–676. https://doi.org/10.1007/s10862-019-09744-z.

Kelly, Y., Zilanawala, A., Booker, C., & Sacker, A. (2018). Social media use and adolescent mental health: Findings from the UK Millennium Cohort Study. *EClinicalMedicine*, *6*, 59–68. https://doi.org/10.1016/j.eclinm.2018.12.005.

Knutson, B., & Bossaerts, P. (2007). Neural antecedents of financial decisions. *Journal of Neuroscience*, *27*(31), 8174–8177. https://doi.org/10.1523/JNEUROSCI.1564-07.2007.

Liu, M., Wu, L., & Yao, S. (2016). Dose-response association of screen time-based sedentary behaviour in children and adolescents and depression: A meta-analysis of observational studies. *British Journal of Sports Medicine*, *50*(20), 1252–1258. https://doi.org/10.1136/bjsports-2015-095084.

Loos, A. (2013). Cyberchondria: Too much information for the health anxious patient? *Journal of Consumer Health on the Internet*, *17*(4), 439–445. https://doi.org/10.1080/15398285.2013.833452.

Makarla, S., Gopichandran, V., & Tondare, D. (2019). Prevalence and correlates of cyberchondria among professionals working in the information technology sector in Chennai, India: A cross-sectional study. *Journal of Postgraduate Medicine*, *65*(2), 87–92. https://doi.org/10.4103/jpgm.JPGM_293_18.

Marino, C., Fergus, T. A., Vieno, A., Bottesi, G., Ghisi, M., & Spada, M. M. (2020). Testing the Italian version of the cyberchondria severity scale and a metacognitive model of cyberchondria. *Clinical Psychology & Psychotherapy*. https://doi.org/10.1002/cpp.2444, cpp.2444.

Massey, C., TenBrook, S., Tatum, C., & Whittaker, S. (2014). PIM and personality: What do our personal file systems say about us? In *Conference on human factors in computing systems—Proceedings* (pp. 3695–3704). New York, NY, USA: Association for Computing Machinery. https://doi.org/10.1145/2556288.2557023.

Mathes, B. M., Norr, A. M., Allan, N. P., Albanese, B. J., & Schmidt, N. B. (2018). Cyberchondria: Overlap with health anxiety and unique relations with impairment, quality of life, and service utilization. *Psychiatry Research*, *261*, 204–211. https://doi.org/10.1016/j.psychres.2018.01.002.

McDaid, D., & Park, A.-L. (2010). *Bupa health pulse 2010. Online health: Untangling the web*. Retrieved from October 1, 2019 https://www.bupa.com.au/staticfiles/Bupa/HealthAndWellness/MediaFiles/PDF/LSE_Report_Online_Health.pdf.

McElroy, E., Kearney, M., Touhey, J., Evans, J., Cooke, Y., & Shevlin, M. (2019). The CSS-12: Development and validation of a short-form version of the cyberchondria severity scale. *Cyberpsychology, Behavior and Social Networking*, *22*(5), 330–335. https://doi.org/10.1089/cyber.2018.0624.

McElroy, E., & Shevlin, M. (2014). The development and initial validation of the cyberchondria severity scale (CSS). *Journal of Anxiety Disorders*, *28*(2), 259–265. https://doi.org/10.1016/j.janxdis.2013.12.007.

McManus, F., Leung, C., Muse, K., & Williams, J. M. G. (2014). Understanding "cyberchondria": An interpretive phenomenological analysis of the purpose, methods and impact of seeking health information online for those with health anxiety. *Cognitive Behaviour Therapist*, *7*. https://doi.org/10.1017/S1754470X14000270.

McMullan, R. D., Berle, D., Arnáez, S., & Starcevic, V. (2019). The relationships between health anxiety, online health information seeking, and cyberchondria: Systematic review and meta-analysis. *Journal of Affective Disorders*. https://doi.org/10.1016/j.jad.2018.11.037.

Monacis, L., De Palo, V., Griffiths, M. D., & Sinatra, M. (2017). Social networking addiction, attachment style, and validation of the Italian version of the Bergen Social Media Addiction Scale. *Journal of Behavioral Addictions*, *6*(2), 178–186. https://doi.org/10.1556/2006.6.2017.023.

Newby, J. M., & McElroy, E. (2020). The impact of internet-delivered cognitive behavioural therapy for health anxiety on cyberchondria. *Journal of Anxiety Disorders*, *69*, 102150. https://doi.org/10.1016/j.janxdis.2019.102150.

Norr, A. M., Albanese, B. J., Oglesby, M. E., Allan, N. P., & Schmidt, N. B. (2014). Anxiety sensitivity and intolerance of uncertainty as potential risk factors for cyberchondria. *Journal of Affective Disorders*, *174*, 64–69. https://doi.org/10.1016/j.jad.2014.11.023.

Norr, A. M., Oglesby, M. E., Raines, A. M., Macatee, R. J., Allan, N. P., & Schmidt, N. B. (2015). Relationships between cyberchondria and obsessive-compulsive symptom dimensions. *Psychiatry Research*, *230*(2), 441–446. https://doi.org/10.1016/j.psychres.2015.09.034.

Pew Research Center. (2018). *Teens, Social Media & Technology*. Retrieved from July 21, 2020 https://www.pewresearch.org/internet/2018/05/31/teens-social-media-technology-2018/50/.

Qudrat Abas, N., & Jaff, D. (2018). Social media as an effective therapeutic tool for addressing obsessive-compulsive disorder: A case study. *Medicine, Conflict, and Survival*. https://doi.org/10.1080/13623699.2018.1527882.

Sachdev, R., Ruparelia, R., Reid, J., Mpavaenda, D., Cinosi, E., & Fineberg, N. (2019). Pharmacological treatments for obsessive-compulsive and related disorders: A transdiagnostic perspective. In *A Transdiagnostic Approach to Obsessions, Compulsions and Related Phenomena* Cambridge University Press. https://doi.org/10.1017/9781108164313.

Schiele, K., & Hughes, M. U. (2013). Possession rituals of the digital consumer: A study of Pinterest | ACR. In G. Cornelissen, E. Reutskaja, & A. Valenzuela (Eds.), *Vol. 10. E - European Advances in consumer research*. Duluth, MN: Association for Consumer Research.

Selvi, Y., Turan, S. G., Sayin, A. A., Boysan, M., & Kandeger, A. (2018). The cyberchondria severity scale (CSS): Validity and reliability study of the Turkish version. *Sleep and Hypnosis*, *20*(4), 241–246. https://doi.org/10.5350/Sleep.Hypn.2018.20.0157.

Shin, Y. C., Choi, S. W., Ha, J., Choi, J. S., & Kim, D. J. (2015). Gambling disorder in financial markets: Clinical and treatment-related features. *Journal of Behavioral Addictions*, *4*(4), 244–249. https://doi.org/10.1556/2006.4.2015.032.

Starčević, V. (1990). Relationship between hypochondriasis and obsessive-compulsive personality disorder: Close relatives separated by nosological schemes? *American Journal of Psychotherapy*, *44*(3), 340–347. https://doi.org/10.1176/appi.psychotherapy.1990.44.3.340.

Starcevic, V. (2017). Cyberchondria: Challenges of problematic online searches for health-related information. *Psychotherapy and Psychosomatics*, *86*(3), 129–133. https://doi.org/10.1159/000465525.

Starcevic, V., Baggio, S., Berle, D., Khazaal, Y., & Viswasam, K. (2019). Cyberchondria and its relationships with related constructs: A network analysis. *Psychiatric Quarterly*, *90*(3), 491–505. https://doi.org/10.1007/s11126-019-09640-5.

Starcevic, V., & Berle, D. (2013). Cyberchondria: Towards a better understanding of excessive health-related internet use. *Expert Review of Neurotherapeutics*. https://doi.org/10.1586/ern.12.162.

Starcevic, V., & Berle, D. (2015). Cyberchondria: An old phenomenon in a new guise? In E. Aboujaoude, & V. Starcevic (Eds.), *Mental health in the digital age: Grave dangers, great promise* (pp. 106–117). New York, NY: Oxford University Press. https://doi.org/10.1093/med/9780199380183.001.0001.

Starcevic, V., Berle, D., Arnáez, S., Vismara, M., & Fineberg, N. A. (2020). The assessment of cyberchondria: Instruments for assessing problematic online health-related research. *Current Addiction Reports*. https://doi.org/10.1007/s40429-020-00308-w.

Stevens, M. W. R., King, D. L., Dorstyn, D., & Delfabbro, P. H. (2019). Cognitive–behavioral therapy for internet gaming disorder: A systematic review and meta-analysis. *Clinical Psychology & Psychotherapy*. https://doi.org/10.1002/cpp.2341.

Sweeten, G., Sillence, E., & Neave, N. (2018). Digital hoarding behaviours: Underlying motivations and potential negative consequences. *Computers in Human Behavior*, *85*, 54–60. https://doi.org/10.1016/j.chb.2018.03.031.

Tatli, Z., Tatli, O., & Kokoc, M. (2019). Development and validity of cyberchondria tendency scale. *World Journal on Educational Technology: Current Issues*, *11*.

te Poel, F., Baumgartner, S. E., Hartmann, T., & Tanis, M. (2016). The curious case of cyberchondria: A longitudinal study on the reciprocal relationship between health anxiety and online health information seeking. *Journal of Anxiety Disorders*, *43*, 32–40. https://doi.org/10.1016/j.janxdis.2016.07.009.

The Harris Pool. (2010). *"Cyberchondriacs" on the rise?*. Retrieved from July 22, 2020 https://theharrispoll.com/the-latest-harris-poll-measuring-how-many-people-use-the-internet-to-look-for-information-about-health-topics-finds-that-the-numbers-continue-to-increase-the-harris-poll-first-used-the-word-cyberch/.

Twenge, J. M., Joiner, T. E., Rogers, M. L., & Martin, G. N. (2018). Increases in depressive symptoms, suicide-related outcomes, and suicide rates among U.S. adolescents after 2010 and links to increased new media screen time. *Clinical Psychological Science*, *6*(1), 3–17. https://doi.org/10.1177/2167702617723376.

Tyrer, P., Cooper, S., Tyrer, H., Wang, D., & Bassett, P. (2019). Increase in the prevalence of health anxiety in medical clinics: Possible cyberchondria. *The International Journal of Social Psychiatry*, 65(7–8), 566–569. https://doi.org/10.1177/0020764019866231.

Uzun, S. U., & Zencir, M. (2018). Reliability and validity study of the Turkish version of cyberchondria severity scale. *Current Psychology*. https://doi.org/10.1007/s12144-018-0001-x.

Van Bennekom, M. J., Blom, R. M., Vulink, N., & Denys, D. (2015). A case of digital hoarding. *BMJ Case Reports*. https://doi.org/10.1136/bcr-2015-210814.

Van Bennekom, M. J., De Koning, P. P., & Denys, D. (2018). Social media and smartphone technology in the symptomatology of OCD. *BMJ Case Reports*. https://doi.org/10.1136/bcr-2017-223662, bcr-2017-223662.

Vismara, M., Caricasole, V., Starcevic, V., Cinosi, E., Dell'Osso, B., Martinotti, G., et al. (2020). Is cyberchondria a new transdiagnostic digital compulsive syndrome? A systematic review of the evidence. *Comprehensive Psychiatry*. https://doi.org/10.1016/j.comppsych.2020.152167.

Ward, S., Smith, N., & Bowden-Jones, H. (2018). The use of naltrexone in pathological and problem gambling: A UK case series. *Journal of Behavioral Addictions*, 7(3), 827–833. https://doi.org/10.1556/2006.7.2018.89.

Watkins, R., & Molesworth, M. (2012). Attachment to digital virtual possessions in videogames. *Research in Consumer Behavior*, 14, 153–170. https://doi.org/10.1108/S0885-2111(2012)0000014012.

White, R. W., & Horvitz, E. (2009). Cyberchondria: Studies of the escalation of medical concerns in web search. *ACM Transactions on Information Systems*, 27(4). https://doi.org/10.1145/1629096.1629101.

Wijesinghe, C. A., Liyanage, U. L. N. S., Kapugama, K. G. C. L., Warsapperuma, W. A. N. P., Williams, S. S., Kuruppuarachchi, K. A. L. A., et al. (2019). "Muddling by googling"—Cyberchondria among outpatient attendees of two hospitals in Sri Lanka. *Sri Lanka Journal of Psychiatry*, 10(1), 11. https://doi.org/10.4038/sljpsyc.v10i1.8202.

Wolniczak, I., Cáceres-DelAguila, J. A., Palma-Ardiles, G., Arroyo, K. J., Solís-Visscher, R., Paredes-Yauri, S., et al. (2013). Association between Facebook dependence and poor sleep quality: A study in a sample of undergraduate students in Peru. *PLoS ONE*, 8(3). https://doi.org/10.1371/journal.pone.0059087, e59087.

World Health Organization. (2014). *Public health implications of excessive use of the internet, computers, smartphones and similar electronic devices meeting report. Main Meeting Hall, foundation for promotion of cancer research, National Cancer Research Centre, Tokyo, Japan 27–29 August 2.*

World Health Organization. (2018). *International classification of diseases for mortality and morbidity statistics (11th Revision)*. Retrieved from October 1, 2019 https://icd.who.int/en.

Wu, A. M. S., Cheung, V. I., Ku, L., & Hung, E. P. W. (2013). Psychological risk factors of addiction to social networking sites among Chinese smartphone users. *Journal of Behavioral Addictions*, 2(3), 160–166. https://doi.org/10.1556/JBA.2.2013.006.

Young, K. S. (1998). Internet addiction: The emergence of a new clinical disorder. *CyberPsychology and Behavior*, 1(3), 237–244. https://doi.org/10.1089/cpb.1998.1.237.

Young, K. S., & Nabuco de Abreu, C. (2010). *Internet addiction: A handbook and guide to evaluation and Treatment*. John Wiley & Sons, Inc.

Internet-use disorders: A theoretical framework for their conceptualization and diagnosis

Elisa Wegmann[a], Joël Billieux[b,c], and Matthias Brand[a,d]
[a]Department of General Psychology: Cognition and Center for Behavioral Addiction Research (CeBAR), University of Duisburg-Essen, Duisburg, Germany, [b]Institute of Psychology, University of Lausanne (UNIL), Lausanne, Switzerland, [c]Centre for Excessive Gambling, Addiction Medicine, Lausanne University Hospitals (CHUV), Lausanne, Switzerland, [d]Erwin L. Hahn Institute for Magnetic Resonance Imaging, Essen, Germany

Introduction

The digitalization of personal and professional daily life is one of the most important developments in the last century. As a result, the distribution of smartphones and the time- and location-independent availability of the Internet have significantly changed our communication behavior. Estimates indicate that 3.9 billion people worldwide used the Internet in 2018, and 4.14 billion people in 2021 (Poleshova, 2019). The number of smartphones has already exceeded the 3 billion mark in 2019 and a further increase is estimated over the next few years (Statista, 2019b). The time spent online has also continued to rise steadily since 2011. For the year 2021, time spent online using a desktop PC is thought to be 37 minutes per day, and time spent using mobile Internet is significantly higher at 155 minutes per day (Statista, 2019a). However, it is worth noting that these estimates are from 2019 and that usage times have significantly increased in 2020 during the COVID-19 pandemic (Statista, 2020). Even though there are regional differences, for example, the proportion of Internet users has been highest in East Asia to date—Internet use has become an essential component of daily and professional life, as well as the main channel for many leisure activities (e.g., video-gaming, TV series watching).

Most people use the Internet in a functional and life-enriching way. However, a subgroup of vulnerable individuals experience negative consequences due to excessive and uncontrolled use of information and communication technologies (Kuss, Griffiths, Karila, & Billieux, 2014). In this chapter, we focus on problematic and addictive behaviors related to Internet use, or Internet-use disorders. The term Internet-use disorder refers to the uncontrolled and dysfunctional use of the Internet in general and may be specified for different types of online applications, for example, gaming, gambling, buying/shopping, pornography use, and the use of social networks (Brand, Wegmann, et al., 2019).

The Diagnostic and Statistical Manual of the American Psychiatry Association (DSM-5; American Psychiatric Association, 2013) included Internet-gaming disorder

Mental Health in a Digital World. https://doi.org/10.1016/B978-0-12-822201-0.00022-8

as a condition for further consideration in the category of substance-related and addictive disorders. In 2019, and in the International Classification System of Diseases (ICD-11) of the World Health Organization (WHO), gaming disorder and gambling disorder were classified as "disorders due to addictive behaviors" and described as conditions involving a pattern of persistent pathological behavior taking place either predominantly online or offline (World Health Organization, 2019). Both types of disorders are defined by three key components: impaired control over the behavior, increasing priority given to the behavior, and continuation or escalation despite the experiences of negative consequences in personal, family, social, education, occupational, or other areas of life resulting in functional impairment in several life domains (World Health Organization, 2019).

Although only these two disorders were included in ICD-11, other disorders due to addictive behaviors, such as the problematic use of online pornography (Stark, Klucken, Potenza, Brand, & Strahler, 2018), buying-shopping disorder (Müller, Brand, 2019), and problematic use of social networks (Wegmann, Mueller, Ostendorf, & Brand, 2018) may also be relevant to consider. These are potential candidates for the ICD-11 category 6C5Y "other specified disorders due to addictive behaviors." In an effort to avoid overpathologizing of everyday behavior, Brand, Rumpf, Demetrovics, et al. (2020) suggested three metalevel criteria to define these other disorders due to addictive behaviors: (1) clinical relevance, (2) theoretical embedding, and (3) empirical evidence of underlying psychological and (neurobiological) mechanisms, which are related to the development and maintenance of the problematic behavior.

Regarding the first criterion (clinical relevance), studies investigating clinical samples as well as prevalence estimates for the different types of Internet-use disorders should be considered. A meta-analysis by Pan, Chiu, and Lin (2020) reported an average prevalence of 7.02% for unspecified Internet-use disorder, although no gold standard for diagnosing unspecified Internet-use disorders exists, and this may result in an overestimation of its prevalence. Further estimates focusing on specific online problematic behaviors also indicate that a minority of vulnerable individuals report symptoms of gaming disorder, gambling disorder, pornography-use disorder, and buying-shopping disorder (e.g., Chóliz, Marcos, & Lázaro-Mateo, 2019; Darvesh et al., 2020; de Alarcón, de la Iglesia, Casado, & Montejo, 2019; Lelonek-Kuleta, Bartczuk, Wiechetek, Chwaszcz, & Niewiadomska, 2020; Liao et al., 2020; Maraz, Griffiths, & Demetrovics, 2016; Mihara & Higuchi, 2017; Wéry & Billieux, 2017).

For problematic use of social networks, there are also some studies indicating that a subgroup of users reports diminished control and negative consequences due to the overuse of social networks (see Guedes et al., 2016; Hussain & Griffiths, 2018). Although no consistent diagnostic instrument or definition has been used, existing data suggest an emerging public health issue.

Furthermore, behavioral as well as neurobiological findings—comprising criterion 3—indicate the importance of specific affective and cognitive components involved in the maintenance and relapse of gaming disorder, gambling disorder, pornography-use disorder, buying-shopping disorder, and problematic use of social networks (for example, Antons & Brand, 2020; Brand, Rumpf, Demetrovics, et al., 2020; Stark et al., 2018; Trotzke, Müller, Brand, Starcke, & Steins-Loeber, 2020; Wegmann & Brand, 2020;

Wölfling, Duven, Wejbera, Beutel, & Müller, 2020). Theoretical frameworks in substance-related addiction research such as dual-process approaches (Bechara, 2005; Everitt & Robbins, 2016; Rochat, Maurage, Heeren, & Billieux, 2019) and the brain disease model of addiction (Volkow, Koob, & McLellan, 2016) are used to describe the mechanisms involved in Internet-use disorders.

We appreciate the advance behavioral addiction research has made, but we would also suggest here that some additional steps are needed to pave the way of the future research, public health efforts, and clinical interventions in this field.

First, we address a debate focusing on diagnosis of specific types of Internet-use disorders. We elaborate on what defines a functional, regular behavior and what are potential criteria that differentiate between a problematic and a pathological use of specific Internet applications. Second, we discuss nosological considerations and the potential distinction between impulsive, compulsive, and addictive behaviors in the context of Internet-use disorders and potential common and divergent mechanisms. Third, we address the special features of the smartphone and other mobile devices and their impact in the conceptualization of a problematic use of social networks.

We present these debates against the background of different theoretical assumptions. We also consider the perspective of a spectrum hypothesis of problems related to overuse of the Internet. The original idea of a spectrum hypothesis was proposed by the mathematicians Georg Cantor in 1878, and illustrates the power of the continuum as a set of natural numbers (see Gillmann, 2002). In physics, the term spectrum refers to phenomena without gaps or interruptions. This also coincides with the semantic meaning of a continuous, gapless connection (Dudenverlag, 2020). It is characterized by a linear function with different extreme or end points, where a continuous back-and-forth movement seems possible. The hypothesis of a spectrum can be applied to mental health and mental disorders, including addictions and Internet-use disorders, and may inspire research questions linked to the relationship between health and disorder, nonuser and excessive user, normal behavior and pathological behavior, symptoms of one disorder, and symptoms of another disorder.

Diagnosis

As Internet-use disorders concern highly ubiquitous behaviors (e.g., gaming, online pornography, social networks use), it is crucial to apply a conservative approach to their diagnosis. In that regard, a crucial question is to define clear boundaries between what constitutes a regular but functional behavior from a potentially problematic and even pathological involvement (Billieux, Flayelle, Rumpf, & Stein, 2019; Kardefelt-Winther et al., 2017). The idea of the dual-continua model of mental health, which is closely linked to the mental health continuum model, seems relevant in the current context. This approach, proposed by Tudor (1996) and developed further by Keyes (2002, 2005), views mental health and psychopathology as two related but distinct states along a linear continuum with two extreme ends (Franken, Lamers, Ten Klooster, Bohlmeijer, & Westerhof, 2018; Keyes, 2005). The notion of a spectrum has been used to investigate the construct of well-being (e.g., Franken et al., 2018;

Tebeka et al., 2018), but has also been used to study different psychological disorders (e.g., Benazzi, 2008; Stenberg, 2016; Watson, Sawrie, Greene, & Arredondo, 2002).

The construct of a spectrum with a healthy, functional end and a dysfunctional, disordered end is relevant to the definition and diagnosis of Internet-use disorders. In our view, four different approaches can be used to define a spectrum of Internet-use disorders: (1) based on the number DSM-5 diagnostic criteria fulfilled, (2) based on the severity of functional impairment, (3) based on specific psychological factors and processes, and (4) based on time spent online (see Fig. 14.1). Notably, this approach combines quantitative (number of criteria fulfilled) and qualitative factors type of criteria fulfilled and underlying psychological dimensions.

A first spectrum approach is based on the nine criteria used to define "Internet-gaming disorder" in the DSM-5: preoccupation, withdrawal, tolerance, loss of control, continued overuse, deception, escape from negative feelings, loss of interest, and jeopardizing (American Psychiatric Association, 2013; Jo et al., 2019; Petry et al., 2014). In the DSM-5, at least five of nine criteria must be met within the last 12 months to diagnose a pathological gaming pattern. Individuals, who fulfill be-

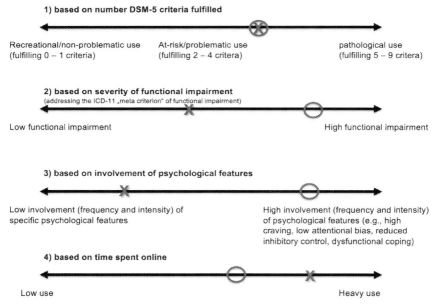

Fig. 14.1 Illustration of the continuum hypothesis. Note: The *red circle* (gray circle in print version) and the *red X* (gray X in print version) represent two different hypothetical individuals characterized by, for example, one specific type of Internet-use disorder such as gaming disorder. On the first continuum, it is shown that both individuals fulfill five of nine DSM-5 criteria, which, however, could differ in their type of criteria. Individuals could also differ in their severity of functional impairment, the involvement of psychological features, and the time spent online. This highlights that even if the number of DSM-5 criteria fulfilled for both individuals, they present with different levels of functional impairment and psychological features.

tween two and four of nine criteria, are considered as at-risk or problematic gamers, whereas equal or less than one criterion is categorized as nonproblematic behavior (American Psychiatric Association, 2013; Jo et al., 2019). Several studies have assessed these criteria covering (Internet) gaming disorder and gambling disorder in different samples (Jiménez-Murcia et al., 2019; Ko, Lin, Lin, & Yen, 2020; Mihara & Higuchi, 2017; Müller, Beutel, Dreier, & Wolfling, 2019; Rennert et al., 2014).[a] Based on this, the extreme ends are "recreational/nonproblematic use" (fulfilling zero criteria) and "pathological use," where an individual fulfills all nine DSM-5 criteria.

A second spectrum approach emphasizes that overall functional impairment is more important than simply adding the number of criteria. Individual criteria may not have equal importance and significance (Grant, Odlaug, & Chamberlain, 2017), and may differ in their clinical validity, clinical utility, and prognostic value (e.g., Besser, Loerbroks, Bischof, Bischof, & Rumpf, 2019; Castro-Calvo et al., 2021; Jo et al., 2019). For example, Müller, Beutel, et al. (2019) found that the criterion "escape from negative feelings" was unable to differentiate between nondisordered and disordered gaming. Billieux et al. (2019) suggested, capitalizing on the previous work by Charlton and Danforth (2007), that DSM-5 criteria encompasses both peripheral features (e.g., deception, mood management) and core features (e.g., loss of control, continuation). Such a proposal has been recently confirmed in the framework of a Delphi study conducted with an internationally representative sample of gaming disorder experts (Castro-Calvo et al., 2021). Crucially, this implies that peripheral features should not be used to diagnose gaming disorder and that high involvement in gaming does not automatically reflect pathological involvement (Billieux et al., 2019). Instead, it is critical to consider the severity of functional impairment (Billieux et al., 2017), ranging from "low functional impairment" to "high functional impairment," based on specific behavioral patterns and considering which criteria are fulfilled and to what degree.

A third spectrum approach to differentiating nondisordered from disordered use of Internet applications is based on the consideration of underlying psychological processes. Indeed, although it is important to capture the number of diagnostic symptoms and their severity, identifying the psychological processes (e.g., affective, cognitive, motivational, interpersonal) sustaining disordered online behaviors is crucial to tailor psychological treatment. The psychological processes and mechanisms potentially involved in functional use of the Internet have been summarized by Brand, Young, and Laier (2014). Achieving a personal goal or satisfying specific needs (e.g., to get informed, to buy something online, to pass time) are considered as the main motivations for using a specific application. Specific cognitions related to positive reinforcement and goal achievement, as well as solution-oriented coping strategies, are characteristic of functional use of applications. When use is controlled, goal achievement is in the foreground (see also Brand et al., 2014), and this is also characterized by efficient

---

[a] It is worth noting that the criteria to define gambling disorder and gaming disorder are not strictly identical in the DSM-5. Furthermore, gambling disorder is recognized as a mental condition in the DSM-5, while Internet gaming-disorder is considered as an emerging condition requiring further research and included in Section 3 of DSM-5.

regulation of online applications. This may be one key aspect for differentiating the controlled (functional) use of a specific from diminished control over use resulting in negative consequences (dysfunctional use). Processes underlying diminished control have been highlighted in recent comprehensive theoretical models of the psychological and neurobiological mechanisms involved in the development and maintenance of addictive behaviors. One example is the recently updated Interaction of Person-Affect-Cognition-Execution model (named I-PACE model) (Brand, Wegmann, et al., 2019). The model also draws on dual-process approaches (Bechara, 2005; Everitt & Robbins, 2005, 2016), incentive-sensitization theory (Robinson & Berridge, 2001, 2008), and reward deficiency models (Blum et al., 1996). Additional theoretical models also address specific types of Internet-use disorders or addictive (online) behaviors, including the pathway model of gambling disorder (Blaszczynski & Nower, 2002), the cognitive behavioral model and the tripartite model for gaming disorder (Dong & Potenza, 2014; Wei, Zhang, Turel, Bechara, & He, 2017), and the specific framework proposed by Wegmann and Brand (2019) in relation to problematic social network use. All these models primarily address affective and cognitive components such as cue reactivity and craving, attentional bias, dysfunctional cognitions, impairment in executive functions and inhibitory control, deficits in decision-making as well as dysfunctional expectancies and motives, and their interactions.

A fourth spectrum approach is based on the time spent online. On this continuum, the extreme points may be "low use" and "heavy use," where "low use" primarily includes reduced time spent online, highly restricted, and low involvement (see Fig. 14.1). Heavy Internet use is often associated with time-consuming involvement and addictive use, even if intensive involvement is not necessarily associated to addiction symptoms (Kiraly, Toth, Urban, Demetrovics, & Maraz, 2017). Empirical findings showed the relationship between time spent online and symptoms of gaming disorder (Buono et al., 2020; Rho et al., 2017; Triberti et al., 2018), pornography-use disorder (Baranowski, Vogl, & Stark, 2019; Wéry, Burnay, Karila, & Billieux, 2016), buying-shopping disorder (Duroy, Gorse, & Lejoyeux, 2014), as well as problematic use of social networks (Lee, Lee, Namkoong, & Jung, 2021). However, the time-consuming behavior is a first indicator only, which should not be considered in an isolated manner but rather in relation to psychological factors underlying maladaptive usage patterns, such as dysfunctional cognitions or emotion regulation strategies (Bodi, Maintenant, & Pennequin, 2021; Chamarro, Oberst, Cladellas, & Fuster, 2020; Drach, Orloff, & Hormes, 2021; Kuss et al., 2014). Moreover, Antons et al. (2019) differentiated individuals using online pornography in recreational-occasional, recreational-frequent, and unregulated users based on time spent online and reported symptoms of a problematic behavior. Results illustrated that recreational-frequent users of online pornography showed positive attitudes toward the online behavior, which was not necessarily linked to addictive tendencies. In the context of social networks use, Coyne, Rogers, Zurcher, Stockdale, and Booth (2020) demonstrated in a longitudinal approach that time spent on social networks was not related to mental health issues. In summary, time spent online may be one indicator reflecting heavy Internet use but is not pathognomonic of a disorder.

As a supplement to the definition of functional Internet use and in distinction to the definition of disordered Internet use, habitual behavior should also be defined.

Similar to functional Internet use, habitual behavior is defined as goal-oriented behavior that balances costs and benefits (Kuem & Ray, 2021). However, in the context of substance use disorders, Everitt and Robbins (2016) emphasize the connectedness of habits and drug-seeking behavior, noting that habits may be a key component of problematic behavior. They stipulate that habitual behavior is not necessarily pathological since it includes, for example, the ability to process information efficiently. However, it may become maladaptive, resulting in drug-seeking or addictive behaviors if it is part of a transition from an exclusively goal-directed behavior to a compulsive habitual behavior (Everitt & Robbins, 2005, 2016). Note, however, the critical view of Hogarth (2020) and Perales et al. (2020) arguing that drug-seeking behavior and high involvement in appetitive activities are more goal directed than habitual. This nuance is of importance given that goal-related behaviors are more frequently functional than dysfunctional.

We propose that the four spectrums, when considered together, allow for subtyping disordered involvement in online activities. For example, and as illustrated in Fig. 14.1 in the context of problem gaming, it could be that for a person fulfilling five out nine DSM-5 criteria (tolerance, deception, mood modification, preoccupation, loss of interest), the functional impairment is low, the expression or impairment of a mechanism such as inhibitory control is present, and the person spends lots of time online. In contrast, a different individual may fulfill five (partially different) DSM-5 criteria (preoccupation, loss of control, jeopardizing, continuation, loss of interest), report severe functional impairment, experience high craving, but not spend very much time online (it may be higher than typical use, but lower than in another individual also fulfilling five criteria). This raises several questions. Which configuration of the continua describes a problematic or disordered behavior? How do we differentiate high involvement in gaming behaviors from disordered behaviors? Accordingly, the future research should conjointly consider the various continua proposed here when investigating and assessing disordered behavior.

Etiology

A second debate addresses potential overlaps between impulsive, compulsive, obsessive-compulsive, and addictive behaviors in the context of Internet-use disorders. What are the potential overlapping and divergent characteristics across these constructs, and is there a possible transition from addictive behaviors to compulsive behaviors? This topic is not a simple debate about classification or diagnostic guidelines. The debate more specifically addresses the actual etiology of Internet-use disorders and whether they have specific defining psychological and neurobiological mechanisms, or whether the underlying mechanisms are more or less transdiagnostic. It may be relevant to consider the diagnostic criteria for compulsive sexual behavior disorder (CSBD), as an example of an impulse-control disorder, and those for gaming disorder, as an example of a disorder due to addictive behaviors in the ICD-11, and then to compare the psychological processes underlying the symptoms of these two disorders.

Table 14.1 ICD-11 criteria for CSBD and gaming disorder and the core convergent criteria.

Criteria for CSBD	Criteria for gaming disorder	Convergent criteria for CSBD and gaming disorder
Persistent pattern of failure to control intense, repetitive sexual impulses or urges resulting in repetitive sexual behavior.	Impaired control over gaming (e.g., onset, frequency, intensity, duration, termination, context).	Diminished control over the behavior
Repetitive sexual activities becoming a central focus of the person's life to the point of neglecting health and personal care or other interests, activities, and responsibilities.	Increasing priority given to gaming to the extent that gaming takes precedence over other life interests and daily activities.	Increasing priority given to the behavior
Numerous unsuccessful efforts to significantly reduce repetitive sexual behavior; continued repetitive sexual behavior despite adverse consequences or deriving little or no satisfaction from it.	Continuation or escalation of gaming despite the occurrence of negative consequences.	Continuation or escalation of the behavior despite negative consequences
The behavior causes marked distress or significant impairment in personal, family, social, educational, occupational, or other important areas of functioning.	The behavior pattern is of sufficient severity to result in marked distress or significant impairment in personal, family, social, educational, occupational, or other important areas of functioning.	Marked distress and/or functional impairment

Modified from in Brand, M., Blycker, G.R., & Potenza, M.N. (2019). When pornography becomes a problem: Clinical insights. *Psychiatric Times, CME section*.

When we look at the phenomenology of CSBD and gaming disorder, as described in the ICD-11 diagnostic guidelines, they converge on four main criteria (see Table 14.1). In other words, although CSBD and gaming disorder are classified in two different diagnostic categories in the ICD-11, they share their main features, which make a clear-cut distinction hazardous and tentative. However, this does not necessarily mean that these two conditions share all underlying psychological and neurobiological mechanisms. One might argue that addictive behaviors are displayed more frequently and habitually without the experience of strong impulses, while impulsive behaviors occur from time to time with a strong impulse to behave in a specific way that increases to a point at which it cannot be controlled. However, the frequency of the behavior is neither a criterion of an impulse-control disorder nor a criterion for addictive behaviors.

When it comes to underlying processes, the debate about commonalities and differences between CSBD and gaming disorder continues (Kraus, Voon, & Potenza, 2016; Stark et al., 2018), and the future studies may systematically compare psychological and neurobiological features of the two disorders.

Another relevant question pertains to how much compulsivity is involved in addictive behaviors. And relatedly, are addictive behaviors compulsive from the onset or does compulsivity in addictive behaviors develop over time? Everitt and Robbins (2005, 2016) argue that within the course of addictions, behaviors change from voluntary actions to habitual behaviors and compulsive behaviors. When we look at the definition of compulsive behaviors, there is one main feature that—at a first glance—does not necessarily fit with the addiction framework, namely the fact that the behavior is repetitive and stereotyped and, more importantly, undertaken to reduce harm and/or to avoid unpleasant consequences (Fineberg et al., 2018). Many authors argue that addictive behaviors are motivated by anticipated gratification, at least at the beginning of the addictive process (e.g., Brand, Wegmann, et al., 2019), and that those behaviors linked to natural or secondary rewards are prone to becoming addictive (Edwards, 2016; Olsen, 2011; Patrono, Gasbarri, Tomaz, & Nishijo, 2016; Robinson, Fischer, Ahuja, Lesser, & Maniates, 2016).

There is a major difference between obsessive-compulsive disorders, which are motivated by avoidance of unpleasant feelings, and addictive behaviors, which are primarily motivated by rewards, at least in the first steps of their evolution. However, in addictive disorders, reward experiences may become less central, and behaviors may become more compulsive. In other words, it is tenable to posit a compulsivity continuum in addictive behaviors that may interact inversely with a reward continuum (Brand, Young, Laier, Wölfling, & Potenza, 2016). In the later stages of substance use and addictive disorders, when the behavior becomes more and more compulsive, many parallels can be observed between addictive behaviors and obsessive-compulsive behaviors. This is, for example, particularly true when considering neurocognitive profiles, which are characterized by deficits in executive functions (inhibitory and motor control, cognitive inflexibility), reversal learning, and habit formation (Fineberg et al., 2018). In addition, research on attentional bias in patients with obsessive-compulsive disorders presents striking similarities to what is found in relation to cue reactivity in individuals with gaming disorder (Kim et al., 2018). Compulsivity in later stages of addictive disorders is mediated by a switch from ventral to dorsal striatum involvement (Vollstädt-Klein et al., 2010), and dorsal striatum is known to play a key role in obsessive-compulsive disorders (Figee et al., 2016; Lipton, Gonzales, & Citri, 2019).

Given the similarities between addictive and obsessive-compulsive disorders, one may argue that they belong to the same cluster of mental disorders. However, there is another important difference, especially when it comes to treatment and early intervention, which pertains to the motivation driving the behavior. Addictive behaviors are mainly driven by rewards—at the beginning of the addictions process; while obsessive-compulsive behaviors are mainly driven by avoidance motivations (Starcevic et al., 2011). However, as outlined above, addictive behaviors may become less rewarding during the addiction process, which means that negative reinforcement becomes more prevalent than positive reinforcement over time. Interestingly, there is evidence that compulsive behaviors may become rewarding during the course of obsessive-compulsive disorders (Fontenelle et al., 2015). Considering these potential reverse continua from positive reinforcement to negative reinforcement in addictive disorders and from negative reinforcement to positive reinforcement in obsessive-compulsive disorders, there are several moments during the courses of these disorders where they may share characteristics and appear similar. However, at least at their early stages, there are also key differences.

One potential disorder that is particularly controversial in terms of its classification and clinical validity is problematic use of social networks (e.g., Brand, Rumpf, Demetrovics, et al., 2020). Notably, there is a recent proposal that differentiates the development and maintenance of problematic social network use according to two different pathways: a fear-driven/compensation-seeking hypothesis and a reward-seeking hypothesis (Wegmann & Brand, 2019). Specific predisposing variables (e.g., need to belong, social anxiety) are thought to promote the behavior in order to experience gratification or to compensate individual deficits (Wegmann & Brand, 2019). Taking the current debate into account, it could be hypothesized that the reward-driven pathway is characterized by addictive-like use, while the fear-driven pathway is characterized by compulsive use. This could also partly account for the inconsistent results when comparing decision-making or craving in problematic social networks use with that in other substance use and addictive disorders (Meshi et al., 2020; Müller et al., 2021; Wegmann, Stodt, & Brand, 2018).

Disordered smartphone use

The worldwide distribution of the smartphone and time spent on the Internet have increased significantly in the last decade. In line with this, the excessive, time-consuming use of the smartphone has become part of addiction research, often mentioned as problematic use of smartphones or smartphone addiction, even if to date not classified as a mental disorder. A body of data shows that addictive smartphone use is related to negative consequences in daily life, impaired control, psychopathological symptoms (e.g., depression and anxiety), and reckless driving (Canale et al., 2021; Elhai, Levine, Dvorak, & Hall, 2016; Hussain, Griffiths, & Sheffield, 2017; Kuss et al., 2018). Echoing past research on the "Internet addiction" construct, it has been suggested that what is important is the content of use, not the medium (e.g., smartphone, Internet, tablets) through which it is performed. Kimberly Young was among the first to emphasize the necessity of considering the content of use and of differentiating addictive involvement in various online activities (Young, 1996, 1998). More recently, it has been more directly argued that "Internet addiction" and "smartphone addiction" are not tenable constructs, and should be replaced by a focus on specific addictive online activities (Starcevic, 2013; Starcevic & Billieux, 2017).

Similarly, there are approaches which emphasize a content-based investigation of smartphone use (Lee, Ahn, Min, & Kim, 2020). This often results in a significant overlap between smartphone addiction, problematic smartphone use, and problematic social networks use (Wegmann & Brand, 2019, 2020). It raises the question of whether the problematic use of smartphones is necessarily a problematic use of social networks. However, in more recent studies, gaming has been described as the "most distracting smartphone-related activity" (p. 939; Moretta, Chen, & Potenza, 2020; Mourra et al., 2020). Empirical studies have found that intensive or problematic smartphone use is often associated with playing online games (Liu, Lin, Pan, & Lin, 2016; Wu, Lin, & Lin, 2021). This point illustrates well the need to differentiate the device vs. the content of use.

Montag, Wegmann, Sariyska, Demetrovics, and Brand (2021) have argued that the method of Internet access should be considered but that the content of use matters more. Elhai, Yang, and Levine (2021) have further specified that the content of mobile Internet use is important, but that the method of access, for example, via smartphone or desktop PC may provide important insights when defining intervention programs or treatment strategies. This means that the device is not at the core of the problematic behavior but should not be neglected. Our view is that both components (device and content) are relevant to consider, but that the content is central in understanding the type of problematic behavior.

A further dimension of this debate, addressed by Moretta et al. (2020) and Starcevic et al. (2021), focuses on underlying mechanisms and individual differences, which are important for differentiating between smartphone usage and specific types of Internet-use disorders. Similarly, Canale et al. (2021) highlighted the need to consider different subtypes of problematic smartphone (for discussion see also Billieux, Maurage, Lopez-Fernandez, Kuss, & Griffiths, 2015; Montag, Wegmann, Sariyska, Demetrovics, & Brand, 2021; Panova & Carbonell, 2018). In the theoretical framework provided by Kardefelt-Winther (2014), it is suggested that dysfunctional use of the Internet mainly reflects a coping strategy, where online activities satisfy basic needs (e.g., social affiliation, competence) that are unmet in offline life. Brand, Rumpf, King, Potenza, and Wegmann (2020) instead argued that coping should not be considered as exclusion or inclusion criteria in the context of addictive behaviors, but rather as a psychological feature or underlying mechanism. In line with this, emotion regulation strategies may play a pivotal role in addictive smartphone use, as supported by several recent studies (Elhai et al., 2018; Extremera, Quintana-Orts, Sánchez-Álvarez, & Rey, 2019; Horwood & Anglim, 2021). Again, however, further research should establish whether this relationship is more relevant or pronounced for certain contents (e.g., gaming, pornography, online communication).

As a next step, we suggest that behavioral patterns and symptoms should be distinguished from hypothesized underlying psychological processes. Using this perspective, Billieux, Maurage, et al. (2015) proposed a theoretical framework to understand problematic mobile phone use. This model posits three distinct pathways associated with specific psychological and psychopathological factors: (1) the excessive reassurance pathway, (2) the impulsive pathways, and (3) the extraversion pathway. The excessive reassurance pathway is linked to factors such as emotional instability, anxiety symptoms, dysfunctional attachment, or low self-esteem, which promote addictive-like mobile phone use [e.g., using the phone to get reassured in the context of unsecure romantic or affective relationship, see Billieux, Philippot, et al., 2015]. The impulsive pathway is related to personal characteristics such as impulsivity, low self-control, or antisocial personality that may lead to various types of problematic mobile phone use [e.g., addictive, risky, and antisocial use, see Canale et al., 2021]. The extraversion pathway addresses risk factors such as sensation-seeking, extraversion, and reward sensitivity, which may result in addictive and risky usage patterns (Billieux, Maurage, et al., 2015; Canale et al., 2021). This model, which illustrates different "pathways" or "routes" leading to specific patterns of dysfunctional mobile phone use, has received empirical sup from the recent studies (see, for example, Canale et al., 2021; Dey et al., 2019).

However, there are other conceptual frameworks that are relevant in the context of problematic smartphone use. The importance of specific expectancies and needs in the context of media use has been demonstrated through the uses and gratification theory (Katz, 1959; Katz, Blumler, & Gurevich, 1974). The idea of considering needs, expectancies, and the experience of gratification and compensation as underlying mechanisms has been elaborated by Wegmann and Brand (2019) in the context of problematic use of social networks. These authors hypothesized two pathways resulting in problematic online behavior: reward-seeking and fear-driven. It is proposed that specific reinforcement mechanisms such as gratification experiences, rewarding experiences, or compensation of deficits and fears mediate the effect of predisposing individual factors (e.g., need to belong, narcissism, or social anxiety) on problematic social networks use. These mechanisms emphasize that the decision to use specific online applications is related to specific expectancies and psychological processes, which include maladaptive emotion regulation and coping strategies.

If we consider the components of the various theoretical approaches discussed here (Billieux, Maurage, et al., 2015; Brand, Rumpf, King, et al., 2020; Kardefelt-Winther, 2014; Wegmann & Brand, 2019), it seems that the investigation of smartphone use and types of Internet-use disorders is less about the device itself than about the content used or predisposing factors (e.g., psychosocial characteristics, personality traits). In line with this, Rumpf, Browne, Brandt, and Rehbein (2021) have specified that besides the consideration of new technologies, which might change the online behavior in terms of availability and access, the underlying mechanisms such as reward sensitivity or social interaction are universal. Moreover, Starcevic et al. (2021) have argued that a focus on devices solely would shift the focus away from further important factors such as usage motives and evidence of functional impairment. We agree that it is important to consider technologies and their development, but they do not simply entail new disorders. Instead, at least three aspects should be studied: (1) method of access, (2) content, and (3) psychological features and underlying processes/mechanisms resulting in problematic use.

Conclusion

These debates reflect some of the current discussions in behavioral addiction research, especially in the context of different Internet-use disorders. For the diagnosis and classification of disorders due to addictive behaviors, we outlined that it would be helpful to combine different approaches, for example, the number of DSM-5 criteria, the severity of functional impairment, the underlying psychological (e.g., cognitive, affective, motivational) processes, and the time spent online, to appreciate the multi-determined nature of these conditions. Our view is that considering the interplay of these components has the potential to pave the way for future clinical research and treatment.

In addition, we have emphasized the importance of examining possible commonal-ities and differences between different disorders, including compulsive and impulsive conditions, which may be helpful in unveiling individual mechanisms and understand-ing how disorders develop over time. In the case of problematic use of social net-works, it may be particularly relevant to consider the psychological characteristics of addictive and compulsive behavior. Importantly, these issues are also relevant in the conceptualization and diagnosis of "smartphone addiction."

Developments in information and communication technologies have long prompted and shaped addiction research. However, as reflected by the research reviewed in this chapter, it is not merely a question of a technology per se leading to an addictive behavior. Instead, our theoretical frameworks should emphasize the hypothesized eti-ological processes leading to the dysfunctional behavior. In conclusion, the current overview aims to pave the way for future research aiming to tackle the multideter-mined nature and heterogeneity of Internet-use disorders.

Disclosure statements

JB and MB are members of the COST Action 16207 "European Network for Problematic Usage of the Internet." EW, JB, and MB declare that they have no conflict of interests concerning this chapter.

References

American Psychiatric Association. (2013). *Diagnostic and statistical manual of mental disor-ders* (5th ed.). American Psychiatric Publishing.

Antons, S., & Brand, M. (2020). Inhibitory control and problematic internet-pornography use—The important balancing role of the insula. *Journal of Behavioral Addictions*, 9(1), 1–13. https://doi.org/10.1556/2006.2020.00010.

Antons, S., Mueller, S. M., Wegmann, E., Trotzke, P., Schulte, M. M., & Brand, M. (2019). Facets of impulsivity and related aspects differentiate among recreational and unregulated use of Internet pornography. *Journal of Behavioral Addictions*, 8(2), 223–233. https://doi.org/10.1556/2006.8.2019.22.

Baranowski, A. M., Vogl, R., & Stark, R. (2019). Prevalence and determinants of problematic online pornography use in a sample of German women. *The Journal of Sexual Medicine*, 16(8), 1274–1282. https://doi.org/10.1016/j.jsxm.2019.05.010.

Bechara, A. (2005). Decision making, impulse control and loss of willpower to resist drugs: A neurocognitive perspective. *Nature Neuroscience*, 8, 1458–1463. https://doi.org/10.1038/nn1584.

Benazzi, F. (2008). The continuum hypothesis of mood disorders. *Journal of Clinical Psychiatry*, 69(7), 1187–1188. https://doi.org/10.4088/jcp.v69n0720b.

Besser, B., Loerbroks, L., Bischof, G., Bischof, A., & Rumpf, H.-J. (2019). Performance of the DSM-5-based criteria for Internet addiction: A factor analytical examination of three samples. *Journal of Behavioral Addictions*, *8*(2), 288–294. https://doi.org/10.1556/2006.8.2019.19.

Billieux, J., Flayelle, M., Rumpf, H.-J., & Stein, D. J. (2019). High involvement versus pathological involvement in video games: A crucial distinction for ensuring the validity and utility of gaming disorder. *Current Addiction Reports*, *6*(3), 323–330. https://doi.org/10.1007/s40429-019-00259-x.

Billieux, J., King, D. L., Higuchi, S., Achab, S., Bowden-Jones, H., Hao, W., et al. (2017). Functional impairment matters in the screening and diagnosis of gaming disorder. *Journal of Behavioral Addictions*, *6*(3), 285–289. https://doi.org/10.1556/2006.6.2017.036.

Billieux, J., Maurage, P., Lopez-Fernandez, O., Kuss, D. J., & Griffiths, M. D. (2015). Can disordered mobile phone use be considered as behavioral addiction? An update on current evidence and a comprehensive model for future research. *Current Addiction Reports*, *2*(2), 156–162. https://doi.org/10.1007/s40429-015-0054-y.

Billieux, J., Philippot, P., Schmid, C., Maurage, P., De Mol, J., & Van der Linden, M. (2015). Is dysfunctional use of the mobile phone a behavioural addiction? Confronting symptom-based versus process-based approaches. *Clinical Psychology & Psychotherapy*, *22*(5), 460–468. https://doi.org/10.1002/cpp.1910.

Blaszczynski, A., & Nower, L. (2002). A pathways model of problem and pathological gambling. *Addiction*, *97*, 487–499. https://doi.org/10.1046/j.1360-0443.2002.00015.x.

Blum, K., Sheridan, P. J., Wood, R. C., Braverman, E. R., Chen, T. J., Cull, J. G., et al. (1996). The D2 dopamine receptor gene as a determinant of reward deficiency syndrome. *Journal of the Royal Society of Medicine*, *89*(7), 396–400.

Bodi, G., Maintenant, C., & Pennequin, V. (2021). The role of maladaptive cognitions in gaming disorder: Differences between online and offline gaming types. *Addictive Behaviors*, *112*, 106595. https://doi.org/10.1016/j.addbeh.2020.106595.

Brand, M., Rumpf, H.-J., Demetrovics, Z., Müller, A., Stark, R., King, D. L., et al. (2020). Which conditions should be considered as disorders in the International Classification of Diseases (ICD-11) designation of "other specified disorders due to addictive behaviors"? *Journal of Behavioral Addictions*. https://doi.org/10.1556/2006.2020.00035.

Brand, M., Rumpf, H.-J., King, D. L., Potenza, M. N., & Wegmann, E. (2020). Clarifying terminologies in research on gaming disorder and other addictive behaviors: Distinctions between core symptoms and underlying psychological processes. *Current Opinion in Psychology*, *36*, 49–54. https://doi.org/10.1016/j.copsyc.2020.04.006.

Brand, M., Wegmann, E., Stark, R., Müller, A., Wölfling, K., Robbins, T. W., et al. (2019). The interaction of person-affect-cognition-execution (I-PACE) model for addictive behaviors: Update, generalization to addictive behaviors beyond internet-use disorders, and specification of the process character of addictive behaviors. *Neuroscience & Biobehavioral Reviews*, *104*, 1–10. https://doi.org/10.1016/j.neubiorev.2019.06.032.

Brand, M., Young, K. S., & Laier, C. (2014). Prefrontal control and internet addiction: A theoretical model and review of neuropsychological and neuroimaging findings. *Frontiers in Human Neuroscience*, *8*, 375. https://doi.org/10.3389/fnhum.2014.00375.

Brand, M., Young, K. S., Laier, C., Wölfling, K., & Potenza, M. N. (2016). Integrating psychological and neurobiological considerations regarding the development and maintenance of specific Internet-use disorders: An Interaction of Person-Affect-Cognition-Execution (I-PACE) model. *Neuroscience & Biobehavioral Reviews*, *71*, 252–266. https://doi.org/10.1016/j.neubiorev.2016.08.033.

Buono, F. D., Paul, E., Sprong, M. E., Smith, E. C., Garakani, A., & Griffiths, M. D. (2020). Gaming and gaming disorder: A mediation model gender, salience, age of gaming onset, and time spent gaming. *Cyberpsychology, Behavior and Social Networking*, *23*(9), 647–651. https://doi.org/10.1089/cyber.2019.0445.

Canale, N., Moretta, T., Pancani, L., Buodo, G., Vieno, A., Dalmaso, M., et al. (2021). A test of the pathway model of problematic smartphone use. *Journal of Behavioral Addictions*, *10*(1), 181–193. https://doi.org/10.1556/2006.2020.00103.

Castro-Calvo, J., King, D. L., Stein, D. J., Brand, M., Carmi, L., Chamberlain, S. R., et al. (2021). Expert appraisal of criteria for assessing gaming disorder: An international Delphi study. *Addiction*. https://doi.org/10.1111/add.15411.

Chamarro, A., Oberst, U., Cladellas, R., & Fuster, H. (2020). Effect of the frustration of psychological needs on addictive behaviors in mobile videogamers—The mediating role of use expectancies and time spent gaming. *International Journal of Environmental Research and Public Health*, *17*(17), 6429. https://doi.org/10.3390/ijerph17176429.

Charlton, J. P., & Danforth, I. D. W. (2007). Distinguishing addiction and high engagement in the context of online game playing. *Computers in Human Behavior*, *23*(3), 1531–1548. https://doi.org/10.1016/j.chb.2005.07.002.

Chóliz, M., Marcos, M., & Lázaro-Mateo, J. (2019). The risk of online gambling: A study of gambling disorder prevalence rates in Spain. *International Journal of Mental Health and Addiction*, *19*, 404–417. https://doi.org/10.1007/s11469-019-00067-4.

Coyne, S. M., Rogers, A. A., Zurcher, J. D., Stockdale, L., & Booth, M. (2020). Does time spent using social media impact mental health?: An eight year longitudinal study. *Computers in Human Behavior*, *104*, 106160. https://doi.org/10.1016/j.chb.2019.106160.

Darvesh, N., Radhakrishnan, A., Lachance, C. C., Nincic, V., Sharpe, J. P., Ghassemi, M., et al. (2020). Exploring the prevalence of gaming disorder and Internet gaming disorder: A rapid scoping review. *Systematic Reviews*, *9*(1), 68. https://doi.org/10.1186/s13643-020-01329-2.

de Alarcón, R., de la Iglesia, J. I., Casado, N. M., & Montejo, A. L. (2019). Online porn addiction: What we know and what we don't—A systematic review. *Journal of Clinical Medicine*, *8*(1), 91. https://doi.org/10.3390/jcm8010091.

Dey, M., Studer, J., Schaub, M. P., Gmel, G., Ebert, D. D., Lee, J. Y.-C., et al. (2019). Problematic smartphone use in young Swiss men: Its association with problematic substance use and risk factors derived from the pathway model. *Journal of Behavioral Addictions*, *8*(2), 326–334. https://doi.org/10.1556/2006.8.2019.17.

Dong, G., & Potenza, M. N. (2014). A cognitive-behavioral model of Internet gaming disorder: Theoretical underpinnings and clinical implications. *Journal of Psychiatric Research*, *58*, 7–11. https://doi.org/10.1016/j.jpsychires.2014.07.005.

Drach, R. D., Orloff, N. C., & Hormes, J. M. (2021). The emotion regulatory function of online social networking: Preliminary experimental evidence. *Addictive Behaviors*, *112*, 106559. https://doi.org/10.1016/j.addbeh.2020.106559.

Dudenverlag, B. I. G. (2020). *Duden*. https://www.duden.de/rechtschreibung/Kontinuum.

Duroy, D., Gorse, P., & Lejoyeux, M. (2014). Characteristics of online compulsive buying in Parisian students. *Addictive Behaviors*, *39*(12), 1827–1830. https://doi.org/10.1016/j.addbeh.2014.07.028.

Edwards, S. (2016). Reinforcement principles for addiction medicine: From recreational drug use to psychiatric disorder. *Progress in Brain Research*, *223*, 63–76. https://doi.org/10.1016/bs.pbr.2015.07.005.

Elhai, J. D., Levine, J. C., Dvorak, R. D., & Hall, B. J. (2016). Fear of missing out, need for touch, anxiety and depression are related to problematic smartphone use. *Computers in Human Behavior*, *63*, 509–516. https://doi.org/10.1016/j.chb.2016.05.079.

Elhai, J. D., Tiamiyu, M. F., Weeks, J. W., Levine, J. C., Picard, K. J., & Hall, B. J. (2018). Depression and emotion regulation predict objective smartphone use measured over one week. *Personality and Individual Differences*, *133*, 21–28. https://doi.org/10.1016/j.paid.2017.04.051.

Elhai, J. D., Yang, H., & Levine, J. C. (2021). Applying fairness in labeling various types of internet use disorders. *Journal of Behavioral Addictions*, *9*(4), 924–927. https://doi.org/10.1556/2006.2020.00071.

Everitt, B. J., & Robbins, T. W. (2005). Neural systems of reinforcement for drug addiction: From actions to habits to compulsion. *Nature Neuroscience*, *8*(11), 1481–1489. https://doi.org/10.1038/nn1579.

Everitt, B. J., & Robbins, T. W. (2016). Drug addiction: Updating actions to habits to compulsions ten years on. *Annual Review of Psychology*, *67*, 23–50. https://doi.org/10.1146/annurev-psych-122414-033457.

Extremera, N., Quintana-Orts, C., Sánchez-Álvarez, N., & Rey, L. (2019). The role of cognitive emotion regulation strategies on problematic smartphone use: Comparison between problematic and non-problematic adolescent users. *International Journal of Enviromental Research and Public Health*, *16*(17), 3142. https://doi.org/10.3390/ijerph16173142.

Figee, M., Pattij, T., Willuhn, I., Luigjes, J., van den Brink, W., Goudriaan, A., et al. (2016). Compulsivity in obsessive-compulsive disorder and addictions. *European Neuropsychopharmacology*, *26*(5), 856–868. https://doi.org/10.1016/j.euroneuro.2015.12.003.

Fineberg, N. A., Apergis-Schoute, A. M., Vaghi, M. M., Banca, P., Gillan, C. M., Voon, V., et al. (2018). Mapping compulsivity on the DSM-5 obsessive compulsive and related disorders: Cognitive domains, neural circuitry, and treatment. *International Journal of Neuropsychopharmacology*, *21*(1), 42–58. https://doi.org/10.1093/ijnp/pyx088.

Fontenelle, L. F., Oostermeijer, S., Ferreira, G. M., Lorenzetti, V., Luigjes, J., & Yücel, M. (2015). Anticipated reward in obsessive-compulsive disorder: Are compulsions rewarding? *Journal of Clinical Psychiatry*, *76*(9), e1134–e1135. https://doi.org/10.4088/JCP.14l09499.

Franken, K., Lamers, S. M. A., Ten Klooster, P. M., Bohlmeijer, E. T., & Westerhof, G. J. (2018). Validation of the mental health continuum-short form and the dual continua model of well-being and psychopathology in an adult mental health setting. *Journal of Clinical Psychology*, *74*(12), 2187–2202. https://doi.org/10.1002/jclp.22659.

Gillmann, L. (2002). Two classical surprises concerning the axiom of choice and the continuum hypothesis. *American Mathematical Monthly*, *109*, 544–553.

Grant, J. E., Odlaug, B. L., & Chamberlain, S. R. (2017). Gambling disorder, DSM-5 criteria and symptom severity. *Comprehensive Psychiatry*, *75*, 1–5. https://doi.org/10.1016/j.comppsych.2017.02.006.

Guedes, E., Sancassiani, F., Carta, M. G., Campos, C., Machado, S., King, A. L. S., et al. (2016). Internet addiction and excessive social networks use: What about Facebook? *Clinical Practice and Epidemiology in Mental Health*, *12*, 43–48. https://doi.org/10.2174/1745017901612010043.

Hogarth, L. (2020). Addiction is driven by excessive goal-directed drug choice under negative affect: Translational critique of habit and compulsion theory. *Neuropsychopharmacology: official publication of the American College of Neuropsychopharmacology*, *45*(5), 720–735. https://doi.org/10.1038/s41386-020-0600-8.

Horwood, S., & Anglim, J. (2021). Emotion regulation difficulties, personality, and problematic smartphone use. *CyberPsychology, Behavior, and Social Networking*, *24*(4), 275–281. https://doi.org/10.1089/cyber.2020.0328.

Hussain, Z., & Griffiths, M. D. (2018). Problematic social networking site use and comorbid psychiatric disorder: A systematic review of recent large-scale studies. *Frontiers in Psychiatry*, *9*, 686. https://doi.org/10.3389/fpsyt.2018.00686.

Hussain, Z., Griffiths, M. D., & Sheffield, D. (2017). An investigation into problematic smartphone use: The role of narcissism, anxiety, and personality factors. *Journal of Behavioral Addictions*, *6*(3), 378–386. https://doi.org/10.1556/2006.6.2017.052.

Jiménez-Murcia, S., Granero, R., Fernández-Aranda, F., Sauvaget, A., Fransson, A., Hakansson, A., et al. (2019). A comparison of DSM-IV-TR and DSM-5 ciagnostic criteria for gambling disorder in a large clinical aample. *Frontiers in Psychology*, *10*, 931. https://doi.org/10.3389/fpsyg.2019.00931.

Jo, Y. S., Bhang, S. Y., Choi, J. S., Lee, H. K., Lee, S. Y., & Kweon, Y. S. (2019). Clinical characteristics of diagnosis for internet gaming disorder: Comparison of DSM-5 IGD and ICD-11 GD diagnosis. *Journal of Clinical Medicine*, *8*(7), 945. https://doi.org/10.3390/jcm8070945.

Kardefelt-Winther, D. (2014). A conceptual and methodological critique of internet addiction research: Towards a model of compensatory internet use. *Computers in Human Behavior*, *31*, 351–354. https://doi.org/10.1016/j.chb.2013.10.059.

Kardefelt-Winther, D., Heeren, A., Schimmenti, A., van Rooij, A., Maurage, P., Carras, M., et al. (2017). How can we conceptualize behavioural addiction without pathologizing common behaviours? *Addiction*, *112*(10), 1709–1715. https://doi.org/10.1111/add.13763.

Katz, E. (1959). Mass communication research and the study of culture: An editorial note on a possible future for this journal. *Studies in Public Communication*, *2*, 1–6.

Katz, E., Blumler, G. J., & Gurevich, M. (1974). Utilization of mass communication by the individual. In G. J. Blumler, & E. Katz (Eds.), *The uses of mass communication: Current perspectives on gratifications research* (pp. 19–32). Sage.

Keyes, C. L. M. (2002). The mental health continuum: From languishing to flourishing in life. *Journal of Health and Social Behavior*, *43*(2), 207–222. https://doi.org/10.2307/3090197.

Keyes, C. L. M. (2005). Mental illness and/or mental health? Investigating axioms of the complete state model of health. *Journal of Consulting and Clinical Psychology*, *73*(3), 539–548. https://doi.org/10.1037/0022-006x.73.3.539.

Kim, S. N., Kim, M., Lee, T. H., Lee, J. Y., Park, S., Park, M., et al. (2018). Increased attentional bias toward visual cues in internet gaming disorder and obsessive compulsive disorder: An event-related potential study. *Frontiers in Psychiatry*, *9*, 315. https://doi.org/10.3389/fpsyt.2018.00315.

Kiraly, O., Toth, D., Urban, R., Demetrovics, Z., & Maraz, A. (2017). Intense video gaming is not essentially problematic. *Psychology of Addictive Behaviors*, *31*(7), 807–817. https://doi.org/10.1037/adb0000316.

Ko, C. H., Lin, H. C., Lin, P. C., & Yen, J. Y. (2020). Validity, functional impairment and complications related to Internet gaming disorder in the DSM-5 and gaming disorder in the ICD-11. *Australian and New Zealand Journal of Medicine*, *54*(7), 707–718. https://doi.org/10.1177/0004867419881499.

Kraus, S. W., Voon, V., & Potenza, M. N. (2016). Should compulsive sexual behavior be considered an addiction? *Addiction*, *111*(12), 2097–2106. https://doi.org/10.1111/add.13297.

Kuem, J., & Ray, S. (2021). Personality antecedents and consequences of internet addiction vis-à-vis Internet habit: A theory and an empirical investigation. *Information Systems Frontiers*. https://doi.org/10.1007/s10796-021-10110-2.

Kuss, D. J., Griffiths, M. D., Karila, M., & Billieux, J. (2014). Internet addiction: A systematic review of epidemiological research for the last decade. *Current Pharmaceutical Design*, *20*, 4026–4052. https://doi.org/10.2174/13816128113199990617.

Kuss, D. J., Kanjo, E., Crook-Rumsey, M., Kibowski, F., Wang, G. Y., & Sumich, A. (2018). Problematic mobile phone use and addiction across generations: The roles of psychopathological symptoms and smartphone use. *Journal of Technology in Behavioral Science*, *3*(3), 141–149. https://doi.org/10.1007/s41347-017-0041-3.

Lee, D., Lee, J., Namkoong, K., & Jung, Y.-C. (2021). Altered functional connectivity of the dorsal attention network among problematic social network users. *Addictive Behaviors*, *116*, 106823. https://doi.org/10.1016/j.addbeh.2021.106823.

Lee, J., Ahn, J. S., Min, S., & Kim, M. H. (2020). Psychological characteristics and addiction propensity according to content type of smartphone use. *International Journal of Enviromental Research and Public Health*, *17*(7), 2292. https://doi.org/10.3390/ijerph17072292.

Lelonek-Kuleta, B., Bartczuk, R. P., Wiechetek, M., Chwaszcz, J., & Niewiadomska, I. (2020). The prevalence of e-gambling and of problem e-gambling in Poland. *International Journal of Environmental Research and Public Health*, *17*(2), 404. https://doi.org/10.3390/ijerph17020404.

Liao, Z., Huang, Q., Huang, S., Tan, L., Shao, T., Fang, T., et al. (2020). Prevalence of Internet gaming disorder and its association with personality traits and gaming characteristics among Chinese adolescent gamers. *Frontiers in Psychiatry*, *11*, 1266. https://doi.org/10.3389/fpsyt.2020.598585.

Lipton, D. M., Gonzales, B. J., & Citri, A. (2019). Dorsal striatal circuits for habits, compulsions and addictions. *Frontiers in Systems Neuroscience*, *13*, 28. https://doi.org/10.3389/fnsys.2019.00028.

Liu, C. H., Lin, S. H., Pan, Y. C., & Lin, Y. H. (2016). Smartphone gaming and frequent use pattern associated with smartphone addiction. *Medicine*, *95*(28). https://doi.org/10.1097/md.0000000000004068, e4068.

Maraz, A., Griffiths, M. D., & Demetrovics, Z. (2016). The prevalence of compulsive buying: A meta-analysis. *Addiction*, *111*(3), 408–419. https://doi.org/10.1111/add.13223.

Meshi, D., Ulusoy, E., Özdem-Mertens, C., Grady, S. M., Freestone, D. M., Eden, A., et al. (2020). Problematic social media use is associated with increased risk-aversion after negative outcomes in the Balloon Analogue Risk Task. *Psychology of Addictive Behaviors*, *34*(4), 549–555. https://doi.org/10.1037/adb0000558.

Mihara, S., & Higuchi, S. (2017). Cross-sectional and longitudinal epidemiological studies of internet gaming disorder: A systematic review of the literature. *Psychiatry and Clinical Neurosciences*, *71*(7), 425–444. https://doi.org/10.1111/pcn.12532.

Montag, C., Wegmann, E., Sariyska, R., Demetrovics, Z., & Brand, M. (2021). How to overcome taxonomical problems in the study of internet use disorders and what to do with "smartphone addiction"? *Journal of Behavioral Addictions*, *9*(4), 908–914. https://doi.org/10.1556/2006.8.2019.59.

Moretta, T., Chen, S., & Potenza, M. N. (2020). Mobile and non-mobile Internet Use Disorder: Specific risks and possible shared Pavlovian conditioning processes. *Journal of Behavioral Addictions*, *9*(4), 938–941. https://doi.org/10.1556/2006.2020.00077.

Mourra, G. N., Sénécal, S., Fredette, M., Lepore, F., Faubert, J., Bellavance, F., et al. (2020). Using a smartphone while walking: The cost of smartphone-addiction proneness. *Addictive Behaviors*, *106*, 106346. https://doi.org/10.1016/j.addbeh.2020.106346.

Müller, K. W., Beutel, M. E., Dreier, M., & Wolfling, K. (2019). A clinical evaluation of the DSM-5 criteria for Internet Gaming Disorder and a pilot study on their applicability to further internet-related disorders. *Journal of Behavioral Addictions*, *8*(1), 16–24. https://doi.org/10.1556/2006.7.2018.140.

Müller, A., Brand, M., Claes, L., Demetrovics, Z., de Zwaan, M., Fernández-Aranda, F., et al. (2019). Buying-shopping disorder—Is there enough evidence to support its inclusion in ICD-11? *CNS Spectrums*, 1–6. https://doi.org/10.1017/S1092852918001323.

Müller, S. M., Wegmann, E., García Arias, M., Bernabéu Brotóns, E., Marchena Giráldez, C., & Brand, M. (2021). Deficits in executive functions but not in decision making under risk in individuals with problematic social-network use. *Comprehensive Psychiatry*, *106*, 152228. https://doi.org/10.1016/j.comppsych.2021.152228.

Olsen, C. M. (2011). Natural rewards, neuroplasticity, and non-drug addictions. *Neuropharmacology*, *61*(7), 1109–1122. https://doi.org/10.1016/j.neuropharm.2011.03.010.

Pan, Y.-C., Chiu, Y.-C., & Lin, Y.-H. (2020). Systematic review and meta-analysis of epidemiology of internet addiction. *Neuroscience & Biobehavioral Reviews*, *118*, 612–622. https://doi.org/10.1016/j.neubiorev.2020.08.013.

Panova, T., & Carbonell, X. (2018). Is smartphone addiction really an addiction? *Journal of Behavioral Addictions*, *7*(2), 252–259. https://doi.org/10.1556/2006.7.2018.49.

Patrono, E., Gasbarri, A., Tomaz, C., & Nishijo, H. (2016). Transitionality in addiction: A "temporal continuum" hypotheses involving the aberrant motivation, the hedonic dysregulation, and the aberrant learning. *Medical Hypotheses*, *93*, 62–70. https://doi.org/10.1016/j.mehy.2016.05.015.

Perales, J. C., King, D. L., Navas, J. F., Schimmenti, A., Sescousse, G., Starcevic, V., et al. (2020). Learning to lose control: A process-based account of behavioral addiction. *Neuroscience & Biobehavioral Reviews*, *108*, 771–780. https://doi.org/10.1016/j.neubiorev.2019.12.025.

Petry, N. M., Rehbein, F., Gentile, D. A., Lemmens, J. S., Rumpf, H. J., Mößle, T., et al. (2014). An international consensus for assessing internet gaming disorder using the new DSM-5 approach. *Addiction*, *109*(9), 1399–1406. https://doi.org/10.1111/add.12457.

Poleshova, A. (2019). *Statistiken zur Internetnutzung weltweit*. Retrieved from 24/02/2021 https://de.statista.com/themen/42/internet/.

Rennert, L., Denis, C., Peer, K., Lynch, K. G., Gelernter, J., & Kranzler, H. R. (2014). DSM-5 gambling disorder: Prevalence and characteristics in a substance use disorder sample. *Experimental and Clinical Psychopharmacology*, *22*(1), 50–56. https://doi.org/10.1037/a0034518.

Rho, M. J., Lee, H., Lee, T. H., Cho, H., Jung, D. J., Kim, D. J., et al. (2017). Risk factors for Internet gaming disorder: Psychological factors and internet gaming characteristics. *International Journal of Environmental Research and Public Health*, *15*(1), 40. https://doi.org/10.3390/ijerph15010040.

Robinson, T. E., & Berridge, K. C. (2001). Incentive-sensitization and addiction. *Addiction*, *96*(1), 103–114. https://doi.org/10.1046/j.1360-0443.2001.9611038.x.

Robinson, T. E., & Berridge, K. C. (2008). The incentive sensitization theory of addiction: Some current issues. *Philosophical Transactions of the Royal Society, B: Biological Sciences*, *363*, 3137–3146. https://doi.org/10.1098/rstb.2008.0093.

Robinson, M. J., Fischer, A. M., Ahuja, A., Lesser, E. N., & Maniates, H. (2016). Roles of "wanting" and "liking" in motivating behavior: Gambling, food, and drug addictions. *Current Topics in Behavioral Neurosciences*, *27*, 105–136. https://doi.org/10.1007/7854_2015_387.

Rochat, L., Maurage, P., Heeren, A., & Billieux, J. (2019). Let's open the decision-making umbrella: A framework for conceptualizing and assessing features of impaired decision making in addiction. *Neuropsychology Review*, *29*(1), 27–51. https://doi.org/10.1007/s11065-018-9387-3.

Rumpf, H.-J., Browne, D., Brandt, D., & Rehbein, F. (2021). Addressing taxonomic challenges for Internet Use Disorders in light of changing technologies and diagnostic classifications. *Journal of Behavioral Addictions*, *9*(4), 942–944. https://doi.org/10.1556/2006.2020.00094.

Starcevic, V. (2013). Is internet addiction a useful concept? *Australian and New Zealand Journal of Psychiatry*, *47*(1), 16–19. https://doi.org/10.1177/0004867412461693.

Starcevic, V., Berle, D., Brakoulias, V., Sammut, P., Moses, K., Milicevic, D., et al. (2011). Functions of compulsions in obsessive-compulsive disorder. *Australian and New Zealand Journal of Medicine*, *45*(6), 449–457. https://doi.org/10.3109/00048674.2011.567243.

Starcevic, V., & Billieux, J. (2017). Does the construct of internet addiction reflect a single entity or a spectrum of disorders? *Clinical Neuropsychiatry*, *14*(1), 5–10.

Starcevic, V., King, D. L., Delfabbro, P. H., Schimmenti, A., Castro-Calvo, J., Giardina, A., et al. (2021). "Diagnostic inflation" will not resolve taxonomical problems in the study of addictive online behaviours. *Journal of Behavioral Addictions*, *9*(4), 915–919. https://doi.org/10.1556/2006.2020.00083.

Stark, R., Klucken, T., Potenza, M. N., Brand, M., & Strahler, J. (2018). A current understanding of the behavioral neuroscience of compulsive sexual behavior disorder and problematic pornography use. *Current Behavioral Neuroscience Reports*, *5*, 218–231. https://doi.org/10.1007/s40473-018-0162-9.

Statista. (2019a). *Daily time spent with the internet per capita worldwide from 2011 to 2021, by device*. Retrieved from 24/02/2021 https://www.statista.com/statistics/319732/daily-time-spent-online-device/.

Statista. (2019b). *Number of smartphone users worldwide from 2016 to 2021*. Retrieved from 24/02/2021 https://www.statista.com/statistics/330695/number-of-smartphone-users-worldwide/.

Statista. (2020). *Additional daily time spent on social media platforms by users in the United States due to coronavirus pandemic as of March 2020*. Retrieved from 24/02/2021 https://www.statista.com/statistics/1116148/more-time-spent-social-media-platforms-users-usa-coronavirus/.

Stenberg, G. (2016). Impulse control disorders—The continuum hypothesis. *Journal of Parkinson's Disease*, *6*(1), 67–75. https://doi.org/10.3233/jpd-150770.

Tebeka, S., Pignon, B., Amad, A., Le Strat, Y., Brichant-Petitjean, C., Thomas, P., et al. (2018). A study in the general population about sadness to disentangle the continuum from well-being to depressive disorders. *Journal of Affective Disorders*, *226*, 66–71. https://doi.org/10.1016/j.jad.2017.08.085.

Triberti, S., Milani, L., Villani, D., Grumi, S., Peracchia, S., Curcio, G., et al. (2018). What matters is when you play: Investigating the relationship between online video games addiction and time spent playing over specific day phases. *Addictive Behaviors Reports*, *8*, 185–188. https://doi.org/10.1016/j.abrep.2018.06.003.

Trotzke, P., Müller, A., Brand, M., Starcke, K., & Steins-Loeber, S. (2020). Buying despite negative consequences: Interaction of craving, implicit cognitive processes, and inhibitory control in the context of buying-shopping disorder. *Addictive Behaviors*, *110*, 106523. https://doi.org/10.1016/j.addbeh.2020.106523.

Tudor, K. (1996). *Mental health promotion: Paradigms and practice*. Routledge.

Volkow, N. D., Koob, G. F., & McLellan, A. T. (2016). Neurobiologic advances from the brain disease model of addiction. *The New England Journal of Medicine*, *374*(4), 363–371. https://doi.org/10.1056/NEJMra1511480.

Vollstädt-Klein, S., Wichert, S., Rabinstein, J., Bühler, M., Klein, O., Ende, G., et al. (2010). Initial, habitual and compulsive alcohol use is characterized by a shift of cue processing from ventral to dorsal striatum. *Addiction*, *105*(10), 1741–1749. https://doi.org/10.1111/j.1360-0443.2010.03022.x.

Watson, P. J., Sawrie, S. M., Greene, R. L., & Arredondo, R. (2002). Narcissism and depression: MMPI-2 evidence for the continuum hypothesis in clinical samples. *Journal of Personality Assessment*, *79*(1), 85–109. https://doi.org/10.1207/s15327752jpa7901_06.

Wegmann, E., & Brand, M. (2019). A narrative overview about psychosocial characteristics as risk factors of a problematic social networks use. *Current Addiction Reports*, *6*, 402–409. https://doi.org/10.1007/s40429-019-00286-8.

Wegmann, E., & Brand, M. (2020). Cognitive correlates in gaming disorder and social networks use disorder: A comparison. *Current Addiction Reports*, *7*, 356–364. https://doi.org/10.1007/s40429-020-00314-y.

Wegmann, E., Mueller, S. M., Ostendorf, S., & Brand, M. (2018). Highlighting Internet-communication disorder as further internet-use disorder when considering neuroimaging studies. *Current Behavioral Neuroscience Reports*, *5*(4), 295–301. https://doi.org/10.1007/s40473-018-0164-7.

Wegmann, E., Stodt, B., & Brand, M. (2018). Cue-induced craving in Internet-communication disorder using visual and auditory cues in a cue-reactivity paradigm. *Addiction Research & Theory*, *26*(4), 306–314. https://doi.org/10.1080/16066359.2017.1367385.

Wei, L., Zhang, S., Turel, O., Bechara, A., & He, Q. (2017). A tripartite neurocognitive model of Internet gaming disorder. *Frontiers in Psychiatry*, *8*, 285. https://doi.org/10.3389/fpsyt.2017.00285.

Wéry, A., & Billieux, J. (2017). Problematic cybersex: Conceptualization, assessment, and treatment. *Addictive Behaviors*, *64*, 238–246. https://doi.org/10.1016/j.addbeh.2015.11.007.

Wéry, A., Burnay, J., Karila, L., & Billieux, J. (2016). The short French internet addiction test adapted to online sexual activities: Validation and links with online sexual preferences and addiction symptoms. *The Journal of Sex Research*, *53*(6), 701–710. https://doi.org/10.1080/00224499.2015.1051213.

Wölfling, K., Duven, E., Wejbera, M., Beutel, M. E., & Müller, K. W. (2020). Discounting delayed monetary rewards and decision making in behavioral addictions—A comparison between patients with gambling disorder and internet gaming disorder. *Addictive Behaviors*, *108*, 106446. https://doi.org/10.1016/j.addbeh.2020.106446.

World Health Organization. (2019). *Website for ICD-11 Beta Draft (Mortality and Morbidity Statistics)*. https://icd.who.int/dev11/l-m/en.

Wu, Y.-L., Lin, S. H., & Lin, Y. H. (2021). Two-dimensional taxonomy of internet addiction and assessment of smartphone addiction with diagnostic criteria and mobile apps. *Journal of Behavioral Addictions*, *9*(4), 928–933. https://doi.org/10.1556/2006.2020.00074.

Young, K. S. (1996). Addictive use of the Internet: A case that breaks the stereotype. *Psychological Reports*, *79*, 899–902.

Young, K. S. (1998). Internet addiction: The emergence of a new clinical disorder. *Cyberpsychology & Behavior*, *3*, 237–244. https://doi.org/10.1089/cpb.1998.1.237.

Cybersex (including sex robots)

Johannes Fuss[a] and Beáta Bőthe[b]
[a]Institute of Forensic Psychiatry and Sex Research, University Duisburg-Essen, Essen, Germany, [b]Department of Psychology, Université de Montréal, Montréal, QC, Canada

Introduction

> *'Virtual Sex' has been celebrated as the ultimate freedom and/or as the ultimate form of oppression.*
>
> *Slavoj Žižek*

The present chapter addresses the many faces of cybersex. But what is cybersex? Most authors used the term "cybersex" to describe sexual activities using new technologies (Shaughnessy, Byers, & Thornton, 2011). While some have limited the use of the term to interactive sexual activities (Daneback, Cooper, & Månsson, 2005), others have also included solitary sexual activities (Cooper & Griffin-Shelley, 2002). Here, we use a broad definition of cybersex, describing many kinds of sexual activities using the internet or new technologies ranging from internet pornography to sex robots. This chapter therefore addresses the intersection of sex and technology. In the past 30 years, three different types of cybersex use have developed in succession. At first, people mainly consumed erotic and pornographic material online. Subsequently, social media emerged and the internet was increasingly used for interactive purposes thus opening new paths for sexual interaction and dating (e.g., with webcams, dating apps, or chat). Lastly, there was a shift toward simulations of sex with a high degree of immersion, including the use of sex robots and virtual reality. This last development is only at its beginning. However, even though the use of technology for sexual gratification has dramatically increased in the past 30 years, technical capabilities of cybersex fall short of what was expected in the past. This becomes clear when recapitulating the words of Rheingold (1990):

> *Twenty years from now, when portable teledidd!ers are ubiquitous, people will use them to have sexual experiences with other people, at a distance, in combinations and configurations undreamt of by precybernetic voluptuaries. Through the synthesis of virtual reality technology and telecommunication networks, you will be able to reach out and touch someone – or an entire population – in ways humans have never before experienced. (p. 319)*

Today, the complete immersion in a sex scene is still a utopian idea only found in science fiction. However, even though the technological advance was smaller than expected, it has led to a cultural shift in human sexualities worldwide. From internet pornography to sex toys controlled via cell phone to virtual realities and sex robots: Technologies are about to change the way humans experience and live their sexuality and has brought about new sexualities such as the digisexuals, whose primary sexual identity is defined by the use of technology (McArthur & Twist, 2017).

This transformation of sexualities has been accompanied by polarized discussions about the risks and benefits of cybersex. Opponents have emphasized the dangers to the mental health of users and society, while proponents have stressed the potential of cybersex to equally promote the sexual health of all people. These discussions are accompanied by emotional reactions that are often not informed by scientific knowledge. For example, in 2016, 17 US states declared pornography a public health crisis, despite relatively few epidemiological data on this issue (Nelson & Rothman, 2020). Others have launched a widely published Campaign Against Sex Robots although there are few studies of sex robots.

It seems to be common wisdom that a new technology's success dramatically increases once it can be used for sexual purposes (Koops, 2009). In the future, we can expect that many successful new technologies will also be used for sexual activities. Many of these will face the same criticism and hyperbole that other technologies have encountered in the past. Scientific investigation of the risks and benefits will always lag behind by a few years, so increasing the risk for polarized discussions. This chapter aims to shed light on how cybersex may be related to mental health, based on current scientific evidence. While many researchers have addressed phenomena such as Internet pornography, other (mostly newer) technologies have hardly been studied so far and will mainly be described here to provide a full picture of today's cybersexualities.

Epidemiology, definitions, and phenomenology

Internet pornography

With widespread internet access and the advent of digital technologies, pornography has become readily accessible, anonymous, and affordable for most people in industrialized countries (Cooper, 1998; Griffiths, 2012). Pornography may mean different things to different people, and it has been defined in various ways in previous scientific studies as well (Kohut et al., 2019). Currently, the following, quite comprehensive definition of pornography use is the most supported one by academics (Kohut et al., 2019):

> *Using pornography means to intentionally look at, read, or listen to (a) pictures, videos, or films that depict nude individuals or people having sex; or (b) written or audio material that describes nude individuals, or people having sex. Using pornography does not involve viewing or interacting with actual, live, nude individuals, or participating in interactive sexual experiences with other human beings in person or online. For example, participating in live sex chat or a camshow, and getting a 'lapdance' in a strip club are not considered pornography use (p. 737).*

Showing the worldwide popularity of pornography, 70%–94% of adults (84%–94% of men, 54%–87% of women) have ever used pornography in their lifetime, based on recent nationally representative studies from Australia, the United States, Norway, and Poland (Grubbs, Kraus, & Perry, 2019; Herbenick et al., 2020; Lewczuk, Glica, Nowakowska, Gola, & Grubbs, 2020; Rissel et al., 2017; Træen, Spitznogle, & Beverfjord, 2004). The occurrence of pornography use in romantic relationships appears similar, 71%–92% of coupled men, and 34%–83% of coupled women reported pornography use (Vaillancourt-Morel, Rosen, Willoughby, Leonhardt, & Bergeron, 2020; Willoughby, Carroll, Busby, & Brown, 2016). While most people in industrialized countries have viewed pornography at some point in their lives, only a smaller number experience problematic pornography use (Bőthe, Tóth-Király, et al., 2018; Grubbs, Kraus, et al., 2019; Rissel et al., 2017; Wéry et al., 2016). Pornography use may become problematic for approximately 3%–4% of men and 1% of women (Grubbs, Kraus, et al., 2019; Lewczuk et al., 2020; Rissel et al., 2017), resulting in adverse consequences, such as romantic relationship problems or job loss (Bergner & Bridges, 2002; Bostwick & Bucci, 2008; Ford, Durtschi, & Franklin, 2012), and treatment-seeking (Gola, Lewczuk, & Skorko, 2016; Lewczuk, Szmyd, Skorko, & Gola, 2017). But what is *"problematic pornography use"* exactly?

Despite the inclusion of Compulsive Sexual Behavior Disorder (CSBD) in the 11th version of *International Statistical Classification of Diseases and Related Health Problems* (ICD-11) (World Health Organization, 2019), there is no specific diagnosis for problematic pornography use. Given that problematic pornography use is often considered as a subcategory of CSBD (Fernandez & Griffiths, 2019; Kafka, 2010), it may be described as repetitive, persistent patterns of intense and uncontrollable pornography use despite significant distress and functional impairment in diverse life domains (Kraus et al., 2018). Nevertheless, it is important to note that despite the growing number of scientific studies in the field of CSBD research (Bőthe, Bartók, et al., 2018; Grubbs et al., 2020; Kowalewska et al., 2018; Kraus, Voon, & Potenza, 2016b; Reid et al., 2012), it cannot be conclusively determined whether CSBD—and thus, problematic pornography use—should be considered as an impulsivity-related, compulsivity-related, or addictive disorder (Fuss, Briken, Stein, & Lochner, 2019; Grubbs et al., 2020; Kraus, Voon, & Potenza, 2016a; Potenza, Gola, Voon, Kor, & Kraus, 2017; Prause, Janssen, Georgiadis, Finn, & Pfaus, 2017).

Concerning the antecedents of problematic pornography use, younger single men may have a higher chance of developing and maintaining problematic pornography use than others (Egan & Parmar, 2013; Grubbs, Kraus, et al., 2019; Lewczuk et al., 2017; Rissel et al., 2017). Regarding personality traits, higher problematic pornography use has been associated with higher neuroticism and lower agreeableness and conscientiousness, but the associations were weak. Openness and extraversion were not related to problematic pornography use (Egan & Parmar, 2013; Grubbs, Volk, Exline, & Pargament, 2015). Given their transdiagnostic features and clinical relevance, impulsivity and compulsivity were also examined in relation to problematic pornography use in a large community sample with more than 13,000 people (Bőthe, Tóth-Király, et al., 2019). Higher levels of impulsivity and compulsivity were associated with higher levels of problematic pornography use among both men and women, but the associations were weak. These results support the view that no single personality trait leads to problematic behavior (Griffiths, 2017; Kerr, 1996). Moreover, using pornography for sexual pleasure, boredom avoidance, and stress reduction were related to higher pornography use frequency, while motivations linked to problematic pornography use differed. Stress reduction was the strongest predictor of problematic pornography use, followed by emotional avoidance, boredom avoidance, fantasy, and sexual pleasure, suggesting that pornography use motivations may provide more essential information about the development of problematic or nonproblematic pornography use than single personality traits (Bőthe, Tóth-Király, Bella, et al., 2021; Reid, Li, Gilliland, Stein, & Fong, 2011; Wéry & Billieux, 2016).

When considering the potential outcomes of pornography use, the most frequently asked question is how pornography use may affect romantic relationships and sexuality. The majority of studies in this field have focused on the associations between pornography use frequency and sexual satisfaction (Vaillancourt-Morel, Daspe, Charbonneau-Lefebvre, Bosisio, & Bergeron, 2019). Findings of systematic reviews, metaanalyses (Dwulit & Rzymski, 2019; Grubbs, Wright, Braden, Wilt, & Kraus, 2019; Vaillancourt-Morel et al., 2019; Wright, Tokunaga, Kraus, & Klann, 2017), and dyadic studies (Brown et al., 2017; Willoughby & Leonhardt, 2020; Yucel & Gassanov, 2010) indicate that men's pornography use frequency is associated with lower sexual satisfaction. Mixed results have been reported among women, but in general, women's pornography use frequency is unrelated to their sexual satisfaction (Bridges & Morokoff, 2011; Muusses, Kerkhof, & Finkenauer, 2015; Willoughby & Leonhardt, 2020; Yucel & Gassanov, 2010). Concerning sexual functioning, multiple studies have reported no significant associations between pornography use frequency and sexual functioning in men (Dwulit & Rzymski, 2019; Grubbs & Gola, 2019; Landripet & Štulhofer, 2015; Prause & Pfaus, 2015), while in women, pornography use frequency has been associated with better sexual functioning (Blais-Lecours, Vaillancourt-Morel, Sabourin, & Godbout, 2016; Bőthe, Tóth-Király, Griffiths, et al., 2021). Less is known about the associations between problematic pornography use and sexual outcomes. However, men and women with problematic pornography use have reported lower sexual and relationship satisfaction (Bőthe, Tóth-Király, Demetrovics, & Orosz, 2017), and higher levels of sexual functioning problems (Bőthe, Tóth-Király, Griffiths, et al., 2021; Grubbs & Gola, 2019; Wéry & Billieux, 2016). Thus, existing results suggest that pornography use frequency in itself may be associated with little or no adverse sexual outcomes (Kohut, Fisher, & Campbell, 2017), while problematic pornography use has been consistently related to worse sexual outcomes.

Nevertheless, it is important to note that some people using pornography may feel that their partner is more critical about their physical appearance, and feel jealous of or try competing with the men and women in the videos (Grov, Gillespie, Royce, & Lever, 2011; Kohut et al., 2017). Also, some forms of pornography may reinforce stereotypes about sex and gender, promote physical or verbal aggression, or depict unsafe sexual activities (Bridges, Wosnitzer, Scharrer, Sun, & Liberman, 2010; Fritz & Paul, 2017; Klaassen & Peter, 2015; Vannier, Currie, & O'Sullivan, 2014). In sum, the context of pornography use may play a crucial role in the potential positive or negative outcomes of pornography use (Bőthe, Vaillancourt-Morel, & Bergeron, 2021; Campbell & Kohut, 2017).

Adolescents' pornography use

The ease of access to pornography has made its use not only common among adults but among adolescents as well (Alexandraki, Stavropoulos, Anderson, Latifi, & Gomez, 2018; Bőthe, Vaillancourt-Morel, Bergeron, & Demetrovics, 2019; Owens, Behun, Manning, & Reid, 2012; Peter & Valkenburg, 2016; Price, Patterson, Regnerus, & Walley, 2016). This is unsurprising, as adolescents are present in the online population, with relatively common exposure to content (Jones & Fox, 2009). Still, prevalence rates of adolescents' pornography use vary widely from one study to another (Peter & Valkenburg, 2016). Based on data from nationally representative and large-scale adolescent studies (9–18-year-olds) from the United States, Canada, and Europe, 23%–63% of adolescents reported having already viewed pornography (Bőthe, Vaillancourt-Morel, et al., 2020; Lobe, Livingstone, Ólafsson, & Vodeb, 2011; Wolak, Mitchell, & Finkelhor, 2007). Of those adolescents who reported pornography use in their lifetime, more than 50% reported using it once a week or more often in the past 3 months (Bőthe, Vaillancourt-Morel, et al., 2020). It is also important to note that exposure to pornography may appear both intentionally (i.e., deliberate search for pornographic materials) and/or unwantedly (e.g., pornographic materials show up in pop-up advertisements). Unwanted pornography exposure seems to be more prevalent among adolescents than wanted exposure, 66%–71% of adolescents reported unwanted exposure to pornography, whereas 29%–34% reported intentional pornography use (Luder et al., 2011; Wolak et al., 2007).

Adolescents tend to have their first experience with pornography in early adolescence, with approximately 30% have their first experience before the age of 11 (Peter & Valkenburg, 2016; Sinković, Štulhofer, & Božić, 2013), and this early exposure to pornography has been increasing. Based on objective website traffic data, computer-based pornography use increased by 10% among preadolescents (aged between 7 and 12) between 2004 and 2016 in Poland (Lewczuk, Wojcik, & Gola, 2019). This ratio is presumably higher, as pornography use via mobile devices (e.g., smartphones) was not assessed and is particularly popular among the visitors of one of the most popular pornography sites (84% of the visitors of this site viewed pornography on their mobile devices in the past year) (Pornhub.com, 2019).

Despite the high percentage of adolescents' pornography use, only a handful of studies have examined problematic pornography use in adolescents. A total of 5%–14% of adolescents (mostly boys) reported excessive, compulsive, or problematic use of pornography (Efrati & Gola, 2018; Bőthe, Vaillancourt-Morel, Dion, Štulhofer, & Bergeron, 2021; Pizzol, Bertoldo, & Foresta, 2016; Štulhofer, Rousseau, & Shekarchi, 2020; Svedin, Åkerman, & Priebe, 2011). However, only 5% of adolescent boys reported problematic pornography use consistently over a 5-month period, suggesting a high "fluidity" in adolescents self-perceived problematic pornography use (Štulhofer et al., 2020).

These experiences with pornography may have an impact on adolescents' development through potential changes in sexual attitudes, beliefs, and behaviors, but the limitations of the conducted studies (e.g., cross-sectional, self-report study designs) should be kept in mind when interpreting the findings (Alexandraki et al., 2018; Owens et al., 2012; Peter & Valkenburg, 2016). For example, more frequent pornography use among adolescents was reported to be related to less strict sexual attitudes and more experience with casual sexual intercourse, but not to greater experience with different sexual practices or risky sexual behaviors (Alexandraki et al., 2018; Owens et al., 2012; Peter & Valkenburg, 2016). Also, some studies suggest that pornography use may have long-term effects on adult sexuality for some, but not for others (Štulhofer, Buško, & Landripet, 2010). Nevertheless, so far, conclusions that can be drawn from prior studies about the potential effects of pornography use on adolescents are limited, and further longitudinal studies are strongly needed for firmer conclusions (Grubbs & Kraus, 2021).

Cyber-grooming and cybersexual solicitation of minors

The internet also increases the risk of minors being approached by adults for (cyber) sexual purposes (Berson, 2003; Dombrowski, Gischlar, & Durst, 2007). This ranges from grooming behaviors [such as establishing trust and compliance with a minor but ultimately aiming for (cyber)sexual abuse] to more direct forms of sexual solicitation (such as encouraging minors to talk about or do something sexual, or to share personal sexual information or pictures). Roughly, 10% of minors report experiencing unwanted online sexual solicitation (Madigan et al., 2018; Sklenarova, Schulz, Schuhmann, Osterheider, & Neutze, 2018). Fortunately, prevalence rates have decreased over the past 30 years (Madigan et al., 2018) but some populations are still at high risk of unwanted cybersexual solicitation (Reed et al., 2019).

In a survey of adult internet users from Germany, Finland, and Sweden (Schulz, Bergen, Schuhmann, Hoyer, & Santtila, 2016), 4.5% reported that they had at least once solicited an adolescent online, while 1% indicated that they had solicited a child. Among those who reported interacting sexually with strangers online, 5.1% reported contacts with more than 20 minors in the past year and 8.2% reported a sexual outcome with a minor (e.g., sending or receiving sexual images, cybersex or sexual acts offline). What is remarkable is the high proportion of women: 30.6% of solicitations to adolescents and 17.2% of solicitations to children happened through women. Such behaviors are associated with mental health issues among perpetrators and victims. People who sexually solicit minors online show higher levels of social anxiety, loneliness, and problematic Internet use (Schulz, Bergen, Schuhmann, & Hoyer, 2017), while victims are more likely to exhibit a posttraumatic stress disorder, anxiety, depression, and developmental disruption (Dombrowski, LeMasney, Ahia, & Dickson, 2004; Wells & Mitchell, 2007). However, most children and adolescents seem to cope well with most undesirable sexual solicitations online by blocking or deleting the perpetrator (see, e.g., Livingstone, Haddon, Görzig, & Ólafsson, 2011; Mitchell, Finkelhor, & Wolak, 2001; Wolak, Mitchell, & Finkelhor, 2006). Low socioeconomic status, being a girl and being younger is associated with a higher risk of being significantly bothered by unwanted sexual solicitations (Livingstone et al., 2011).

Dating applications

Showing the popularity of online dating, 35% of people who married between 2005 and 2012 met on an online venue, based on the findings of a US nationally representative study with more than 19,000 people (Cacioppo, Cacioppo, Gonzaga, Ogburn, & Vanderweele, 2013). In 2018, there were almost 8000 different dating sites world-wide, with a business worth nearly 2 billion US dollars per year (Matthews, 2018). Thus, it is clear that since the widespread availability of smartphones, a new era of online dating has begun, presumably due to the advantages of smartphones, such as availability, portability, locatability, and multimediality (Schrok, 2015). Despite the popularity of online dating and dating applications, research examining the potential mental health issues related to online dating or problematic use of online dating is limited by the examination of cross-sectional, convenience samples (Bonilla-Zorita, Griffiths, & Kuss, 2020).

Young adult men are reported to be the most active users of online dating platforms, while people with higher sensation-seeking, sociability, sexual permissiveness, social anxiety, anxious attachment style, and lower conscientiousness also tend to use online dating applications and sites more frequently (Bonilla-Zorita et al., 2020). Moreover, people with higher levels of CSBD may be more likely to engage in online dating (Zlot, Goldstein, Cohen, & Weinstein, 2018). Despite the popularity and common use of these platforms, users generally consider online dating more dangerous than tradi-tional dating. This notion is supported by empirical results as some studies found that dating application users may engage in more condomless sex, and users may feel ex-posed to risks of deceit and financial exploitation and may experience fear of physical harassment and self-objectification (Bonilla-Zorita et al., 2020).

Only one study has examined problematic online dating and its potential predictors with a focus on Tinder, one of the most popular online dating applications (Orosz et al., 2018). The findings of this three-study investigation suggest that using Tinder to enhance one's self-esteem was the strongest predictor of problematic use compared to other motivations, such as using Tinder to find casual sex partners, find love, or avoid boredom. Of importance, personality traits (i.e., agreeableness, conscientious-ness, neuroticism, openness, and extraversion), self-esteem, and basic psychological needs satisfaction and frustration were also examined in relation to problematic Tinder use. However, no direct association was identified between these characteristics and problematic Tinder use when motivations were included in the model.

Webcams

Webcam use for cybersexual activities has become a common behavior among internet-using populations and seems to be more prevalent among men compared to women (Albright, 2008; Shaughnessy, Byers, & Walsh, 2011). Nevertheless, it was hypothesized that webcam cybersex could become particularly prevalent among women in the future (Ferree, 2003) because of their preference for activities that allow interaction compared to solitary sexual activities. Posing or performing sexual acts in front of webcams is also prevalent among adolescents with roughly 10% reporting posing naked and 5% reporting masturbation in front of a webcam in various surveys from Northern Europe (Koops, Dekker, & Briken, 2018).

A qualitative study found various reasons for cybersexual use of webcams (Couch & Liamputtong, 2008). Interestingly, some emphasize that webcams are also useful for relationship formation as they are helpful to assess if others are trustworthy before beginning a cybersexual relationship or an off-line affair. In contrast, in existing long-distance relationships, webcams for cybersex seem to play a minor role (Neustaedter & Greenberg, 2012). In contrast, they are increasingly used for sex work as it can be safer than offline sex work (Döring, 2008). However, there are also reports of pimps using webcams to monitor and control offline sex workers from remote locations (Hughes, 2004), involuntary recording of cybersex via webcams, hacking of personal information, and verbal harassment online (Jones, 2016). The use of anonymous ways to pay for cybersex (e.g., with Bitcoins) also opens the way to criminal behaviors such as online auctions of women and children, live videos of sexual torture and rape, or other forms of extremely violent and humiliating cybersexual acts (Koops et al., 2018). Webcams are used to circumvent legal restrictions in some countries. For example, Hughes documented a case of smuggling and trafficking Japanese women into Honolulu (United States) to perform cybersex in front of webcams for a Japanese audience because of stricter laws on pornography in Japan compared to the United States (Hughes, 2002). Another example is so-called "webcam child sex tourism," which is the sexual exploitation of children in other countries using webcams. Few data offer a glimpse of the relevance of such phenomena as they mainly become public through law enforcement agencies (Açar, 2017). The international children's rights humanitarian organization Terre des Hommes addressed the problem of "webcam child sex tourism" by developing a 3D model of a 10-year old girl called "Sweetie" from the Philippines that could be approached via chat rooms and dating sites. Over 10 weeks, more than 20,000 people tried to approach Sweetie online and more than 1000 people from 71 countries offered money for sexual acts (Açar, 2017). Currently, in a follow-up project called Sweetie 2.0 a chatbot is developed to map, measure, and finally combat child sexual exploitation online (Henseler & de Wolf, 2019). These reports illustrate that the use of webcams for cybersex can be problematic in some circumstances, while it may promote sexual health in others.

Sex robots

Although the development of humanoid sex robots is currently being promoted by only a few companies in the United States and the interactive features using artificial intelligence are still limited, the commercial marketing of such robots has already begun. First in Barcelona, and later also in Turin, and Moscow (The Sun, 2018), the company LumiDolls opened the first brothels in which customers can only rent highly realistic silicone dolls with body heat and voice function for sexual acts. The opening of these houses was accompanied by controversy. In Barcelona, LumiDolls had to move to the outskirts due to protests by sex workers, in Turin LumiDolls was closed by the police after 14 days (New York Post, 2018), in Houston, Texas, the city administration prevented the opening of a sex doll brothel by the Canadian company KinkySDollS (CNBC, 2018) who had already opened a branch in Toronto. The central arguments of the controversy about the use of highly realistic sex dolls and robots can be roughly assigned to two camps. On the one hand, opponents warn of the consequences of using sex robots for real-life sex. They stress that sex robots contribute to objectification (especially of women) and that human-robot interactions may replace or impair real-life interpersonal contact. Often extreme examples are cited in this context, such as the case of a Chinese man, who married a robot instead of a human (The Guardian, 2017). The leitmotif that robot sex leads to "cold and cruel" sex with robots (Sharkey, van Wynsberghe, Robbins, & Hancock, 2017) can also be found in the latest film receptions on the subject, such as the HBO series *Westworld* and the film *Ex Machina*. The opponents of robot sex, such as the British ethicist Kathleen Richardson, see above all the danger that robot sex will increase the likelihood that people objectify others in real life. The same attitude that would enable sex with robots would have led to the spread of slavery and prostitution (Richardson, 2015). Richardson and others thus oppose sex robots and founded the Campaign Against Sex Robots.

Proponents emphasize that robots could be tailored to human desires and used in sexual practices for which it is difficult to find human partners (McArthur & Twist, 2017). They would therefore contribute to greater sexual satisfaction and new sexual experiences and be particularly helpful for sexual minorities. Stigmatized groups of people in certain regions (such as homosexual people in countries where homosexuality is prohibited) would therefore benefit from sex robots (McArthur & Twist, 2017). The Canadian sexologist James Cantor, for example, responds to the argument of objectification by pointing out that sex robots are just a "piece of latex" and not humans (Cantor, 2018). McArthur and Twist (2017) cite as another example the possibility of satisfying zoophile desires by animal robots in the future to enable those affected to have sexual experiences that are not in conflict with the law. The topic of pedophilia and child-like sex robots is left out of the article. However, on June 13, 2018, the US House of Representatives passed a law prohibiting child-like sex robots, which would be inextricably linked to the objectification and sexual abuse of children. Currently, there is no scientific evidence for this assumption and others call for the therapeutic use of sex robots for people with pedophilia comparing child-like sex robots to the use of methadone to treat people with drug addiction (Danaher & McArthur, 2017). The sexologist Michael Seto also weighed in on the subject that for some people with pedophilia "access to artificial child pornography or to child sex dolls could be a safer outlet for their sexual urges, reducing the likelihood that they would seek out child pornography or sex with real children. For others, having these substitutes might only aggravate their sense of frustration." (The Atlantic, 2016).

Surveys among the general population also show how divided people's attitudes toward robot sex are. In a representative online panel survey conducted by the Huffington Post and YouGov, 42% of respondents indicated that people in monogamous relationships who sexually interact with a robot cheated, while only 31% said they did not (Huffington Post, 2013). At least 9% of the respondents also said that they would have sex with robots if they were available. Another survey of Americans showed that two-thirds of men generally advocated robot sex, while two-thirds of women opposed it (Scheutz et al., 2016). Thus, although many people have apparently already formed an opinion about the consequences of robot sex, the technical options available so far are limited and sex robots have so far only been used by a small group of people. Empirical data on the long-term consequences of robot sex are missing. It is known, however, that humans as well as other primates can develop an attachment to inanimate objects (Harlow, 1961) and recent research demonstrates that humans form an attachment to others online (Coulson, Barnett, Ferguson, & Gould, 2012; Levine & Stekel, 2016), virtual characters that were created by themselves (Lewis, Weber, & Bowman, 2008), and social robots (Sharkey, 2008; Tanaka, Cicourel, & Movellan, 2007). The ethical and societal implications of such bonds will be an ongoing matter of debate (Peeters & Haselager, 2019) and it is still unclear when empirical data on human-robot sex will be available.

Virtual reality

Virtual reality (VR) pornography reached the mass market in 2016. With the release of several VR goggles within a few months and the opening of a free VR channel at the world's largest provider of streaming pornography—Pornhub—the use of VR pornography has increased significantly. For example, on Christmas Day 2016, the number of daily users of VR pornography on the Pornhub website jumped from around 400,000 to 900,000 (Wired, 2018). The market has grown steadily since then. According to a forecast by investment bank Piper Jaffray, VR pornography revenues will be $ 1 billion in 2025 (Piper Jaffrey, 2015). VR pornography is characterized by a high level of immersion. Some claim that users are experiencing that they are part of the sex scene that they are watching and that they are actually interacting with their sexual partners and would report the feeling of "human intimacy" (Wired, 2018). Many commentators on popular online media have expressed high hopes in VR pornography due to these experiences. They see a potential in VR pornography of people using this to have meaningful experiences that would become part of their own lives and thus satisfy their sexual desires in the long term. Today, VR pornography differs from Rheingold's initial visionary quote in three aspects: (i) the immersion is limited to seeing and hearing (Hall, 2016); (ii) interactions between viewer and porn actors/other viewers are not possible yet so that viewers merely watch a three-dimensional (3D) movie; and (iii) the user's radius of action is restricted to movements of the head: Viewers thus are not able to walk within the 3D scene. Novel VR sex games offer more ways to interact, but their usage is only emerging (Orel, 2020).

Against the optimistic views about the future of VR pornography represented by popular media, a pessimistic vision about the consequences of virtual sex has been discussed since the 1990s. For example, the philosopher Slavoj Žižek stressed the dangers of virtual sexualities (Žižek, 1996) and argued that if technological developments make the desired object more and more easily accessible through simulation, sexual desire will cease. If all that is desired becomes immediately available, it would be deprived of its substance and at the same time of its perceived value. Therefore, the possibility of virtual sexualities would in the long run transform human sexualities beyond recognition. Žižek further predicts that virtual sexualities would intensify a "pathological narcissism"—a sexual relationship to oneself—and that every other desiring subject and one's own body would eventually become a burden because it would only disturb the dwelling in perfect virtual worlds. The subject would be freed from the "flaw" of his physical existence in virtual sexualities (Žižek, 1996). This pessimistic view is also present in the scientific community with a recent review concluding that "we might see a steady rise in escaping our dominant reality and seeking alternative ways to fulfil our desires."

For those who fear negative consequences, the rise of virtual sexualities may seem particularly alarming against the background of empirical findings in recent years, which on the one hand suggest a slight decrease in partnered sexuality and on the other hand an increase in solo sexual acts since the start of the spread of internet pornography (Beutel et al., 2018; Helsinki Times, 2016; Mercer et al., 2013; Youth Risk Behavior Survey, 2015). A solid empirical relation between both trends is however lacking.

Diagnostic criteria

In many cases, cybersex use is not problematic and not associated with personal distress or functional impairment (Wéry & Billieux, 2017). Only in those cases where people lose control over their cybersexual behavior and experience-related distress and negative consequences, a compulsive sexual behavior disorder (CSBD) may be diagnosed. This is conceptualized as an impulse control disorder in ICD-11. CSBD is not specific to cybersexual behavior but may be also expressed through a variety of other sexual behaviors, such as masturbation, partnered sex, telephone sex, and other forms of repetitive sexual behavior. According to the guidelines, CSBD is characterized by.

A persistent pattern of failure to control intense, repetitive sexual impulses or urges, resulting in repetitive sexual behavior over an extended period (e.g., 6 months or more) that causes marked distress or impairment in personal, family, social, educational, occupational or other important areas of functioning.

The pattern is manifested in one or more of the following:

(a) *engaging in repetitive sexual activities has become a central focus of the person's life to the point of neglecting health and personal care or other interests, activities, and responsibilities;*
(b) *the person has made numerous unsuccessful efforts to control or significantly reduce repetitive sexual behavior;*
(c) *the person continues to engage in repetitive sexual behavior despite adverse consequences (e.g., repeated relationship disruption, occupational consequences, negative impact on health); or*
(d) *the person continues to engage in repetitive sexual behavior even when he/she derives little or no satisfaction from it.*

Even though the ICD-11 conceptualizes CSBD as an impulse control disorder, there is no consensus regarding the conceptualization and others understand it as a behavioral addiction (comparable to other behavioral addictions such as pathological gambling) (Fuss, Lemay, et al., 2019). The absence of diagnostic criteria in the past led to multiple definitions that were used simultaneously in research. The introduction of the ICD-11 guidelines will hopefully harmonize research efforts to understand the phenomenology, neurobiological underpinnings as well as effective treatments.

Importantly, to diagnose CSBD, the diagnostic guidelines require the exclusion of other disorders that may be responsible for the excessive use of cybersex. Among others, manic or hypomanic episodes in bipolar disorder may be associated with an increased interest in and impaired control of sexual behaviors. Moreover, certain medications (e.g., dopaminergic agonists to treat Parkinson's disease or restless legs syndrome) and substances (such as methamphetamine) and conditions (e.g., dementia syndrome) have an effect on the central nervous system in a way that may lead to excessive sexual behavior. CSBD should not be diagnosed if the impaired control over sexual impulses, urges, or behaviors is entirely attributable to the direct effects of drugs, medications, or certain disorders on the central nervous system. Lastly, distress completely related to moral judgments and disapproval of sexual impulses, urges, or behaviors is not sufficient to meet the CSBD diagnosis.

Differential diagnoses

Assessment of comorbid disorders

Approximately 50% of individuals with compulsive sexual behaviors report some types of psychiatric disorders besides CSBD (Kraus et al., 2016b), with mood disorders (31%–72%), anxiety disorders (33%–47%), attention deficit hyperactivity disorder (17%–67%), and substance use disorder (14%–41%) being the most commonly reported ones (Blankenship & Laaser, 2004; Kafka & Hennen, 2002; Raymond, Coleman, & Miner, 2003; Reid, 2007; Reid, Carpenter, Gilliland, & Karim, 2011; Reid, Davtian, Lenartowicz, Torrevillas, & Fong, 2013; Scanavino et al., 2013; Wéry et al., 2016), while only 10% of self-diagnosed individuals with CSBD report any type of personality disorder (Raymond et al., 2003). Similarly, mood disorders (71%), substance use disorders (41%), and anxiety disorders (40%) were reported to be the most prevalent among problematic pornography users; while for example, attention deficit hyperactivity disorder was reported only by 3% of the participants in a sample of treatment-seeking men (Bőthe, Koós, Tóth-Király, Orosz, & Demetrovics, 2019; Grubbs et al., 2015; Kraus, Potenza, Martino, & Grant, 2015; Willoughby, Busby, & Young-Petersen, 2019; Willoughby, Carroll, Nelson, & Padilla-Walker, 2014). Thus, thorough clinical assessments are needed to identify whether the presenting symptoms of cybersexual activities are the primary problem or whether they appeared as a secondary problem.

Does quantity equal problematic use?

The quantity of use (e.g., frequency of use or engagement in a given online sexual activity) has been considered as an important indicator of problematic use. However, recent findings suggest that, for example, pornography use frequency in itself may not be a reliable indicator of problematic pornography use (Bőthe, Lonza, Štulhofer, & Demetrovics, 2020; Bőthe, Tóth-Király, Potenza, Orosz, & Demetrovics, 2020; Grubbs, Perry, Wilt, & Reid, 2019). Self-reported problematic pornography use may be present with a relatively low frequency of pornography use, as a result of moral incongruence toward pornography use (Grubbs, Perry, et al., 2019; Kraus & Sweeney, 2019), or high-frequency pornography use may be present without problematic use, as a result of intense sexual desire (Bőthe, Tóth-Király, Potenza, et al., 2020; Štulhofer, Bergeron, & Jurin, 2016; Štulhofer, Jurin, & Briken, 2016). Thus, in accordance with prior theoretical models (Billieux, Flayelle, Rumpf, & Stein, 2019; Grubbs, Perry, et al., 2019) and empirical work (Bőthe, Lonza, et al., 2020), although the quantity or frequency of use can provide valuable information on the intensity of engagement in a given activity, it cannot by itself be used to determine whether a given individual's behavior should be considered problematic or not or whether it could lead to negative consequences or not. Thus, it is important to distinguish between the frequency of use and problematic use when examining associations with potential antecedents and outcomes in research and clinical work as well.

Problematic pornography use due to dysregulation and/or moral incongruence

Two pathways of *perceived* problematic pornography use may be present in treatment-seeking individuals, one stemming from behavioral dysregulation (e.g., compulsive use), another deriving from moral incongruence concerning pornography use (e.g., engaging in pornography use despite that it violates one's values), based on the moral incongruence model of problematic pornography use (Grubbs, Perry, et al., 2019). Both pathways include significant distress that may be a trigger for treatment-seeking; however, only people with control problems (dysregulation pathway) meet the diagnostic criteria for CSBD, given that *"distress that is entirely related to moral judgments and disapproval about sexual impulses, urges, or behaviors is not sufficient"* to diagnose someone with CSBD. Nonetheless, people from both pathways seek treatment for their pornography use, and all of them should be diagnosed and treated appropriately (Chen, Jiang, Luo, Kraus, & Bőthe, 2021).

A precise and accurate differential diagnosis is needed to determine whether the perceived problematic pornography use stems from control problems, moral incongruence toward pornography use, or from both. This is especially important because different interventions or therapeutic approaches may be effective, depending on whether control problems, moral incongruence or both are present (Kraus & Sweeney, 2019). To understand the reasons why a given individual seeks treatment for problematic pornography use, it is necessary to examine in detail the nature of problematic pornography use. For this reason, (i) distress and/or impaired functioning due to pornography; (ii) moral incongruence in relation to pornography use; and (iii) control over use should be assessed. For a more detailed guide, see the recommendations of Kraus and Sweeney (2019).

Assessment and evaluation

The assessment of compulsive sexual behaviors and problematic cybersexual activities is diverse, and several scales have been adapted and developed to assess compulsive sexual behaviors in general or a specific behavior, such as problematic pornography use (Fernandez & Griffiths, 2019; Marshall & Briken, 2010; Montgomery-Graham, 2017; Stewart & Fedoroff, 2014; Wéry & Billieux, 2017). To date, the only scale that can assess CSBD based on the ICD-11 diagnostic guidelines is the Compulsive Sexual Behavior Disorder Scale (CSBD-19) (Bőthe, Potenza, et al., 2020). The scale was developed with more than 9000 participants from the United States, Germany, and Hungary. The CSBD-19 (see Box 15.1) assesses CSBD symptoms via five factors (control, salience, relapse, dissatisfaction, and negative consequences), demonstrated strong psychometric properties (i.e., factor structure, reliability, measurement invariance, and associations with theoretically relevant constructs), and a cutoff score was determined that can identify individuals at high risk of CSBD. These initial findings suggest that the CSBD-19 is a short, reliable, and valid measure of CSBD, and can distinguish between individuals at elevated and lower risk of CSBD. However, further research is in process to test the CSBD-19 with clinical samples.

Regarding specific problematic cybersexual activities, most scales have been developed to assess problematic pornography use. So far, more than 20 scales have been developed or adapted to evaluate problematic pornography use (Fernandez & Griffiths, 2019). Considering the strengths and limitations of these scales, the Problematic Pornography Consumption Scale (PPCS-18) (Bőthe, Tóth-Király, et al., 2018; Chen et al., 2021), its short version the PPCS-6 (Bőthe, Tóth-Király, Demetrovics, & Orosz, 2021) (see Box 15.2), and its short, adolescent version (PPCS-6-A; (Bőthe, Vaillancourt-Morel, Dion, et al., 2021)) have demonstrated the strongest psychometric properties, and they were recommended for use in both research and clinical settings, given their solid theoretical background, strong psychometric properties, and the brevity and clarity of the items (Bőthe, Tóth-Király, Demetrovics, et al., 2021; Fernandez & Griffiths, 2019). The PPCS-18, PPCS-6, and PPCS-6-A assesses six dimensions of problematic pornography use: salience, tolerance, mood modification, relapse, withdrawal, and conflict (Griffiths, 2005).

Importantly, when the prevalence of problematic behavior is low (which is the case for CSBD and problematic cybersexual activities), the most appropriate use of screening measures is to *rule out* a condition, not to establish a diagnosis to avoid misdiagnosis and overpathologization (Billieux, Schimmenti, Khazaal, Maurage, & Heeren, 2015; Maraz, Király, & Demetrovics, 2015; Streiner, 2003). Thus, a two-step evaluation process may be ideal. Reliable and valid self-report scales may be used as the first step of a diagnostic procedure, accompanied by several questions regarding different sexual behaviors (e.g., frequency of pornography use, frequency of casual sexual relationships, sexual desire). If the self-report scales and questions suggest that problematic cybersexual activities may be present in the individual's life, thorough clinical interviews should be conducted. Only clinical interviews can determine whether the symptoms in fact indicate problematic cybersexual activities or whether other underlying problems cause the symptoms, such as comorbid psychiatric disorders (as described in the "Differential diagnoses" section) or moral incongruence regarding pornography use (Grubbs, Perry, et al., 2019; Kraus & Sweeney, 2019). Using this multimethod approach, practitioners are able to obtain a more accurate and comprehensive view of the individual's condition.

Box 15.1 The Compulsive Sexual Behavior Disorder Scale (CSBD-19) and scoring information—English Version.

Below are a number of statements that describe various thoughts, feelings, and behaviors about sex. Please, think back to the **past 6 months** and indicate on the following four-point scale to what extent the statements apply to you. There are no right or wrong answers. *For the purpose of this questionnaire, sex is defined as any activity or behavior that stimulates or arouses a person with the intent to produce an orgasm or sexual pleasure (e.g., self-masturbation or solosex, using pornography, intercourse with a partner, oral sex, anal sex, etc.). Sexual behaviors may or may not involve a partner.*

1—totally disagree 2—somewhat disagree 3—somewhat agree 4—totally agree

	1	2	3	4
1. Even though my sexual behavior was irresponsible or reckless, I found it difficult to stop.	O	O	O	O
2. Sex has been the most important thing in my life.	O	O	O	O
3. I was able to resist my sexual urges for only a little while before I surrendered to them.	O	O	O	O
4. I had sex even when I did not enjoy it anymore.	O	O	O	O
5. My sexual urges and impulses changed me in a negative way.	O	O	O	O
6. I could not control my sexual cravings and desires.	O	O	O	O
7. I would rather have had sex than to have done anything else.	O	O	O	O
8. Trying to reduce the amount of sex I had almost never worked.	O	O	O	O
9. Although sex was not as satisfying for me as before, I engaged in it.	O	O	O	O
10. I did not accomplish important tasks because of my sexual behavior.	O	O	O	O
11. My sexual desires controlled me.	O	O	O	O
12. When I could have sex, everything else became irrelevant.	O	O	O	O

Continued

Box 15.1   Continued

13. I was not successful in reducing the amount of sex I had. ○ ○ ○

14. Although my sex life was not as satisfying as it had been before, I had sex. ○ ○ ○

15. My sexual activities interfered with my work and/or education. ○ ○ ○

16. My sexual behaviors had negative impact on my relationships with others. ○ ○ ○

17. I have been upset because of my sexual behaviors. ○ ○ ○

18. My sexual activities interfered with my ability to experience healthy sex. ○ ○ ○

19. I often found myself in an embarrassing situation because of my sexual behavior. ○ ○ ○

Scoring: Add the scores of the items. Fifty points or more indicate high risk of compulsive sexual behavior disorder.

Factors of the scale: *Control:* 1., 6., 11. *Salience:* 2., 7., 12. *Relapse:* 3., 8., 13. *Dissatisfaction:* 4., 9., 14. *Negative consequences:* 5., 10., 15., 16., 17., 18., 19.

Cite as: Bőthe, B., Potenza, M. N., Griffiths, M. D., Kraus, S. W., Klein, V., Fuss, J., & Demetrovics, Z. (2020). The development of the Compulsive Sexual Behavior Disorder Scale (CSBD-19): An ICD-11 based screening measure across three languages. *Journal of Behavioral Addictions, 9*(2), 247–258.

Box 15.2 The long and short version of the Problematic Pornography Consumption Scale (PPCS-18 and PPCS-6) and scoring information—English Version.

Please, think back to the last 6months and indicate on the following seven-point scale how often or to what extent the statements apply to you. There is no right or wrong answer. Please indicate the answer that most applies to you. *For the purpose of this questionnaire, pornography is defined as material (e.g., text, picture, video) that (1) creates or elicits sexual feelings or thoughts and (2) contains explicit exposure or descriptions of sexual acts involving the genitals, such as vaginal or anal intercourse, oral sex, or masturbation.*

	1	2	3	4	5	6	7
1 - 2- 3- 4- 5- 6- 7- Never Rarely Occasionally Sometimes Often Very often All the time							
1. I felt that porn is an important part of my life.	O	O	O	O	O	O	O
2. I used porn to restore the tranquility of my feelings.	O	O	O	O	O	O	O
3. I felt porn caused problems in my sexual life.	O	O	O	O	O	O	O
4. I felt that I had to watch more and more porn for satisfaction.	O	O	O	O	O	O	O
5. I unsuccessfully tried to reduce the amount of porn I watch.	O	O	O	O	O	O	O
6. I became stressed when something prevented me from watching porn.	O	O	O	O	O	O	O
7. I thought about how good it would be to watch porn.	O	O	O	O	O	O	O
8. Watching porn got rid of my negative feelings.	O	O	O	O	O	O	O
9. Watching porn prevented me from bringing out the best in me.	O	O	O	O	O	O	O
10. I felt that I needed more and more porn in order to satisfy my needs.	O	O	O	O	O	O	O
11. When I vowed not to watch porn anymore, I could only do it for a short period of time.	O	O	O	O	O	O	O
12. I became agitated when I was unable to watch porn.	O	O	O	O	O	O	O
13. I continually planned when to watch porn.	O	O	O	O	O	O	O
14. I released my tension by watching porn.	O	O	O	O	O	O	O
15. I neglected other leisure activities as a result of watching porn.	O	O	O	O	O	O	O

Continued

Box 15.2 Continued

16. I gradually watched more "extreme" porn, because the porn I watched before was less satisfying. ○ ○ ○ ○ ○
17. I resisted watching porn for only a little while before I relapsed. ○ ○ ○ ○ ○
18. I missed porn greatly when I didn't watch it for a while. ○ ○ ○ ○ ○

Note: Italics indicate the items of the PPCS-6.

PPCS-18 scoring: Add the scores of the items of each factor. For the total score add all the scores of the items. In all, 76 points or more indicate possible problematic pornography use.

Factors of the PPCS-18: *Salience:* 1., 7., 13. *Mood modification:* 2., 8., 14. *Conflict:* 3., 9., 15. *Tolerance:* 4., 10., 16. *Relapse:* 5., 11., 17. *Withdrawal:* 6., 12., 18.

PPCS-6 scoring: Add the scores of the items. 20 points or more indicate possible problematic pornography use.

Cite PPCS-18 as: Bőthe, B., Tóth-Király, I., Zsila, Á., Griffiths, M. D. Demetrovics, Z., & Orosz, G. (2018). The development of the problematic pornography consumption scale (PPCS). *Journal of Sex Research,* 55(3), 395–406. https://doi.org/10.1080/00224499.2017.1291798

Cite PPCS-6 as: Bőthe, B., Tóth-Király, I., Demetrovics, Z., & Orosz, G. (2021). The short version of the Problematic Pornography Consumption Scale (PPCS-6). *Journal of Sex Research,* 58(3), 342–352. https://doi.org/10.1080/00224499.2020.1716205

Psychobiology

Most research addressing the psychobiology of cybersex has investigated the effects of viewing sexual stimuli or long-term consequences of pornography use on brain and behavior. Currently, there is also emerging research that scrutinizes the use of virtual reality for cybersexual purposes (see below). Sex with robots, albeit passionately discussed, has not been subject of psychobiological research at the time of writing this chapter.

Functional brain imaging

Central processing of visual sexual stimuli (VSS) has been investigated with functional brain imaging using cue-reactivity paradigms in people suffering from CSBD or problematic pornography consumption and healthy controls. Cue-reactivity is an experimental paradigm from addiction research. Cues are conditioned stimuli that are related to reward anticipation. For example, in alcohol use disorder entering a bar could be a cue, while drinking a beer would constitute the following reward. There is ample evidence from addiction research that cues facilitate substance use because they stimulate craving in subjects and the brain response toward a cue is more pronounced in people suffering from addiction (that is somehow related to this cue). Neuroimaging studies have repeatedly demonstrated that people suffering from CSBD show greater blood oxygenation level-dependent (BOLD) responses in the brain reward system when watching visual sexual stimuli (Stark, Klucken, Potenza, Brand, & Strahler, 2018). Such BOLD responses are related to higher subjective sexual desire in people with CSBD toward these stimuli (Seok & Sohn, 2015; Voon et al., 2014) but also self-reported symptoms of problematic pornography consumption (Brand, Snagowski, Laier, & Maderwald, 2016). Only one study found conflicting results in a sample of the general population (Kühn & Gallinat, 2014). These findings could be interpreted as signs of brain responses comparable to addiction; however, for sexual stimuli it is unclear whether these are cues or rewards (Gola, Lewczuk, & Skorko, 2016; Gola, Wordecha, Marchewka, & Sescousse, 2016). Watching sexual stimuli can be seen as an unconditioned reward, especially for those who experience and report high sexual desire toward these stimuli. Interpretation of functional brain imaging data is dependent on this conceptualization of cue vs reward, with data interpreted as supporting or contradicting the addiction hypothesis. Some experts have therefore called for a "reexamination—and possibly reinterpretation—of the results" reported in earlier functional neuroimaging studies that assess cue-reactivity in response to visual sexual stimuli (Gola, Wordecha, et al., 2016).

Structural brain imaging

Associations between brain structure and CSBD as well as average porn use have been investigated in few studies. Three studies assessed gray matter volume (GMV) using voxel-based morphometry as well as resting-state functional connectivity (Kühn & Gallinat, 2014; Schmidt et al., 2017; Seok & Sohn, 2018) and one study measured structural connectivity using diffusion tensor imaging (Miner, Raymond, Mueller, Lloyd, & Lim, 2009). A recent preprint also reports about GMV in people with CSBD

(Draps et al., 2020). Imaging data are somehow inconclusive showing a negative correlation between excessive pornography use and right caudate GMV (Kühn & Gallinat, 2014), an increased GMV in the left amygdala (Schmidt et al., 2017), reduced GMV in the left superior temporal gyrus and right middle temporal gyrus (Seok & Sohn, 2018), and reduced GMV in the right anterior cingulate cortex as well as the left orbitofrontal cortex (Draps et al., 2020) in people with CSBD. Most structural findings have thus not been replicated and may well be incidental to rather than causal of CSBD symptoms.

Neuropsychology

Several personality traits have been linked to a higher risk of excessive (cyber)sexual behavior. Among these are difficulties with attachment to other humans (Gilliland, Blue Star, Hansen, & Carpenter, 2015) making it more likely that people seek cybersexual outlets instead of interpersonal sexualities. Attachment difficulties can arise from childhood sexual abuse leading to persistent sexual avoidance with real people and also sexual compulsivity (Vaillancourt-Morel et al., 2015). In addition to avoidant attachment style, excessive cybersex use was also related to higher levels of sexual desire and depressive mood (Varfi et al., 2019) as well as higher sexual excitability and dysfunctional coping (Laier & Brand, 2014).

Neuroendocrinology

Plasma levels of luteinizing hormone were found to be elevated in people suffering from CSBD, while other sex hormones were comparable to healthy controls (Chatzittofis et al., 2020). Moreover, a dysfunction of the hypothalamus-pituitary-adrenal (HPA) axis was observed in men with CSBD showing an insufficient suppression after dexamethasone intake (Chatzittofis et al., 2016). Given the strong relation between sex hormones and HPA axis regulation (Fuss, Claro, et al., 2019), these findings may implicate a complex neuroendocrinological disturbance in people suffering from CSBD. However, further research is needed to disentangle whether these disturbances are the cause or consequence of excessive (cyber)sexual behavior.

Virtual reality pornography

So far, few studies have investigated the psychobiology of VR pornography by experimentally comparing the perception of VR to traditional pornography. As expected, VR pornography was found to elicit a stronger feeling of presence and sexual arousal (Dekker, Wenzlaff, Biedermann, Briken, & Fuss, 2020; Elsey, van Andel, Kater, Reints, & Spiering, 2019). In addition to subjective measures of sexual arousal, skin conductance levels as an objective measure of bodily arousal are also higher during VR compared to traditional pornography (Simon & Greitemeyer, 2019). Another essential difference between VR and traditional pornography is the perception of the interaction with actors. In an experimental study, participants felt more desired, more flirted with, more looked into the eyes when watching VR pornography. They were also more likely to feel connected with the actors and more likely to feel the urge to interact with them. Salivary oxytocin levels were related to the perceived eye contact with the actors in VR indicating that oxytocin may promote such virtual interactions in VR (Dekker et al., 2020).

Pharmacotherapy

Pharmacological treatment of cybersexual behavior should only be an option if it is perceived as being problematic <u>and</u> CSBD can be diagnosed according to ICD-11 guidelines. Cybersexual behavior should not be treated pharmacologically if the distress is related to real or feared social disapproval of cybersexual behavior when there is no indication of further psychopathology. Moreover, if an underlying condition or substance use is solely responsible for the excessive use of cybersex, the underlying condition should be treated, and substance use should be addressed. Certain medications are associated with increased sexual impulses and therefore a thorough evaluation of the patient's medication should precede any pharmacological intervention. After ruling out other factors, several substances may be suitable for the treatment of problematic cybersexual behavior as these medications showed efficacy in the treatment of CSBD in clinical trials and case reports. Ideally, pharmacological treatment should be accompanied by psychotherapeutic care.

Selective serotonin reuptake inhibitors

Selective serotonin reuptake inhibitors (SSRIs) block the reuptake of serotonin into neurons and thus increase serotonin availability in the synaptic cleft. They are typically used to treat anxiety disorders and depression and often have side effects related to sexual functioning and desire. These sexual side effects are however one rationale for using SSRIs in the treatment of CSBD. In addition to several case reports, two clinical studies have shown that SSRIs may be effective in the treatment of compulsive sexual behavior, in some cases. In an open-label trial, men with paraphilic and nonparaphilic compulsive sexual behavior received between 20 and 40 mg of the SSRI fluoxetine (Kafka & Prentky, 1992). After 4 weeks, compulsive sexual behaviors were reduced, indicating that fluoxetine may be helpful in the treatment of people with CSBD. Subsequently, a 12-week, double-blind trial compared the SSRI citalopram with placebo using dosages between 20 and 60 mg/day in 28 men who have sex with men (MSM). They found that citalopram significantly reduced sexual desire, masturbation frequency, and pornography use, while the number of sex partners was not affected (Wainberg et al., 2006). It should be noted that, in some patients, use of SSRI has been associated with paradoxical increase in the riskiness of sexual acts.

Naltrexone

Naltrexone is an opioid antagonist and decreases the amount of the neurotransmitter dopamine released from the nucleus accumbens thus directly acting on the brain reward system. Naltrexone is typically used for the treatment of alcohol use disorder as well as opioid dependence. In a recent trial (Savard et al., 2020), 20 men seeking treatment for compulsive sexual behavior disorder in an outpatient setting received 25–50 mg naltrexone for 4 weeks. A reduction of compulsive sexual behavior during treatment with naltrexone was observed, as well as an increase in symptoms following discontinuation of the treatment.

Other pharmacological treatments such as testosterone-lowering medication (e.g., cyproterone acetate, GnRH analogs or antagonists) have been explored in case reports, and may potentially lower sexual desire. They are used, in some cases, for the treatment of people with severe paraphilic disorders with a high risk of sexual offending. Given the serious side effects (e.g., on bone density) and lack of high quality evidence, these medications are usually not appropriate for the treatment of excessive cybersexual behavior and may only be suitable when severe risks are present; and even then with caution and in expert prescriber settings (see, e.g., Thibaut et al., 2020).

Psychotherapy

Traditional psychotherapy

Regardless of debates about the proper classification, definition, etiology, and assessment of CSBD and problematic cybersexual activities, these are existing problems that many practitioners encounter. Thus, there is a need for effective intervention strategies for the management and treatment of problematic cybersexual activities. However, the available scientific evidence regarding the psychotherapeutic treatment options and their efficacy for problematic online sexual activities is limited, due to small sample sizes, lack of proper assessment, lack of control groups, and homogeneous samples (for more details, see Dhuffar & Griffiths, 2015; Garcia et al., 2016; Goslar, Leibetseder, Muench, Hofmann, & Laireiter, 2020; Grubbs et al., 2020; Hook, Reid, Penberthy, Davis, & Jennings, 2014; Kaplan & Krueger, 2010; Sniewski, Farvid, & Carter, 2018; von Franqué, Klein, & Briken, 2015; Wéry & Billieux, 2017).

A diverse set of psychological interventions, including individual, couple, family, and group therapies in off-line and online settings were reported in the literature, based on cognitive behavior therapy (CBT), acceptance and commitment therapy (ACT), motivational interviewing techniques, experiential therapy, art therapy, emotionally focused therapy, and this list is still not exhaustive. Based on the findings of recent literature reviews discussing the treatment approaches for problematic pornography use, problematic cybersexual activities, and CSBD (Dhuffar & Griffiths, 2015; Garcia et al., 2016; Goslar et al., 2020; Hook et al., 2014; Kaplan & Krueger, 2010; Sniewski et al., 2018; von Franqué et al., 2015; Wéry & Billieux, 2017), cognitive behavior therapy (CBT), acceptance and commitment therapy (ACT), motivational interviewing techniques, and mindfulness-based approaches might be the most effective in the treatment of problematic cybersexual activities. However, the evidence is mostly based on case reports and uncontrolled studies with few exceptions (Dhuffar & Griffiths, 2015; Garcia et al., 2016; Hook et al., 2014; Kaplan & Krueger, 2010; Sniewski et al., 2018; von Franqué et al., 2015; Wéry & Billieux, 2017); thus, results and recommendations should be dealt with care.

Only one randomized controlled trial study examined the efficacy of a group-based CBT in a relatively large sample of men with hypersexuality (Hallberg et al., 2019). Participants were randomized between a treatment and a waitlist control group, and self-report scales (e.g., sexual compulsivity, psychological distress) were administered before, during, and right after the treatment as well as at 3- and 6-month follow-ups. Aiming to reduce hypersexuality, this intervention provided seven CBT-based modules over a period of 7 weeks for the participants. The modules included psychoeducational and behavioral activation content (e.g., how to challenge dysfunctional thoughts and beliefs, conflict management). Based on the longitudinal comparison of the treatment and the waitlist control group, a significant decrease in hypersexuality symptoms and sexual compulsivity were observed with medium to large effects sizes. The achieved improvement was maintained even 6 months after the end of the intervention. Moreover, a significant decrease in depressive symptoms was also observed; however, this improvement was not maintained at the 6-month follow-up. The results of this short, group-based CBT for improving hypersexuality symptoms are promising. Nevertheless, it has to be noted that the primary outcome measure of the study was a nonvalidated scale, the response rates were low at the 3-month (35% for the treatment group and 41% for the control group) and 6-month follow-ups (24% for the treatment group and 20% for the control group), and only men were included in the study, limiting the generalizability of the findings (Klein, Savaş, & Conley, 2021).

As can be seen, current scientific evidence is scarce to determine or guide practitioners in terms of the best settings and techniques of treatment for people with problematic cybersexual activities. However, some general recommendations may be formulated (for more details, see Grubbs et al., 2017). Appropriate assessment of the problematic cybersexual behaviors (e.g., not only the frequency of the given behavior but the subjective feelings, problematic engagement, and consequences as well) is crucial, and the determination of the intervention aims are essential to provide a solid foundation for the treatment (Grubbs et al., 2017). Importantly, as it was demonstrated in the previous sections of this chapter, psychiatric comorbidities (especially mood disorders) may be common among individuals with problematic cybersexual activities and may affect their prognosis. Thus, comorbid disorders or accompanying problems should be assessed and treated before or simultaneously with problematic cybersexual activities (Garcia et al., 2016; Grubbs et al., 2017). Also, interventions should be structured to promote healthy sexual behaviors and eliminate those thoughts and behavioral patterns that are related to the development and maintenance of the problematic behavior and the deriving distress and functional impairment (Bőthe, Baumgartner, Schaub, Demetrovics, & Orosz, 2020; Grubbs et al., 2017). Therefore, the main goal of the interventions is to provide techniques and teach people with problematic cybersexual behaviors how to regulate their behaviors and to develop a healthy, enjoyable, and fulfilling sexual life.

Online problems, online solutions?

Given social and individual barriers of traditional (off-line, face-to-face) treatment approaches for problematic cybersexual activities, such as feelings of shame and stigma or unaffordable costs (Dhuffar & Griffiths, 2016), scalable, science-based online interventions may be considered as an alternative for traditional interventions. Online self-help interventions may reduce traditional treatment barriers by providing a free and easy-to-use tool with high anonymity, privacy, flexibility, and short or no waiting time; and supporting participants' autonomy and self-efficacy, as it was demonstrated, for example, in the case of substance use and problematic gambling (Baumgartner et al., 2019; Haug, Castro, Wenger, & Schaub, 2018; Herrero et al., 2019; Weisel et al., 2018). However, online interventions have their disadvantages as well, such as high dropout rates (Rooke, Copeland, Norberg, Hine, & McCambridge, 2013; Schaub et al., 2015), or lower levels of adherence due to the "distant" nature of the interventions (e.g., lack of personal relationships, or limited individualization options) (Amann et al., 2018; Haug et al., 2018; Schaub et al., 2016). Thus, online interventions should not be considered as replacements for traditional, face-to-face therapies but as an additional method that may provide treatment for those people who are hesitant or cannot afford to seek traditional treatment.

There are only two online interventions for problematic cybersexual activities in the literature, where effectiveness has already been or is currently examined. The first online intervention aiming to reduce hypersexuality and problematic pornography use is the Candeo program, which is based on a CBT approach and includes 10 self-paced, psychoeducational modules (Hardy, Ruchty, Hull, & Hyde, 2010). The modules concentrate on the development and maintenance of the problematic behavior, provide a way to "break free" from problematic pornography use (e.g., the ABCD model of CBT), and promote a healthy sexual mindset. Based on retrospective (i.e., not experimental or longitudinal study design), self-reported responses of 138 participants, participation in the program resulted in higher levels of perceived recovery, more constructive reactions to temptation, positive emotions, self-control, abilities to be in a relationship, and less pornography use, masturbation, obsessive sexual thoughts, negative emotions, and tendencies to deny the problematic sexual behavior. However, it should be noted that no control group was included in the study, no well-validated measures were assessed, and the results are completely based on the participants' retrospective reports.

The second online intervention aiming to reduce problematic pornography use is the Hands-off program, which is based on motivational interviewing, cognitive-behavioral therapy, mindfulness techniques, and "wise" social-psychological interventions (Bőthe, Baumgartner, et al., 2020). The program includes six core modules and one booster module that can be accessed 1 month after the end of the core modules. The effectiveness of this preregistered program is currently being examined in a two-armed randomized controlled trial study design with 242 participants. Psychiatric disorders are controlled for in the study. Well-validated, self-report scales are assessed at baseline, right after the end of the intervention, at 1-month, and at 3-month follow-ups after the end of the program. The study's primary outcome is the level of problematic pornography use, while the secondary outcomes include pornography use frequency, pornography craving, pornography use-avoidance self-efficacy, sex mindset, sexual satisfaction, negative and positive emotions, and life satisfaction.

Conclusion

This chapter provides a framework for understanding the relationship between mental health and cybersex. For a long time, cybersex was a topic for future utopias, but in recent years, it has become a part of many people's lives. As sexual and mental health interact, the increasing focus of psychiatry and psychology on these issues reflects this development. Some people may benefit from the new possibilities of cybersexualities, and those who develop mental health problems in relation to cybersex will hopefully benefit from the introduction of CSBD in ICD-11 and an increasing understanding of cybersex. In recent years, the number of psychotherapeutic and pharmacological studies, screening tools, and studies on the neurobiology of cybersex has steadily increased (Grubbs et al., 2020). However, most of the prior work in the field is characterized by rudimentary methodological designs, a lack of theoretical integration, and an absence of quality measurement and treatment-related research (Grubbs et al., 2020). Therefore, further studies are necessary to (1) refine the assessment of cybersex; (2) study mechanisms underlying compulsive cybersexual behaviors, contributing to the identification of prevention and intervention targets; and (3) develop innovative, intervention strategies to reduce compulsive cybersexual behaviors. Mental health professionals will benefit from understanding the nature of cybersex and how to deal with it therapeutically.

References

Açar, K. V. (2017). Webcam child prostitution: An exploration of current and futuristic methods of detection. *International Journal of Cyber Criminology*, *11*(1), 98–109.

Albright, J. M. (2008). Sex in America online: An exploration of sex, marital status, and sexual identity in Internet sex seeking and its impacts. *Journal of Sex Research*, *45*(2), 175–186.

Alexandraki, K., Stavropoulos, V., Anderson, E., Latifi, M. Q., & Gomez, R. (2018). Adolescent pornography use: A systematic literature review of research trends 2000-2017. *Current Psychiatry Reviews*, *14*(1), 47–58. https://doi.org/10.2174/2211556007666180606073617.

Amann, M., Haug, S., Wenger, A., Baumgartner, C., Ebert, D. D., Berger, T., … Schaub, M. P. (2018). The effects of social presence on adherence-focused guidance in problematic cannabis users: Protocol for the CANreduce 2.0 randomized controlled trial. *JMIR Research Protocols*, *7*(1), e30. https://doi.org/10.2196/resprot.9484.

Baumgartner, C., Bilevicius, E., Khazaal, Y., Achab, S., Schaaf, S., Wenger, A., … Schaub, M. P. (2019). Efficacy of a web-based self-help tool to reduce problem gambling in Switzerland: Study protocol of a two-armed randomised controlled trial. *BMJ Open*, *9*(12). https://doi.org/10.1136/bmjopen-2019-032110, e032110.

Bergner, R. M., & Bridges, A. J. (2002). The significance of heavy pornography involvement for romantic partners: Research and clinical implications. *Journal of Sex and Marital Therapy*, *28*(3), 193–206. https://doi.org/10.1080/009262302760328235.

Berson, I. R. (2003). Grooming cybervictims: The psychosocial effects of online exploitation for youth. *Journal of School Violence*, *2*(1), 5–18.

Beutel, M. E., Burghardt, J., Tibubos, A. N., Klein, E. M., Schmutzer, G., & Brahler, E. (2018). Declining sexual activity and desire in men-findings from representative German surveys, 2005 and 2016. *The Journal of Sexual Medicine*, *15*(5), 750–756. https://doi.org/10.1016/j.jsxm.2018.03.010.

Billieux, J., Flayelle, M., Rumpf, H.-J., & Stein, D. J. (2019). High involvement versus pathological involvement in video games: A crucial distinction for ensuring the validity and utility of gaming disorder. *Current Addiction Reports*, *6*(3), 323–330. https://doi.org/10.1007/s40429-019-00259-x.

Billieux, J., Schimmenti, A., Khazaal, Y., Maurage, P., & Heeren, A. (2015). Are we overpathologizing everyday life? A tenable blueprint for behavioral addiction research. *Journal of Behavioral Addictions*, *4*(3), 119–123. https://doi.org/10.1556/2006.4.2015.009.

Blais-Lecours, S., Vaillancourt-Morel, M.-P., Sabourin, S., & Godbout, N. (2016). Cyberpornography: Time use, perceived addiction, sexual functioning, and sexual satisfaction. *Cyberpsychology, Behavior and Social Networking*, *19*(11), 649–655.

Blankenship, R., & Laaser, M. (2004). Sexual addiction and ADHD: Is there a connection? *Sexual Addiction and Compulsivity*, *11*(1–2), 7–20. https://doi.org/10.1080/10720160490458184.

Bonilla-Zorita, G., Griffiths, M. D., & Kuss, D. J. (2020). Online dating and problematic use: A systematic review. *International Journal of Mental Health and Addiction*, 1–34. https://doi.org/10.1007/s11469-020-00318-9.

Bostwick, J. M., & Bucci, J. A. (2008). Internet sex addiction treated with naltrexone. *Mayo Clinic Proceedings*, *83*(2), 226–230. https://doi.org/10.4065/83.2.226.

Bőthe, B., Bartók, R., Tóth-Király, I., Reid, R. C., Griffiths, M. D., Demetrovics, Z., & Orosz, G. (2018). Hypersexuality, gender, and sexual orientation: A large-scale psychometric survey study. *Archives of Sexual Behavior*, *47*(8), 2265–2276. https://doi.org/10.1007/s10508-018-1201-z.

Bőthe, B., Baumgartner, C., Schaub, M. P., Demetrovics, Z., & Orosz, G. (2020). Hands-off: Study protocol of a two-armed randomized controlled trial of a web-based self-help tool to reduce problematic pornography use. *Journal of Behavioral Addictions*, *9*(2), 433–445.

Bőthe, B., Koós, M., Tóth-Király, I., Orosz, G., & Demetrovics, Z. (2019). Investigating the associations of adult ADHD symptoms, hypersexuality, and problematic pornography use among men and women on a largescale, non-clinical sample. *The Journal of Sexual Medicine*, *16*(4), 489–499. https://doi.org/10.1016/J.JSXM.2019.01.312.

Bőthe, B., Lonza, A., Štulhofer, A., & Demetrovics, Z. (2020). Symptoms of problematic pornography use in a sample of treatment considering and treatment non-considering men: A network approach. *The Journal of Sexual Medicine*, *17*(10), 2016–2028.

Bőthe, B., Potenza, M. N., Griffiths, M. D., Kraus, S. W., Klein, V., Fuss, J., & Demetrovics, Z. (2020). The development of the compulsive sexual behavior disorder scale (CSBD-19): An ICD-11 based screening measure across three languages. *Journal of Behavioral Addictions*, *9*(2), 247–258.

Bőthe, B., Tóth-Király, I., Bella, N., Potenza, M. N., Demetrovics, Z., & Orosz, G. (2021). Why do people watch pornography? The motivational basis of pornography use. *Psychology of Addictive Behaviors*, *35*(2), 172–186. https://doi.org/10.1037/adb0000603.

Bőthe, B., Tóth-Király, I., Demetrovics, Z., & Orosz, G. (2017). The pervasive role of sex mindset: Beliefs about the malleability of sexual life is linked to higher levels of relationship satisfaction and sexual satisfaction and lower levels of problematic pornography use. *Personality and Individual Differences*, *117*, 15–22. https://doi.org/10.1016/j.paid.2017.05.030.

Bőthe, B., Tóth-Király, I., Demetrovics, Z., & Orosz, G. (2021). The short version of the problematic pornography consumption scale (PPCS-6): A reliable and valid measure in general and treatment-seeking populations. *The Journal of Sex Research*, *58*(3), 342–352. https://doi.org/10.1080/00224499.2020.1716205.

Bőthe, B., Tóth-Király, I., Griffiths, M. D., Potenza, M. N., Orosz, G., & Demetrovics, Z. (2021). Are sexual functioning problems associated with frequent pornography use and/or problematic pornography use? Results from a large community survey including males and females. *Addictive Behaviors*, *112*(106603), 1–9.

Bőthe, B., Tóth-Király, I., Potenza, M. N., Griffiths, M. D., Orosz, G., & Demetrovics, Z. (2019). Revisiting the role of impulsivity and compulsivity in problematic sexual behaviors. *Journal of Sex Research*, *56*(2), 166–179. https://doi.org/10.1080/00224499.2018.1480744.

Bőthe, B., Tóth-Király, I., Potenza, M. N., Orosz, G., & Demetrovics, Z. (2020). High-frequency pornography use may not always be problematic. *The Journal of Sexual Medicine*, *17*(4), 793–811. https://doi.org/10.1016/j.jsxm.2020.01.007.

Bőthe, B., Tóth-Király, I., Zsila, Á., Griffiths, M. D., Demetrovics, Z., & Orosz, G. (2018). The development of the problematic pornography consumption scale (PPCS). *Journal of Sex Research, 55*(3), 395–406.

Bőthe, B., Vaillancourt-Morel, M. P., & Bergeron, S. (2021). Associations between pornography use frequency, pornography use motivations, and sexual wellbeing in couples. *The Journal of Sex Research,* 1–15.

Bőthe, B., Vaillancourt-Morel, M.-P., Bergeron, S., & Demetrovics, Z. (2019). Problematic and non-problematic pornography use among LGBTQ adolescents: A systematic literature review. *Current Addiction Reports, 6*(4), 478–494. https://doi.org/10.1007/s40429-019-00289-5.

Bőthe, B., Vaillancourt-Morel, M-P., Dion, J., Štulhofer, A., & Bergeron, S. (2021). Validity and reliability of the short version of the Problematic Pornography Consumption Scale (PPCS-6-A) in adolescents. *Psychology of Addictive Behaviors,* 1–15.

Bőthe, B., Vaillancourt-Morel, M. P., Girouard, A., Štulhofer, A., Dion, J., & Bergeron, S. (2020). A large-scale comparison of Canadian sexual/gender minority and heterosexual, cisgender adolescents' pornography use characteristics. *The Journal of Sexual Medicine, 17*(6), 1156–1167.

Brand, M., Snagowski, J., Laier, C., & Maderwald, S. (2016). Ventral striatum activity when watching preferred pornographic pictures is correlated with symptoms of Internet pornography addiction. *NeuroImage, 129,* 224–232.

Bridges, A. J., & Morokoff, P. J. (2011). Sexual media use and relational satisfaction in heterosexual couples. *Personal Relationships, 18*(4), 562–585. https://doi.org/10.1111/j.1475-6811.2010.01328.x.

Bridges, A. J., Wosnitzer, R., Scharrer, E., Sun, C., & Liberman, R. (2010). Aggression and sexual behavior in best-selling pornography videos: A content analysis update. *Violence Against Women, 16*(10), 1065–1085. https://doi.org/10.1177/1077801210382866.

Brown, C. C., Carroll, J. S., Yorgason, J. B., Busby, D. M., Willoughby, B. J., & Larson, J. H. (2017). A common-fate analysis of pornography acceptance, use, and sexual satisfaction among heterosexual married couples. *Archives of Sexual Behavior, 46*(2), 575–584. https://doi.org/10.1007/s10508-016-0732-4.

Cacioppo, J. T., Cacioppo, S., Gonzaga, G. C., Ogburn, E. L., & Vanderweele, T. J. (2013). Marital satisfaction and break-ups differ across on-line and off-line meeting venues. *Proceedings of the National Academy of Sciences of the United States of America, 110*(25), 10135–10140. https://doi.org/10.1073/pnas.1222447110.

Campbell, L., & Kohut, T. (2017). The use and effects of pornography in romantic relationships. *Current Opinion in Psychology, 13,* 6–10. https://doi.org/10.1016/j.copsyc.2016.03.004.

Cantor, J. (2018). The question of "sex doll brothels". In J. White (Ed.), *For the record.* http://bcitnews.com/2018/10/05/the-ethics-of-sex-doll-brothels-for-the-record/.

Chatzittofis, A., Arver, S., Öberg, K., Hallberg, J., Nordström, P., & Jokinen, J. (2016). HPA axis dysregulation in men with hypersexual disorder. *Psychoneuroendocrinology, 63,* 247–253.

Chatzittofis, A., Boström, A. E., Öberg, K. G., Flanagan, J. N., Schiöth, H. B., Arver, S., & Jokinen, J. (2020). Normal testosterone but higher luteinizing hormone plasma levels in men with hypersexual disorder. *Sexual Medicine.*

Chen, L., Jiang, X., Luo, S., Kraus, S. W., & Bőthe, B. (2021). The role of impaired control in screening problematic pornography use: Evidence from cross-sectional and longitudinal studies in a large help-seeking male sample. *Psychology of Addictive Behaviors,* 1–11.

Chen, L., Luo, X. L., Bőthe, B., Jiang, X., Demetrovics, Z., & Potenza, M. N. (2021). Properties of the Problematic Pornography Consumption Scale (PPCS-18) in community and subclinical samples in China and Hungary. *Addictive Behaviors, 112*(106591), 1–9.

CNBC. (2018). *Proposed 'sex robot brothel' blocked by Houston government: 'We are not Sin City'*. https://www.cnbc.com/2018/10/04/houston-blocks-sex-robot-brothel-from-opening. html. Retrieved 25 July 2020.

Cooper, A. (1998). Sexuality and the internet: Surfing into the new Millenium. *Cyberpsychology & Behavior, 1*(2), 187–193. https://doi.org/10.1080/09505430220137252.

Cooper, A., & Griffin-Shelley, E. (2002). Introduction. The internet: The next sexual revolution. In *Sex and the Internet: A guidebook for clinicians* (pp. 1–15).

Couch, D., & Liamputtong, P. (2008). Online dating and mating: The use of the internet to meet sexual partners. *Qualitative Health Research, 18*(2), 268–279.

Coulson, M., Barnett, J., Ferguson, C. J., & Gould, R. L. (2012). Real feelings for virtual people: Emotional attachments and interpersonal attraction in video games. *Psychology of Popular Media Culture, 1*(3), 176–184. https://doi.org/10.1037/a0028192.

Danaher, J., & McArthur, N. (2017). *Robot sex: Social and ethical implications* (p. 133). Cambridge, MA: MIT Press.

Daneback, K., Cooper, A., & Månsson, S. A. (2005). An internet study of cybersex participants. *Archives of Sexual Behavior, 34*(3), 321–328.

Dekker, A., Wenzlaff, F., Biedermann, S., Briken, P., & Fuss, J. (2020). VR porn as 'empathy machine'? Perception of self and others in virtual reality pornography. *Journal of Sex Research* (in press).

Dhuffar, M. K., & Griffiths, M. D. (2015). A systematic review of online sex addiction and clinical treatments using CONSORT evaluation. *Current Addiction Reports, 2*(2), 163–174. https://doi.org/10.1007/s40429-015-0055-x.

Dhuffar, M. K., & Griffiths, M. D. (2016). Barriers to female sex addiction treatment in the UK. *Journal of Behavioral Addictions, 5*(4), 562–567. https://doi.org/10.1556/2006.5.2016.072.

Dombrowski, S. C., Gischlar, K. L., & Durst, T. (2007). Safeguarding young people from cyber pornography and cyber sexual predation: A major dilemma of the Internet. *Child Abuse Review: Journal of the British Association for the Study and Prevention of Child Abuse and Neglect, 16*(3), 153–170.

Dombrowski, S. C., LeMasney, J. W., Ahia, C. E., & Dickson, S. A. (2004). Protecting children from online sexual predators: Technological, psychoeducational, and legal considerations. *Professional Psychology: Research and Practice, 35*(1), 65.

Döring, N. (2008). Sexualität im Internet. *Zeitschrift für Sexualforschung, 21*(04), 291–318. https://doi.org/10.1055/s-0028-1098728.

Draps, M., Sescousse, G., Potenza, M. N., Duda, A., Lew-Starowicz, M., Kopera, M., … Gola, M. (2020). Gray matter volume differences in impulse control and addictive disorders. *PsyArXiv*. https://doi.org/10.31234/osf.io/qyem5.

Dwulit, A. D., & Rzymski, P. (2019). The potential associations of pornography use with sexual dysfunctions: An integrative literature review of observational studies. *Journal of Clinical Medicine, 8*(7), 914. https://doi.org/10.3390/jcm8070914.

Efrati, Y., & Gola, M. (2018). Understanding and predicting profiles of compulsive sexual behavior among adolescents. *Journal of Behavioral Addictions, 7*(4), 1004–1014. https://doi.org/10.1556/2006.7.2018.100.

Egan, V., & Parmar, R. (2013). Dirty habits? Online pornography use, personality, obsessionality, and compulsivity. *Journal of Sex and Marital Therapy, 39*(5), 394–409. https://doi.org/10.1080/0092623X.2012.710182.

Elsey, J. W., van Andel, K., Kater, R. B., Reints, I. M., & Spiering, M. (2019). The impact of virtual reality versus 2D pornography on sexual arousal and presence. *Computers in Human Behavior, 97*, 35–43.

Fernandez, D. P., & Griffiths, M. D. (2019). Psychometric instruments for problematic pornography use: A systematic review. *Evaluation & the Health Professions*, 1–71. https://doi.org/10.1177/0163278719861688.

Ferree, M. (2003). Women and the web: Cybersex activity and implications. *Sexual and Relationship Therapy*, *18*(3), 385–393.

Ford, J. J., Durtschi, J. A., & Franklin, D. L. (2012). Structural therapy with a couple battling pornography addiction. *American Journal of Family Therapy*, *40*(4), 336–348. https://doi.org/10.1080/01926187.2012.685003.

Fritz, N., & Paul, B. (2017). From orgasms to spanking: A content analysis of the agentic and objectifying sexual scripts in feminist, for women, and mainstream pornography. *Sex Roles*, *77*(9–10), 639–652. https://doi.org/10.1007/s11199-017-0759-6.

Fuss, J., Briken, P., Stein, D. J., & Lochner, C. (2019). Compulsive sexual behavior disorder in obsessive–compulsive disorder: Prevalence and associated comorbidity. *Journal of Behavioral Addictions*, 1–7. https://doi.org/10.1556/2006.8.2019.23.

Fuss, J., Claro, L., Ising, M., Biedermann, S. V., Wiedemann, K., Stalla, G. K., … Auer, M. K. (2019). Does sex hormone treatment reverse the sex-dependent stress regulation? A longitudinal study on hypothalamus-pituitary-adrenal (HPA) axis activity in transgender individuals. *Psychoneuroendocrinology*, *104*, 228–237.

Fuss, J., Lemay, K., Stein, D. J., Briken, P., Jakob, R., Reed, G. M., & Kogan, C. S. (2019). Public stakeholders' comments on ICD-11 chapters related to mental and sexual health. *World Psychiatry*, *18*(2), 233.

Garcia, F. D., Assumpção, A. A., Malloy-diniz, L., De Freitas, A. A. C., Delavenne, H., & Thibaut, F. (2016). A comprehensive review of psychotherapeutic treatment of sexual addiction. *Journal of Groups in Addiction & Recovery*, *11*(1), 59–71. https://doi.org/10.1080/1556035X.2015.1066726.

Gilliland, R., Blue Star, J., Hansen, B., & Carpenter, B. (2015). Relationship attachment styles in a sample of hypersexual patients. *Journal of Sex & Marital Therapy*, *41*(6), 581–592.

Gola, M., Lewczuk, K., & Skorko, M. (2016). What matters: Quantity or quality of pornography use? Psychological and behavioral factors of seeking treatment for problematic pornography use. *The Journal of Sexual Medicine*, *13*(5), 815–824.

Gola, M., Wordecha, M., Marchewka, A., & Sescousse, G. (2016). Visual sexual stimuli—Cue or reward? A perspective for interpreting brain imaging findings on human sexual behaviors. *Frontiers in Human Neuroscience*, *10*, 402.

Goslar, M., Leibetseder, M., Muench, H. M., Hofmann, S. G., & Laireiter, A.-R. (2020). Treatments for internet addiction, sex addiction and compulsive buying: A meta-analysis. *Journal of Behavioral Addictions*, *9*(1), 14–43. https://doi.org/10.1556/2006.2020.00005.

Griffiths, M. D. (2005). A "components" model of addiction within a biopsychosocial framework. *Journal of Substance Use*, *10*(4), 191–197. https://doi.org/10.1080/14659890500114359.

Griffiths, M. D. (2012). Internet sex addiction: A review of empirical research. *Addiction Research and Theory*, *20*(2), 111–124. https://doi.org/10.3109/16066359.2011.588351.

Griffiths, M. D. (2017). The Myth of the addictive personality. *Addiction & Rehabilitation Medicine*, *3*(2), 1–4. https://doi.org/10.1002/ijc.28807.

Grov, C., Gillespie, B. J., Royce, T., & Lever, J. (2011). Perceived consequences of casual online sexual activities on heterosexual relationships: A U.S. online survey. *Archives of Sexual Behavior*, *40*(2), 429–439. https://doi.org/10.1007/s10508-010-9598-z.

Grubbs, J. B., & Gola, M. (2019). Is pornography use related to erectile functioning? Results from cross-sectional and latent growth curve analyses. *The Journal of Sexual Medicine*, *16*(1), 111–125. https://doi.org/10.1016/j.jsxm.2018.11.004.

Grubbs, J. B., Grant, J. T., Lee, B. N., Hoagland, K. C., Davidson, P., Reid, R. C., & Kraus, S. W. (2020). Sexual addiction 25 years on: A systematic and methodological review of empirical literature and an agenda for future research. *Clinical Psychology Review*, 101925.

Grubbs, J. B., Hook, J. P., Griffin, B. J., Cushman, M. S., Hook, J. N., & Penberthy, J. K. (2017). Treating hypersexuality. In *The wiley handbook of sex therapy* (pp. 115–128). https://doi.org/10.1002/9781118510384.ch8.

Grubbs, J. B., & Kraus, S. W. (2021). Pornography use and psychological science: A call for consideration. *Current Directions in Psychological Science*, *30*(1), 68–75.

Grubbs, J. B., Kraus, S. W., & Perry, S. L. (2019). Self-reported addiction to pornography in a nationally representative sample: The roles of use habits, religiousness, and moral incongruence. *Journal of Behavioral Addictions*, *8*(1), 88–93.

Grubbs, J. B., Perry, S. L., Wilt, J. A., & Reid, R. C. (2019). Pornography problems due to moral incongruence: An integrative model with a systematic review and meta-analysis. *Archives of Sexual Behavior*, *48*(2), 397–415. https://doi.org/10.1007/s10508-018-1248-x.

Grubbs, J. B., Volk, F., Exline, J. J., & Pargament, K. I. (2015). Internet pornography use: Perceived addiction, psychological distress, and the validation of a brief measure. *Journal of Sex and Marital Therapy*, *41*(1), 83–106. https://doi.org/10.1080/0092623X.2013.842192.

Grubbs, J. B., Wright, P. J., Braden, A. L., Wilt, J. A., & Kraus, S. W. (2019). Internet pornography use and sexual motivation: A systematic review and integration. *Annals of the International Communication Association*, *43*(2), 117–155. https://doi.org/10.1080/23808985.2019.1584045.

Hall, L. (2016). Sex with robots for love free encounters. In A. D. Cheok, K. Devlin, & D. Levy (Eds.), *Love and sex with robots. Second international conference. Revised, selected papers* (pp. 128–136). Springer.

Hallberg, J., Kaldo, V., Arver, S., Dhejne, C., Jokinen, J., & Öberg, K. G. (2019). A randomized controlled study of group-administered cognitive behavioral therapy for hypersexual disorder in men. *The Journal of Sexual Medicine*. https://doi.org/10.1016/j.jsxm.2019.03.005.

Hardy, S. A., Ruchty, J., Hull, T. D., & Hyde, R. (2010). A preliminary study of an online psychoeducational program for hypersexuality. *Sexual Addiction and Compulsivity*, *17*(4), 247–269. https://doi.org/10.1080/10720162.2010.533999.

Harlow, H. F. (1961). The development of affectional patterns in infant monkeys. In B. M. Foss (Ed.), *Determinants of infant behaviour I* (pp. 75–97). London, UK/New York, NY: Methuen/Wiley.

Haug, S., Castro, R. P., Wenger, A., & Schaub, M. P. (2018). Efficacy of a mobile phone-based life-skills training program for substance use prevention among adolescents: Study protocol of a cluster-randomised controlled trial. *BMC Public Health*, *18*(1102), 1–9.

Helsinki Times. (2016). *Nationwide sex survey finds increase in masturbation, decrease in sex*. http://www.helsinkitimes.fi/finland/finland-news/domestic/14163-nationwide-sex-survey-finds-increase-in-masturbation-decrease-in-sex.html. Retrieved 25 July 2020.

Henseler, H., & de Wolf, R. (2019). Sweetie 2.0 technology: Technical challenges of making the sweetie 2.0 Chatbot. In *Sweetie 2.0* (pp. 113–134). The Hague: TMC Asser Press.

Herbenick, D., Fu, T.-C., Wright, P., Paul, B., Gradus, R., Bauer, J., & Jones, R. (2020). Diverse sexual behaviors and pornography use: Findings from a nationally representative probability survey of Americans aged 14 to 60 years. *The Journal of Sexual Medicine*, 1–11. https://doi.org/10.1016/j.jsxm.2020.01.013.

Herrero, R., Mira, A., Cormo, G., Etchemendy, E., Baños, R., García-Palacios, A., … Botella, C. (2019). An internet based intervention for improving resilience and coping strategies in university students: Study protocol for a randomized controlled trial. *Internet Interventions*, *16*, 43–51. https://doi.org/10.1016/j.invent.2018.03.005.

Hook, J. N., Reid, R. C., Penberthy, J. K., Davis, D. E., & Jennings, D. J. (2014). Methodological review of treatments for nonparaphilic hypersexual behavior. *Journal of Sex and Marital Therapy*, *40*(4), 294–308. https://doi.org/10.1080/0092623X.2012.751075.

Huffington Post. (2013). *Robot sex poll reveals Americans' attitudes about robotic lovers, servants, soldiers*. https://www.huffingtonpost.com/2013/04/10/robot-sex-poll-americans-robotic-lovers-servants-soldiers_n_3037918.html. Retrieved 25 July 2020.

Hughes, D. M. (2002). The use of new communications and information technologies for sexual exploitation of women and children. *Hastings Women's Law Journal*, *13*, 127.

Hughes, D. M. (2004). Prostitution online. *Journal of Trauma Practice*, *2*(3–4), 115–131.

Jaffrey, P. (2015). Next mega tech theme is virtual reality. Piper Jaffray Investment Research (Ed.) In *Guides for the journey*. Minneapolis (US).

Jones, A. (2016). "I get paid to have orgasms": Adult webcam models' negotiation of pleasure and danger. *Signs: Journal of Women in Culture and Society*, *42*(1), 227–256.

Jones, S., & Fox, S. (2009). *Generations online in 2009*. Pew Research Center. https://www.pewinternet.org/2009/01/28/generations-online-in-2009/.

Kafka, M. P. (2010). Hypersexual disorder: A proposed diagnosis for DSM-V. *Archives of Sexual Behavior*, *39*(2), 377–400. https://doi.org/10.1007/s10508-009-9574-7.

Kafka, M. P., & Hennen, J. (2002). A DSM-IV axis I comorbidity study of males (n = 120) with paraphilias and paraphilia-related disorders. *Sexual Abuse: A Journal of Research and Treatment*, *14*(4), 349–366. https://doi.org/10.1177/107906320201400405.

Kafka, M. P., & Prentky, R. (1992). Fluoxetine treatment of nonparaphilic sexual addictions and paraphilias in men. *The Journal of Clinical Psychiatry*, *53*(10), 351–358.

Kaplan, M. S., & Krueger, R. B. (2010). Diagnosis, assessment, and treatment of hypersexuality. *Journal of Sex Research*, *47*(2–3), 181–198. https://doi.org/10.1080/00224491003592863.

Kerr, J. S. (1996). Two myths of addiction: The addictive personality and the issue of free choice. *Human Psychopharmacology: Clinical and Experimental*, *11*(S1), S9–S13. https://doi.org/10.1002/(SICI)1099-1077(199602)11:1+<S9::AID-HUP747>3.0.CO;2-6.

Klaassen, M. J. E., & Peter, J. (2015). Gender (in)equality in internet pornography: A content analysis of popular pornographic internet videos. *The Journal of Sex Research*, *52*(7), 721–735. https://doi.org/10.1080/00224499.2014.976781.

Klein, V., Savaş, Ö., & Conley, T. D. (2021). How WEIRD and androcentric is sex research? Global inequities in study populations. *The Journal of Sex Research*, 1–8.

Kohut, T., Balzarini, R. N., Fisher, W. A., Grubbs, J. B., Campbell, L., & Prause, N. (2019). Surveying pornography use: A shaky science resting on poor measurement foundations. *Journal of Sex Research*, 1–21. https://doi.org/10.1080/00224499.2019.1695244.

Kohut, T., Fisher, W. A., & Campbell, L. (2017). Perceived effects of pornography on the couple relationship: Initial findings of open-ended, participant-informed, "bottom-up" research. *Archives of Sexual Behavior*, *46*(2), 585–602. https://doi.org/10.1007/s10508-016-0783-6.

Koops, B. J. (2009). Sex, kids, and crime in cyberspace: Some reflections on crossing boundaries. In A. R. Lodder, & A. Oskamp (Eds.), *Caught in the cyber crime act* Kluwer.

Koops, T., Dekker, A., & Briken, P. (2018). Online sexual activity involving webcams—An overview of existing literature and implications for sexual boundary violations of children and adolescents. *Behavioral Sciences & the Law*, *36*(2), 182–197.

Kowalewska, E., Grubbs, J. B., Potenza, M. N., Gola, M., Draps, M., & Kraus, S. W. (2018). Neurocognitive mechanisms in compulsive sexual behavior disorder. *Current Sexual Health Reports*, *10*(4), 255–264. https://doi.org/10.1007/s11930-018-0176-z.

Kraus, S. W., Krueger, R. B., Briken, P., First, M. B., Stein, D. J., Kaplan, M. S., … Reed, G. M. (2018). Compulsive sexual behaviour disorder in the ICD-11. *World Psychiatry*, *17*(1), 109–110. https://doi.org/10.1002/wps.20499.

Kraus, S. W., Potenza, M. N., Martino, S., & Grant, J. E. (2015). Examining the psychometric properties of the Yale-Brown obsessive-compulsive scale in a sample of compulsive pornography users. *Comprehensive Psychiatry*, *59*, 117–122. https://doi.org/10.1016/j.comppsych.2015.02.007.

Kraus, S. W., & Sweeney, P. J. (2019). Hitting the target: Considerations for differential diagnosis when treating individuals for problematic use of pornography. *Archives of Sexual Behavior*, *48*(2), 431–435.

Kraus, S. W., Voon, V., & Potenza, M. N. (2016a). Additional challenges and issuesin classifying compulsive sexual behavior as an addiction. *Journal of Sex Research*, *111*(9), 181–198.

Kraus, S. W., Voon, V., & Potenza, M. N. (2016b). Should compulsive sexual behavior be considered an addiction? *Addiction*, *111*(12), 2097–2106. https://doi.org/10.1111/add.13297.

Kühn, S., & Gallinat, J. (2014). Brain structure and functional connectivity associated with pornography consumption: The brain on porn. *JAMA Psychiatry*, *71*(7), 827–834.

Laier, C., & Brand, M. (2014). Empirical evidence and theoretical considerations on factors contributing to cybersex addiction from a cognitive-behavioral view. *Sexual Addiction & Compulsivity*, *21*(4), 305–321.

Landripet, I., & Štulhofer, A. (2015). Is pornography use associated with sexual difficulties and dysfunctions among younger heterosexual men? *The Journal of Sexual Medicine*, *12*(5), 1136–1139. https://doi.org/10.1111/jsm.12853.

Levine, D. T., & Stekel, D. J. (2016). So why have you added me? Adolescent girls' technology mediated attachments and relationships. *Computers in Human Behavior*, *63*, 25–34. https://doi.org/10.1016/j.chb.2016.05.011.

Lewczuk, K., Glica, A., Nowakowska, I., Gola, M., & Grubbs, J. B. (2020). Evaluating pornography problems due to moral incongruence model. *The Journal of Sexual Medicine*, *17*(2), 300–311. https://doi.org/10.1016/j.jsxm.2019.11.259.

Lewczuk, K., Szmyd, J., Skorko, M., & Gola, M. (2017). Treatment seeking for problematic pornography use among women. *Journal of Behavioral Addictions*, *6*(4), 445–456. https://doi.org/10.1556/2006.6.2017.063.

Lewczuk, K., Wojcik, A., & Gola, M. (2019). *Increase in the prevalence of online pornography use—Objective data analysis from the period between 2004 and 2016 in Poland* (pp. 1–45). https://doi.org/10.31234/osf.io/tmn4r.

Lewis, M., Weber, R., & Bowman, N. (2008). "They may be pixels, but they're MY pixels": Developing a metric of character attachment in role-playing video games. *Cyberpsychology & Behavior*, *11*(4), 515–518. https://doi.org/10.1089/cpb.2007.0137.

Livingstone, S., Haddon, L., Görzig, A., & Ólafsson, K. (2011). *Risks and safety on the internet: The perspective of European children. Full findings*. LSE, London: EU Kids Online.

Lobe, B., Livingstone, S., Ólafsson, K., & Vodeb, H. (2011). *Cross-national comparison of risks and safety on the internet: Initial analysis from the EU kids online survey of European children*.

Luder, M.-T., Pittet, I., Berchtold, A., Akré, C., Michaud, P.-A., & Surís, J.-C. (2011). Associations between online pornography and sexual behavior among adolescents: Myth or reality? *Archives of Sexual Behavior*, *40*(5), 1027–1035.

Madigan, S., Villani, V., Azzopardi, C., Laut, D., Smith, T., Temple, J. R., … Dimitropoulos, G. (2018). The prevalence of unwanted online sexual exposure and solicitation among youth: A meta-analysis. *Journal of Adolescent Health*, *63*(2), 133–141.

Maraz, A., Király, O., & Demetrovics, Z. (2015). Commentary on: Are we overpathologizing everyday life? A tenable blueprint for behavioral addiction research. *Journal of Behavioral Addictions*, *4*(3), 151–154. https://doi.org/10.1556/2006.4.2015.026.

Marshall, L. E., & Briken, P. (2010). Assessment, diagnosis, and management of hypersexual disorders. *Current Opinion in Psychiatry*, *23*(6), 570–573. https://doi.org/10.1097/YCO.0b013e32833d15d1.

Matthews, H. (2018). 27 online dating statistics and what they mean for the future of dating. *Dating News*. https://www.datingnews.com/industry-trends/online-dating-statistics-what-they-mean-for-future/.

McArthur, N., & Twist, M. L. (2017). The rise of digisexuality: Therapeutic challenges and possibilities. *Sexual and Relationship Therapy*, *32*(3–4), 334–344.

Mercer, C. H., Tanton, C., Prah, P., Erens, B., Sonnenberg, P., Clifton, S., … Johnson, A. M. (2013). Changes in sexual attitudes and lifestyles in Britain through the life course and over time: Findings from the National Surveys of Sexual Attitudes and Lifestyles (Natsal). *Lancet*, *382*(9907), 1781–1794. https://doi.org/10.1016/S0140-6736(13)62035-8.

Miner, M. H., Raymond, N., Mueller, B. A., Lloyd, M., & Lim, K. O. (2009). Preliminary investigation of the impulsive and neuroanatomical characteristics of compulsive sexual behavior. *Psychiatry Research: Neuroimaging*, *174*(2), 146–151.

Mitchell, K. J., Finkelhor, D., & Wolak, J. (2001). Risk factors for and impact of online sexual solicitation of youth. *JAMA*, *285*(23), 3011–3014.

Montgomery-Graham, S. (2017). Conceptualization and assessment of hypersexual disorder: A systematic review of the literature. *Sexual Medicine Reviews*, *5*(2), 146–162. https://doi.org/10.1016/j.sxmr.2016.11.001.

Muusses, L. D., Kerkhof, P., & Finkenauer, C. (2015). Internet pornography and relationship quality: A longitudinal study of within and between partner effects of adjustment, sexual satisfaction and sexually explicit internet material among newly-weds. *Computers in Human Behavior*, *45*(February 2016), 77–84. https://doi.org/10.1016/j.chb.2014.11.077.

Nelson, K. M., & Rothman, E. F. (2020). Should public health professionals consider pornography a public health crisis? *American Journal of Public Health*, *110*(2), 151–153.

Neustaedter, C., & Greenberg, S. (2012). Intimacy in long-distance relationships over video chat. In *Proceedings of the SIGCHI conference on human factors in computing systems* (pp. 753–762). New York, NY: ACM.

New York Post. (2018). *Police shut down sex robot brothel two weeks after it opened*. https://nypost.com/2018/09/14/police-shut-down-sex-robot-brothel-two-weeks-after-it-opened/. Retrieved 25 July 2020.

Orel, M. (2020). Escaping reality and touring for pleasure: The future of virtual reality pornography. *Porn Studies*, 1–5.

Orosz, G., Benyo, M., Berkes, B., Nikoletti, E., Gál, É., Tóth-Király, I., & Bőthe, B. (2018). The personality, motivational, and need-based background of problematic tinder use. *Journal of Behavioral Addictions*, *7*(2), 301–316. https://doi.org/10.1556/2006.7.2018.21.

Owens, E. W., Behun, R. J., Manning, J. C., & Reid, R. C. (2012). The impact of internet pornography on adolescents: A review of the research. *Sexual Addiction and Compulsivity*, *19*(1–2), 99–122.

Peeters, A., & Haselager, P. (2019). Designing virtuous sex robots. *International Journal of Social Robotics*, 1–12.

Peter, J., & Valkenburg, P. M. (2016). Adolescents and pornography: A review of 20 years of research. *Journal of Sex Research*, *53*(4–5), 509–531.

Pizzol, D., Bertoldo, A., & Foresta, C. (2016). Adolescents and web porn: A new era of sexuality. *International Journal of Adolescent Medicine and Health*, *28*(2), 169–173. https://doi.org/10.1515/ijamh-2015-0003.

Pornhub.com. (2019). *The 2019 year in review*. https://www.pornhub.com/insights/2019-year-in-review.

Potenza, M. N., Gola, M., Voon, V., Kor, A., & Kraus, S. W. (2017). Is excessive sexual behaviour an addictive disorder? *Lancet Psychiatry*, *4*(9), 663–664. https://doi.org/10.1016/S2215-0366(17)30316-4.

Prause, N., Janssen, E., Georgiadis, J., Finn, P., & Pfaus, J. (2017). Data do not support sex as addictive. *The Lancet Psychiatry*, *4*(12), 899. https://doi.org/10.1016/S2215-0366(17)30441-8.

Prause, N., & Pfaus, J. (2015). Viewing sexual stimuli associated with greater sexual responsiveness, not erectile dysfunction. *Sexual Medicine*, *3*(2), 90–98. https://doi.org/10.1002/sm2.58.

Price, J., Patterson, R., Regnerus, M., & Walley, J. (2016). How much more XXX is generation X consuming? Evidence of changing attitudes and behaviors related to pornography since 1973. *Journal of Sex Research*, *53*(1), 12–20. https://doi.org/10.1080/00224499.2014.1003773.

Raymond, N. C., Coleman, E., & Miner, M. H. (2003). Psychiatric comorbidity and compulsive/impulsive traits in compulsive sexual behavior. *Comprehensive Psychiatry*, *44*(5), 370–380. https://doi.org/10.1016/S0010-440X(03)00110-X.

Reed, E., Salazar, M., Behar, A. I., Agah, N., Silverman, J. G., Minnis, A. M., … Raj, A. (2019). Cyber sexual harassment: Prevalence and association with substance use, poor mental health, and STI history among sexually active adolescent girls. *Journal of Adolescence*, *75*, 53–62.

Reid, R. C. (2007). Assessing readiness to change among clients seeking help for hypersexual behavior. *Sexual Addiction and Compulsivity*, *14*(3), 167–186. https://doi.org/10.1080/10720160701480204.

Reid, R. C., Carpenter, B. N., Gilliland, R., & Karim, R. (2011). Problems of self-concept in a patient sample of hypersexual men with attention-deficit disorder. *Journal of Addiction Medicine*, *5*(2), 134–140. https://doi.org/10.1097/ADM.0b013e3181e6ad32.

Reid, R. C., Carpenter, B. N., Hook, J. N., Garos, S., Manning, J. C., Gilliland, R., … Fong, T. (2012). Report of findings in a DSM-5 field trial for hypersexual disorder. *The Journal of Sexual Medicine*, *9*(11), 2868–2877. https://doi.org/10.1111/j.1743-6109.2012.02936.x.

Reid, R. C., Davtian, M., Lenartowicz, A., Torrevillas, R. M., & Fong, T. W. (2013). Perspectives on the assessment and treatment of adult ADHD in hypersexual men. *Neuropsychiatry*, *3*(3), 295–308. https://doi.org/10.2217/npy.13.31.

Reid, R. C., Li, D. S., Gilliland, R., Stein, J. A., & Fong, T. (2011). Reliability, validity, and psychometric development of the pornography consumption inventory in a sample of hypersexual men. *Journal of Sex and Marital Therapy*, *37*(5), 359–385.

Rheingold, H. (1990). Teledildonics—Reach out and touch someone. In D. D. Waskul (Ed.), *Net.SeXXX. Readings on Sex, Pornography, and the Internet* (pp. 319–322). Peter Lang (2004).

Richardson, K. (2015). The asymmetrical 'relationship': Parallels between prostitution and the development of sex robots. *Computers & Society*, *45*(3), 290–293.

Rissel, C., Richters, J., de Visser, R. O., McKee, A., Yeung, A., & Caruana, T. (2017). A profile of pornography users in Australia: Findings from the second Australian study of health and relationships. *Journal of Sex Research*, *54*(2), 227–240.

Rooke, S., Copeland, J., Norberg, M., Hine, D., & McCambridge, J. (2013). Effectiveness of a self-guided web-based cannabis treatment program: Randomized controlled trial. *Journal of Medical Internet Research*, *15*(2). https://doi.org/10.2196/jmir.2256, e26.

Savard, J., Öberg, K. G., Chatzittofis, A., Dhejne, C., Arver, S., & Jokinen, J. (2020). Naltrexone in compulsive sexual behavior disorder: A feasibility study of twenty men. *The Journal of Sexual Medicine*.

Scanavino, M. D. T., Ventuneac, A., Helena, C., Abdo, N., Tavares, H., Amaral, M. L., … Parsons, J. T. (2013). Compulsive sexual behavior and psychopathology among treatment-seeking men in Sao Paulo, Brazil. *The Journal of Sexual Medicine*, *10*, 310. https://doi.org/10.1016/j.psychres.2013.01.021.

Schaub, M. P., Blankers, M., Lehr, D., Boss, L., Riper, H., Dekker, J., … Ebert, D. D. (2016). Efficacy of an internet-based self-help intervention to reduce co-occurring alcohol misuse and depression symptoms in adults: Study protocol of a three-arm randomised controlled trial. *BMJ Open*, *6*(5). https://doi.org/10.1136/bmjopen-2016-011457, e011457.

Schaub, M. P., Wenger, A., Berg, O., Beck, T., Stark, L., Buehler, E., & Haug, S. (2015). A web-based self-help intervention with and without chat counseling to reduce cannabis use in problematic cannabis users: Three-arm randomized controlled trial. *Journal of Medical Internet Research*, *17*(10). https://doi.org/10.2196/jmir.4860, e232.

Scheutz, M., Arnold, T., & 11th Annual ACM/IEEE International Conference on Human-Robot Interaction. (2016). Are we ready for sex robots? In *ACM/IEEE international conference on human-robot interaction* (pp. 351–358).

Schmidt, C., Morris, L. S., Kvamme, T. L., Hall, P., Birchard, T., & Voon, V. (2017). Compulsive sexual behavior: Prefrontal and limbic volume and interactions. *Human Brain Mapping*, *38*(3), 1182–1190.

Schrok, A. R. (2015). Communicative affordances of mobile media: Portability, availability, locatability, and multimediality. *International Journal of Communication*, *9*, 1229–1246. https://ijoc.org/index.php/ijoc/article/view/3288.

Schulz, A., Bergen, E., Schuhmann, P., & Hoyer, J. (2017). Social anxiety and loneliness in adults who solicit minors online. *Sexual Abuse*, *29*(6), 519–540.

Schulz, A., Bergen, E., Schuhmann, P., Hoyer, J., & Santtila, P. (2016). Online sexual solicitation of minors: How often and between whom does it occur? *Journal of Research in Crime and Delinquency*, *53*(2), 165–188.

Seok, J. W., & Sohn, J. H. (2015). Neural substrates of sexual desire in individuals with problematic hypersexual behavior. *Frontiers in Behavioral Neuroscience*, *9*, 321.

Seok, J. W., & Sohn, J. H. (2018). Gray matter deficits and altered resting-state connectivity in the superior temporal gyrus among individuals with problematic hypersexual behavior. *Brain Research*, *1684*, 30–39.

Sharkey, N. (2008). The ethical frontiers of robotics. *Science*, *322*(5909), 1800–1801.

Sharkey, N., van Wynsberghe, A., Robbins, S., & Hancock, E. (2017). *Our sexual future with robots*. (A foundation for responsible robotics consultation report).

Shaughnessy, K., Byers, E. S., & Walsh, L. (2011). Online sexual activity experience of heterosexual students: Gender similarities and differences. *Archives of Sexual Behavior*, *40*(2), 419–427.

Shaughnessy, K., Byers, S., & Thornton, S. J. (2011). What is cybersex? Heterosexual students' definitions. *International Journal of Sexual Health*, *23*(2), 79–89.

Simon, S. C., & Greitemeyer, T. (2019). The impact of immersion on the perception of pornography: A virtual reality study. *Computers in Human Behavior*, *93*, 141–148.

Sinković, M., Štulhofer, A., & Božić, J. (2013). Revisiting the association between pornography use and risky sexual behaviors: The role of early exposure to pornography and sexual sensation seeking. *Journal of Sex Research*, *50*(7), 633–641. https://doi.org/10.1080/0022 4499.2012.681403.

Sklenarova, H., Schulz, A., Schuhmann, P., Osterheider, M., & Neutze, J. (2018). Online sexual solicitation by adults and peers—Results from a population based German sample. *Child Abuse & Neglect*, *76*, 225–236.

Sniewski, L., Farvid, P., & Carter, P. (2018). The assessment and treatment of adult heterosexual men with self-perceived problematic pornography use: A review. *Addictive Behaviors*, *77*, 217–224. https://doi.org/10.1016/j.addbeh.2017.10.010.

Stark, R., Klucken, T., Potenza, M. N., Brand, M., & Strahler, J. (2018). A current understanding of the behavioral neuroscience of compulsive sexual behavior disorder and problematic pornography use. *Current Behavioral Neuroscience Reports*, *5*(4), 218–231.

Stewart, H., & Fedoroff, J. P. (2014). Assessment and treatment of sexual people with complaints of hypersexuality. *Current Sexual Health Reports*, *6*(2), 136–144. https://doi.org/10.1007/s11930-014-0017-7.

Streiner, D. L. (2003). Diagnosing tests: Using and misusing diagnostic and screening tests. *Journal of Personality Assessment*, *81*(3), 209–219. https://doi.org/10.1207/S15327752JPA8103_03.

Štulhofer, A., Bergeron, S., & Jurin, T. (2016). Is high sexual desire a risk for women's relationship and sexual well-being? *Journal of Sex Research*, *53*(7), 882–891. https://doi.org/10.1080/00224499.2015.1084984.

Štulhofer, A., Buško, V., & Landripet, I. (2010). Pornography, sexual socialization, and satisfaction among young men. *Archives of Sexual Behavior*, *39*(1), 168–178. https://doi.org/10.1007/s10508-008-9387-0.

Štulhofer, A., Jurin, T., & Briken, P. (2016). Is high sexual desire a facet of male hypersexuality? Results from an online study. *Journal of Sex and Marital Therapy*, *42*(8), 665–680. https://doi.org/10.1080/0092623X.2015.1113585.

Štulhofer, A., Rousseau, A., & Shekarchi, R. (2020). A two-wave assessment of the structure and stability of self-reported problematic pornography use among male croatian adolescents. *International Journal of Sexual Health*, 1–14. https://doi.org/10.1080/19317611.2020.1765940.

Svedin, C. G., Åkerman, I., & Priebe, G. (2011). Frequent users of pornography. A population based epidemiological study of Swedish male adolescents. *Journal of Adolescence*, *34*(4), 779–788. https://doi.org/10.1016/j.adolescence.2010.04.010.

Tanaka, F., Cicourel, A., & Movellan, J. R. (2007). Socialization between toddlers and robots at an early childhood education center. *Proceedings of the National Academy of Sciences*, *104*(46), 17954–17958.

The Atlantic. (2016). *Can child dolls keep pedophiles from offending?*. https://www.theatlantic.com/health/archive/2016/01/can-child-dolls-keep-pedophiles-from-offending/423324/. Retrieved 25 July 2020.

The Guardian. (2017). *Chinese man 'marries' robot he built himself.* https://www.theguardian.com/world/2017/apr/04/chinese-man-marries-robot-built-himself. Retrieved 25 July 2020.

The Sun. (2018). *Russia's first sex robot brothel opens in Moscow offering dolls with heated privates who'll 'talk dirty' and 'moan with pleasure'.* https://www.thesun.co.uk/news/7412317/russias-first-sex-robot-brothel-opens-in-moscow-offering-dolls-with-heated-privates-wholl-talk-dirty-and-moan-with-pleasure. Retrieved 25 July 2020.

Thibaut, F., Cosyns, P., Fedoroff, J. P., Briken, P., Goethals, K., Bradford, J. M., & WFSBP Task Force on Paraphilias. (2020). The World Federation of Societies of Biological Psychiatry (WFSBP) 2020 guidelines for the pharmacological treatment of paraphilic disorders. *The World Journal of Biological Psychiatry*, 1–79.

Træen, B., Spitznogle, K., & Beverfjord, A. (2004). Attitudes and use of pornography in the Norwegian population 2002. *Journal of Sex Research*, *41*(2), 193–200. https://doi.org/10.1080/00224490409552227.

Vaillancourt-Morel, M.-P., Daspe, M.-È., Charbonneau-Lefebvre, V., Bosisio, M., & Bergeron, S. (2019). Pornography use in adult mixed-sex romantic relationships: Context and correlates. *Current Sexual Health Reports*, *11*(1), 35–43. https://doi.org/10.1007/s11930-019-00190-2.

Vaillancourt-Morel, M. P., Godbout, N., Labadie, C., Runtz, M., Lussier, Y., & Sabourin, S. (2015). Avoidant and compulsive sexual behaviors in male and female survivors of childhood sexual abuse. *Child Abuse & Neglect*, *40*, 48–59.

Vaillancourt-Morel, M.-P., Rosen, N. O., Willoughby, B. J., Leonhardt, N. D., & Bergeron, S. (2020). Pornography use and romantic relationships: A dyadic daily diary study. *Journal of Social and Personal Relationships*, *37*(10–11), 2802–2821.

Vannier, S. A., Currie, A. B., & O'Sullivan, L. F. (2014). Schoolgirls and soccer moms: A content analysis of free "teen" and "MILF" online pornography. *The Journal of Sex Research*, *51*(3), 253–264. https://doi.org/10.1080/00224499.2013.829795.

Varfi, N., Rothen, S., Jasiowka, K., Lepers, T., Bianchi-Demicheli, F., & Khazaal, Y. (2019). Sexual desire, mood, attachment style, impulsivity, and self-esteem as predictive factors for addictive cybersex. *JMIR Mental Health*, *6*(1), e9978.

von Franqué, F., Klein, V., & Briken, P. (2015). Which techniques are used in psychotherapeutic interventions for nonparaphilic hypersexual behavior? *Sexual Medicine Reviews*, *3*(1), 3–10. https://doi.org/10.1002/smrj.34.

Voon, V., Mole, T. B., Banca, P., Porter, L., Morris, L., Mitchell, S., … Irvine, M. (2014). Neural correlates of sexual cue reactivity in individuals with and without compulsive sexual behaviours. *PLoS ONE*, *9*(7), e102419.

Wainberg, M. L., Muench, F., Morgenstern, J., Hollander, E., Irwin, T. W., Parsons, J. T., … O'Leary, A. (2006). A double-blind study of citalopram versus placebo in the treatment of compulsive sexual behaviors in gay and bisexual men. *The Journal of Clinical Psychiatry*, *67*(12), 1968–1973. https://doi.org/10.4088/JCP.v67n1218.

Weisel, K., Lehr, D., Heber, E., Zarski, A. C., Berking, M., Riper, H., & Ebert, D. D. (2018). Severely burdened individuals do not need to be excluded from internet-based and mobile-based stress management: Effect modifiers of treatment outcomes from three randomized controlled trials. *Journal of Medical Internet Research*, *20*(6). https://doi.org/10.2196/jmir.9387.

Wells, M., & Mitchell, K. J. (2007). Youth sexual exploitation on the internet: DSM-IV diagnoses and gender differences in co-occurring mental health issues. *Child and Adolescent Social Work Journal*, *24*(3), 235–260.

Wéry, A., & Billieux, J. (2016). Online sexual activities: An exploratory study of problematic and non-problematic usage patterns in a sample of men. *Computers in Human Behavior*, *56*, 257–266.

Wéry, A., & Billieux, J. (2017). Problematic cybersex: Conceptualization, assessment, and treatment. *Addictive Behaviors*, *64*, 238–246. https://doi.org/10.1016/j.addbeh.2015.11.007.

Wéry, A., Vogelaere, K., Challet-Bouju, G., Poudat, F.-X., Caillon, J., Lever, D., … Grall-Bronnec, M. (2016). Characteristics of self-identified sexual addicts in a behavioral addiction outpatient clinic. *Journal of Behavioral Addictions*, *5*(4), 623–630. https://doi.org/10.1556/2006.5.2016.071.

Willoughby, B. J., Busby, D. M., & Young-Petersen, B. (2019). Understanding associations between personal definitions of pornography, using pornography, and depression. *Sexuality Research & Social Policy*, *16*(3), 342–356. https://doi.org/10.1007/s13178-018-0345-x.

Willoughby, B. J., Carroll, J. S., Busby, D. M., & Brown, C. C. (2016). Differences in pornography use among couples: Associations with satisfaction, stability, and relationship processes. *Archives of Sexual Behavior*, *45*(1), 145–158. https://doi.org/10.1007/s10508-015-0562-9.

Willoughby, B. J., Carroll, J. S., Nelson, L. J., & Padilla-Walker, L. M. (2014). Associations between relational sexual behaviour, pornography use, and pornography acceptance among US college students. *Culture, Health and Sexuality*, *16*(9), 1052–1069. https://doi.org/10.1080/13691058.2014.927075.

Willoughby, B. J., & Leonhardt, N. D. (2020). Behind closed doors: Individual and joint pornography use among romantic couples. *Journal of Sex Research*, *57*(1), 77–91. https://doi.org/10.1080/00224499.2018.1541440.

Wired. (2018). *Coming attractions: The rise of VR porn*. https://www.wired.com/story/coming-attractions-the-rise-of-vr-porn/. Retrieved 25 July 2020.

Wolak, J., Mitchell, K., & Finkelhor, D. (2007). Unwanted and wanted exposure to online pornography in a national sample of youth internet users. *Pediatrics*, *119*(2), 247–257. https://
doi.org/10.1542/peds.2006-1891.

Wolak, J., Mitchell, K. J., & Finkelhor, D. (2006). *Online victimization of youth: Five years
later*. Alexandria, VA: National Center for Missing and Exploited Children. http://www.
unh.edu/ccrc/pdf/CV138.pdf.

World Health Organization. (2019). *International statistical classification of diseases and related health problems* (11th ed.).

Wright, P. J., Tokunaga, R. S., Kraus, A., & Klann, E. (2017). Pornography consumption and
satisfaction: A meta-analysis. *Human Communication Research*, *43*(3), 315–343. https://
doi.org/10.1111/hcre.12108.

Youth Risk Behavior Survey. (2015). *Trends in the prevalence of sexual behaviors and HIV
testing national YRBS: 1991–2015*. Retrieved 24 November 2018.

Yucel, D., & Gassanov, M. A. (2010). Exploring actor and partner correlates of sexual satisfaction among married couples. *Social Science Research*, *39*(5), 725–738. https://doi.
org/10.1016/j.ssresearch.2009.09.002.

Žižek, S. (1996). Sex in the age of virtual reality. *Science as Culture*, *5*(4), 506–525.

Zlot, Y., Goldstein, M., Cohen, K., & Weinstein, A. (2018). Online dating is associated with sex
addiction and social anxiety. *Journal of Behavioral Addictions*, *7*(3), 821–826. https://doi.
org/10.1556/2006.7.2018.66.

Developmental aspects (including cyberbullying)

Gemma Mestre-Bach[a], Fernando Fernández-Aranda[b,c,d], Susana Jiménez-Murcia[b,c,d], and Marc N. Potenza[e,f,g,h,i,j]

[a]Universidad Internacional de La Rioja, Logroño, La Rioja, Spain, [b]Department of Psychiatry, Bellvitge University Hospital-IDIBELL, Barcelona, Spain, [c]Ciber Fisiopatología Obesidad y Nutrición (CIBERObn), Instituto de Salud Carlos III, Madrid, Spain, [d]Department of Clinical Sciences, School of Medicine, University of Barcelona, Barcelona, Spain, [e]Department of Psychiatry, Yale University School of Medicine, New Haven, CT, United States, [f]Department of Neuroscience, Yale University School of Medicine, New Haven, CT, United States, [g]Yale Child Study Center, Yale University School of Medicine, New Haven, CT, United States, [h]Connecticut Mental Health Center, New Haven, CT, United States, [i]Connecticut Council on Problem Gambling, Wethersfield, CT, United States, [j]Wu Tsai Institute, Yale University, New Haven, CT, United States

Introduction

According to the self-regulation theories, the use of the Internet may satisfy the needs of autonomy, competence, and relatedness (Barnes & Pressey, 2011). In addition, the Internet allows individuals to be exposed to social interactions in a relatively controlled manner (El Asam, Samara, & Terry, 2019). Internet use differs across age groups (Seifert & Schelling, 2016), with adolescents and young adults often being highly involved.

Regarding problematic Internet use, it may begin early in life and manifest in particular ways during adolescence and early adulthood (Jelenchick & Christakis, 2014; Rial Boubeta, Gómez Salgado, Isorna Folgar, Araujo Gallego, & Varela Mallou, 2015). This chapter attempts, therefore, to provide an overview of Internet use and problematic Internet use from a developmental perspective, focusing mostly on behavioral development and neurodevelopment associated with common online behaviors.

Behavioral development

Social networking

Conceptualization

The use of interactive digital devices is increasing at the early stages of development, and media use rapidly evolves between childhood and adolescence (Coyne et al., 2017). In the specific case of social networks, in recent years they have become a

Mental Health in a Digital World. https://doi.org/10.1016/B978-0-12-822201-0.00007-1

powerful tool that facilitates immediate contact between individuals around the world (Roberts, Callahan, & O'leary, 2017). Numerous social networks additionally involve public exposure of their users' experiences and lifestyles (Shumaker, Loranger, & Dorie, 2017). More specifically, social networking sites have been defined as "virtual communities where users can create individual public profiles, interact with real-life friends, and meet other people based on shared interests" (Kuss & Griffiths, 2011).

Currently, there are numerous networks that have grown in popularity, such as Facebook, Instagram, Snapchat, WeChat, and Tik Tok, and individuals at different developmental stages have different preferences. For example, adolescents currently show a greater interest in Snapchat, possibly because its ephemeral nature (messages are automatically deleted in short periods of time) generates a perception of security (Kuss & Griffiths, 2017). Nowadays, adolescents appear to be more aware, therefore, of potential risks associated with their own privacy, and at the same time seem to desire greater control over audiences for their messages on these networks (Kuss & Griffiths, 2017).

Prevalence

A total of 2.34 billion social network users were reported in 2016 worldwide (Kuss & Griffiths, 2017). However, regarding problematic use of social networking, some studies have reported that 4.5% of adolescents could be considered at risk (Bányai et al., 2017). Relatedly, among young adults, it has been reported that 29.5% may exhibit problematic social networking use (Tang & Koh, 2017). However, it should be noted that these prevalence estimates may vary widely given means of assessment and other factors, and may change over time with changes in social network access and use within and across countries and cultures.

Motives

Social network applications are often used more frequently in adolescence (relative to childhood), and use may be related to important aspects of human psychosocial development (Eckstrand et al., 2017; Hussong et al., 2018; Jacobs et al., 2017). Adolescence is a critical period both at individual and social levels, and individuals at this life stage are expected to develop mechanisms to face possible difficulties that may be encountered as adults (Meeus, 2016). During adolescence, the development of one's identity and self-esteem, relationships with parents and interactions with peers contribute importantly to the use of social networks (Gittins & Hunt, 2019; King, McLaughlin, Silk, & Monahan, 2018; Sherman, Payton, Hernandez, Greenfield, & Dapretto, 2016; Smink et al., 2018).

In reference to personal identity development, previous studies have reported that some advantages of social networks for adolescents include promotion of self-esteem, exploration of one's own identity and self-disclosure (Best, Manktelow, & Taylor, 2014; Uhls, Ellison, & Subrahmanyam, 2017). Some authors claim that showing preferences online and openly and trying to manage the impression they give to viewers could help adolescents discover themselves and develop their self-concepts (Bartsch & Subrahmanyam, 2015; Fullwood, James, & Chen-Wilson, 2016).

Social networks also may become a tool that facilitates adolescent searches for autonomy (Uhls et al., 2017). They, therefore, may provide an environment in which many adolescents may perceive that they have more complete control, without parental supervision (Shehu & Zhurda, 2017). Indeed, most social networks set a minimum age of 13, based on the Children's Online Privacy Protection Act (COPPA) (O'Keeffe, 2016). These sites assume that at this age adolescents have the developmental skills necessary to understand and manage the content to which they may be exposed (O'Keeffe, 2016). Understanding how parenting influences the use of social networks and vice versa is essential to understanding adolescent development (Lauricella, Wartella, & Rideout, 2015). Along this line, it has been suggested that adolescents who have had more contact with their parents on social networks may show lower levels of delinquency and emotional problems (Coyne, Padilla-Walker, Day, Harper, & Stockdale, 2014). Parental supervision of an adolescent's online world may be, therefore, adaptive for them (Barry, Sidoti, Briggs, Reiter, & Lindsey, 2017), although research in this line is limited.

For many, identity is also partially built with social approval derived from publishing content on social networks, which in turn is generating social changes with respect to privacy considerations (Nardis & Panek, 2019). The social component of social networks enhances the need for belonging and for popularity, and these may be particularly salient and potentially adaptive during adolescence (Barry et al., 2017). Another motivation that for using social networks is a "fear of missing out" (Kuss & Griffiths, 2017). This phenomenon has been described as "a pervasive apprehension that others might be having rewarding experiences from which one is absent" and has been associated with, among other factors, greater involvement in social networks (Przybylski, Murayama, Dehaan, & Gladwell, 2013). Moreover, other psychological mechanisms such as social comparison, self-disclosure, and impression management have been also related to the use of social networks among adolescents (Uhls et al., 2017).

Studies on social networking in adulthood have mostly focused on young adults. In emerging adulthood, corresponding roughly to the period between 18 and 25 years, individuals experience identity uncertainty and tend to experiment with diverse identities in different social contexts (Arnett, 2005). Therefore, social networks have become an essential tool by allowing individuals at this stage to take a more active role in creating their experience and shaping their online identity (Bartsch & Subrahmanyam, 2015; Subrahmanyam & Šmahel, 2011). Additionally, young people are establishing or breaking relationships online and may be frequently transforming social and cultural norms in online environments (Michikyan & Suárez-Orozco, 2015).

In the case of individuals over 60 years, many use the Internet, and it allows them to access information, as well as contact with family, friends, and caregivers even if geographically distant (Vroman, Arthanat, & Lysack, 2015). Such contact may promote social participation and positive attitudes and decrease mental problems (Afsar, 2013; Yuan, 2020). However, when studying the use of social networks, limitations of this developmental stage should be considered. For example, experiencing impairments, both physical and mental, may impact skills required for social contact, which could lead individuals to become isolated (Domènech-Abella, Mundó, Haro, & Rubio-Valera, 2019). In addition, individuals may exhibit disadvantageous behaviors (e.g., selfishness) when they experience loneliness, according to the Evolutionary Theory of Loneliness (ETL), so social relationships may be even more affected (Cacioppo & Cacioppo, 2018).

Consequences

While there are potential benefits of the use of social networks, their use during relatively early stages of life, including in middle and high school students, may accompany poor concentration and academic performance (Kuss & Griffiths, 2017; Sampasa-Kanyinga, Chaput, & Hamilton, 2019). In addition, adolescent use of social networking sites may promote unhealthy behaviors, such as substance use, lack of physical activity, and altered eating patterns (Sampasa-Kanyinga & Chaput, 2016a, 2016b). A worsening of sleep quality associated with the use of social networks, and especially with nighttime-specific social media use, has also been observed in adolescents (Woods & Scott, 2016).

In the case of young adults, when considering associations between social networks use and mental health, it has been reported that both the need to belong and the perceived conflicts with parents may be risk factors for the development of mental disorders associated with the use of social networks, while perceived social support may be a protective factor (Berryman, Ferguson, & Negy, 2018). Importantly, not all users of social networks develop problematic use. However, some young people may be particularly prone to problematic use and experiencing depression and anxiety, relating to, among other things, their engagement in attention-seeking behaviors, such as frequent status updates and checking for "likes" (Shensa, Sidani, Dew, Escobar-Viera, & Primack, 2018). In some adult populations, such as sexual minority men, a link has also been identified between social networks use, eating disorder symptomatology, and body dissatisfaction, with this association greater in the case of image-centric social media platforms (Griffiths, Murray, Krug, & McLean, 2018).

Apart from a worsening of mental health in adolescents and young adults, a deterioration of social skills in these populations has also been described with skills being sacrificed for a need to be "constantly connected" perhaps leading to poor sustained attentional capacities (Kuss & Griffiths, 2017).

Online sex: Sexting and online pornography

Exposure to online pornography and online sexual solicitation, both voluntarily and involuntarily, have also become emerging public health concerns, especially for adolescents and young adults (Chang et al., 2016).

Sexting and sex-related online behaviors

Conceptualization
There is still no fully agreed-upon conceptualization of sexting. The National Center for Missing and Exploited Children (2009) defined sexting as "writing sexually explicit messages, taking sexually explicit photos of themselves or others in their peer group, and transmitting those photos and/or messages to their peers by smartphone,

computer, video camera, digital camera, or video game." When considering sexting, Barrense-Dias, Surís, and Akre (2019) noted that most adolescents and young adults considered it as, "an activity that could be positive and respectful between two consenting persons."

One of the classifications that have been proposed is to divide sexting into consensual and nonconsensual forms. Consensual sexting may include both purely consensual sexting between two individuals of similar ages, and consensual but coerced sexting (with coercion eroding the notion of consensuality), which would be characterized by some pressure from one of the members. Nonconsensual sexting may include disseminated sexts without the consent of one of the members, sextortion (threats of dissemination), or teen sexts requested by an adult (Strasburger, Zimmerman, Temple, & Madigan, 2019).

Sexting is a behavior particularly studied in adolescents and young adults. It has been suggested that sexting in adolescence increases with age until early adulthood and progressively decreases when adult individuals have stable affective relationships (Mitchell, Finkelhor, Jones, & Wolak, 2012; Wysocki & Childers, 2011).

Prevalence

In terms of prevalence estimates, a review examining 18 studies found that between 0.9% and 27.6% of adolescents acknowledged having conducted sexting (Barrense-Dias, Berchtold, Surís, & Akre, 2017). This heterogeneity in the prevalences may reflect the lack of an agreed-upon definition of the construct. In addition, it should be taken into account that sexting may be underreported in younger populations (Barrense-Dias et al., 2017).

A meta-analysis of 39 studies focused on youth specified that 14.8% had sent a sext, 27.4% had received a sext, 12.0% had forwarded a sext without consent and 8.4% had a sext forwarded without consent (Madigan, Ly, Rash, Van Ouytsel, & Temple, 2018). In the case of adulthood, one study found that 53% of adults had sent sexts and 57% had received them (Klettke, Hallford, & Mellor, 2014). Among US veterans, 68.9% reported having sexted (Turban, Shirk, Potenza, Hoff, & Kraus, 2020).

Motives

The construction of one's own identity as an adolescent includes the exploration of sexuality (Davis, 2013), and new technologies have allowed online interactions of a sexual nature, such as sexting (Chalfen, 2009). Therefore, consensual sexting could be considered a development issue, especially relevant to adolescence (Strasburger et al., 2019). The sending of nonconsensual sexts among adolescent boys (13–17 years) have been linked to pornography and instrumental attitudes toward sex (that is, for excitement rather than intimacy) (van Oosten & Vandenbosch, 2020).

Differences in sexting have been identified according to the age of adolescents, with older adolescents being more likely to sext. This tendency may reflect biological changes (pubertal changes in late adolescence, which increase sexual interest and activity), psychological considerations (including the development of personality features), and social factors (including peer influences) (Barrense-Dias et al., 2017; Baumgartner, Sumter, Peter, Valkenburg, & Livingstone, 2014; Handschuh, La Cross,

& Smaldone, 2019; Kar, Choudhury, & Singh, 2015). Consequently, adolescents have greater tendencies to engage in risky sexual behaviors and to act impulsively often without adequately considering consequences (Chambers, Taylor, & Potenza, 2003), possibly making them less aware of potential risks of sexting (Strasburger et al., 2019).

With respect to adults, most studies have focused on young adults. Brodie, Wilson, and Scott (2019) reported that sexting in adults between 17 and 58 years within romantic relationships was mostly conducted to seek implicit or explicit reinforcement and by imitating friends, perceiving the behavior as normative and healthy within affective relationships. The authors also observed a reduction in sexting behavior as age increases and hypothesized that older adults might show generational differences with the use of new technologies, reductions in sexual behaviors, and/or more negative perceptions of their bodies, and these factors could limit sexting. In addition, other authors have suggested that such age differences may reflect older adults tending to be more risk averse and aware of possible negative consequences of sexting (Garcia et al., 2016).

Consequences

Sexting in adolescents and young adults may lead to different consequences, such as increased likelihood of being cyber-victimized, of being a cyberbullying victim, and of engaging in risky sexual behaviors (Benotsch, Snipes, Martin, & Bull, 2013; Reyns, Burek, Henson, & Fisher, 2013; Van Ouytsel, Lu, Ponnet, Walrave, & Temple, 2019). In addition, sexting can become an online version of offline forms of sexual coercion and may be a risk factor for dating violence (Choi, Van Ouytsel, & Temple, 2016; Morelli, Bianchi, Baiocco, Pezzuti, & Chirumbolo, 2016). Sexting has also been associated with experiences of unwanted sexting and pressure (Van Ouytsel, Punyanunt-Carter, Walrave, & Ponnet, 2020).

Regarding psychological distress, it has been observed that receiving unwanted sexts or experiencing sexting under coercion is associated with symptoms of anxiety and depression, as well as decreased self-esteem and increased alcohol use (Frankel, Bass, Patterson, Dai, & Brown, 2018; Klettke, Hallford, Clancy, Mellor, & Toumbourou, 2019). Other authors have also highlighted a significant association between suicidal ideation and sexting, cyber-victimization, and depressive symptomatology (Medrano, Lopez Rosales, & Gámez-Guadix, 2018). Possible legal consequences of sexting in which minors are involved should also be highlighted, since it may be considered as child pornography (Barrense-Dias et al., 2017).

Cybersex and online pornography use

Conceptualization

Sexually explicit potentially stimulating materials (such as films, video clips, photos, or books) are currently online both for a fee and free of charge (Döring, 2009). The perceived anonymity, affordability, and accessibility of these sexually explicit materials have made them increasingly available to people (Cooper, 1998). The Internet has also been used for sexual contacts, both in cyberspace (cybersex) and offline for "hookups" or other behaviors (Döring, 2009). However, there are some differences in definitions of online pornography and potential confusion between terms, and online pornography has been considered an element of cybersex for some authors and an independent element for others (Short, Black, Smith, Wetterneck, & Wells, 2012).

Prevalence

In the case of children and adolescents, the use of online pornography increases with age, with 1% of consumers reported in children aged 10–11 and 40% in male adolescents aged 16–17. In the case of girls, the use of pornography seems to start later, at 16–17 years of age, with a prevalence of 8% (Wolak, Mitchell, & Finkelhor, 2007). More recent data suggest that children and adolescents are showing increases in pornography viewing (Dwulit & Rzymski, 2019; Mattebo, Tydén, Häggström-Nordin, Nilsson, & Larsson, 2013) and such viewing may include harder-core ("gonzo") pornography and lead to copying of sexual acts and other concerning behaviors (Donevan & Mattebo, 2017; Mattebo, Tydén, Häggström-Nordin, Nilsson, & Larsson, 2016; Rothman & Adhia, 2015; Rothman, Kaczmarsky, Burke, Jansen, & Baughman, 2015). Adolescent pornography viewing has also been linked to poor body image, poorer family function, psychosomatic symptoms, and less positive youth development prospectively (Cranney, 2015; Mattebo, Tydén, Häggström-Nordin, Nilsson, & Larsson, 2018; Shek & Ma, 2012).

Among young adults, approximately 80% of university students have been exposed to pornography, with earlier age of onset linked to relational and sexual concerns (Dwulit & Rzymski, 2019). In another study, 78% of men reported performing cybersex at least once a month (Studer, Marmet, Wicki, & Gmel, 2019).

Motives

With regard to adolescents, multiple motives have been proposed that lead them to watch pornography online. Frequent reasons in this age group are, in addition to involuntary exposure to this sexual contents, sexual curiosity, the search for information about sex, and peer pressure (Braun-Courville & Rojas, 2009; Romito & Beltramini, 2011; Wallmyr & Welin, 2006).

In the case of adults, reasons for use of pornography may differ, with solitary masturbation for men being a main reason and for sexual relations with an affective partner for women (Bothe et al., 2020; Bridges & Morokoff, 2011), although other motivations exist. Adults may use pornography in attempts to reduce negative emotions such as stress, loneliness, and boredom, to make sex more interesting, or to excite the sexual partner (Foubert & Bridges, 2017). It has been suggested that cybersex is used as a maladaptive coping strategy involving escaping from negative emotions, as well as for social motives and enhancement (i.e., sexual gratification) (Doornwaard et al., 2017; Franc et al., 2018; Laier & Brand, 2014).

Consequences

The impact of online pornography use on teens and adults has been a matter of debate. Some authors have argued that exposure to pornography during adolescence is not related to risky sexual behaviors (Luder et al., 2011), although previous literature has highlighted an association between pornography and more permissive sexual norms, less progressive gender role attitudes, and sexual harassment perpetration (Brown & L'Engle, 2009). In addition, given that pornography content often contains violence toward and objectification of women (Bridges, Wosnitzer, Scharrer, Sun, & Liberman, 2010), may include racist themes (Fritz, Malic, Paul, & Zhou, 2020), and has genres related to incest and rape (Rothman et al., 2015), the impact on developing youth may be more substantial than is currently known.

In addition to potential impacts on sexual motivations, functioning, and behaviors, there is a growing understanding of problematic pornography use in both adolescents and adults (Brand, Blycker, & Potenza, 2019). In adolescents, an association between the frequency of pornography use, alcohol use, and diminished mental health has been reported (Svedin, Åkerman, & Priebe, 2011). Regarding young adults, similar findings have been observed. For example, links between frequent use of online pornography and problematic behaviors, such as gambling, gaming, and alcohol and cannabis use, have been described (Harper & Hodgins, 2016).

Other consequences that are beginning to be studied especially in adolescents and young adults are the nonconsensual pornography, also termed revenge pornography or cyber rape, a specific type of cyber-harassment (Kamal & Newman, 2016). With the development of online pornography, many couples have recorded their sexual activities. Although this may be done with the consent of both members and typically in the context of an intimate relationship, the materials can be disseminated by one member without the prior consent of the other, as a form of revenge or to obtain a profit (Recupero, 2016). If the victim's contact information is also displayed, as is often the case, the victim may receive harassment by strangers, both online and offline (Citron & Franks, 2014). In addition, it has been described that victims may experience significant psychological damage, such as anxiety, depression, or posttraumatic stress disorder (Bates, 2017).

Online gambling and gaming

The nature of gambling and gaming has undergone considerable transformations recently, especially after the arrival of the Internet. Both gambling and gaming have become relevant factors in the development and also public concerns (Ferguson, 2013; Lenhart & Project, 2008).

Online gambling

Conceptualization

Although many have considered gambling as an adult behavior, it often begins in childhood and adolescence, often with family members or peers (Derevensky & Gilbeau, 2015). Gambling may constitute a risk behavior that begins earlier than many other adolescent risk behaviors (Derevensky & Gilbeau, 2015). Some studies indicate that young individuals, and especially males, gamble frequently and may be at particular risk of developing problems with gambling behavior (Ricijas, Dodig Hundric, & Huic, 2016; Yau & Potenza, 2015). Gambling trends may change over time for different age groups. For example between 2007 and 2011, in the 18–24 age group, a reduction in regular gambling was observed, as well as an increase in occasional gambling, especially in women aged 18–24 and 45–54 years (Salonen, Alho, & Castrén, 2015).

Although there are numerous types of gambling, online gaming may provide perceived anonymity, rapid feedback, and accessibility at most times and places (Brevers, Sescousse, Maurage, & Billieux, 2019; Lelonek-Kuleta, Bartczuk, Wiechetek, Chwaszcz, & Niewiadomska, 2020). Therefore, the Internet may be used preferentially by adolescents and young adults, and individuals who gamble online are younger than those gambling offline (Estévez et al., 2017). While interest in online gambling may decrease with age (Lelonek-Kuleta et al., 2020), use of the Internet for gambling has also increased in men aged 55–64 years (Salonen, Alho, & Castrén, 2017).

In adolescence, gambling usually occurs with friends, and sports wagering is usually a gambling preference (Assanangkornchai, McNeil, Tantirangsee, & Kittirattanapaiboon, 2016). However, peer influences may be less substantial with online gambling in adolescents (Potenza et al., 2011). In addition, adolescents may engage in many types of gambling (Carbonneau, Vitaro, Brendgen, & Tremblay, 2015), and being young, highly educated, and male are factors linked to online gambling (Griffiths, Wardle, Orford, Sproston, & Erens, 2009; Petry & Weinstock, 2007).

Prevalence

Prevalence estimates for online gambling vary by country and stage of development. The prevalence of adolescents with problematic gambling may be increasing, and this has been associated with increased likelihoods of gambling problems during adulthood. For example, a recent study found that 6.5% of 12–17 year-olds gambled online, with 9 out of 10 of them being males with a mean age of 15 years old (Gómez, Feijóo, Braña, Varela, & Rial, 2019). Among adults, one study found that 4.1% gambled online (Lelonek-Kuleta et al., 2020). However, online gambling prevalence in the elderly has not yet been reported (Sauvaget et al., 2015).

Among people who gamble online, a recent survey noted that sports betting was the most common type of gambling (26.9%) and that smartphones (via Mobile apps) were the most frequently used devices (68.6%) (Columb & O'Gara, 2018). In addition, among users of gambling-related online communities, 54.33% may have at-risk/problem gambling (Sirola, Kaakinen, & Oksanen, 2018). More specifically, a study in Germany found that the replacement of 10% of offline gambling with online gambling increased the probability of developing problem gambling behavior by 8.8%–12.6% (Effertz, Bischof, Rumpf, Meyer, & John, 2018). More specifically, it has been described that 18% of people who gamble offline present with problematic gambling behavior, compared to 31% of those who gamble online (Yazdi & Katzian, 2017).

Motives

By analyzing the motives that lead individuals to gamble, a three-dimensional model has been proposed (Stewart & Zack, 2008). The search for positive emotions or enhancement would be a central motivation, in which gambling may be used as positive internal reinforcement. The second motivation may be to use gambling as negative internal reinforcement, namely as a maladaptive coping strategy to deal with negative emotions. Finally, it has been proposed that gambling may be motivated by social aspects that could provide external positive reinforcement (Stewart & Zack, 2008).

In the case of adolescents, these three gambling motives have been identified (Grande-Gosende, Martínez-Loredo, & Fernández-Hermida, 2019). Online gambling has become accessible for adolescents (especially due to the lax age restrictions of most gambling websites), a population frequently engaged in digital communications (Cotte & Latour, 2009; Amanda Lenhart, 2015; Romer & Moreno, 2017). Considering that adolescence is a stage in which it is common to present with elevated impulsivity, which typically decreases with age thereafter, the presence of impulsive and even risky behaviors is not surprising (Huang, Hu, & Li, 2017). Elevated impulsivity and poor control may lead adolescents, especially males, to seek immediate rewards and uncertainty in gambling (Canale, Scacchi, & Griffiths, 2016).

In adolescents, online gambling may also be promoted by negative reinforcement with the intention of relieving negative emotions. It may be powerful considering that adolescence is an emotionally turbulent developmental stage in which coping skills are still maturing (King, Delfabbro, & Griffiths, 2010).

Finally, considering the third gambling motivation, it has been observed that adolescents and youth with limited family and peer support are more likely to gamble problematically (Hardoon, Gupta, & Derevensky, 2004). Online gambling has been linked to the development of social networking communities that have become discussion forums for individuals who gamble (Caputo, 2015). Therefore, these platforms may address the socialization needs typical of adolescents, but they can also constitute a potential risk factor for the development of problematic gambling (Sirola et al., 2018).

During adulthood, personal and working situations evolve, leading to, among other things, greater financial responsibilities. Therefore, some have suggested adding to the theoretical model of gambling motivations the desire to win an immediate economic reward, which could become an even more central motivation during adulthood (Dechant, 2014; Dechant & Ellery, 2011). This gambling motivation to earn money may be linked to adult wishes to improve their social status or assert themselves (Dechant, 2014). Some individuals consider gambling as a lucrative financial option with more advantages than depositing money in bank accounts or other low-interest investments (Chevalier, Geoffrion, Allard, & Audet, 2002). Although it seems that during adolescence it is not as central a reason motivating gambling (Grande-Gosende et al., 2019), the current media's promotion of gambling could be also encouraging adolescents to perceive it as a strategy to get money easily and possibly even as a job option (Derevensky & Gilbeau, 2015).

Other central motivations for gambling that have been observed in adults, especially young adults, have been easy access to online gambling, pressure or suggestions from friends, and the economic prizes announced by online gambling operators (Kim, Wohl, Gupta, & Derevensky, 2017). In the case of young adults, a migration from social casino games to online gambling has been observed related to, among other factors, advertisements. Additionally, and winnings from offline gambling may promote perceptions of having appropriate skills to win during online gambling (Kim et al., 2017).

Regarding older adults, it has been suggested that gambling could be a maladaptive attempt to satisfy needs of autonomy, competence, and relatedness. These motivations fit within the self-determination theory (SDT) and may be particularly relevant during retirement transitions (Martin, Lichtenberg, & Templin, 2011). More specifically, self-determined motives for gambling, such as enjoyment, would be associated with greater gambling, as opposed to other reasons, such as for financial gain (Martin et al., 2011). Another reason identified in older adults has been to escape from feelings of boredom, loneliness, and loss due to the death of a loved one (Granero et al., 2019, 2020; Martin et al., 2011).

Although the reasons that induce different populations to engage in gambling behavior are relatively well known, the reasons that promote transitions from offline to online gambling have been less well studied (Kim et al., 2017).

Consequences

Excessive online gambling and related negative consequences may be experienced differently based on individuals' developmental stages. Further, it should be noted that online gambling may have a greater addictive potential than offline gambling, and therefore individuals with problematic gambling, especially young ones, may show greater proclivities to gambling online (Yazdi & Katzian, 2017).

Some adolescents may develop gambling problems (Derevensky & Gilbeau, 2015). In a study involving individuals from 15 to 25 years of age, youth between 18 and 21 years old were most likely to exhibit problematic gambling behavior or a gambling disorder (Sirola et al., 2018). However, adolescents and young adults often do not recognize problematic gambling and its possible consequences, or they may hide it (Gainsbury & Blaszczynski, 2011; Mudry & Strong, 2013; Sirola et al., 2018).

Online gaming

Conceptualization

Online gaming has experienced considerable growth recently among both adolescents and adults (Rho et al., 2018). Recent technological advances have allowed online video games to become increasingly sophisticated (Feng, Ramo, Chan, & Bourgeois, 2017). Online videogames, unlike offline ones, are usually played interactively with others, which typically involves cooperation and/or competition, as well as team responsibilities. On the other hand, offline video games are often played individually. Another characteristic of online games is that they are usually endless, while offline games typically have an established end point (Hsu, Wen, & Wu, 2009; Smohai et al., 2017).

Prevalence

Most (88%) children and adolescents between the ages of 8 and 18 years play electronic video games, and 23% play daily (Gentile, 2009). As for the problematic use of video games, prevalence estimates between 1% and 9% have been reported (Gentile et al., 2017), although even wider estimates have been described (Petry & O'Brien, 2013). When studying the trajectories of video game use from adolescence to emerging adulthood, Coyne et al. (2020) found that approximately 10% of the adolescents presented moderate symptomatology of problematic gaming, with increases in symptomatology at 6 years of age.

Motives
The most studied reasons for online gaming both in adolescents and adults have been to escape from reality, the fantasy generated by identities, the development of skills, the use of gaming as a coping strategy to cope with emotional distress, competition, social aspects such as the creation of new relationships or recreational purposes (Demetrovics et al., 2011). Some authors have suggested that escape and competition are the most predictable reasons for the development of problematic online gaming (Király et al., 2015; Montag et al., 2019). Others have observed that the only motivation that does not correlate with Internet gaming disorder is for recreational purposes (Moudiab & Spada, 2019).

In the case of adolescents, Başol and Kaya (2018) did not find an association between online gaming behaviors and the reasons for seeking success, economic profits, or relevance to a group. However, the most prominent reasons were achievement and immersion.

Consequences
Although controversial, some suggest that children may be particularly vulnerable to the effects of video games and online gaming (Lobel, Engels, Stone, Burk, & Granic, 2017). Additionally, problematic online gaming has been associated with depressive and anxious symptoms, lower academic achievement, loneliness, poor self-esteem or fatigue, among other concerns, especially in adolescents and young adults (Brunborg, Mentzoni, & Frøyland, 2014; Männikkö, Billieux, & Kääriäinen, 2015).

When comparing profiles of individuals with problematic gambling and gaming, Sanders and Williams (2019) found that they were similar, although those with gaming problems tended to be younger and more likely to have depression, while those with gambling problems were more impulsive.

Cyberbullying

Conceptualization

In the last decade, cyberbullying has become a public health concern, especially at school, college, and university levels (Garett, Lord, & Young, 2016; Myers & Cowie, 2019). Cyberbullying encompasses repeated psychological violence, especially against children and adolescents, within the framework of digital social networks (using usually text messages, photos, audios, or videos). Some authors consider that cyberbullying is the bullying that occurs in the digital sphere, characterized by three essential aspects: intention, power imbalance, and repetition (Englander, Donnerstein, Kowalski, Lin, & Parti, 2017; Hutson, 2016). It occurs in the cyber sphere, without the need for a specific physical environment (Brochado, Soares, & Fraga, 2017). Therefore, this implies that victims do not feel safe in contexts where traditional bullying would allow them to feel relief (Bauman, 2010). However, as cyberbullying is a relatively recent phenomenon linked to the development of new technologies, there is no clear consensus on the definition of the construct and its nature (Ferreira & Deslandes, 2018).

Cyberbullying may be interrelated with other online behaviors, such as the use of social networks, sexting, and online gambling and gaming (Chang et al., 2014; Van Ouytsel et al., 2019). Considering the nature of the violence, the following behaviors have been contemplated by using social networking: written verbal attacks (usually through phone calls, emails, or text messages), spreading rumors, deliberate exclusion of a member from an online group, threats, visual attacks by sending embarrassing images, sending intimate information of the victim (sexting without consent), or representation; that is, using the identity of another to make private information public (Nocentini et al., 2010). Furthermore, cyberbullying can occur in the context of online gambling and gaming, for example, by monitoring the victim's computer or camera without consent, entering the victim's account without consent, blocking the victim from chats related to the gaming or gambling contexts, or stealing gaming-related items (Chisholm, 2014; Ferreira & Deslandes, 2018). In addition, cyberbullying is closely related to other harmful behaviors, such as online harassment and online sexual harassment (Parti & Magyar, 2015).

Some potential risk factors to be a victim of cyberbullying include behavioral problems, school-related, attention or relational difficulties, use of instant messaging, 3 or more hours a day of Internet use, and risky behaviors on the Internet, such as publishing personal information (Sara Mota Borges, Cássio, Caroline Gomez, Aline Villa Lobo, & Wagner Silva, 2015). Furthermore, there seems to be an overlap between traditional bullying and cyberbullying, so that between 50% and 90% of students who have been victims of cyberbullying have also been victims of other forms of bullying (Olweus & Limber, 2018).

In recent years, a categorization of the types of victims of bullying and cyberbullying has been developed, due to the complexity of the victimization processes. Although there are several classifications, the proposal that seems to have more consensus is the distinction between those adolescents who bully other peers but are in turn victims of bullying or cyberbullying (bully-victims), those who are not victimized but victimize other adolescents (bullies), and those who are exclusively victims (Runions et al., 2019; van Dijk, Poorthuis, & Malti, 2017).

Prevalence

Due to the heterogeneity of conceptualizations of the phenomenon of cyberbullying, the ranges of prevalence oscillate remarkably among studies, usually ranging from 6.5% to 35.4% (Sara Mota Borges et al., 2015). In a review of 36 studies, it was observed that most have focused on adolescents between 12 and 18 years old, obtaining a median prevalence of cyberbullying of 23.0% (Hamm et al., 2015).

Among the types of cyberbullying, figures of 13.4% of pure cybervictims, 0.7% of pure cyberbullies, and 3.1% of cyberbully-victims were observed among students between the ages of 9 and 13 years (Machimbarrena & Garaigordobil, 2018).

For university students, a review of 14 studies reported estimates of between 3.8% and 9.9% of cyberbullying perpetration (Lund & Ross, 2017). In addition, cyber-harassment is beginning to emerge in adulthood, especially in work environments, with prevalence estimates of between 9% and 21% (Muhonen, Jönsson, & Bäckström, 2017).

Motives

Cyberspace has certain characteristics such as perceived anonymity, wide audiences, limited supervision, and the lack of time and space limits, thus providing an easy scenario for the perpetuation of cyberbullying (Hu, 2016). In addition, the absence of nonverbal communication reduces empathy in interpersonal relationships, and this may be especially relevant to social control in adolescent relationships (Ferreira & Deslandes, 2018). During adolescence, a common goal involves obtaining social power, and therefore, strategies in which there is control over peers, such as cyber-bullying, may facilitate social dominance (Brandau & Evanson, 2018; Thornberg & Knutsen, 2011).

Other common reasons for cyberbullying include disliking the victim, entertainment, seeking attention, revenge and harm, acceptance in a social group, social popularity, and defense against inferiority (Fluck, 2017; Johnston et al., 2014; Rafferty & Vander Ven, 2014; Zhou et al., 2013). Therefore, cyberbullying may cover several social motivations during adolescence.

Focusing on the Uses and Gratifications Theory (UGT), Tanrikulu and Erdur-Baker (2019) hypothesized that certain personality traits may motivate individuals to harm others through cyberbullying. The authors found that those individuals who showed higher levels of online disinhibition tended to engage in cyberbullying for entertainment, without considering the possible negative consequences of their conduct. Moreover, those individuals who showed higher levels of aggression and moral disengagement would use cyberbullying more often as a form of revenge against past bullies. Individuals with more narcissistic traits and more moral disengagement, on the other hand, could use cyberbullying as a strategy of domination, with the aim of demonstrating their skills in the use of cyberspace.

Consequences

Both bullying and cyberbullying have been associated with multiple adverse consequences, especially for the victim's mental health, such as substance use or academic problems, which may persist into adulthood (Pham & Adesman, 2015). Furthermore, it has been highlighted that being a victim of cyberbullying, compared to traditional bullying, has worse consequences in terms of self-esteem problems, anxious and depressive symptomatology, physical health, school absenteeism, and suicidal ideation (Giumetti & Kowalski, 2015; Van Geel, Vedder, & Tanilon, 2014). One of the most relevant protective factors against the development of depressive and anxious symptomatology is the social support perceived by the adolescent victim, especially on the part of the family and teachers (Hellfeldt, López-Romero, & Andershed, 2020).

It should be noted that experiencing cyberbullying repeatedly in early adolescence may lead victims to develop maladaptive behaviors and patterns of socialization that make them even more vulnerable to further episodes of victimization in adolescence or adulthood (Calvete, Fernández-González, González-Cabrera, & Gámez-Guadix, 2018). Therefore, although cyberbullying is a problem that has been especially studied in children and adolescents, due to its high prevalence estimates, it should be noted that concerns may persist as individuals mature (Jenaro, Flores, & Frías, 2018).

Cyberbullying is being studied in adults, especially in college students (Orel, Campbell, Wozencroft, Leong, & Kimpton, 2017; Sargent, Krauss, Jouriles, & McDonald, 2016). Arguably the most studied topics in adults are psychological processes involved in cyberbullying and risky behaviors associated with the use of technologies, instead of effects of cyberbullying on mental health, a recurrent topic in children and adolescents (Jenaro et al., 2018). Moreover, situations of cyberbullying or cyber-harassment are being studies in adults, especially in work contexts. Being a victim of cyber-harassment may not have considerable direct impacts on well being and work engagement or on intentions to quit (Muhonen et al., 2017). However, cyberbullying or cyber-harassment may significantly influence victims' perceptions of social support from superiors and coworkers (Muhonen et al., 2017).

Neurodevelopment

Developmental aspects of the online behaviors outlined above should be considered within a neurodevelopmental framework. Four basic principles may be kept in mind when considering neurodevelopment in adolescents (Dow-Edwards et al., 2019): (1) brain development is not linear; (2) in adolescence, the brain becomes more connected and specialized; (3) adolescent behavior is significantly influenced by changes between limbic/arousal/reward and frontal/executive/control regions; and (4) brain malleability leads to neuroplasticity and learning, but also potentially to greater vulnerability to various disorders.

Other features to consider in adolescence are a pronounced hypothalamic-pituitary-adrenal axis, increased testosterone levels and the impact of testosterone and cortisol on the adolescent brain, changes in biogenic aminergic systems, striatal and limbic circuits, and immature prefrontal cortex (Brown & Wisco, 2019; Chambers et al., 2003).

During adolescence, brain reorganization occurs and areas associated with planning, internal control, and multitasking undergo considerable changes (Blakemore, 2012). Likewise, risky decision-making in adolescence could relate to differential development of reward and control systems (Blakemore, 2012).

Maturation of motivational substrates

Adolescence is a developmental stage characterized by, among other things, a high novelty-seeking, and therefore brain regions involved in the representation of novelty may influence the behavior of adolescents more than in adults (Chambers & Potenza, 2003). Novelty-seeking/impulsivity and incentive-motivational processes characteristic of adolescence may be derived from developmental alterations in primary motivation circuitry (Chambers & Potenza, 2003), with multiple neurotransmitter systems contributing (Chambers et al., 2003). Both serotonin metabolites and cerebrospinal fluid dopamine concentrations begin to decline in childhood, reaching adult-like levels by age 16 (Takeuchi et al., 2000). Furthermore, adolescents experience hormonal changes, influencing motivational systems.

Maturation of inhibitory substrates

As the abovementioned brain changes occur, the prefrontal cortex also develops. During adolescence, the ability of the prefrontal cortex to inhibit impulses is not fully maximized (Chambers & Potenza, 2003). Therefore, problem-solving, logical thinking, and capacity to inhibit impulses may be still developing, although they improve from childhood to late adolescence (Feinberg, 1982; Woo, Pucak, Kye, Matus, & Lewis, 1997; Yates, 1996). Additionally, adolescents develop a motivational interest in engage in novel adult-like experiences, which may also affect the maturation of the prefrontal cortex (Chambers et al., 2003).

Neurodevelopment and online behaviors

Neurodevelopmental factors are associated with the maladaptive behaviors reported in the previous sections.

Social networking and cyberbullying

The existing literature examining associations between brain development and social networking and cyberbullying in adolescents and young adults is sparse. It should be noted that the socio-affective development of adolescents is associated with relevant brain changes, such as a greater number of white matter connections that facilitate better communication between the striatum and the prefrontal cortex (Crone & Konijn, 2018). Furthermore, changes in gray-matter volume have been described throughout adolescence, especially in those brain regions relevant to social understanding (e.g., temporal-parietal junction, medial prefrontal cortex, and superior temporal cortex) (Crone & Konijn, 2018). Finally, it seems that children, adolescents, and adults show greater activation in the ventral striatum derived from receiving "likes" and, therefore, from being socially accepted (Crone & Konijn, 2018).

In the case of cyberbullying, McLoughlin et al. (2020) studied how the brains of young adults react to witnessing cyberbullying. Numerous brain regions were activated by cyberbullying stimuli, evidencing what the authors have called a "socio-emotional/self-referential network." While no age-related differences were identified, differences were observed according to gender and whether participants had previously been victims of cyberbullying or not. More specifically, males relative to females showed a lower BOLD response to cyberbullying in the anterior cingulate cortex. Moreover, individuals who had not previously experienced cyberbullying showed a greater BOLD response in the precuneus than those with previous experience.

Pornography use

Brown and Wisco (2019) recently proposed that the stimulation of the hypothalamic-pituitary-adrenal axis and the amygdala may be increased in adolescents (relative to adults) exposed to pornography. Such exposures could lead to higher activation of the basal ganglia and a greater curtailment of the prefrontal cortex, and could interfere with executive functions, promote impulsivity, and reduce self-control.

In the case of adults, it has been observed that pornography use is associated with reduced gray-matter volume in the right caudate (Kühn & Gallinat, 2014). Previous studies have highlighted the role of the striatum in reward processing (Delgado, 2007; Heinz, Grace, & Beck, 2009). Kühn and Gallinat (2014) hypothesized that those adults with lower striatal volumes may require higher levels of external stimulation in order to feel pleasure.

Gambling and gaming

In the case of gambling and gaming, multiple cognitive impairments have been highlighted, such as poor error monitoring, diminished reward sensitivity, and impaired delaying of gratification (Goudriaan, Yücel, & van Holst, 2014; Yücel et al., 2017). More specifically, alterations in functional connectivity within central executive networks have been observed in late adolescence with Internet gaming disorder (Yuan et al., 2016). In addition, alterations have been identified in the interaction between executive and salience networks (Yuan et al., 2016).

In adults, those with a gambling disorder may show decreased activation of certain brain regions compared to controls, such as basal ganglionic, cortical, and thalamic regions (Potenza et al., 2003). In addition, compared to the controls, hypo-activation of the reward system has been observed in adults (Goudriaan, De Ruiter, Van Den Brink, Oosterlaan, & Veltman, 2010; Luijten, Schellekens, Kühn, MacHielse, & Sescousse, 2017; Miedl, Peters, & Büchel, 2012).

Conclusions

Interest in the impact of Internet use on stages of development has been growing, given recent increases in accessibility and availability of the Internet. Some groups, especially children and adolescents, have been considered at risk, being particularly vulnerable to the consequences of Internet use. Although most online behaviors (e.g., gambling, gaming, pornography use, etc.) are manifested across a wide range of ages, the motivations for engaging in such behaviors, as well as their possible consequences, often vary by age. Therefore, it is important to consider a developmental perspective in order to understand types and patterns of Internet use and their impacts.

Funding

Financial support was received through the Ministerio de Ciencia, Innovación y Universidades (Grant RTI2018-101837-B-100). FIS PI14/00290 and FIS PI17/01167 received aid from the Ministerio de Sanidad, Servicios Sociales e Igualdad. The research was also funded by the Delegación del Gobierno para el Plan Nacional sobre Drogas (2017I067), CIBER Fisiología Obesidad y Nutrición (CIBERobn), ISCIII. We thank CERCA Programme/Generalitat de Catalunya for institutional support. Fondo Europeo de Desarrollo Regional (FEDER) "Una manera de hacer Europa"/"a way to build Europe." Dr. Mestre-Bach was supported by a postdoctoral grant by FUNCIVA. Dr. Potenza's involvement was supported by the NIH grant R01 DK121551 and by the Connecticut Council on Problem Gambling and the Connecticut Department of Mental Health and Addiction Services.

Conflict of interest

None of the authors have any conflicts of interest. Marc Potenza has consulted for Rivermend Health, Opiant Therapeutics, Game Day Data, Addiction Policy Forum, Idorisa Pharmaceuticals and AXA; has received research support from Mohegan Sun Casino and the National Center for Responsible Gaming; has participated in surveys, mailings, or telephone consultations related to drug addiction, impulse-control disorders, or other health topics; has consulted for and/or advised gambling, health, and legal entities on issues related to impulse-control/addictive disorders; has provided clinical care in a problem gambling services program; has performed grant reviews for research-funding agencies; has edited journals and journal sections; has given academic lectures in grand rounds, CME events, and other clinical or scientific venues; and has generated books or book chapters for publishers of mental health texts.

References

Afsar, B. (2013). The relation between Internet and social media use and the demographic and clinical parameters, quality of life, depression, cognitive function and sleep quality in hemodialysis patients. Social media and hemodialysis. *General Hospital Psychiatry*, *35*(6), 625–630.

Arnett, E. J. (2005). The developmental context of substance use in emerging adulthood. *Journal of Drug Issues*, *35*(2), 235–254.

Assanangkornchai, S., McNeil, E. B., Tantirangsee, N., & Kittirattanapaiboon, P. (2016). Gambling disorders, gambling type preferences, and psychiatric comorbidity among the Thai general population: Results of the 2013 national mental health survey. *Journal of Behavioral Addictions*, *5*(3), 410–418.

Bányai, F., Zsila, Á., Király, O., Maraz, A., Elekes, Z., Griffiths, M. D., … Demetrovics, Z. (2017). Problematic social media use: Results from a large-scale nationally representative adolescent sample. *PLoS ONE*, *12*(1).

Barnes, S. J., & Pressey, A. D. (2011). Who needs cyberspace? Examining drivers of needs in second life. *Internet Research, 21*(3), 236–254.

Barrense-Dias, Y., Berchtold, A., Surís, J. C., & Akre, C. (2017). Sexting and the definition issue. *Journal of Adolescent Health, 61*(5), 544–554.

Barrense-Dias, Y., Surís, J. C., & Akre, C. (2019). "When it deviates it becomes harassment, doesn't it?" A qualitative study on the definition of sexting according to adolescents and young adults, parents, and teachers. *Archives of Sexual Behavior, 48*(8), 2357–2366.

Barry, C. T., Sidoti, C. L., Briggs, S. M., Reiter, S. R., & Lindsey, R. A. (2017). Adolescent social media use and mental health from adolescent and parent perspectives. *Journal of Adolescence, 61*, 1–11.

Bartsch, M., & Subrahmanyam, K. (2015). Technology and self-presentation. In *The Wiley handbook of psychology, technology, and society* (pp. 339–357). Hoboken, NJ: Wiley-Blackwell.

Başol, G., & Kaya, A. B. (2018). Motives and consequences of online game addiction: A scale development study. *Noropsikiyatri Arsivi, 55*(3), 225–232.

Bates, S. (2017). Revenge porn and mental health: A qualitative analysis of the mental health effects of revenge porn on female survivors. *Feminist Criminology, 12*(1), 22–42.

Bauman, S. (2010). Cyberbullying in a rural intermediate school: An exploratory study. *Journal of Early Adolescence, 30*(6), 803–833.

Baumgartner, S. E., Sumter, S. R., Peter, J., Valkenburg, P. M., & Livingstone, S. (2014). Does country context matter? Investigating the predictors of teen sexting across Europe. *Computers in Human Behavior, 34*, 157–164.

Benotsch, E. G., Snipes, D. J., Martin, A. M., & Bull, S. S. (2013). Sexting, substance use, and sexual risk behavior in young adults. *Journal of Adolescent Health, 52*(3), 307–313.

Berryman, C., Ferguson, C. J., & Negy, C. (2018). Social media use and mental health among young adults. *Psychiatric Quarterly, 89*(2), 307–314.

Best, P., Manktelow, R., & Taylor, B. (2014). Online communication, social media and adolescent wellbeing: A systematic narrative review. *Children and Youth Services Review, 41*, 27–36.

Blakemore, S. J. (2012). Development of the social brain in adolescence. *Journal of the Royal Society of Medicine, 105*(3), 111–116.

Bothe, B., Tóth-Király, I., Bella, N., Potenza, M. N., Demetrovics, Z., & Orosz, G. (2020). Why do people watch pornography? The motivational basis of pornography use. *Psychology of Addictive Behaviors*.

Brand, M., Blycker, G. R., & Potenza, M. N. (2019). When pornography becomes a problem: Clinical insights. *Psychiatric Times, 36*(12), 48–51.

Brandau, M., & Evanson, T. A. (2018). Adolescent victims emerging from cyberbullying. *Qualitative Health Research, 28*(10), 1584–1594.

Braun-Courville, D. K., & Rojas, M. (2009). Exposure to sexually explicit web sites and adolescent sexual attitudes and Behaviors. *Journal of Adolescent Health, 45*(2), 156–162.

Brevers, D., Sescousse, G., Maurage, P., & Billieux, J. (2019). Examining neural reactivity to gambling cues in the age of online betting. *Current Behavioral Neuroscience Reports, 6*(3), 59–71.

Bridges, A. J., & Morokoff, P. J. (2011). Sexual media use and relational satisfaction in heterosexual couples. *Personal Relationships, 18*(4), 562–585.

Bridges, A. J., Wosnitzer, R., Scharrer, E., Sun, C., & Liberman, R. (2010). Aggression and sexual behavior in best-selling pornography videos: A content analysis update. *Violence Against Women, 16*(10), 1065–1085.

Brochado, S., Soares, S., & Fraga, S. (2017). A scoping review on studies of cyberbullying prevalence among adolescents. *Trauma, Violence & Abuse, 18*(5), 523–531.

Brodie, Z. P., Wilson, C., & Scott, G. G. (2019). Sextual intercourse: Considering social–cognitive predictors and subsequent outcomes of sexting behavior in adulthood. *Archives of Sexual Behavior, 48*(8), 2367–2379.

Brown, J. A., & Wisco, J. J. (2019). The components of the adolescent brain and its unique sensitivity to sexually explicit material. *Journal of Adolescence, 72*, 10–13.

Brown, J. D., & L'Engle, K. L. (2009). Sexual attitudes and behaviors exposure to sexually explicit media. *Communication Research, 36*(1), 129–151.

Brunborg, G. S., Mentzoni, R. A., & Frøyland, L. R. (2014). Is video gaming, or video game addiction, associated with depression, academic achievement, heavy episodic drinking, or conduct problems? *Journal of Behavioral Addictions, 3*(1), 27–32.

Cacioppo, J. T., & Cacioppo, S. (2018). Loneliness in the modern age: An evolutionary theory of loneliness (ETL). *Advances in Experimental Social Psychology, 58*, 127–197.

Calvete, E., Fernández-González, L., González-Cabrera, J. M., & Gámez-Guadix, M. (2018). Continued bullying victimization in adolescents: Maladaptive schemas as a mediational mechanism. *Journal of Youth and Adolescence, 47*(3), 650–660.

Canale, N., Scacchi, L., & Griffiths, M. D. (2016). Adolescent gambling and impulsivity: Does employment during high school moderate the association? *Addictive Behaviors, 60*, 37–41.

Caputo, A. (2015). Sharing problem gamblers' experiences: A text analysis of gambling stories via online forum. *Mediterranean Journal of Clinical Psychology, 3*(1), 1–26.

Carbonneau, R., Vitaro, F., Brendgen, M., & Tremblay, R. E. (2015). Variety of gambling activities from adolescence to age 30 and association with gambling problems: A 15-year longitudinal study of a general population sample. *Addiction, 110*(12), 1985–1993.

Chalfen, R. (2009). 'It's only a picture': Sexting, 'smutty' snapshots and felony charges 1. *Visual Studies, 24*(3), 258–268.

Chambers, R. A., & Potenza, M. N. (2003). Neurodevelopment, impulsivity, and adolescent gambling. *Journal of Gambling Studies, 19*(1), 53–84.

Chambers, R. A., Taylor, J. R., & Potenza, M. N. (2003). Developmental neurocircuitry of motivation in adolescence: A critical period of addiction vulnerability. *American Journal of Psychiatry, 160*(6), 1041–1052.

Chang, F. C., Chiu, C. H., Miao, N. F., Chen, P. H., Lee, C. M., & Chiang, J. T. (2016). Predictors of unwanted exposure to online pornography and online sexual solicitation of youth. *Journal of Health Psychology, 21*(6), 1107–1118.

Chang, F. C., Chiu, C. H., Miao, N. F., Chen, P. H., Lee, C. M., Huang, T. F., & Pan, Y. C. (2014). Online gaming and risks predict cyberbullying perpetration and victimization in adolescents. *International Journal of Public Health, 60*(2), 257–266.

Chevalier, S., Geoffrion, C., Allard, D., & Audet, C. (2002). Motivations for gambling as tools for prevention and treatment of pathological gambling. In *Vol. 18. Conference proceedings 5th European conference on gambling studies and policy issues (October 2-5, 2002). Retrieved electronically Sept* (p. 2004).

Chisholm, J. F. (2014). Review of the status of cyberbullying and cyberbullying prevention. *Journal of Information Systems Education, 25*(1), 77–87.

Choi, H. J., Van Ouytsel, J., & Temple, J. R. (2016). Association between sexting and sexual coercion among female adolescents. *Journal of Adolescence, 53*, 164–168.

Citron, D., & Franks, M. (2014). Criminalizing revenge porn. *Wake Forest Law Review, 49*, 345–391.

Columb, D., & O'Gara, C. (2018). A national survey of online gambling behaviours. *Irish Journal of Psychological Medicine, 35*(4), 311–319.

Cooper, A. L. (1998). Sexuality and the internet: Surfing into the new millennium. *CyberPsychology and Behavior, 1*(2), 187–193.

Cotte, J., & Latour, K. A. (2009). Blackjack in the kitchen: Understanding online versus casino gambling. *Journal of Consumer Research*, *35*(5), 742–758.

Coyne, S. M., Padilla-Walker, L. M., Day, R. D., Harper, J., & Stockdale, L. (2014). A friend request from dear old dad: Associations between parent-child social networking and adolescent outcomes. *Cyberpsychology, Behavior and Social Networking*, *17*(1), 8–13.

Coyne, S. M., Radesky, J., Collier, K. M., Gentile, D. A., Linder, J. R., Nathanson, A. I., … Rogers, J. (2017). Parenting and digital media. *Pediatrics*, *140*, S112–S116.

Coyne, S. M., Stockdale, L. A., Warburton, W., Gentile, D. A., Yang, C., & Merrill, B. M. (2020). Pathological video game symptoms from adolescence to emerging adulthood: A 6-year longitudinal study of trajectories, predictors, and outcomes. *Developmental Psychology*.

Cranney, S. (2015). Internet pornography use and sexual body image in a Dutch sample. *International Journal of Sexual Health*, *27*(3), 316–323.

Crone, E. A., & Konijn, E. A. (2018). Media use and brain development during adolescence. *Nature Communications*, *9*(1), 1–10.

Davis, K. (2013). Young people's digital lives: The impact of interpersonal relationships and digital media use on adolescents' sense of identity. *Computers in Human Behavior*, *29*(6), 2281–2293.

Dechant, K. (2014). Show me the money: Incorporating financial motives into the gambling motives questionnaire. *Journal of Gambling Studies*, *30*(4), 949–965.

Dechant, K., & Ellery, M. (2011). The effect of including a monetary motive item on the gambling motives questionnaire in a sample of moderate gamblers. *Journal of Gambling Studies*, *27*(2), 331–344.

Delgado, M. R. (2007). Reward-related responses in the human striatum. *Annals of the New York Academy of Sciences*, *1104*, 70–88.

Demetrovics, Z., Urbán, R., Nagygyörgy, K., Farkas, J., Zilahy, D., Mervó, B., … Harmath, E. (2011). Why do you play? The development of the motives for online gaming questionnaire (MOGQ). *Behavior Research Methods*, *43*(3), 814–825.

Derevensky, J. L., & Gilbeau, L. (2015). Adolescent gambling: Twenty-five years of research. *Canadian Journal of Addiction*, *6*(2), 4–12.

Domènech-Abella, J., Mundó, J., Haro, J. M., & Rubio-Valera, M. (2019). Anxiety, depression, loneliness and social network in the elderly: Longitudinal associations from The Irish Longitudinal Study on Ageing (TILDA). *Journal of Affective Disorders*, *246*, 82–88.

Donevan, M., & Mattebo, M. (2017). The relationship between frequent pornography consumption, behaviours, and sexual preoccupancy among male adolescents in Sweden. *Sexual & Reproductive Healthcare*, *12*, 82–87.

Doornwaard, S. M., den Boer, F., Vanwesenbeeck, I., van Nijnatten, C. H. C. J., ter Bogt, T. F. M., & van den Eijnden, R. J. J. M. (2017). Dutch adolescents' motives, perceptions, and reflections toward sex-related internet use: Results of a web-based focus-group study. *Journal of Sex Research*, *54*(8), 1038–1050.

Döring, N. M. (2009). The Internet's impact on sexuality: A critical review of 15 years of research. *Computers in Human Behavior*, *25*(5), 1089–1101.

Dow-Edwards, D., MacMaster, F. P., Peterson, B. S., Niesink, R., Andersen, S., & Braams, B. R. (2019). Experience during adolescence shapes brain development: From synapses and networks to normal and pathological behavior. *Neurotoxicology and Teratology*, *76*.

Dwulit, A. D., & Rzymski, P. (2019). Prevalence, patterns and self-perceived effects of pornography consumption in polish university students: A cross-sectional study. *International Journal of Environmental Research and Public Health*, *16*(10), 1861.

Eckstrand, K. L., Choukas-Bradley, S., Mohanty, A., Cross, M., Allen, N. B., Silk, J. S., … Forbes, E. E. (2017). Heightened activity in social reward networks is associated with adolescents' risky sexual behaviors. *Developmental Cognitive Neuroscience*, *27*, 1–9.

Effertz, T., Bischof, A., Rumpf, H. J., Meyer, C., & John, U. (2018). The effect of online gambling on gambling problems and resulting economic health costs in Germany. *The European Journal of Health Economics*, *19*(7), 967–978.

El Asam, A., Samara, M., & Terry, P. (2019). Problematic internet use and mental health among British children and adolescents. *Addictive Behaviors*, *90*, 428–436.

Englander, E., Donnerstein, E., Kowalski, R., Lin, C. A., & Parti, K. (2017). Defining cyberbullying. *Pediatrics*, *140*, S148–S151.

Estévez, A., Rodríguez, R., Díaz, N., Granero, R., Mestre-Bach, G., Steward, T., … Jiménez-Murcia, S. (2017). How do online sports gambling disorder patients compare with land-based patients? *Journal of Behavioral Addictions*, *6*(4), 639–647.

Feinberg, I. (1982). Schizophrenia: Caused by a fault in programmed synaptic elimination during adolescence? *Journal of Psychiatric Research*, *17*(4), 319–334.

Feng, W., Ramo, D. E., Chan, S. R., & Bourgeois, J. A. (2017). Internet gaming disorder: Trends in prevalence 1998–2016. *Addictive Behaviors*, *75*, 17.

Ferguson, C. J. (2013). Violent video games and the supreme court: Lessons for the scientific community in the wake of brown v. entertainment merchants association. *American Psychologist*, *68*(2), 57–74.

Ferreira, T. R.d. S. C., & Deslandes, S. F. (2018). Cyberbullying: Concepts, dynamics, characters and health implications. *Ciencia E Saude Coletiva*, *23*(10), 3369–3379.

Fluck, J. (2017). Why do students bully? An analysis of motives behind violence in schools. *Youth and Society*, *49*(5), 567–587.

Foubert, J. D., & Bridges, A. J. (2017). What is the attraction? Pornography use motives in relation to bystander intervention. *Journal of Interpersonal Violence*, *32*(20), 3071–3089.

Franc, E., Khazaal, Y., Jasiowka, K., Lepers, T., Bianchi-Demicheli, F., & Rothen, S. (2018). Factor structure of the cybersex motives questionnaire. *Journal of Behavioral Addictions*, *7*(3), 601–609.

Frankel, A. S., Bass, S. B., Patterson, F., Dai, T., & Brown, D. (2018). Sexting, risk behavior, and mental health in adolescents: An examination of 2015 Pennsylvania youth risk behavior survey data. *Journal of School Health*, *88*(3), 190–199.

Fritz, N., Malic, V., Paul, B., & Zhou, Y. (2020). Worse than objects: The depiction of Black women and men and their sexual relationship in pornography. *Gender Issues*, 1–21.

Fullwood, C., James, B. M., & Chen-Wilson, C. H. J. (2016). Self-concept clarity and online self-presentation in adolescents. *Cyberpsychology, Behavior and Social Networking*, *19*(12), 716–720.

Gainsbury, S., & Blaszczynski, A. (2011). Online self-guided interventions for the treatment of problem gambling. *International Gambling Studies*, *11*(3), 289–308.

Garcia, J. R., Gesselman, A. N., Siliman, S. A., Perry, B. L., Coe, K., & Fisher, H. E. (2016). Sexting among singles in the USA: Prevalence of sending, receiving, and sharing sexual messages and images. *Sexual Health*, *13*(5), 428–435.

Garett, R., Lord, L. R., & Young, S. D. (2016). Associations between social media and cyberbullying: A review of the literature. *mHealth*, *2*, 46.

Gentile, D. (2009). Pathological video-game use among youth ages 8 to 18: A national study: Research article. *Psychological Science*, *20*(5), 594–602.

Gentile, D. A., Bailey, K., Bavelier, D., Brockmyer, J. F., Cash, H., Coyne, S. M., … Young, K. (2017). Internet gaming disorder in children and adolescents. *Pediatrics*, *140*, S81–S85.

Gittins, C. B., & Hunt, C. (2019). Parental behavioural control in adolescence: How does it affect self-esteem and self-criticism? *Journal of Adolescence*, *73*, 26–35.

Giumetti, G. W., & Kowalski, R. M. (2015). Cyberbullying matters: Examining the incremental impact of cyberbullying on outcomes over and above traditional bullying in North America. In *Cyberbullying across the globe* (pp. 117–130). Cham: Springer.

Gómez, P., Feijóo, S., Braña, T., Varela, J., & Rial, A. (2019). Minors and online gambling: Prevalence and related variables. *Journal of Gambling Studies*, 1–11.

Goudriaan, A. E., De Ruiter, M. B., Van Den Brink, W., Oosterlaan, J., & Veltman, D. J. (2010). Brain activation patterns associated with cue reactivity and craving in abstinent problem gamblers, heavy smokers and healthy controls: An fMRI study. *Addiction Biology*, *15*(4), 491–503.

Goudriaan, A. E., Yücel, M., & van Holst, R. J. (2014). Getting a grip on problem gambling: What can neuroscience tell us? *Frontiers in Behavioral Neuroscience*, *8*, 141.

Grande-Gosende, A., Martínez-Loredo, V., & Fernández-Hermida, J. R. (2019). Gambling motives questionnaire validation in adolescents: Differences based on gambling severity and activities. *Adicciones*, *31*(3), 212–220.

Granero, R., Jiménez-Murcia, S., del Pino-Gutiérrez, A., Mena-Moreno, T., Mestre-Bach, G., Gómez-Peña, M., … Fernández-Aranda, F. (2019). Gambling phenotypes in older adults. *Journal of Gambling Studies*, 1–20.

Granero, R., Jiménez-Murcia, S., Fernández-Aranda, F., Del Pino-Gutiérrez, A., Mena-Moreno, T., Mestre-Bach, G., … Menchón, J.M. (2020). Presence of problematic and disordered gambling in older age and validation of the South Oaks Gambling Scale. *PLoS ONE*, *15*(5).

Griffiths, M., Wardle, H., Orford, J., Sproston, K., & Erens, B. (2009). Sociodemographic correlates of internet gambling: Findings from the 2007 British gambling prevalence survey. *CyberPsychology and Behavior*, *12*(2), 199–202.

Griffiths, S., Murray, S. B., Krug, I., & McLean, S. A. (2018). The contribution of social media to body dissatisfaction, eating disorder symptoms, and anabolic steroid use among sexual minority men. *Cyberpsychology, Behavior and Social Networking*, *21*(3), 149–156.

Hamm, M. P., Newton, A. S., Chisholm, A., Shulhan, J., Milne, A., Sundar, P., … Hartling, L. (2015). Prevalence and effect of cyberbullying on children and young people. *JAMA Pediatrics*, *169*(8), 770.

Handschuh, C., La Cross, A., & Smaldone, A. (2019). Is sexting associated with sexual behaviors during adolescence? A systematic literature review and meta-analysis. *Journal of Midwifery and Women's Health*, *64*(1), 88–97.

Hardoon, K. K., Gupta, R., & Derevensky, J. L. (2004). Psychosocial variables associated with adolescent gambling. *Psychology of Addictive Behaviors*, *18*(2), 170–179.

Harper, C., & Hodgins, D. C. (2016). Examining correlates of problematic internet pornography use among university students. *Journal of Behavioral Addictions*, *5*(2), 179–191.

Heinz, A., Grace, A. A., & Beck, A. (2009). The intricacies of dopamine neuron modulation. *Biological Psychiatry*, *65*(2), 101.

Hellfeldt, K., López-Romero, L., & Andershed, H. (2020). Cyberbullying and psychological well-being in young adolescence: The potential protective mediation effects of social support from family, friends, and teachers. *International Journal of Environmental Research and Public Health*, *17*(1), 45.

Hsu, S. H., Wen, M. H., & Wu, M. C. (2009). Exploring user experiences as predictors of MMORPG addiction. *Computers & Education*, *53*(3), 990–999.

Hu, S. (2016). *Why cyberbullies choose cyberspace: From the perspective of uses and gratifications.*

Huang, Y., Hu, P., & Li, X. (2017). Undervaluing delayed rewards explains adolescents' impulsivity in inter-temporal choice: An ERP study. *Scientific Reports*, *7*.

Hussong, A. M., Ennett, S. T., Neish, D. M., Berg, W. A. R., Cole, V., Gottfredson, N. C., & Faris, R. W. (2018). Teen social networks and depressive symptoms-substance use associations: Developmental and demographic variation. *Journal of Studies on Alcohol and Drugs*, *79*(5), 770–780.

Hutson, E. (2016). Cyberbullying in adolescence: A concept analysis. *Advances in Nursing Science*, *39*(1), 60–70.

Jacobs, W., Goodson, P., Barry, A. E., McLeroy, K. R., McKyer, E. L. J., & Valente, T. W. (2017). Adolescent social networks and alcohol use: Variability by gender and type. *Substance Use and Misuse*, *52*(4), 477–487.

Jelenchick, L. A., & Christakis, D. A. (2014). Problematic internet use during adolescence and young adulthood. *Adolescent Medicine: State of the Art Reviews*, *25*(3), 605.

Jenaro, C., Flores, N., & Frías, C. P. (2018). Systematic review of empirical studies on cyberbullying in adults: What we know and what we should investigate. *Aggression and Violent Behavior*, *38*, 113–122.

Johnston, P., Tankersley, M., Joenson, T., Hupp, M., Buckley, J., Redmond-McGowan, M., … Walsh, A. (2014). Motivations behind "bullies then offenders" versus "pure bullies": Further suggestions for anti-bully education and practice. *Education*, *134*(3), 316–325.

Kamal, M., & Newman, W. J. (2016). Revenge pornography: Mental health implications and related legislation. *The Journal of the American Academy of Psychiatry and the Law*, *44*(3), 359–367.

Kar, S., Choudhury, A., & Singh, A. (2015). Understanding normal development of adolescent sexuality: A bumpy ride. *Journal of Human Reproductive Sciences*, *8*(2), 70.

Kim, H. S., Wohl, M. J. A., Gupta, R., & Derevensky, J. L. (2017). Why do young adults gamble online? A qualitative study of motivations to transition from social casino games to online gambling. *Asian Journal of Gambling Issues and Public Health*, *7*(1), 6.

King, D., Delfabbro, P., & Griffiths, M. (2010). The convergence of gambling and digital media: Implications for gambling in young people. *Journal of Gambling Studies*, *26*(2), 175–187.

King, K. M., McLaughlin, K. A., Silk, J., & Monahan, K. C. (2018). Peer effects on self-regulation in adolescence depend on the nature and quality of the peer interaction. *Development and Psychopathology*, *30*(4), 1389–1401.

Király, O., Urbán, R., Griffiths, M. D., Ágoston, C., Nagygyörgy, K., Kökönyei, G., & Demetrovics, Z. (2015). The mediating effect of gaming motivation between psychiatric symptoms and problematic online gaming: An online survey. *Journal of Medical Internet Research*, *17*(4), e88.

Klettke, B., Hallford, D. J., Clancy, E., Mellor, D. J., & Toumbourou, J. W. (2019). Sexting and psychological distress: The role of unwanted and coerced sexts. *Cyberpsychology, Behavior and Social Networking*, *22*(4), 237–242.

Klettke, B., Hallford, D. J., & Mellor, D. J. (2014). Sexting prevalence and correlates: A systematic literature review. *Clinical Psychology Review*, *34*(1), 44–53.

Kühn, S., & Gallinat, J. (2014). Brain structure and functional connectivity associated with pornography consumption the brain on porn. *JAMA Psychiatry*, *71*(7), 827–834.

Kuss, D. J., & Griffiths, M. D. (2011). Online social networking and addiction—A review of the psychological literature. *International Journal of Environmental Research and Public Health*, *8*(9), 3528–3552.

Kuss, D. J., & Griffiths, M. D. (2017). Social networking sites and addiction: Ten lessons learned. *International Journal of Environmental Research and Public Health*, *14*(3), 311.

Laier, C., & Brand, M. (2014). Empirical evidence and theoretical considerations on factors contributing to cybersex addiction from a cognitive-behavioral view. *Sexual Addiction and Compulsivity, 21*(4), 305–321.

Lauricella, A. R., Wartella, E., & Rideout, V. J. (2015). Young children's screen time: The complex role of parent and child factors. *Journal of Applied Developmental Psychology, 36,* 11–17.

Lelonek-Kuleta, B., Bartczuk, R. P., Wiechetek, M., Chwaszcz, J., & Niewiadomska, I. (2020). The prevalence of e-gambling and of problem e-gambling in Poland. *International Journal of Environmental Research and Public Health, 17*(2), 404.

Lenhart, A. (2015). *Teens, Social Media & Technology Overview 2015 | Pew Research Center* (pp. 9–12). Pew Research Center.

Lenhart, A., & Project, P. I. A. L. (2008). *Teens, video games, and civics: Teens' gaming experiences are diverse and include significant social interaction and civic engagement.* Pew Internet & American Life Project.

Lobel, A., Engels, R. C. M. E., Stone, L. L., Burk, W. J., & Granic, I. (2017). Video gaming and children's psychosocial wellbeing: A longitudinal study. *Journal of Youth and Adolescence, 46*(4), 884–897.

Luder, M. T., Pittet, I., Berchtold, A., Akré, C., Michaud, P. A., & Surís, J. C. (2011). Associations between online pornography and sexual behavior among adolescents: Myth or reality? *Archives of Sexual Behavior, 40*(5), 1027–1035.

Luijten, M., Schellekens, A. F., Kühn, S., MacHielse, M. W. J., & Sescousse, G. (2017). Disruption of reward processing in addiction: An image-based meta-analysis of functional magnetic resonance imaging studies. *JAMA Psychiatry, 74*(4), 387–398.

Lund, E. M., & Ross, S. W. (2017). Bullying perpetration, victimization, and demographic differences in college students: A review of the literature. *Trauma, Violence & Abuse, 18*(3), 348–360.

Machimbarrena, J. M., & Garaigordobil, M. (2018). Prevalence of bullying and cyberbullying in the last stage of primary education in the Basque Country. *Spanish Journal of Psychology, 21.*

Madigan, S., Ly, A., Rash, C. L., Van Ouytsel, J., & Temple, J. R. (2018). Prevalence of multiple forms of sexting behavior among youth: A systematic review and meta-analysis. *JAMA Pediatrics, 172*(4), 327–335.

Männikkö, N., Billieux, J., & Kääriäinen, M. (2015). Problematic digital gaming behavior and its relation to the psychological, social and physical health of Finnish adolescents and young adults. *Journal of Behavioral Addictions, 4*(4), 281–288.

Martin, F., Lichtenberg, P. A., & Templin, T. N. (2011). A longitudinal study: Casino gambling attitudes, motivations, and gambling patterns among urban elders. *Journal of Gambling Studies, 27*(2), 287–297.

Mattebo, M., Tydén, T., Häggström-Nordin, E., Nilsson, K. W., & Larsson, M. (2013). Pornography consumption, sexual experiences, lifestyles, and self-rated health among male adolescents in Sweden. *Journal of Developmental and Behavioral Pediatrics, 34*(7), 460–468.

Mattebo, M., Tydén, T., Häggström-Nordin, E., Nilsson, K. W., & Larsson, M. (2016). Pornography consumption among adolescent girls in Sweden. *The European Journal of Contraception & Reproductive Health Care, 21*(4), 295–302.

Mattebo, M., Tydén, T., Häggström-Nordin, E., Nilsson, K. W., & Larsson, M. (2018). Pornography consumption and psychosomatic and depressive symptoms among Swedish adolescents: A longitudinal study. *Upsala Journal of Medical Sciences, 123*(4), 237–246.

McLoughlin, L. T., Shan, Z., Broadhouse, K. M., Winks, N., Simcock, G., Lagopoulos, J., & Hermens, D. F. (2020). Neurobiological underpinnings of cyberbullying: A pilot functional magnetic resonance imaging study. *Human Brain Mapping, 41*(6), 1495–1504.

Medrano, J. L. J., Lopez Rosales, F., & Gámez-Guadix, M. (2018). Assessing the links of sexting, cybervictimization, depression, and suicidal ideation among university students. *Archives of Suicide Research, 22*(1), 153–164.

Meeus, W. (2016). Adolescent psychosocial development: A review of longitudinal models and research. *Developmental Psychology, 52*(12), 1969–1993.

Michikyan, M., & Suárez-Orozco, C. (2015). Adolescent media and social media use: Implications for development. *Journal of Adolescent Research, 31*(4), 411–414.

Miedl, S. F., Peters, J., & Büchel, C. (2012). Altered neural reward representations in pathological gamblers revealed by delay and probability discounting. *Archives of General Psychiatry, 69*(2), 177–186.

Mitchell, K. J., Finkelhor, D., Jones, L. M., & Wolak, J. (2012). Prevalence and characteristics of youth sexting: A national study. *Pediatrics, 129*(1), 13–20.

Montag, C., Schivinski, B., Sariyska, R., Kannen, C., Demetrovics, Z., & Pontes, H. M. (2019). Psychopathological symptoms and gaming motives in disordered gaming—A psychometric comparison between the WHO and APA diagnostic frameworks. *Journal of Clinical Medicine, 8*(10), 1691.

Morelli, M., Bianchi, D., Baiocco, R., Pezzuti, L., & Chirumbolo, A. (2016). Sexting, psychological distress and dating violence among adolescents and young adults. *Psicothema, 28*(2), 137–142.

Moudiab, S., & Spada, M. M. (2019). The relative contribution of motives and maladaptive cognitions to levels of Internet Gaming Disorder. *Addictive Behaviors Reports, 9*.

Mudry, T. E., & Strong, T. (2013). Doing recovery online. *Qualitative Health Research, 23*(3), 313–325.

Muhonen, T., Jönsson, S., & Bäckström, M. (2017). Consequences of cyberbullying behaviour in working life. *International Journal of Workplace Health Management, 10*(5), 376–390.

Myers, C. A., & Cowie, H. (2019). Cyberbullying across the lifespan of education: Issues and interventions from school to university. *International Journal of Environmental Research and Public Health, 16*(7), 1217.

Nardis, Y., & Panek, E. (2019). Explaining privacy control on Instagram and Twitter: The roles of narcissism and self-esteem. *Communication Research Reports, 36*(1), 24–34.

National Center for Missing and Exploited Children. (2009). *Policy statement on sexting*. www.missingkids.com/home.

Nocentini, A., Calmaestra, J., Schultze-Krumbholz, A., Scheithauer, H., Ortega, R., & Menesini, E. (2010). Cyberbullying: Labels, behaviours and definition in three European countries. *Australian Journal of Guidance and Counselling, 20*(2), 129–142.

O'Keeffe, G. S. (2016). Social media: Challenges and concerns for families. *Pediatric Clinics of North America, 63*(5), 841–849.

Olweus, D., & Limber, S. P. (2018). Some problems with cyberbullying research. *Current Opinion in Psychology, 19*, 139–143.

Orel, A., Campbell, M., Wozencroft, K., Leong, E., & Kimpton, M. (2017). Exploring university students' coping strategy intentions for cyberbullying. *Journal of Interpersonal Violence, 32*(3), 446–462.

Parti, K., & Magyar, K. (2015). Section VII: How effective are bullying prevention programs in addressing cyberbullying? In E. Englander (Ed.), *Cyberbullying: Current & future research & directions: A white paper submitted to the Institute of Digital Media and Child Development*, Institute of Digital Media and Child Development.

Petry, N. M., & O'Brien, C. P. (2013). Internet gaming disorder and the DSM-5. *Addiction*, *108*(7), 1186–1187.

Petry, N. M., & Weinstock, J. (2007). Internet gambling is common in college students and associated with poor mental health. *American Journal on Addictions*, *16*(5), 325–330.

Pham, T., & Adesman, A. (2015). Teen victimization: Prevalence and consequences of traditional and cyberbullying. *Current Opinion in Pediatrics*, *27*(6), 748–756.

Potenza, M. N., Leung, H. C., Blumberg, H. P., Peterson, B. S., Fulbright, R. K., Lacadie, C. M., … Gore, J. C. (2003). An fMRI stroop task study of ventromedial prefrontal cortical function in pathological gamblers. *American Journal of Psychiatry*, *160*(11), 1990–1994.

Potenza, M. N., Wareham, J. D., Steinberg, M. A., Rugle, L., Cavallo, D. A., Krishnan-Sarin, S., & Desai, R. A. (2011). Correlates of at-risk/problem internet gambling in adolescents. *Journal of the American Academy of Child and Adolescent Psychiatry*, *50*(2), 150–159.e3.

Przybylski, A. K., Murayama, K., Dehaan, C. R., & Gladwell, V. (2013). Motivational, emotional, and behavioral correlates of fear of missing out. *Computers in Human Behavior*, *29*(4), 1841–1848.

Rafferty, R., & Vander Ven, T. (2014). "I hate everything about you": A qualitative examination of cyberbullying and on-line aggression in a college sample. *Deviant Behavior*, *35*(5), 364–377.

Recupero, P. R. (2016). New technologies, new problems, new laws. *The Journal of the American Academy of Psychiatry and the Law*, *44*(3), 322–327.

Reyns, B. W., Burek, M. W., Henson, B., & Fisher, B. S. (2013). The unintended consequences of digital technology: Exploring the relationship between sexting and cybervictimization. *Journal of Crime and Justice*, *36*(1), 1–17.

Rho, M. J., Lee, H., Lee, T. H., Cho, H., Jung, D. J., Kim, D. J., & Choi, I. Y. (2018). Risk factors for internet gaming disorder: Psychological factors and internet gaming characteristics. *International Journal of Environmental Research and Public Health*, *15*(1), 40.

Rial Boubeta, A., Gómez Salgado, P., Isorna Folgar, M., Araujo Gallego, M., & Varela Mallou, J. (2015). PIUS-a: Problematic Internet Use Scale in adolescents. Development and psychometric validation. *Adicciones*, *27*(1), 47–63.

Ricijas, N., Dodig Hundric, D., & Huic, A. (2016). Predictors of adverse gambling related consequences among adolescent boys. *Children and Youth Services Review*, *67*, 168–176.

Roberts, M., Callahan, L., & O'leary, C. (2017). Social media: A path to health literacy. *Studies in Health Technology and Informatics*, *240*, 464–475.

Romer, D., & Moreno, M. (2017). Digital media and risks for adolescent substance abuse and problematic gambling. *Pediatrics*, *140*, S102–S106.

Romito, P., & Beltramini, L. (2011). Watching pornography: Gender differences, violence and victimization. An exploratory study in Italy. *Violence Against Women*, *17*(10), 1313–1326.

Rothman, E. F., & Adhia, A. (2015). Adolescent pornography use and dating violence among a sample of primarily black and hispanic, urban-residing, underage youth. *Behavioral Science*, *6*(1), 1.

Rothman, E. F., Kaczmarsky, C., Burke, N., Jansen, E., & Baughman, A. (2015). "Without porn. I Wouldn't know half the things I know now": A qualitative study of pornography use among a sample of urban, low-income, black and hispanic youth. *Journal of Sex Research*, *52*(7), 736–746.

Runions, K. C., Shaw, T., Bussey, K., Thornberg, R., Salmivalli, C., & Cross, D. S. (2019). Moral disengagement of pure bullies and bully/victims: Shared and distinct mechanisms. *Journal of Youth and Adolescence*, *48*(9), 1835–1848.

Salonen, A. H., Alho, H., & Castrén, S. (2015). Gambling frequency, gambling problems and concerned significant others of problem gamblers in Finland: Cross-sectional population studies in 2007 and 2011. *Scandinavian Journal of Public Health*, *43*(3), 229–235.

Salonen, A. H., Alho, H., & Castrén, S. (2017). Attitudes towards gambling, gambling participation, and gambling-related harm: Cross-sectional Finnish population studies in 2011 and
2015. *BMC Public Health*, *17*(1), 122.

Sampasa-Kanyinga, H., & Chaput, J. P. (2016a). Use of social networking sites and adherence
to physical activity and screen time recommendations in adolescents. *Journal of Physical
Activity and Health*, *13*(5), 474–480.

Sampasa-Kanyinga, H., & Chaput, J. P. (2016b). Use of social networking sites and alcohol
consumption among adolescents. *Public Health*, *139*, 88–95.

Sampasa-Kanyinga, H., Chaput, J. P., & Hamilton, H. A. (2019). Social media use, school connectedness, and academic performance among adolescents. *Journal of Primary Prevention*,
40(2), 189–211.

Sanders, J., & Williams, R. (2019). The relationship between video gaming, gambling, and
problematic levels of video gaming and gambling. *Journal of Gambling Studies*, *35*(2),
559–569.

Sara Mota Borges, B., Cássio, M. C. B., Caroline Gomez, R., Aline Villa Lobo, C., & Wagner
Silva, R. (2015). Cyberbullying and adolescent mental health: Systematic review. *Cadernos
de Saúde Pública*, *31*, 463–475.

Sargent, K. S., Krauss, A., Jouriles, E. N., & McDonald, R. (2016). Cyber victimization, psychological intimate partner violence, and problematic mental health outcomes among first-
year college students. *Cyberpsychology, Behavior and Social Networking*, *19*(9), 545–550.

Sauvaget, A., Jiménez-Murcia, S., Fernández-Aranda, F., Fagundo, A. B., Moragas, L., Wolz, I.,
… Menchón, J. M. (2015). Unexpected online gambling disorder in late-life: A case report.
Frontiers in Psychology, *6*, 655.

Seifert, A., & Schelling, H. R. (2016). Old and offline?: Findings on the use of the Internet by
people aged 65 years and older in Switzerland. *Zeitschrift fur Gerontologie und Geriatrie*,
49(7), 619–625.

Shehu, M., & Zhurda, Y. (2017). Social networks used by teens and parental control of their online communication. *Bulgarian Journal of Science and Education Policy*, *11*(1), 121–131.

Shek, D. T. L., & Ma, C. M. S. (2012). Consumption of pornographic materials among Hong
Kong early adolescents: A replication. *The Scientific World Journal*, *2012*.

Shensa, A., Sidani, J. E., Dew, M. A., Escobar-Viera, C. G., & Primack, B. A. (2018). Social
media use and depression and anxiety symptoms: A cluster analysis. *American Journal of
Health Behavior*, *42*(2), 116–128.

Sherman, L. E., Payton, A. A., Hernandez, L. M., Greenfield, P. M., & Dapretto, M. (2016). The
power of the *Like* in adolescence. *Psychological Science*, *27*(7), 1027–1035.

Short, M. B., Black, L., Smith, A. H., Wetterneck, C. T., & Wells, D. E. (2012). A review of
internet pornography use research: Methodology and content from the past 10 years.
Cyberpsychology, Behavior and Social Networking, *15*(1), 13–23.

Shumaker, C., Loranger, D., & Dorie, A. (2017). Dressing for the internet: A study of female
selfpresentation via dress on instagram. *Fashion, Style and Popular Culture*, *4*(3), 365–382.

Sirola, A., Kaakinen, M., & Oksanen, A. (2018). Excessive gambling and online gambling communities. *Journal of Gambling Studies*, *34*(4), 1313–1325.

Smink, F. R. E., van Hoeken, D., Dijkstra, J. K., Deen, M., Oldehinkel, A. J., & Hoek, H. W.
(2018). Self-esteem and peer-perceived social status in early adolescence and prediction
of eating pathology in young adulthood. *International Journal of Eating Disorders*, *51*(8),
852–862.

Smohai, M., Urbán, R., Griffiths, M. D., Király, O., Mirnics, Z., Vargha, A., & Demetrovics,
Z. (2017). Online and offline video game use in adolescents: Measurement invariance and
problem severity. *American Journal of Drug and Alcohol Abuse*, *43*(1), 111–116.

Stewart, S. H., & Zack, M. (2008). Development and psychometric evaluation of a three-dimensional Gambling Motives Questionnaire. *Addiction, 103*(7), 1110–1117.

Strasburger, V. C., Zimmerman, H., Temple, J. R., & Madigan, S. (2019). Teenagers, sexting, and the law. *Pediatrics, 143*(5).

Studer, J., Marmet, S., Wicki, M., & Gmel, G. (2019). Cybersex use and problematic cybersex use among young Swiss men: Associations with sociodemographic, sexual, and psychological factors. *Journal of Behavioral Addictions, 8*(4), 794–803.

Subrahmanyam, K., & Šmahel, D. (2011). Digital youth: The role of media in development. *Choice Reviews Online, 48*(10), 48-5768.

Svedin, C. G., Åkerman, I., & Priebe, G. (2011). Frequent users of pornography. A population based epidemiological study of Swedish male adolescents. *Journal of Adolescence, 34*(4), 779–788.

Takeuchi, Y., Matsushita, H., Sakai, H., Kawano, H., Yoshimoto, K., & Sawada, T. (2000). Developmental changes in cerebrospinal fluid concentrations of monoamine-related substances revealed with a Coulochem electrode array system. *Journal of Child Neurology, 15*(4), 267–270.

Tang, C. S., & Koh, Y. Y. W. (2017). Online social networking addiction among college students in Singapore: Comorbidity with behavioral addiction and affective disorder. *Asian Journal of Psychiatry, 25*, 175–178.

Tanrikulu, I., & Erdur-Baker, Ö. (2019). Motives behind cyberbullying perpetration: A test of uses and gratifications theory. *Journal of Interpersonal Violence*, 0886260518819882.

Thornberg, R., & Knutsen, S. (2011). Teenagers' explanations of bullying. *Child & Youth Care Forum, 40*(3), 177–192.

Turban, J. L., Shirk, S. D., Potenza, M. N., Hoff, R. A., & Kraus, S. W. (2020). Posting sexually explicit images or videos of oneself online is associated with impulsivity and Hypersexuality but not measures of psychopathology in a sample of US veterans. *The Journal of Sexual Medicine, 17*(1), 163–167.

Uhls, Y. T., Ellison, N. B., & Subrahmanyam, K. (2017). Benefits and costs of social media in adolescence. *Pediatrics, 140*, S67–S70.

van Dijk, A., Poorthuis, A. M. G., & Malti, T. (2017). Psychological processes in young bullies versus bully-victims. *Aggressive Behavior, 43*(5), 430–439.

Van Geel, M., Vedder, P., & Tanilon, J. (2014). Relationship between peer victimization, cyberbullying, and suicide in children and adolescents a meta-analysis. *JAMA Pediatrics, 168*(5), 435–442.

van Oosten, J. M. F., & Vandenbosch, L. (2020). Predicting the willingness to engage in non-consensual forwarding of sexts: The role of pornography and instrumental notions of sex. *Archives of Sexual Behavior, 49*(4), 1121–1132.

Van Ouytsel, J., Lu, Y., Ponnet, K., Walrave, M., & Temple, J. R. (2019). Longitudinal associations between sexting, cyberbullying, and bullying among adolescents: Cross-lagged panel analysis. *Journal of Adolescence, 73*, 36–41.

Van Ouytsel, J., Punyanunt-Carter, N. M., Walrave, M., & Ponnet, K. (2020). Sexting within young adults' dating and romantic relationships. *Current Opinion in Psychology*.

Vroman, K. G., Arthanat, S., & Lysack, C. (2015). "Who over 65 is online?" Older adults' dispositions toward information communication technology. *Computers in Human Behavior, 43*, 156–166.

Wallmyr, G., & Welin, C. (2006). Young people, pornography, and sexuality: Sources and attitudes. *The Journal of School Nursing: The Official Publication of the National Association of School Nurses, 22*(5), 290–295.

Wolak, J., Mitchell, K., & Finkelhor, D. (2007). Unwanted and wanted exposure to online pornography in a national sample of youth internet users. *Pediatrics, 119*(2), 247–257.

Woo, T. U., Pucak, M. L., Kye, C. H., Matus, C. V., & Lewis, D. A. (1997). Peripubertal refinement of the intrinsic and associational circuitry in monkey prefrontal cortex. *Neuroscience*, *80*(4), 1149–1158.

Woods, H. C., & Scott, H. (2016). #Sleepyteens: Social media use in adolescence is associated with poor sleep quality, anxiety, depression and low self-esteem. *Journal of Adolescence*, *51*, 41–49.

Wysocki, D. K., & Childers, C. D. (2011). "Let my fingers do the talking": Sexting and infidelity in cyberspace. *Sexuality and Culture*, *15*(3), 217–239.

Yates, T. (1996). Theories of cognitive development. In L. M. Baltimore (Ed.), *Child and adolescent psychiatry* (pp. 134–155).

Yau, Y. H. C., & Potenza, M. N. (2015). Gambling disorder and other behavioral addictions. *Harvard Review of Psychiatry*, *23*(2), 134–146.

Yazdi, K., & Katzian, C. (2017). Addictive potential of online-gambling. A prevalence study from Austria. *Psychiatria Danubina*, *29*(3), 376–378.

Yuan, H. (2020). Internet use and mental health problems among older people in Shanghai, China: The moderating roles of chronic diseases and household income. *Aging and Mental Health*, 1–7.

Yuan, K., Qin, W., Yu, D., Bi, Y., Xing, L., Jin, C., & Tian, J. (2016). Core brain networks interactions and cognitive control in internet gaming disorder individuals in late adolescence/early adulthood. *Brain Structure and Function*, *221*(3), 1427–1442.

Yücel, M., Carter, A., Allen, A. R., Balleine, B., Clark, L., Dowling, N. A., … Hall, W. (2017). Neuroscience in gambling policy and treatment: An interdisciplinary perspective. *The Lancet Psychiatry*, *4*(6), 501–506.

Zhou, Z., Tang, H., Tian, Y., Wei, H., Zhang, F., & Morrison, C. M. (2013). Cyberbullying and its risk factors among Chinese high school students. *School Psychology International*, *34*(6), 630–647.

Section D

Interventions

Internet-based psychotherapies

17

Gerhard Andersson
Department of Behavioural Sciences and Learning, Department of Biomedical
and Clinical Sciences, Linköping University, Linköping, Sweden

Background

Major advances in information technology have had an impact on the clinical management of mental health problems. While the field is new there are numerous research studies and clinical implementations of technology-supported interventions, mainly in the form of psychological treatments that have been developed and tested during a time period that is now over 20 years (Andersson, 2018).

There are important historical background factors that have facilitated the growth of what is now often referred to as Internet-based psychological interventions. First, there is vast literature on text-based treatments under the name of bibliotherapy (Watkins & Clum, 2008). Several controlled bibliotherapy trials have been conducted for a range of problems showing that self-help books based on cognitive-behavior therapy (CBT) can be effective (Marrs, 1995), in particular, when supported by a clinician (over phone or in meetings). However, while self-help books based on CBT have been disseminated widely most have not been underpinned by research (Rosen, 1987). A second background is telephone-based psychological treatments (Haas, Benedict, & Kobos, 1996), which are commonly practiced and also studied in research to some extent (Leach & Christensen, 2006). This is also the case for video consultations for which there is some but still limited research (Varker, Brand, Ward, Terhaag, & Phelps, 2019). A final background that precede the Internet CD-ROM and computerized treatments on stand-alone computers (Marks, Shaw, & Parkin, 1998). Research on earlier forms of computerized psychotherapy stopped when the Internet was introduced and now most research and clinical practice involving self-help text material, video consultations, telephone (smartphone), and computers delivered online.

The introduction of the Internet in the 1990s changed society worldwide and also had an impact on various aspects of psychotherapy. A majority of people in the world now access the Internet frequently, but do not benefit from the Internet its capabilities connecting people and providing access to information (Krotoski, 2013). Having said that it is important to note that online support groups and more recently social media (for example, Facebook and twitter) have a major impact on help seeking, advice on treatment options, and potential support (Mehta & Atreja, 2015). Clinicians need to consider this when seeing clients as there is limited evidence for their benefits and also possibilities for negative effects (for example, instructions on self-harm). It is also a moving target with earlier open peer-support groups (Griffiths, Calear, & Banfield, 2009) now often being replaced by more closed communities in social media (Giustini, Ali, Fraser, & Kamel Boulos, 2018).

Mental Health in a Digital World. https://doi.org/10.1016/B978-0-12-822201-0.00008-3

The impact of the Internet on psychotherapy and other psychological treatments has been unprecedented and has had consequences for knowledge dissemination, assessment procedures, treatment evaluation, intervention research, and generating an evidence base (Andersson, 2018). While most of the activities have been based on CBT (see below for other orientations), there are several other implementations and also treatments that are based on methods than talking therapies such as cognitive bias modification programs delivered online (Carlbring et al., 2012) and virtual reality (Lindner et al., 2017).

In this chapter, the focus will be on Internet-delivered psychological treatments and their application for mental health problems. I will not cover smartphone applications, bias modification, or virtual reality. The aim of the chapter is to provide an updated overview of the field of Internet-delivered psychotherapies including the role of the clinician delivering the intervention. I will also comment on ongoing research and possible future directions.

Procedures

In this section, I will cover the basics of how a treatment platform can be organized, how assessments are made within systems, various treatment contents including theoretical orientations, and the role of the supporting clinician.

Treatment platform

There are not many detailed descriptions of the treatment platforms on which treatment material is presented and communication is handled with clients. One early paper focused on security considerations (Bennett, Bennett, & Griffiths, 2010), and more recently a system hosted in Sweden has been described (Vlaescu, Alasjö, Miloff, Carlbring, & Andersson, 2016). There are, however, papers on how system design can be informed by behavioral theory (Ritterband, Thorndike, Cox, Kovatchev, & Gonder-Frederick, 2009), how to boost engagement (Yardley et al., 2016), uptake (van Gemert-Pijnen et al., 2011), and the role of design features (Radomski et al., 2019).

Most contemporary treatment platforms are able to present video and audio files, and can also support text and video chat within the system. As with the Internet and data communication in general, *security* is a crucial aspect in the interaction between client and a therapist via text or video chat, in particular when collecting sensitive data such as symptom ratings. Open web pages used for information without any interaction with patients do not require this but when it comes to treatment and interaction security is crucial. Technical solutions tend to resemble Internet banking (e.g., when bills are payed online), and include encryption of all data traffic. There are strict regulations in many countries and it is often not to access a system. Instead, systems are encrypted and use a double-authentication procedure at login. In some countries and states in the United States, it is also required that the server is placed locally and not in another country. People who access the Internet need to be able to reach the system regardless of device used and should, for example, be able to use and switch between computers, smartphones, and tablets in a seamless manner. Increasingly, treatment platforms have this function and respond automatically to the mode of presentation (Vlaescu et al., 2016). This is not the same thing as smartphone applications which require installation. In sum, technology changes rapidly and while not a topic in this chapter it should be mentioned that sensors and other applications increasingly are embedded in treatment platforms (Mohr, Zhang, & Schueller, 2017). It is also increasingly possible, given security considerations, to transfer data to medical filing systems and quality assurance registers. This is a topic for which there are different technical solutions and legal requirements across the world (Dever Fitzgerald, Hunter, Hadjistavropoulos, & Koocher, 2010).

Assessments

I move on to Internet-based computerized assessments which basically follow the emergence of Internet therapies and have been around for more than 20 years (Buchanan, 2002). All Internet research including clinical implementations use online questionnaires to collect outcome measures, but also for screening, epidemiological, and online psychological experiments. With regards to questionnaires, there is ample evidence showing that psychometric properties and characteristics of measures remain stable and also have advantages such as reducing the possibility skip items (van Ballegooijen, Riper, Cuijpers, van Oppen, & Smit, 2016). Moreover, it is also possible to use stepwise procedures with, for example, screening questions leading to further questions. Online assessment procedures are increasingly incorporated in clinical practice (Zimmerman & Martinez, 2012). One cautionary note is, however, that the format should not change between paper-and-pencil and online questionnaires in research studies (Carlbring et al., 2007). With regards to diagnostic procedures, self-report questionnaires cannot replace diagnostic interviews (Eaton, Neufeld, Chen, & Cai, 2000), but increasingly video consultations are and have the benefit of not requiring the client to visit a clinic (Chakrabarti, 2015).

Treatment content

Treatment content in Internet-based psychotherapies varies widely across disorders, conditions, and research groups. Most treatment programs are derived from text-based self-help materials (often described in books or treatment manuals), but adapted for online presentation. Indeed, a typical CBT program might contain 150 pages of text divided into modules. Not only text but also video and audio files can be included and various interactive features for illustration of techniques. Internet-based treatments can also be presented as online lectures with slide shows alongside a presenter. The CBT programs often include homework and tasks to be performed in real life. Reports about homework can be made in the treatment platform and for some problems such as insomnia diaries may be used and calculated on the platform (for example, sleep efficiency). The programs tend to follow face-to-face psychotherapies in terms of duration but can sometimes be shorter. A typical treatment for depression can, for example, last 10 weeks, but there are several examples of both longer and shorter treatments

(Andersson, 2015). Given the rapid development of new programs, it is beyond the scope of this chapter to describe even a fraction of all evidence-based treatments in any detail, but here it can be mentioned that there are programs for most common psychiatric conditions and also transdiagnostic and tailored programs, which can be suitable across anxiety and mood disorders. There are also an increasing number of programs for psychological problems such as loneliness and perfectionism that are often comorbid with psychiatric problems.

While most Internet treatments are derived from CBT treatment protocols, it should be mentioned that there are programs based on psychodynamic psychotherapy (Johansson, Frederick, & Andersson, 2013), interpersonal psychotherapy (Donker et al., 2013), and also treatments based on certain methods and techniques such as mindfulness (Sevilla-Llewellyn-Jones, Santesteban-Echarri, Pryor, McGorry, & Alvarez-Jimenez, 2018), applied relaxation (Stefanopoulou, Lewis, Taylor, Broscombe, & Larkin, 2019), and physical activity (Nyström et al., 2017). Within the CBT umbrella, there are also programs based on acceptance and commitment therapy (Brown, Glendenning, Hoon, & John, 2016).

Another aspect that is suitable for online interventions is the possibility translate and culturally adapt treatments (Salamanca-Sanabria, Richards, & Timulak, 2019), and this can be done more rapidly than is usually the case in treatment research. This can be in the form of studies with countries collaborating using different versions of the same treatment program (but in different languages), or providing treatment within countries for individuals who prefer their native language or might not even know the language in the country where they reside. Given migration and limited access to translators in face-to-face psychotherapy, this has opened up new possibilities. An example of a screenshot for a translated program into Kurdish is shown in Fig. 17.1 (Lindegaard et al., 2019).

Support and blending

Internet psychotherapy often involves clinicians. The input from the clinician can range from absent in fully *self-guided* treatments (with no diagnostic procedures or interviews and no support) to video interactions and even blended treatments in which clinical face-to-face sessions are mixed with online treatment programs (Erbe, Eichert, Riper, & Ebert, 2017). Most research has been on therapist-guided Internet treatments with minimal weekly text-based guidance based on reports sent by clients and their questions. This support is often asynchronous, which facilitates supervision and also possibility to check previous conversations. Automated messages can be used as well but more personalized specific feedback is most often provided by a clinician.

There is a growing literature on the role of the clinician and how clients respond to the interaction in Internet psychotherapies. First, while debated, there are clear indications that support yields better adherence and less dropout from treatment and possibly better outcomes (Baumeister, Reichler, Munzinger, & Lin, 2014), even if there are exceptions of studies showing that support-on-demand (Hadjistavropoulos et al., 2017), and even largely automated treatment can work when treatment is completed (Titov et al., 2013). On the other hand, it needs to be said that even if automated treatments

بۆ پرۆژەی سەفین

Fig. 17.1 Screenshot from kurdish ICBT study (Lindegaard et al., 2019).

might work for suitable clients it may still be that both clients and clinicians prefer treatments that are guided, in particular for more severe problems and vulnerable groups (Topooco et al., 2017). Second, many studies have investigated the role of therapeutic alliance in Internet psychotherapies (Berger, 2017), and have found that clients rate the alliance as high (in spite of much less contact with their therapist and often only via text), and that higher alliance ratings can be associated with better outcomes as in face-to-face psychotherapies (Probst, Berger, & Flückiger, 2019). Adding to this, there are also qualitative studies on how clients experience Internet psychotherapies and in a meta-synthesis of 24 studies it was concluded that personal support was valued highly as a major component of the treatments and when they worked (Patel et al., 2020). Finally, there are also studies on how therapists act in Internet treatments indicating that what they write in the messages can be both helpful and sometimes less so (Paxling et al., 2013). However, most of the correspondence between clients and their therapists consist of encouragement and clarification of the treatment components and procedures, and to a lesser extent therapeutic interactions and conversations about the therapy relation (Hadjistavropoulos, Schneider, Klassen, Dear, & Titov, 2018). While not yet, there are studies on what clients ask (Soucy, Hadjistavropoulos, Pugh, Dear, & Titov, 2019), and write about in their correspondence with their therapists (Svartvatten, Segerlund, Dennhag, Andersson, & Carlbring, 2015). Again, as expected most of this is related to the treatment but what is less known is how clients approach their treatment. For example, a therapy session in real life can hardly be repeated unless recorded, whereas a text message in the Internet treatment can be read several times and also the intervention itself. Qualitative studies finding that some clients only read assignments, whereas others make major changes in their lives as a result of the intervention (Bendelin et al., 2011).

A typical treatment case

One way to describe Internet psychotherapy is to illustrate with a case. There are very few published case studies on Internet treatments and the information provided in research papers is often limited with a focus on outcomes. Before moving on to research support, I will briefly give an example of a case here (based on actual clients but here fictional). Louise was a 42-year-old female, mother of two and divorced 2 years ago. She had an episode of depression in her youth but now suffered from worry about her situation including family, work, and her brother who has an addiction problem. She also worried about her health, but not in the form of health anxiety but rather fear of accidents. She decided to seek help at the local GP clinic and was referred to a psychologist. Following an interview and a screening based on the MINI interview, the psychologist concluded that generalized anxiety disorder was a probable diagnosis, which also corresponded with what she had discussed in a previous meeting with her GP. The psychologist told her that the clinic now could provide online treatment and asked if she might be interested. This was an attractive option for her as she would find it hard to get off work and with the children also that she has read about Internet treatments in the paper. She also had a friend who had participated in a research study a few years found the treatment helpful. As the clinic also would evaluate the intervention, she gave informed consent that her data would be used later on for evaluation. The first step was to complete a set of self-report questionnaires online at home after instructions and introduction to the treatment platform with the psychologist. The following week they had a short telephone call during which the psychologist told her about the GAD program and how they would work for the 9 weeks. He told her that they would communicate via the system but that it would be possible to schedule appointments if needed. Then, they scheduled a follow-up visit at the clinic 2 months later when the treatment had ended. The subsequent weeks were focused on a GAD treatment program called "Oroshjälpen" and which has been tested in controlled trials (Dahlin et al., 2016). The treatment is based on CBT but has an orientation toward acceptance and commitment therapy (ACT). The first module is called "What is worry?" and includes psychoeducation about anxiety and worry and how it can be treated. An overview of the treatment program is also presented. A homework task was given to describe how perceived her anxiety and worry and how she had handled it previously. In the second module, functional analysis was presented. This involved information on how to practice functional analysis as a way to understand her behaviors and anxiety. Values and value-based activities were presented in the third module. She was instructed to work with her own values and schedule meaningful activities based on those values. In the fourth module, mindfulness was presented in terms of the theory behind and through different exercises. She was encouraged to practice mindfulness and write down the experiences during the week and later report to her therapist. In the fifth module, Louise was asked to review worry as a constant struggle based on avoidance and to take a new stance regarding unpleasant thoughts and feelings. The work with mindfulness, thoughts, and feelings was continued and reported on a weekly basis. In the sixth module, acceptance was introduced as an alternative to avoidance and struggle to take control over thoughts and feelings. She was instructed to incorporate the practice of acceptance in the mindfulness exercises and daily living and to describe the experiences later on in the correspondence. The final last module included a brief review of the treatment and the importance of continued work. A relapse prevention plan was also presented.

With regards to the process, Louise had a good collaboration with the psychologist and did not view the treatment as too hard or difficult to understand. She had thought about mindfulness previously and was thus motivated to give it a try. When reaching the end, the psychologist sent her instructions for the outcome questionnaires. In the final meeting, face to face they discussed the treatment and outcome (on the Penn State Worry Questionnaire her scores had gone down from 66 to 42 points). While most of had been positive, she had experienced some sadness when realizing that she had spent too much time worrying and that her kids might have suffered from her GAD. The psychologist and she discussed this and she also realized that the treatment might be applied for this problem as well (e.g., functional analysis).

Research support

Conditions and target groups

As I mentioned in the introduction of this chapter, Internet interventions research is a rapidly growing field with new controlled trials being published every month. I will focus here on an overview and give examples mainly based on systematic reviews and meta-analyses as they are almost as abundant as the controlled trials. We recently published an umbrella review (review of reviews), which focused on meta-analyses on anxiety and mood disorders in adults (Andersson, Carlbring, Titov, & Lindefors, 2019). Following the identification of 618 meta-analytic reviews, we selected the nine most recent reviews of controlled trials for conditions such as panic disorder, GAD, social anxiety disorder (SAD), posttraumatic stress disorder, major depression, and transdiagnostic studies. Between group effect sizes against control conditions in these meta-analyses ranged between very large ($d = 1.31$ for panic disorder) to small ($d = 0.44$ in one of the reviews on depression), but were overall moderate to large and in line with what has been found in face-to-face research. Quality of the meta-analyses also varied as well as the amount of therapist guidance. In addition to the work on adults, there are reviews of studies on Internet treatments for children and adolescents (Vigerland et al., 2016) and older adults (Xiang et al., 2020). There are also systematic reviews and meta-analyses on eating disorders (Loucas et al., 2014), addictions (Boumparis et al., 2019; Boumparis, Karyotaki, Schaub, Cuijpers, & Riper, 2017), stress (Heber et al., 2017), insomnia (Soh, Ho, Ho, & Tam, 2020), and numerous studies on health problems such as chronic pain, tinnitus, cancer, heart problems, diabetes, and other somatic conditions (S. Mehta, Peynenburg, & Hadjistavropoulos, 2019). Here are also conditions and target groups for which there are not yet enough studies for systematic reviews. This includes OCD and specific phobias, and also problems such as loneliness and procrastination, which are not contained within a diagnostic nomenclature but commonly seen in health-care settings. Another line of research focus on prevention of psychiatric illness shows some initial support (Ebert, Cuijpers, Muñoz, & Baumeister, 2017). There is also work on Internet programs for the reduction of suicidal ideation (Büscher, Torok, Terhorst, & Sander, 2020) showing promising results.

While meta-analyses have their value, another complementary way to assess research is to collect all data and combine them across studies in an individual patient-level meta-analysis (IPDMA). These reviews are dependent on researchers sharing data, which can cause bias but they are helpful when investigating predictors and estimating effects across trials (Stewart & Tierney, 2002). There are some IPDMAs published on Internet interventions, for example, on problems drinking (Riper et al., 2018) and depression (Karyotaki et al., 2018). Based on our own trials across disorders, we aggregated data from 2866 patients in 29 Swedish clinical trials of Internet interventions (Andersson, Carlbring, & Rozental, 2019). We covered a range of conditions we categorized as either anxiety disorders, depression, or other. When focusing on reliable change for the primary outcomes, we found that 65.6% of the clients receiving treatment were classified as achieving recovery. The categorization was based on Jacobson and Truax's (1991) reliable change index (RCI) (Jacobson & Truax, 1991). Using a stricter criteria for remission with the additional requirement of having improved substantially, we found that 35.0% could be classified as reaching remission. Using the same data set, we have also reported deterioration rates of 5.8% in treatment condition (Rozental, Magnusson, Boettcher, Andersson, & Carlbring, 2017), and in another report we focused on nonresponse and found that 26.8% could be classified as nonresponders (Rozental, Andersson, & Carlbring, 2019). Thus, roughly and across trials and conditions it can be estimated that 65% improve, 35% improve to the extent that they "recover," 25% experience no change, and a minority of 6% may even deteriorate over a treatment period. These estimates will vary across conditions and trials and are based on different calculations (not summing up to 100%), but most likely they do not represent an overestimation of effects.

Compared to face to face

With the promising results of Internet treatments, the question was raised early to what extent guided Internet treatments are as effective as face-to-face psychotherapy.

At this stage, it was only CBT that had been tested and with regards to direct comparisons (controlled trials) it is still the case that a majority of trials are based on CBT. Comparative trials are more difficult to conduct as they require that participants are willing to be randomized to either Internet treatment or to live therapy sessions individually or in groups. Preferences may be in either direction but it can also be for practical reasons hard to participate if allocated to face-to-face treatment. Thus are not many studies and most are small. The most recent meta-analysis included 20 studies in which participants had been randomly assigned to guided Internet treatment (CBT) for psychiatric and somatic conditions or to face-to-face CBT (Carlbring, Andersson, Cuijpers, Riper, & Hedman-Lagerlöf, 2018). The pooled between-group effect size at posttreatment was Hedge's $g = 0.05$, suggesting that ICBT and face-to-face treatment produce equivalent effects. While the controlled trials clearly suggest that Internet treatments work, it is still premature to conclude noninferiority against face-to-face CBT (O'Kearney, Kim, Dawson, & Calear, 2019. It is increasingly the case that there are no evidence-based face-to-face treatments to compare with as treatment development often is done using Internet interventions (Andersson, Titov, Dear, Rozental, & Carlbring, 2018). The paradoxical question may then be if face-to-face treatments work as well as evidence-based Internet treatments.

Long-term effects

Several studies on Internet interventions have included 1-year follow-up data or shorter follow-ups of 6 months. To my knowledge, these have not been summarized in a systematic review. Longer follow-ups of at least 2 years are less common but have been reviewed (Andersson, Rozental, Shafran, & Carlbring, 2018). The focus was on follow-up data at least 2 years after treatment completion and 14 studies were included with 902 participants. The average follow-up period was 3 years. Long-term outcome studies on panic disorder, social anxiety disorder, generalized anxiety disorder, depression, mixed anxiety and depression, obsessive-compulsive disorder, pathological gambling, stress, and chronic fatigue were included. The pre- to follow-up within-group effect size was Hedge's $g = 1.52$. This large effect corresponds well with short-term outcomes but must be interpreted with caution given the small number of studies, the uncontrolled nature of the effects, and uncertainties regarding the naturalistic course of some conditions.

Implementation and evidence in clinical settings

A separate literature on implementation and evidence in real-life clinical settings has been published. One early review concluded that effects of clinical service-provided Internet treatments tended to be the same as in research studies based on community recruitment (Andersson & Hedman, 2013). A more recent systematic review focused on nonrandomized pre-post studies conducted in routine care settings (Etzelmueller et al., 2020). These included 19 studies (with 30 groups) and reported pooled effects of $g = 1.78$ for depression studies and $g = 0.94$ for anxiety studies. Deterioration rates were low (3%) and moderate to high acceptability were reported. Another systematic review compared studies using community vs clinical service recruitment. In that review, anxiety outcomes were larger in studies with community recruitment (Romijn et al., 2019). Large studies are now being reported (Titov et al., 2020), and while the research to date clearly indicates that clinical delivery of Internet treatments can work it may be important to further investigate subgroup differences which can lie behind recruitment and referral routes. Service delivery models differ and are important to consider (Titov et al., 2018).

In the context of service delivery practice guidelines and ethical considerations are embedded and while they have been mentioned in the literature it is still the case that there are major differences between countries and settings (Borgueta, Purvis, & Newman, 2018; Dever Fitzgerald et al., 2010; Mendes-Santos, Weiderpass, Santana, & Andersson, 2020). Data security is only one aspect but client safety including risk management is also an important aspect (Nielssen et al., 2015).

Future and ongoing developments

In this section, I will comment on ongoing research and suggest future research challenges. First, a comment on cost effectiveness. There are clear indications that Internet treatments, even when guided by a clinician, can be cost effective (Donker et al., 2015), with important factors being reduced costs for society and increased capacity to function and work. However, more work needs to be done and also from an international perspective as Internet treatments can reach persons across borders, which make cost calculations and cost savings a complicated matter. A classical question is the balance between effects and scalability, which regular psychotherapy rarely achieves but which is possible with Internet treatments (Fairburn & Patel, 2017).

Second point concerns technology advances which may occur rapidly. Not only ways to handle large data sets using machine learning but also so-called embodied conversational agents (Provoost, Lau, Ruwaard, & Riper, 2017) and chatbots (Ly, Ly, & Andersson, 2017) can be used as adjuncts or even replacements for clinicians. However, the development of a product does not necessarily mean that clients will use it or prefer to use it. It will be important to investigate if an alliance can be formed with such technical solutions (Miloff et al., 2020), and also how much machine learning algorithms can be used to improve the quality of the therapeutic interaction. Another angle in relation to Internet psychotherapies is to use persuasive technology (Radomski et al., 2019) and serious games (Lindner et al., 2020; Sardi, Idri, & Fernandez-Aleman, 2017) to boost the treatment. As stated earlier in this chapter, virtual reality and smartphone applications are also part of this development.

My third point is that treatments might work for a majority of clients but there is always variation in response making predictors of outcome important to investigate and report. There are numerous studies on predictors of outcome of Internet treatments but unfortunately few consistently replicated findings. For example, cognitive function does not appear to predict outcome (Lindner et al., 2016), and gene are also not significantly related to outcome (Rayner et al., 2019). Promising findings have emerged regarding brain imaging but there are yet few studies (Månsson et al., 2015; Webb et al., 2018). Other ways to do research on predictors include ecological momentary assessments and using machine learning algorithms (Colombo et al., 2019). One potentially promising approach is to develop and study adaptive treatments to handle possible treatment failures (Forsell et al., 2019). In line with the research on moderators, there are also studies on variables that might mediate treatment outcome (Andersson, Titov, et al., 2018). As with the prediction studies, there are few consistent findings to date but this will hopefully change with larger data sets and participants recruited in clinical settings. Another approach mentioned earlier is to combine data sets in IPDMAs to achieve more statistical power.

My final point will focus on topics I believe will be investigated further in future research. This includes research on knowledge about treatment and how much clients learn in their treatments, and also the pedagogical aspects of Internet treatments can be boosted (Berg et al., 2020). There will also be more research on treatments other than psychological physical activity and medication adherence. Further, while research on psychological problems such as loneliness and procrastination has begun other urgent matters like pandemic may merit specifics that are easy to develop and test using Internet research (Wahlund et al., 2020). Finally, training in psychotherapy as well as research on how to best train and supervise psychotherapists (Cooper et al., 2017).

Conclusion

In conclusion, Internet-based psychotherapy has existed only a short time but during these 20 years a large number of treatments have been developed, tested in research, and a few have also been implemented. It can be argued that the Internet medium has resulted in more rapid knowledge development rapid progression technical solutions. Overall, the research suggests that Internet-based psychotherapies can be as effective as face-to-face psychotherapies that the treatments work in regular clinics and that most mild to moderate psychiatric and some somatic conditions.

References

Andersson, G. (2015). *The internet and CBT: A clinical guide*. Boca Raton: CRC Press.

Andersson, G. (2018). Internet interventions: Past, present and future. *Internet Interventions*, *12*, 181–188. https://doi.org/10.1016/j.invent.2018.03.008.

Andersson, G., Carlbring, P., & Rozental, A. (2019). Response and remission rates in internet-based cognitive behavior therapy: An individual patient data meta-analysis. *Frontiers in Psychiatry*, *10*, 749. https://doi.org/10.3389/fpsyt.2019.00749.

Andersson, G., Carlbring, P., Titov, N., & Lindefors, N. (2019). Internet interventions for adults with anxiety and mood disorders: A narrative umbrella review of recent meta-analyses. *Canadian Journal of Psychiatry*, *64*, 465–470. https://doi.org/10.1177/0706743719839381.

Andersson, G., & Hedman, E. (2013). Effectiveness of guided internet-delivered cognitive behaviour therapy in regular clinical settings. *Verhaltenstherapie*, *23*, 140–148. https://doi.org/10.1159/000354779.

Andersson, G., Rozental, A., Shafran, R., & Carlbring, P. (2018). Long-term effects of internet-supported cognitive behavior therapy. *Expert Review of Neurotherapeutics*, *18*, 21–28. https://doi.org/10.1080/14737175.2018.1400381.

Andersson, G., Titov, N., Dear, B. F., Rozental, A., & Carlbring, P. (2018). Internet-delivered psychological treatments: From innovation to implementation. *World Psychiatry*, *18*, 20–28. https://doi.org/10.1002/wps.20610.

Baumeister, H., Reichler, L., Munzinger, M., & Lin, J. (2014). The impact of guidance on internet-based mental health interventions – A systematic review. *Internet Interventions*, *1*, 205–215. https://doi.org/10.1016/j.invent.2014.08.003.

Bendelin, N., Hesser, H., Dahl, J., Carlbring, P., Zetterqvist Nelson, K., & Andersson, G. (2011). Experiences of guided Internet-based cognitive-behavioural treatment for depression: A qualitative study. *BMC Psychiatry*, *11*, 107. https://doi.org/10.1186/1471-244X-11-107.

Bennett, K., Bennett, A. J., & Griffiths, K. M. (2010). Security considerations for e-mental health interventions. *Journal of Medical Internet Research*, *12*. https://doi.org/10.2196/jmir.1468, e61.

Berg, M., Rozental, A., de Brun Mangs, J., Näsman, M., Strömberg, K., Viberg, L., et al. (2020). The role of learning support and chat-sessions in guided internet-based cognitive behavioural therapy for adolescents with anxiety: A factorial design study. *Frontiers in Psychiatry*, *11*, 503. https://doi.org/10.3389/fpsyt.2020.00503.

Berger, T. (2017). The therapeutic alliance in internet interventions: A narrative review and suggestions for future research. *Psychotherapy Research*, *27*, 511–524. https://doi.org/10.1080/10503307.2015.1119908.

Borgueta, A. M., Purvis, C. K., & Newman, M. G. (2018). Navigating the ethics of internet-guided self-help interventions. *Clinical Psychology: Science and Practice*, *25*(2), e12235. https://doi.org/10.1111/cpsp.12235.

Boumparis, N., Karyotaki, E., Schaub, M. P., Cuijpers, P., & Riper, H. (2017). Internet interventions for adult illicit substance users: A meta-analysis. *Addiction*, *112*, 1521–1532. https://doi.org/10.1111/add.13819.

Boumparis, N., Loheide-Niesmann, L., Blankers, M., Ebert, D. D., Korf, D., Schaub, M. P., et al. (2019). Short- and long-term effects of digital prevention and treatment interventions for cannabis use reduction: A systematic review and meta-analysis. *Drug and Alcohol Dependence*, *200*, 82–94. https://doi.org/10.1016/j.drugalcdep.2019.03.016.

Brown, M., Glendenning, A., Hoon, A. E., & John, A. (2016). Effectiveness of web-delivered acceptance and commitment therapy in relation to mental health and well-being: A systematic review and meta-analysis. *Journal of Medical Internet Research*, *18*. https://doi.org/10.2196/jmir.6200, e221.

Buchanan, T. (2002). Online assessment: Desirable or dangerous? *Professional Psychology: Research and Practice*, *33*, 148–154.

Büscher, R., Torok, M., Terhorst, Y., & Sander, L. (2020). Internet-based cognitive behavioral therapy to reduce suicidal ideation: A systematic review and meta-analysis. *JAMA Network Open*, *i3*, e203933. https://doi.org/10.1001/jamanetworkopen.2020.3933.

Carlbring, P., Andersson, G., Cuijpers, P., Riper, H., & Hedman-Lagerlöf, E. (2018). Internet-based vs. face-to-face cognitive behavior therapy for psychiatric and somatic disorders: An updated systematic review and meta-analysis. *Cognitive Behaviour Therapy*, *47*, 1–18. https://doi.org/10.1080/16506073.2017.1401115.

Carlbring, P., Apelstrand, M., Sehlin, H., Amir, N., Rousseau, A., Hofmann, S., et al. (2012). Internet-delivered attention training in individuals with social anxiety disorder – a double blind randomized controlled trial. *BMC Psychiatry*, *12*, 66.

Carlbring, P., Brunt, S., Bohman, S., Austin, D., Richards, J. C., Öst, L.-G., et al. (2007). Internet vs. paper and pencil administration of questionnaires commonly used in panic/agoraphobia research. *Computers in Human Behavior*, *23*, 1421–1434. https://doi.org/10.1016/j.chb.2005.05.002.

Chakrabarti, S. (2015). Usefulness of telepsychiatry: A critical evaluation of videoconferencing-based approaches. *World Journal of Psychiatry*, *5*(3), 286–304. https://doi.org/10.5498/wjp.v5.i3.286.

Colombo, D., Fernandez-Alvarez, J., Patane, A., Semonella, M., Kwiatkowska, M., Garcia-Palacios, A., et al. (2019). Current state and future directions of technology-based ecological momentary assessment and intervention for major depressive disorder: A systematic review. *Journal of Clinical Medicine*, *8*, 465. https://doi.org/10.3390/jcm8040465.

Cooper, Z., Bailey-Straebler, S., Morgan, K. E., O'Connor, M. E., Caddy, C., Hamadi, L., et al. (2017). Using the internet to train therapists: Randomized comparison of two scalable methods. *Journal of Medical Internet Research*, *19*(10). https://doi.org/10.2196/jmir.8336, e355.

Dahlin, M., Andersson, G., Magnusson, K., Johansson, T., Sjögren, J., Håkansson, A., et al. (2016). Internet-delivered acceptance-based behaviour therapy for generalized anxiety disorder: A randomized controlled trial. *Behaviour Research and Therapy*, *77*, 86–95. https://doi.org/10.1016/j.brat.2015.12.007.

Dever Fitzgerald, T., Hunter, P. V., Hadjistavropoulos, T., & Koocher, G. P. (2010). Ethical and legal considerations for internet-based psychotherapy. *Cognitive Behaviour Therapy*, *39*, 173–187. https://doi.org/10.1080/16506071003636046.

Donker, T., Bennett, K., Bennett, A., Mackinnon, A., van Straten, A., Cuijpers, P., et al. (2013). Internet-delivered interpersonal psychotherapy versus internet-delivered cognitive behavioral therapy for adults with depressive symptoms: Randomized controlled noninferiority trial. *Journal of Medical Internet Research*, *15*. https://doi.org/10.2196/jmir.2307, e82.

Donker, T., Blankers, M., Hedman, E., Ljótsson, B., Petrie, K., & Christensen, H. (2015). Economic evaluations of internet interventions for mental health: A systematic review. *Psychological Medicine*, *45*, 3357–3376. https://doi.org/10.1017/s0033291715001427.

Eaton, W. W., Neufeld, K., Chen, L.-S., & Cai, G. (2000). A comparison of self-report and clinical diagnostic interviews for depression. Diagnostic interview schedule and schedules for clinical assessment in neuropsychiatry in the Baltimore epidemiologic catchment area follow-up. *Archives of General Psychiatry*, *57*, 217–222.

Ebert, D. D., Cuijpers, P., Muñoz, R. F., & Baumeister, H. (2017). Prevention of mental health disorders using internet- and mobile-based interventions: A narrative review and recommendations for future research. *Frontiers in Psychiatry*, *8*, 116. https://doi.org/10.3389/fpsyt.2017.00116.

Erbe, D., Eichert, H. C., Riper, H., & Ebert, D. D. (2017). Blending face-to-face and internet-based interventions for the treatment of mental disorders in adults: Systematic review. *Journal of Medical Internet Research*, *19*. https://doi.org/10.2196/jmir.6588, e306.

Etzelmueller, A., Vis, C., Karyotaki, E., Baumeister, H., Titov, N., Berking, M., et al. (2020). Effects of internet-based cognitive behavioral therapy in routine care for adults in treatment for depression and anxiety: Systematic review and meta-analysis. *Journal of Medical Internet Research*, *22*. https://doi.org/10.2196/18100, e18100.

Fairburn, C. G., & Patel, V. (2017). The impact of digital technology on psychological treatments and their dissemination. *Behaviour Research and Therapy*, *88*, 19–25. https://doi.org/10.1016/j.brat.2016.08.012.

Forsell, E., Jernelöv, S., Blom, K., Kraepelien, M., Svanborg, C., Andersson, G., et al. (2019). Proof of concept for an adaptive treatment strategy to prevent failures in internet-delivered CBT: A single-blind randomized clinical trial with insomnia patients. *American Journal of Psychiatry*, *176*, 315–323. https://doi.org/10.1176/appi.ajp.2018.18060699.

Giustini, D., Ali, S. M., Fraser, M., & Kamel Boulos, M. N. (2018). Effective uses of social media in public health and medicine: A systematic review of systematic reviews. *Online Journal of Public Health Informatics, 10*(2). https://doi.org/10.5210/ojphi.v10i2.8270, e215.

Griffiths, K. M., Calear, A. L., & Banfield, M. (2009). Systematic review on internet support groups (ISGs) and depression (1): Do ISGs reduce depressive symptoms? *Journal of Medical Internet Research, 11.* https://doi.org/10.2196/jmir.1270, e40.

Haas, L. J., Benedict, J. G., & Kobos, J. C. (1996). Psychotherapy by telephone: Risks and benefits for psychologists and consumers. *Professional Psychology: Research and Practice, 27,* 154–160.

Hadjistavropoulos, H. D., Schneider, L. H., Edmonds, M., Karin, E., Nugent, M. N., Dirkse, D., et al. (2017). Randomized controlled trial of internet-delivered cognitive behaviour therapy comparing standard weekly versus optional weekly therapist support. *Journal of Anxiety Disorders, 52,* 15–24. https://doi.org/10.1016/j.janxdis.2017.09.006.

Hadjistavropoulos, H. D., Schneider, L. H., Klassen, K., Dear, B. F., & Titov, N. (2018). Development and evaluation of a scale assessing therapist fidelity to guidelines for delivering therapist-assisted Internet-delivered cognitive behaviour therapy. *Cognitive Behaviour Therapy, 47,* 447–461. https://doi.org/10.1080/16506073.2018.1457079.

Heber, E., Ebert, D. D., Lehr, D., Cuijpers, P., Berking, M., Nobis, S., et al. (2017). The benefit of web- and computer-based interventions for stress: A systematic review and meta-analysis. *Journal of Medical Internet Research, 19.* https://doi.org/10.2196/jmir.5774, e32.

Jacobson, N. S., & Truax, P. (1991). Clinical significance: A statistical approach to defining meaningful change in psychotherapy research. *Journal of Consulting and Clinical Psychology, 59,* 12–19. https://doi.org/10.1037/0022-006X.59.1.12.

Johansson, R., Frederick, R. J., & Andersson, G. (2013). Using the Internet to provide psychodynamic psychotherapy. *Psychodynamic Psychiatry, 41,* 385–412. https://doi.org/10.1521/pdps.2013.41.4.513.

Karyotaki, E., Ebert, D. D., Donkin, L., Riper, H., Twisk, J., Burger, S., et al. (2018). Do guided internet-based interventions result in clinically relevant changes for patients with depression? An individual participant data meta-analysis. *Clinical Psychology Review, 63,* 80–92. https://doi.org/10.1016/j.cpr.2018.06.007.

Krotoski, A. (2013). *Untangling the web. What the internet is doing to you.* London: Guardian Books.

Leach, L. S., & Christensen, H. (2006). A systematic review of telephone-based interventions for mental disorders. *Journal for Telemedicine and Telecare, 12,* 122–129.

Lindegaard, T., Brohede, D., Koshnawa, K., Osmana, S. S., Johansson, R., & Andersson, G. (2019). Internet-based treatment of depressive symptoms in a Kurdish population: A randomized controlled trial. *Journal of Clinical Psychology, 75,* 985–998. https://doi.org/10.1002/jclp.22753.

Lindner, P., Carlbring, P., Flodman, E., Hebert, A., Poysti, S., Hagkvist, F., et al. (2016). Does cognitive flexibility predict treatment gains in internet-delivered psychological treatment of social anxiety disorder, depression, or tinnitus? *PeerJ, 4.* https://doi.org/10.7717/peerj.1934, e1934.

Lindner, P., Miloff, A., Hamilton, W., Reuterskiöld, L., Andersson, G., Powers, M., et al. (2017). Creating state of the art, next-generation virtual reality exposure therapies for anxiety disorders using consumer hardware platforms: Design considerations and future direction. *Cognitive Behaviour Therapy, 46,* 404–420. https://doi.org/10.1080/16506073.2017.1280843.

Lindner, P., Rozental, A., Jurell, A., Reuterskiöld, L., Andersson, G., Hamilton, W., et al. (2020). Experiences of gamified and automated Virtual Reality exposure therapy for spider phobia: Qualitative study. *JMIR Serious Games, 8,* e17807. https://doi.org/10.2196/17807.

Loucas, C. E., Fairburn, C. G., Whittington, C., Pennant, M. E., Stockton, S., & Kendall, T. (2014). E-therapy in the treatment and prevention of eating disorders: A systematic review and meta-analysis. *Behaviour Research and Therapy*, *63C*, 122–131. https://doi.org/10.1016/j.brat.2014.09.011.

Ly, K. H., Ly, A.-M., & Andersson, G. (2017). A fully automated conversational agent for promoting mental well-being: A pilot RCT using mixed methods. *Internet Interventions*, *10*, 39–46. https://doi.org/10.1016/j.invent.2017.10.002.

Månsson, K. N. T., Frick, A., Boraxbekk, C.-J., Marquand, A. F., Williams, S. C. R., Carlbring, P., et al. (2015). Predicting long-term outcome of Internet-delivered cognitive behavior therapy for social anxiety disorder using fMRI and support vector machine learning. *Translational Psychiatry*, *5*. https://doi.org/10.1038/tp.2015.22, e530.

Marks, I. M., Shaw, S., & Parkin, R. (1998). Computer-assisted treatments of mental health problems. *Clinical Psychology: Science and Practice*, *5*, 51–170. https://doi.org/10.1111/j.1468-2850.1998.tb00141.x.

Marrs, R. W. (1995). A meta-analysis of bibliotherapy studies. *American Journal of Community Psychology*, *23*, 843–870.

Mehta, N., & Atreja, A. (2015). Online social support networks. *International Review of Psychiatry*, *27*, 118–123. https://doi.org/10.3109/09540261.2015.1015504.

Mehta, S., Peynenburg, V. A., & Hadjistavropoulos, H. D. (2019). Internet-delivered cognitive behaviour therapy for chronic health conditions: A systematic review and meta-analysis. *Journal of Behavioral Medicine*, *42*, 169–187. https://doi.org/10.1007/s10865-018-9984-x.

Mendes-Santos, C., Weiderpass, E., Santana, R., & Andersson, G. (2020). Portuguese psychologists' attitudes toward internet interventions: Exploratory cross-sectional study. *JMIR Mental Health*, *7*(4). https://doi.org/10.2196/16817, e16817.

Miloff, A., Carlbring, P., Hamilton, W., Andersson, G., Reuterskiöld, L., & Lindner, P. (2020). Measuring alliance toward embodied virtual therapists in the era of automated treatments: The virtual therapist alliance scale (VTAS). *Journal of Medical Internet Research*, *22*. https://doi.org/10.2196/16660, e16660.

Mohr, D. C., Zhang, M., & Schueller, S. M. (2017). Personal sensing: Understanding mental health using ubiquitous sensors and machine learning. *Annual Review of Clinical Psychology*, *13*, 23–47. https://doi.org/10.1146/annurev-clinpsy-032816-044949.

Nielssen, O., Dear, B. F., Staples, L. G., Dear, R., Ryan, K., Purtell, C., et al. (2015). Procedures for risk management and a review of crisis referrals from the MindSpot Clinic, a national service for the remote assessment and treatment of anxiety and depression. *BMC Psychiatry*, *15*, 304. https://doi.org/10.1186/s12888-015-0676-6.

Nyström, M. B. T., Stenling, A., Sjöström, E., Neely, G., Lindner, P., Hassmén, P., et al. (2017). Behavioral activation versus physical activity via the Internet: A randomized controlled trial. *Journal of Affective Disorders*, *215*, 85–93. https://doi.org/10.1016/j.jad.2017.03.018.

O'Kearney, R., Kim, S., Dawson, R. L., & Calear, A. L. (2019). Are claims of non-inferiority of Internet and computer-based cognitive-behavioural therapy compared with in-person cognitive-behavioural therapy for adults with anxiety disorders supported by the evidence from head-to-head randomised controlled trials? A systematic review. *Australian and New Zealand Journal of Psychiatry*, *53*, 851–865. https://doi.org/10.1177/0004867419864433.

Patel, S., Akhtar, A., Malins, S., Wright, N., Rowley, E., Young, E., et al. (2020). The acceptability and usability of digital health interventions for adults with depression, anxiety, and somatoform disorders: Qualitative systematic review and meta-synthesis. *Journal of Medical Internet Research*, *22*. https://doi.org/10.2196/16228, e16228.

Paxling, B., Lundgren, S., Norman, A., Almlöv, J., Carlbring, P., Cuijpers, P., et al. (2013). Therapist behaviours in Internet-delivered cognitive behaviour therapy: Analyses of e-mail correspondence in the treatment of generalized anxiety disorder. *Behavioural and Cognitive Psychotherapy*, *41*, 280–289. https://doi.org/10.1017/S1352465812000240.

Probst, G. H., Berger, T., & Flückiger, C. (2019). The alliance-outcome relation in internet-based interventions for psychological disorders: A correlational meta-analysis. *Verhaltenstherapie*. https://doi.org/10.1159/000503432.

Provoost, S., Lau, H. M., Ruwaard, J., & Riper, H. (2017). Embodied conversational agents in clinical psychology: A scoping review. *Journal of Medical Internet Research*, *19*. https://doi.org/10.2196/jmir.6553, e151.

Radomski, A. D., Wozney, L., McGrath, P., Huguet, A., Hartling, L., Dyson, M. P., et al. (2019). Design and delivery features that may improve the use of internet-based cognitive behavioral therapy for children and adolescents with anxiety: A realist literature synthesis with a persuasive systems design perspective. *Journal of Medical Internet Research*, *21*(2). https://doi.org/10.2196/11128, e11128.

Rayner, C., Coleman, J. R. I., Purves, K. L., Hodsoll, J., Goldsmith, K., Alpers, G. W., et al. (2019). A genome-wide association meta-analysis of prognostic outcomes following cognitive behavioural therapy in individuals with anxiety and depressive disorders. *Translational Psychiatry*, *9*(1), 150. https://doi.org/10.1038/s41398-019-0481-y.

Riper, H., Hoogendoorn, A., Cuijpers, P., Karyotaki, E., Boumparis, N., Pastor, A. M., et al. (2018). Effectiveness and treatment moderators of internet interventions for adult problem drinking: An individual patient data meta-analysis of 19 randomised controlled trials. *PLoS Medicine*, *15*. https://doi.org/10.1371/journal.pmed.1002714, e1002714.

Ritterband, L. M., Thorndike, F. P., Cox, D. J., Kovatchev, B. P., & Gonder-Frederick, L. A. (2009). A behavior change model for internet interventions. *Annals of Behavioral Medicine*, *38*, 18–27. https://doi.org/10.1007/s12160-009-9133-4.

Romijn, G., Batelaan, N., Kok, R., Koning, J., van Balkom, A., Titov, N., et al. (2019). Internet-delivered cognitive behavioral therapy for anxiety disorders in open community versus clinical service recruitment: Meta-analysis. *Journal of Medical Internet Research*, *21*. https://doi.org/10.2196/11706, e11706.

Rosen, G. M. (1987). Self-help treatment books and the commercialization of psychotherapy. *American Psychologist*, *42*, 46–51.

Rozental, A., Andersson, G., & Carlbring, P. (2019). In the absence of effects: An individual patient data meta-analysis of non-response and its predictors in internet-based cognitive behavior therapy. *Frontiers in Psychology*, *10*, 589. https://doi.org/10.3389/fpsyg.2019.00589.

Rozental, A., Magnusson, K., Boettcher, J., Andersson, G., & Carlbring, P. (2017). For better or worse: An individual patient data meta-analysis of deterioration among participants receiving internet-based cognitive behavior therapy. *Journal of Consulting and Clinical Psychology*, *85*, 160–177. https://doi.org/10.1037/ccp0000158.

Salamanca-Sanabria, A., Richards, D., & Timulak, L. (2019). Adapting an internet-delivered intervention for depression for a Colombian college student population: An illustration of an integrative empirical approach. *Internet Interventions*, *15*, 76–86. https://doi.org/10.1016/j.invent.2018.11.005.

Sardi, L., Idri, A., & Fernandez-Aleman, J. L. (2017). A systematic review of gamification in e-Health. *Journal of Biomedical Informatics*, *71*, 31–48. https://doi.org/10.1016/j.jbi.2017.05.011.

Sevilla-Llewellyn-Jones, J., Santesteban-Echarri, O., Pryor, I., McGorry, P., & Alvarez-Jimenez, M. (2018). Web-based mindfulness interventions for mental health treatment: Systematic review and meta-analysis. *JMIR Mental Health*, *5*. https://doi.org/10.2196/10278, e10278.

Soh, H. L., Ho, R. C., Ho, C. S., & Tam, W. W. (2020). Efficacy of digital cognitive behavioural therapy for insomnia: A meta-analysis of randomised controlled trials. *Sleep Medicine, 75,* 315–325. https://doi.org/10.1016/j.sleep.2020.08.020.

Soucy, J. N., Hadjistavropoulos, H. D., Pugh, N. E., Dear, B. F., & Titov, N. (2019). What are clients asking their therapist during therapist-assisted internet-delivered cognitive behaviour therapy? A content analysis of client questions. *Behavioural and Cognitive Psychotherapy, 47,* 407–420. https://doi.org/10.1017/S1352465818000668.

Stefanopoulou, E., Lewis, D., Taylor, M., Broscombe, J., & Larkin, J. (2019). Digitally delivered psychological interventions for anxiety disorders: A comprehensive review. *Psychiatric Quarterly, 90*(1), 197–215. https://doi.org/10.1007/s11126-018-9620-5.

Stewart, L. A., & Tierney, J. F. (2002). To IPD or not to IPD? Advantages and disadvantages of systematic reviews using individual patient data. *Evaluation & the Health Professions, 25,* 76–97. https://doi.org/10.1177/0163278702025001006.

Svartvatten, N., Segerlund, M., Dennhag, I., Andersson, G., & Carlbring, P. (2015). A content analysis of client e-mails in guided internet-based cognitive behavior therapy for depression. *Internet Interventions, 2,* 121–127. https://doi.org/10.1016/j.invent.2015.02.004.

Titov, N., Dear, B., Nielssen, O., Staples, L., Hadjistavropoulos, H., Nugent, M., et al. (2018). ICBT in routine care: A descriptive analysis of successful clinics in five countries. *Internet Interventions, 13,* 108–115. https://doi.org/10.1016/j.invent.2018.07.006.

Titov, N., Dear, B. F., Johnston, L., Lorian, C., Zou, J., Wootton, B., et al. (2013). Improving adherence and clinical outcomes in self-guided internet treatment for anxiety and depression: Randomised controlled trial. *PLoS One, 8.* https://doi.org/10.1371/journal.pone.0062873, e62873.

Titov, N., Dear, B. F., Nielssen, O., Wootton, B., Kayrouz, R., Karin, E., et al. (2020). User characteristics and outcomes from a national digital mental health service: An observational study of registrants of the Australian MindSpot Clinic. *Lancet Digital Health, 2,* e582–e593.

Topooco, N., Riper, H., Araya, R., Berking, M., Brunn, M., Chevreul, K., et al. (2017). Attitudes towards digital treatment for depression: A European stakeholder survey. *Internet Interv, 8,* 1–9. https://doi.org/10.1016/j.invent.2017.01.001.

van Ballegooijen, W., Riper, H., Cuijpers, P., van Oppen, P., & Smit, J. H. (2016). Validation of online psychometric instruments for common mental health disorders: A systematic review. *BMC Psychiatry, 16,* 45. https://doi.org/10.1186/s12888-016-0735-7.

van Gemert-Pijnen, J. E., Nijland, N., van Limburg, M., Ossebaard, H. C., Kelders, S. M., Eysenbach, G., et al. (2011). A holistic framework to improve the uptake and impact of eHealth technologies. *Journal of Medical Internet Research, 13*(4). https://doi.org/10.2196/jmir.1672, e111.

Varker, T., Brand, R. M., Ward, J., Terhaag, S., & Phelps, A. (2019). Efficacy of synchronous telepsychology interventions for people with anxiety, depression, posttraumatic stress disorder, and adjustment disorder: A rapid evidence assessment. *Psychological Services, 16,* 621–635. https://doi.org/10.1037/ser0000239.

Vigerland, S., Lenhard, F., Bonnert, M., Lalouni, M., Hedman, E., Ahlen, J., et al. (2016). Internet-delivered cognitive behavior therapy for children and adolescents: A systematic review and meta-analysis. *Clinical Psychology Review, 50,* 1–10. https://doi.org/10.1016/j.cpr.2016.09.005.

Vlaescu, G., Alasjö, A., Miloff, A., Carlbring, P., & Andersson, G. (2016). Features and functionality of the Iterapi platform for internet-based psychological treatment. *Internet Interventions, 6,* 107–114. https://doi.org/10.1016/j.invent.2016.09.006.

Wahlund, T., Mataix-Cols, D., Olofsdotter Lauri, K., de Schipper, E., Ljótsson, B., Aspvall, K., et al. (2020). Brief online cognitive behavioural intervention for dysfunctional worry related to the COVID-19 pandemic: A randomised controlled trial. *Psychotherapy and Psychosomatics*. https://doi.org/10.1159/000512843.

Watkins, P. L., & Clum, G. A. (Eds.). (2008). *Handbook of self-help therapies*. New York: Routledge.

Webb, C. A., Olson, E. A., Killgore, W. D. S., Pizzagalli, D. A., Rauch, S. L., & Rosso, I. M. (2018). Rostral anterior cingulate cortex morphology predicts treatment response to internet-based cognitive behavioral therapy for depression. *Biological Psychiatry. Cognitive Neuroscience and Neuroimaging*, *3*, 255–262. https://doi.org/10.1016/j.bpsc.2017.08.005.

Xiang, X., Wu, S., Zuverink, A., Tomasino, K. N., An, R., & Himle, J. A. (2020). Internet-delivered cognitive behavioral therapies for late-life depressive symptoms: A systematic review and meta-analysis. *Aging & Mental Health*, *24*(8), 1196–1206. https://doi.org/10.1080/13607863.2019.1590309.

Yardley, L., Spring, B. J., Riper, H., Morrison, L. G., Crane, D. H., Curtis, K., et al. (2016). Understanding and promoting effective engagement with digital behavior change interventions. *American Journal of Preventive Medicine*, *51*(5), 833–842. https://doi.org/10.1016/j.amepre.2016.06.015.

Zimmerman, M., & Martinez, J. H. (2012). Web-based assessment of depression in patients treated in clinical practice: Reliability, validity, and patient acceptance. *Journal of Clinical Psychiatry*, *73*, 333–338. https://doi.org/10.4088/JCP.10m06519.

Apps for mental health

18

John Strauss[a,b,c], Jasmine Zhang[d,e], Madeleine L. Jarrett[a,f],
Beth Patterson[d,e], and Michael Van Ameringen[d,e]

[a]Child, Youth and Emerging Adult Program, Cundill Centre for Child and Youth Depression, Centre for Addiction and Mental Health, Toronto, ON, Canada, [b]Shannon Centennial Informatics Lab, Centre for Addiction and Mental Health, Toronto, ON, Canada, [c]Department of Psychiatry, Faculty of Medicine, University of Toronto, Toronto, ON, Canada, [d]MacAnxiety Research Centre, McMaster University, Hamilton, ON, Canada, [e]Department of Psychiatry and Behavioural Neurosciences, McMaster University, Hamilton, ON, Canada, [f]Human Biology Program, Faculty of Arts and Science, University of Toronto, Toronto, ON, Canada

Introduction

Technological advances in the 21st century have led to the nearly ubiquitous use of mobile devices around the world. The global population is becoming increasingly reliant on mobile technology, with 3.5 billion smartphone users globally in 2020 (Statista, 2020). The widespread adoption of smartphones and tablets in combination with increased internet access present unique opportunities for mobile health (mHealth) applications (apps) to be utilized as novel interventions for medical conditions. Mobile apps refer to programs designed for smartphone, tablet, and other digital platforms, enabling such technologies to support medicine and public health practices (Van Ameringen, Turna, Khalesi, Pullia, & Patterson, 2017). This expands the scope of health-care services beyond clinical and hospital settings, providing patients with additional supports and means of communication. Interest in mHealth apps has grown particularly for mental health (MH) conditions, which are becoming increasingly prevalent worldwide. Estimates from large-scale epidemiological studies suggest approximately 20.6% of US adults suffer from mental illness annually (NSDUH Annual National Report, 2020). The prevalence of mental illness is also high in children and adolescents, ranging from 10% to 20% worldwide (World Health Organization, 2020). Moreover, children, adolescents, and families affected by mental illness suffer various degrees of distress and experience a lower quality of life (Evans, Banerjee, Leese, & Huxley, 2007; Hansson, 2006; Orley, Saxena, & Herrman, 1998; Walton-Moss, Gerson, & Rose, 2005). There are also significant economic burdens associated with mental illness, which the Lancet Commission on Global Mental Health and Sustainable Development projects will cost the global economy $16 trillion by 2030 (The Carter Center, 2018). The negative impact of mental illness is thus widespread and extends beyond those who are diagnosed. It is critical to overcome treatment barriers for the well-being of the global population. Improved access to MH care and alternative interventions are necessary from a public health standpoint, and mobile apps offer a promising solution.

Mental Health in a Digital World. https://doi.org/10.1016/B978-0-12-822201-0.00006-X

The potential of MH apps

Apps can potentially alleviate many significant barriers to MH treatment. In a large global sample of 63,678 individuals with a DSM-IV disorder, the most common reason for not initiating treatment was low perceived need (Andrade et al., 2014). This issue is particularly striking for children and adolescents, who rely on adults to access MH resources and treatment (Logan & King, 2001). Apps can address this issue as they may bolster awareness and subsequently reduce the stigma around MH (Levin, Krafft, & Levin, 2018). Additionally, young people have become very well versed in technology, making MH apps highly accessible for this population.

For those who are aware of treatment needs, many experience difficulties in seeking help. A prominent issue lies in the lack of reliable MH information (Moroz, Moroz, & Slovinec D'Angelo, 2020) as the health-care system is complex and patients often struggle to find appropriate resources. MH apps which focus on resources may help patients quickly navigate the health-care system, find useful information, and connect with professionals. The high cost of traditional MH care is another major concern for treatment-seeking individuals (Moroz et al., 2020). Among participants in the National Comorbidity Study with a mood, anxiety, or substance use disorder, 47% of those who believed they needed treatment reported concerns with high cost or lack of health insurance as a barrier to care (Sareen et al., 2007). This is a particularly concerning issue as individuals with mental illness are less likely to have health insurance than those without MH problems (Rowan, McAlpine, & Blewett, 2013). Even for those who have insurance, many plans only cover partial treatment costs, thereby resulting in fragmented or discontinued care. MH apps are a promising solution to cost-effective service delivery. Many apps are free with optional paid components, and fully paid apps remain significantly cheaper than traditional therapy and medical interventions. MH apps may thus help overcome socioeconomic inequities in treatment accessibility.

Another significant barrier to MH treatment is the low availability of care facilities and trained professionals (Moroz et al., 2020). The demand for care heavily outweighs the amount of resources available, resulting in extremely delayed treatment access for many patients. In many parts of the world, currently available estimates suggest that wait times for psychiatric services are much longer than the recommended (Loebach & Ayoubzadeh, 2017). Follow-up visits by physicians are also lacking, leading to higher rates of repeated emergency department visits and rehospitalizations. Given that apps can be used remotely and at any time, they allow access to care during vulnerable periods when at-risk patients are awaiting treatment. Apps may further provide immediate assistance in times of stress or crisis when clinicians are unavailable. Therefore, while MH apps cannot replace direct intervention from clinicians, they may supplement treatment and facilitate increased clinician availability.

The integration of smartphones into MH treatment may also empower patients and encourage them to become involved in their care, leading to more favorable outcomes. This is especially true for young patients, who are the most active users of smartphones and social media. Research suggests that adolescents may be more inclined to seek remote rather than in-person care (Huberty et al., 2019), which can be facilitated by MH apps. Smartphones and their frequent use among young people, therefore, provide an opportunity for faster access to care with fewer restrictions.

Functions of MH apps

Many patients, including those who are older or experience serious mental illness, are willing to try MH apps, and clinicians have also expressed interest in incorporating MH apps to complement traditional treatments (Ben-Zeev, Davis, Kaiser, Krzsos, & Drake, 2013; Erbes et al., 2014; Torous, Friedman, & Keshvan, 2014). MH apps generally serve at least one of three major functions: providing assessment tools, tracking and monitoring symptoms, and delivering interventions. To assess MH status and provide potential diagnoses for users, apps can incorporate preset algorithms to assess subjectively reported symptoms (Labrique, Vasudevan, Kochi, Fabricant, & Mehl, 2013; Van Ameringen et al., 2017). Some apps include standardized assessments such as the Generalized Anxiety Disorder-7 (GAD-7) and Patient Health Questionnaire-9 (PHQ-9), while others incorporate customized questionnaires. Although conclusions cannot be derived from app assessments alone, this information may help patients understand their symptoms and confirm diagnoses for clinicians-in-training (Labrique et al., 2013; Torous & Powell, 2015). Many applications also include tracking functions, which help clinicians and patients monitor symptoms remotely. Data may be collected actively by asking users to answer questionnaires, write diary entries, or complete subjective symptom ratings (Torous & Powell, 2015). Passive data, on the other hand, are tracked automatically using embedded sensors. These include GPS locations, accelerometers, monitoring phone calls and texting activity, and microphones for detecting social engagement (Torous & Powell, 2015). Done properly, information from symptom tracking provides clinicians with valuable insight into the potential prognosis of illnesses and the effects of treatment regimens. Lastly, many MH apps claim to treat disorders by providing evidence-based interventions. Most intervention-based apps incorporate aspects of traditional face-to-face psychological treatments such as acceptance and commitment therapy (ACT), cognitive-behavioral therapy (CBT), and exposure and response prevention (ERP). However, it is important to note that transitions of these interventions to the smartphone interface are in their infancy. Nonetheless, the various functions of apps hold much promise and have the potential to drastically alter the landscape of MH treatment.

An immense number of health-related apps have become available to the public in recent years, and recent estimates suggest that over 10,000 are specifically designed for mental well-being (Torous & Roberts, 2017). Apps also vary widely in their intended audience and purpose. Some are designed for specific age groups (e.g., older adults, young adults, adolescents, and children), while others are appropriate for all ages. With regard to function, many apps target specific MH conditions including anxiety disorders, mood disorders, obsessive-compulsive disorder (OCD), substance use disorders, posttraumatic stress disorder (PTSD), eating disorders, and schizoaffective disorders. Others claim to improve general well-being through mindfulness and stress reduction techniques. The extreme volume and variety of apps available can make the selection an extremely overwhelming experience for patients and clinicians, especially if they do not possess ample background knowledge in this area. Additionally, no regulatory bodies currently oversee app development and marketing, leaving many questions regarding the validity of their efficacy claims unanswered. The accuracy of information provided and the safety of interventions are also not guaranteed.

The most notable setback against the widespread adoption of MH apps lies in the lack of high-quality evidence on their efficacy; almost all apps claim to be effective, but few are supported by empirical research (Agarwal et al., 2016; Bauer et al., 2020; Chan, Torous, Hinton, & Yellowlees, 2015; Chandrashekar, 2018; Donker et al., 2013; Wang, Varma, & Prosperi, 2018). This stands in stark contrast with the rapid rate of app development and the vast number of apps currently available. Furthermore, mHealth apps must meet criteria in a number of other domains, including safety, privacy, and usability, to be considered appropriate for use. These aspects often go unaddressed in randomized control trials (RCTs) and feasibility studies or are overlooked by patients and clinicians. To combat this issue, researchers and professional organizations have devised frameworks for evaluating apps, some of which are for mHealth apps in general and others are specific to MH. Such frameworks should be used by developers to guide the design of high-quality apps. Implementing app evaluation frameworks is also particularly important for patients and clinicians, as many app users are doing so without professional guidance. The following sections identify key areas of app evaluation and review currently available frameworks. Additionally, the extent to which evidence-based app recommendations are possible is considered.

Key aspects of mobile apps evaluation

Efficacy

Perhaps the most important area to evaluate is an app's efficacy, which refers to the empirical support and evidence base underlying app functions and interventions. Many apps claim to be empirically effective as they incorporate scientifically supported interventions, but differences in intervention platforms and delivery methods prevent such conclusions from being drawn. Each app must therefore be considered as a novel intervention and individually undergo rigorous evaluations. Many different research methods may be utilized to evaluate app efficacy, including RCTs, N-of-1 studies, and optimization strategies (Jake-Schoffman et al., 2017; Ondersma & Walters, 2020). Although a wide variety of MH apps have been assessed in feasibility studies, few have been evaluated in high-quality clinical trials. Notable weaknesses in extant clinical trials have also been identified, including small sample sizes, high risk of bias, and unclear knowledge regarding long-term use (Bauer et al., 2020; Chan et al., 2015; Chandrashekar, 2018; Donker et al., 2013; Wang et al., 2018). Given the rapid evolution of technology and frequent updates involved in app maintenance, it is key to continuously reevaluate apps, especially following major updates that involve changes in the intervention. The specificity of the proposed interventions must also be considered, given the wide range of functions that apps serve. Lastly, evaluation frameworks should consider the extent to which apps incorporated clinician and patient input during intervention development. This aspect is often neglected in apps, making interventions inappropriate to the groups who are using them. Though the process of evaluating the evidence base behind apps can be costly and time-consuming, it is paramount to the well-being of app users. Using apps with little or no supporting evidence may not only waste time and resources but may also put users at risk of negative consequences, such as delays in seeking care. We have divided evidence from evaluation frameworks and reviews into three tables—Table 18.1 for adults, Table 18.2 for multipurpose apps, and Table 18.3 for children and youth.

Safety

Every app comes with inherent safety risks. These are particularly important to consider when patients choose to use MH apps without adequate empirical support or clinician guidance. This may potentially worsen symptoms and conditions, which poses grave dangers for user health and safety (Akbar, Coiera, & Magrabi, 2020). Thus, apps must be evaluated for potential negative effects, and these must be monitored closely throughout the course of app usage. Lewis and Wyatt (2014) outlined three main dimensions that affect the risk level associated with mHealth apps. These involve the probability and the severity of harm, the inherent complexity of the app, and additional risk factors (Lewis & Wyatt, 2014). Safety outcomes are also particularly important to incorporate for children and youth, considering the developmental vulnerabilities present during these ages. However, MH apps for young people are generally underevaluated, and safety is among the dimensions that are not thoroughly assessed.

Privacy and security

Another key area to consider when evaluating MH apps is data privacy and security. MH data should be kept confidential and often include identifying information. Not only should patients be aware of how their data is collected and stored, they should also have full control over other people who have access to and how their data is being used. Furthermore, many apps lack a privacy policy, leaving no protection for personal information or safeguards against the misuse of data. It is thus critical to enforce health data protection acts and ensure that app developers are utilizing data ethically and transparently.

Usability

App usability encompasses features which make usage a smooth and enjoyable experience. This dimension must be met in order for users to actually benefit from the intervention. A major component of usability involves whether patients find apps easy and accessible to use, which can be evaluated based on user ratings and reviews, as well as surveys of user experiences. App usability is particularly important for understanding whether apps are accessible and friendly toward users with various levels of technological knowledge, disabilities, and symptom severity. Ideally, apps should also cater to individuals from a variety of socioeconomic and cultural backgrounds. Evaluating app usability is particularly important to understanding the currently poor adherence to MH apps. In apps specifically designed for young people, high attrition rates for trials assessing the efficacy of digital interventions indicate that while some applications may be effective

Table 18.1 Empirically supported and reviewed apps for various MH symptoms and conditions in adults.

Name	Availability and pricing	Functionality and features	Research evidence	Frameworks which have assessed this app
General anxiety				
Flowy	Google Play and App Store; Free	Involves breathing retraining to break the user's attention away from the source of panic and anxiety to calm the body	(2016) 4-week RCT showed reduced in anxiety, panic, and self-report hyperventilation scores in both trial arms. Those in the intervention arm experienced higher quality of life. No significant decreases in clinical measures	PsyberGuide
Mind Shift CBT—Anxiety Canada	Google Play and App StoreFree	Provides strategies to deal with everyday anxiety and offers specific tools to tackle issues like social anxiety and perfectionism	(2019) Reduced somatic anxiety, general anxiety, and depression symptoms in 18 college students following 3 weeks of use (2019). Focus group with 23 young people aged 13–25 years, thematic analysis of the apps' content. Found that young people value personalization and autonomy when choosing mHealth apps	ADAAHealth NavigatorPsyberGuide
Self-help Anxiety Management	Google Play and App Store; Free	Provides users with a symptom tracker, educational articles, self-help techniques, and social support through a closed networking function	(2018) Data mining from 105,380 users showed markedly reduced anxiety in the first few days of usage, with some reversals thereafter. A small group of users showed long-term reductions in anxiety	ADAAHealth NavigatorPsyberGuide

PTSD			
PTSD Coach	Google Play and App Store; Free	Provides information about PTSD, self-assessment tools, support opportunities, and tools to manage posttraumatic stress	(2017) RCT of 120 individuals with PTSD used the app for 3 months or were in a wait-listed control. Users showed significantly greater improvements in PTSD, depression, and psychosocial functioning than waitlist controls. No significant differences were found in outcomes between conditions posttreatment. A greater proportion of PTSD Coach participants achieved clinically significant improvements in PTSD symptoms than waitlist controls (2016). Twenty veterans with PTSD symptoms in primary care were randomized to engage in either self-managed PTSD coach consisting of one 10-min session, or clinician-supported PTSD coach consisting of four 20-min sessions. Both treatments led to reductions in PTSD symptoms, and more participants receiving clinician-supported PTSD coach reported clinically significant improvements	ADAAHealth NavigatorPsyberGuide
PE Coach 2	Google Play and App Store; Free	Intended to be an add-on to prolonged exposure therapy. Contains tools for recording sessions, helping patients complete homework, and practice skills gained during the treatment	(2015) Two soldiers completed eight sessions of PE, four of which integrated PE coach, finding positive ratings and higher levels of satisfaction during combined treatment (2015) Investigated 271 clinicians' use of PE coach. In the past year, half of clinicians practicing PE reported using PE coach, and 93.6% intended to continue use 77.6% of clinicians who did not use PE Coach at the time of the survey intended do so the future (2017). Conducted semistructured interviews with 25 PE providers, who used PE Coach with 450 patients with PTSD identified positive and negative features of PE coach	PsyberGuide

Continued

Table 18.1 Continued

Name	Availability and pricing	Functionality and features	Research evidence	Frameworks which have assessed this app
CBT-i coach	Google Play and App Store; Free	For individuals who are engaged in CBT-i with a health provider, or who have experienced symptoms of insomnia and would like to improve their sleep habits	(2016) Two surveys of CBT-I trained clinicians regarding their perceptions of CBT-i coach before its release ($n = 138$) and after its release ($n = 176$). Two years following app release, 59.9% of the clinicians who used the app with patients saw positive impacts on homework adherence and outcomes	Practical AppsPsyberGuide
OCD				
GGOC: OCD Relief	Google Play and App Store; Free version Paid version	Aims to improve OCD symptoms, specifically negative thinking, by increasing the user's awareness of negative thoughts and training the brain to challenge them	(2018) Case study of a patient with severe contamination and washing/cleaning OCD symptoms, who completed 47 levels of GGOC to target OCD-relevant maladaptive beliefs OBQ-20, OCI-R, and Y-BOCS scores decreased following GGOC use (2018) 20 undergraduate students completed 3 min of training daily for 15 days. Showed significant reduction on OCD symptoms and OCD-beliefs. No reductions in depression	PsyberGuide
Mood disorders				
Daylio	Google Play and App Store; Free	Designed to help users record and track mood over time	(2016) Provides an overview of the app and identifies strengths (2018). Case study of a patient with mood disorders who used Daylio. Found the app to be informative, which increased engagement during therapy sessions. Shared the information from the app with his therapist and used the data in order to inform treatment decisions	PsyberGuide

App	Platform; Cost	Description	Research findings	Rating
Schizophrenia Storylines	Google Play and App Store; Free	Helps user to record details about symptoms, medication, moods, and other relevant information	(2017) Analyzed 43,451 mood, medication, and symptom entries from 622 registered app users 71% tried mood-tracking. 49% tried symptom tracking, 36% tried medication-tracking. Overall use was low; a small proportion of participants were highly engaged with the app and $\leq$35% of all entries for each app feature were accounted for by the top 10 users for that feature	PsyberGuide

Eating disorders

App	Platform; Cost	Description	Research findings	Rating
Recovery Record (RR): Eating Disorder Management	Google Play Store and App Store; Free	Designed to aid recovery from eating disorders, and to assist individuals with general concerns about eating, weight, and body shape. Features include a meal log, check-ins, and a "Clinician Connect" option which allows users to share their RR entries with a clinician	Kim et al. (2018) 8-day pilot study of the app, found the app to be acceptable and feasible Users selectively used features they found helpful (2019). Individuals with eating disorders were recruited to use a tailored self-help version of the app (n=292) or a standard version of the app (n=285). Both groups showed significant improvements based on the EDE-Q, but no between-group differences emerged. The remission rate at 8 weeks was significantly greater in those who completed the tailored version of the app (2018). Evaluated whether the 1280 RR app users cluster in clinically meaningful groups. Hierarchical cluster analysis showed five groups of participants who approximated diagnostic categories of DSM-5 eating disorders (2017). Clinicians (N=31) participated in field studies and interviews to assess the interdisciplinary clinical perspective and impact on treatment of RR "Access to app data between treatment sessions," and "The patient-clinician relationship" were the two overarching themes (2018). Patients (N=31) from an eating disorder treatment facility were observed in treatment sessions, and some participated in interviews. Patients' experiences with RR dependent on app features, the impact of said features on patients, and specific app usage (2019). Female patients with anorexia nervosa (N=40) were randomized either to 8 weeks of RR with treatment as usual, or treatment as usual alone. Patients adhered to and accepted the app well. Small-to-moderate between-group effect sizes emerged favoring the treatment group postintervention, but these were not statistically significant. No differences emerged at a 6-month follow-up	PsyberGuide

Table 18.2 Multipurpose apps

Name	Conditions	Availability and Pricing	Functionality	Research evidence	Frameworks which have assessed this app
T2 Mood Tracker	Stress Anxiety Mood	Google Play and App Store; Free	Helps users track their emotional experiences across the areas of anxiety, depression, general well-being, head injury, PTSD, and stress. Creates reports that can be shared with a health-care provider	(2014) Field-tested the app with eight redeployed soldiers under treatment for behavioral health issues, who used the app an average of 10 different days over 2–3-weeks. The app was easy to use and beneficial for participants	Psyberguide ADAA Health Navigator
Happify: For Stress and Worry	Stress Anxiety Mood PTSD	Google Play and App Store; Free version Paid version: $14.95/month	Aims to help adults improve overall well-being and happiness using positive psychology, CBT, and mindfulness concepts. Users earn points and enter to win prizes by completing happiness activities	(2016) Drew data from 152,747 Happify users to assess the relationship between usage and well-being, and analyzed free text responses from 10,818 of these users to explore the underlying processes that accompany improvement. On average, users' scores on a measure of positive emotion increased 27% over 8 weeks. Within users, more usage predicted more positive emotion (2019). Participants who used Happify during recovery after a laboratory stressor showed significantly lower levels of salivary alpha amylase compared to those who did not use the app. No between-groups differences in salivary cortisol levels or self-reported stress were found during recovery (2018).	ADAA PsyberGuide w/ professional review

Online trial of first-time Happify registrants, randomly assigned to access the full app platform or a psychoeducation comparison condition for 8 weeks. Those who used Happify at a recommended level (2–3 activities per week) reported lower depressive and anxiety symptoms, greater resilience, and greater net benefits than those with lower usage or those in the psychoeducation condition (2018). RCT comparing change in resilience over time among employees who were assigned to use Happify, a psychoeducational version of the platform, and employees who did not use their assigned platform. In employees with high emotional distress or high workplace distress, those who used Happify showed significantly greater increases in resilience over 8 weeks the two other groups (2020). Drew data from participants with and without chronic conditions who used Happify for at least 6 weeks. Users with a chronic condition reported significantly lower subjective well-being compared to those without a chronic condition at baseline. Both groups experienced similar improvements in well-being during app. Completing more activities was associated with increasingly longer periods of improved well-being scores

Continued

Table 18.2 Continued

Name	Conditions	Availability and Pricing	Functionality	Research evidence	Frameworks which have assessed this app
Headspace: Guided Meditation	Stress Anxiety MoodSleep	Google Play and App Store; Free w/in-app purchases	Includes guided meditations covering a wide range of topics, such as sleep, focus, and exercise. Users can track their progress and time spent meditating	(2016) Participants were randomly assigned to engage with a Headspace intervention ($n=57$) or a control intervention ($n=64$) for 10 days Headspace users showed significant increases in positive affect and reduced depressive symptoms. The control condition did not exhibit statistically significant improvements (2017). Inpatients at an acute care state hospital ($N=13$) used Headspace for 1 week. All participants reported the app was engaging and easy to use; 83% felt comfortable using it and 83% would recommend it to others (2019). Focus group with 23 young people aged 13–25 years, thematic analysis of the apps' content. Found that young people value personalization and autonomy when choosing mHealth apps	ADAAPsyberGuide w/ professional review Health Navigator

| Sanvello (previously Pacifica) | StressAnxietyMood | Google Play and App Store, online; Free w/in-app purchases | Provides tools for easing stress and anxiety, such as a daily mood tracker and audio recordings for relaxation | (2019) Adults with mild-to-moderate anxiety ($N=200$) participated in a randomized waitlist-controlled trial of Pacifica. Those in the active condition showed significantly greater decreases in depression, anxiety, and stress, as well as increased self-efficacy, though no relationship were found between overall app engagement and symptom reductions. Users who completed more thought recording exercises showed greater sustained improvements in their symptoms at a 2-month follow-up compared to those who completed fewer exercises (2019). Focus group with 23 young people aged 13–25 years, thematic analysis of the apps' content. Found that young people value personalization and autonomy when choosing mHealth apps | ADAAHealth NavigatorPractical AppsPsyberGuide |
| Wysa: Stress, depression and anxiety therapy chatbot | Stress Depression Anxiety | Google Play Store and App Store; Free | A chatbot that keeps track of users' moods and helps alleviate stress and anxiety. Provides calming meditation and mindfulness exercises | (2018) Collected data from anonymous global users based on in-app texting and self-reported depression symptoms on the PHQ-9. Average mood improvement was higher for high users. A majority (67.7%) of user feedback responses found the app experience helpful and encouraging | PsyberGuide |

Continued

Table 18.2 Continued

Name	Conditions	Availability and Pricing	Functionality	Research evidence	Frameworks which have assessed this app
Woebot	Stress Anxiety Mood	Google Play Store and App Store; Free	A chatbot that guides users in managing distressing thoughts and feelings using CBT principles. Offers tools, skills, and strategies by inferring the users' most immediate needs. Emergency resources available through "SOS" mode	(2017) Individuals ($N=70$) were randomized to receive either 2 weeks of Woebot CBT ($n=34$) or received the NIMH "Depression in College Students" ebook as a control group ($n=36$). Those who used Woebot showed significantly reduced depression symptoms over the study period, based on the PHQ-9	PsyberGuide
WhatsMyM3	Mood Anxiety PTSD	Google Play Store and App Store; Free	Screening tool for clients with MH concerns. Users complete a brief checklist to identify problems with mood, anxiety, and/ or PTSD, and results are intended to help clients and doctors to make decisions about treatment. Also allows users to track changes in their symptoms over time	(2010) 647 participants were assessed with the M3 checklist and clinicians reviewed the tool. Overall sensitivity and specificity were high for all modules (sensitivity=0.84–0.88; specificity=0.76–0.80). When using the app to screen for a psychiatric disorder, sensitivity, and specificity were also high at 0.83 and 0.76, respectively	ADAA PsyberGuide

Catch it	Mood Anxiety Stress PTSD	Google Play Store and App Store; Free	Helps users achieve a stronger understanding of their moods using an ongoing diary. Illustrates key CBT-based approaches to improve MH	(2016) Individuals ($N=285$) downloaded the app, and most (65%) used the app only once. Most (84%) user-generated content was consistent with the basic CBT concepts. Users showed significant reductions in negative mood intensity and increases in positive mood intensity	NHS App Library
Talkspace Counselling & Therapy	Stress Anxiety PTSD Mood Phobias Eating disorders Sleep	Google Play Store and App Store; Free with IAP	Users answer questions in a free consultation and are paired with licensed therapists, who provide support for stress and anxiety, depression, PTSD, LGBTQ issues, work/life issues, and couples' therapy	(2019) Retrospective within-subjects study to evaluated app effects on MH outcomes and engagement with employment. Adults seeking text therapy treatment ($N=51$) used the app for 14–15 weeks. Posttreatment, participants reported significantly lower depression and anxiety and stronger engagement with work (2017). Adults seeking text therapy treatment ($N=57$) used the app for 15 weeks. Almost half (46%) of participants showed clinically significant symptom remission; participants reported satisfaction with affordability, convenience, and effectiveness. Therapeutic alliance was weaker than in traditional treatment settings but predicted symptom improvement nonetheless	PsyberGuide

Continued

Table 18.2 Continued

Name	Conditions	Availability and Pricing	Functionality	Research evidence	Frameworks which have assessed this app
Good Days Ahead	Stress Anxiety Mood	Google Play Store and App Store; $50	Teaches CBT techniques to enable better management of depression and anxiety. Users complete lessons in which they follow a character who works to better manage her depression across various settings	(2002) Ninety-six subjects used the software, 78.1% of whom completed the entire program. Cognitive therapy knowledge scores were improved significantly following app use (2005). Participants with MDD ($N=45$) were randomly assigned to a waitlist control, cognitive therapy, or therapy through Good Days Ahead for nine sessions over 8 weeks. Those completing computer-assisted cognitive therapy and standard cognitive therapy showed superior improvements in depression outcomes compared to waitlist controls; benefits remained at 3- and 6-month follow-ups	PsyberGuide w/ professional review
MoodKit	Stress Anxiety Mood	App Store; $4.99	CBT-based app with tools designed to help users experiencing depression. Also helps target stress and anxiety	(2018) Assessed three MH apps, MoodKit, MoodPrism, MoodMission vs controls. All MH app groups showed increases in well-being when compared to controls. No groups showed decreases in anxiety, but those who used MoodKit and MoodMission groups experienced lower depression (2019). Compared Moodivate, MoodKit (active control), or no app for 8 weeks. Users of both apps showed significant, sustained decreases in depressive symptoms	PsyberGuide w/ professional review

| Virtual Hope Box | Google Play Store and App Store; Free | A multimedia coping skill app designed for individuals, particularly military service members, struggling with depression. Includes four main features sections for distraction, inspiration, relaxation, and coping skills | (2015) High-risk patients and their clinicians who used the app more regularly found it to be beneficial, useful, easy to set up, and easily integrated into treatment. Users and clinicians also were likely to use the app in the future and recommend it to others (2017). Parallel-group RCT of VHB vs control for 12 weeks. App users reported significantly greater coping abilities for unpleasant emotions and thoughts at 3 and 12 weeks of use (2019). Veterans with suicidal ideation ($N=117$) completed measures of coping self-efficacy and suicidal ideation during 12 weeks of using the app or treatment as usual. Coping self-efficacy in app users was associated with lower suicidal ideation severity, compared to controls | Health NavigatorPsyberGuide |
| PTSDMood | | | | |

Continued

Table 18.2 Continued

Name	Conditions	Availability and Pricing	Functionality	Research evidence	Frameworks which have assessed this app
Intellicare	StressAnxietyMood	Google Play; Free	A suite of apps designed to address thought patterns or behaviors related to depression and anxiety	(2017) Patients with depression or anxiety (N=99) completed an 8-week 2-arm RCT using the IntelliCare apps. Participants showed substantial reductions in symptoms on the PHQ-9 and GAD-7 (2019). Participants with depression or anxiety (N=301) were randomized to one of four treatments with different methods of maintaining engagement for 8 weeks, 6 month follow-up. Significant symptom reductions in the PHQ-9 and GAD-7 were found in all treatment arms (2020) 146 participants with anxiety and/ or depression used IntelliCare vs waitlist controls for 8 weeks. More participants in the treatment group recovered from depression. Sustained effects were observed for depression and anxiety scores during follow-up	PsyberGuide
MindMax	Stress Anxiety Mood	Google Play Store and App Store; Free	Aims to help users build resilience through training sessions, games, and social sharing features. User undergo well-being training undertaken by AFL players	(2020) Naturalistic trial of participants who used the app across 2 months. Observed significant 1- and 2-month increases in help-seeking intentions and sense of connection to the MindMax community (2017). A case study of app users found that apps such as MindMax can engage people in well-being training and goal setting. Video games and connections with sports stars and fellow fans through the app help foster engagement and support well-being goals	PsyberGuide

Table 18.3 Empirically supported and reviewed apps for various MH symptoms and conditions in children and youth.

Name	Availability and pricing	Functionality and features	Research evidence	Frameworks which have assessed this app
Music eScape	Currently unavailable	Engages young people in identifying and managing emotions using music	(2019) A Randomized Controlled Trial of 169 young people with mental distress to determine the effects of using the app on distress and well-being at 1, 2, 3, and 6 months. Found no changes after 1 month, some significant changes in the longer trials (2019). Focus group with 23 young people aged 13–25 years, thematic analysis of the apps' content. Found that young people value personalization and autonomy when choosing mHealth apps	PsyberGuide
Jourvie Research App	Currently unavailable	Allows users to track meals, answer prompts and deliver skills from their clinicians	(2017) Study protocol for a randomized controlled trial published for 30 adolescents with anorexia to prevent further weight loss during the waiting time for treatment	PsyberGuide
Calm	Free for download on App Store and Google Play, however Calm Premium is required to extend the free trial ($69.99 CAD)	An 8-week mindfulness and meditation program	(2019) A Randomized Controlled Trial of 88 University students with elevated stress to compare Calm to a wait-list control for effects on stress, mindfulness and self-compassion. Overall, they demonstrated between-group differences for all the variables	PsyberGuide

Continued

Table 18.3 Empirically supported and reviewed apps for various MH symptoms and conditions in children and youth.—Cont'd

Name	Availability and pricing	Functionality and features	Research evidence	Frameworks which have assessed this app
PowerUp	Currently unavailable	This app supports patient activation and encourages shared decision-making	(2019) A feasibility trial was completed to determine the parameters for a randomized controlled trial. Studied 270 young people from 8 mental health services to determine the acceptability of this app. They found the app was acceptable and it would be feasible to perform a larger randomized controlled trial	N/A
BRITE	Available on Google Play for research purposes	Facilitated an app-supported in-patient intervention for suicidal youth	(2018) Pilot study of 68 adolescents who have been hospitalized for suicidal ideation or suicide attempts. Determined their intervention to be acceptable and feasible	N/A
Crisis Care	Currently unavailable	A smartphone intervention for adolescents with suicidal ideation and their parents	(2017) Pilot tested with 20 patient-adult groups. Demonstrated preliminary acceptability and usability	N/A
Companion App	Currently unavailable	An interactive peer-mentoring system that incorporates health-relevant content to foster positive peer culture and reduce stress	(2016) Control study group to gauge the effectiveness of the app. Intervention arm did not produce any measurable effect	N/A
ESM App	Currently unavailable	Experience sampling method for auditory verbal hallucinations	(2019) Small exploratory study with three adolescents. Mixed experiences with feasibility and acceptability were reported	N/A

Continued

App	Availability	Description	Study	Rating
PROMIS App	This version currently unavailable	An interactive app with animal cartoons and prompts for children to reflect on their mental health	(2020) Pilot trial with 15 students aged 5–7. In phase two they tested the usability and determined it demonstrated good usability and was acceptable	N/A
SmartCat 2.0	Available for research purposes only	An mHealth platform with an app and clinical portal	(2020) A feasibility trial with 34 anxious youth ages 9–14. Determined to be feasible to use with clinicians and patients in this way	N/A
REACH	Currently unavailable	An early intervention for anxiety in youth, exposure-based CBT delivered through an app	(2017) An initial usability trial in which 132 children and 45 service providers rated the app. Found that the app was highly positively rated by users	N/A
Affective Control Training App	Currently unavailable	App to improve affective control capacity in adolescents	(2020) Protocol for a randomized controlled trial with 200 adolescents. Attempt to determine the impact of improving affective control capacity in adolescents on their mental health	N/A
Pocket Helper 2.0	Currently unavailable	App with daily surveys, daily tips sent to users, provides access to live emotional support	(2019) Study with 100 homeless youth between the ages of 16–25. Seemed to be acceptable for use in this population	N/A
Mood Mission	Available on App Store and Google Play	Provides you with evidence-based "missions" to cope with depression and anxiety	(2019) Focus group with 23 young people aged 13–25 years, thematic analysis of the apps' content. Found that young people value personalization and autonomy when choosing mHealth apps	PsyberGuide
What's Up?	Available on App Store and Google Play	Uses CBT and ACT to cope with depression and anxiety	(2019) Focus group with 23 young people aged 13–25 years, thematic analysis of the apps' content. Found that young people value personalization and autonomy when choosing mHealth apps	Psyberguide

Table 18.3 Continued

Name	Availability and pricing	Functionality and features	Research evidence	Frameworks which have assessed this app
BYOTS App	Currently unavailable	Guides users to create a self-written and recorded theme song	(2019) Aimed to evaluate the effectiveness with 72 adolescent black or biracial eighth-grade females. Determined the app useful for reducing negative thinking in this underserved population	N/A
SPRS App	Currently unavailable	Uses positive words during video playback to increase motivation and improve self-confidence in young adults	(2017) Aimed to evaluate preliminary app efficacy with 22 participants aged 18–24 years with subthreshold depression. Determined the app was safe and may be effective, but further research is needed	N/A
The Toolbox	N/A	A web-based app-recommendation service for mental health and well-being apps	(2017) Aimed to assess the efficacy of The Toolbox at improving well-being in 387 participants between 16 and 25 years old. Determined their intervention may not lead to improvements but may stop a decline in well-being	N/A
POD Adventures	Currently unavailable	Smartphone delivered game to provide low-intensity human support	(2019) App was developed and tested in consultation with 50 youth. Participants valued reliability and simplicity. RCT planned for this app to evaluate its effectiveness	N/A
The Blue App	Currently unavailable	Smartphone app to address gaps in patient care after discharge	(2018) A study protocol aimed at evaluating this app	N/A

BeSafe	Available on App Store and Google Play	Smartphone app that helps young adults make a safety plan and make decisions in crisis	(2017) Sought to determine the feasibility of integrating this app into safety planning at time of discharge. Determined it may be feasible and that download of the app earlier in admission may improve app experience	N/A
Lawson SMART Records App	Currently unavailable	Allows individuals access to their personal health information on their smartphone.	(2016) Evaluation of 41 patients with depressive symptoms aged 16–21 to determine the usability and acceptability of this app for youth experiencing depressive symptoms. It was determined to be useful, but could have been simpler for easier use	N/A
myAssessment	Currently unavailable	An assessment application on your device to quickly obtain information for use in therapy	(2015) A quasi-experimental study to determine the acceptability and effect of the intervention for 339 young people at their first appointment. Determined to be widely acceptable by young people and clinicians	N/A
BlueIce	Available on App Store	Uses evidenced-based CBT approaches to help young people who self-harm	(2018) Evaluate the acceptability, use, and safety of BlueIce in 40 young people 12–17 years old. Determined BlueIce was acceptable for users, easy to use and convenient for them (2018). Preliminary evaluation of BlueIce with 40 young people 12–17 years old. Determine that BlueIce is useful for managing self-harm along with face-to-face intervention	N/A

(Garrido et al., 2019), their lack of usability may prevent them from being used to their full potential (Garrido et al., 2019). It is also important to incorporate patient perspectives, particularly those from children and adolescents, in the app development process to improve usability (Wilansky et al., 2016).

Integration

Lastly, evaluations must consider the extent to which an MH app can be integrated into clinical care (Agarwal et al., 2016; Torous, Chan, Yellowlees, & Boland, 2016; Torous, Luo, & Chan, 2018). Otherwise known as interoperability, mHealth interventions must be integrated into existing health information systems (HISs) and align with electronic records. The data collected by apps should also be easily accessible to clinicians. Additionally, the data collected by apps should bear clinical relevance and inform care. Smartphones and tablets have sensors and processing abilities that enable them to collect self-report, behavioral, and physiological data (Sequeira, Battaglia, Perrotta, Merikangas, & Strauss, 2019). Although many of these measures are impossible to capture through traditional methods, this data should only be collected if it is accessible and useful in the clinical setting. The HL7 FHIR standard (https://www.hl7.org/fhir/) and App Launch Framework (https://hl7.org/fhir/smart-app-launch/) serve to connect apps and HIS data.

Current app evaluation frameworks

Frameworks for general mHealth apps

mHealth evidence reporting and assessment checklist

In recognizing the need for regulations and standards for the growing body of apps, global experts were convened by the World Health Organization to develop the mHealth evidence reporting and assessment (mERA) checklist (Agarwal et al., 2016; Agarwal, Lefevre, & Labrique, 2017). This qualitative tool asks 16 questions to assess the quality of an mHealth intervention and its associated research, covering the areas of app intervention content, context, and technical features. The mERA also includes an optional 29-item checklist for reporting on study design and methods (Agarwal et al., 2016). The research-focused nature of this tool enables the synthesis of high-quality evidence and critical assessments of the transparency and completeness of mHealth studies. Another major advantage of the mERA lies in its flexibility and applicability to a wide variety of research, ranging from descriptive studies to more rigorous experimental designs. It is important to note that the core items of the mERA should be used alongside other study design checklists, such as CONSORT for RCTs and STROBE for observational studies (Agarwal et al., 2016, 2017). Furthermore, the psychometric properties of the mERA checklist have not been documented, and evaluations of its reliability and validity should be conducted before widespread adoption by policymakers, reviewers, and editors.

The enlight framework

The Enlight framework (Baumel, Faber, Mathur, Kane, & Muench, 2017) is a two-section set of criteria-based measurements which enable researchers to objectively rate online health interventions, including mobile apps. Enlight addresses the areas of persuasive design, behavior change, and therapeutic alliance/principles across various delivery media and clinical aims. The quality assessment section consists of six core constructs: usability, visual design, user engagement, content, therapeutic persuasiveness, and therapeutic alliance (Baumel et al., 2017). These cover 25 items, each of which is rated on a five-point Likert scale ($1 = very\ poor$ to $5 = very\ good$). The areas covered by this first section items are particularly beneficial as they bear relevance to patient and clinician experiences. The second section of the Enlight program involves a checklist with items assessing whether the app shows adequate credibility, evidence-based content, privacy explanations, and basic security (Baumel et al., 2017). Though these items are more technical, they are critical for clinicians to consider in recommending apps. Taken together, the areas evaluated by the two sections of the Enlight framework are highly applicable to MH apps and thus provide comprehensive evaluations. The qualitative nature of the Enlight framework also enables direct comparisons of multiple apps. Psychometric evaluation of the Enlight framework yielded strong internal consistency (Cronbach's $\alpha = 0.83–0.90$) and interrater reliability (ICC $= 0.77–0.98$) (Baumel et al., 2017), though more studies may be necessary. Overall, this framework offers a strong evaluation of mHealth apps and most areas are applicable to MH apps.

Mobile app rating scale

The Mobile App Rating Scale (MARS) is an increasingly popular tool for evaluating the quality of mHealth apps. Using four objective quality scales, the MARS assesses app engagement, functionality, aesthetics, and information quality (Stoyanov et al., 2015). An additional subjective quality scale asks raters to evaluate the program holistically after completing core concept ratings. Each quality scale contains several subcategories, resulting in a total of 23 subcategories used to formulate the items of the scale. Items are rated on a five-point Likert scale ranging from $1 = Inadequate$ to $5 = Excellent$. Although the MARS can be used for all mHealth apps, its psychometric properties were specifically tested using 50 mobile MH and well-being apps. Interrater reliability was excellent (ICC $= 0.79$), and total scores also showed high internal consistency (Cronbach's $\alpha = 0.90$). The internal consistencies and interrater reliabilities of each subscale were also high, with Cronbach's $\alpha = 0.80–0.89$ and ICC $= 0.50–0.80$. It is important to note that training and expertise is required for administering the MARS, which limits the populations that it is available for. To expand the accessibility of the MARS, a consumer version, the uMARS, was developed by simplifying the initial scale (Stoyanov, Hides, Kavanagh, & Wilson, 2016). This modified 16-item scale yielded also strong psychometric properties, showing excellent internal consistency ($\alpha = 0.90$) and strong test-retest reliability over several months. Thus, the MARS and uMARS are another currently available framework for evaluating mHealth apps and have been demonstrated to be applicable to MH apps specifically.

The American Psychiatric Association app evaluation model

As the collection of MH applications has grown, the American Psychiatric Association (APA) developed a hierarchical rating system with an embedded rubric, which highlights key clinician and patient considerations for selecting appropriate MH apps (Lagan et al., 2020; Torous, Chan, et al., 2018; Torous, Luo, et al., 2018). The model is organized in a four-level pyramid such that users should progress to higher levels only if the app being evaluated satisfies the requirements of the previous stage.

The ground level of the APA App Evaluation Model now entitled "App Advisor" (American Psychiatric Association, 2020) involves gathering background information about the app, including its developers, costs, and technological requirements. In doing so, the credibility of the app's creator is established by questioning his or her reputation, the ability to update the app, and funding sources (Torous, Chan, et al., 2018). Then, users must consider the privacy and security features of the app. This is particularly important as MH data is highly confidential and sensitive, and many apps do not guarantee the proper protection of this information. If the app demonstrates strong privacy and security, then users should evaluate the clinical foundation of the app, which includes elements such as face validity, relevant sources, and references, evidence of validation, as well as the efficacy of interventions and functions. This step is critical as many apps may appear useful but hold very little clinical efficacy. There is also evidence that some applications may tout efficacy but lead to adverse outcomes (Torous, Chan, et al., 2018). As such, it is paramount to seek an app with scientific support, and it is recommended that clinicians try an app before recommending it to a patient. In cases where an app without formal evidence may be effective, patients must be made aware that efficacy claims have not been verified. Once an app is deemed to have a reasonable clinical foundation, its usability must be considered. This is particularly important given that many MH apps are often downloaded but left unused (Schueller, Neary, O'Loughlin, & Adkins, 2018). Furthermore, app engagement generally declines rapidly within 2 weeks of download (Carlo, Hosseini Ghomi, Renn, & Areán, 2019; Dorsey et al., 2017). As such, applications that involve patients during development may lead to stronger user-friendly features that lead to higher engagement (Torous, Chan, et al., 2018). At the highest level of the pyramid is data integration toward a therapeutic goal. This level examines interoperability, the availability of the data collected or generated by the app to patients, clinicians, and others involved in the patient's care. Apps should minimize fragmentation of care, and those that support integrated treatment modalities will be most useful for patients (Torous, Chan, et al., 2018).

The reliability of the APA App Evaluation Model was tested with five psychiatrists who were presented with three mood tracking apps (MoodTrack, MoodTools, and T2 Mood Tracker) and asked to rate the app for use in two clinical situations (Torous, Chan, et al., 2018). Each reviewer downloaded the apps and used each one for at least 15 min before reviewing and searching for empirical studies on the apps. Results indicated strong interrater reliability, as Kendall's coefficient of concordance ranged from 0.67 to 0.93 and reached statistical significance for all stages (Torous, Chan, et al., 2018). However, further psychometric testing should be conducted on apps with various functions beyond mood tracking. To date, the APA App Evaluation Model

(App Advisor) is the only framework that offers a hierarchical method of assessing apps, making it a particularly useful framework for clinicians and patients (Lagan et al., 2020; Torous, Chan, et al., 2018; Torous, Luo, et al., 2018).

The ASPECTS framework

To further guide clinicians in choosing MH apps, Torous et al. (2016) devised the ASPECTS framework. This model was designed to assist clinicians in making informed decisions regarding whether apps are actionable, secure, professional, evidence based, customizable, and transparent. The actionable aspect refers to whether the app collects meaningful data and produces valuable results. Given that apps can now capture tremendous amounts of self-report, behavioral, and physiological data, the information collected should be ideally limited to that which is clinically relevant and useful (Torous et al., 2016). Security refers to patient data protection measures. Given the sensitive nature of MH information, apps should implement passcodes, biometric authentication, or other security features. Additionally, clinicians should check whether patient data is stored and encrypted on the device itself, which prevents others from reading confidential information a device is stolen or hacked. Another key security consideration is whether an app clearly states its patient data encryption, transmission, and storage processes. In addition, clinicians must educate patients and inform them to take protective measures, including understanding permission dialog boxes, not entering personal information into apps, and using third-party security applications and built-in safety features. MH apps must also be Professional, meaning that they should ensure that use is in line with professional and ethical standards (Torous et al., 2016). This is particularly important to consider as many apps do not comply with health body regulations and rules. Another key aspect of app evaluation is whether it is evidence based. When recommending MH apps, clinicians must seek out those with robust empirical support, while considering potential unintended consequences, risks, and harm (Torous et al., 2016). This is particularly important as ineffective apps could lead patients or clinicians to think the patient is treatment refractory when the app is simply ineffective. If apps with no or little empirical support are selected, clinicians should initiate discussions with the patient regarding the potential risks involved. Customization is another important aspect to evaluate MH apps, as each patient has unique clinical needs and responses to treatment (Torous et al., 2016). Thus, apps with more customizable and flexible elements should be favored. Lastly, app Transparency must be considered. This involves understanding how apps utilize the data they collect, and patients need to understand how their data are being used, as trust is always necessary for accurate reporting of symptoms (Torous et al., 2016). Clinicians and patients must select apps that not only guarantee data security but also have clear privacy policies. Ideally, apps should adopt policies in which the patient has control over the use and sharing of their health-care data.

One mind PsyberGuide app reviews

Another recently emerging tool for evaluating MH apps is PsyberGuide, a nonprofit, noncommercial website dedicated to helping users make informed decisions. Apps are evaluated based on credibility, user experience, data transparency, and ease of use, and reviews include a professional opinion on the usefulness of the app in question (Lipczynska, 2019). Credibility considers multiple aspects of empirical support; this includes the degree of research support for an app, the level of expert clinical input in its development, and the specificity of interventions. User experience is evaluated using the MARS based on app engagement, functionality, aesthetics, and information (Lipczynska, 2019; Stoyanov et al., 2015). Lastly, app transparency concerns whether apps provide adequate policies on data storage and collection. How readily available this information is to users and is rated on three levels: acceptable, questionable, unacceptable. The PsyberGuide website is neutral and does not advocate for any biases or agenda, making it a particularly valuable tool for individuals seeking mobile interventions for a wide range of MH symptoms and disorders (Lipczynska, 2019).

Other app review websites include Practicalapps.ca and Health Navigator. Powered by the Ontario Telemedicine Network, Practicalapps.ca provides physician reviews of mobile applications for a variety of physical and mental health problems, including anxiety, insomnia, PTSD, and depression (Ontario Telemedicine Network, 2020). The aspects of features, effectiveness, usability, privacy and security, reliability, and accessibility are rated on a five-point scale, with a justification for each rating. Although fewer apps are reviewed than on other websites, Practicalapps.ca directly compares applications with each other and provides overviews of disorders and patient experiences to compliment app information. Similarly, Health Navigator, an organization in New Zealand, provides a list of mobile apps reviewed by health-care professionals (Health Navigator, 2020). The advantages and disadvantages of each app are listed to help potential users make informed decisions, and empirical evidence is listed where applicable.

Evidence-based recommendations regarding the effectiveness of MH app interventions can only be made after assessing app efficacy. Overall, the evidence base for MH apps. Meta-analyses and systematic reviews indicate that very few apps for adult MH have been evaluated in RCTs, and trials which have been conducted exhibit poor quality due to high risk of bias and low sample sizes (Byambasuren, Sanders, Beller, & Glasziou, 2018; Firth et al., 2017; Lui, Marcus, & Barry, 2017; Seppälä et al., 2019). Studies evaluating the efficacy of apps for child and adolescent MH have shown similarly mixed results. Some evidence suggests that mHealth interventions for young people have a small but significant effect on health behavior outcomes. Seko, Kidd, Wiljer, and McKenzie (2014) conducted a scoping review evaluating evidence on the efficacy of various mobile phone interventions for youth, including mobile apps. After reviewing 17 articles that met inclusion criteria, the authors noted insufficient evidence supporting the efficacy of mobile phone interventions. All studies demonstrated that mobile phones are potentially effective for improving MH interventions among young people, but significant gaps in the literature undermined the making of any firm conclusions on the subject. In a similar study, Grist, Porter, and Stallard (2017) also found virtually no evidence supporting the effectiveness of MH apps for children and adolescents, largely due to a lack of RCTs. Overall, the low evidence of effectiveness greatly limits the prescribability of MH apps and the extent to which evidence-based recommendations are possible. There is a clear need for robust RCTs with strong methodology and the use of more standardized, comprehensive evaluation frameworks. Making such improvements will improve both the scientific standings of mobile MH apps and open new avenues for treatment for both patients and clinicians.

Conclusions and future directions

At present, frameworks offer acceptable assessments of mobile MH applications for both adults and youth, but improvements are required to achieve a more comprehensive uptake of the frameworks and, more importantly, of their results. Overall, the literature suggests that there is insufficient evidence underlying most MH apps, and although there are many well-designed evaluation frameworks that may be utilized to illustrate this issue, there appear to be barriers in knowledge translation.

A critical next step is to promote the adoption of app evaluation frameworks to inform research, treatment, and app development. Current frameworks seem to be targeted toward clinicians and are only useable by professionals who are well-versed in the area of mobile apps. However, it is unclear whether professionals are actively utilizing this resource; most seem to prefer having other experts offer guidance on which apps to use. Additionally, several frameworks recommend that clinicians test apps and become familiar with them before making recommendations to patients. Given the time constraints experienced by clinicians, this may not be a realistic plan of action.

Most app evaluation frameworks are published in scientific literature, rendering them inaccessible to app users without specialized knowledge of MH apps and research. Although more curated app libraries and accessible reviews are being developed, most consumers continue to discover apps through personal searches. Thus, app store descriptions are an important informant of consumer choice, but these may not always be reliable sources of information (Larsen et al., 2019). In coding the descriptions of 73 top-rated MH apps, Larsen et al. (2019) found that developers most frequently use scientific language to appeal to potential users. However, very little research evidence was provided to uphold claims of efficacy. Consumers also rely on app reviews largely consisting of anecdotal information focusing more on app user interface and user-friendliness (Alqahtani & Orji, 2020). Thus, consumers often overlook the efficacy of apps, indicating a need to more effectively communicate the scientific legitimacy of an app to its target audience.

A responsible approach for the industry would be to adopt and implement an app evaluation framework with the release of their app and display not just individual reviews, but framework ratings. App developers have also largely neglected using evaluation frameworks, partially due to the cost and time constraints involved during app development. Given the vast number of apps available, developers may feel pressured to get apps onto the market as soon as possible, then make changes through updates. Not only does this lower the quality of newly available apps, it also encourages repeated updating. This process reduces the time available for apps to be assessed using evaluation frameworks, and resources to continuously run updates through evaluation frameworks. The updating process also affects the empirical basis of the app, as substantial updates may alter aspects of interventions, tracking, and assessment functions. As a result of these financial and practical constraints, it is unlikely that app developers, will use an evaluation framework nor provide efficacy data for their app unless mandated by a government regulator. This issue must be addressed given that end users often lack technical understanding, and that there are no objective measures to assist them when deciding on which app to utilize.

Evidence-based recommendations about the effectiveness of MH apps for youth and adults are largely not possible at this point. The results indicate there is some evidence for the efficacy of mobile MH apps, and there is evidence that these app interventions may be feasible and acceptable—however, the paucity of completed clinical trials focusing on outcomes, especially for young people, limits what we can determine about the effectiveness. Now that it is repeatedly documented that these smartphone application interventions are feasible, the focus will shift to effectiveness. The number of study protocols and pilot trials, however, does confirm a recent increase in trial research in this area, likely in response to the well-documented gap in the literature surrounding apps for youth and adult MH.

References

Agarwal, S., Lefevre, A. E., & Labrique, A. B. (2017). A call to digital health practitioners: New guidelines can help improve the quality of digital health evidence. *JMIR mHealth and uHealth, 5*(10). https://doi.org/10.2196/mhealth.6640, e136.

Agarwal, S., Lefevre, A. E., Lee, J., L'engle, K., Mehl, G., Sinha, C., et al. (2016). Guidelines for reporting of health interventions using mobile phones: Mobile health (mHealth) evidence reporting and assessment (mERA) checklist. *BMJ, 352*, 1–10. https://doi.org/10.1136/bmj.i1174.

Akbar, S., Coiera, E., & Magrabi, F. (2020). Safety concerns with consumer-facing mobile health applications and their consequences: A scoping review. *Journal of the American Medical Informatics Association, 27*(2), 330–340. https://doi.org/10.1093/jamia/ocz175.

Alqahtani, F., & Orji, R. (2020). Insights from user reviews to improve mental health apps. *Health Informatics Journal, 26*(3), 2042–2066. https://doi.org/10.1177/1460458219896492.

American Psychiatric Association. (2020). *App Advisor: An American Psychiatric Association initiative.* https://www.psychiatry.org/psychiatrists/practice/mental-health-apps.

Andrade, L. H., Alonso, J., Mneimneh, Z., Wells, J. E., A-Hamzawi, A., Borges, G., et al. (2014). Barriers to mental health treatment: Results from the WHO World Mental Health (WMH) surveys. *Psychological Medicine, 44*(6), 1303–1317. https://doi.org/10.1017/S0033291713001943.

Bauer, M., Glenn, T., Geddes, J., Gitlin, M., Grof, P., Kessing, L. V., et al. (2020). Smartphones in mental health: A critical review of background issues, current status and future concerns. *International Journal of Bipolar Disorders, 8*(2), 1–19. https://doi.org/10.1186/s40345-019-0164-x.

Baumel, A., Faber, K., Mathur, N., Kane, J. M., & Muench, F. (2017). Enlight: A comprehensive quality and therapeutic potential evaluation tool for mobile and web-based eHealth interventions. *Journal of Medical Internet Research, 19*(3). https://doi.org/10.2196/jmir.7270.

Ben-Zeev, D., Davis, K. E., Kaiser, S., Krzsos, I., & Drake, R. E. (2013). Mobile technologies among people with serious mental illness: Opportunities for future services. *Administration and Policy in Mental Health, 40*(4), 340–343. https://doi.org/10.1007/s10488-012-0424-x.

Byambasuren, O., Sanders, S., Beller, E., & Glasziou, P. (2018). Prescribable mHealth apps identified from an overview of systematic reviews. *NPJ Digital Medicine*, *1*(1), 1–12. https://doi.org/10.1038/s41746-018-0021-9.

Carlo, A. D., Hosseini Ghomi, R., Renn, B. N., & Areán, P. A. (2019). By the numbers: Ratings and utilization of behavioral health mobile applications. *NPJ Digital Medicine*, *2*(1), 1–8. https://doi.org/10.1038/s41746-019-0129-6.

Chan, S., Torous, J., Hinton, L., & Yellowlees, P. (2015). Towards a framework for evaluating mobile mental health apps. *Telemedicine and e-Health*, *21*(12), 1038–1041. https://doi.org/10.1089/tmj.2015.0002.

Chandrashekar, P. (2018). Do mental health mobile apps work: Evidence and recommendations for designing high-efficacy mental health mobile apps. *mHealth*, *4*, 6. https://doi.org/10.21037/mhealth.2018.03.02.

Donker, T., Petrie, K., Proudfoot, J., Clarke, J., Birch, M. R., & Christensen, H. (2013). Smartphones for smarter delivery of mental health programs: A systematic review. *Journal of Medical Internet Research*, *15*(11), 1–13. https://doi.org/10.2196/jmir.2791.

Dorsey, E. R., Chan, Y. F., Mcconnell, M. V., Shaw, S. Y., Trister, A. D., & Friend, S. H. (2017). The use of smartphones for health research. *Academic Medicine*, *92*(2), 157–160. https://doi.org/10.1097/ACM.0000000000001205.

Erbes, C. R., Stinson, R., Kuhn, E., Polusny, M., Urban, J., Hoffman, J., et al. (2014). Access, utilization, and interest in mHealth applications among veterans receiving outpatient care for PTSD. *Military Medicine*, *179*(11), 1218–1222. https://doi.org/10.7205/MILMED-D-14-00014.

Evans, S., Banerjee, S., Leese, M., & Huxley, P. (2007). The impact of mental illness on quality of life: A comparison of severe mental illness, common mental disorder and healthy population samples. *Quality of Life Research*, *16*(1), 17–29. https://doi.org/10.1007/s11136-006-9002-6.

Firth, J., Torous, J., Nicholas, J., Carney, R., Rosenbaum, S., & Sarris, J. (2017). Can smartphone mental health interventions reduce symptoms of anxiety? A meta-analysis of randomized controlled trials. *Journal of Affective Disorders*, *218*(April), 15–22. https://doi.org/10.1016/j.jad.2017.04.046.

Garrido, S., Cheers, D., Boydell, K., Nguyen, Q. V., Schubert, E., Dunne, L., et al. (2019). Young people's response to six smartphone apps for anxiety and depression: Focus group study. *Journal of Medical Internet Research.*. https://doi.org/10.2196/14385.

Garrido, S., Millington, C., Cheers, D., Boydell, K., Schubert, E., Meade, T., et al. (2019). What works and what doesn't work? A systematic review of digital mental health interventions for depression and anxiety in young people. *Frontiers in Psychiatry*, *10*(November), 1–19. https://doi.org/10.3389/fpsyt.2019.00759.

Grist, R., Porter, J., & Stallard, P. (2017). Mental health mobile apps for preadolescents and adolescents: A systematic review. *Journal of Medical Internet Research*, *19*(5). https://doi.org/10.2196/jmir.7332, e176.

Hansson, L. (2006). Determinants of quality of life in people with severe mental illness. *Acta Psychiatrica Scandinavica*, *113*(suppl. 429), 46–50. https://doi.org/10.1111/j.1600-0447.2005.00717.x.

Huberty, J., Green, J., Glissmann, C., Larkey, L., Puzia, M., & Lee, C. (2019). Efficacy of the mindfulness meditation mobile app "calm" to reduce stress among college students: Randomized controlled trial. *Journal of Medical Internet Research*, *21*(6). https://doi.org/10.2196/14273.

Jake-Schoffman, D. E., Silfee, V. J., Waring, M. E., Boudreaux, E. D., Sadasivam, R. S., Mullen, S. P., et al. (2017). Methods for evaluating the content, usability, and efficacy of commercial mobile health apps. *JMIR mHealth and uHealth*, 5(12). https://doi.org/10.2196/mhealth.8758, e190.

Kim, J. P., Sadeh-Sharvit, S., Darcy, A. M., Neri, E., Vierhile, M., Robinson, A., et al. (2018). The utility and acceptability of a self-help smartphone application for eating disorder behaviors. *Journal of Technology in Behavioral Science*, 3(3), 161–164.

Labrique, A. B., Vasudevan, L., Kochi, E., Fabricant, R., & Mehl, G. (2013). Mhealth innovations as health system strengthening tools: 12 common applications and a visual framework. *Global Health Science and Practice*, 1(2), 160–171. https://doi.org/10.9745/GHSP-D-13-00031.

Lagan, S., Aquino, P., Emerson, M. R., Fortuna, K., Walker, R., & Torous, J. (2020). Actionable health app evaluation: Translating expert frameworks into objective metrics. *NPJ Digital Medicine*, 3(1), 1–8. https://doi.org/10.1038/s41746-020-00312-4.

Larsen, M. E., Huckvale, K., Nicholas, J., Torous, J., Birrell, L., Li, E., et al. (2019). Using science to sell apps: Evaluation of mental health app store quality claims. *NPJ Digital Medicine*, 2(1). https://doi.org/10.1038/s41746-019-0093-1.

Levin, M. E., Krafft, J., & Levin, C. (2018). Does self-help increase rates of help seeking for student mental health problems by minimizing stigma as a barrier? *Journal of American College Health*, 66(4), 302–309.

Lewis, T. L., & Wyatt, J. C. (2014). MHealth and mobile medical apps: A framework to assess risk and promote safer use. *Journal of Medical Internet Research*, 16(9), 1–8. https://doi.org/10.2196/jmir.3133.

Lipczynska, S. (2019). Psyberguide: A path through the app jungle. *Journal of Mental Health*, 28(1), 104. https://doi.org/10.1080/09638237.2017.1417574.

Loebach, R., & Ayoubzadeh, S. (2017). Wait times for psychiatric care in Ontario. *University of Western Ontario Medical Journal*, 86(2), 48–50. https://doi.org/10.5206/uwomj.v86i2.2027.

Logan, D. E., & King, C. A. (2001). Parental facilitation of adolescent mental health service utilization: A conceptual and empirical review. *Clinical Psychology: Science and Practice*, 8(3), 319–333. https://doi.org/10.1093/clipsy.8.3.319.

Lui, J. H. L., Marcus, D. K., & Barry, C. T. (2017). Evidence-based apps? A review of mental health mobile applications in a psychotherapy context. *Professional Psychology: Research and Practice*, 48(3), 199–210. https://doi.org/10.1037/pro0000122.

Moroz, N., Moroz, I., & Slovinec D'Angelo, M. (2020). Mental health services in Canada: Barriers and cost-effective solutions to increase access. *Healthcare Management Forum*, 1–6. https://doi.org/10.1177/0840470420933911.

Health Navigator. (2020). Health Navigator. https://www.healthnavigator.org.nz/.

NSDUH Annual National Report, 2020. SAMHSA, September 11. https://www.samhsa.gov/data/report/2019-nsduh-annual-national-report.

Ontario Telemedicine Network. (2020). *Practical apps*. https://practicalapps.ca/.

Ondersma, S. J., & Walters, S. T. (2020). Clinician's guide to evaluating and developing eHealth interventions for mental health. *Psychiatric Research and Clinical Practice*. https://doi.org/10.1176/appi.prcp.2020.20190036, appi.prcp.2020.

Orley, J., Saxena, S., & Herrman, H. (1998). Quality of life and mental illness. Reflections from the perspective of the WHOQOL. *The British Journal of Psychiatry: The Journal of Mental Science*, 172(May), 291–293. https://doi.org/10.1192/bjp.172.4.291.

Rowan, K., McAlpine, D. D., & Blewett, L. A. (2013). Access and cost barriers to mental health care, by insurance status, 1999-2010. *Health Affairs*, 32(10), 1723–1730. https://doi.org/10.1377/hlthaff.2013.0133.

Sareen, J., Jagdeo, A., Cox, B. J., Clara, I., Ten Have, M., Belik, S. L., et al. (2007). Perceived barriers to mental health service utilization in the United States, Ontario, and the Netherlands. *Psychiatric Services*, 58(3), 357–364. https://doi.org/10.1176/ps.2007.58.3.357.

Schueller, S. M., Neary, M., O'Loughlin, K., & Adkins, E. C. (2018). Discovery of and inter-est in health apps among those with mental health needs: Survey and focus group study. *Journal of Medical Internet Research*, *20*(6). https://doi.org/10.2196/10141.

Seko, Y., Kidd, S., Wiljer, D., & McKenzie, K. (2014). Youth mental health interventions via mobile phones: A scoping review. *Cyberpsychology, Behavior and Social Networking*, *17*(9), 591–602. https://doi.org/10.1089/cyber.2014.0078.

Seppälä, J., De Vita, I., Jämsä, T., Miettunen, J., Isohanni, M., Rubinstein, K., et al. (2019). Mobile phone and wearable sensor-based mHealth approach for psychiatric disorders and symptoms: Systematic review and link to the M-REsist project. *Journal of Medical Internet Research*, *21*(2), 1–14. https://doi.org/10.2196/mental.9819.

Sequeira, L., Battaglia, M., Perrotta, S., Merikangas, K., & Strauss, J. (2019). Digital phenotyp-ing with mobile and wearable devices: Advanced symptom measurement in child and ado-lescent depression. *Journal of the American Academy of Child and Adolescent Psychiatry*, *58*(9), 841–845. https://doi.org/10.1016/j.jaac2019.04.011.

Statista. (2020). Number of smartphone users worldwide from 2016 to 2021 (in billions). https://www.statista.com/statistics/330695/number-of-smartphone-users-worldwide/.

Stoyanov, S. R., Hides, L., Kavanagh, D. J., & Wilson, H. (2016). Development and validation of the user version of the Mobile Application Rating Scale (uMARS). *JMIR mHealth and uHealth*, *4*(2). https://doi.org/10.2196/mhealth.5849, e72.

Stoyanov, S. R., Hides, L., Kavanagh, D. J., Zelenko, O., Tjondronegoro, D., & Mani, M. (2015). Mobile app rating scale: A new tool for assessing the quality of health mobile apps. *JMIR mHealth and uHealth*, *3*(1). https://doi.org/10.2196/mhealth.3422, e27.

The Carter Center. (2018). Mental illness will cost the world $16 USD trillion by 2030. https://www.psychiatrictimes.com/view/mental-illness-will-cost-world-16-usd-trillion-2030.

Torous, J. B., Chan, S. R., Yee-Marie Tan Gipson, S., Kim, J. W., Nguyen, T. Q., Luo, J., et al. (2018). A hierarchical framework for evaluation and informed decision making regard-ing smartphone apps for clinical care. *Psychiatric Services*, *69*(5), 498–500. https://doi.org/10.1176/appi.ps.201700423.

Torous, J. B., Chan, S. R., Yellowlees, P. M., & Boland, R. (2016). To use or not? Evaluating ASPECTS of smartphone apps and mobile technology for clinical care in psychia-try. *Journal of Clinical Psychiatry*, *77*(6), e734–e738. https://doi.org/10.4088/JCP.15com10619.

Torous, J. B., Friedman, R., & Keshvan, M. (2014). Smartphone ownership and interest in mobile applications to monitor symptoms of mental health conditions. *JMIR mHealth and uHealth*, *2*(1). https://doi.org/10.2196/mhealth.2994, e2.

Torous, J. B., Luo, J., & Chan, S. R. (2018). Mental health apps: What to tell patients. *Current Psychiatry*, *17*(3), 21–25.

Torous, J. B., & Powell, A. C. (2015). Current research and trends in the use of smartphone applications for mood disorders. *Internet Interventions*, *2*(2), 169–173. https://doi.org/10.1016/j.invent.2015.03.002.

Torous, J. B., & Roberts, L. W. (2017). Needed innovation in digital health and smartphone applications for mental health transparency and trust. *JAMA Psychiatry*. https://doi.org/10.1001/jamapsychiatry.2017.0262.

Van Ameringen, M., Turna, J., Khalesi, Z., Pullia, K., & Patterson, B. (2017). There is an app for that! The current state of mobile applications (apps) for DSM-5 obsessive-compulsive dis-order, posttraumatic stress disorder, anxiety and mood disorders. *Depression and Anxiety*, *34*(6), 526–539. https://doi.org/10.1002/da.22657.

Walton-Moss, B., Gerson, L., & Rose, L. (2005). Effects of mental illness on fam-ily quality of life. *Issues in Mental Health Nursing*, *26*(6), 627–642. https://doi.org/10.1080/01612840590959506.

Wang, K., Varma, D. S., & Prosperi, M. (2018). A systematic review of the effectiveness of mobile apps for monitoring and management of mental health symptoms or disorders. *Journal of Psychiatric Research*, *107*(October), 73–78. https://doi.org/10.1016/j.jpsychires.2018.10.006.

Wilansky, P., Eklund, J. M., Milner, T., Kreindler, D., Cheung, A., Kovacs, T., et al. (2016). Cognitive behavior therapy for anxious and depressed youth: Improving homework adherence through mobile technology. *JMIR Research Protocols*, *5*(4). https://doi.org/10.2196/resprot.5841, e209.

World Health Organization. (2020). *Child and Adolescent Mental Health*. https://www.who.int/mental_health/maternal-child/child_adolescent/en/.

Further reading

Bakker, D., Kazantzis, N., Rickwood, D., & Rickard, N. (2018). A randomized controlled trial of three smartphone apps for enhancing public mental health. *Behaviour Research and Therapy*, *109*, 75–83. https://doi.org/10.1016/j.brat.2018.08.003.

Bidargaddi, N., Musiat, P., Winsall, M., Vogl, G., Blake, V., Quinn, S., et al. (2017). Efficacy of a web-based guided recommendation service for a curated list of readily available mental health and well-being mobile apps for young people: Randomized controlled trial. *Journal of Medical Internet Research*, *19*(5). https://doi.org/10.2196/jmir.6775, e141.

Bohleber, L., Crameri, A., Eich-Stierli, B., Telesko, R., & von Wyl, A. (2016). Can we foster a culture of peer support and promote mental health in adolescence using a web-based app? A control group study. *JMIR Mental Health*, *3*(3). https://doi.org/10.2196/mental.5597, e45.

Bradford, S., & Rickwood, D. (2015). Acceptability and utility of an electronic psychosocial assessment (myAssessment) to increase self-disclosure in youth mental healthcare: A quasi-experimental study. *BMC Psychiatry*, *15*(1), 305. https://doi.org/10.1186/s12888-015-0694-4.

Bush, N. E., Dobscha, S. K., Crumpton, R., Denneson, L. M., Hoffman, J. E., Crain, A., et al. (2015). A virtual hope box smartphone app as an accessory to therapy: Proof-of-concept in a clinical sample of veterans. *Suicide and Life-Threatening Behavior*, *45*(1), 1–9. https://doi.org/10.1111/sltb.12103.

Bush, N. E., Ouellette, G., & Kinn, J. (2014). Utility of the T2 mood tracker mobile application among army warrior transition unit service members. *Military Medicine*, *179*(12), 1453–1457. https://doi.org/10.7205/MILMED-D-14-00271.

Bush, N. E., Smolenski, D. J., Denneson, L. M., Williams, H. B., Thomas, E. K., & Dobscha, S. K. (2017). A virtual hope box: Randomized controlled trial of a smartphone app for emotional regulation and coping with distress. *Psychiatric Services*, *68*(4), 330–336. https://doi.org/10.1176/appi.ps.201600283.

Carpenter, J., Crutchley, P., Zilca, R. D., Schwartz, H. A., Smith, L. K., Cobb, A. M., et al. (2016). Seeing the "big" picture: Big data methods for exploring relationships between usage, language, and outcome in internet intervention data. *Journal of Medical Internet Research*, *18*(8). https://doi.org/10.2196/jmir.5725, e241.

Chaudhry, B. M. (2016). Daylio: Mood-quantification for a less stressful you. *mHealth*, *2*. https://doi.org/10.21037/mhealth.2016.08.04.

Cheng, V. W. S., Davenport, T., Johnson, D., Vella, K., Mitchell, J., & Hickie, I. B. (2020). Naturalistic evaluation of a sport-themed mental health and wellbeing app aimed at men

(MindMax), that incorporates applied video games and gamification. *Internet Interventions*, *20*. https://doi.org/10.1016/j.invent.2020.100306.

Cristol, S. (2018). Patient's perspective on using mobile technology as an aid to psychotherapy. *JMIR Mental Health*, *5*(4). https://doi.org/10.2196/10015, e10015.

Dahne, J., Lejuez, C. W., Diaz, V. A., Player, M. S., Kustanowitz, J., Felton, J. W., et al. (2019). Pilot randomized trial of a self-help behavioral activation mobile app for utilization in primary care. *Behavior Therapy*, *50*(4), 817–827. https://doi.org/10.1016/j.beth.2018.12.003.

DellaCrosse, M., Mahan, K., & Hull, T. D. (2019). The effect of messaging therapy for depression and anxiety on employee productivity. *Journal of Technology in Behavioral Science*, *4*(1), 1–5. https://doi.org/10.1089/tmj.2016.0114.

Denneson, L. M., Smolenski, D. J., Bauer, B. W., Dobscha, S. K., & Bush, N. E. (2019). The mediating role of coping self-efficacy in hope box use and suicidal ideation severity. *Archives of Suicide Research*, *23*(2), 234–246. https://doi.org/10.1080/13811118.2018.1456383.

Edbrooke-Childs, J., Edridge, C., Averill, P., Delane, L., Hollis, C., Craven, M. P., et al. (2019). A feasibility trial of power up: Smartphone app to support patient activation and shared decision making for mental health in young people. *JMIR mHealth and uHealth*, *7*(6). https://doi.org/10.2196/11677, e11677.

Fitzpatrick, K. K., Darcy, A., & Vierhile, M. (2017). Delivering cognitive behavior therapy to young adults with symptoms of depression and anxiety using a fully automated conversational agent (Woebot): A randomized controlled trial. *JMIR Mental Health*, *4*(2). https://doi.org/10.2196/mental.7785, e19.

Forchuk, C., Reiss, J., Eichstedt, J., Singh, D., Collins, K., Rudnick, A., et al. (2016). The youth-mental health engagement network: An exploratory pilot study of a smartphone and computer-based personal health record for youth experiencing depressive symptoms. *International Journal of Mental Health*, *45*(3), 205–222. https://doi.org/10.1080/0020741 1.2016.1204823.

Gao, W., Yuan, C., Zou, Y., & Lin, H. (2020). Development and pilot testing a self-reported pediatric PROMIS app for young children aged 5–7 years. *Journal of Pediatric Nursing*, *53*, 74–83. https://doi.org/10.1016/j.pedn.2020.04.003.

Gaynes, B. N., DeVeaugh-Geiss, J., Weir, S., Gu. H., MacPherson, C., Schulberg, H. C., et al. (2010). Feasibility and diagnostic validity of the M-3 checklist: A brief, self-rated screen for depressive, bipolar, anxiety, and post-traumatic stress disorders in primary care. *The Annals of Family Medicine*, *8*(2), 160–169. https://doi.org/10.1370/afm.1092.

Glover, A. C., Schueller, S. M., Winiarski, D. A., Smith, D. L., Karnik, N. S., & Zalta, A. K. (2019). Automated Mobile phone-based mental health resource for homeless youth: Pilot study assessing feasibility and acceptability. *JMIR Mental Health*, *6*(10). https://doi.org/10.2196/15144, e15144.

Gonsalves, P. P., Hodgson, E. S., Kumar, A., Aurora, T., Chandak, Y., Sharma, R., et al. (2019). Design and development of the 'POD adventures' smartphone game: A blended problem-solving intervention for adolescent mental health in India. *Frontiers in Public Health*, *7*, 238. https://doi.org/10.3389/fpubh.2019.00238.

Graham, A. K., Greene, C. J., Kwasny, M. J., Kaiser, S. M., Lieponis, P., Powell, T., et al. (2020). Coached mobile app platform for the treatment of depression and anxiety among primary care patients: A randomized clinical trial. *JAMA Psychiatry*, *77*(9), 906–914. https://doi.org/10.1001/jamapsychiatry.2020.1011.

Gregory, J. M., Sukhera, J., & Taylor-Gates, M. (2017). Integrating smartphone technology at the time of discharge from a child and adolescent inpatient psychiatry unit. *Journal of the Canadian Academy of Child and Adolescent Psychiatry*, *26*(1), 45.

Grist, R., Porter, J., & Stallard, P. (2018). Acceptability, use, and safety of a mobile phone app (BlueIce) for young people who self-harm: Qualitative study of service users' experience. *JMIR Mental Health*, 5(1). https://doi.org/10.2196/mental.8779, e16.

Hansson, K., Johansson, B. A., Andersson, C., Rastam, M., & Eberhard, S. (2018). Issues in child and adolescent inpatient assessment and evaluation after discharge: Protocol for app development and a randomized controlled trial. *JMIR Research Protocols*, 7(11). https://doi.org/10.2196/10121, e10121.

Hides, L., Dingle, G., Quinn, C., Stoyanov, S. R., Zelenko, O., Tjondronegoro, D., et al. (2019). Efficacy and outcomes of a music-based emotion regulation mobile app in distressed young people: Randomized controlled trial. *JMIR mHealth and uHealth*, 7(1). https://doi.org/10.2196/11482, e11482.

Howells, A., Ivtzan, I., & Eiroa-Orosa, F. J. (2016). Putting the 'app' in happiness: A randomised controlled trial of a smartphone-based mindfulness intervention to enhance wellbeing. *Journal of Happiness Studies*, 17(1), 163–185. https://doi.org/10.1007/s10902-014-9589-1.

Hull, T. D., & Mahan, K. (2017). A study of asynchronous mobile-enabled SMS text psychotherapy. *Telemedicine and e-Health*, 23(3), 240–247. https://doi.org/10.1089/tmj.2016.0114.

Hunter, J. F., Olah, M. S., Williams, A. L., Parks, A. C., & Pressman, S. D. (2019). Effect of brief biofeedback via a smartphone app on stress recovery: Randomized experimental study. *JMIR Serious Games*, 7(4), e15974.

Inkster, B., Sarda, S., & Subramanian, V. (2018). An empathy-driven, conversational artificial intelligence agent (Wysa) for digital mental well-being: Real-world data evaluation mixed-methods study. *JMIR mHealth and uHealth*, 6(11), e12106.

Kennard, B. D., Goldstein, T., Foxwell, A. A., McMakin, D. L., Wolfe, K., Biernesser, C., et al. (2018). As safe as possible (ASAP): A brief app-supported inpatient intervention to prevent postdischarge suicidal behavior in hospitalized, suicidal adolescents. *American Journal of Psychiatry*, 175(9), 864–872. https://doi.org/10.1176/appi.ajp.2018.17101151.

Kolar, D. R., Hammerle, F., Jenetzky, E., & Huss, M. (2017). Smartphone-enhanced low-threshold intervention for adolescents with anorexia nervosa (SELTIAN) waiting for outpatient psychotherapy: Study protocol of a randomised controlled trial. *BMJ Open*, 7(10). https://doi.org/10.1136/bmjopen-2017-018049, e018049.

Kuhn, E., Crowley, J. J., Hoffman, J. E., Eftekhari, A., Ramsey, K. M., Owen, J. E., et al. (2015). Clinician characteristics and perceptions related to use of the PE (prolonged exposure) coach mobile app. *Professional Psychology: Research and Practice*, 46(6), 437. https://doi.org/10.1037/pro0000051.

Kuhn, E., Kanuri, N., Hoffman, J. E., Garvert, D. W., Ruzek, J. I., & Taylor, C. B. (2017). A randomized controlled trial of a smartphone app for posttraumatic stress disorder symptoms. *Journal of Consulting and Clinical Psychology*, 85(3), 267. https://doi.org/10.1037/ccp0000163.

Kuhn, E., Weiss, B. J., Taylor, K. L., Hoffman, J. E., Ramsey, K. M., Manber, R., et al. (2016). CBT-I coach: A description and clinician perceptions of a mobile app for cognitive behavioral therapy for insomnia. *Journal of Clinical Sleep Medicine*, 12(4), 597–606. https://doi.org/10.5664/jcsm.5700.

Lindgreen, P., Clausen, L., & Lomborg, K. (2018). Clinicians' perspective on an app for patient self-monitoring in eating disorder treatment. *International Journal of Eating Disorders*, 51(4), 314–321.

Lindgreen, P., Lomborg, K., & Clausen, L. (2018). Patient experiences using a self-monitoring app in eating disorder treatment: Qualitative study. *JMIR mHealth and uHealth*, 6(6). https://doi.org/10.2196/10253, e10253.

Matthews, P., Topham, P., & Caleb-Solly, P. (2018). Interaction and engagement with an anxiety management app: Analysis using large-scale behavioral data. *JMIR Mental Health*, 5(4). https://doi.org/10.2196/mental.9235, e58.

McManama O'Brien, K. H., LeCloux, M., Ross, A., Gironda, C., & Wharff, E. A. (2017). A pilot study of the acceptability and usability of a smartphone application intervention for suicidal adolescents and their parents. *Archives of Suicide Research*, 21(2), 254–264. https://doi.org/10.1080/13811118.2016.1182094.

Mistler, L. A., Ben-Zeev, D., Carpenter-Song, E., Brunette, M. F., & Friedman, M. J. (2017). Mobile mindfulness intervention on an acute psychiatric unit: Feasibility and acceptability study. *JMIR Mental Health*, 4(3). https://doi.org/10.2196/mental.7717, e34.

Moberg, C., Niles, A., & Beermann, D. (2019). Guided self-help works: Randomized waitlist controlled trial of Pacifica, a mobile app integrating cognitive behavioral therapy and mindfulness for stress, anxiety, and depression. *Journal of Medical Internet Research*, 21(6). https://doi.org/10.2196/12556, e12556.

Mohr, D. C., Schueller, S. M., Tomasino, K. N., Kaiser, S. M., Alam, N., Karr, C., et al. (2019). Comparison of the effects of coaching and receipt of app recommendations on depression, anxiety, and engagement in the IntelliCare platform: Factorial randomized controlled trial. *Journal of Medical Internet Research*, 21(8). https://doi.org/10.2196/13609, e13609.

Mohr, D. C., Tomasino, K. N., Lattie, E. G., Palac, H. L., Kwasny, M. J., Weingardt, K., et al. (2017). IntelliCare: An eclectic, skills-based app suite for the treatment of depression and anxiety. *Journal of Medical Internet Research*, 19(1). https://doi.org/10.2196/jmir.6645, e10.

Neal-Barnett, A., Stadulis, R., Ellzey, D., Jean, E., Rowell, T., Somerville, K., et al. (2019). Evaluation of the effectiveness of a musical cognitive restructuring app for black inner-city girls: Survey, usage, and focus group evaluation. *JMIR mHealth and uHealth*, 7(6). https://doi.org/10.2196/11310, e11310.

Neumayr, C., Voderholzer, U., Tregarthen, J., & Schlegl, S. (2019). Improving aftercare with technology for anorexia nervosa after intensive inpatient treatment: A pilot randomized controlled trial with a therapist-guided smartphone app. *International Journal of Eating Disorders*, 52(10), 1191–1201.

Parks, A. C., Williams, A. L., Kackloudis, G. M., Stafford, J. L., Boucher, E. M., & Honomichl, R. D. (2020). The effects of a digital well-being intervention on patients with chronic conditions: Observational study. *Journal of Medical Internet Research*, 22(1), e16211.

Parks, A. C., Williams, A. L., Tugade, M. M., Hokes, K. E., Honomichl, R. D., & Zilca, R. D. (2018). Testing a scalable web and smartphone based intervention to improve depression, anxiety, and resilience: A randomized controlled trial. *International Journal of Wellbeing*, 8(2).

Pascual-Vera, B., Roncero, M., Doron, G., & Belloch, A. (2018). Assisting relapse prevention in OCD using a novel mobile app-based intervention: A case report. *Bulletin of the Menninger Clinic*, 82(4), 390–406. https://doi.org/10.1521/bumc.2018.82.4.390.

Paul, A. M., & Fleming, C. E. (2019). Anxiety management on campus: An evaluation of a mobile health intervention. *Journal of Technology in Behavioral Science*, 4(1), 58–61. https://doi.org/10.1007/s41347-018-0074-2.

Peever, N., Vella, K., Johnson, D., Ploderer, B., Klarkowski, M., & Mitchell, J. (2017, November). Understanding initial experiences with Mindmax, an mHealth app that draws on shared interests in sports and video games. In *Proceedings of the 29th Australian conference on computer-human interaction* (pp. 438–442). https://doi.org/10.1145/3152771.3156152.

Pham, Q., Khatib, Y., Stansfeld, S., Fox, S., & Green, T. (2016). Feasibility and efficacy of an mHealth game for managing anxiety: "Flowy" randomized controlled pilot trial and design evaluation. *Games for Health Journal*, 5(1), 50–67. https://doi.org/10.1089/g4h.2015.0033.

Possemato, K., Kuhn, E., Johnson, E., Hoffman, J. E., Owen, J. E., Kanuri, N., et al. (2016). Using PTSD coach in primary care with and without clinician support: A pilot randomized controlled trial. *General Hospital Psychiatry*, *38*, 94–98. https://doi.org/10.1016/j.genhosppsych.2015.09.005.

Reger, G. M., Browne, K. C., Campellone, T. R., Simons, C., Kuhn, E., Fortney, J. C., et al. (2017). Barriers and facilitators to mobile application use during PTSD treatment: Clinician adoption of PE coach. *Professional Psychology: Research and Practice*, *48*(6), 510. https://doi.org/10.1037/pro0000153.

Reger, G. M., Skopp, N. A., Edwards-Stewart, A., & Lemus, E. L. (2015). Comparison of prolonged exposure (PE) coach to treatment as usual: A case series with two active duty soldiers. *Military Psychology*, *27*(5), 287–296. https://doi.org/10.1037/mil0000083.

Roncero, M., Belloch, A., & Doron, G. (2018). A novel approach to challenging OCD related beliefs using a mobile-app: An exploratory study. *Journal of Behavior Therapy and Experimental Psychiatry*, *59*, 157–160. https://doi.org/10.1016/j.jbtep.2018.01.008.

Sadeh-Sharvit, S., Kim, J. P., Darcy, A. M., Neri, E., Vierhile, M., Robinson, A., et al. (2018). Subgrouping the users of a specialized app for eating disorders. *Eating Disorders*, *26*(4), 361–372.

Schweizer, S., Leung, J. T., Kievit, R., Speekenbrink, M., Trender, W., Hampshire, A., et al. (2019). Protocol for an app-based affective control training for adolescents: Proof-of-principle double-blind randomized controlled trial. *Wellcome Open Research*, *4*. https://doi.org/10.12688/wellcomeopenres.15229.2.

Silk, J. S., Pramana, G., Sequeira, S. L., Lindhiem, O., Kendall, P. C., Rosen, D., et al. (2020). Using a smartphone app and clinician portal to enhance brief cognitive behavioral therapy for childhood anxiety disorders. *Behavior Therapy*, *51*(1), 69–84.

Smelror, R. E., Bless, J. J., Hugdahl, K., & Agartz, I. (2019). Feasibility and acceptability of using a mobile phone app for characterizing auditory verbal hallucinations in adolescents with early-onset psychosis: Exploratory study. *JMIR Formative Research*, *3*(2). https://doi.org/10.2196/13882, e13882.

Stallard, P., Porter, J., & Grist, R. (2018). A smartphone app (BlueIce) for young people who self-harm: Open phase 1 pre-post trial. *JMIR mHealth and uHealth*, *6*(1). https://doi.org/10.2196/mhealth.8917, e32.

Stoll, R. D., Pina, A. A., Gary, K., & Amresh, A. (2017). Usability of a smartphone application to support the prevention and early intervention of anxiety in youth. *Cognitive and Behavioral Practice*, *24*(4), 393–404.

Takahashi, K., Takada, K., & Hirao, K. (2019). Feasibility and preliminary efficacy of a smartphone application intervention for subthreshold depression. *Early Intervention in Psychiatry*, *13*(1), 133–136. https://doi.org/10.1111/eip.12540.

Torous, J., Staples, P., Slaters, L., Adams, J., Sandoval, L., Onnela, J. P., et al. (2017). Characterizing smartphone engagement for schizophrenia: Results of a naturalist mobile health study. *Clinical Schizophrenia & Related Psychoses*. https://doi.org/10.3371/CSRP.JTPS.071317.

Tregarthen, J., Kim, J. P., Sadeh-Sharvit, S., Neri, E., Welch, H., & Lock, J. (2019). Comparing a tailored self-help mobile app with a standard self-monitoring app for the treatment of eating disorder symptoms: Randomized controlled trial. *JMIR Mental Health*, *6*(11). https://doi.org/10.2196/14972, e14972.

Williams, A. L., Parks, A. C., Cormier, G., Stafford, J., & Whillans, A. (2018). Improving resilience among employees high in depression, anxiety, and workplace distress. *International Journal of Management and Business Research*, *9*(1–2), 4–22.

Wright, J. H., Wright, A. S., Albano, A. M., Basco, M. R., Goldsmith, L. J., Raffield, T., et al. (2005). Computer-assisted cognitive therapy for depression: Maintaining efficacy while reducing therapist time. *American Journal of Psychiatry*, *162*(6), 1158–1164. https://doi.org/10.1176/appi.ajp.162.6.1158.

Wright, J. H., Wright, A. S., Salmon, P., Beck, A. T., Kuykendall, J., Goldsmith, L. J., et al. (2002). Development and initial testing of a multimedia program for computer-assisted cognitive therapy. *American Journal of Psychotherapy*, *56*(1), 76–86. https://doi.org/10.1176/appi.psychotherapy.2002.56.1.76.

Clinical interventions for technology-based problems

19

Daniel L. King[a], Joël Billieux[b,c], Kai Mueller[d], and Paul H. Delfabbro[e]
[a]College of Education, Psychology, & Social Work, Flinders University, Adelaide, Australia, [b]Institute of Psychology, University of Lausanne (UNIL), Lausanne, Switzerland, [c]Centre for Excessive Gambling, Addiction Medicine, Lausanne University Hospitals (CHUV), Lausanne, Switzerland, [d]Outpatient Clinic for Behavioral Addictions, Department of Psychosomatic Medicine and Psychotherapy at the University Medical Center, Mainz, Germany, [e]School of Psychology, The University of Adelaide, Adelaide, Australia

Introduction

Multibillion-dollar electronic entertainment industries continue to innovate and expand on a global scale. While digital media can have personal and social benefits, excessive use of smartphones, laptops, computers, and gaming consoles can also have major negative health consequences for vulnerable individuals, particularly young people. In some extreme cases, excessive use may develop into a pattern of dysfunctional behavior with symptoms consistent with behavioral addiction (e.g., gambling disorder) (Brand, Rumpf, King, Potenza, & Wegmann, 2020; Higuchi et al., 2017; Saunders et al., 2017). While individuals vary in their level of risk or susceptibility to developing such problems, due to upbringing, personality, cognitive, and/or neurobiological factors (Brand et al., 2019), it is recognized that aspects of the activity itself can contribute to technology-based problems (King, Delfabbro, Deleuze, et al., 2019). For example, many digital media activities, including social media and online games, are designed to employ behavioral tracking, social data manipulation, and other tactics to deliver optimized content to incentivize users to constantly think about and habitually engage with and spend money on digital media devices (King, Delfabbro, Gainsbury, et al., 2019). A challenge to developing effective clinical and public health responses to digital technology problems has been identifying modifiable areas to effect potential positive, long-term change (Király et al., 2018). The main aim of this chapter is to review and discuss the literature on interventions for digital technology-based problems, with a focus on identifying current evidence-based approaches in this area.

From a public health perspective, involvement in digital media activities may be viewed along a spectrum, where most individuals tend to participate at "safe" recreational levels (i.e., involvement that does not produce any significant negative consequences for the user or others and may also confer benefits). A small proportion of individuals may "misuse" digital media in different ways and to varying degrees of regularity. Misuse may involve, for example, compulsively checking or engaging with social media to the extent that it has negative consequences for the user or others. At the furthest end of the spectrum is a very small proportion of the population who could be considered problematic users, due to the manifestation of a pattern of statistically abnormal use that generates harm. In the case of video gaming, with the WHO's official recognition of gaming disorder (GD) as an addictive disorder, some extreme users may be considered "pathological" users. Research suggests that some individuals, particularly adolescents, are more vulnerable than others to developing unhelpful technology habits that can progress to addiction in the absence of protective countermeasures (Kwon, 2011). Public health recommendations have included delaying the age of involvement in certain activities (e.g., online gaming) and restricting screen time during early developmental periods of life. However, the high accessibility and affordability of digital devices and activities across home, work, and school domains have often made such recommendations difficult to implement. There is also increasing demand for clinical interventions, including specialized individual and group-based treatments.

Effective interventions aim to cater and respond to the unique needs of different groups based on level of risk and required support. Interventions typically aim to prevent the onset of problems and the progression of existing problems to more severe manifestations. The evidence base for interventions for digital technology problems is currently still developing. This is due to the significantly greater expense, special expertise, and time required to conduct this research as compared to basic survey research on the nature, severity, and/or correlates of problematic digital media use. There may also be some uncertainty among researchers about appropriate targets (e.g., individual vs family) and strategies for intervention. To date, some interventions have been adapted from preexisting protocols for gambling and substance use disorders, on the assumption that problematic use of digital media (gaming, social media) is sufficiently similar to these conditions. There have been few programmatic responses and recommendations for managing individuals with lower or less risky levels of problem use. This may be because frequent electronic media use, particularly among young people, is highly prevalent and generally does not have the same negative health consequences associated with low to moderate use of substances such as tobacco, cannabis, and alcohol. It can be difficult, therefore, to determine whether certain high levels of use reflect a transient absorption (or "healthy obsession") in the activity or a riskier form of involvement that could lead to significant negative consequences. Further, some problems related to habitual overuse of digital media may also be masked by other concurrent problems (e.g., depression).

Reflecting priorities to address the more severe end of the spectrum, research on interventions for problem gaming has had a strong focus on therapies for individuals who have experienced major life problems (e.g., unemployment, disengagement from the study, social isolation) due to excessive digital media use (King et al., 2017; Wölfling et al., 2019). Treatments for GD have been provided in countries across Europe, North America, and Asia, where much of this research has been conducted (King et al., 2018; Liu, Nie, & Wang, 2017), and usually with a focus on cognitive-behavioral therapies and other psychotherapies (King et al., 2017; Stevens, Dorstyn, Delfabbro, & King, 2021). Many of these treatment providers report that they also deal with general overuse of the Internet, or consider gaming problems under the umbrella of general terms like "Internet addiction." Other treatments and support modalities include peer supports, such as through Computer Gamers Anonymous (https://cgaa.info/) and GameQuitters (https://gamequitters.com/), and group therapies at hospitals and universities. Examples of these are the residential in-hospital treatment program for video gaming dependency at Hotel-Dieu Grace in Windsor, problem gaming group therapies for gamers and family members at the Center for Addiction Mental Health in Toronto, and the digital detox summer camp at the UCSB campus in Santa Barbara. Some drug therapies, including methylphenidate and bupropion, have also been used with some limited success (Zajac, Ginley, Chang, & Petry, 2017; King & Delfabbro, 2019a, 2019b). Currently, the literature is still publishing studies that provide insight into the potential value, feasibility, and level of support for prevention options among diverse groups of regular and problem users of digital media (Busiol & Lee, 2015).

Social perceptions of problems and interventions

The extent to which interventions are perceived to have value and will be implemented effectively is likely to depend on multiple factors, including issues of cost, access, and feasibility. Another important but overlooked issue in the behavioral addictions field is the general public perception of the severity of behavioral conditions relative to other mental health issues. Many activities (e.g., social media, shopping, eating) proposed to be "addictive" may be seen as small, even trivial, problems because most people tend to engage in these activities at safe, recreational levels. This issue is also relevant to problematic gaming which, due to its widespread popularity and acceptance in popular culture, may be perceived as relatively harmless (notwithstanding sensationalistic media stories that contribute to "moral panic" about new technologies, including games; see Markey & Ferguson, 2017; Orben, 2020). This may extend to some individuals and groups (e.g., organizations, governments) focusing only on the potential benefits of gaming and downplaying its potential addictiveness for some users.

Social judgments of the relative "addictiveness" of certain behaviors and substances were examined in Thege et al.'s (2015) study. The authors surveyed a representative sample of 4000 participants about the perceived addiction risk and etiology of four substances (alcohol, tobacco, marijuana, and cocaine) and six behaviors (problematic gambling, eating, shopping, sexual behavior, video gaming, and work). Respondents tended to consider substances as having greater addiction liability than behaviors, whereas character flaws (e.g., moral failures) were viewed as more associated with behavioral addictions. However, the perceptions of each individual activity indicated a more complex picture. Gaming was rated by participants as having comparable addictiveness to gambling and eating, as well as alcohol and marijuana, but lower than tobacco and cocaine. In another study by Colder Carras et al. (2018), regular gamers expressed mixed views on the concept of gaming "addiction." They tended to support the view that problematic gaming could involve continued use despite harm, unsuccessful attempts to quit, and loss of interest in other activities. However, addiction concepts such as tolerance, withdrawal, and secrecy received much less support.

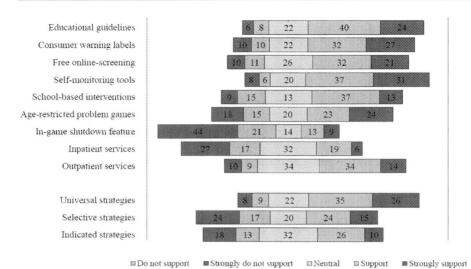

Fig. 19.1 Support for interventions among adult gamers ($N=992$).
From Internet Gaming Disorder. (c. 2019). Elsevier. https://doi.org/10.1016/
B978-0-12-812924-1.00008-3.

Further evidence suggests that certain types of interventions for digital technology-based problems may be considered more favorably than others by the individuals intended to use them. Stevens, Delfabbro, and King (2021a, 2021b) examined regular gamers' views of the value and feasibility of different types of intervention for problematic gaming. Participants were asked to rate their degree of support for a list of various interventions. Overall, the respondents were more favorable toward prevention measures that involved informed decision-making, autonomy, and self-directed actions. These views seemed to align with the cultural values of Western individualized societies and were consistent with previous studies undertaken with gamblers (Harris & Griffiths, 2017). Fig. 19.1 presents a summary of the key findings from this study, highlighting participants' preferences for broad prevention measures as compared to more targeted, specialized measures. About two-thirds of participants were opposed to modifications to video games (e.g., timers, shutdown features that restrict access and time spent on the activity). Overall, this research base suggests that there are diverse views on the status of digital technology-related problems and such views may underlie support and engagement with interventions.

Types of intervention

Interventions aim to: (1) prevent or delay the onset of the problem behavior; (2) reduce the severity of the problem; and (3) improve psychological and emotional well-being in individuals to help them cope more effectively (Romano & Hage, 2000). Interventions encompass three main levels: primary, secondary, and tertiary (Table 19.1).

Table 13.1 Interventions for digital technology-based problems (King et al., 2018, reproduced in revised format).

Strategic target	Intervention type		
	Primary	Secondary	Tertiary
Risky or hazardous use of digital technology (i.e., excessive or risky levels of use, unhealthy levels of use)	**Legislation and enforcement** – Shutdown/fatigue systems – Ban or restriction on Internet use – Retail restrictions (e.g., R18 + rating) **Technological measures** – Use of appropriate media – Parental locks and limit-setting – Smartphone apps – Internet speed restriction/"throttling" – In-game feedback for breaks **Education and guidelines** – Physical activity recommendations – Engagement in alternative activities – Digital media literacy training – Safe Internet use orientation courses – Avoid/minimize riskier game types	**Education and programs** – Education on healthy Internet use – Address comorbid mental health issues – Youth empowerment approaches **Legislation and enforcement** – Reduce opening hours for Internet cafes – Regulations for safe use **Regular examination and screening** – Screening risky use (health providers) – Stress management – Self-monitoring online activity **Parental role** – Family media agreements, limit-setting – Facilitate alternatives to Internet use	**Support groups** – Online self-help communities – Community groups **National Health Guidelines** – Exercise and diet – Screen time restrictions **Education and awareness** – Self-monitoring/Limit-setting – Harm reduction – Awareness days **Mental health services** – Treatment for primary disorders
Problematic or disordered use of digital technology (i.e., meets criteria for DSM-5 or ICD-11 guidelines, diagnosed issues)	**Legislation and enforcement** – Restrictions on riskier games – Shutdown/fatigue systems **Technological measures** – Online monitoring of use – Game account deactivation – Device-free environments (e.g., bedrooms) **Education and guidelines** – Internet addiction education – Understanding links to other disorders – Target student population – Interactive lectures/workshops	**Education and programs** – Education for users/carers – Self-control/self-regulation strategies – Contingency management – Exercise/outdoor activities **Regular examination and screening** – Mental health checks – Epidemiological surveys **Technological measures** – Limit-setting software **Parental role** – Family media agreements, limit-setting – Facilitate alternatives to Internet use	**Outpatient medical services** – Treatment for medical disorders (inc. pain, injury, other illness) – Psychosocial rehabilitation **Support groups** – Online self-help – Community groups – Community engagement/mentors **Rehabilitation programs** – "Digital detox" – Boot camps and retreats – Hospitalization – Psychosocial rehabilitation – Exercise programs **Psychological therapy/pharmacology** – CBT/ACT/MI therapy – Group/individual-based – Medication (e.g., antidepressants)

Primary preventions

Primary prevention is based on the notion that all members of the general population can benefit from certain interventions. For digital technology-based problems, this includes education campaigns, which promote awareness of the harms associated with excessive use, adherence to moderate levels of use, and encouraging healthy lifestyle choices related to diet and physical exercise (Chau, Tsui, & Cheng, 2019; Vondráčková & Gabrhelik, 2016). In Hong Kong, for example, the Wise-IT Use program has been employed widely to increase awareness of the potential harms of excessive gaming and to promote moderate use and engage in physical exercise (Chau et al., 2019).

Examples of primary prevention include:

(1) educational resources, such as guidelines on healthy levels of use (e.g., restricting total hours of use per day), digital literacy courses to increase productive Internet use, physical activity recommendations (e.g., 30 min of moderate exercise per day), and the promotion of structured outdoor activities;
(2) legislative or regulatory actions, such as the mandated shutdown of online gaming services at certain times of the day, and the prevention of sale of certain gaming products to certain age groups;
(3) technological measures, such as parental locks, inappropriate content filters, and time-limit settings on gaming consoles, wearing watches instead of carrying smartphones, pop-up notifications for time spent on a device;
(4) public awareness messages, such as national days that encourage nonuse of digital technology, and campaigns to provide information on relevant services; and
(5) environmental measures, such as reducing accessibility to gaming devices, including removing devices from bedrooms.

Secondary prevention

Secondary strategies are targeted at more vulnerable individuals at risk of developing problems, including gamers who show signs of problem gaming, or those with comorbid mood disorders, low self-esteem, and social competence (Király et al., 2018; Yeun & Han, 2016). Common secondary strategies include screening tools for adolescent gamers; legislature (e.g., shutdown laws) preventing younger people from gaming at specific times; in-game lockout features (e.g., parental controls and limit-setting features); and school programs aimed at teaching protective skills such as stress and time management, self-regulation, and social skills. School-based educational programs have been developed and implemented widely in Asia. For example, Mun and Lee (2015) developed an eight-session school-based program for vulnerable youth in South Korea based on empowerment and cognitive-behavioral principles, which they reported reduced GD symptoms and improved self-regulation. Similarly, Walther, Hanewinkel, and Morgenstern (2014) trial evaluated a program for 1843 students in Germany who participated in an educational program, covering topics of self-regulation, self-monitoring, and positive gaming motivations, which they reported reduced excessive gaming.

Examples of secondary prevention include:

(1) regular screening, including epidemiological research to identify at-risk populations, typically in schools and universities;
(2) medical checks, including consultation with medical practitioners to screen for emotional distress or underlying problems that may increase the risk of gaming as a maladaptive coping strategy;
(3) school-based educational programs, such as programs that teach healthy technology use, promote real-world social interaction, and support hobbies and physical exercise to increase self-esteem and empowerment; and
(4) workplace Internet policy, or rules for Internet access privileges for nonessential purposes in vocational settings, to prevent individuals from browsing gaming-related websites and accessing online gaming servers.

Tertiary prevention

Tertiary prevention strategies are targeted at individuals who are either at high risk of or have already developed, problematic gaming tendencies. Common tertiary strategies include support groups and communities, outpatient treatment options, and inpatient clinics or rehabilitation centers. Several reviews have highlighted the short-term effectiveness of psychotherapeutic and psychopharmacological treatment for problem gaming, although there are limitations of this evidence base (e.g., lack of standard measures and control groups) (Stevens et al., 2021; Winkler, Dörsing, Rief, Shen, & Glombiewski, 2013). Similarly, some drug therapies, such as methylphenidate and bupropion, have also been shown to reduce GD symptoms (see Zajac et al., 2017).

Examples of tertiary prevention include:

(1) support groups, including community groups and online self-help communities;
(2) outpatient medical and mental health services, including treatment of mental disorders (e.g., mood disorders, personality issues, insomnia) and medical problems (e.g., pain issues, injuries that prevent employment) that may underlie or contribute to gaming problems;
(3) psychosocial rehabilitation, including "digital detox" and other structured programs with a focus on increasing face-to-face socialization, time spent in nature, and developing alternative interests; and
(4) psychoeducation, including specialized information about symptoms and strategies for regulating gaming to minimize harm.

Prevention and treatment evidence

There is increasing demand for interventions to address digital technology-based problems (Humphreys, 2019; Nakayama & Higuchi, 2015), but the lack of evidence-based guidelines (King, Delfabbro, Griffiths, & Gradisar, 2012; Rodda, Booth, Vacaru, Knaebe, & Hodgins, 2018) means there is some uncertainty about optimal treatment approaches. A survey of 289 psychiatrists reported that 43% were not confident in their ability to manage problem gaming in their practice (Dullur & Hay, 2017). However, despite this uncertainty, psychological treatment was considered the first-line therapy approach and most (75%) reportedly did not prescribe medication for these issues.

The evidence base on interventions for digital technology-based problems has been developing steadily over the last decade. It is perhaps not surprising that most of the available treatment studies have focused on gaming disorder (King et al., 2017), with its greater recognition in the literature and status as a mental disorder in the ICD-11. However, there is an emerging literature on interventions for other issues, in particular, problematic social media use (Zhou, Rau, Yang, & Zhou, 2020) and "smartphone addiction" (Lan et al., 2018). Most of the published research on treatment has been undertaken in South Korea, China, Japan, and Germany (King et al., 2017), where there are established treatment centers to address online-related problems.

Available research suggests that cognitive-behavioral therapy (CBT) is a promising first-line approach for problematic use (King et al., 2017; Winkler et al., 2013; Zajac et al., 2017). As a recent example, Fig. 19.2 presents Wölfling et al.'s (2019) manualized CBT program that was evaluated in a randomized controlled trial. Their multicenter clinical trial was conducted in 4 outpatient clinics in Germany and Austria that involved 143 male problem gamers and reported that 69% of participants in the treatment group showed remission as compared to 24% in the wait-list control group. Treatment effects, including reductions in problem gaming symptoms, time spent gaming, and depression were estimated to be moderate to large.

Other studies involving CBT have reported similar positive results. A meta-analysis by Stevens, King, Dorstyn, and Delfabbro (2019) examined 12 independent studies. CBT demonstrated high efficacy in reducing GD symptoms and depression and showed moderate efficacy in reducing anxiety at posttest. CBT for GD may be an effective short-term intervention for reducing GD and depressive symptoms but more studies with follow-ups are needed to assess long-term gains. Many treatment studies have fundamental design and reporting limitations. Many studies do not have control groups, and there is a general lack of compliance with the CONSORT statement (i.e., gold standard for reporting trials). Recommendations to improve studies include (1) extending follow-up assessment from 1 month to at least 3–6 months; (2) including an assessment of diagnostic (i.e., clinical) change, rather than differences in mean symptom score; (3) conducting a broader assessment of treatment outcomes, including quality of life, and measuring cognitions in CBT studies; and (4) examining post-treatment adjustment, including social and environmental changes.

CBT recommendations appear to be consistent with models of behavioral addiction (i.e., Brand, Young, Laier, Wölfling, & Potenza, 2016; Dong & Potenza, 2014; King & Delfabbro, 2019a, 2019b). For example, the I-PACE model proposed by Brand et al. (2016) proposed that these conditions are maintained by diminished cognitive control, which inhibits decision-making processes resulting in the decision to play video games. Young and Brand (2017) argued that CBT techniques may be particularly useful to target the maladaptive processes that contribute to internet use disorders as described in the I-PACE model and related models. An apparent advantage of CBT over other therapies, including pharmacological treatment, is its ability to target and modify maladaptive cognitions that underlie behaviors that generate harm and/or distress.

Another benefit of CBT is that this approach is consistent with the therapies used to address comorbid conditions and other psychological issues likely to arise in

Intervention stages	Examples of major intervention strategies applied
Early phase (sessions 1–3)	Additional diagnostics regarding psychopathological symptoms, level of functioning, and psychosocial resources
	Assessing individual characteristics for the motivation to change, enhancing problem awareness and the motivational status for behavioral change
	Development of realistic and personally meaningful treatment goals (including, but not limited to, the abstinence or a substantial reduction of the problematic online behavior)
	Psychoeducation (e.g., introduction of models on the development and maintenance of addictive behaviors, including neurobiological and psychological perspectives)
	Working on a trustful alliance between therapist and patient
Behavior modification (sessions 4–12)	Conceptualization of an individual model explaining specific pathways in the development and maintenance of the addictive behavior. Identification of triggers (internal and external ones that act as conditioned cues leading to craving); behavioral analyses (according to SORKC-schemes) and cognitive restructuring resp. stepwise modification of conditioned (automatic) responses to triggers
	Elaborating awareness for emotional states and skills for effective mood regulation (without using the internet); stress analyses and functional stress management; social skills and reestablishment of alternative behaviors and interests (including elements of well-being therapy)
	Initiating a temporary full abstinence from any internet use (lasting for 6 weeks) in order to facilitate exploring alternative activities. Exposure training with reaction prevention under therapeutic guidance
Stabilization and relapse prevention (sessions 13–15)	Reestablishment of alternative behavioral strategies and interests
	Relapse prevention (e.g., identifying stopping techniques, craving skills, and working on emergency plans)
	Identification of critical conditions associated with a heightened risk for relapse; development of individualized strategies to face such conditions (creation of an individual "emergency plan")

Fig. 19.2 Treatment phases and intervention strategies of STICA (Wölfling et al., 2019).

behavioral addictions (Thorens et al., 2014; Wölfling, Beutel, Dreier, & Müller, 2014). This includes depression (Wang, Cho, & Kim, 2018), general anxiety (Bargeron & Hormes, 2017), social anxiety (Wei, Chen, Huang, & Bai, 2012), attention deficits (Yen et al., 2017), elevated stress (Batthyany, Müller, Benker, & Wölfling, 2009), sleep problems (Dworak, Schierl, Bruns, & Strüder, 2007), maladaptive coping

(Batthyany et al., 2009), loneliness (Lemmens, Valkenburg, & Peter, 2011), and suicidal ideation (Rehbein, Kleimann, & Mößle, 2010).

Research evidence on early interventions for internet-related problems is quite limited. A review by Rumpf et al. (2018) concluded that the literature was insufficient to generate recommendations on specific interventions and/or statements about potential efficacy. However, this review suggested that several approaches may be potential candidates for further testing, such as eHealth interventions, counseling, motivational interviewing, and cognitive-behavioral therapy. Recent meta-analyses of prevention programs for youth in East Asian countries (Liu et al., 2017; Yeun & Han, 2016) have reported promising results. In a review of 58 studies ($N=2871$ participants) by Liu et al. (2017), group counseling programs, CBT, and sports intervention were reported to significantly reduce Internet addiction levels. Group counseling programs were reportedly effective in improving time management, interpersonal and health issues, and reducing compulsive Internet use. CBT yielded a positive change in depression, anxiety, aggression, somatization, social insecurity, phobic anxiety, paranoid ideation, and psychoticism. Sports intervention demonstrated improvements in all symptoms of Internet addiction, particularly withdrawal symptoms.

Government responses

Governments around the world have begun, or already committed, to address digital technology-based problems as an issue of importance. In this section, we provide a brief overview of some of the recent developments in policy and preventative measures in different countries.

South Korea

South Korea has developed a complex governmental system to respond to the region's high prevalence of gaming and Internet-related problems (Koh, 2015; Ministry of Science, ICT, & Future Planning, 2016). This region is unique in that its government has been at the forefront of prevention efforts, particularly in contrast to the United States, Western Europe, and Oceania, where private services and nonprofit organizations provide diverse prevention measures. The region opened the Internet Addiction Prevention Center (IAPC) in 2002 and has established numerous Internet addiction centers across 13 regional governments. For more extreme cases, the IAPC offers rehabilitation camps through the National Center for Youth Internet Addiction Treatment (NYIT) that involves total Internet abstinence for users. Besides these tertiary level initiatives, there have been numerous universal prevention measures, such as public education to promote a healthy online gaming culture. Several agencies including the Korea Education and Research Information Service (KERIS, comprising 178 Wee Centers national wide) and Seoul Metropolitan Government (including six "I Will" Centers in Seoul City) promote a healthy online culture. Large epidemiological and treatment studies involving young people have been conducted via the longitudinal iCURE study (see Jeong et al., 2017).

China

China's legislative approach to technology-related problems has been its selective restriction and censorship of online activities (Stone, 2009). For example, from 2000 to 2014, foreign gaming consoles, such as the Sony PlayStation system, were banned from commercial sale in China. In 2007, the Ministry of Culture (MoC) was responsible for the implementation of the Online Game AntiAddiction System (OGAAS). This system requires all Internet game service developers to collect age-verification data and monitor individuals' usage. Individuals under the age of 18 years are restricted from playing Internet games for more than 3 h a day, with longer playtime resulting in automatic deactivation or compromised in-game reward mechanisms (i.e., "fatigue system'"). Players are required to log in using their verified ID. In April 2011, the Ministry of Culture implemented the Interim Provisions on the Administration of Internet Culture, as a means of gaining more control over Internet-based services. Under these regulations, Internet games (and any online products) are not permitted to include gambling, pornography, or violence, or any content considered to erode social morals or violate laws. The regulations also forbid underage players from purchasing virtual currency in Internet games.

As a secondary prevention measure, the Ministry of Culture proposed the Comprehensive Prevention Program Plan for Minors' Online Gaming Addition in 2013 and highlighted conducting research on prevalence, diagnostic tools, and addiction development models as one of the major measures. The central and local governments have funded independent research undertaken by various institutes, such as the National Key Laboratory of Cognitive Neuroscience and Learning at Beijing Normal University and the School of Public Health and Primary Care at the Chinese University of Hong Kong, to investigate the prevalence of IA across multiple regions in China (Li, 2013; Li, Zhang, Lu, Zhang, & Wang, 2014; Mak et al., 2014; Wang, Wu, & Lau, 2016). Gaming disorder or Internet gaming addiction is a recognized disorder in mainland China, and affected individuals may seek treatment at specialist outpatient clinics at public hospitals. Therefore, epidemiological research enables the government to better plan and coordinate its systemic responses. Private hospitals, NGOs, and private practitioners provide mental health services for at-risk populations (Su, Fang, Miller, & Wang, 2011).

Japan

The Japanese government recognizes both Internet use and content as potentially harmful under certain conditions, and particularly for young populations (Sakuma et al., 2017). Several prevention initiatives have been supported in Japan. In 2012, the MIC launched an initiative that aimed to increase information technology literacy in the population via lectures and training resources, while also educating about the hazards of Internet misuse. In 2014, the region launched the "IT moral developing project for children" which raised awareness of hazardous Internet use, particularly in relation to smartphone use. Since 2014, the Japan Internet Safety Promotion Association (JISPA) has had a campaign that teaches safe Internet use to children. JISPA is a nonprofit organization that receives government funding. The campaign also targets parents and involves lectures and promotion of filtering and monitoring of the Internet. The region also launched a clinical trial for internet addiction for young people in 2014. The trial offers a multitherapeutic approach with an outdoor program that is overseen by the National Institution for Youth Education in collaboration with the Kurihama Medical and Addiction Center, which launched its own treatment section in 2011 and receives hundreds of patients each year, primarily with problems related to excessive gaming (Humphreys, 2019).

Germany

Germany has had an increasing number of referrals for disordered gaming or Internet use registered in its traditional addiction treatment centers over the past decade (Dau, Hoffman, & Banger, 2015). This presented a major challenge for medical and psychiatric treatment providers because treatment of these problems could only be provided if it also presented with a comorbid disorder (e.g., depression, substance use). However, in 2012, the Federal Ministry of Health updated its drug and addiction policy to specify new initiatives for internet use disorders. The Ministry's report outlined goals, including (1) further training and qualification of teachers and professionals in the field of parental and family counseling; (2) education for parents about possible risks of online activities, including technological measures (e.g., parental locks) to protect children on home computers; (3) improved protection of children and young people in relation to computer games; (4) criteria to identify risky and pathological Internet use and adopting these criteria in rating systems for Internet games; and (5) diagnostic instruments for Internet and gaming addiction, for implementation in treatment settings (Drug Commissioner of the Federal Ministry of Health, 2012).

Germany has a range of public services for addiction treatment, in addition to self-help and support services. There are numerous websites in the field of addiction support, which provide information, self-report IA tests, consultation webchats and email support, and brief self-help interventions and strategies. There are several university institutions engaged in treatment and prevention research on disordered or hazardous gaming or Internet use, investigating, for example, selective prevention programs in schools (Dreier, Wölfling, Beutel, & Müller, 2015). A professional association has been established ("Fachverband Medienabhängigkeit e.V." or Media Addiction Association) and the German Association for Psychiatry, Psychotherapy, and Psychosomatics (Deutsche Gesellschaft für Psychiatrie, Psychosomatik und Nervenheilkunde) has founded a group for the investigation and classification of Internet-related problems. In addition to this, the German Federal Parliament's Office for Technology-Outcome Assessment (Büro für Technikfolgen-Abschätzung) advises the Parliament and its committees regarding questions concerning technological and social change, including questions on new electronic media and behavioral addictions (Evers-Wölk, Opielka, & Sonk, 2016).

Several outpatient treatment centers have emerged in Germany over the past decade. The Schwerin Media Addiction Counseling center for "excessive media use and media addiction" was established in 2006 as a joint project between the Mecklenburg-Vorpommern Evangelical Addiction Help and the Schwerin Helios medical centers. The Computer Game Addiction Outpatient Clinic of the University Hospital in Mainz was opened in 2008. The service delivers cognitive-behavioral therapy in manualized individual and group formats and provides free telephone support for friends and families of clients. Another service is the independent consulting and treatment service for media dependency in the outpatient clinic of the Department of Addictions and Psychotherapy, at the LVR Clinic in Bonn, which was established in 2009.

United Kingdom, United States, and Australia

The United Kingdom, United States, and Australia have much in common with respect to their national approaches to gaming disorder and Internet addiction prevention and treatment. Historically, governments in these regions have not generally funded specialized gaming or other Internet-related disorder treatment services, but have offered funding to nonprofit organizations for universal and secondary prevention efforts. As an exception, in the United Kingdom, the National Health Service recently established the National Center for Behavioral Addictions, which was preceded by the Center for Compulsive and Addictive Behaviors, to provide treatment for problem gambling and problem gaming. For gaming-related problems, the NHS clinic provides individual and/or group treatment of up to a 12-week program, family therapy, and practical support and advice for the young person's family or people close to them who may also be affected. The service is promoted as available for individuals aged 13 years and over.

In the United States and Australia, there has been a rapid increase in private providers (e.g., the reSTART Internet Addiction Recovery Programme in Seattle), including online psychological practices (e.g., www.netaddiction.com in the United States, established by the late Dr. Kimberly Young) and independent residential programs. These regions have a strong network of independent councils and international societies dedicated to educating parents and users about problems and general risks stemming from gaming and Internet use. In the United States, there are private, nonprofit organizations including the National Center for Missing & Exploited Children (NCMEC) and the Family Online Safety Institute. Collectively, these bodies provide practical parenting resources for hazardous Internet use and have a strong focus on supporting law enforcement in tackling illegal online activities involving children.

The bulk of research into treatment and prevention is generally undertaken by university institutions in these regions. However, competitive funding opportunities for gaming or Internet-related research appear to be limited, which has negatively affected the overall scope and quality of the research base and its compliance with international standards for health and clinical research (King et al., 2017; King, Delfabbro, Griffiths, & Gradisar, 2011). Australia's leading expert body for health and medical research, the National Health and Medical Research Council (NHMRC) has not funded a project on gaming disorder or other digital technology-based problems in its history. The main Australian governmental body concerned with gaming and Internet-related issues is the Australian Communications and Media Authority (ACMA). The ACMA is an independent statutory authority tasked with ensuring media and communications legislation operates effectively and efficiently, and in the public interest. To date, the ACMA has acknowledged excessive gaming and Internet use and provided warnings and parenting resources, and supported epidemiological research. More recently, in Australia, gambling researchers and research organizations have taken more interest in problem gaming, both in terms of its similarity to problem gambling as well as its overlap and convergence with gambling activities (e.g., esports betting).

The role of industry and online content providers

Some authors have argued that digital entertainment and social media industries have a social responsibility to address issues related to excessive use and offer more user protections (King and Gaming Industry Response Consortium, 2018; Shi, Renwick, Turner, & Kirsh, 2019; Swanton, Blaszczynski, Forlini, Starcevic, & Gainsbury, 2021; Van Rooij, Meerkerk, Schoenmakers, Griffiths, & Van de Mheen, 2010). A common focal point of this discussion has included a focus on the industry's use of monetization features, including features that resemble gambling (loot boxes) (Drummond, Sauer, Hall, Zendle, & Loudon, 2020; King, Delfabbro, Deleuze, et al., 2019; King, Delfabbro, Gainsbury, et al., 2019; King, Koster, & Billieux, 2019). Some recent papers have drawn comparisons between paid random rewards in games and electronic gambling machines, as well as virtual currencies (skins) that facilitate financial gambling (Greer, Rockloff, Browne, Hing, & King, 2019), and the lack of regulation or protective countermeasures (Brooks & Clark, 2019; Drummond, Sauer, & Hall, 2019; King & Delfabbro, 2018, 2019b). Some countries (e.g., Belgium, the Netherlands) have taken steps to legally classify and regulate these activities as gambling, and other regions (e.g., China and Japan) have mandated the industry to disclose the odds associated with random item purchases (Drummond et al., 2019; Király et al., 2018).

To date, the industry has generally not directly acknowledged the existence of excessive use of digital technologies and has expressed opposition to mental disorders involving digital technology, including ICD-11 gaming disorder (European Games Developer Foundation, 2018; King and Gaming Industry Response Consortium, 2018). Two main types of industry responses to digital technology-based problems warrant acknowledgement: (i) age classification systems and (ii) safety guidelines for online services and products. The age classification of digital games intended for commercial sale is undertaken by different regulatory bodies depending on the region. For example, all video games intended for commercial sale in the United States must first be reviewed by the Entertainment Software Rating Board (ESRB), an industry body that provides consumer advice and warnings in relation to the age appropriateness of gaming material. Similar age rating systems operate in other jurisdictions, such as the Pan European Gaming Information (PEGI) ratings system. In some regions, such as Australia and South Korea, the rating system is administered by a statutory classification body. Rating systems often recommend parental guidance or adult use only for some games, but they lack reference to specific game content or types of games (e.g., MMORPGs and MOBAs) with stronger research evidence on hazardous use.

Several major software companies with international markets have provided user guidelines for safe Internet use. For example, Microsoft (2016) developed an online "Healthy Gaming Guide" that states *repetitive movements, poor posture and over-indulgence…can sometimes cause numbness, tingling and other issues that might escalate into serious health problems.*" Recommendations for safe use primarily concern the physical action of use (e.g., posture, viewing distance, method of pressing buttons), with suggestions of taking breaks, managing stress, making healthy lifestyle choices, and consulting health professionals as required. Similarly, Microsoft, Sony, and Nintendo provide online guides and video demonstrations on setting time limits and content restrictions on their gaming systems. Major online service companies, such as Apple and Google, have developed safe use guidelines for parents that explain privacy, filtering, and monitoring options, but these guides also lack acknowledgment of excessive use.

Future research directions

There is a continued need for high-quality epidemiological and intervention studies of digital technology-based problems. Studies should include more refined measurements of gaming-related harms, as well as measures of comorbidity to address questions regarding the contribution of other mental disorders, such as depression, anxiety, attention-deficit/hyperactivity, or other factors that may affect digital media use. Similarly, future work should consider alternative perspectives and concepts to understand how problems digital technology use arises and persists, such as theories of habit, impulsivity, and compulsivity. This extends to problematic behaviors that are diagnostically subthreshold entities, such as "hazardous gaming" (QE22) in the ICD-11.

Future studies may benefit from the inclusion of measures that are sensitive to improvements in quality of life, such as the social benefits of online activities. For example, problem gaming symptoms and negative consequences of gaming should be weighed against reported benefits of gaming (i.e., cost/benefit analysis). This may help determine whether some individuals classified within "low risk" categories might experience a net benefit for their quality of life and psychological well-being.

Another avenue for future research is the use of behavioral tracking data in combination with screening tools and related measures. The field has often relied on self-report approaches to validate tools, which has unavoidable limitations (e.g., biased recall, denial/defensiveness, lack of insight). Conventional survey and interview approaches may be supplemented by user data (e.g., social media account data) to provide an objective historical account; i.e., to describe or corroborate patterns of behavior that may otherwise be difficult to recall. Such data may be acquired by using an app or similar monitoring device or software. Such work relies on the cooperation of industry partners (King, Billieux, & Delfabbro, 2021) and should be transparent and independent to ensure scientific integrity (Griffiths & Pontes, 2019; King & Delfabbro, 2019a, 2019b; Muggleton et al., 2021).

Another area for future research concerns the monetization of online content in online games and social media (e.g., sponsored posts, advertising, in-game purchasing, microtransactions, and "loot boxes"; see King, Delfabbro, Deleuze, et al., 2019; King, Delfabbro, Gainsbury, et al., 2019; Zendle & Cairns, 2018). Problematic gaming that involves interactions with monetized content may be more financially involved and share features in common with gambling disorder (e.g., spending more than one can afford, borrowing, or stealing money) (King & Delfabbro, 2018; King, Delfabbro, Deleuze, et al., 2019; King, Delfabbro, Gainsbury, et al., 2019). Screening tools may need to reflect some of these structural elements in these activities, such as additional questions to examine different behaviors and consequences related to different types of activities and modes of access (e.g., smartphones, virtual reality) (King, Koster, & Billieux, 2019).

Practical steps to raise the public profile of behavioral addictions include (1) recognizing behavioral addictions (gambling, gaming, and internet use disorders) within national addiction policy and health research priorities, to enable more coordinated efforts in areas of research and intervention; (2) the inclusion of questions about the problematic use of digital technologies in national epidemiological studies; (3) support for prevention campaigns and resources, such as school-based programs for young people as well as older users at-risk of developing significant gaming problems. Such programs could be designed to complement existing digital health programs about managing screen time and appropriate use of online technologies. This may ensure that discussion of problem use occurs alongside other priority areas including cyber-safety, "sexting," and privacy issues. Fact sheets and resources (including online materials) and intervention options in mental health and medical settings would be helpful.

Educating the general public using clear and concise descriptions of problem digital technology use based on scientific models and guidelines (e.g., references to "loss of control") (Gainsbury, Tobias-Webb, & Slonim, 2018). Screening instruments for problem digital technology use could be made more accessible and translatable to a general audience, such as in the form of a self-report checklist on an app or a website. This would enable individuals to monitor their usage or the usage of others, with the potential option of tailored and normative feedback about patterns of use and digital well-being (see Auer & Griffiths, 2014). Example feedback may include "You have checked your phone 500 times this week, which is about the same as 30% of the population."

Discussion

This chapter provides a summary of various interventions for problematic digital technology use and the available research evidence. Perhaps the most established literature base at this time related to the treatment of problem gaming and gaming disorder, which includes some RCTs conducted in Europe and Asia. To date, there have been more prevention studies conducted in South Korea and China, reflecting the greater prioritization and expenditure of resources to combat these issues in these regions. Research on prevention has had a strong focus on school-based programs to train healthier Internet use habits in children. The efficacy of selective prevention approaches in combating gaming and Internet disorders appears promising but warrants further empirical attention and evaluation. There is also a need for empirical data on the efficacy and cost-effectiveness of targeted government and independent services, such as "boot camps" and similar youth-targeted initiatives and programs. There is only limited evidence of digital entertainment industries taking steps to introduce preventative countermeasures. Similarly, outside of the gambling industry, there is little evidence of the industry providing funding or collaboration with public health bodies or research institutions for epidemiological (e.g., data-sharing) and intervention studies.

A notable feature of East Asian approaches to interventions has been their formal acknowledgment of problematic technology use as a public health issue (Fang et al., 2015; King & Delfabbro, 2017; Koo, Wati, Lee, & Oh, 2011; Lim, 2012). This was in contrast to policy in other regions, particularly the United States and Australia, which acknowledge indirect harms related to excessive screen time but have limited acknowledgment of behavioral addictions beyond gambling disorder. The South Korean model of gaming disorder prevention is an exemplar of a coordinated response to a public health threat, with extensive government initiatives and long-term strategic plans at all three levels of prevention. A major advantage of their approach has been their organization of services and strategies with a long-term plan. South Korea's government initiatives also enable a greater geographical reach of services and links with existing service providers.

The Chinese government has invested heavily in developing technological measures aimed to restrict the hours of under-18 access to Internet gaming services. It is pertinent, however, to evaluate so-called "shutdown laws" in relation to their impact on incidence and prevalence of problems, and to consider the potential for these measures to be used to suppress information and content. Laboratory-based evidence suggests that these measures could be counterproductive (Davies & Blake, 2016) or even ineffectual given potential loopholes. Understanding these systems would be helpful in regions like Australia, where there have previously been (unsuccessful) proposals to introduce (likely, ineffective) Internet filters and/or "broadband-throttling" to reduce Internet access (Joint Select Committee on Cyber-Safety, 2011).

Western regions are dominated by prevention and treatment approaches led by non-profit organizations and private enterprises. On the one hand, this may place a lower burden on government-funded services and infrastructure if they provide effective solutions. However, an objective evaluation is required to appraise whether a network of independent private service providers is actually effective. Another concern in the Western context is the general lack of competitive research funding opportunities for researchers to pursue more rigorous epidemiological, prevention, and intervention research agendas. Although there may be significant public interest and media attention on problematic technology use, without high-quality scientific investigation it may be difficult to elevate public understanding and discussion of risks beyond unqualified opinion and moral panic. The German prevention model would suggest that one way forward for governments may be to develop a strategic plan outlining various initiatives to standardize efforts (e.g., treatment models, assessment tools, and training). This could be especially advantageous for countries which do not have a detailed national health policy on such issues (e.g., Australia).

Conclusions

All individuals born into industrialized societies will be raised in environments where digital technologies are ever-present, easily accessible, and an integral part of everyday life. A major challenge is to identify effective measures that can prevent as many of these individuals from engaging in levels of use that cause significant negative consequences. There is a need for greater empirical evaluation of interventions and policies to identify best practice approaches across populations and regions. It is important for researchers to work together with relevant stakeholders to apply their knowledge and assist in the development and testing of models of care and prevention. Digital entertainment and social media industries have largely not introduced substantial user welfare measures, and they appear to be mostly silent on their role in public health issues. There is great potential for academic-industry research on digital technology habits to advance knowledge of the well-being risks of digital media during and enhance organized efforts to help vulnerable users. The way forward in prevention ultimately rests upon all stakeholders working together in the public interest, confronting the reality of the evidence base and developing practical, ethical, and sustainable countermeasures.

Conflict of interest

The authors declare no conflict of interest with respect to the content of this chapter.

References

Auer, M., & Griffiths, M. D. (2014). Personalised feedback in the promotion of responsible gambling: A brief overview. *Responsible Gambling Review*, *1*, 27–36.

Bargeron, A. H., & Hormes, J. M. (2017). Psychosocial correlates of internet gaming disorder: Psychopathology, life satisfaction, and impulsivity. *Computers in Human Behavior*, *68*, 388–394.

Batthyany, D., Müller, K. W., Benker, F., & Wölfling, K. (2009). Computer game playing: Clinical characteristics of dependence and abuse among adolescents. *Wiener Klinische Wochenschrift*, *121*(15–16), 502–509.

Brand, M., Rumpf, H. J., King, D. L., Potenza, M. N., & Wegmann, E. (2020). Clarifying terminologies in research on gaming disorder and other addictive behaviors: Distinctions between core symptoms and underlying psychological processes. *Current Opinion in Psychology*, *36*, 49–54.

Brand, M., Wegmann, E., Stark, R., Müller, A., Wölfling, K., Robbins, T. W., et al. (2019). The interaction of person-affect-cognition-execution (I-PACE) model for addictive behaviors: Update, generalization to addictive behaviors beyond internet-use disorders, and specification of the process character of addictive behaviors. *Neuroscience and Biobehavioral Reviews*, *104*, 1–10.

Brand, M., Young, K. S., Laier, C., Wölfling, K., & Potenza, M. N. (2016). Integrating psychological and neurobiological considerations regarding the development and maintenance of specific internet-use disorders: An interaction of person-affect-cognition-execution (I-PACE) model. *Neuroscience & Biobehavioral Reviews*, *71*, 252–266.

Brooks, G. A., & Clark, L. (2019). Associations between loot box use, problematic gaming and gambling, and gambling-related cognitions. *Addictive Behaviors*, *96*, 26–34.

Busiol, D., & Lee, T. Y. (2015). Prevention of internet addiction: The PATHS program. Student well-being in Chinese adolescents in Hong. In *Kong* (pp. 185–193). Singapore: Springer.

Chau, C. L., Tsui, Y. Y. Y., & Cheng, C. (2019). Gamification for internet gaming disorder prevention: Evaluation of a wise IT-use (WIT) program for Hong Kong primary students. *Frontiers in Psychology, 10*, 2468.

Colder Carras, M., Porter, A. M., van Rooij, A. J., King, D. L., Lange, A., …. (2018). Gamers' insights into the phenomenology of normal gaming and game "addiction": A mixed methods study. *Computers in Human Behavior, 79*, 238–246.

Dau, W., Hoffman, J. D. G., & Banger, M. (2015). Therapeutic interventions in the treatment of problematic internet use: Experiences from Germany. In C. Montag, & M. Reuter (Eds.), *Internet addiction: Neuroscientific approaches and therapeutical interventions* (pp. 183–217). Springer International Publishing.

Davies, B., & Blake, E. (2016). Evaluating existing strategies to limit video game playing time. *IEEE Computer Graphics and Applications. 36*, 47–57.

Dong, G., & Potenza, M. N. (2014). A cognitive-behavioral model of internet gaming disorder: Theoretical underpinnings and clinical implications. *Journal of Psychiatric Research, 58*, 7–11.

Dreier, M., Wölfling, K., Beutel, M. E., & Müller, K. W. (2015). Prävention der Internetsucht. Workshop für Kinder und Jugendliche mit digitalen Methodenkoffern [Internet addiction prevention. Workshop for children and adolescents using digital methods]. *Pädiatrie und Pädologie, 50*, 200–205.

Drug Commissioner of the Federal Ministry of Health. (2012). *National strategy on drug and addiction policy*. Berlin: Federal Ministry of Health.

Drummond, A., Sauer, J. D., & Hall, L. C. (2019). Loot box limit-setting: A potential policy to protect video game users with gambling problems? *Addiction, 114*, 935–936.

Drummond, A., Sauer, J. D., Hall, L. C., Zendle. D., & Loudon, M. R. (2020). Why loot boxes could be regulated as gambling. *Nature Human Behaviour, 4*, 986–988.

Dullur, P., & Hay, P. (2017). Problem internet use and internet gaming disorder: A survey of health literacy among psychiatrists from Australia and New Zealand. *Australasian Psychiatry, 25*, 140–145.

Dworak, M., Schierl, T., Bruns, T., & Strüder, H. K. (2007). Impact of singular excessive computer game and television exposure on sleep patterns and memory performance of school-aged children. *Pediatrics, 120*(5), 978–985.

Environment and Communications References Committee. (November, 2018). *Gaming micro-transactions for chance-based items*. The Senate: Commonwealth of Australia.

European Games Developer Foundation. (2018). Statement on WHO ICD-11 list and the inclusion of gaming. Available at: http://www.egdf.eu/wp-content/uploads/2018/06/Industry-Statement-on-18-June-WHO-ICD-11.pdf (archived at http://www.webcitation.org/70U6I0i4S).

Evers-Wölk, M., Opielka, M., & Sonk, M. (2016). *Neue elektronische Medien und Suchtverhalten. Endbericht zum TA Projekt [New electronic media and behavioural addiction. Final report for the TA project] (Vol. TAB Arbeitsbericht Nr. 166)*. Berlin: Büro für Technologieabschätzung beim Deutschen Bundestag.

Fang, X., Liu, L., Deng, L., Liu, Q., Su, W., & Lan, J. (2015). The prevention and intervention of adolescent internet addiction. *Psychological Development and Education, 31*, 100–107.

Gainsbury, S. M., Tobias-Webb, J., & Slonim, R. (2018). Behavioral economics and gambling: A new paradigm for approaching harm-minimization. *Gaming Law Review, 22*, 608–617.

Greer, N., Rockloff, M., Browne, M., Hing, N., & King, D. L. (2019). Esports betting and skin gambling: A brief history. *Journal of Gambling Issues, 43*, 128–146.

Griffiths, M. D., & Pontes, H. M. (2019). The future of gaming disorder research and player protection: What role should the video gaming industry and researchers play? *International
Journal of Mental Health and Addiction*, 1–7.

Harris, A., & Griffiths, M. D. (2017). A critical review of the harm-minimisation tools available
for electronic gambling. *Journal of Gambling Studies*, *33*, 187–221.

Higuchi, S., Nakayama, H., Mihara, S., Maezono, M., Kitayuguchi, T., & Hashimoto, T.
(2017). Inclusion of gaming disorder criteria in ICD-11: A clinical perspective in favor:
Commentary on: Scholars' open debate paper on the World Health Organization ICD-11
gaming disorder proposal (Aarseth et al.). *Journal of Behavioral Addictions*, *6*, 293–295.

Humphreys, G. (2019). Sharpening the focus on gaming disorder. World Health Organization.
Bulletin of the World Health Organization, *97*(6), 382–383.

Jeong, H., Yim, H. W., Jo, S. J., Lee, S. Y., Kim, E., Son, H. J., et al. (2017). Study protocol of
the internet user cohort for unbiased recognition of gaming disorder in early adolescence
(iCURE), Korea, 2015–2019. *BMJ Open*, *7*(10).

Joint Select Committee on Cyber-Safety. (2011). *High-wire act: Cyber-safety and the young*.
Commonwealth of Australia.

King, D. L., Billieux, J., & Delfabbro, P. H. (2021). COVID-19: Science of tech habits needs
industry support. *Nature*, *589*, 198.

King, D. L., & Delfabbro, P. H. (2017). Prevention and policy related to internet gaming disorder. *Current Addiction Reports*, *4*, 284–292.

King, D. L., & Delfabbro, P. H. (2018). Predatory monetization features in video games (e.g.,
'loot boxes') and internet gaming disorder. *Addiction*, *113*, 1967–1969.

King, D. L., & Delfabbro, P. H. (2019a). *Internet gaming disorder: Theory, assessment, treatment, and prevention*. Cambridge, MA: Elsevier Academic Press.

King, D. L., & Delfabbro, P. H. (2019b). Loot box limit-setting is not sufficient on its own to
prevent players from overspending: A reply to Drummond, Sauer, and Hall. *Addiction*,
114, 1324–1325.

King, D. L., Delfabbro, P. H., Deleuze, J., Perales, J. C., Király, O., Krossbakken, E., et al.
(2019). Maladaptive player-game relationships in problematic gaming and gaming disorder: A systematic review. *Clinical Psychology Review*, *73*, 101777.

King, D. L., Delfabbro, P. H., Doh, Y. Y., Wu, A. M. S., Kuss, D. J., Mentzoni, R., et al. (2018).
Policy and prevention approaches for disordered and hazardous gaming and internet use:
An international perspective. *Prevention Science*, *19*, 233–249.

King, D. L., Delfabbro, P. H., Gainsbury, S. M., Dreier, M., Greer, N., & Billieux, J. (2019).
Unfair play? Video games as exploitative monetized services: An examination of game pat-
ents from a consumer protection perspective. *Computers in Human Behavior*, *101*, 131–143.

King, D. L., Delfabbro, P. H., Griffiths, M. D., & Gradisar, M. (2011). Assessing clinical trials
of internet addiction treatment: A systematic review and CONSORT evaluation. *Clinical
Psychology Review*, *31*, 1110–1116.

King, D. L., Delfabbro, P. H., Griffiths, M. D., & Gradisar, M. (2012). Cognitive-behavioral approaches to outpatient treatment of internet addiction in children and adolescents. *Journal
of Clinical Psychology*, *68*, 1185–1195.

King, D. L., Delfabbro, P. H., Wu, A. M. S., Doh, Y. Y., Kuss, D. J., Mentzoni, R., et al. (2017).
Treatment of internet gaming disorder: An international systematic review and CONSORT
evaluation. *Clinical Psychology Review*, *54*, 123–133.

King, D. L., & Gaming Industry Response Consortium. (2018). Comment on the global gaming
industry's statement on ICD-11 gaming disorder: A corporate strategy to disregard harm
and deflect social responsibility? *Addiction*, *113*, 2145–2146.

King, D. L., Koster, E., & Billieux, J. (2019). Study what makes games addictive. *Nature*, *573*, 346.

Király, O., Griffiths, M. D., King, D. L., Lee, H.-K., Lee, S.-Y., Bányai, F., et al. (2018). Policy responses to problematic video game use: A systematic review of current measures and future possibilities. *Journal of Behavioral Addictions*, *7*, 503–517.

Koh, Y.-S. (2015). The Korean national policy for internet addiction. In C. Montag, & M. Reuter (Eds.), *Internet addiction: Neuroscientific approaches and therapeutic interventions* (pp. 219–233). Springer International Publishing.

Koo, C., Wati, Y., Lee, C. C., & Oh, H. Y. (2011). Internet-addicted kids and South Korea government efforts: Boot-camp case. *Cyberpsychology, Behavior and Social Networking*, *14*, 391–394.

Kwon, J.-H. (2011). Toward the prevention of adolescent internet addiction. In K. Young, & N. de Abreu (Eds.), *Internet addiction: A handbook and guide to evaluation and treatment* (pp. 223–243).

Lan, Y., Ding, J. E., Li, W., Li, J., Zhang, Y., Liu, M., et al. (2018). A pilot study of a group mindfulness-based cognitive-behavioral intervention for smartphone addiction among university students. *Journal of Behavioral Addictions*, *7*(4), 1171–1176.

Lemmens, J. S., Valkenburg, P. M., & Peter, J. (2011). Psychosocial causes and consequences of pathological gaming. *Computers in Human Behavior*, *27*(1), 144–152.

Li, L. (2013). Prevention of adolescents' internet addiction: Based on the evidence from research. *Advances in Psychological Science*, *20*, 791–797.

Li, Y., Zhang, X., Lu, F., Zhang, Q., & Wang, Y. (2014). Internet addiction among elementary and middle school students in China: A nationally representative sample study. *Cyberpsychology, Behavior and Social Networking*, *17*, 111–116.

Lim, S. S. (2012). Regulatory initiatives for managing online risks and opportunities for youths—The East Asian experience. In M. Walrave (Ed.), *e-Youth: Balancing between opportunities and risks?* (pp. 271–290). Brussels: Peter Lang.

Liu, J., Nie, J., & Wang, Y. (2017). Effects of group counseling programs, cognitive behavioral therapy, and sports intervention on internet addiction in East Asia: A systematic review and meta-analysis. *International Journal of Environmental Research and Public Health*, *14*(12), 1470.

Mak, K. K., Lai, C. M., Watanabe, H., Kim, D. I., Bahar, N., Ramos, M., et al. (2014). Epidemiology of internet behaviors and addiction among adolescents in six Asian countries. *Cyberpsychology, Behavior and Social Networking*, *17*, 720–728.

Markey, P. M., & Ferguson, C. J. (2017). Internet gaming addiction: Disorder or moral panic? *American Journal of Psychiatry*, *174*, 195–196.

Microsoft. (2016). *Windows 10 health gaming guide*. Retrieved online: https://support.xbox.com/en-AU/xbox-on-windows/family-safety-and-security/healthy-gaming-guide.

Ministry of Science, ICT and Future Planning. (2016). *National master plan for implementing healthy use of smartphone and internet (2016–2018)*.

Muggleton, N., Parpart, P., Newall, P., Leake, D., Gathergood, J., & Stewart, N. (2021). The association between gambling and financial, social and health outcomes in big financial data. *Nature Human Behaviour*, 1–8.

Mun, S. Y., & Lee, B. S. (2015). Effects of an integrated internet addiction prevention program on elementary students' self-regulation and internet addiction. *Journal of Korean Academy of Nursing*, *45*, 251–261.

Nakayama, H., & Higuchi, S. (2015). Internet addiction. *Nihon rinsho. Japanese Journal of Clinical Medicine*, *73*(9), 1559–1566.

Orben, A. (2020). The Sisyphean cycle of technology panics. *Perspectives on Psychological Science*. https://doi.org/10.1177/1745691620919372.

Rehbein, F., Kleimann, M., & Mößle, T. (2010). Prevalence and risk factors of video game dependency in adolescence: Results of a German nationwide survey. *Cyberpsychology, Behavior and Social Networking*, *13*(3), 269–277.

Rodda, S. N., Booth, N., Vacaru, M., Knaebe, B., & Hodgins, D. C. (2018). Behaviour change strategies for internet, pornography and gaming addiction: A taxonomy and content analysis of professional and consumer websites. *Computers in Human Behavior*, *84*, 467–476.

Romano, J. L., & Hage, S. M. (2000). Prevention and counseling psychology: Revitalizing commitments for the 21st century. *The Counseling Psychologist*, *28*, 733–763.

Rumpf, H. J., Bischof, A., Bischof, G., Besser, B., Brand, D., & Rehbein, F. (2018). Early intervention in gaming disorder: What can we learn from findings in the substance abuse field? *Current Addiction Reports*, *5*(4), 511–516.

Sakuma, H., Mihara, S., Nakayama, H., Miura, K., Kitayuguchi, T., Maezono, M., et al. (2017). Treatment with the self-discovery camp (SDiC) improves internet gaming disorder. *Addictive Behaviors*, *64*, 357–362.

Saunders, J., Hao, W., Long, J., King, D. L., Mann, K., et al. (2017). Gaming disorder: Its delineation as a serious condition for diagnosis, management and prevention. *Journal of Behavioral Addictions*, *6*, 271–279.

Shi, J., Renwick, R., Turner, N. E., & Kirsh, B. (2019). Understanding the lives of problem gamers: The meaning, purpose, and influences of video gaming. *Computers in Human Behavior*, *97*, 291–303.

Stevens, M. W., Delfabbro, P. H., & King, D. L. (2021a). Prevention approaches to problem gaming: A large-scale qualitative investigation. *Computers in Human Behavior*, *115*, 106611.

Stevens, M. W. R., Delfabbro, P. H., & King, D. L. (2021b). Prevention strategies to address problematic gaming: An evaluation of strategy support among habitual and problem gamers. *The Journal of Primary Prevention*, *42*, 183–201.

Stevens, M. W. R., Dorstyn, D., Delfabbro, P. H., & King, D. L. (2021). Global prevalence of gaming disorder: A systematic review and meta-analysis. *Australian and New Zealand Journal of Psychiatry*, *55*, 553–568.

Stevens, M. W., King, D. L., Dorstyn, D., & Delfabbro, P. H. (2019). Cognitive–behavioral therapy for internet gaming disorder: A systematic review and meta-analysis. *Clinical Psychology & Psychotherapy*, *26*(2), 191–203.

Stone, R. (2009). China reins in wilder impulses in treatment of "internet addiction. *Science*, *324*, 1630–1631.

Su, W., Fang, X., Miller, J. K., & Wang, Y. (2011). Internet-based intervention for the treatment of online addiction for college students in China: A pilot study of the healthy online self-helping center. *Cyber Psychology, Behavior, & Social Networking*, *14*, 497–503.

Swanton, T. B., Blaszczynski, A., Forlini, C., Starcevic, V., & Gainsbury, S. M. (2021). Problematic risk-taking involving emerging technologies: A stakeholder framework to minimize harms. *Journal of Behavioral Addictions*, *9*, 869–875.

Thege, B. K., Colman, I., el-Guebaly, N., Hodgins, D. C., Patten, S. B., Schopflocher, D., et al. (2015). Social judgments of behavioral versus substance-related addictions: A population-based study. *Addictive Behaviors*, *42*, 24–31.

Thorens, G., Achab, S., Billieux, J., Khazaal, Y., Khan, R., Pivin, E., et al. (2014). Characteristics and treatment response of self-identified problematic internet users in a behavioral addiction outpatient clinic. *Journal of Behavioral Addictions*, *3*, 78–81.

Van Rooij, A. J., Meerkerk, G. J., Schoenmakers, T. M., Griffiths, M., & Van de Mheen, D. (2010). Video game addiction and social responsibility. *Addiction Research and Theory*, *18*, 489–493.

Vondráčková, P., & Gabrhelik, R. (2016). Prevention of internet addiction: A systematic review. *Journal of Behavioral Addictions*, *5*, 568–579.

Walther, B., Hanewinkel, R., & Morgenstern, M. (2014). Effects of a brief school-based media literacy intervention on digital media use in adolescents: Cluster randomized controlled trial. *Cyberpsychology, Behavior and Social Networking, 17*, 616–623.

Wang, H. R., Cho, H., & Kim, D. J. (2018). Prevalence and correlates of comorbid depression in a nonclinical online sample with DSM-5 internet gaming disorder. *Journal of Affective Disorders, 226*, 1–5.

Wang, Y., Wu, A. M. S., & Lau, J. T. (2016). The health belief model and number of peers with internet addiction as inter-related factors of internet addiction among secondary school students in Hong Kong. *BMC Public Health, 16*, 272.

Wei, H. T., Chen, M. H., Huang, P. C., & Bai, Y. M. (2012). The association between online gaming, social phobia, and depression: An internet survey. *BMC Psychiatry, 12*(1), 1–7.

Winkler, A., Dörsing, B., Rief, W., Shen, Y., & Glombiewski, J. A. (2013). Treatment of internet addiction: A meta-analysis. *Clinical Psychology Review, 33*(2), 317–329.

Wölfling, K., Beutel, M. E., Dreier, M., & Müller, K. W. (2014). Treatment outcomes in patients with internet addiction: A clinical pilot study on the effects of a cognitive-behavioral therapy program. *BioMed Research International, 425924*.

Wölfling, K., Müller, K. W., Dreier, M., Ruckes, C., Deuster, O., Batra, A., et al. (2019). Efficacy of short-term treatment of internet and computer game addiction: A randomized clinical trial. *JAMA Psychiatry, 76*(10), 1018–1025.

Yen, J. Y., Liu, T. L., Wang, P. W., Chen, C. S., Yen, C. F., & Ko, C. H. (2017). Association between internet gaming disorder and adult attention deficit and hyperactivity disorder and their correlates: Impulsivity and hostility. *Addictive Behaviors, 64*, 308–313.

Yeun, Y. R., & Han, S. J. (2016). Effects of psychosocial interventions for school-aged children's internet addiction, self-control and self-esteem: Meta-analysis. *Healthcare Informatics Research, 22*, 217–230.

Young, K. S., & Brand, M. (2017). Merging theoretical models and therapy approaches in the context of internet gaming disorder: A personal perspective. *Frontiers in Psychology, 8*, 1853.

Zajac, K., Ginley, M. K., Chang, R., & Petry, N. M. (2017). Treatments for internet gaming disorder and internet addiction: A systematic review. *Psychology of Addictive Behaviors, 31*, 979.

Zendle, D., & Cairns, P. (2018). Video game loot boxes are linked to problem gambling: Results of a large-scale survey. *PLoS One, 13*(11). e0206767.

Zhou, X., Rau, P. L. P., Yang, C. L., & Zhou, X. (2020). Cognitive behavioral therapy-based short-term abstinence intervention for problematic social media use: Improved well-being and underlying mechanisms. *Psychiatric Quarterly*, 1–19.

Scaling up of mental health services in the digital age: The rise of technology and its application to low- and middle-income countries

Saher Siddiqui[a], Pattie P. Gonsalves[b,c,d], and John A. Naslund[e]
[a]Harvard College, Harvard University, Cambridge, MA, United States, [b]Sangath, Saket, New Delhi, India, [c]Sangath, Bardez, Goa, India, [d]School of Psychology, University of Sussex, Brighton, United Kingdom, [e]Department of Global Health and Social Medicine, Harvard Medical School, Boston, MA, United States

Introduction

As highlighted in the preceding chapters in this book, digital technologies offer a wide range of approaches for supporting mental health services. To date, much of the literature on the clinical effectiveness of digital mental health interventions has come from higher income settings, including systematic reviews and meta-analyses of smartphone applications for depression, anxiety, and other mental disorders (Firth et al., 2017a, 2017b; Linardon, Cuijpers, Carlbring, Messer, & Fuller-Tyszkiewicz, 2019), but there is less evidence from low-resource settings. Notwithstanding varied access and gaps in access or connectivity, especially in rural areas, digital technologies offer unparalleled opportunities for transforming the delivery and use of mental health interventions in low-income and middle-income countries (LMICs).

There is wide variation among LMICS, and the World Bank defines low-income countries as those with a GNI per capita of $1035 or less, lower middle-income countries as those with a GNI per capita of $1036 to $4,045, and upper middle-income countries as those with a GNI per capita of $4,046 to $12,535, all in US dollars (World Bank Group, 2020). According to the World Health Organization (WHO), 75% of those living with mental disorders reside in LMICs, with most located in regions with less than 1 psychiatrist per 100,000 people (Bruckner et al., 2011). This burden is exacerbated in LMICs where stigma and lack of awareness, limited resources, and insufficient research capacity result in low prioritization of mental health services in health systems, reluctance to seek care among patients and families, and inadequate access to evidence-based services (Sweetland et al., 2014). Furthermore, social factors such as poverty, urbanization, migration, and lifestyle changes due to rapid industrialization contribute to the high morbidity rate (Rathod et al., 2017).

Mental Health in a Digital World. https://doi.org/10.1016/B978-0-12-822201-0.00004-6

One major effect of globalization is the widespread distribution of digital technologies, such as mobile phones, particularly in LMICs. For example, the rise in mobile phones has largely overshadowed the use of landline phones in many LMICs. While the reach of state-provided landline telecommunication networks has been limited in many low-income countries due to high costs, mobile phones allow for greater coverage and accessibility and overcome many of the costly infrastructure requirements to install landlines (Brookings, 2016). As of 2020, there were over 5 billion unique mobile phone users worldwide (We Are Social, 2020), representing roughly two-thirds of the global population. There has been rapid growth in telecommunications in many regions of the globe; for instance, in India, mobile phone penetration is now at 78%, while in Mexico roughly 89% of the population has access to mobile phones (We Are Social, 2020). In recent years sub-Saharan Africa has seen one of the largest rises in mobile technology use, where upwards of 90% of the population had at least 2G coverage by the end of 2017 (Radcliffe, 2018). Consequently, this rapid diffusion of digital technologies around the globe has resulted in increasing mobile internet coverage (We Are Social, 2020), which yields new opportunities to potentially deliver mental health services that would otherwise be inaccessible in most LMICs.

With the rise in digital technology in LMICs, the application of its use to promote mental well-being has also become more prevalent. These technologies include mobile phone apps, websites, wearable devices, and other online digital interventions to deliver mental health support. A recent review on the implementation of eMental health in low-resource settings spanning both high-income and lower income countries found 67 studies, with depression and general mental well-being representing the most common mental health issues addressed (Kaonga & Morgan, 2019). Among the included studies, 31 were from LMICs, and primarily from three countries: India, China, and South Africa. The prominent intervention modalities included online platforms and text messaging, largely focused on improving service delivery, promoting behavior change, and supporting data collection. This review ultimately concluded that eMental health interventions in low-resource settings show promise for supporting treatment adherence, providing direct interventions in a patient's current location, and educating both clients and health-care workers, though it is clear that studies from many LMICs are underrepresented in this synthesis of the evidence (Kaonga & Morgan, 2019).

Another recent systematic review identified studies of Internet-based interventions for the prevention, treatment, and management of mental disorders across Latin America (Jiménez-Molina et al., 2019). The review summarized 22 Internet-based studies that focused primarily on depression, substance misuse, anxiety, and mental health literacy for education and health professionals. The primary countries included Brazil, Mexico, and Chile. Furthermore, the primary intervention methods included telepsychiatry/psychology, guided Internet-based self-help programs, unguided Internet-based self-help programs, and Internet-based programs for education and training of health/education workers. The authors concluded that while there was certainly a rise in Internet-based interventions for the treatment of mental health disorders across Latin America, there were not enough rigorous studies on effectiveness and cost-effectiveness, making it difficult at present to draw conclusions on effectiveness necessary to justify scaling up of these intervention programs (Jiménez-Molina et al., 2019).

A consistent finding highlighted across these reviews is the acceptability and feasibility of using new technologies for supporting mental health care in low-resource settings, which has been similarly reflected in prior reviews of the digital mental health literature from LMICs (Naslund et al., 2017). However, there remains a paucity of clinical effectiveness data for these digital interventions. One recent meta-analysis of digital psychological interventions in LIMCs offers the first quantitative synthesis of findings from the scientific literature (Fu, Burger, Arjadi, & Bockting, 2020). Across 22 included studies primarily targeting depression and substance misuse among young adults, the pooled results showed that digital psychological interventions appear moderately effective when compared to control conditions including usual care. Nevertheless, the heterogeneity in the analysis of their study suggested the need to carry out more studies with a standardized implementation of digital psychological intervention programs to ensure reproducibility and efficiency (Fu et al., 2020).

Consequently, despite a growing number of studies using digital mental health interventions in LMICs, as reflected by these recent reviews and initial promising signs of effectiveness for digital psychological interventions as demonstrated in a recent meta-analysis (Fu et al., 2020), the implementation and sustained use of these technologies in real-world clinical settings pose major challenges (Naslund et al., 2019; Naslund, Bartels, & Marsch, 2019). There remain significant gaps in the evidence, and in particular with regards to tailoring digital mental health interventions to local settings and aligning these programs with health system and community goals, while ensuring consistent delivery of program content necessary to allow reproducibility of the findings. These limitations highlight the need for continued efforts to evaluate digital mental health interventions across diverse low-resource settings, as well as the need to further expand the reach of promising technologies to regions with minimal access to even basic mental health services.

This chapter seeks to illustrate key targets for digital mental health interventions, and where there may be a promise to advance the scale-up of mental health services in LMICs. Specifically, we draw from recent reviews of the literature to propose five broad targets where digital mental health interventions could play an important role spanning community outreach, to primary care services and care for more complex disorders. Across five recent reviews (Carter, Araya, Anjur, Deng, & Naslund, 2021; Fu et al., 2020; Jiménez-Molina et al., 2019; Kaonga & Morgan, 2019; Naslund et al., 2017), we found over 100 studies of digital mental health interventions from 24 different LMICs. These are illustrated in Fig. 20.1. We present promising case examples for each target area with the goal to inform the selection, adaptation, and implementation of similar programs in other low-resource settings, as illustrated in Fig. 20.2. These include (1) technology for community outreach, raising awareness, and challenging stigma; (2) interventions for youth mental health; (3) technology

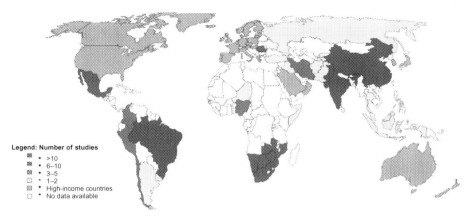

Fig. 20.1 Distribution of the number of studies on digital mental health technologies in LMICs.

Note: The studies in this map were extracted from the following recent reviews: Carter, H., Araya, R., Anjur, K., Deng, D., & Naslund, J.A. (2021). The emergence of digital mental health in low-income and middle-income countries: A review of recent advances and implications for the treatment and prevention of mental disorders. *Journal of Psychiatric Research, 122*, 223–246; Fu, Zhongfang, Burger, H., Arjadi, R., & Bockting, C. L. (2020). Effectiveness of digital psychological interventions for mental health problems in low-income and middle-income countries: A systematic review and meta-analysis. *The Lancet Psychiatry, 7*, 851–864. doi: 10.1016/S2215-0366(20)30256-X; Jiménez-Molina, Á, Franco, P., Martínez, V., Martínez, P., Rojas, G., & Araya, R. (2019). Internet-based interventions for the prevention and treatment of mental disorders in Latin America: A scoping review. *Frontiers in Psychiatry, 10*, 664. doi:10.3389/fpsyt.2019.00664; Kaonga, N. N., & Morgan, J. (2019). Common themes and emerging trends for the use of technology to support mental health and psychosocial well-being in limited resource settings: A review of the literature. *Psychiatry Research, 281*, 112594. doi:10.1016/j.psychres.2019.112594; Naslund, J. A., Aschbrenner, K. A., Araya, R., Marsch, L. A., Unutzer, J., Patel, V., & Bartels, S. J. (2017). Digital technology for treating and preventing mental disorders in low-income and middle-income countries: A narrative review of the literature. *Lancet Psychiatry, 4*(6), 486–500. doi:10.1016/S2215-0366(17)30096-2. In total, there were over 100 studies of digital mental health interventions from LMICs after the removal of duplicates, with studies from 24 different countries.

for mental health in humanitarian settings; (4) technology for supporting clinical care and building capacity of frontline health workers; and (5) technology for severe mental disorders.

These five targets are essential to address toward facilitating increased access to evidence-based mental health care. Furthermore, these broad categories have gained recognition as critically important aspects of successful mental health services delivery, and have experienced significant growth in digital interventions in recent years in parallel with the surging capacity of emerging technologies. Nevertheless, the case examples detailed in the following sections are not exhaustive and provide a brief illustration of various promising and cutting edge projects across the globe, and the use of different forms of technology.

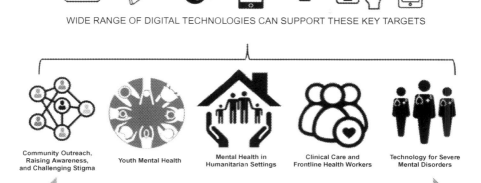

WIDE RANGE OF DIGITAL TECHNOLOGIES CAN SUPPORT THESE KEY TARGETS

| Community Outreach, Raising Awareness, and Challenging Stigma | Youth Mental Health | Mental Health in Humanitarian Settings | Clinical Care and Frontline Health Workers | Technology for Severe Mental Disorders |

SPECTRUM OF COMMUNITY AND CLINICAL APPLICATIONS

Fig. 20.2 Digital mental health interventions for scaling up mental health care across key target areas.
Note: All graphics and images are Creative Commons Licensed resources.

Technology for community outreach, raising awareness, and challenging stigma

Technology for outreach and challenging stigma are essential when taking into context the rise in the double burden of disease, in which both communicable and noncommunicable diseases become prominent, in LIMCs. Unfortunately, the stigma and global burden of mental illness are greatest in LMICs. Technology holds promise as it not only offers capabilities to facilitate connections across the globe where stories can be shared and support provided but also allows for anonymity of users of these platforms (Naslund, Aschbrenner, Marsch, & Bartels, 2016). This section discusses key examples for challenging stigma and promoting well-being.

The Indian youth-focused "It's Ok to Talk" campaign (It's Ok to Talk) by Sangath, a nongovernmental organization (www.sangath.in), aims to increase awareness about mental health and well-being by encouraging its beneficiaries to engage in dialogues about mental health and seek help when needed (http://itsoktotalk.in). This creative online platform provides the opportunity to share personal narratives in multimedia format documenting real experiences of mental health needs. A qualitative analysis of submissions to the platform from young persons from across India identified four major themes: (1) living through difficulties, (2) mental health in context, (3) managing one's mental health, and (4) breaking stigma and sharing hope (Gonsalves et al., 2019). Overall, participants expressed strong feelings of distress and hopelessness as a result of their mental health problems and a desire to overcome prejudice and discrimination. The authors concluded that these personal narratives offered a window into the mind of young people, allowing us to identify their priorities and challenges related to mental health problems and recovery. These insights can inform antistigma initiatives and other public awareness activities pertaining to youth mental health (Gonsalves, Hodgson, Michelson, et al., 2019).

Atmiyata is a program based in Maharashtra, India and organized by the Center for Mental Health Law and Policy (https://cmhlp.org/project/atmiyata/), that utilizes community-led interventions in rural areas to address common mental disorders. This program involves using smartphone technology for training Champions, local community volunteers, to provide support and basic counselling to community members with common mental disorders, to facilitate access to mental health care and social benefits, to improve community awareness of mental health issues, and to promote well-being (Shields-Zeeman, Pathare, Walters, Kapadia-Kundu, & Joag, 2017). A recent study assessed the feasibility of the Atmiyata program and showed that this model of capacity building to train Champions resulted in the identification of common mental disorders with proficient accuracy. Further, the researchers found that after a number of counselling sessions, there was a trend that pointed to a reduction in the severity of depression and anxiety symptoms. The qualitative and quantitative findings show that the intervention is feasible for implementation across rural settings in India and that short films accessible from mobile phones can facilitate conversations and the sharing of information on prevalent mental health issues. Finally, collaboration among local stakeholders enhanced the acceptability and feasibility of delivering the intervention (Joag et al., 2020).

An innovative project in Bangladesh studied the effect of "Meen," a popular animated television program named after a young female lead character (Hasan & Thornicroft, 2018). Since the start of the program, the researchers found a significant change in the educational inclusion of girls in hard-to-reach rural areas and in attitudes and practices related to religious beliefs, cultural practices, and social conditions that lead to everyday discrimination, though programs like this require more rigorous evaluation to assess their effects on mental health and cost-effectiveness (Hasan & Thornicroft, 2018).

Technology for mental health in humanitarian settings

In humanitarian settings, instability and lack of structure may deter the efforts of those attempting to provide or seek mental health support. To overcome this, technology epitomizes a strategy that is flexible, portable, and potentially adaptable to a variety of settings experiencing conflicts. This section discusses some illustrative examples of humanitarian assistance through digital technology.

"Tell Your Story" is a digital intervention that seeks to reduce stigma in traumatized male refugees (Black Dog Institute, 2020). It is an online educational program that constitutes a total of 12 sessions and features stories of male refugees who sought help for their posttraumatic stress disorder (PTSD) symptoms. These stories challenge common misconceptions about mental illness and encourage constituents to share their stories on the platform. A study was conducted and showed that those who actively participated in the intervention program demonstrated decreased levels of shame, self-blame, avoidance of help-seeking, and feelings of social inadequacy in comparison to those who did not participate in the program (Black Dog Institute, 2020).

A randomized, controlled trial was carried out at the outpatient clinic of Sadr Hospital in Tehran, Iran, where 66 war veterans were allocated to either a control or intervention group (Darvish, Khodadadi-Hassankiadeh, Abdoosti, & Kashani, 2019). The intervention group received psychiatric support from short text messages for 6 months whereas the control group received routine hospital care. The team of researchers found a significant improvement in PTSD in the intervention group compared to the control. Furthermore, the recurrence frequency in the intervention group was significantly lower. The authors concluded that their text messaging-based psychiatric nursing program was effective in reducing the severity of symptoms in veterans with PTSD and improved their quality of life (Darvish et al., 2019).

Another study examined the use of a Web-based self-help program, the Chinese version of My Trauma Recovery (CMTR), among Chinese trauma survivors of the 2008 Sichuan earthquake (Wang, Wang, & Maercker, 2016). The study included 56 urban survivors of different trauma types and 90 rural survivors. One of the major findings was that the use of triggers and self-talk modules showed a consistent positive association with improvement in the posttraumatic diagnostic scale, Symptom Checklist 90-Depression, social functioning impairment questionnaire, and trauma coping self-efficacy scale. The authors concluded that both individual (demographic, health problems, psychological) and social factors (social functioning, social support) should be considered when delivering Web-based interventions, specifically in collectivist cultures. Furthermore, they concluded that specific program adherence indicators (webpages completed in each module, activity types completed) rather than general program usage (total time) should be developed to examine the effectiveness of program modules and other elements (Wang et al., 2016).

A study in Iraq assessed the efficacy of a cognitive behavioral Internet-based intervention for war-traumatized patients (Knaevelsrud, Brand, Lange, Ruwaard, & Wagner, 2015). A total of 159 participants were randomized to the treatment or control group. The treatment group received 2 weekly 45-min cognitive behavioral interventions through the Internet over a 5-week period, which came out to 10 sessions. The researchers found that posttraumatic stress symptoms were significantly reduced from baseline to posttreatment in the treatment group relative to the control group and these results were consistent during a 3-month follow-up. They concluded that individuals experiencing posttraumatic stress symptoms can benefit from a cognitive behavioral treatment provided via the Internet (Knaevelsrud et al., 2015).

Another study assessed the feasibility of SMS-based methods to screen for depression risk among refugees in South Africa utilizing mental health services in addition to comparing its reliability and acceptability with face-to-face consultation (Tomita, Kandolo, Susser, & Burns, 2016). The authors concluded that using SMS to screen for risk of depression was both viable for social service agencies and refugees in low-resource settings. While participants reported a preference for face-to-face interaction with health providers in discussing psychological challenges, there was no significant difference in preference regarding methods of assessment. Finally, there was high acceptance with respect to using SMS-based methods for depression screening and it was found to be reliable as well (Tomita et al., 2016).

Digital Interventions for youth mental health

Mental health problems account for nearly half of the burden of disease in adolescents, with depressive, anxiety and conduct disorders together accounting for over 75% of this burden (Reiner et al., 2019; UNFPA, 2014). The impact of youth mental health problems falls most heavily on LMICs. The large mental health care gap in LMICs coincides with a rapid boom in telecommunications and internet access (Naslund et al., 2017). Young people typically adopt new technologies and use mobile devices and the internet more frequently than older age groups, including for the purpose of accessing health-related information. Digital technologies have therefore been advocated as an important platform for scaling up youth mental health care (Mei et al., 2020), with the potential to increase reach, reduce stigma, and lower costs compared with conventional clinic-based service models (Firth et al., 2017a, 2017b; Hollis et al., 2017). This section discusses some examples that embody the ability of emerging technologies to alleviate the burden of mental distress in youth from various settings in LMICs.

"POD Adventures" is a problem-solving app intervention delivered in Indian secondary schools with guidance provided by lay counsellors (Gonsalves et al., 2019). This approach integrates face-to-face contact with self-guided digital content and is consistent with findings that human facilitation can optimize engagement with and outcomes of digital interventions. POD Adventures is part of the PRIDE research program (2016–2021) that has been developing and evaluating transdiagnostic psychological interventions for common adolescent mental health problems in India. Previous PRIDE studies (Michelson et al., 2020a, 2020b; Parikh et al., 2019) revealed a high demand for psychological support among secondary school pupils, the majority of whom did not meet conventional clinical thresholds for mental disorders. Keeping this wider group in mind, POD Adventures was conceptualized as an open-access, early intervention to promote adaptive coping and to mitigate risks for developing more severe and socially disabling mental health problems in the longer term. The app was collaboratively designed with adolescents recruited from schools in New Delhi and Goa through an iterative and person-centered approach, incorporating insights from a range of user consultations across a period of 18 months prior to conducting this study (Gonsalves, Hodgson, Kumar, et al., 2019). Key findings were that participants most valued relatability and interactivity within real-world stories with the support of an in-app guide, and the use of concrete examples of concepts to enhance engagement. This formative research shaped the design of POD Adventures and informed a forthcoming randomized controlled trial to evaluate the platform as a tool to deliver support to students in low-resource settings (Gonsalves, Hodgson, Kumar, et al., 2019).

A program was initiated in Araucania Region, Chile to assess the feasibility, acceptability, and effectiveness of remote collaborative depression care (RCDC) intervention for adolescents with major depressive disorder (MDD) (Martínez et al., 2018). A cluster-randomized trial was carried out at 16 primary care centers with 143 participants aged 13–19 years. One-third of participants showed an optimal adherence to psychopharmacological treatment and adolescents in the RCDC group were more satisfied with psychological assistance than those in the enhanced usual care comparison group. There were no significant differences in depressive symptoms between groups. The authors concluded that the intervention showed comparable effectiveness to an already established nationwide treatment program (Martínez et al., 2018).

A randomized clinical trial was carried out to investigate the efficacy of Internet-based behavioral activation with lay counsellor support (termed Guided Act and Feel Indonesia [GAF-ID]) compared with online minimal psychoeducation without support for depression in Indonesia. In total, 313 participants with an average age of 25 were enrolled. They found that depressive symptoms were reduced in the GAF-ID group compared with the online psychoeducation group at 3 months and 6 months. The findings suggest the potential of online behavioral activation interventions combined with task-shifting by lay counsellor support to bridge the mental health gap for young adults in LMICs (Arjadi et al., 2018). Furthermore, this type of program could be scaled up and efficiently delivered to a larger population group.

There have also been mixed findings in recent studies using digital technology for youth mental health in LMICs. For instance, in a quasiexperimental feasibility study conducted in Thailand with adolescents, a total of 180 participants were recruited from three high schools (Anttila, Sittichai, Katajisto, & Välimäki, 2019). Students were either assigned to a control group with no intervention or the experimental group with the web-based program known as DepisNet-Thai. The program included a 2-week orientation and five weekly modules (psychological stress, physical well-being, and modules about family, friendships, and other social relationship). These modules lasted 50 min and the entire program took 7 weeks to complete. In addition, individuals are given weekly assignments that hone self-reflection skills and teach self-management skills. There were no statistically significant changes between the groups regarding depression, stress, or satisfaction. One explanation may be the low completion rate for the program among adolescents (Anttila et al., 2019). This reflects a common challenge for digital mental health interventions, where low engagement can impede successful outcomes, highlighting the need to engage stakeholders throughout the development and implementation of interventions to ensure that these programs sufficiently capture the interests and priorities of the target population (Yardley, Morrison, Bradbury, & Muller, 2015).

The STARS project aims to create a digital psychological intervention that will be used by adolescents experiencing high levels of psychological distress (aged 15–18 years) globally, to increase access to mental health treatment (Hall & Carswell, 2019). The design of this digital intervention utilizes a human-centered approach by drawing from the experiences of adolescents across five diverse settings: Jamaica, Nepal, Pakistan, South Africa, and West Bank and Gaza Strip. A key strategy in its approach has been to take advantage of the fact that adolescents are very technologically driven and use it for multiple purposes. For example, messaging platforms are quite popular among this age group, thus this has led to the development of "chatbots," a messaging agent which mimics human interaction through speaking (Hall & Carswell, 2019).

Technology for supporting clinical care and building capacity of frontline health workers

In most LMICs, frontline health workers, such as nonspecialist providers, lay health workers, or community health workers, deliver the bulk of primary care services, particularly in rural and underserved settings (Vasan, Mabey, Chaudhri, Epstein, & Lawn, 2017). Referred to as "task sharing," a growing body of evidence suggests that utilizing nonspecialist health workers to deliver psychosocial treatments for common mental health disorders in primary settings is clinically effective (Raviola, Naslund, Smith, & Patel, 2019). Therefore, training and building the capacity of frontline health workers and offering ongoing supervision and support is a key strategy to address the mental health care gap in LMICs due to the lack of available specialty mental health personnel, such as psychiatrists or psychologists. Technology holds promise for supporting task sharing by offering opportunities to overcome some of these barriers in providing access to mental health training programs, as well as facilitating the supervision of frontline health workers and supporting them in effectively delivering care in remote settings (Naslund, Shidhaye, & Patel, 2019). These digital platforms can be used to train health workers, provide digital tools for diagnosis, guide treatment, and facilitate supervision and integration of services into existing clinics or community facilities.

For instance, a phone app known as CONEMO, a low-intensity psychoeducational 6-week intervention delivered via mobile phones with the assistance of a nurse, was launched (Menezes et al., 2019). The aim of CONEMO is to reduce depressive symptoms among individuals with diabetes or hypertension. Three pilot studies were launched to measure the effectiveness of the intervention in which two were based in Lima, Peru (one in a primary care center and one in a cardiology and endocrinology outpatient consultation area of a tertiary level hospital). The third pilot study took place in Sao Paulo, Brazil in a Family Health Care Strategies Clinic. Across all three pilot studies, there were a total of 66 primarily female participants between the ages of 41 and 60 years. At the conclusion of the study, a reduction in depressive symptoms was observed in all three pilot studies. Furthermore, the following percentage of participants achieved treatment success from each study: 62% in Sao Paulo, 62% in the first pilot in Lima, and 50% from the second pilot in Lima. Overall, 58% of the total participants across all three pilot studies reached treatment success. The intervention emerged as feasible and effective in reducing participants' depressive symptoms (Menezes et al., 2019).

DIADA (Detection and Integrated Care for Depression and Alcohol Use in Primary Care) is a research project that aims to evaluate the implementation of technology-supported screening, diagnosis, and care of depression and alcohol use disorder among adults presenting for primary care visits at six sites spanning urban and rural communities in Colombia (Torrey et al., 2020). While it was first launched in 2018 and is still in its early stages, there is currently data reported on its potential impact for supporting detection of depression and alcohol use disorder. For example, in its first year, DIADA was able to screen thousands of individuals which allowed primary care doctors to diagnose patients with depression or alcohol use disorder. Specifically, DIADA utilizes a kiosk and tablet to communicate screening results to primary care physicians. As a result, the rate of diagnosis of depression increased from 0% to 17%, while the rate of diagnosis of alcohol use increased from 0% to 2%. The authors of the study concluded that the project has led to higher diagnoses of depression and alcohol use disorder in primary care settings and can inform policymakers and other stakeholders who seek to scale up mental health care in primary care settings in the country (Torrey et al., 2020).

In Zimbabwe, the Friendship Bench program aims to address common mental health disorders within primary care settings (Chibanda et al., 2016). In this program, trained lay health workers deliver a six-session intervention focused on problem-solving techniques on a bench outside the clinic. The lay health workers used text messages and phone calls to reinforce program content and to promote adherence among patients while the clinical team used voice calls and text messaging to provide supervision and guidance to lay health workers. The effectiveness of the program was reflected by significant reductions in symptoms of depression when compared to a control group (Chibanda et al., 2016).

The ESSENCE (Enabling translation of Science to Service to ENhance Depression CarE) project utilizes digital technologies for training nonspecialist health workers to deliver an evidence-based brief psychological treatment for depression in primary care in rural India (Muke et al., 2019). The project involved developing a smartphone app digital training program with content adapted to the local context in Sehore, a rural district in Madhya Pradesh (see sample content in Fig. 20.3) (Khan et al., 2020). The digital training program in the ESSENCE project follows the Healthy Activity Program (HAP) treatment for depression, and by doing so, the program was able to encompass the core principles of behavioral activation, an evidence-based approach to treating depression (Khan et al., 2020). In an initial pilot study, the digital training program when enhanced with remote support appeared to contribute to comparable improvements in knowledge acquisition as conventional face-to-face training among nonspecialist health workers (Muke et al., 2020). Efforts are needed to demonstrate the generalizability of this digital approach to training nonspecialist health workers, and that it is possible to develop skills and competencies of these essential health workers in a low-cost and scalable manner across diverse settings in India. If success-ful, this approach can potentially be adapted to other global settings and can offer a template for guiding the development of digital training programs for frontline health workers (Muke et al., 2019).

Fig. 20.3 Sample content from digital interventions for global mental health.
Note: Mobile app interface for a digital program for training community health workers to deliver an evidence-based psychological treatment for depression in primary care in rural India. Khan, A., Shrivastava, R., Tugnawat, D., Singh, A., Dimidjian, S., Patel, V., . . . Naslund, J. A. (2020). Design and development of a digital program for training non-specialist health workers to deliver an evidence-based psychological treatment for depression in primary care in India. *Journal of Technology in Behavioral Science*, 5(1), 1–14. 10.1007/s41347-020-00154-7.

Technology for severe mental disorders

Severe mental disorders can be debilitating and in countries where the health-care infrastructure is poor, this can lead to negative consequences for this particular population, including homelessness, suicide, incarceration, and reduced life expectancy (Naslund & Aschbrenner, 2019; Young, 2015). There is emerging evidence that digital interventions could be used to support care delivery and symptom management for those living with severe mental disorders in LMICs. For example, a recent review found that we are lacking in studies evaluating digital interventions for those living with severe mental disorders in LMICs, emphasizing the urgency of the matter during the COVID-19 pandemic (Merchant, Torous, Rodriguez-Villa, & Naslund, 2020). Using technology to scale up treatment is essential to providing support in LMICs where there may be no other options. This section considers examples of technological support for those living with severe mental disorders.

LEAN (Lay health supporters, E-platform, Award, and iNtegration) is a program that features recruitment of a lay health supporter and text messages for medication reminders, health education, monitoring of early signs of relapses, and facilitated linkage to primary health care (Xu et al., 2019). A two-arm randomized controlled trial was run where 278 community-dwelling villagers were randomly selected from individuals with schizophrenia from nine townships of Hunan, China. Participants were randomized to LEAN or a control group, both of which received a nationwide community-based mental health program that provided free antipsychotic medications. The study showed that the addition of the LEAN program was more effective than just the free-medicine program, as reflected by improved medication adherence and reduced relapses and rehospitalizations (Xu et al., 2019).

Another study was conducted to determine whether patients with first-episode psychosis who were seeking treatment at a regional tertiary psychiatric facility for the first time would be more likely to attend their next scheduled clinic visit after receiving short message service (SMS) reminders about their upcoming appointment (Thomas, Lawani, & James, 2017). In this trial, 200 patients from a psychiatric hospital in Nigeria seeking treatment for their first psychotic episode were randomly assigned to either a control or intervention group. While both groups received appointment dates on appointment cards, only the intervention group received an additional SMS text reminder. Individuals who received SMS reminders were almost twice as likely to attend their appointment compared to the control group. Even after adjusting for sociodemographic and clinical variables, the SMS reminder independently reduced the risk of a missed next appointment by 50%. The researchers concluded that SMS reminders of appointments were an effective intervention to improve clinic attendance among individuals treated for first-episode psychosis at the Federal Neuro-Psychiatric Hospital in Benin City, Nigeria (Thomas et al., 2017).

In another study, 77 participants were recruited from a psychiatric hospital in Cape Town, South Africa (Sibeko et al., 2017). The intervention group underwent treatment-partner contracting and psychoeducation and received monthly text message reminders of clinic appointments. The study showed that the treatment-partner and psychoeducation components were acceptable and feasible, the text message component was acceptable, and efficacy outcomes favored the intervention but did not reach statistical significance (Sibeko et al., 2017).

SHARP (Smartphone Health Assessment for Relapse Prevention) is a research project using a digital platform to predict and prevent relapse for those living with schizophrenia. The goal of the project is to guide development and adaptation of LAMP, an open-source smartphone application and digital dashboard, across diverse cultures in a patient-centered and transparent manner to ensure personalized care (Rodriguez-Villa et al., 2021). This study, which spans across multiple sites in India and the US, is still ongoing, though the findings will highlight the potential for digital mental health tools to inform and contribute to meaningful clinical care for a high-risk patient group, with important implications for both low-income settings in both high-income and lower income countries toward closing gaps in accessibility to care and ensuring timely response to relapse (Torous et al., 2019).

Ethical considerations

While the benefits of using digital technology to increase accessibility of mental health care are potentially great, there are also important ethical considerations that must be taken into account. For instance, patient privacy and security is at risk when we attempt to understand behavioral patterns by tracking daily digital activities. This data may be sold in the marketplace and eventually be used to classify people, potentially resulting in discrimination. Furthermore, there is potential harm related to poor quality online information, self-diagnosis and self-treatment, passive monitoring, and the use of invalidated smartphone apps. To mitigate these negative consequences, health providers must be educated about and aware of possible risks with using digital programs for mental health, while patients or persons in need of support must be provided with information on the use and limitations of these websites and apps (Bauer et al., 2017).

Another study highlights key areas that may lead to ethical dilemmas when prescribing these technologies to patients. These key areas include (1) regulatory issues in which rapidly changing technologies raises concerns about their accuracy and safety, (2) privacy and data security in which the personal data of a person may be compromised, (3) the constant monitoring and assessing of risks and benefits due to the constantly evolving nature of technology, (4) the inclusion of the target audience during the entire development process of the digital technology, (5) ensuring research ethics boards properly oversee research carried out on digital health, and (6) obtaining informed consent from the beneficiary of the product. The following recommendations are made in response to the previous concerns: ensuring developers design safe and trustworthy systems that align with the values and expectations of the beneficiaries, encouraging researchers to consider ethical standards more broadly, informing clinicians on what technologies are safe and effective, removing misleading and false messages in technology advertisements through government regulation, educating individuals about the use and risks of these technologies, and finally considering ethics for the development and monitoring of digital technologies (Wykes, Lipshitz, & Schueller, 2019).

Finally, and perhaps most importantly, ethical risks in the distribution of mental health technology in LMICs may be more pronounced. For instance, poorly regulated marketplaces could be a potential avenue for predatory companies to distribute ineffective and potentially harmful digital products to patients (Clifford, 2017). Furthermore, there remains a substantial gender divide in LMICs with regards to access to digital technology. Particularly, in households, this includes limited access to technology among women, with mobile devices largely in the hands of males (GMSA, 2020). Third, there remains an ongoing threat to the spread of misinformation and fake news (UNESCO). In LMICs, this could have extremely detrimental consequences where education and literacy may be sparse. Furthermore, victimization of individuals may occur if others discover they have mental illness, a particularly stigmatized diagnosis. Further, the most impoverished settings or remote areas still have very low access to technology, and may not realize the benefits from emerging digital mental health interventions. This may potentially exacerbate disparities and widen the gap in accessibility for mental health support.

Mental health during pandemics and the need for digital interventions

During the height of the COVID-19 pandemic, there was a rapid surge of reports high-lighting mental health impacts. While the virus itself ignited fear and hopelessness, there was a whole other realm of distress stemming from increasing inequalities, economic recessions, and the emotional burden of social distancing (Holmes et al., 2020; Moreno et al., 2020). There was evidence of disruption of mental health care in many parts of the world, making it difficult to address new-onset symptoms of depression and anxiety or worsening preexisting mental health problems (Patel, 2020). We can expect similar pandemics in the future.

The universal exacerbation of mental health during such pandemics has demonstrated the necessity for digital mental health technologies in the modern age (Rodriguez-Villa, Naslund, Keshavan, Patel, & Torous, 2020). One review emphasizes the importance of deploying two key mental health strategies in LMICs: the use of task-shifting within community health worker models and the use of digital technologies, particularly mobile phones. Task-shifting can be utilized to build a provider base, provide service delivery at the community level, within homes, schools, workplaces, and care centers. Furthermore, these settings can serve essential roles for mental health promotion and awareness programs, and for service distribution via community engagement with trained lay mental health workers. Additionally, digital technology can be used to strengthen health systems, as demonstrated in previous sections of this chapter. Health-care settings across the world have come to increasingly rely on digital technologies during this age of the pandemic to minimize the contraction of the virus. In particular, mobile phones can assist with the delivery of care by facilitating access to training, supervision, support among care providers, and making health records readily available remotely (Kola, 2020).

Ultimately, disruptive global events such as pandemics force the world to adapt to a new normal and shift our perspectives on the traditional methods of delivery of care. Such pandemics include not only infectious disease but growing numbers of non-communicable diseases in LMIC settings. In a world where technology is rapidly advancing, it should be a priority to maximize its potential and allow it to penetrate and enhance the field of mental health care. Low-resource settings, in particular, can leverage these technologies to minimize health disparities and increase access to services. To begin the implementation of these digital technologies in mental health practice, researchers have emphasized various key steps, including training medical professionals to use these technologies, ensuring patients have digital literacy to secure equity and justice and taking into account economic disparities and the accessibility of these digital resources (Torous, Myrick, Rauseo-Ricupero, & Firth, 2020).

Discussion and conclusion

The global rise in digital technology has disseminated throughout various fields, particularly mental health. As reflected in this chapter, we see the application of a multitude of digital technologies to address existing issues in both availability and access to mental health care, particularly in low-resource settings. For instance, these technologies have been used to support frontline health-care workers, train nonspecialist workers, promote youth health, challenge stigma, provide support in humanitarian settings, and treat and support individuals living with severe mental disorders. Despite this positive influence, ethical considerations must be taken into account and fully addressed (see also chapter by Hartford). It is important to note that this chapter provides an overview of promising current and future directions for digital mental health across diverse LMICs. The examples described here represent only a small fraction of global efforts using digital technology for mental health, and therefore do not offer a comprehensive synthesis of the entire field. As this is a rapidly evolving field, we anticipate that there will be many new advances and exciting applications of digital mental health technologies in LMICs in the months and years to come.

A potential future direction for the global application of mental health technology is to increase collaboration across diverse contexts, cultures, and countries. This collaboration should take place between researchers, clinicians, persons with lived experience of mental health needs, engineers, technologists and designers, policymakers, and other stakeholders who design or deliver interventions across both high- and low-income countries. In this collaboration, rigorous randomized controlled trials with larger sample sizes will be essential to ensure generalizability of results. Finally, researchers should take into account barriers to accessing care such as stigma, discrimination, and financial difficulties (Carter et al., 2021).

References

Anttila, M., Sittichai, R., Katajisto, J., & Välimäki, M. (2019). Impact of a web program to support the mental wellbeing of high school students: A quasi experimental feasibility study. *International Journal of Environmental Research and Public Health, 16*(14), 2473. https://doi.org/10.3390/ijerph16142473.

Arjadi, R., Nauta, M. H., Scholte, W. F., Hollon, S. D., Chowdhary, N., Suryani, A. O., … Bockting, C.L.H. (2018 Sep). Internet-based behavioural activation with lay counsellor support versus online minimal psychoeducation without support for treatment of depression: a randomised controlled trial in Indonesia. *Lancet Psychiatry, 5*(9), 707–716. https://doi.org/10.1016/S2215-0366(18)30223-2. Epub 2018 Jul 11. PMID: 30006262.

Bauer, M., Glenn, T., Monteith, S., Bauer, R., Whybrow, P. C., & Geddes, J. (2017). Ethical perspectives on recommending digital technology for patients with mental illness. *International Journal of Bipolar Disorders, 5*(1). https://doi.org/10.1186/s40345-017-0073-9.

Black Dog Institute. (2020, May 4). *Tell your story*. Black Dog Institute. https://www.blackdoginstitute.org.au/research-projects/tell-your-story/.

Brookings.edu. (2016, July 6). Advancing Technological Diffusion in Developing Countries. Brookings.edu. https://www.brookings.edu/wp-content/uploads/2016/07/Aspen14_Brookings_Blum_Roundtable_Technology-5.pdf.

Bruckner, T. A., Scheffler, R. M., Shen, G., Yoon, J., Chisholm, D., Morris, J., … Saxena, S. (2011 Mar 1). The mental health workforce gap in low- and middle-income countries: a needs-based approach. *Bull World Health Organ, 89*(3), 184–194. https://doi.org/10.2471/BLT.10.082784. Epub 2010 Nov 22. PMID: 21379414; PMCID: PMC3044251.

Carter, H., Araya, R., Anjur, K., Deng, D., & Naslund, J. A. (2021). The emergence of digital mental health in low-income and middle-income countries: A review of recent advances and implications for the treatment and prevention of mental disorders. *Journal of Psychiatric Research*, *122*, 223–246.

Chibanda, D., Weiss, H. A., Verhey, R., Simms, V., Munjoma, R., Rusakaniko, S., … Araya, R. (2016 Dec 27). Effect of a Primary Care-Based Psychological Intervention on Symptoms of Common Mental Disorders in Zimbabwe: A Randomized Clinical Trial. *JAMA*, *316*(24), 2618–2626. https://doi.org/10.1001/jama.2016.19102. PMID: 28027368.

Clifford, G. D. (2017). E-health in low to middle income countries. *Journal of Medical Engineering & Technology*, *40*(7–8), 336–341. https://doi.org/10.1080/03091902.2016.1256081.

Darvish, A., Khodadadi-Hassankiadeh, N., Abdoosti, S., & Kashani, M. G. (2019). Effect of text messaging-based psychiatric nursing program on quality of life in veterans with post-traumatic stress disorder: A randomized controlled trial. *International Journal of Community Based Nursing & Midwifery*, *7*(1), 52–62.

Firth, J., Torous, J., Nicholas, J., Carney, R., Pratap, A., Rosenbaum, S., & Sarris, J. (2017a). The efficacy of smartphone-based mental health interventions for depressive symptoms: A meta-analysis of randomized controlled trials. *World Psychiatry*, *16*(3), 287–298. https://doi.org/10.1002/wps.20472.

Firth, J., Torous, J., Nicholas, J., Carney, R., Rosenbaum, S., & Sarris, J. (2017b). Can smartphone mental health interventions reduce symptoms of anxiety? A meta-analysis of randomized controlled trials. *Journal of Affective Disorders*, *218*, 15–22. https://doi.org/10.1016/j.jad.2017.04.046.

Fu, Z., Burger, H., Arjadi, R., & Bockting, C. L. (2020). Effectiveness of digital psychological interventions for mental health problems in low-income and middle-income countries: A systematic review and meta-analysis. *The Lancet Psychiatry*, *7*, 851–864. https://doi.org/10.1016/S2215-0366(20)30256-X.

GMSA. (2020). *Gender gap—Mobile for development*. GMSA. https://www.gsma.com/r/gender-gap/.

Gonsalves, P. P., Hodgson, E. S., Kumar, A., Aurora, T., Chandak, Y., Sharma, R., … Patel, V. (2019). Design and Development of the *"POD Adventures"* Smartphone Game: A Blended Problem-Solving Intervention for Adolescent Mental Health in India. *Frontiers in public health*, *7*, 238. https://doi.org/10.3389/fpubh.2019.00238.

Gonsalves, P. P., Hodgson, E. S., Michelson, D., Pal, S., Naslund, J., Sharma, R., & Patel, V. (2019). What are young Indians saying about mental health? A content analysis of blogs on the it's ok to talk website. *BMJ Open*, *9*(6), e028244. https://doi.org/10.1136/bmjopen-2018-028244.

Hall, J., & Carswell, K. (2019). *STARS: Developing a new WHO psychological digital intervention for adolescents*. Retrieved from https://www.mhinnovation.net/blog/2019/may/24/stars-developing-new-who-psychological-digital-intervention-adolescents.

Hasan, M. T., & Thornicroft, G. (2018). Mass media campaigns to reduce mental health stigma in Bangladesh. *The Lancet Psychiatry*, *5*(8), 616. https://doi.org/10.1016/s2215-0366(18)30219-0.

Hollis, C., et al. (2017). Annual research review: Digital health interventions for children and young people with mental health problems – A systematic and meta-review. *Journal of Child Psychology and Psychiatry*, *58*(4), 474–503.

Holmes, E. A., O'Connor, R. C., Perry, V. H., Tracey, I., Wessely, S., Arseneault, L., … Bullmore, E. (2020 Jun). Multidisciplinary research priorities for the COVID-19 pandemic: a call for action for mental health science. *Lancet Psychiatry*, *7*(6), 547–560. https://doi.org/10.1016/S2215-0366(20)30168-1. Epub 2020 Apr 15. PMID: 32304649; PMCID: PMC7159850.

Jiménez-Molina, Á., Franco, P., Martínez, V., Martínez, P., Rojas, G., & Araya, R. (2019). Internet-based interventions for the prevention and treatment of mental disorders in Latin America: A scoping review. *Frontiers in Psychiatry*, *10*, 664. https://doi.org/10.3389/fpsyt.2019.00664.

Joag, K., Shields-Zeeman, L., Kapadia-Kundu, N., Kawade, R., Balaji, M., & Pathare, S. (2020). Feasibility and acceptability of a novel community-based mental health intervention delivered by community volunteers in Maharashtra, India: The Atmiyata programme. *BMC Psychiatry*, *20*(1), 48. https://doi.org/10.1186/s12888-020-2466-z.

Kaonga, N. N., & Morgan, J. (2019). Common themes and emerging trends for the use of technology to support mental health and psychosocial well-being in limited resource settings: A review of the literature. *Psychiatry Research*, *281*, 112594. https://doi.org/10.1016/j.psychres.2019.112594.

Khan, A., Shrivastava, R., Tugnawat, D., et al. (2020). Design and Development of a Digital Program for Training Non-specialist Health Workers to Deliver an Evidence-Based Psychological Treatment for Depression in Primary Care in India. *J. technol. behav. sci.*, *5*, 402–415. https://doi.org/10.1007/s41347-020-00154-7.

Knaevelsrud, C., Brand, J., Lange, A., Ruwaard, J., & Wagner, B. (2015). Web-based psychotherapy for posttraumatic stress disorder in war-traumatized Arab patients: Randomized controlled trial. *Journal of Medical Internet Research*, *17*(3), e71. https://doi.org/10.2196/jmir.3582.

Kola, L. (2020). Global mental health and COVID-19. *The Lancet*, *7*(8), 655–657. https://doi.org/10.1016/S2215-0366(20)30235-2.

Linardon, J., Cuijpers, P., Carlbring, P., Messer, M., & Fuller-Tyszkiewicz, M. (2019). The efficacy of app-supported smartphone interventions for mental health problems: A meta-analysis of randomized controlled trials. *World Psychiatry*, *18*(3), 325–336. https://doi.org/10.1002/wps.20673.

Martínez, V., Rojas, G., Martínez, P., Zitko, P., Irarrázaval, M., Luttges, C., & Araya, R. (2018). Remote collaborative depression care program for adolescents in Araucanía region, Chile: Randomized controlled trial. *Journal of Medical Internet Research*, *20*(1), e38. https://doi.org/10.2196/jmir.8021.

Mei, C., et al. (2020). Global research priorities for youth mental health. *Early Intervention in Psychiatry*, *14*(1), 3–13.

Menezes, P., Quayle, J., Garcia Claro, H., da Silva, S., Brandt, L. R., Diez-Canseco, F., … Araya, R. (2019 Apr 26). Use of a Mobile Phone App to Treat Depression Comorbid With Hypertension or Diabetes: A Pilot Study in Brazil and Peru. *JMIR Ment Health*, *6*(4), e11698. https://doi.org/10.2196/11698. PMID: 31025949; PMCID: PMC6658291.

Merchant, R., Torous, J., Rodriguez-Villa, E., & Naslund, J. A. (2020). Digital technology for management of severe mental disorders in low-income and middle-income countries. *Current Opinion in Psychiatry*, *33*(5), 501–507. https://doi.org/10.1097/yco.0000000000000626.

Michelson, D., et al. (2020a). Development of a transdiagnostic, low-intensity, psychological intervention for common adolescent mental health problems in Indian secondary schools. *Behaviour Research and Therapy*, *130*, 103439.

Michelson, D., et al. (2020b). Effectiveness of a brief lay counsellor-delivered, problem-solving intervention for adolescent mental health problems in urban, low-income schools in India: A randomised controlled trial. *The Lancet Child & Adolescent Health*, *4*(8), 571–582.

Moreno, C., Wykes, T., Galderisi, S., Nordentoft, M., Crossley, N., Jones, N., … Arango, C. (2020 Sep). How mental health care should change as a consequence of the COVID-19 pandemic. *Lancet Psychiatry*, *7*(9), 813–824. https://doi.org/10.1016/S2215-0366(20)30307-2. Epub 2020 Jul 16. PMID: 32682460; PMCID: PMC7365642.

Muke, S. S., Shrivastava, R. D., Mitchell, L., Khan, A., Murhar, V., Tugnawat, D., … Naslund, J.A. (2019). Acceptability and feasibility of digital technology for training community health workers to deliver brief psychological treatment for depression in rural India. *Asian Journal of Psychiatry*, *45*, 99–106. https://doi.org/10.1016/j.ajp.2019.09.006.

Muke, S. S., Tugnawat, D., Joshi, U., Anand, A., Khan, A., Shrivastava, R., … Naslund, J.A. (2020 Sep 1). Digital Training for Non-Specialist Health Workers to Deliver a Brief Psychological Treatment for Depression in Primary Care in India: Findings from a Randomized Pilot Study. *Int J Environ Res Public Health*, *17*(17), 6368. https://doi.org/10.3390/ijerph17176368. PMID: 32883018; PMCID: PMC7503742.

Naslund, J. A., & Aschbrenner, K. A. (2019). Digital technology for health promotion: Opportunities to address excess mortality in persons living with severe mental disorders. *Evidence-Based Mental Health*, *22*(1), 17–22.

Naslund, J. A., Aschbrenner, K. A., Marsch, L. A., & Bartels, S. J. (2016). The future of mental health care: Peer-to-peer support and social media. *Epidemiology and Psychiatric Sciences*, *25*(2), 113–122.

Naslund, J. A., Aschbrenner, K. A., Araya, R., Marsch, L. A., Unutzer, J., Patel, V., & Bartels, S. J. (2017). Digital technology for treating and preventing mental disorders in low-income and middle-income countries: A narrative review of the literature. *Lancet Psychiatry*, *4*(6), 486–500. https://doi.org/10.1016/S2215-0366(17)30096-2.

Naslund, J. A., Bartels, S. M., & Marsch, L. A. (2019). Digital technology, including telemedicine, in the management of mental illness. In *Revolutionizing tropical medicine: Point-of-care tests, new imaging technologies and digital health* (pp. 505–530).

Naslund, J. A., Shidhaye, R., & Patel, V. (2019). Digital technology for building capacity of non-specialist health workers for task sharing and scaling up mental health care globally. *Harvard Review of Psychiatry*, *27*(3), 181–192. https://doi.org/10.1097/HRP.0000000000000217.

Naslund, J. A., Gonsalves, P. P., Gruebner, O., Pendse, S. R., Smith, S. L., Sharma, A., & Raviola, G. (2019). Digital innovations for global mental health: Opportunities for data science, task sharing, and early intervention. *Current Treatment Options in Psychiatry*, *6*(4), 337–351.

Parikh, R., et al. (2019). Priorities and preferences for school-based mental health services in India: A multi-stakeholder study with adolescents, parents, school staff, and mental health providers. *Global Mental Health*, *6*, E18.

Patel, V. (2020). *Global mental health in the time of COVID-19*. 16 June. Retrieved from https://www.health.harvard.edu/blog/global-mental-health-in-the-time-of-covid-19-2020061620194.

Radcliffe, D. (2018). *Mobile in Sub-Saharan Africa: Can world's fastest-growing mobile region keep it up?*. Retrieved from https://www.zdnet.com/article/mobile-in-sub-saharan-africa-can-worlds-fastest-growing-mobile-region-keep-it-up/.

Rathod, S., Pinninti, N., Irfan, M., Gorczynski, P., Rathod, P., Gega, L., & Naeem, F. (2017). Mental health service provision in low- and middle-income countries. *Health Services Insights*, *10*. https://doi.org/10.1177/1178632917694350, 117863291769435.

Raviola, G., Naslund, J. A., Smith, S. L., & Patel, V. (2019). Innovative models in mental health delivery systems: Task sharing care with non-specialist providers to close the mental health treatment gap. *Current Psychiatry Reports*, *21*(6), 44. https://doi.org/10.1007/s11920-019-1028-x.

Reiner, R. C., Olsen, H. E., Ikeda, C. T., Echko, M. M., Ballestreros, K. E., Manguerra, H., … Kassebaum, N. J. (2019). Diseases, injuries, and risk factors in child and adolescent health, 1990 to 2017. *JAMA Pediatrics*, *173*(6). https://doi.org/10.1001/jamapediatrics.2019.0337.

Rodriguez-Villa, E., Naslund, J., Keshavan, M., Patel, V., & Torous, J. (2020). Making mental health more accessible in light of COVID-19: Scalable digital health with digital navigators in low and middle-income countries. *Asian Journal of Psychiatry*, *54*, 102433.

Rodriguez-Villa, E., Mehta, U. M., Naslund, J., Tugnawat, D., Gupta, S., Thirtalli, J., ... Keshavan, M. (2021). Smartphone Health Assessment for Relapse Prevention (SHARP): a digital solution toward global mental health. *BJPsych Open*, 7(1).

Shields-Zeeman, L., Pathare, S., Walters, B. H., Kapadia-Kundu, N., & Joag, K. (2017). Promoting wellbeing and improving access to mental health care through community champions in rural India: The Atmiyata intervention approach. *International Journal of Mental Health Systems*, 11(1). https://doi.org/10.1186/s13033-016-0113-3.

Sibeko, G., Temmingh, H., Mall, S., Williams-Ashman, P., Thornicroft, G., Susser, E. S., ... Milligan, P.D. (2017 Nov 9). Improving adherence in mental health service users with severe mental illness in South Africa: a pilot randomized controlled trial of a treatment partner and text message intervention vs. treatment as usual. *BMC Res Notes*, 10(1), 584. https://doi.org/10.1186/s13104-017-2915-z. PMID: 29121999; PMCID: PMC5679373.

Sweetland, A. C., Oquendo, M. A., Sidat, M., Santos, P. F., Vermund, S. H., Duarte, C. S., ... Wainberg, M.L. (2014). Closing the mental health gap in low-income settings by building research capacity: perspectives from Mozambique. *Annals of global health*, 80(2), 126–133. https://doi.org/10.1016/j.aogh.2014.04.014.

Thomas, I. F., Lawani, A. O., & James, B. O. (2017). Effect of short message service reminders on clinic attendance among outpatients with psychosis at a psychiatric hospital in Nigeria. *Psychiatric Services*, 68(1), 75–80. https://doi.org/10.1176/appi.ps.201500514.

Tomita, A., Kandolo, K. M., Susser, E., & Burns, J. K. (2016). Use of short messaging services to assess depressive symptoms among refugees in South Africa: Implications for social services providing mental health care in resource-poor settings. *Journal of Telemedicine and Telecare*, 22(6), 369–377. https://doi.org/10.1177/1357633x15605406.

Torous, J., Wisniewski, H., Bird, B., et al. (2019). Creating a Digital Health Smartphone App and Digital Phenotyping Platform for Mental Health and Diverse Healthcare Needs: an Interdisciplinary and Collaborative Approach. *J. technol. behav. sci.*, 4, 73–85. https://doi.org/10.1007/s41347-019-00095-w.

Torous, J., Myrick, K. J., Rauseo-Ricupero, N., & Firth, J. (2020). Digital mental health and COVID-19: Using technology today to accelerate the curve on access and quality tomorrow. *JMIR Mental Health*, 7(3), e18848. https://doi.org/10.2196/18848.

Torrey, W. C., Cepeda, M., Castro, S., Bartels, S. M., Cubillos, L., Obando, F. S., ... Marsch, L.A. (2020 Jul 1). Implementing Technology-Supported Care for Depression and Alcohol Use Disorder in Primary Care in Colombia: Preliminary Findings. *Psychiatr Serv.*, 71(7), 678–683. https://doi.org/10.1176/appi.ps.201900457. Epub 2020 Mar 10. PMID: 32151216; PMCID: PMC7332379.

UNFPA. (2014). *The power of 1.8 billion adolescents, youth and the transformation of the future.*

Vasan, A., Mabey, D. C., Chaudhri, S., Epstein, H. B., & Lawn, S. D. (2017). Support and performance improvement for primary health care workers in low- and middle-income countries: A scoping review of intervention design and methods. *Health Policy and Planning*, 32(3), 437–452. https://doi.org/10.1093/heapol/czw144.

Wang, Z., Wang, J., & Maercker, A. (2016). Program use and outcome change in a web-based trauma intervention: Individual and social factors. *Journal of Medical Internet Research*, 18(9), e243. https://doi.org/10.2196/jmir.5839.

We Are Social, USA. https://wearesocial.com/.

World Bank Group. (2020). *International development, poverty, & sustainability*. Retrieved from https://www.worldbank.org/.

Wykes, T., Lipshitz, J., & Schueller, S. M. (2019). Towards the design of ethical standards related to digital mental health and all its applications. *Current Treatment Options in Psychiatry*, 6(3), 232–242. https://doi.org/10.1007/s40501-019-00180-0.

Xu, D. R., Xiao, S., He, H., Caine, E. D., Gloyd, S., Simoni, J., … Gong, W. (2019). Lay health supporters aided by mobile text messaging to improve adherence, symptoms, and functioning among people with schizophrenia in a resource-poor community in rural China (LEAN): A randomized controlled trial. *PLoS medicine*, *16*(4), e1002785. https://doi.org/10.1371/journal.pmed.1002785.

Yardley, L., Morrison, L., Bradbury, K., & Muller, I. (2015). The person-based approach to intervention development: Application to digital health-related behavior change interventions. *Journal of Medical Internet Research*, *17*, e30. https://doi.org/10.2196/jmir.4055.

Young, J. (2015). *Untreated mental illness*. Retrieved from https://www.psychologytoday.com/us/blog/when-your-adult-child-breaks-your-heart/201512/untreated-mental-illness.

Addiction, autonomy, and the Internet: Some ethical considerations

Anna Hartford[a] and Dan J. Stein[b]
[a]Brain-Behaviour Unit, Neuroscience Institute, University of Cape Town, Cape Town, South Africa, [b]SA MRC Unit on Risk & Resilience in Mental Disorders, Department of Psychiatry & Neuroscience Institute, University of Cape Town, Cape Town, South Africa

Introduction

Concerns about "Internet addiction" have existed since the first years of its public use. In 1996 *The New York Times* ran an article headlined "The Symptoms of Internet Addiction," in which they spoke of a self-described Internet addict who spent "more than 6 h a day online and more than an hour reading his email" (Belluck, 1996). Needless to say, nowadays this sounds unremarkable (if not restrained). The average American teenager now spends over 7h a day on digital devices, not including school or homework (Common Sense Media, 2019). The anecdote serves to illustrate some of the difficulties in drawing boundaries between "normal" and "excessive" (or even pathological) behavior. These difficulties are exacerbated when it comes to new behaviors, such as those involved in our interactions with newly developed technologies, where the relevant understandings and frames of reference are in perpetual flux and development.

There are many reasons for caution. Social and moral panics regularly accompany the emergence of new technologies, which are often initially perceived as corrupting; it is, therefore, necessary to guard against this tendency, which has so often proved short-sighted and unduly conservative with hindsight (Hier, 2011). Nevertheless, as Internet use has proliferated across the globe and into all aspects of our lives, problematic behaviors with regard to Internet use have become an increasing source of concern both medically and socially, and certain governments have declared problematic Internet use a major public health issue. Estimates regarding prevalence rates vary widely (as do the criteria for inclusion) but it is now indisputable that there is a significant global population who engage with the Internet in a manner that fundamentally and chronically disrupts their other interests, life goals, and close relationships, and who experience enormous distress with regard to their level of use and their struggle to control it.

Of course, the vast majority of Internet users will not experience such pronounced difficulties. Nevertheless, many of us will be unsurprised by the lure to excessive use and the addictive qualities of the Internet. The compulsive checking of certain Internet platforms and the incessant engagement with smartphones have become facts of life in many

Mental Health in a Digital World. https://doi.org/10.1016/B978-0-12-822201-0.00003-4

parts of the world. One report indicates that the average smartphone user checks their device over 70 times a day, and swipes and interacts with it thousands of times (dscout, 2016). While efforts to limit or reduce time spent on devices, even among "ordinary" users, can require significant self-control, and often results in failure (Deloitte, 2018).

Despite growing understanding of the addictive qualities of the Internet, and rising concerns about the effects of excessive Internet use on personal well-being and mental health, the corresponding ethical debate is still in its infancy, and many of the relevant philosophical and conceptual frameworks are still underdeveloped. Our goal in this chapter is to explore some of this evolving terrain, even if we are only able to touch the surface of these complex and multifaceted issues, which now permeate so many aspects of our lives and societies. We hope to thereby contribute to the growing (and very necessary) conversation reflecting on how we ought to develop and adapt these now ubiquitous technologies in order to better promote the well-being of those who use them.

There are immediate complexities to this ethical discussion: in the first place, as we have already indicated, there are unique ethical considerations that pertain to the formalization of a clinical disorder related to excessive Internet use. In "Distinguishing clinical and ethical debates" section, we will begin by briefly looking at some of these considerations. However, it is important to distinguish social and ethical debates about the addictive qualities of the Internet from clinical debates about the appropriateness of particular diagnostic categories (Hanin, 2020; Williams, 2018). Our ethical concerns (and indeed our mental health concerns) about whether certain technologies undermine well-being can and should be far broader than the debate concerning the formalization of a psychiatric disorder.

With this in mind, we proceed (in "The ethics of persuasive design" section) by exploring some of these broader ethical debates with regard to persuasive (and even coercive) digital technologies, particularly those which aim to maximize use or even encourage compulsion. In "The nature of the harm" section we consider the conceptual difficulty in articulating the harms involved in excessive Internet use, especially where such use has not led to functional impairment: are we merely being "distracted" by these technologies or, as some have argued, is our autonomy being fundamentally undermined by them? We will emphasize the spectrum between these extremes: we need not endorse "techno-determinism" in order to raise concerns about the effects of these technologies on our agency. Following these broader conversations, we will end, in "Ethical implications" section, by briefly considering some of the more practical ethical implications generated by the addictive qualities of the Internet, including the prospect of regulation on certain design features, concerns about growing inequalities in the burden of online services (where users reliant on free services are subjected to far more toxic and manipulative Internet environment than users who can pay), and whether there should be a "right to disconnect."

Distinguishing clinical and ethical debates

As it stands, no diagnosis has been formalized with regard to excessive Internet use, and debate continues concerning the appropriateness of such a diagnosis, as well as its defining features. Some have contended that the Internet is merely an interface and that the focus should therefore be directed toward particular problematic behaviors, such as sexual preoccupations and social networking. There is also no end to what can be pursued online, including essential and otherwise worthwhile undertakings, and therefore no straightforward relationship between time spent on the Internet and excessive or pathological use. Within this debate, the terms "Internet Addiction," "Internet Addiction Disorder," "Internet Use Disorder," "Pathological Internet Use Disorder," "Maladaptive Internet Use," and "Problematic Use of the Internet" (among many others) are in use (see chapter by Wegmann).

A range of unique ethical considerations pertain to the formalization of a psychiatric disorder, as well as to when it is appropriate to categorize someone as having a psychiatric disorder. On the one hand, insertion of a diagnosis into the nosology can encourage appropriate diagnosis and treatment, as well as research, and so formalization of a disorder may have real benefits to individuals and society. At the level of individual patients, there may also be consolation and validation in having their condition scientifically and medically recognized.

On the other hand, such a diagnosis may hold pejorative connotations that are potentially stigmatizing to individuals and can have long-term negative effects on both how someone perceives themselves, and how they are perceived within their communities. Where disorders are related to particular activities or behaviors—as in the case of excessive Internet use—there is a risk of stigmatizing not only individuals but also the relevant behaviors themselves (Aarseth et al., 2017; van Rooij et al., 2018). Furthermore, diagnosing too widely risks trivializes psychiatric disorders and undermines social recognition of the severity of psychiatric conditions. These points are related to fundamental concerns within psychiatry, including the legitimacy of psychiatric categories, and concerns about diagnostic overreach.

There are therefore good reasons for having appropriate evidentiary, pragmatic, and clinical grounds for the formalization of a new disorder, which warrant the extensive and ongoing debate this issue has elicited. But the mental health concerns, as well as the social and ethical concerns, associated with the addictive qualities of the Internet do not begin and end at the point of formal classification alone. This is an important point to emphasize because (as we will indicate throughout the chapter) these two conversations often get intertwined in both public and professional debates. In clinical debates it is sometimes assumed that diagnostic formalization is necessary in order to raise particular ethical concerns (i.e., regarding the need for government policy or regulation); while in public debates, it is sometimes assumed that ethical concerns are only warranted insofar as there is diagnostic formalization.

As we reflect on the effects of these increasingly ubiquitous technologies both for ourselves and for our societies and imagine the new ways that they could better serve us, it is important to uncouple these concerns and aspirations from the confines of clinical categories. As the growing ethical literature on digital well-being explores, the ethical justifications for our technologies should be aligned to much higher goals, including "the impact of digital technologies on what it means to live a life that is *good for* a human being" within our present societies (cf. Burr, Taddeo, & Floridi, 2020 for a thematic review). This is echoed in public health debates which emphasize the spectrum between wellness and illness, and the need for public (mental) health which is concerned with the needs of the general population, in addition to those with clinically significant disorders (Patel, Saxena, Frankish, & Boyce, 2016).

One area which has generated considerable interest, in terms of the tension between certain digital technologies and human well-being, has concerned the proliferation of persuasive design features which endeavor to maximize use. While these features might sometimes be implicated in clinical cases of Internet addiction, the ethical concerns they raise apply far more broadly.

The ethics of persuasive design

Broadly speaking, persuasive design is a process of creating technologies in order to generate behavioral change. One can distinguish between the intended and unintended effects of persuasive design (Verbeek, 2006), and also between persuasive design and outright manipulative, deceptive or coercive design (Bech, 2020; Fogg, 2003), though in many cases these distinctions will be vague.

The so-called "attention economy" that has come to dominate the provision of many online services has meant that success and profitability often rely on maximizing user engagement: the more often and the longer users engage with your product, the more data you are able to collect on them and the longer you have them as an audience for potential advertisers. In turn, the goal of many software developers has been to design products that generate habitual engagement and maximize use, even to the point of compulsion, drawing on techniques from applied psychology, neuroscience, and behavioral economics in their efforts.

Certain pervasive design features—such as "like" buttons (or the equivalent), push notifications, "streaks," auto-play, and infinite scroll—have been especially successful in this regard, and have proliferated across platforms. Some of these features generate intermittent variable reward (Eyal, 2014), which has long been linked to compulsive behavior, and is also associated with the addictive quality of slot machines (Schüll, 2014). At the level of our neural reward system, an unreliable reward generates a more significant dopamine response than a reliable reward. On prominent Internet platforms, sophisticated machine learning technologies now endeavor to randomize rewards for each user.

Take the example of a search engine: usually, someone would consult a search engine because they have something specific to look up; this constitutes the user's goal. But in many respects the search engine's goal is to keep them online long after they have achieved these ends (or even to make them forget these ends altogether): perhaps by luring them in with a dropdown list of "trending searches" which invariably involve high arousal topics, or by populating the homepage with clickbait news, or by displaying search results which are algorithmically calibrated to generate more engagement; all the while having one's use tracked, and being followed by targeted advertising.

Persuasive design is not necessarily unethical, and it can be used in beneficial ways: a wide range of health and wellness apps claim to do just that (though even these uses have been challenged, Cf. Verbeek, 2009; Sullivan & Reiner, 2019). The ethical concerns about persuasive design largely turn on its extent and effectiveness, as well as the uses that it is put to. There is therefore an essential interplay between this section and the next in which we consider the sorts of costs and harms associated with excessive Internet use, or with extensive attentional loss; we will draw out these connections further in the next section.

Persuasive design focused on maximizing use has come under particular scrutiny in recent years. Public interest about the effects of these designs on our behavior, and on our mental health and well-being, has grown significantly, informed by a public conversation featuring tech-insiders (notably the former Google design ethicist Tristin Harris), policy-makers, health specialists and educators, among others. Harris, in particular, has argued that widespread persuasive design features have crossed over from acceptable methods to those which undermine agency and generate compulsion. "They are shaping the thoughts and feelings and actions of people," he said in an interview with Anderson Cooper. "They are programming people" (quoted in Aswad, 2020).

The concept of addiction has played a significant part in this public debate, where these design features are sometimes presented as transforming us all into powerless addicts, or mindless zombies. This perspective of "techno-determinism" has been criticized for giving altogether too much credit to the powers of software design, and altogether too little credit to the human capacities for self-control and deliberation, and indeed to our own complicities within our use (Seymour, 2020). Despite the effects of persuasive design and targeted content, most of us routinely disengage our attention (we get bored or fed up, or we are drawn away by those things we value more and consider more important).

But, importantly, concerns about autonomy can be more nuanced, and exist on more of a continuum, than these strict binaries presume: our autonomy can be threatened, and even compromised, without being defeated. And the burden of having to exert self-control, or having to assert deliberative control, against powerful competing forces is not itself insignificant.

Some have argued that the increasing sophistication of persuasive digital technologies, and its personalized nature, makes them a far deeper and more considerable threat than more longstanding and familiar forms of persuasive design (Williams, 2018). Another distinguishing aspect is the scale of the effect: there are ever more countries in which the vast majority of the population own these devices and interact with these platforms and services (and where, in many cases, their use is almost mandatory; a point to which we will soon return).

As we have already noted, a central factor in appraising persuasive design features is to consider the uses they are put to. Where design encourages behavior that we would reflectively endorse, for instance, it seems altogether more justifiable than where it does not, even if it is extremely effective and takes place at a significant scale. To this end, some have suggested the concept of trust as the crucial feature by which to distinguish ethical and unethical uses of persuasive design, where unethical design betrays or erodes trust (Brennan, 2020). So what is the nature of persuasion when we are being encouraged to spend ever more time online? Are these ends that we might reflectively endorse (do we often share these goals of high engagement?), or are they not? Exploring these questions is intimately tied to how we understand the potential harms implicit in excessive time online.

The nature of the harm

Implicit in these calls for concern is the idea that there is some sort of harm involved in excessive time online, especially time which far exceeds the user's deliberative aims, goals, and intentions. But here we hit ill-articulated terrain: for what is the harm, if any, in directing your time and attention to one place rather than another? There are many ways to live a life, and being on the Internet is one of them; there is nothing about that, on its own, that makes it a less worthwhile or meaningful life than the alternative.

Unlike various substance addictions which have clear deleterious effects on physical health and brain function, there is no straightforward relationship between excessive Internet use and physical harm. The main physical effect associated with excessive Internet use is sleep disturbance and deprivation (Choi et al., 2009). And unlike behavioral addictions such as pathological gambling, there is also no straightforward relationship between excessive Internet use and financial harm; indeed, many of the Internet services associated with problematic use are free. (Naturally, this excludes online gambling and monetization schemes in video games, such as "loot boxes"; there may also be a financial opportunity costs even to "free" services, in the form of lost income).

When exploring these questions not only at the extreme end of the continuum of excessive use but in a broader range of cases, the nature of the harm is more evasive still. At the point of functional impairment, one can easily point to the damaging consequences of excessive use within an individual's life: from failed degrees to lost jobs to ruined relationships. But there are many other users who feel distressed or dismayed at how much time they spend online, or alienated from the sorts of things they pursue there, who nevertheless manage to function adequately. Is there any harm in these more prevalent cases? And if so, what is it?

A first consideration is that there might be emotional harms involved with excessive time online. Research has indicated a relationship between increased Internet use (particularly social media) and increased anxiety and depression, as well as decreased well-being, although disagreement remains about the significance of these findings (Kross et al., 2013; Lin et al., 2016; Sagioglou & Greitemeyer, 2014; see Orben & Przybylski, 2019 for a skeptical take). Internet addiction has also been associated with a range of psychiatric disorders, including depression (Carli et al., 2013). The research is currently inconclusive with regard to the causal relationships: the extent to which depression leads people to spend more time online, and the extent to which more time online leads people to experience depression (or the interplay of both). Some have argued that panics about disordered use are misguided and that our first efforts should be to address the underlying circumstances and conditions that might lead people to excessive online behavior in the first place (van Rooij et al., 2018).

Aside from potential emotional harms, we might endeavor to explore the ill-articulated terrain with regard to attention itself, and what it matters (if it matters) to spend one's attention one way rather than another. As we explored in the previous section, the present nature and omnipresence of the Internet has made it an extraordinary draw on human attention, which has been amplified by design and commodification.

The value of our attention—our ability to direct our attention in meaningful ways, and our capacity for sustained attention—is, as yet, underexplored and undertheorized territory (Hanin, 2020; Williams, 2018). But as the power of digital distractions reach such staggering scales, and as our ability to focus our attention on our own considered ends erodes even further, the need to understand and articulate what is at stake has become pressing. Yet the necessary ethical frameworks (and even vocabularies) for understanding the significance of these forces are underdeveloped.

A similar lack of articulation attends discussions on neuromarketing, which also draws on how we process reward and other aspects of our decision-making in order to affect behavior. As Adina Roskies (2016) writes, exploring the question of "cognitive liberty" with regard to neuromarketing: "The precise threats posed by understanding the neural mechanisms of decision-making have yet to be fully articulated. Is neuromarketing being used merely to design products that satisfy our desires more fully or is it being used to manipulate us? Depending on how you see it, it could be construed as "good or evil.""

The same framing can be applied to the debate at hand, and the question of using persuasive design to maximize engagement. Construed as a good, we might think that the draw on attention is indicative of interest and worth (or at least pleasure and satisfaction). Call this the hedonic defense. From this perspective, one might argue that targeted content and persuasive design enhance preference satisfaction, by helping you find just what you like. Insofar as this is so, it might encourage behavior which (though subject to persuasion) we would nevertheless reflectively endorse.

Construed as an evil, we might think that these forces pose a serious threat to agency and personal autonomy. Taking the latter position, Williams writes: "To date, the problems of 'distraction' have been minimized as minor annoyances. Yet the competition for attention and the 'persuasion' of users ultimately amounts to a project of the manipulation of the will. We currently lack a language for talking about, and thereby recognizing, the full depth of these problems. At individual levels, these problems threaten to frustrate one's authorship of one's own life" (2018). Amplifying this sentiment Daniel Dennett has said that "this is perhaps the greatest risk to human political freedom that we've ever seen," and that "an agent who controls your attention controls you" (Dennett, 2020).

Some philosophers, drawing on Susan Wolf, have emphasized the importance of the construction of worth and meaning to human well-being, and argued that persistent distraction undermines the pursuit of these goals (Sullivan & Reiner, 2019; Wolf, 1997). Others have drawn on Martha Nussbaum's capabilities approach—which asserts the moral importance of the freedom to achieve well-being, and understands well-being in terms of individual capabilities—to argue that the harms of excessive time online undermine the human capabilities central to human dignity (Bhargava & Velasquez, 2020).

These vying frameworks of good and evil are both prevalent within public debates endeavoring to understand the relationship between engagement and worth. Responding to criticism of persuasive design, Nir Eyal (the author of *Hooked: How to Build Habit-Forming Products*) said that "you can't sell something to people if they don't want that thing" (quoted in Schulson, 2015); Eyal and other proponents of persuasive design have been careful to say these techniques should be used for the good.

On the face of it, this point has normative significance: while coercing people to do what they *do not want* seems straightforwardly morally suspect (including potentially undermining their autonomy and agency), providing people with what they *do want* seems closer to a service. That is to say: where an individual's engagement is construed as indicative of what they value, then there seems to be little moral concern in generating more of that engagement. However, if there is a more complicated relationship between engagement and worth (where we can engage obsessively even with what we do not value) then the grounds for moral concern become far more substantive.

What we mean by "wanting" is an interesting question, both within philosophy and psychiatry. After all, we can find ourselves wanting what we do not want to want. Our lower-order wants can clash fundamentally with our higher-order wants; a recovering alcoholic might simultaneously really want a drink, while also never wanting to drink again (Frankfurt, 1988). Williams draws on Harry Frankfurt to argue that the persuasive lures to maximize time online further undermine our ability to "want what we want to want"; an ability central to living the lives we want to live (Frankfurt, 1988; Williams, 2018).

The question of "wanting" has also been important within addiction research. In some respects, we think of "wanting" something interchangeably with liking and valuing it. But in other respects, they are clearly distinct, and the relevant neurological distinctions have now been explored extensively (Berridge, 2009). Understanding addiction in terms of dopamine and reward cycles has often led to assumptions about its hedonic nature, where dopamine corresponds to "liking" some reward. But a variety of findings have contested this association: Berridge and Robinson's research points to the fact that dopamine does not produce "liking" so much as to generate "wanting" (Berridge & Kringelbach, 2015; Robinson & Berridge, 2008). You can want something you do not like; you can even want something while knowing you do not like it, and you can be driven by those wants while deriving no sincere satisfaction from the source of your desire.

While animal models of wanting and liking are clearly relevant to substance use, they may also be applicable to behavioral addictions (Holton & Berridge, 2013). People with addictive disorders might experience wanting without liking to particularly high degrees, with regard to certain substances or behaviors. But once again, these findings are not only relevant at the point of clinical addiction alone. If behavioral addictions are conceptualized as one extreme on a continuum, many people might be deeply adversely affected by the same psychological-neural processes, even if they have not passed the thresholds for clinical diagnosis. While these thresholds are rightly stringent (including for the reasons we discussed in "Distinguishing clinical and ethical debates" section), they do not limit the scope of our ethical concerns, nor our concerns regarding mental health and well-being.

These findings are relevant to ethical debates which endeavor to understand the relationship between engagement and subjective worth, including those concerning persuasive design. While it might often be the case that engagement is indicative of subjective worth, there is no necessary connection here, and high engagement can be compelled by forces that are utterly distinct from sincere preference-satisfaction or assessments of value. If this conception is accurate, then the hedonic defense for endeavoring to generate maximum engagement is undermined.

Ethical implications

With this broader discussion in place, we would now like to consider more practical ethical questions which arise from the addictive qualities of the Internet, and concerns about the negative effects that excessive use can have on mental health and well-being.

Regulation on design

Even if we can agree that something needs to change in our relationship with these technologies, it is not clear who ought to change it, or how. Is it up to individuals to better control their use? Is it up to technology companies to change the nature of their services so that they are less likely to generate excessive use? Or is it up to governments to intervene with laws, policies, and regulations? How do we justify any of these alternatives?

Some have argued for technology-based solutions, contending that "the same design principles that create addiction could be leveraged to mitigate it" (Purohit, Barclay, & Hozer, 2020). Such interventions could potentially use design to reinstate deliberative engagement in the same way that design has been used to forestall it. For example, the design might generate friction instead of lowering it, provide feedback and reminders on use, and shift default settings to those which reduce rather than amplify use (Purohit et al., 2020).

In some quarters this tech-solutionism, and the ethos of "ethical design," is gaining momentum. Recent iPhones now allow greater control over time spent on the device and specific apps. Elsewhere, new apps and plugins are proliferating to help users control their time online, or to undermine the default designs which facilitate extended, nondeliberative engagement [though sometimes these habit-breaking apps are rejected from app stores (Aswad, 2020)].

Others are more cynical about tech solutionism, especially when it is ultimately left up to the humanist or ethical impulses of technology giants (Mackinnon & Shade, 2020; Sullivan & Reiner, 2019). From this vantage, if these companies start grudgingly paying lip service to "ethical design" and "time well spent," it is only to preserve their reputations, positions, and profits in the face of growing public scrutiny.

Another prominent suggestion is that change ought to be forced through regulation (see chapter by King). Although the focus of government regulation on technology has mostly been on other areas (including data privacy, national security, electoral manipulation, and false information), the question of regulation has also arisen with regard to certain design features which exacerbate excessive use.

All debates about regulation must contend with concerns about paternalism, restricted liberty, and undue interference. In this context: does the imposition of regulation with regard to design and other features constitute an undue restriction of freedom and choice from either individual users of online services, or their corporate produces?

Antipaternalists contend that it is up to individual users to make their own choices about how to engage with digital platforms and devices, just as they ought to make their own choices with regard to a range of other behaviors and pastimes, including those which might have associated risks or ill effects.

The debate is complicated by the fact that persuasive design features are sometimes intended precisely to forestall or undermine deliberative choice. With this in mind, some have argued that when undertaken appropriately regulation can be choice enhancing rather than choice diminishing (Schulson, 2015). Others have drawn on Thaler and Sunstein's notion of "libertarian paternalism," which endeavors to balance the freedom to make the widest range of choices, while still facilitating better choices (and "better" not only objectively but also as judged by themselves) (Thaler & Sunstein, 2008).

Another factor in this debate is what has been called the "indispensability thesis" (Hanin, 2020). The all-purpose nature of digital devices (which include a range of essential and work-related functions) means that the use of such devices is increasingly becoming a requirement in our both personal and professional lives. Having ready access to the Internet has become central to many of life's activities, including school, work, communication, civic administration, hailing a taxi, banking, ordering food, job-hunting, following current affairs, or finding a home. In response to antipaternalists, some have suggested that this indispensability undermines full-fledged consent to the risks and deleterious effects of such engagement, given that there is increasingly no realistic alternative (Hanin, 2020).

The question of design regulation again evokes parallels with the machine gambling industry, where regulation has been implemented or recommended in various countries (Schüll, 2014). Clinical conceptions of addiction played into regulatory debates with regard to machine gambling. According to Natasha Schüll, representatives of the machine gambling industry seized on psychiatric diagnosis as a defense strategy. She writes: "By the mid-1990s, the gambling industry had already grasped (as the alcohol industry had some decades earlier) that a medical diagnosis linked to the excessive consumption of its product by some individuals could serve to deflect attention away from the product's potentially problematic role in promoting that consumption, and onto the biological and psychological vulnerabilities of a small minority of its customers" (Schüll, 2014).

These conversations regarding regulation have scarcely begun when it comes to prominent Internet platforms, apps, and services. There are immense practical and other limitations to regulate online services, which are rapidly changing and available on a global scale. A further concern is whether regulatory interventions will be equal to the task, especially insofar as the broader incentive structures remain the same. Given that these persuasive technologies are intractably intertwined with the economic structure of online services—which will remain incentivized to keep users engaged for as long as possible—it is hard to see how any small-scale regulations and design modifications will have a truly meaningful effect. However, if we endeavor to address the problem of these broader structures, we are not merely posing something as modest as "regulation," but rather a full restructuring of the nature of many online services.

New "digital divides": Growing socioeconomic inequalities

Access to the Internet has increasingly become a necessity for economic, civic, and social participation, as well as an indispensable educational tool. In turn, there has been long-standing and warranted concern about "digital divides" which generate or exacerbate social inequalities. Initially, research on these digital divides focused predominantly on the question of access or nonaccess to the Internet. But as access has widened, and as the field has developed, it has become clear that more complex and multidimensional analysis of digital inequalities are necessary.

Questions of inequality also pertain to the concerns we have raised within this chapter. The potential burdens of online access (including the psychological, attentional, and self-regulatory burdens we have been exploring) will be very differently felt by different Internet users, depending on their device, their digital literacy, and their ability to pay for premium apps and services.

The ability to afford a more expensive smartphone, for instance, provides a far higher degree of data privacy, and greater control over which apps and services can be removed from a device, or controlled within it, including those that someone might find distressingly habit-forming. A parent who can afford to buy their child an iPhone is therefore given a far greater range of control over their child's time on their device, and other use limits, than a parent who cannot (Mackinnon & Shade, 2020). Android phones (which cost a third of iPhones) have also been reported to collect 10 times as much personal data (Schmidt, 2018). This increased data collection generates a vicious cycle in which data can be deployed to better maximize use (through AI-driven personalized recommendations and randomized rewards), which in turn allows more data to be gathered (Hanin, 2020).

Socioeconomic inequalities in the burdens of attentional harms are liable to increase in coming years, as divisions emerge concerning who is aware of these harms, and as wealthier Internet users buy their way out of some of the more noxious aspects of the online attention economy (Castro & Pham, 2020). In considering ways to move away from the attention economy model, the most obvious suggestion is to pay for services. In recommending regulations on persuasive technologies, Williams suggests that "companies could be expected (or compelled, if necessary) to give users a choice about how to 'pay' for content online—that is, with their money or with their attention" (Williams, 2018). Aspects of this choice are already prevalent online, with the distinction between "free" and "premium" services. As Kevin Roose writes: "today's Internet is full of premium subscriptions, walled gardens and virtual VIP rooms, all of which promise a cleaner, more pleasant experience than their free counterparts" (Roose, 2019).

In societies that have largely overcome inequalities with regard to Internet access, socioeconomic vulnerability is sometimes correlated with more rather than less time on certain platforms, including social media and digital gaming. Research has also suggested that lower socioeconomic status is a risk factor for developing Internet addiction (Müller, Glaesmer, Brahler, Wolfling, & Beutel, 2014; Rumpf et al., 2014). In some quarters "tech-lite" environments are becoming the ultimate privilege: take the much-reported fact that many Silicon Valley insiders send their children to a deliberately tech-lite school (Richtel, 2011). Motivating for government-provided "tech-lite" environments, Hanin emphasizes that "poor and rich alike should have access to such settings, which may otherwise risk becoming a luxury for the few" (Hanin, 2020).

Those societies still addressing earlier digital divides should do so with cognizance of these emerging complexities, and new stratifications, with regard to the potential attentional costs and burdens of access. That is to say: the most empowering forms of connectivity we can provide are those which also empower us with strategies and effective methods to *disengage* and *disconnect* when we recognize—and are enabled to recognize (Castro & Pham, 2020)—that time online is impeding, rather than serving, our own considered ends.

A right to disconnect?

Ordinarily, someone struggling with addictive or otherwise excessive behaviors would be advised to stay away from environments and circumstances which serve as triggers: a gambling addict, for instance, should stay away from casinos. But it is near impossible to implement similar advice with regard to the Internet. As we introduced with regard to the "indispensability thesis," with the proliferation of the Internet through our societies and our educational and professional lives, it has become increasingly ordinary to expect others to have ready access to the Internet and to even consider such access a requirement.

The current nature of the Internet seems to exacerbate this difficulty: you cannot keep only the "essential" Internet on you (the parts you need to function); you must always have access to the whole thing, including those parts that might be sources of compulsion, angst, and regret. As Hanin (2020) puts it: "Whereas no sane adult must smoke, use drugs, consume sugary foods, or gamble as a precondition to leading a fulfilling life or excelling in a profession, many sane adults have no practical way of avoiding often prolonged entanglement with digital ecosystems in the workplace and their personal lives. This entanglement poses formidable psychological challenges for self-regulation."

Growing understanding of the potential burdens of constant Internet access leads us to recognize that expectations of constant connectivity warrant reconsideration. This is most pressing for people who exhibit pathological use (or who are at risk of developing it), but it is also relevant for anyone who finds constant access to the Internet an impediment to the attainment of their own goals, or to the parts of their lives from which they derive lasting meaning.

As we explored above, most often when rights are evoked with regard to the Internet it is with regard to the right to have access (and given how essential the Internet has become to social and economic participation, this argument has immense strength). But should there also be a right to *disconnect*? A right not to have the Internet in your home, or in your pocket? This question is particularly relevant with regard to employment requirements, but it could also be relevant in other contexts (for instance, a requirement that certain essential services and opportunities remain available offline). In the employment context, the right to disconnect has recently been asserted in French Labor Law, as a measure against growing expectations to be available online after hours (Rubin, 2017). Insofar as particular ethical concerns emerge, or are exacerbated by, the increasing indispensability of the Internet, there might be considerable value in resisting or at least limiting this indispensability.

Conclusion

This chapter has briefly surveyed some of the ethical terrains that correspond to our growing understanding with regard to the addictive qualities of the Internet. We touched on a few of the complexities implicit in this debate, as well as some of the potential ethical implications although there are many considerations we were not able to address here. Our hope has been to contribute to the growing conversation reflecting on how we can and should intervene in order to better align digital technologies with human well-being.

While there was a great deal of utopian promise (some of it realized) in the early years of the Internet, the last several years have ushered in an era of reckoning, as we grapple with some of the unintended consequences of these new interfaces and forms of engagement. This reckoning is a moment of great opportunity, in which we might be able to better preserve the many beneficial aspects of these technologies, while still finding ways to mitigate against their more harmful aspects. Finding the right ways to understand and intervene in these complicated interactions is one of the great public health challenges of our time.

Persuasive technologies, as we have seen, can exploit our psychological biases. Another bias we suffer from is the tendency to accept as inevitable certain features of the status quo: to feel that because things are a certain way, they could never be otherwise. And although so many of these technologies, and the forms they have taken within our societies, are incredibly new, we nevertheless often feel that they are too entrenched to alter. But the mere fact that something is a certain way does not generate a moral reason to preserve it; these reasons must appeal to worth in a much deeper sense and must contend against many possible alternatives. In this respect, it is crucial to encourage public conversation that allows us to recognize that we are able to, and capable of, intervening in these technologies in ways that allow them to better serve us as individuals and as societies, and in ways that acknowledge and respect both our human strengths and our human weaknesses.

References

Aarseth, E., Bean, A. M., Boonen, H., Colder Carras, M., Coulson, M., Das, D., … Van Rooij, A. J. (2017). Scholars' open debate paper on the World Health Organization ICD-11 gaming disorder proposal. *Journal of Behavioral Addictions, 6*(3), 267–270.

Aswad, E. M. (2020). Losing the freedom to be human. *Columbia Human Rights Law Review, 52.*

Bech, C. J. (2020). The need for focused research on coercion, deception and manipulation in persuasive use of social media. In *Paper for conference Persuasive Technology 2020.*

Belluck, P. (1996). The symptoms of internet addiction. *The New York Times.* 1 December. Retrieved from: https://www.nytimes.com/1996/12/01/weekinreview/the-symptoms-of-internet-addiction.html.

Berridge, K. C. (2009). Wanting and liking: Observations from the neuroscience and psychology laboratory. *Inquiry, 52*(4), 378–398.

Berridge, K. C., & Kringelbach, M. L. (2015). Pleasure Systems in the Brain. *Neuron, 86,* 646–664.

Bhargava, V. R., & Velasquez, M. (2020). Ethics of the attention economy: The problem of social media addiction. *Business Ethics Quarterly.*

Brennan, J. (2020). Trust as a test for unethical persuasive design. *Philosophy & Technology.* https://doi.org/10.1007/s13347-020-00431-6.

Burr, C., Taddeo, M., & Floridi, L. (2020). The ethics of digital well-being: A thematic review. *Science and Engineering Ethics, 26*(4), 2313–2343.

Carli, V., Durkee, T., Wasserman, D., Hadlaczky, G., Despalins, R., Kramarz, E., ... Kaess, M. (2013). The association between pathological internet use and comorbid psychopathology: A systematic review. *Psychopathology, 46*(1), 1–13.

Castro, C., & Pham, A. K. (2020). Is the attention economy noxious? *Philosophers' Imprint, 20*(17), 1–13.

Choi, K., Son, H., Park, M., Han, J., Kim, K., Lee, B., & Gwak, H. (2009). Internet overuse and excessive daytime sleepiness in adolescents. *Psychiatry and Clinical Neurosciences, 63*(4), 455–462.

Common Sense Media. (2019). *The common sense census: Media use by tweens and teens.* Retrieved from https://www.commonsensemedia.org/sites/default/files/uploads/research/2019-census-8-to-18-full-report-updated.pdf.

Deloitte. (2018). *2018 Global Mobile Consumer Survey: US Edition.* Retrieved from: https://www2.deloitte.com/content/dam/Deloitte/us/Documents/technology-media-telecommunications/us-tmt-global-mobile-consumer-survey-exec-summary-2018.pdf.

Dennett, D. C. (2020). Herding cats and free will inflation. In *Romanell lecture delivered at the one hundred seventeenth annual Central Division meeting of the American Philosophical Association, Chicago, February 28th, 2020.*

dscout. (2016). *Mobile Touches: dscout's inaugural study on humans and their tech. Research Report.* Retrieved from: https://blog.dscout.com/hubfs/downloads/dscout_mobile_touches_study_2016.pdf.

Eyal, N. (2014). *Hooked: How to build habit-forming products.* Portfolio.

Fogg, B. J. (2003). *Persuasive technology: Using computers to change what we think and do.* Morgan Kaufmann.

Frankfurt, H. G. (1988). *The importance of what we care about: Philosophical essays.* Cambridge University Press.

Hanin, M. L. (2020). *Theorizing digital distraction.* Philosophy & Technology.

Hier, S. (2011). *Moral panic and the politics of anxiety.* Routledge.

Holton, R., & Berridge, K. C. (2013). Addiction between compulsion and choice. In N. Levy (Ed.), *Addiction and self-control: Perspectives from philosophy, psychology and neuroscience* Oxford University Press.

Kross, E., Verduyn, P., Demiralp, E., Park, J., Lee, D. S., Lin, N., ... Ybarra, O. (2013). Facebook use predicts declines in subjective well-being in young adults. *PLoS One, 8*(8), 1–6.

Lin, L. Y., Sidani, J. E., Shensa, A., Radovic, A., Miller, E., Colditz, J. B., ... Primack, B. A. (2016). Association between social Media use and depression among U.S. young adults. *Depression & Anxiety, 33*(4), 323–331.

Mackinnon, K., & Shade, L. R. (2020). 'God only knows what It's doing to our Children's brains': A closer look at internet addiction discourse. *Jeunesse: Young People, Texts, Cultures, 12*(1), 16–38.

Müller, K. W., Glaesmer, H., Brähler, E., Wolfling, K., & Beutel, M. E. (2014). Prevalence of Internet addiction in the general population: Results from a German population-based survey. *Behaviour & Information Technology, 33*(7), 757–766.

Orben, A., & Przybylski, A. K. (2019). The association between adolescent well-being and digital technology use. *Nature Human Behaviour, 3,* 173–182.

Patel, V., Saxena, S., Frankish, H., & Boyce, N. (2016). Sustainable development and global mental health—A *Lancet* commission. *The Lancet, 387*(10024), 1143–1145.

Purohit, A. K., Barclay, L., & Hozer, A. (2020). Designing for digital detox: Making social media less addictive with digital nudges. In *Extended abstracts of the 2020 CHI conference on human factors in computing systems.*

Richtel, M. (2011). A Silicon Valley school that Doesn't compute. *The New York Times*. 22 October. Retrieved from: https://www.nytimes.com/2011/10/23/technology/at-waldorf-school-in-silicon-valley-technology-can-wait.html.

Robinson, T. E., & Berridge, K. C. (2008). The incentive sensitization theory of addiction: Some current issues. *Philosophical transactions of the Royal Society of London Series B, Biological sciences, 363*(1507), 3137–3146.

Roose, K. (2019). Online cesspool got you down? You can clean it up, for a price. *New York Times Magazine*. 13 November. Retrieved from: https://www.nytimes.com/interactive/2019/11/13/magazine/internet-premium.html.

Roskies, A. (2016). Neuroethics. In *Stanford Encyclopedia of Philosophy* (Spring 2016 Edition).

Rubin, A. J. (2017). France lets workers turn off, tune out and live life. *The New York Times*. 3 January. Retrieved from: https://www.nytimes.com/2017/01/02/world/europe/france-work-email.html.

Rumpf, H. J., Bischof, G., Bischof, A., Besser, B., Glorius, S., de Brito, S., … Petry, N. M. (2014). *Applying DSM-5 criteria for Internet Gaming Disorder to Different Internet Activities*. Manuscript draft Lübeck, Germany: University of Lübeck.

Sagioglou, C., & Greitemeyer, T. (2014). Facebook's emotional consequences: Why Facebook causes a decrease in mood and why people still use it. *Computers in Human Behavior, 35*, 359–363.

Schmidt, D. C. (2018). *Google data collection*. Retrieved from: . https://digitalcontentnext.org/wp-content/uploads/2018/08/DCN-Google-Data-Collection-Paper.pdf.

Schüll, N. (2014). *Addiction by design: Machine gambling in Las Vegas*. Princeton University Press.

Schulson, M. (2015). User behaviour: Websites and apps are designed for compulsion, even addiction. Should the net be regulated like drugs or casinos? *Aeon*. 24 November. Retrieved from: https://aeon.co/essays/if-the-internet-is-addictive-why-don-t-we-regulate-it.

Seymour, R. (2020). *The twittering machine*. Verso.

Sullivan, L. S., & Reiner, P. (2019). *Digital wellness and persuasive technologies*. Philosophy & Technology.

Thaler, R. H., & Sunstein, C. R. (2008). *Nudge: Improving decisions about health, wealth and happiness*. Penguin.

van Rooij, A. J., Ferguson, C. J., Carras, M. C., Kardefelt-Winther, D., Shi, J., Aarseth, E., … Przybylski, A. K. (2018). A weak scientific basis for gaming disorder: Let us err on the side of caution. *Journal of Behavioral Addictions, 7*(1), 1–9.

Verbeek, P. P. (2006). Persuasive technology and moral responsibility: Toward an ethical framework for persuasive technologies. In *Paper for conference Persuasive Technology 2006*Eindhoven University of Technology.

Verbeek, P. P. (2009). Ambient intelligence and persuasive technology: The blurring boundaries between human and technology. *NanoEthics, 3*(3), 231–242.

Williams, J. (2018). *Stand out of our light: Freedom and resistance in the attention economy*. Cambridge University Press.

Wolf, S. (1997). Happiness and meaning: Two aspects of the good life. *Social Philosophy and Policy, 14*(1), 207–225.

Index

Note: Page numbers followed by *f* indicate figures, *t* indicate tables, and *b* indicate boxes.

Printed in the United States
by Baker & Taylor Publisher Services